# Historical Destiny and National Socialism in Heidegger's *Being and Time*

# Historical Destiny and National Socialism in Heidegger's *Being and Time*

## Johannes Fritsche

University of California Press

Berkeley / Los Angeles / London

University of California Press
Berkeley and Los Angeles, California

University of California Press, Ltd.
London, England

©1999 by
The Regents of the University of California

Library of Congress Cataloging-in-Publication Data

Fritsche, Johannes.
  Historical destiny and national socialism in
Heidegger's "Being and time" / Johannes Fritsche.
    p.  cm.
  Includes bibliographical references (p.  ) and index
  ISBN 0-520-21002-6 (alk. paper)
    1. Heidegger, Martin, 1889–1976.  Sein und Zeit.
  2. National socialism and philosophy.  I. Title.
  B3279.H48S4434  1999
  111—dc21                                   98-21750
                                                  CIP

Printed in the United States of America

9  8  7  6  5  4  3  2  1

# Contents

121200 - 5280p8

# Preface

The German verb «übersetzen» is used in several ways. Most of the time, it means «to translate,» as in translating from one language into another. The English word «to translate» also has several meanings, but it does not signify what by virtue of its Latin root, transferre, it might be expected to mean and what the German übersetzen may in fact mean, namely, to carry somebody over a river or an ocean. Thus, in probably all German lexica on Greek mythology one reads that Charon setzte the souls of the dead über the Styx to carry them to the doors of Hades. However, as one is promised in the Welcome Area of John F. Kennedy Airport, not every Übersetzung over a body of water is an Übersetzung into death. By coming to the «New World,» the United States, many begin a new life; they have new experiences, can change themselves or can become what for this or that reason they couldn't be in the «Old World» they came from. When Michel Foucault setzte über from France to the United States, he too changed. An American expert in such Übersetzungen from Europe, Richard Rorty, refers to a European expert, Vincent Descombes, to point out that in France Foucault is considered to be a Nietzschean, but in the United States he is viewed as a liberal democrat.[1] With Jim Miller's biography of Foucault,[2] a further Foucault setzte über. At least this is what, if I am not mistaken, a commentator on New York Public Radio maintained when he concluded his review of Miller's book by saying—probably against Miller's intentions—that Foucault was a fascist just as Heidegger was a Nazi.

Foucault was by no means a fascist. However, Heidegger was a Nazi, and he was strongly involved in National Socialism. This has to be admitted after Victor Farías's and Hugo Ott's intensive research, the results of which have been published in several articles since 1983 and, in 1987 and 1988, in two books.[3] But does this mean that Heidegger's writings bear some relation to his political commitment? Farías's and Ott's research completely changed the terms of the debate. Already prior to their work, literature on the political aspects and implications of Heidegger's writings had been published, notably, Alexander Schwan's book in 1965 and Pierre Bourdieu's *L'Ontologie politique du Martin Heidegger* in 1975.[4] However, since Farías and Ott, countless texts on the subject have been produced, and the debate has often become highly controversial. In 1987 Jacques Derrida published his *De l'esprit: Heidegger et la question,*[5] which David F. Krell hailed in the strongest terms.[6] For Richard Wolin, however, the book is «awry,»[7] and it as well as Derrida's other writings on the issue are a «quasi-exoneration»[8] of Heidegger. In his own book, Wolin argues that Heidegger's commitment to National Socialism «was *rooted in the innermost tendencies of his thought*» (PB 66), that is, of his book *Being and Time*. Tom Rockmore also maintains that Heidegger turned to National Socialism «on the basis of his philosophy,»[9] and he traces the issue of Nazism even in Heidegger's latest works. In 1993 a Heidegger scholar and Heideggerian philosopher as distinguished as John D. Caputo published a book entitled *Demythologizing Heidegger*.[10] Meanwhile, the ship of Heidegger's philosophical politics seems to have reached less turbulent waters.[11] Fred R. Dallmayr was even «struck by . . . the complete absence of any sinister fascist overtones,»[12] though he leaves it a little bit up in the air whether fascist overtones—or, for that matter, clear fascist voices—are by definition sinister or not.

To me it seemed necessary to give a very detailed interpretation of section 74 of *Being and Time*. In doing so, I refer to only three texts—with the exception of section C of chapter 5, where I draw on several sources—that deal with that section in more detail, texts that, as far as I know, are representative of the American literature on this section. One of the three is Wolin's book, *The Politics of Being: The Political Thought of Martin Heidegger* (PB), whose thesis I have already mentioned. The second is an article by Charles Guignon, "History and Commitment in the Early Heidegger" (HC), according to which Heidegger develops a theory of the political in *Being and Time* that is neutral regarding the specific political options available at Heidegger's time. Third, I refer to Peg Birmingham's article, "The Time of the Political" (TP), in which she presents Heidegger as a kind of anarchist. In other words, at least in my understanding of her article, according to her, Heidegger politically belonged neither to the Center nor to the Right but definitely to the Left.

A discussion of a major work in German and its English translations will necessarily often refer to German terms. To avoid a proliferation of italics, all German and other foreign words are set in roman type. Italics are used only for titles of books and for emphasis, either my own or, in quotations, that of the original. Quotations from translations often include insertions, emendations, or comments by the translator, typically enclosed in brackets. My own insertions and comments, such as the German wording in a translation or explanatory material, are enclosed in curly brackets ({ }) throughout.

Quotation marks present another complication in any discussion of Heidegger's work. To avoid confusion, I have used guillemets («») as my quotation marks throughout. Thus, the quotation marks used in the texts cited are reproduced here exactly, except that the inverted guillemets used in German texts have been changed to American double quotation marks as is standard practice. Regular quotation marks are also used for article and chapter titles as well as for titles of songs and poems. If an English translation of a German text is not followed by a reference to an English edition, the translation is my own. Sometimes, I insert the German word or phrase into an English translation without commenting on the translation. These insertions are meant as a reminder of similar vocabulary of different authors or of different texts by the same author that don't surface in the English translations but that should not be overlooked.

*Being and Time* was published in 1927. As Rockmore says, the book «as a whole culminates» in sections 72–77, that is, in the chapter entitled "Temporality and Historicality" (BT 424ff.; SZ 372ff.).[13] Within this passage section 74 is crucial. It consists of four parts, in the first of which Heidegger returns to a notion he has developed at length in sections 61–63 (BT 349ff.; SZ 301ff.), namely, that of *«anticipatory* resoluteness» (BT 434f., «Dasein factically has its . . . as a basic attribute of care,» SZ 382f.). Subsequently he considers authentic Dasein as it chooses a possibility (BT 435–437; «As thrown, Dasein has . . . *that is to say, authentic historicality,»* SZ 383–385). In this part Heidegger develops the concepts of heritage, fate, destiny, community of the people, and struggle. In the third part of this section, he elaborates the theme of the second part in terms of the notion of repetition («It is not necessary . . . indifferent to both these alternatives,» BT 437f.; SZ 385f.). The fourth part, the remainder of section 74, more or less summarizes the preceding passages.

Toward the end of the third part Heidegger uses three German words with the component «wider,» namely, the verb «erwidern» and the nouns «Erwiderung» and «Widerruf» (SZ 386), which have been translated as «[to make a] *reciprocative rejoinder,»* «rejoinder,» and *«disavowal»*: «Rather, the repetition makes a *reciprocative rejoinder* to the possibility of that existence which has-been-there. But when such a rejoinder is made to this possibility in a resolution, it is made *in a moment of vision*; *and as such* it is at the same time a *disavowal* of that which in the "today", is working itself out as the 'past'» (BT 438). This very short passage has been singled out in the literature as crucial to the significance of the entire section and, therefore, to the political import of *Being and Time*—and rightly so. Indeed, how one reads this passage can determine whether the entire section on historicality ends up on the Right or the Left or is neutral toward both as well as toward the Center. Unfortunately, Macquarrie and Robinson's translation of this short passage is, at best, misleading, if not simply wrong. What is more, the passage is one of the very few in the entire book to which the translators have added a note in which they not only comment on Heidegger's German text but also offer an interpretation of the passage based on their extremely questionable, if not wrong, translation (BT 438, n. 1). Yet most of the American literature on this section has been based on their translation and their commentary. The fault is not so much with the translators, because Heidegger's language at that point is even more intricate than in other passages. Nevertheless, one might wish that one or the other of the native German speakers whom the translators thank in their preface (BT 16) might have insisted on a more detailed note pointing out that their rendering of the sentences and the meaning they suggest are by no means the only possible ones. In this sense, my entire book is just a continuation of their note. However, this is certainly not the only reason why the entire section 74 requires a very detailed interpretation. In chapter 1 of this book, I mainly interpret the third part of section 74. In section A, I begin with some comments on the two notions of which the phrase «*anticipatory* resoluteness» is an amalgam, namely, those of «anticipation of death» and «resoluteness,» which characterize Dasein when it becomes authentic. In section B, I comment on the sentence with the verb erwidern («[to make] a *reciprocative rejoinder*») and the various meanings of this verb in German. In section C, I discuss the passage on repetition in the third part and some aspects of the second part of section 74, and in section D, the sentence with «*reciprocative rejoinder*» and the one with «*disavowal*» from the third part of section 74.

In *Being and Time,* Heidegger unfolds a drama in three acts, the drama of Dasein's historicality. In the first act the necessary conditions of the dramatic conflict are developed. In the second act, a critical situation develops that calls for a dramatic solution, which is presented in the third act. The third act of the drama is section 74. As I show already in chapter 1, the solution of the drama consists in authentic Dasein stepping out of the world in which it has been living as ordinary Dasein, turning back to this world, and canceling it. Authentic Dasein does so because it has been called upon by the past to rerealize the past, which has been pushed aside by the world in which Dasein has been living as ordinary Dasein. The rerealization of the past requires that authentic Dasein cancel, destroy, or disavow the world it has been living in as ordinary Dasein. Ordinary Dasein is living in a downward plunge in which it is falling away from and has left behind or canceled a world in which the principle—Montesquieu might say, the spirit—of the past—or, in Heideggerian terms, «what-has-been-there»—has been properly realized. At some point in the downward plunge the second part of the drama begins, and a buzzing in the air—the «anschwellender Bocksgesang,» the emerging tragedy, song of the he-goats—indicates a crisis. The solution of the crisis lies in the cancellation of the downward plunge and the world of ordinary Dasein so as to make room for a world in which the past and its principle are revitalized and properly present.

In chapter 2, I present the main features of the entire drama and work out the details of its final resolution in section 74. In section A, I look at some more general notions of Heidegger's in *Being and Time*—those of origin, primordial temporality, authenticity, and wholeness—and their dynamics in regard to the concept of historicality. In section B, I take up passages and notions from Division One of *Being and Time* as well as from the section on historicality prior to section 74—such as the work of ambiguity and the different meanings of «world» and «history»—by means of which Heidegger makes clear that, indeed, at the beginning of section 74 we are in the second part of the drama of historicality, that is, at the point in the downward plunge where the buzzing in the air begins. In section C, I show how in the second part of section 74— the part on heritage, fate, etc.—the second part of the drama is briefly summarized and the third part begins to unfold whose conclusion at the end of the third part of section 74 I have discussed in my chapter 1.

Though a huge amount of literature on the topic has been published, to my knowledge no one—neither critics of Heidegger nor, as it were, his defenders—has undertaken what is most naheliegend, obvious, namely, a detailed comparison between Heidegger's text and other texts on history and politics of his time. This is done in chapters 3 and 4. In chapter 3, I relate Heidegger to rightist authors and in chapter 4 to leftist authors. In section A of chapter 3, I summarize Adolf Hitler's thoughts on history and politics in *Mein Kampf* (MK; MKe), the first book of which, 406 pages long, was published in 1925 and followed by the second and last one, 376 pages long, in 1927. The beginning of World War I was regarded by many rightist authors as a major opportunity for realizing their agenda. According to their view, God, fate, destiny, or providence had sent World War I in order to call on the German people to put the rightist agenda to work. Thus, in section B of chapter 2 I present an enthusiastic hymn on World War I, 483 pages long, by Max Scheler, *Der Genius des Krieges und der Deutsche Krieg* (The genius of war and the German war) (in PPS), the preface of which is dated November 1914 and which was published in early 1915. How could Scheler finish such a long book a mere three months after the beginning of the war? The answer is simple. According to Scheler, World War I was both the «natural» outcome of and the equally «natural» break with modern history; a break every «true» German and every member of the «true» European community of culture had hoped for and desired. He presented the conceptual framework of modern history in his well-known book *Formalism in Ethics and Non-Formal Ethics of Values: A new Attempt Toward the Foundation of An Ethical Personalism* (FEe; FE). The first part of that work was published already in 1913 and the second one was finished in manuscript form in the same year, as Scheler emphasized in the preface to the first edition in 1916 (FEe xvii; FE 9).

In other writings of the time around World War I, for instance, his book entitled *Ressentiment* (RE; in UW), Scheler spelled out in more detail the implications of his work on formalism for a theory of modern history and the emergence and decline of capitalism. I turn to these writings in section D of chapter 3. By the end of that section it will have become clear, I hope, that the general framework of Hitler's and Scheler's theories on history and the task of politics is the same. Modernity—that is, society or Gesellschaft—is a downward plunge in which the «real» principle of history—namely, Gemeinschaft or community—has been pushed aside by the former. At some point in this downward plunge—with the beginning of World War I, for instance— fate raises its voice and demands that people demolish Gesellschaft in order to rerealize the proper Gemeinschaft.

At the beginning of section E, I point out the two major directions of thinking on the Right. Hitler and Scheler belong to what one might label the revolutionary rightists. Revolutionary rightists and conservative rightists both share the above-mentioned concept of history and politics in terms of fate, Gesellschaft, and the rerealization of Gemeinschaft. They differ insofar as conservative rightists want to rerealize the respective Gemeinschaft more or less in its premodern state, that is, without modern technology, etc. Revolutionary rightists, however, insist that the rerealization of the community must integrate features—modern technology and private property of means of production on a large scale—that, historically, have developed along with modern society.[14] However, by that point in section E it will already be clear that there are great differences between the specifics of revolutionary rightist politics in Hitler on the one hand and in Scheler on the other. As I will point out in section F, these differences enabled Scheler in the twenties to abandon any rightist politics and to turn to the center and the social democrats. With Heidegger it is different.

In the remainder of section E, I present the entire narrative of section 74 in light of the preceding presentation of Hitler and Scheler for two purposes. First, section 74 of Heidegger's *Being and Time* is as brilliant a summary of revolutionary rightist politics as one could wish for. Second, there were not only National Socialists but other revolutionary rightists as well. Several of the latter had indeed strong conceptual means to distance themselves from National Socialism. As was mentioned, Scheler finally even turned away from all rightist politics. However, any such conceptual means that would have enabled Heidegger to distance himself from National Socialism and criticize its basic assumptions are not only absent from *Being and Time* but are also explicitly criticized by him. It is in this sense that one has to say that Heidegger's *Being and Time* makes a direct case for the most revolutionary rightists, the National Socialists, and their Gemeinschaft, namely, the Volksgemeinschaft, the community of the people.

In chapter 4, I discuss leftist theories of history and politics of Heidegger's time. In section A—the section on Georg Lukács's book *History and Class Consciousness* (HI; GK), published in 1923—it is shown that liberals, social democrats as well as communists, relied on a notion of history that is the exact opposite of the rightist one. They were not concerned with a repetition of this or that past; rather, each of them maintained that history and politics were about the realization of a state of society, Gesellschaft, that was unprecedented and in which there was no room for a revitalization of this or that Gemeinschaft. As I show in section B of chapter 4—the one on Paul Tillich's *The Socialist Decision* (SD; SE), published in 1933—it was precisely in this negative relation to the past and the powers and needs embodied in its different Gemeinschaften that Tillich saw the basic flaw of leftist politics and the reason for the disastrous losses of the Left and the massive gains of the National Socialists in the elections in the last years of the Weimar Republic. On the basis of the fundamental difference between the Right and the Left, Tillich proposed to the Left a revision of its politics, and at the same time proposed to the Right to end its decisionistic politics, that is, to end its disavowal of Gesellschaft and its principle, and to acknowledge that the Right can realize its own ends only through Gesellschaft and the principle of Gesellschaft, which in Tillich's words, is the demand for justice.

In chapter 5, I discuss some of Heidegger's texts dating from the years after Hitler's Machtergreifung on January 30, 1933: in section A, part of a speech given by Heidegger on November 30, 1933, in Tübingen as well as his usage of some of its terms in later texts up to the fifties; in section B, Heidegger's lecture course on Hölderlin in the winter semester 1934–35 (HH) and his famous lecture course *An Introduction to Metaphysics* (IM; EM) in summer 1935. In these sections, an indirect proof for the thesis developed in chapters 1 through 4 is offered. For it is shown that the key motif of section 74 of *Being and Time* remains unchanged after the Machtergreifung. For three reasons I turn in section C to Heidegger's reception in the 1990s in the United States. First, I elaborate on the phenomenon that, in some way, the question of politics in *Being and Time* hinges on how one reads the sentences on Erwiderung and Widerruf at the end of the third part of section 74. Second, I develop some details of my interpretation of section 74, notably those surrounding the concept of Held, hero, as used by Heidegger in section 74 (BT 437; SZ 385). Third, I try to show that, indeed, it is extremely difficult for Americans to understand Heidegger's notion of historicality and authentic Dasein. For there could not be a more marked difference than the one between the «German» rightist notions of Held and fate on the one hand and the «American» understanding of what it means to be authentic on the other.

In chapter 6, for the same reason as in sections A and B of chapter 5, I turn to the conversation between Karl Löwith, a Jew, and Heidegger in Rome in 1936 and to Heidegger's own Machtergreifung, his rectorate address on May 27, 1933. Section B returns to the beginning of the book, the brown soil of the woods and forests around Langemarck in order to look for an exit other than the one taken by Heidegger and other rightists.

The topic under discussion here is unpleasant and painful. Therefore, I have looked for some relief for myself as well as the readers and wrote this book as a kind of novel or detective story. One can read it, so to speak, on the subway. (As it will turn out, the case is pretty easy and requires no elaborate arguments. Still, English readers not familiar with German might find the process of securing the evidence in chapters 1 and 2 somewhat laborious. However, from the beginning of chapter 3 on the narrative proceeds very smoothly. Indeed, some readers might want to begin with chapter 3 and read chapters 1 and 2 along with section E of chapter 3.) In addition, a smile or laugh is usually healthy for both mind and body. In fact, smiling is an epistemological category as it carries one into a different Stimmung (mood) and thus allows one to step back, to pause, and to keep a critical distance toward the text and its topic. Thus, here and there I made some jokes. If, in the end, they only have helped me to make the way through, I ask in advance for leniency. Every reader probably knows novels and detective stories that are just too long. However, hermeneutically it is a deeply embarrassing phenomenon that, according to several commentators, whether the concept of historicality, and consequently that of decision goes to the Left, the Right, the Center, or stays neutral regarding all these possibilities hinges on only three sentences. Furthermore, these short sentences determine the content of the section in which the entire book *Being and Time* culminates. In addition, *Being and Time* as a whole does not deal with this or that academic speciality but rather has turned out to be one of the major philosophical books of this century. Last but not least, it was published at the dawn of German National Socialism, and what is at stake in the passages in question is the book's contribution to this. Thus, one might acknowledge that it is necessary to look very closely at the words Heidegger uses, even if one maintains I could have done so in fewer pages.

However, one might justify the length of this volume in a less defensive manner. Many contemporary philosophers have become humble and no longer draw on the gifts of theology and metaphysics, which are often regarded as poisonous. In this situation, two disciplines become especially important, namely, philology and hermeneutics. If one translates the hermeneutical problem of the whole and the parts into a metaphor appropriate to Heidegger, one might say that each sentence, or each section, is a tree in the copse of the text, and the copse of the text is part of a larger forest consisting of all the other texts existing at the same time. One cannot understand the tree without an understanding of the copse and vice versa. In addition, to understand the copse one needs to know something of the forest of which it is a part. We no longer live in the forest of the twenties in Germany, and we are no longer familiar with all the movements in it. It is National Socialism that separates the Germans from the twenties, and many Germans did much to pull themselves out of National Socialism and their involvement with it. For various reasons, after World War II Heidegger himself, and Heideggerians, practiced, so to speak, negative philology with regard to Heidegger's trees and copses. They took the trees out of *Sein und Zeit* and replanted them in the soil of Heidegger's later writings as they understood them. In that soil, those trees looked quite familiar to German philosophers, namely, like a further Entwurf in the series of grand narratives known from German idealism, albeit with reversed premises. According to this story, although in *Sein und Zeit* Heidegger did not yet really get to the point, he had always been exclusively concerned with the history of Being and the distinguished position of the pre-Socratics in that history. In his later writings he added a certain touch of German Besinnlichkeit, pensiveness, a certain smell of the Feldwege[15] around his Hütte. When he joined the National Socialist Party, it was his wife, or some other contingent impulse from the world of the «they,» that dragged him into this. However, as a true philosopher he soon realized that philosophy is, and always has been, incompatible with that sort of politics. Since the seventies planters and gardeners with more sophisticated tools have appeared. Often, these gardeners have not only been quite ignorant of the forest of the twenties in Germany, but they have even cultivated this ignorance by making procedures of decontextualization their primary tool, and they have been harvesting the sweet grapes of postmetaphysical plurality and recognition of the other as irreducible other from the notion of historicality in *Being and Time*. In this situation, philology, that is, chapters 1 and 2 of my book and also some passages in other chapters, is necessary to lead us back into the forest of the twenties and show us that the soil of *Being and Time* is völkisch. Eigentliche philology teaches humility! Heidegger would be the first to cheer this sentence. From the perspective of eigentliche philology, one realizes how often, in negative philology, one behaves the way in which, according to Heideggerians, the modern subject behaves, that is, it just forces its own standards onto the object and the other.[16] Philology teaches respect for the trees and forests and is, so to speak, environmentally correct. In brief, Heidegger always claimed to respond to the situation, and one should do him justice. When one reads *Sein und Zeit* in its context, one sees that, as Scheler put it, in the kairos of the twenties *Sein und Zeit* was a highly political and ethical work, that it belonged to the revolutionary Right, and that it contained an argument for the most radical group on the revolutionary Right, namely, the National Socialists.

Let me mention that in the few years I have known Reiner Schürmann he didn't like to talk much about philosophy outside the New School for Social

Research. We went out for dinners and movies. Still, it was easy to see how extremely serious he was about sentences such as: «'Heidegger', then, will take the place here of a certain discursive regularity. It will not be the proper name, which refers to a man from Meßkirch, deceased in 1976.»[17] One day, I briefly explained my understanding of section 74 and other passages in Heidegger. He just smiled—a long and bright smile. Several people have read the first draft of chapters 1 and 2, among them in Berlin, Germany, Lothar Busch, Ingeborg Ermer, Friedrich Glauner, Christa Hackenesch, Konrad Honsel, and Rosalinde Sartorti; here in New York Talal Asad, Kenneth Bronfenbrenner, Felix Ensslin, April Flakne, Aaron Garrett, Agnes Heller, Emilie Kutash, David Taffel, and David Whitaker. I thank them for their comments. Of course, I am responsible for the product in all of its aspects. In addition, I presented much of the material in a lecture course in spring 1995. It was a pleasure to discuss these and related issues with Jack Ben-Levy, as it was always a pleasure to talk to Aaron Garrett. Tom Rockmore recommended that I send the manuscript to Edward Dimendberg at University of California Press, where it was handled by Laura Pasquale and Rose Anne White. Sabine Seiler edited it with extreme diligence and sensitivity. Morgan Meis helped me review the edited manuscript and read the proofs. I thank all of them for their interest and care for the publication. I also thank two anonymous readers for the press. They have pointed out, as it were, the right means to be faithful to the fact that even detectives and other experts in the field appreciate a certain amount of *Wegmarken* (WM), path markings, signposts, along the way (so to speak, in order not to waste time on *Holzwege*:[18] «da bist'e uff'm Holzweg,» you're barking up the wrong tree). Caitlin Dempsey has gone through the entire manuscript and has corrected my English. I very much enjoyed working with her.

New York City, December 1997
Johannes Fritsche

# Abbreviations

BT    Martin Heidegger, *Being and Time,* trans. John Macquarrie &
Edward Robinson (New York: Harper & Row, 1962).

BW    Martin Heidegger, *Basic Writings,* ed. D. F. Krell (San Francisco:
Harper & Row, 1976).

EM    Martin Heidegger, *Einführung in die Metaphysik* (Tübingen: Max
Niemeyer, 1953 reprinted 1959).

FE    Max Scheler, *Der Formalismus in der Ethik und die materiale
Wertethik: Neuer Versuch der Grundlegung eines ethischen Perso-
nalismus,* 5th ed. (Bern: A. Francke, 1966).

FEe    Max Scheler, *Formalism in Ethics and Non-Formal Ethics of Values: A new Attempt toward the Foundation of an Ethical Personalism,* trans. M. S. Frings and R. L. Funk (Evanston: Northwestern
University Press, 1973).

GK    Georg Lukács, *Geschichte und Klassenbewußtsein: Studien über
marxistische Dialektik* (Berlin: Malik-Verlag, 1923). The pagination
of the first edition is identical to that of the reprint of 1967 (Amster-
dam: Thomas de Munter) and is reprinted in *Geschichte und
Klassenbewußtsein: Studien über marxistische Dialektik,* Georg
Lukács, *Werke,* vol. 2 (Berlin and Neuwied: Luchterhand, 1968).

HC    Charles Guignon, "History and Commitment in the Early Heidegger," *Heidegger: A Critical Reader,* eds. H. L. Dreyfus and H. Hall
(Cambridge, Mass/Oxford: Blackwell, 1992), 130–142.

HH    Martin Heidegger, *Hölderlins Hymnen "Germanien" und "Der Rhein," Gesamtausgabe*, vol. 39 (Frankfurt: Klostermann, 1980).

HI    Georg Lukács, *History and Class Consciousness: Studies in Marxist Dialectics*, trans. Rodney Livingstone (Cambridge/Mass.: MIT Press, 1971).

IM    Martin Heidegger, *An Introduction to Metaphysics*, trans. Ralph Manheim (New Haven and London: Yale University Press, 1959).

MH    E. Kettering and G. Neske, eds., *Martin Heidegger and National Socialism: Questions and Answers*, trans. Lisa Harries (New York: Paragon House, 1990).

MK    Adolf Hitler, *Mein Kampf* (Munich: Zentralverlag der NSDAP, 1925 [first book] and 1927 [second book]. Reprint, Munich: Frz. Eher Nachf., 1940).

MKe   Adolf Hitler, *Mein Kampf*, trans. Ralph Manheim, 23d ed. (Boston: Houghton Mifflin, 1971).

PB    Richard Wolin, *The Politics of Being: The Political Thought of Martin Heidegger* (New York: Columbia University Press, 1990).

PPS   Max Scheler, *Politisch-Pädagogische Schriften*, ed. M. S. Frings, *Gesammelte Werke*, vol. 4 (Bern and Munich: Francke Verlag, 1982).

RE    Max Scheler, *Ressentiment*, trans. William W. Holdheim (New York: The Free Press of Glencoe, 1961).

SB    Martin Heidegger, *Die Selbstbehauptung der deutschen Universität: Rede, gehalten bei der feierlichen Übernahme des Rektorats der Universität Freiburg i. Br. am 27.5.1933. Das Rektorat 1933/34. Tatsachen und Gedanken*, ed. Hermann Heidegger (Frankfurt: Klostermann, 1983).

SD    Paul Tillich, *The Socialist Decision*, trans. Franklin Sherman (New York: Harper & Row, 1977).

SE    Paul Tillich, *Die sozialistische Entscheidung*, (Berlin: Medusa Verlag Wölk, 1980; first edition 1933).

SZ    Martin Heidegger, *Sein und Zeit*, reprint of the 9th edition (Tübingen: Max Niemeyer, 1972).

TP    Peg Birmingham, "The Time of the Political," *Graduate Faculty Philosophy Journal* 14 no. 2–15 no. 1 (1991): 25–45.

UW    Max Scheler, *Vom Umsturz der Werte: Abhandlungen und Aufsätze*, ed. Maria Scheler, *Gesammelte Werke*, vol. 3, 4th ed. (Bern and Munich: Francke Verlag, 1955).

VA    Martin Heidegger, *Vorträge und Aufsätze* (Pfullingen: Neske 1954; 6th reprint, 1990).

WA   Max Scheler, "Der Mensch im Weltalter des Ausgleichs," in *Späte Schriften,* ed. M. S. Frings, *Gesammelte Werke,* vol. 9 (Bern and Munich: Francke Verlag, 1976), 145–170.

WM   Martin Heidegger, *Wegmarken* (Frankfurt: Klostermann, 1967).

# Being and Time, Section 74

geschnürten leibs, geschminkten angesichts, nichts
haben sie gesundes zu erwidern, wo man sie
anfaszt, morsch in allen gliedern.
wiltu solche liebe mit ungehorsam erwiedrigen?
Im augenblick ich gar erwildet.
jederman ist zum krieg erwilt.
> *Deutsches Wörterbuch von Jacob und Wilhelm
> Grimm,* vol. 3 (Leipzig 1836), 1063f.

Es ist nicht tragisch, wenn einer als Schüler *wieder*
und *wider* oder *Tod* und *tot* nicht scharf genug
differenzieren kann.
> Ernst Jünger, *Tagebücher,* quoted according to
> the weekly *Die Zeit,* no.13, March 31, 1995.

## A. «*Anticipation of Death,*» and «*Resoluteness*»

In his *Foundations of the Entire Science of Knowledge,* Fichte elaborates on all those acts of the self that do not appear among the empirical states of consciousness but rather make empirical consciousness possible. Among them is an act Fichte refers to in the sentence «*The self posits itself as determined by the not-self.*»[1] This act gives rise to the assumption that in the self the opposite of «activity»[2] is posited. Fichte calls this opposite «Leiden.»[3] In everyday language, Leiden (suffering) or leiden (to suffer) is a straightforward word signifying experiences of pain. A person can «leiden an einer Krankheit» (suffer an illness) or «Schmerz leiden» (suffer pain), either physically or mentally. However, we mustn't think of these meanings when it comes to the acts of the self. Thus, Fichte adds a note in which he not only points to the inappropriateness of «painful feeling» with regard to pure consciousness but even declares «painful feeling» to be a mere «connotation» of Leiden.[4] At a significant point, the English translators of Heidegger's *Sein und Zeit,* John Macquarrie and Edward Robinson, thought one should keep a phrase of Heidegger's clean of its everyday meaning. In contrast to Fichte, however, they did not use the corresponding English everyday word in order, thereafter, to cleanse it of its everyday meaning. Rather, they translated it in such a way that its everyday meaning could no longer be recognized at all. They translated as *«anticipation,»* *«anticipatory resoluteness,»* and *«anticipation* of death» (BT 349, 349, 350, 353) what in the German text reads as *«Vorlaufen,»* *«vorlaufende Entschlossenheit,»* and *«Vorlaufen* zum Tode» (SZ 302), or «Vorlaufen in den Tod» (SZ 305). They cannot be blamed for this, since in a note they remark on the German word «vorlaufen» and its literal meaning, «running ahead» (BT 350, n. 1). Heidegger's language is difficult even for native German speakers and even more difficult to translate into other languages. Yet, one might regret that in the English translation the emphasis has shifted or has even been reversed. «Anticipation» and «to anticipate» refer primarily to a mental activity, whereas the phrase «to run (ahead)» is primarily used for a physical motion. In German this difference is even more pronounced, for antizipieren (also vorwegnehmen and vorhersehen) exclusively designates mental activities and never physical motions, whereas «vorlaufen» is used exclusively for physical motions and never for mental ones.[5]

Furthermore, if one anticipates (antizipiert, vorhersieht) some situation or event, one assumes that there is a temporal difference between the moment of anticipation and the occurrence of the anticipated situation. It is this time difference that allows one to prepare oneself in thought or action for this situation in order to get out of its way or to benefit from it or even to garner support from others. However, with vorlaufen one does just the opposite. Someone läuft vor when he leaves a group, a place, or a house he has been in so far and runs out, alone, into the open. In doing so one often exposes oneself to insecurities and dangers from which one had previously been protected by the group or house. Thus, vorlaufen is often the crossing of a line that, as in the case of the Greek city wall (the περίβολος, the ὅρος, ὁρισμός, the definition), provides the individual inside with shelter from, and identity in opposition to, the dangerous, undefined outside. As long as I am inside the walls, I am able to anticipate the moves of the enemy outside who beleaguers me; correspondingly, I can anticipate and strategically plan my future moves. However, as soon as I laufe vor, I deprive myself of this safety zone as well as of the time difference and expose myself immediately to the dangers of the outside from which I had previously been protected. Thus, a Vorlaufen is an Übersetzung from one's secure place, one's οἰκεῖος τόπος within one's own city, into the insecure and dangerous open. A Vorlaufen is by no means an anticipation of danger. Rather, I immediately expose myself to the danger precisely by abandoning the security I had hitherto relied on in my earlier acts of anticipation. To summarize: When one läuft vor, one annihilates the interval between the moment of anticipation and the occurrence of the anticipated situation; one abandons the shelter of the wall, which enabled one to anticipate dangers and to prepare oneself for them, and one runs straight ahead into the dangers outside the wall. Detractors of the security within walls and definitions, however, will say that in the moment of danger, or decision, one's οἰκεῖος τόπος, one's proper, or authentic, place is outside where the danger is, amid the seductions and dangers of war, madness, and eros. The place within, the actual city, they say, is either boring or has already become endangered by some foe outside or inside itself. (That the inhabitants don't notice this danger is just a further proof of how threatening the situation has become.) Thus, one has to run ahead, to run out, in order to get rid of the city or in order to return and save, or reshape, the city.

Since «to anticipate» does not have the sense of physical motion, the translation forecloses the associations that could hardly have been avoided by German readers who «ran into» Heidegger's phrase in the years between World War I and World War II. «Entschlossen in den Tod vorlaufen» (to resolutely run ahead into death) was how the acts of those who were later called the «Helden von Langemarck» (heroes of Langemarck) were characterized. World War I was the first war characterized largely by trench warfare. The front lines hardened quickly. Entrenched, the armies lay opposite each other. This situation could have gone on for years and years, with sufficient materiel and Daseine as, in the later Heidegger's term, «standing-reserve [*Bestand*]» (BW 298; VA 20)[6] or «human resources» (BW 299; «Menschenmaterial,» VA 21). Already in November 1914, however, the «Helden von Langemarck,» young German students, most of them Freiwillige (volunteers), had stepped out of the trenches into the open and, with the German national anthem on their lips, had run toward the French trenches. In terms of military strategy, this was sheer suicide and completely counterproductive. Nonetheless, or precisely because of this, they became the paradigm—the myth in the sense of Georges Sorel's *Reflections on Violence*—for all other German soldiers. As one can read in books on World War I written by conservative or right-wing authors, every German soldier was supposed to be capable of doing the same and had to follow, to imitate, or to repeat the actions of these «Helden von Langemarck» in order to become himself a «Held.» The most outstanding ones proved to be the «Helden von Verdun» (heroes of Verdun). Through their actions, these «Helden» gave rise to one of the most powerful myths of the political Right in the years of the Weimar Republic. The «Helden von

Langemarck» and the «Helden von Verdun» symbolized the resoluteness and the gallantry of «der deutsche Soldat» (the German soldier). He would have won the war if only he had received sufficient support from the «Heimatfront» (the home front). Such was the stuff of the so-called Dolchstoßlegende (the legend of the «stab in the back») according to which the Helden were not killed by French bullets coming toward them from the front, but were stabbed in the back by those at home. In this way the German loss of the First World War could be attributed to the «vaterlandslose Gesellen» (unpatriotic knaves), including communists, social democrats, Jews, and liberals, who— as those who propagated the legend of the «stab in the back» maintained— through lack of enthusiasm, subversive activities, and creeping apathy reneged upon the brave promise represented by the «Helden von Langemarck.»[7]

One might feel tempted to use the situation of the «Helden von Langemarck» as the methodological ideal type to interpret Heidegger's concept of resoluteness (Entschlossenheit). Yet, even without it, one cannot overlook an ambivalence of the German word Entschlossenheit that Heidegger entschlossen exploits and that many of his concepts share, namely, to have an active as well as a passive aspect. Entschlossenheit is the noun form of entschlossen (sein) (to be determined or to be resolute). Entschlossen, in turn, is the perfect participle of (sich) entschließen for instance, ins Kino zu gehen (to determine [oneself] to go to a movie, to decide to go to a movie). Entschließen consists of the prefix «ent-» and the verb «schließen» (to close, to shut, to lock, to finish, to end, to terminate). Looking back on one's decision one says, «Ich habe mich (dazu) entschlossen (, ins Kino zu gehen)» (I have decided [to go to a movie]). As the result of such a decision, «man ist entschlossen» (one is determined, one is resolved). One uses this phrase, «Ich bin entschlossen» (I am resolved) mainly to indicate that one's mind is made up. Thus, if someone doubts my decision, I reply by adding to «Ich bin entschlossen» the adverb «unwiderruflich!» (Ruf is call, thus, irrevocably! Or beyond recall; one might also say «Unwiderruflich! Diese Sache ist für mich abgeschlossen.» Beyond recall! For me this issue is settled, or finished.) As already the grammar of this sequence shows, by making a decision one brings oneself into a stable state, the state of resoluteness (Entschlossenheit). Being in the state of resoluteness, that is, having made the final decision, a person manifests activity and strength. In the state of resoluteness, he can no longer be seduced by the many voices talking to him. That is, «er hat sich *ab*geschlossen (gegen diese Stimmen).» Abgeschlossen is the perfect participle of the verb «abschließen,» which consists of the prefix «ab-» and the verb «schließen»; thus, «abschließen» is «to lock up» or «to seal off» (and also to close, to end, to terminate). Thus, «Er hat sich abgeschlossen gegen diese Stimmen» is: He has locked himself up, or closed himself off, against these voices. (One might also say, he has sich selbst verschlossen [locked up himself] against these voices; thus, he is verschlossen against them, he has become «unzugänglich [inaccessible] to these voices.») In an old metaphor, having made the decision, the resolute person no longer belongs to the «δίκρανοι,» as Parmenides says,[8] to the two-headed mortals, the many, or the «they.» The two-headed crowd, or rather, each Dasein that has been living and continues to live in the mode of the «they» does not have the strength to make a decision. Thus, such a Dasein vacillates between being and non-being; it vacillates between several voices, now listening to this one and now to that. In the architecture and aesthetics during Nazism, Arnold Breker's sculptures were the most obvious incarnations of the resolute person. They call on the viewer to make a decision and to remain entschlossen.

As for its active aspect, Entschlossenheit testifies to strength and steadfastness as well as to the ability to remain closed to, or inaccessible to, the many promptings of the multiple voices here and there. At the same time, however, one has also opened oneself. With the decision one has become inaccessible to the many voices and has opened oneself to one particular voice. One has «sich entschlossen,» that is, opened up, or unlocked, oneself. Be-decken or zu-decken means «to cover (up),» «to shield,» or «to protect,» and ent-decken means «to discover.» Ver-schleiern, or ver-hüllen, means «to veil» or «to disguise,» and ent-schleiern, or ent-hüllen, means «to unveil» or «to reveal.»[9] Thus, the prefix «ent-» often indicates an opening or uncovering. One has «sich entschlossen,» that is, «sich *auf*geschlossen.» «Auf-geschlossen» is the perfect participle of the composite aufschließen, which consists of the prefix «auf-» and the verb schließen. When one is in the state of Entschlossenheit, one has «sich aufgeschlossen für» (unlocked oneself for, or opened oneself for), one is «geöffnet» (opened for) or «offen für» (open for), or one has opened oneself for something; for example, Christians have opened themselves to grace; those on the political Right of the Weimar Republic had opened themselves to «die Stimme des Volkes» (the voice of the people), to the people, or even to the race. By opening oneself one becomes the receptive vessel into which mysterious entities like grace or race pour, mysterious entities calling for obedience, giving one clear directions, and providing one with the identity, spirit, and life that, consciously or unconsciously, one has lacked until one heard their call. (In fact, in these cases the perfect participles are identical in the active and the passive voice; thus, «ich habe mich entschlossen» is «I have decided/resolved/ unlocked myself»; «Ich bin entschlossen» is «I am resolved,» in the sense of «I have made up my mind,» but it might also be read as «I have been decided upon/resolved upon/unlocked [by someone for something]»; equally, «Ich bin aufgeschlossen» might be read as «I have been unlocked [by someone for something]»; as «Ich bin abgeschlossen» might be read as «I have been locked up/closed [by someone against something]»; in this sense, one might read «Ich bin offen» as «I have been opened/unlocked [by someone for something].») Thus, Heidegger's concept of Entschlossenheit might contain a promise, namely, the promise that one would get rid of the loneliness and isolation of bourgeois subjectivity and of the necessity to make decisions for oneself, by becoming a passive vessel and member of the community of the people. It was this promise that made the Jugendbewegung (Youth Movement) and other right-wing groups so attractive.[10]

I commented on Heidegger's notions of «Vorlaufen in den Tod» and «Entschlossenheit» because, after an introductory paragraph, it is with an amalgam of these two notions that Heidegger begins his discussion of historicality:

> We have defined "resoluteness" {Entschlossenheit} as a projecting of oneself upon one's own Being-guilty—a projecting which is reticent and ready for anxiety. Resoluteness gains its authenticity as *anticipatory* resoluteness {*vorlaufende* Entschlossenheit}. In this, Dasein understands itself with regard to its potentiality-for-Being, and it does so in such a manner that it will go right under the eyes of Death in order thus to take over in its thrownness that entity which it is itself, and to take it over wholly. (BT 434; SZ 382)

As is probably hard to imagine for readers in the United States at the end of this century, with the associations surrounding these sentences Heidegger, right at the beginning of his discussion, in a way sets the tone, creates the atmosphere, or evokes—to use one of his pet terms—the «mood» typical of conservative or right-wing thinking about history and politics at the time. In addition, the two notions «Vorlaufen in den Tod» and «Entschlossenheit» contain, as it were, in a nutshell the right-wing understanding of history and the individual's position in it. For reasons that will become clear, in the next sections I turn to the end of Heidegger's argument in section 74 in order then to make my way back to the beginning and into the context of section 74.

From the viewpoint of the resolute person, the two-headed crowds, with all their vacillating, are verschlossen against the call. Due to their inability and pigheadedness they are not able, or are not willing, to open themselves up and to make themselves free for the one voice they should listen to and obey, namely, that of the people. Being verschlossen to the one and real voice, they are, one might say, verfallen to the many voices.[11] From their viewpoint, in turn, the resolute person might look as though he has given up his identity and autonomy, as though, in an extreme formulation, he has sacrificed himself to some «higher» entity. Anyway, as is known, Heidegger assumes that Dasein lives for the most part in the mode of the «they,» that is, as ordinary Dasein. Ordinary Dasein just takes over what parents, peer group, etc., have instilled into it. Heidegger's usage of the terms «ordinary» and «inauthentic» seems not always to be consistent. As I will justify and elaborate in chapter 2, I use the notions with reference to the situation when the call raises its voice. Prior to the call, all Daseine are ordinary Daseine. Once the call raises its voice, some ordinary Daseine don't listen to the call or try to evade it (BT 318f., 323, 335ff., 443f.; SZ 274, 278, 289ff., 391). These Daseine become inauthentic. Other ordinary Daseine, however, listen to the call (BT

317ff.; SZ 272ff). These Daseine become authentic Daseine. How do they respond to the call? In section 74 Heidegger encapsulates his answer in a short and enigmatic sentence: «Die Wiederholung *erwidert* vielmehr die Möglichkeit der dagewesenen Existenz» (SZ 386; «Rather, the repetition makes a *reciprocative rejoinder* to the possibility of that existence which has-been-there,» BT 438). The German verb «erwidern» can have several and even contradictory meanings. Only a careful examination of the context will show what Heidegger meant.[12]

## B. *«Erwidert»* (*«reciprocative rejoinder»*)

In an interview with Andreas Isenschmidt for Swiss radio, broadcast on 9 October 1987, Hans Jonas remarked upon the characteristic of «authenticity» («Eigentlichkeit») as resoluteness: «You must resolve something for yourself. Resoluteness as such, not *for what* or *against what* one resolves oneself, but *that* one resolves oneself becomes the *authentic* signature of *authentic* Dasein. Opportunities to resolve oneself are, however, offered by historicity» (MH 201). Richard Wolin seems to give this a twist: «A philosophy of existence such as Heidegger's presupposes that all traditional contents and truths have lost their substance; and thus all that remains is *naked facticity,* that is, the sheer fact of existence. Thus, unlike traditional hermeneutics, which believes that the past contains a store of semantic potentials that are inherently worthy of redemption, *Existenzphilosophie* in its Heideggerian variant tends to be inherently destructive of tradition» (PB 32). At the beginning of his essay "History and Commitment in the Early Heidegger," Charles Guignon quotes this passage from Wolin as well as Habermas's characterization of resoluteness as «the decisionism of empty resoluteness»[13] and sets his interpretation of Heidegger's concept of action against that backdrop. According to Guignon, Wolin and Habermas assume «that Heidegger regards choice and action as resting on a kind of "leap," in a "moment of vision," cut off from all bonds to traditional social standards and moral ideals» (HC 130). Guignon, on the other hand, argues that *«Being and Time* is working toward a notion of what Charles Taylor calls "situated freedom," an understanding of action as nested in and guided by a range of meaningful, historically constituted possibilities, which are binding on us because they define who we are» (HC 131). He presents comments on several concepts in Heidegger and concludes with an interpretation of section 74 that consists of three passages. Two of these I quote here completely since I will refer to them several times later on. In the first passage, Guignon claims that

> Heidegger's account of authentic historicity expands the conception of authentic agency by (1) showing how we draw guidance from the past, and (2) providing an account of action as the transmission and realization of a tradition.

First, the discussion of the individual's grounding in the past comes across in the description of authenticity as involving "repetition" or "retrieval." When Dasein "explicitly" grasps its indebtedness to "the way in which Dasein has been traditionally understood," according to Heidegger, it grasps its own actions as drawing on and making manifest the possibilities opened by a shared heritage. Authentic Dasein "chooses its hero" and is "free for the struggle of loyally following in the footsteps of that which can be repeated" (*BT,* 437). What is suggested here is that, when one understands oneself as relying on "the Dasein which has been there," one draws a role-model or exemplar from the heroes and heroines of the past and uses that model as a guide for orienting one's life. The paradigmatic stories of our predecessors provide plot-lines, so to speak, for articulating our own lives into coherent, focused happenings. This is most apparent, of course, in the way religious people draw on the lives of the saints or on Old Testament stories in defining their aims. But it is also true for people in professions (Socrates for philosophers, Florence Nightingale for nurses), for cultural groups (Sitting Bull for Native Americans, Martin Luther King for American blacks), and so on. Following the guidelines of the life of the Dasein who came before, the authentic individual finds a sense of direction and an awareness of his or her place in the wider drama of the historical culture. Only in this way, Heidegger claims, can one achieve genuine "self-constancy" and "connectedness" (*BT,* 439, 442).

Secondly, authentic historicity shows how our agency contributes to the transmission of a tradition. This aspect of historicity is worked out in the account of authentic historiography. Heidegger starts from the familiar observation that writing history always involves "selection," and that the ability to select what can count as historically relevant requires that we operate with some understanding of the overall outcome or impact of the unfolding course of events. For this reason, "Even the disclosure of *historiography* {*sic*} temporalizes itself *in terms of the future*" (*BT,* 447). Our ability to identify what genuinely matters in the events of the past depends on our ability to grasp history as a "context of effectiveness and development"[12] which is seen as adding up to something as a totality—as going somewhere or making sense overall. (HC 136f.; n. 12 refers to Heidegger, *Frühe Schriften* [Frankfurt: Klostermann, 1972], 369)

In the second passage, Guignon comments on these two points in terms of Heidegger's reference to Nietzsche's *The Use and Abuse of History for Life* in section 76 (HC 137f.). In the third passage, he interprets authentic Dasein's attitude toward its present and future as follows:

Finally, authentic historiography is critical. But it is critical not in Nietzsche's sense of "judging and annihilating a past." Instead, for Heidegger, critique is aimed at the "today": authentic historiography "becomes a way in which the 'today' gets deprived of its character as present; in other words, it becomes a way of painfully detaching oneself from the fallen {*sic*} publicness of the 'today'" (*BT,* 449). As critical, authentic historiography requires a "*disavowal*

of that which in the 'today' is working itself out as the past," that is, a "destruc-
turing" of the hardened interpretations circulating in the public world in order
to recover "those primordial experiences in which we achieved our first ways
of determining the nature of Being—the ways which have guided us ever since"
(*BT,* 438, 44). The critical stance *"deprives* the 'today' of its character *as present,* and weans one from the conventionalities of the 'they' " (*BT,* 444). Heidegger's claim here is that it is only on the basis of utopian ideals together with
a sense of alternative ways of living discovered by antiquarian preservation that
we can have a standpoint for criticizing calcified forms of life of the present.
The present can be seen as deformed or defective only in contrast to an understanding of the potential built into our heritage and the truest aims definitive of
our destiny. The account of authentic historiography in *Being and Time* is clearly
not just a recipe for writing better history books. Rather, historiography becomes
a model for authentic action. Authentic Dasein understands its fundamental
task as the preservation and transmission of its historical culture for the purposes of realizing a shared destiny. As transmitters of a tradition, it is incum-
bent on us to seize on the defining possibilities of our common world, to creatively reinterpret them in the light of the demands of the present, and to take
a stand on realizing the prospects for the future. As always, the future is primary. Just as the life of the individual is primarily defined by its "being-towards-
the-end," so the community's being is defined by its directedness towards its
"destiny," that is, the task of working out the basic experiences that define it.
(HC 138)

Clearly, according to Guignon, Heidegger stresses the need for utopian
ideals for a critique of the forms of life of the present, and, ontologically, the
primacy of utopian ideals is grounded in the primacy of the future. It seems
to be clear as well that there are several heroes, Socrates, Martin Luther King,
Florence Nightingale, Sitting Bull, and others. However, how and from where
we get the utopian ideals is not so clear. Also, Guignon's use of the singular
and the plural seems to be confusing. In the second quote, he speaks first of
«alternative ways of living discovered by antiquarian preservation,» then of
«a tradition,» after this of «defining possibilities of our common world,» which
we have to «creatively reinterpret . . . in the light of the demands of the present.» However, given the necessity of utopian ideals, Guignon's use of the
singular and the plural is fully justified. Only the utopian ideals enable us to
discover several alternative ways the past offers and then to choose among
them that one way or that one tradition we establish as binding for ourselves.
Both the utopian ideals and this single tradition we choose enable us to criticize the forms of life of the present. But Guignon's interpretation may have
a second aspect, namely, that there is no single binding way, or tradition, at
all. Rather, the utopian ideals enable us to «creatively reinterpret» not only
the forms of life of the present but also the different ways of life of the past
that still exist, albeit in calcified forms. Thus, according to one's utopian ideal
one might choose not Sitting Bull, but rather Socrates as his hero. Socrates

himself, however, does not determine what use his adherent makes of him or how he interprets and, maybe, at a later time reinterprets Socrates. In this second aspect, it is clear that the utopian ideals enable us to distance ourselves not only from the present but also from the past. However, even without the second aspect the utopian ideals make our distancing from the past possible insofar as it is only on the basis of those ideals that we can see the multiplicity of possible heroes offered by the past. And only because of that can we then choose among them and select that one tradition we regard as binding for ourselves. Even if one leaves aside the process of singling out a tradition from several alternative ways of life by means of an utopian ideal and looks only at the last paragraph of the second quotation, our relationship to the tradition we transmit entails the ability to distance ourselves from its specific forms in the present and thus from the past itself. For the utopian ideals also enable us to «creatively reinterpret» the specific forms in which the tradition we transmit is alive. Thus, Guignon seems to focus on a distancing from the past as the bottom line of Heidegger's concept of historicality. In the light of our utopian ideals we distance ourselves from the present and the past as from some monolithic bloc. In so doing, we see that the past contains several different possibilities and heroes. The choice of one single hero requires that we can distance ourselves from all the other possible heroes, and we can do this only thanks to our utopian ideal. The utopian ideal, in turn, is not derived from the past but enables us to choose among all possible heroes the one who fits our ideal. Without this utopian ideal we would remain immersed in an unchallenged present or in a multifariousness of heroes without being able to distance ourselves from them and to single out the tradition we regard as binding for ourselves.

If this is a fair summary of Guignon's interpretation, he seems to interpret the very important sentence on «erwidert» («reciprocative rejoinder») preceding the one with the phrase he quotes («a *disavowal* of that which in the "today", is working itself out as the 'past'») as Macquarrie and Robinson do in their translation of *Sein und Zeit*. Their translation reads:

> Arising, as it does, from a resolute projection of oneself, repetition does not let itself be persuaded of something by what is 'past', just in order that this, as something which was formerly actual, may recur. Rather, the repetition makes a *reciprocative rejoinder* to the possibility of that existence which has-been-there. But when such a rejoinder is made to this possibility in a resolution, it is made *in a moment of vision; and as such* it is at the same time a *disavowal* of that which in the "today", is working itself out as the 'past'. (BT 437f.)

In the note accompanying this passage, the translators give Heidegger's German text and add their comment on the entire passage:

> 'Die Wiederholung lässt sich, einem entschlossenen Sichentwerfen entspringend, nicht vom "Vergangenen" überreden, um es als das vormals Wirkliche nur

wiederkehren zu lassen. Die Wiederholung *erwidert* vielmehr die Möglichkeit der dagewesenen Existenz. Die Erwiderung der Möglichkeit im Entschluss ist aber zugleich *als augenblickliche* der *Widerruf* dessen, was in {*sic*} Heute sich als "Vergangenheit" auswirkt.' The idea seems to be that in resolute repetition one is having, as it were, a conversation with the past, in which the past proposes certain possibilities for adoption, but in which one makes a rejoinder to this proposal by 'reciprocating' with the proposal of other possibilities as a sort of rebuke to the past, which one now disavows. (The punning treatment of 'wieder' and 'wider' is presumably intentional.) (BT 438, n. 1)

To be in a position of having a conversation with the past with its several possibilities that we can adopt, reject, or reinterpret presupposes that we are in a free relationship to the past, whether or not we are so only through utopian ideals. Only this position of free distance from the past, that is, one in which the past does not determine us—at least not completely—enables us to have this conversation, that is, to consider all the possibilities offered by the past, to reject several, to adopt some, and to reinterpret them.

To be sure, the first sentence on the denial of a simple recurrence of the past awakens the expectation that in the following sentence, this distance between the present and the past that cannot simply recur is further explained, stressed, and deepened. Furthermore, the German word «erwidern» seems to fit this purpose exactly. For if we are in a position to be able to make an Erwiderung (response, reciprocation, reciprocative rejoinder), we are free to reject, that is, we can choose freely between several possibilities in the sense of Macquarrie and Robinson's «conversation with the past.» However, in German, in cases like these, one uses «erwidern» not in the accusative but rather in the dative; that is, one would have expected Heidegger to write *«erwidert* vielmehr *der* Möglichkeit der dagewesenen Existenz.»* For, grammatically, the recipient of an Erwiderung in this sense is the dative object of the sentence. For example, someone has told me to leave the room, but I «erwidere *ihm* "Nein!"»* (I respond *to him* "No!"), «Ich erwidere *ihm,* daß ich den Raum nicht verlassen werde» (I respond *to him* that I will not leave the room). The other person, in turn, might erwidern something to my Erwiderung and so on until we reach an agreement. Thus, we would have, as it were, conversations with all the heroes and would then erwidern to all but one of them that we have considered them but have decided not to adopt them and instead will adopt another one with whom we also had a conversation and who has convinced us. However, in Heidegger's sentence the addressee of the Erwiderung is the accusative object of the sentence («*erwidert* vielmehr *die* Möglichkeit der dagewesenen Existenz»).

There is a usage of the German verb «erwidern,» not in the dative, but in the accusative that meets the expectation that in the sentence in question Heidegger heightens the distance between the present and the past and according to which this distance would be even more pronounced than is suggested in the interpretation of Guignon and the translators who allow Dasein finally to adopt or to identify itself with some hero offered by the past. For «erwidern» in the accusative can be used in the sense of «defending oneself against» or «fighting back.» For instance, in a sports competition, party A, a soccer team or a fencer, launches an attack against party B, and if B can defend itself or even launch a counterattack against A, one might summarize this by saying, «B has erwidert A's attack.» Wolin does not comment on the sentence with «erwidert,» but he might have thought of this sentence in connection with his argument that Heidegger's philosophy of existence «tends to be inherently destructive of tradition» (PB 32). Birmingham, however, has explicitly adopted this interpretation, or rather an even stronger one, in her essay "The Time of the Political." Inserting «(Erwidert)» after «reciprocative rejoinder,» she quotes Macquarrie and Robinson's translation from «The repeating of that which is possible does not bring again . . .» to «a *disavowal* of that which in the "today", is working itself out as the 'past'» (BT 437–438; SZ 385–386), and comments on it as follows:

> Macquarrie and Robinson's translation of *Erwidert* as "reciprocative rejoinder" conveys too great a sense of a return understood as identity: I reply to you in the same way that you did to me. In more militaristic terms, I return the strike in the same way that I received it. But clearly the passage above suggests something different. The response to repeatable historical possibilities is one which *disavows* any notion of continuity or identity with the past. Here a reference to the preposition "*wider*" meaning "contrary to or against" is helpful in grasping Heidegger's sense of reply as *Erwidert*. The reply or response to historical possibilities is precisely that which disrupts identity and continuity. *Dasein*'s authentic reply in the *Augenblick* to historical possibilities (*Erwidert*), is the site of resistance and displacement. In still other words, *Dasein*'s critical reply in the *Augenblick* marks the hiatus between the no-longer and not-yet, refuting the notion of history as a continuum.
>
> Therefore, *Dasein*'s critical reply (*Erwidert*) to repeatable historical possibilities calls into question the repetitive, narrative mode of legitimation. (TP 31)[14]

However, these are not the only ways to use erwidern in the accusative. Most of the time, erwidern in the accusative is used in the sense of the Greek ἀντιχαρίζεσθαι. Someone has done me a favor, and now I'm obliged to return that favor, as the second act within the old institution of χάρις, grace, charity, as the binding glue of each society and between different societies.[15] Someone has given me a present, has sent me a letter, or has visited me. According to the rules of charity, I am obliged to give a gift, write a letter, or pay a visit in return, that is, «I will erwidern the present, letter, or visit.» Since Heidegger elsewhere talks about «Ruf» (call) and «Anruf» (appeal, phone call) and since «Anruf» is used mainly for making a phone call, one might have had one's answering machine switched on: «Ich erwidere Ihren

Anruf so bald es mir möglich ist» (I'll return your call as soon as possible) if there had been answering machines in the 1920s. Anyway, «einen Anruf erwidern» was a common phrase at that time.[16] Or, suppose Mr. Jones has fallen in love with Ms. Smith and, hoping she would love him too, declares his love to her. However, Ms. Smith doesn't love him at all, but rather feels somewhat annoyed by his declaration and tells him so. Thus, in a narrative to her friend, Ms. Smith might use erwidern in the dative and tell her «And I erwiderte ihm "No! I'm sorry, I don't love you at all".» However, if she did love him and let him know her love, one would use erwidern in the accusative in a narrative about this: «And she erwiderte his love.» Or take the German sentence «Die Berge erwidern meinen Ruf» (the mountains erwidern my call). It is a common, somewhat poetical, German expression for «echo.» Finally, «Sie erwiderte meinen Hilferuf» (She erwiderte my call for help). One might use this sentence to summarize that when person A called for help, person B (that is, B is the one who «erwidert A's call for help») actually helped A deal with his or her predicament. This is the opposite of erwidern as counterattack and of erwidern in the dative as well. For in a counterattack one erwidert if one resists some attack or demand, defends oneself against it, or even launches an attack of one's own. In cases like the call for help, however, one erwidert this call precisely by complying with it. Heidegger's sentence does not give any indication of which sense of «erwidern» in the accusative he meant. However, as I will show in what follows, the context of this sentence rules out not only Guignon's but also Birmingham's interpretation.

## C. «*Repetition,*» «*Handing down,*» and «*Erwidert*»

Right at the beginning of section 74, Heidegger reminds readers that «resoluteness gains its authenticity as *anticipatory* resoluteness. In this, Dasein understands itself with regard to its potentiality-for-Being, and it does so in such a manner that it will go right under the eyes of Death in order thus to take over in its thrownness that entity which it is itself, and to take it over wholly. The resolute taking over of one's factical 'there', signifies, at the same time, that the Situation is one which has been resolved upon» (BT 434; SZ 382f.). Concerning possible resolutions in particular cases, he then says that «we must ask whence, *in general,* Dasein can draw those possibilities upon which it factically projects itself» (BT 434; SZ 383). It is within this context that Heidegger writes the notorious passages on heritage, destiny, fate, struggle, and «the community, of a {*sic*} people» (BT 435–437; SZ 383–385),[17] on which I will comment in chapters 2 and 3. However, I would like to point out already here that it is important to note that probably already «Erbe» (SZ 383; «heritage» BT 435), but at any rate surely «Schicksal» (SZ 384; «fate,» BT 435) and «Geschick,» that is, «das Geschehen der Gemeinschaft, des Volkes» (SZ 384; «*destiny* . . . the historizing of the community, of {the} people,» BT 436) are something only authentic Dasein gets in touch with by detaching itself from the «they» and by running ahead toward death. Furthermore, those terms («heritage,» «fate,» «community,» «people») appear only in the singular and mainly with the definite article. The plural, «individual fates,» «our fates,» occurs only so that these individual fates can be tied back to «*destiny*» in the singular (SZ 384; BT 436). Finally, in this entire section on «*destiny*» there is not the slightest hint of any concept of an utopian ideal that is different from the past and might guide the conversation with the past. What Heidegger concretely means by «*vorlaufende* Entschlossenheit» (SZ 382; «*anticipatory* resoluteness,» BT 434), would be closer to what Hans Jonas characterizes as the «tormented self» (MH 199). Every Dasein—the ordinary, the authentic, and the inauthentic Dasein—is ecstatic and futural, and some ordinary Dasein might have some futural utopia. But ordinary Dasein is what authentic Dasein must detach itself from. However, «painfully detaching oneself from the falling {verfallenden} publicness of the "today"» (BT 449; SZ 397) authentic Dasein runs into something that in itself cannot offer any positive utopian ideals: «One's anticipatory projection of oneself on that possibility of existence which is not to be outstripped—on death—guarantees only the totality and authenticity of one's resoluteness. But those possibilities of existence which have been factically disclosed are not to be gathered from death» (BT 434; SZ 383). Therefore, either there is no utopian ideal at all, or this utopian ideal is the very past itself, the community of the people that discloses itself to authentic Dasein in Dasein's running ahead to death, and to which Dasein «hands itself down» (BT 437; SZ 385). Thus, one completely misinterprets the entire passage if one makes a distinction between an utopian ideal and the past and maintains that the utopian ideal enables one to keep a distance from the past, to criticize it, or to choose among the different possibilities it offers. Rather, the utopian ideal is the past itself, which discloses itself to Dasein in Dasein's moment of running ahead to death.

After the passage on heritage and destiny, Heidegger rephrases the relation of past and Dasein in terms of «Wiederholung» and «Überlieferung» (SZ 385; «repetition» and «handing down» BT 437). «Überlieferung» most often means tradition, and the loss of tradition was what haunted German intellectuals between World War I and World War II—and by no means only them. This theme has found one of its most concise expressions in a passage in Walter Benjamin's 1936 essay "The Storyteller." Using the notion of «Erfahrung» (experience) for a way of life in which, with the authority of age, the elders can pass on their experiences to the younger generation in proverbs and stories, he writes:

Experience has fallen in value. . . . With the [First] World War a process began to become apparent which has not halted since then. Was it not noticeable at the end of the war that men returned from the battlefield grown silent—not richer, but poorer in communicable experience? What ten years later was poured out in the flood of war books was anything but experience that goes from mouth to mouth. And there was nothing remarkable about that. For never has experience been contradicted more thoroughly than strategic experience by tactical warfare, economic experience by inflation, bodily experience by mechanical warfare, moral experience by those in power. A generation that had gone to school on a horse-drawn streetcar now stood under the open sky in a countryside in which nothing remained unchanged but the clouds, and beneath these clouds, in a field of force of destructive torrents and explosions, was the tiny, fragile human body.[18]

Already by December 1933, in a journal edited in Prague, *Die Welt im Wort,* Benjamin had published an essay entitled, "Erfahrung und Armut" (Experience and poverty). It contains a passage almost identical to the one quoted above,[19] and presents Benjamin's interpretation of the works of Adolf Loos, Paul Klee, Paul Scheerbart, and others as efforts «to get rid of experience.» To get rid of experience is the new «dream of human beings today,» one we can dream of by reading «Mickey Mouse.»[20]

For conservatives, this destruction of Überlieferung took place in the parliament of Weimar and in the big cities, notably Berlin, with their nightbars, with all their different sorts of strange Mickey Mouses, with «Asphalt-Literaten» («asphalt writers») and «Neger-Jazz» («nigger jazz»), and, of course, with social democrats and communists and Jews. It is this situation that is addressed in sections 35–37 of *Being and Time*—the sections on idle talk, curiosity, and ambiguity[21]—and that is implicitly evoked in section 74. Prone to the distractions of the «they,» having lost stable traditions, Dasein must detach itself from the distractions of the «they» to realize its own nullity and finitude, which are ignored by the «they.» It is only this authentic Dasein that becomes the promise of a resurrection, or of a defense, of the threatened tradition:

> The resoluteness which comes back to itself and hands itself down {Die auf sich zurückkommende, sich überliefernde Entschlossenheit}, then becomes the *repetition* of a possibility of existence that has come down to us {*Wiederholung einer überkommenen Existenzmöglichkeit*}. *Repeating is handing down explicitly* {Die *Wiederholung ist die ausdrückliche Überlieferung*}—that is to say, going back into the possibilities of the Dasein that has-been-there. The authentic repetition of a possibility of existence that has been—the possibility that Dasein may choose its hero—is grounded existentially in anticipatory resoluteness; for it is in resoluteness that one first chooses the choice which makes one free for the struggle of loyally following in the footsteps of that which can be repeated. (BT 437; SZ 385)

In the note, the translators comment on the German verb «wiederholen»: «While we usually translate 'wiederholen' as 'repeat', this English word is hardly adequate to express Heidegger's meaning. Etymologically, 'wiederholen' means 'to fetch again'; in modern German usage, however, this is expressed by the cognate separable verb 'wieder . . . holen', while 'wiederholen' means simply 'to repeat' or 'do over again'» (BT 437, n. 1). According to their view, Heidegger intends none of these meanings, however: «Heidegger departs from both these meanings, as he is careful to point out. For him 'wiederholen' does not mean either a mere mechanical repetition or an attempt to reconstitute the physical past; it means rather an attempt to go back to the past and retrieve former *possibilities,* which are thus 'explicitly handed down' or 'transmitted'» (BT 437, n. 1).

Whatever Heidegger concretely means by «repetition,» there is some distance, some gap, between the past and Dasein that has to be bridged so that Dasein can become the repetition. Heidegger fills this gap with a very subtle as well as nasty play with the words «Überlieferung» (SZ 385; «handing down,» BT 437) and «sich überliefernde Entschlossenheit» (SZ 385; «The resoluteness which . . . hands itself down,» BT 437). «Überlieferung» means tradition, and with the exception of liberals, leftists, and analytical philosophers avant la lettre, hardly anyone, at least at Heidegger's time, objected to sentences in which «Überlieferung» was the active subject. In fact, conservatives liked such sentences very much, for example, «Die Überlieferung sagt uns, daß . . .» (tradition tells us to . . .) or «Überlieferung hat uns gelehrt und fordert von uns, daß wir ihr gehorchen» (tradition has taught us and demands from us that we obey it). Only by detaching itself from the «they» and by becoming «free for its death» (BT 437; SZ 385) does Dasein become the site of the repetition of the past. Only in this moment can Dasein relate itself to the past, only now can it, so to speak, grasp the past. Dasein actively appropriates the past, «*sich selbst die ererbte Möglichkeit überliefernd*» (SZ 385; «*by handing down to itself the possibility it has inherited,*» BT 437). The past, the «heritage» (BT 435; «Erbe,» SZ 383) that Dasein appropriates, has already disappeared or is in danger of disappearing because the ordinary Daseine have ignored and have removed themselves from this past. However, by detaching itself from the ordinary Daseine and actively appropriating the vanished or vanishing past, Dasein's activity is transformed into an act of submission to the heritage and the past. Heidegger indicates this by switching from «*sich selbst die ererbte Möglichkeit überliefernd*» (SZ 385; «*handing down to itself the possibility it has inherited,*» BT 436) to «sich überliefernde Entschlossenheit» (SZ 385; «The resoluteness which . . . hands itself down,» BT 437). The grammatical subject of the first sentence is Dasein («*Only an entity which . . . of* **having been,**» BT 437; SZ 385), and that of the second sentence is its resoluteness («The resoluteness which . . . ,» BT 437; SZ 385). However, in the first sentence («*sich selbst die ererbte Möglichkeit überliefernd*») the accusative object of this act is the heritage, and that to which the past is handed down (the dative object) is the Dasein and its resoluteness. In the second sentence («sich überliefernde Entschlossenheit»), however, the accusative object of the act of handing down is the Dasein and its resoluteness, and that to which Dasein hands itself down (the dative object) is the past, which we have to add as the dative object to «sich über-liefernde Entschlossenheit.» Just because Heidegger did not explicitly insert «the possibility it has inherited,» that is «heritage,» as the dative object into the phrase «sich überliefernde Entschlossenheit» (that is, he did not write «sich der ererbten Möglichkeit überliefernde Entschlossenheit,» «The resoluteness which . . . hands itself down to the possibility it has inherited») does not mean that it should not be added but is merely a matter of his discursive strategies. In section 74 Heidegger talks about «struggling» and «struggle.» Even if he did not, one needs a lot of Verschlossenheit against what Heidegger means by «sich überliefern.» The verb «überliefern» is used mainly in the passive voice as participle perfect, often in impersonal constructions. «Es ist überliefert (or über-lieferte Sitte), daß wir jeden Sonntag in die Kirche gehen» (It is a tradition [or a custom handed down] that we go to church every Sunday). However, the reflexive form with an accusative and a dative object, «Ich überliefere mich jemandem» (I hand myself over to someone), is used much less frequently and means simply «to surrender oneself to someone.» The expression «sich jeman-dem überliefern» grows into «sich an jemanden ausliefern,» «sich jemandem übergeben,» or «sich jemandem ergeben»—all of them expressions for «to deliver, surrender, subdue, hand over, subjugate oneself to someone else.»[22] In its act of subjugation to the inherited possibility, Dasein itself, as Heidegger continues, becomes the Überlieferung:

> The resoluteness which comes back to itself and hands itself down {to the pos-sibility it has inherited}, then becomes the *repetition* of a possibility of exis-tence that has come down to us. *Repeating is handing down explicitly.* (BT 437; Die auf sich zurückkommende, sich {selbst der ererbten Existenzmöglichkeit} überliefernde Entschlossenheit wird dann zur *Wiederholung* einer überkomme-nen Existenzmöglichkeit. Die *Wiederholung ist die ausdrückliche Überlie-ferung,* SZ 385)

Dasein surrenders itself to the past and through this act is transformed into the past. The phrase «*Repeating is handing down explicitly*» is explained as follows: «that is to say, going back into the possibilities of the Dasein that has-been-there {das heißt der Rückgang in Möglichkeiten des dagewesenen Daseins}» (BT 437; SZ 385). Therefore, one might say that «Wiederholung» means indeed «fetching again» some past that was ignored as long as Dasein lived ordinarily. Anyway, this aspect also presupposes the act of subjugation, or of being appropriated by the past, as it is developed in the preceding sen-tence («sich überliefernde Entschlossenheit»). In this process, Dasein becomes passive and opens itself up to surrendering itself to the past. These are the two aspects of Entschlossenheit I mentioned in the first section of this chap-ter. It is into these aspects that the concept of resoluteness from the begin-ning of section 74 develops, because it «has always already» contained them.

As will become clear in chapter 3, Heidegger's usage of these terms is completely in line with that of conservatives and people on the extreme right wing of his time. He explicitly distinguishes both aspects from each other in the subordinate clause of the next sentence. In resoluteness one links and, as it were, subdues oneself to a past calling for its repetition: «For it is in resoluteness that one first chooses the choice which makes one free for the struggle of loyally following in the footsteps of that which can be repeated {denn in ihr wird allererst die Wahl gewählt, die für die kämpfende Nachfolge und Treue zum Wiederholbaren frei macht}» (BT 437; SZ 385).[23] Upon becoming authentic, Dasein experiences the possibility of Treue. Prior to becoming authentic, Dasein as ordinary Dasein has already repeated, namely, it has repeated what parents, peer group, society—the «they»—have instilled into it. However, it has performed this repetition in a self-evident manner, without much thought and more often than not without enthusiasm. Upon becoming authentic, it realizes that what it has repeated is ordinary and inauthentic. The authentic possibility having been revealed to the Dasein, the latter understands that it has to dedicate itself to the former. It has to be treu, true, loyal, and devoted to what can be repeated. In other words, what can be repeated has a claim on Dasein, namely, that Dasein must actualize what can be repeated as faithfully as possible and thus must place itself at the service of what can be repeated. Therefore, from the beginning of this passage on, there is a sense of a demanding past—a past in the singular—for which Dasein has to open itself, to make itself free, and into which Dasein itself is transformed in order then to fight for this past and rerealize it.[24]

It is true that Heidegger speaks here of possibilities in the plural: «in Möglichkeiten des dagewesenen Daseins» (SZ 385; BT 437, «into the possibilities of the Dasein that has-been-there»). But what does this mean? The possibilities are the possibilities of an entity in the singular, namely «des dagewesenen Daseins» (SZ 385; «of the Dasein that has-been-there,» BT 437), which one has to equate with «destiny,» «Überlieferung,» that is, with tradition or past. The possibilities of the Dasein that has-been-there are not only those this Dasein actually lived but also those it has not yet lived but is capable of actualizing in the future. Both kinds of possibilities are meant by «Rückgang in Möglichkeiten» (SZ 385; «going back into the possibilities,» BT 437). The reason why Dasein, detaching itself from the «they,» running ahead toward death and surrendering itself to the past, chooses and must choose options for the past that the past itself has not yet actualized is introduced in the next passage: subjugating itself to the past, Dasein has to be «free for the struggle of loyally following in the footsteps of that which can be repeated» (BT 437). The emphasis here is on «struggle.» As is well known from anthropology and sociology, a tradition confronted with a threat to its existence reinterprets itself by intensifying the distinction between friend and foe so as to give rise to the violence that can then be used in the struggle against that foe.

Thus, when in danger of being outstripped by the «they,» the past has to develop possibilities it did not need before. The past has to realize these unrealized possibilities to defend itself against those who are about to destroy it or have already destroyed it.

Thus, we arrive at the exact opposite of Guignon's thesis. According to Guignon, in the light of the utopian ideal there is no single past; rather, what we call the past contains several possibilities, some of which we can choose while rejecting others. In so doing, we dissolve, so to speak, the unity of the past. According to my interpretation, however, there is a strong single past to which we have to subjugate ourselves. The possibilities in plural are the ones for the future into which Dasein has to project itself in order to preserve the past's unity or to regain its existence in the future. Furthermore, Heidegger's passage shows already that out of the subjugation, as a passivity resulting from Dasein's act of detaching itself from the «they,» a new activity of the Dasein arises—the loyal struggle for the past.

Heidegger's text continues:

> But when one has, by repetition, handed down to oneself a possibility that has been, the Dasein that has-been-there is not disclosed in order to be actualized over again. The repeating of that which is possible does not bring again [Wiederbringen] something that is 'past', nor does it bind the 'Present' back to that which has already been 'outstripped'. Arising, as it does, from a resolute projection of oneself, repetition does not let itself be persuaded {überreden} of something by what is 'past', just in order that this, as something which was formerly actual, may recur. (BT 437; SZ 385)[25]

To be sure, Heidegger here says that repetition, as the translators put it, «does not mean either a mere mechanical repetition or an attempt to reconstitute the physical past» (BT 437, n. 1). However, a deliberating conversation with the past in Macquarrie and Robinson's sense is not the only alternative to a «mere mechanical repetition» and «reconstitution of a physical past.» First, authentic repetition is not a «mere mechanical repetition» since ordinary Dasein constantly performs mere mechanical repetitions. Ordinary Dasein without any further thought just takes over and repeats what the «they» has instilled into it. Second, this passage may simply make explicit what, according to my interpretation, is implied in the sentence immediately preceding it, namely, that by repeating the past, Dasein has to develop all those hitherto unrealized possibilities in the past that are necessary to fight for the endangered past. This gives the past a very strong, demanding character vis-à-vis the Dasein, a demanding character Heidegger has already hinted at with the switch to Dasein that «hands itself down {to the possibility it has inherited}» and with the words «struggle» and «loyally» in the preceding sentences and will bring out more clearly through a subtle switch from the prefix «wieder» to the prefix or root, «wider.» Third, independent of this interpretation, ever since Hegel's criticism of the romantic movement, anyone interested in any kind of resurrection of the past, return to the past, or defense of the past against progress, had to defend this project against the charge of nostalgic romanticism. Thus, Heidegger accordingly pays his due by telling readers that «repetition» does not mean a simple return to the past. Again, he will make clear the sense of this negation in the sentences on «erwidert» and «Widerruf.» However, the passage with wiederbringen and überreden has a subtext referring to the idea of the subjugation of Dasein to the past as indicated by the exchange of the two objects of «überliefernd»; this subtext will be even clearer in the subsequent sentences on erwidert and Widerruf.

The German word «überreden» (to talk a person into) is not «überzeugen» (to convince). One überredet others only if one has no good reasons with which to convince them. Now, according to Heidegger, the past does not überreden Dasein. So, might the past überzeugen Dasein? This is the option Macquarrie and Robinson chose. If one says, «I have been überzeugt by,» one regards oneself as a reasonable and autonomous person who cannot be überredet (talked into) but only be convinced by compelling arguments in a free exchange. However, as pointed out above, this would have required Heidegger to use «erwidert vielmehr» (SZ 386; BT 438) in the dative. Thus, since the past does not überzeugen us, we are not autonomous vis-à-vis the past. However, the past does not überreden us either (in that case we would be autonomous too but, so to speak, caught in a moment of inattention). What then does the past do? If überreden is in the middle, and if it is not the extreme überzeugen, it must be the other extreme: «Und bist Du nicht willig, so brauch' ich Gewalt.»[26] It is precisely this violence, or command, that is at the other extreme. What Heidegger says here, then, is that the past does not überzeugen us, and at the same time the past is not in so weak a position that it would need the not quite kosher means of Überredung. Indeed, the past is in a much stronger position, for it has a claim on us. Therefore, the past Heidegger is writing about here is not a vanished past without any claim on us but one that is alive and has a powerful hold on us. This is the reason why Heidegger puts the word «'past'» (BT 438; «"Vergangenheit",» SZ 385) into quotation marks. It is only from the vantage point of those not interested in any sort of resurrection of the past that this past can be said to have disappeared and to have no claims on us anymore. However, this is the perspective of the «they.» From the viewpoint of authentic Dasein, this past has not disappeared at all, but is very present. It is not past at all, and it demands of us that we subjugate ourselves to it and defend or re-realize it. Thus, the way from «nicht . . . überreden» (SZ 386; «not . . . be persuaded,» BT 437) does not lead to überzeugen but rather to überwältigen (overpower, overwhelm).

This is made more explicit in the following sentence with «erwidert»: «Rather, the repetition makes a *reciprocative rejoinder* to {*erwidert*} the possibility of that existence which has-been-there» (BT 438; SZ 386). As mentioned above, Macquarrie and Robinson's interpretation of this sentence as proposing a deliberating conversation with the different ways of having-been-there in the past, or with the different heroes, would be right if Heidegger had used «erwidert» in the dative. Also, the transition from Dasein as «handing down to itself the possibility it has inherited» to Dasein as «resoluteness which . . . hands itself down {to the possibility it has inherited}» (BT 437) shows that there is no conversation with the past. Rather, «erwidert» means either a subjugation to the past or, as Birmingham would have it, a counterattack against the past. However, Heidegger's next sentence makes clear that he does not mean a counterattack.

## D. «*Erwidert*» and «*Widerruf*» («*Disavowal*»)

The different usages of «erwidern» can be summarized in the following scheme. Person A turns to person B and proposes *a* to B. B turns to A (and her *a*) and answers *b*. Thus, B erwidert or makes an Erwiderung. One uses «erwidern» in the dative in cases in which *b* contradicts *a,* as for instance, in statements about disputes, or altercations. In these cases, A and *a* are the dative object of «erwidern,» and *b* is the accusative object of «erwidern» and, most of the time, appears in a subordinate clause. Thus, «A told B to leave the room. However, B erwiderte ihm/ihr (auf seinen/ihren Vorschlag = und ihrem/seinem Vorschlag) (B responded to A [and to A's proposal]) that B would stay in the room.» Or, «A told B that A loved B. However, B erwiderte ihm/ihr (auf seinen/ihren Antrag) (B responded to A [and to A's proposal]) that B didn't love A.» Also in the case of «erwidern» in the accusative in the sense of «to fight back» *b* contradicts *a.* For A attacks B and wants B to be defeated, but B fights back. However, the opposite is the case concerning «erwidern» in the accusative in the sense of «to return a favor» or «to comply with a request.» B erwidert A's call for help only if B actually helps A; that is, if B complies with A's call and thus *b* is in agreement with *a.* In other words, one uses «erwidern» in the sense of «to return a favor» or «to comply with a demand» when one talks about an act in which B identifies himself or herself with A's intention. However, whenever B acts counter to A's intention and thus distances herself from A, one uses «erwidern» in the dative or in the sense of «to fight back.» Since B distances herself from A, the phrase, «B erwiderte ihm/ihr,» is an incomplete sentence. It must be followed by a subordinate clause or some other phrase indicating the *b* that B responds to A. Similarly, a story usually does not end with the sentence, «A attacked B. B erwiderte A's attack.» For one is curious to know what happened next. B might have even defeated A, or A might have launched a second attack. However, since in the case of «erwidern» in the sense of «to return a favor» *b* harmonizes with *a* and meets A's expectation, the phrase «B erwidert A's *a*» can indeed be a complete sentence (as is Heidegger's sentence: «Rather, the repetition *erwidert* the possibility of that existence which has-been-there»). In some cases, it can also close a story, and nothing more is expected. In fact, anything in addition would be just annoying. Therefore, the sequence, «A declared his/her love to B. And B erwiderte A's love» in fairy tales is usually followed only by, «And they lived happily ever after.» If Heidegger thought of «to fight back,» or «to defend oneself successfully,» Birmingham is right. If «B erwidert A's love» is Heidegger's paradigm, then he proposes some happy union between the past and the authentic Dasein. If «B erwidert A's call for help» is Heidegger's paradigm, there would be a union between the past and authentic Dasein, albeit not yet an undisturbed and happy one. Rather, he would say that once one has chosen «the choice which makes one free for the struggle of loyally following in the footsteps of that which can be repeated,» Dasein gets captured by the past, has surrendered itself to the past, or has transformed itself into the medium, or the agent, of the past. This might entail a strong, positive emotional bond, some love or deep affiliation. However, Dasein can not yet really enjoy this love. For this identification, or repetition, is not a mere mechanical repetition of the past without any resistance. Nor is it a reconstitution of a physical past, since, at least for now, the past calls Dasein at the same time into a situation of struggle—struggle against the danger to the past, against the false present that threatens the past's existence or has already destroyed it. The struggle is against the false present ordinary Dasein lives in as long as it has not yet made the choice, the false present that exercises its influence even upon authentic Dasein as long as the latter has not yet destroyed it. That this second option, the Erwiderung of a call for help in a situation of danger, is actually Heidegger's paradigm is clear from his next sentence: «But when such a rejoinder is made to this possibility in a resolution, it is made *in a moment of vision; and as such* it is at the same time a *disavowal* of that which in the "today", is working itself out as the 'past'» (BT 438; SZ 386). As already mentioned, in their accompanying note Macquarrie and Robinson give the German text as well as their interpretation of it as a conversation with the past (BT 438, n. 1). In their note, the German version of the last sentence quoted above reads: «'Die Erwiderung der Möglichkeit im Entschluss ist aber zugleich *als augenblickliche* der *Widerruf* dessen, was in {sic} Heute sich als "Vergangenheit" auswirkt'» (BT 438, n. 1). The «in» instead of «im» is obviously a misprint. The reader should keep in mind that double quotation marks (for instance, «"today",» BT 438) are neither a misprint nor Heidegger's. As the translators explain, «our single quotation marks represent Heidegger's double ones. But we have felt free to introduce double ones of our own wherever we feel that they may be helpful to the reader» (BT 15). Furthermore, in other places Heidegger uses «Heute» (today) with double quotation marks, as for instance in: «Unständig als Man-selbst gegenwärtigt das Dasein sein "Heute"» (SZ 391; thus, Macquarrie and Robinson have: «With the inconstancy of the they-self Dasein makes present its 'today',» BT 443). Macquarrie and Robinson «have chosen the third edition (1931) as typical of the earlier editions, and the eighth (1957) as typical of the later ones» (BT 15). So far, I have quoted the German text from the twelfth edition (1972), which is a reprint of the seventh edition. The translators will perhaps excuse the following train of thought: As they mention in the preface, Heidegger's revisions in later editions of *Sein und Zeit* «went beyond the simple changes in punctuation and citation which Heidegger mentions in his preface» (BT 15). In addition to the misprint in the above quotation, there is also one in the sentence «it becomes a way of painfully detaching oneself from the falling publicness of the 'today"» (BT 449), where an opening single quotation mark has been used instead of the correct double one (see SZ 397). Given all this, one might get the idea that concerning the sentence with Widerruf the translators, typesetters, and proofreaders somehow mixed up all these quotation marks, and that up to the third edition Heidegger might have used «today» with quotation marks and/or «past» without quotation marks, while in later editions he used «today» without quotation marks and «past» with quotation marks. After all, Guignon in his quotation of this sentence left out Heidegger's quotation marks, that is, the single quotation marks of the English translation, at «past,» and he put «today» in single quotation marks: «As critical, authentic historiography requires a *"disavowal"* of that which in the 'today' is working itself out as the past"» (HC 138). Naturally, readers familiar with the Macquarrie and Robinson translation will conclude that the single quotation marks at «today» represent one of the quotation marks added by the translators, while readers not familiar with Macquarrie and Robinson's translation will assume that they represent Heidegger's quotation marks. In addition, both kinds of readers will assume that Heidegger used «Vergangenheit» (past) without quotation marks. In other words, on the basis of Guignon's citation we would expect Heidegger's text either to contain no quotation marks at all or to read as follows: «was im "Heute" sich als Vergangenheit auswirkt.»[27] However, the first edition agrees with the eighth and the ninth editions, namely, «was im Heute sich als "Vergangenheit" auswirkt» (SZ 386). Thus, in this sentence in all the editions Heidegger used «Heute» (today) without his quotation marks and «"Vergangenheit"» («'past'») with his quotation marks.

Now I must apologize to the readers for this digression. It was prompted by the fact that Heidegger makes his point not only by means of the very subtle sequence Wieder-holung (wieder-holen), Er-widerung (er-widern), and Widerruf (wider-rufen) but also, as the readers might already sense, by a very subtle, if not tricky, use of quotation marks. Note that in section 74 up to the sentence with Widerruf Heidegger always uses as the object of «repetition» and similar nouns and verbs either the phrase «the possibility of that existence which-has-been-there» (or, «a possibility that has been») without quotation marks, or he uses «des "Vergangenen"» (SZ 385; «something that is 'past',» BT 437) (or, «das "Überholte"» [SZ 386], «that which has already been 'outstripped'» [BT 437]) with quotation marks. In the sentence with Erwiderung, he uses the former expression (the repetition erwidert «the possibility of that existence which has-been-there,» BT 438; SZ 386), and he also does so in the first part of the sentence with Widerruf («But when such a rejoinder is made to this possibility . . .» [BT 438; SZ 386]). However, with regard to the object of the Widerruf he doesn't use any of those expressions, but rather for the first time the phrase, «dessen, was im Heute sich als "Vergangenheit" auswirkt» (SZ 386; thus, since the translators use single quotation marks for Heidegger's double ones, and since they prefer double quotation marks for «today,» their sentence reads: «of that which in the "today", is working itself out as the 'past'» [BT 438]). For Birmingham, there is obviously no difference between Heidegger's «erwidert» and his «disavowal» («Widerruf»).[28] Now, she might be right if Heidegger had said «Widerruf der Vergangenheit» («disavowal of the past») or «Widerruf der gewesenen Möglichkeit» («disavowal of the possibility that-has-been-there»). Each phrase might have been the climax in the sequence beginning with «But when one has . . .» (BT 437; SZ 385), and might have entitled us to read «*erwidert* . . . die» in «*erwidert* vielmehr die Möglichkeit der dagewesenen Existenz» (SZ 386; BT 438) as one of those instances of «erwidern» in the accusative meaning «to fight back» or «to launch a counterattack.»

The entire passage would then say: repetition does not simply repeat the past; rather, it fights back, defends itself against the past («erwidert»), and it even fights back and cancels, destroys, the past («disavowal»). However, if that is what Heidegger wanted to convey, it would have been necessary for him to make unambiguously clear that the object of the Erwiderung and the object of the Widerruf is one and the same. Regarding the sentence with Widerruf, this would have required two things. First, he would have had to use a conjunction clearly indicating that the sentence with Widerruf intensifies the sentence with erwidert. Quite naturally, the conjunction «ja, sogar» (nay) (or only «sogar» [even]) would have recommended itself. However, Heidegger doesn't use «ja, sogar» or a similar expression. Rather, he uses the conjunction «aber zugleich» («But . . . at the same time»), which most of the time introduces a new point or a counter move to the one in the preceding sentence. Second, in an extremely relaxed mode of writing «aber zugleich» might indeed be used in the sense of «nay.» However, in the case of «ja, sogar» and especially in the case of «aber zugleich» in the sense of «ja, sogar» Heidegger would have had to use as the objects of erwidern and Widerruf the same expression or sufficiently similar ones to make sure that the readers understand that the object of Widerruf is identical with the object of erwidern. He could have easily done so by saying, for instance, «der Widerruf eben dieser Möglichkeit» («the disavowal of that very/same possibility [we have talked about in the sentence with erwidert and the phrase with Erwiderung]»). However, Heidegger says no such thing.

Rather, he uses «aber zugleich,» and he uses the phrase «Widerruf dessen, was im Heute sich als "Vergangenheit" auswirkt» (SZ 386). This use shows that the object of the «Widerruf» («disavowal») differs from the object of the Erwiderung in the sentence with «erwidert.»[29] Now, the «Heute» is the present as seen by authentic Dasein.[30] If the object of «erwidert» is the past as heritage and community of the people, and if the object of «erwidert» differs from the object of the «Widerruf,» the object of the «Widerruf»—that is, that «was im Heute sich als "Vergangenheit" auswirkt»—is, as I will elaborate further in chapters 2 and 3, not «destiny» or «community, of {the} people» (BT 436; SZ 384), but Dasein as ordinary or what determines ordinary Dasein or the past with reference to which ordinary Dasein legitimates its way of life. This past has to be destroyed by the authentic Dasein, since this past is not the «real» one. Heidegger uses «Heute» without quotation marks and «"Vergangenheit"» with quotation marks because this past is not the real past but rather what ordinary or inauthentic Dasein regards as the real past.[31] This train of thought might be paraphrased as follows: Having been recalled from ordinary existence, and having made oneself free for destiny, people, and community of the people— that is, having transformed oneself into the echo of this «real» past, namely, community of the people and destiny—one is called upon to destroy the present, or that «false» past or tradition that has replaced the «real» past. The «false» past or tradition has established itself as the «real» past and as the «real» present with reference to which ordinary and inauthentic Daseine legitimate their way of living. In resoluteness, Dasein experiences the demanding call of the «real» past, which has been destroyed by the «false» past and present. The «real» past calls upon Dasein to rerealize it. This requires that the «false» past and present must be destroyed to make room for the rebirth of the «real» past.

The same point can be made without reference to the quotation marks. «Erwidern» is an ambiguous term; first, it can be regarded as an act of negation of any claim the past might have on me, a very strong negation, as in Birmingham; second, the translators and Guignon pluralize, so to speak, the claims in question and thus, as it were, soften the character of this negation. Within the conversation with the past that has become pluralized by Dasein's utopian ideals, several possibilities are rejected and one is adopted. Since the adoption of one possibility presupposes the refusal of all the others and since the plurality of offers made by the past is the result of Dasein's capacity to distance itself from the present and the past as it lives on in the present, this second interpretation too emphasizes the aspect of negation, as distancing, despite the fact that, in contrast to Birmingham's interpretation, it assumes that, finally, Dasein positively identifies itself with some possibility offered by the past. Third, «erwidert vielmehr» means not some act of negation of the past, but rather the submission to the past. «Widerruf,» however, is unambiguously an act of negation. It is a stronger negation than «erwidern» and is, in fact, the strongest and most intense expression of negation in academic discourse, calling to mind that a Widerruf was required of Galileo and other heretics if they wanted to avoid being sentenced to death.

Thus, a Widerruf is a complete cancellation of the object of this Widerruf. What has to be disavowed must be canceled completely, never resurface again. Since «Widerruf» is a stronger negation than «erwidert,» one might say that both refer to one and the same possibility offered by the past. However, as was said above, in that case Heidegger would have had to apply the two mentioned devices, in the ways described above, to make sure that readers understand that the object of the Widerruf is identical with that of the Erwiderung.

Therefore, one must not conflate the object of «erwidert» and that of «Widerruf.» Rather, authentic Dasein «erwidert» (to) *a* and makes a «Widerruf» of *b*, with *b* being different from *a*. Guignon makes this distinction when he interprets «erwidert» as referring to possibilities within the past and interprets as the object of the «Widerruf» the present in which Dasein has lived while it was still ordinary and did not yet relate to the past as a pool of choices for authentic Dasein:

> Instead, for Heidegger, critique is aimed at the "today": authentic historiography "becomes a way in which the 'today' gets deprived of its character as present; in other words, it becomes a way of painfully detaching oneself from the fallen {*sic*} publicness of the 'today'" (*BT,* 449). As critical, authentic historiography requires a "*disavowal* of that which in the 'today' is working itself out as the past," that is, a "destructuring" of the hardened interpretations circulating in the public world in order to recover "those primordial experiences in which we achieved our first ways of determining the nature of Being—the ways which have guided us ever since" (*BT,* 438, 44). The critical stance "*deprives* the 'today' of its character *as present,* and weans one from the conventionalities of the 'they'" (*BT,* 444). (HC 138)

Being capable of going «right under the eyes of Death» (BT 434; SZ 383), I realize that the past offers several heroes. In the light of my utopian ideal I choose, not Socrates or Martin Luther King, but rather Sitting Bull (HC 137). This act includes that I disavow, not Sitting Bull, but rather, say, my career on Wall Street, which my family and my peer group have prompted me to engage in before I ran «right under the eyes of Death» (BT 434; SZ 382), turned back, and realized that there were several heroes to choose from. Guignon developed his interpretation of «erwidert» since he wanted to argue against the «"decisionism of empty resoluteness"» (HC 130) that would result if Dasein «erwidert» in the sense of «negates» and makes a «Widerruf»; that is, he wanted to argue against an interpretation in which Dasein, as in Birmingham, exclusively negates, regardless of whether the objects of the two acts of negation are the same or not. Though one might say that the two sentences themselves don't exclude the possibility that Dasein, in this or that way, negates («erwidert») something and disavows («Widerruf») something else, Guignon is right in implicitly rejecting this interpretation. For, as I will show in chapters 2 and 3, the context of these two sentences precludes their interpretation as two negations. However, Guignon's own interpretation cannot be right because, as mentioned above, his version of «erwidert» requires the dative. Thus, since «Widerruf» is unmistakably a negation, one is left with «erwidert» not as negation but rather as submission. Since—pace Birmingham—the object of the Erwiderung differs from the object of the Widerruf and since—pace Guignon as well as Birmingham—Dasein submits itself to the past, Dasein submits itself to the suppressed or vanished «real» past, and Dasein cancels all the possibilities of the present it has lived in complacently before the call. The call demands that Dasein hand itself over to the call—that is, to «the possibility of that existence which has-been-there»—and cancel the possibilities Dasein has lived in while still in the mode of the «they,» that is, cancel «that which in the "today" is working itself out as the 'past'» (BT 438; SZ 386).

In his discussion of guilt Heidegger rejects the model of pre-Christian χάρις, grace, and the model of just exchange as being the ordinary, or inauthentic, interpretation of guilt.[32] Furthermore, the use of «erwidern» in the accusative in the sense of «to fight back» usually indicates that there may be some sort of violence or coercion at work. Leaving aside the echo,[33] since it refers to inanimate beings, one might say that all the other examples of «erwidern» in the accusative do indeed show some sort of obligation but only a relatively weak one. In a somewhat frivolous interpretation of «erwidern» in the accusative, one might even say its paradigmatic use is in the following casual[34] situation: On the street, en passant person A looks at person B, and, en passant, B looks back at A, just for some sort of tiny flirtation. In German, one would refer to this situation by «erwidern» in the accusative: «B erwiderte A's glance.»[35] Thus, in that case «erwidern» in the accusative means some small exchange in passing, enjoyable for both parties, or it means some sort of weak obligation. Therefore, one must not insinuate, as I did, that in Heidegger it would mean violence, subjugation, and the like. However, I might erwidern, one also uses the phrase «B erwidert A's glance» if this is, as the saying goes, «love at first sight.» Nonetheless, one might erwidern, love—whether sexual, erotic, agapic, or anything else and whether lukewarm or as passionate as imaginable—is not an issue, neither in *Being and Time* in general nor in the chapter on historicality in particular. However, I might erwidern, do we really know what was at work in Heidegger's love for the Black Forest and the Volksgemeinschaft? In his love for the «Volksgemeinschaft»—the composite of «Gemeinschaft, des Volkes» (SZ 384; «the community, of {the} people,» BT 436)—the word commonly used on the extreme Right? Furthermore (in order that in this exchange of Erwiderungen—to translate word-for-word a German phrase—«I have the last word»): First, as in the case of «überreden,» the possible negations of χάρις not only lead to a level of obligation lower than that in the usual institutions of grace. Heidegger is great at intensifying the meanings of words by their context, great in producing a Stimmung (mood) that pervades the entire text without being in any particular single word. Second, even if one takes only the passage in question, «erwidert» receives additional intensity due to the «Widerruf» following it. For, as mentioned above, in academic discourse, of all the words for an act of negation, Widerruf is the most intense and forceful. Third «erwidert» and «Widerruf» accrue additional force from the surrounding «struggle» and so forth, which in turn get intensified by the entire sequence of sections 72–77 and its context, which I turn to in the next chapter. «Period! No Er-wider-ung! (or: No Wider-rede! No Wider-spruch!) At least for the time being.»[36]

**2**

# Being and Time,
# Sections 72–77

## A. On the Run

In *Being and Time* Heidegger elucidates the structures and activities of Dasein that make it possible for Dasein to be in a world. In the conventional metaphysical fashion, Heidegger develops a hierarchical order of these structures according to different degrees of primordiality. Within this hierarchy, the level of historicality is the most primordial one, that is, historicality is the ultimate level. In accordance with this hierarchical order, Heidegger unfolds a drama, the drama of Dasein's historicality. Again in quite a conventional fashion, the drama consists of three acts. There is a first act, in which the necessary conditions of the dramatic conflict are set up. In the second act, a critical situation emerges that calls for a dramatic solution. In the third act, finally, we witness the solution of the crisis Heidegger recommends. This third act of the drama is section 74. In this sense, the entire book *Being and Time,* as Rockmore says, «as a whole culminates in» the section on historicality.[1] The privileged position of section 74 within the hierarchical as well as the dramatic order shows that, indeed, as Rockmore puts it,

Heidegger's conception of ontology commits him, as a condition of thinking through the problem of the meaning of "Being," to a political understanding of human being, that is, to an idea of the person as mainly inauthentic but as possibly authentic in a concrete fashion. The very concern with fundamental ontology requires a political turn since an authentic thought of Being can only arise on the basis of concrete authenticity. Heidegger's concern with the problem of the meaning of Being is not apolitical; nor is it indifferent to theory and practice in virtue of its concern with the *Seinsfrage*. Rather, the concern with "Being" is itself intrinsically political.[2]

In chapter 1, I examined two of the three parts of the solution of the drama presented in section 74, the first part, the «anticipatory resoluteness» (BT 434; SZ 382) and then the end of the third part—the passage on erwidern and Widerruf—and the entire third part. As I have already shown there, the solution of the drama consists in authentic Dasein stepping out of the world in which it has been living so far as ordinary Dasein and then turning back to this world and canceling it. It does so because it has been called upon by the past to rerealize the past, which has been pushed aside by the world in which Dasein as ordinary Dasein has been living, and the past cannot be rerealized without ordinary Dasein's world being canceled. This motif suggests that Heidegger's concept of historicality is informed by a temporalized version of a metaphysics of falling and recovering. There was a state in which the origin was properly realized. However, then a development began in which the world of the Daseine fell away from that state. A new world emerged in which the origin is no longer present or is present only in a distorted way. At some point in this downward plunge, the origin raises its voice and demands that the Daseine disavow and destroy the new world and replace it with a world in which the origin is once again properly present.

As to the metaphysical aspect of this theory, one must keep in mind several important points, however. Traditional metaphysics—maybe with the exception of Plato in Syracuse—and, for that matter, Christianity never presumed to fully realize the origin here on earth. Heidegger's metaphysics definitely transgresses this limit of traditional metaphysics. Furthermore, one must keep in mind that in the twenties of this century fundamental ontology and metaphysics were definitely not the only philosophical options. That is not to say that Heidegger's philosophy was prone to Nazism because of the old metaphysical motifs continued in his philosophy. Rather, Heidegger revitalized a radicalized or distorted version of metaphysics at a time when there was certainly no need for doing so. Furthermore, we could also leave out the notion of metaphysics. For, as will become clear in chapter 3, Heidegger's concept of historicality is identical with the right-wing one of history and politics. As to the genesis of this latter concept, however, it doesn't seem very reasonable—to me at least—to regard it as a manifestation of the epoch of metaphysics in the way Heideggerians use that term. Moreover, as I will explain in more detail in chapters 3 and 4, one must keep in mind that the right-wing concept of history is not teleological in the same sense the development of a plant through its different phases might be considered teleological. There is nothing in the new world, which is now canceled, that is necessary for the proper rerealization of the origin. Correspondingly, there is nothing in the new world that deserves to be preserved in the world of the properly realized origin. If it happens that the world of the properly realized origin takes on features of the world that is canceled, this is merely a matter of convenience and generosity on the part of the origin. In this section of this chapter 2, I examine several more general concepts of Heidegger's in *Being and Time*—those of origin, primordial temporality, authenticity, and wholeness—and their dynamics in regard to the concept of historicality. In section B, I take up passages and concepts from Division One of *Being and Time*[3] as well as from the section on historicality preceding section 74—those of the work of ambiguity and the different meanings of the terms «world» and «history»—by means of which Heidegger makes clear that, indeed, at the beginning of section 74 we are in the second part of the drama of historicality. In section C, I show that in the second part of section 74—the section on heritage, fate, etc.—the second part of the drama is briefly summarized and the third part begins to unfold whose end in the third part of section 74 I have already discussed in chapter 1.

In section 73 Heidegger develops what he calls «the ordinary understanding of history, and Dasein's historizing» (BT 429; SZ 378); section 74 is entitled "The Basic Constitution of Historicality" (BT 434; SZ 382). De facto, Heidegger develops authentic historicality in this section. In the last paragraph of section 74, Heidegger leads into section 75 by saying that we have to study «Dasein's inauthentic historicality» (BT 439; SZ 387) in order to complete the exposition of the ontological problem of history. Thus, in section 75 ("Dasein's Historicality, and World-History," BT 439; SZ 387) he elucidates inauthentic historicality. Already from this brief outline we might expect that in the entire passage Heidegger describes something like a crisis, a κρίσις in the Greek sense, namely, a separation or a decision or the decisive turning point in a political development or in the course of a disease. The combatants—political parties opposed to each other or the «forces of life» versus the «forces of death»—are pitted against each other in the decisive battle. Within ordinary Dasein's historizing as developed in section 73 there is a more or less hidden potential or conflict that gives rise to the two opposite modes of Dasein, its authentic and its inauthentic historicality. This is the aspect I want to focus on.

However, a few preliminary remarks are necessary. In the first four paragraphs of section 72 («All our efforts . . . when we learn not to take problems too lightly,» BT 424–425; SZ 372–373), Heidegger exposes the problem of the «'connectedness of life'» (BT 425; «"Zusammenhang des Lebens",» SZ 373). In the next three paragraphs («What seems 'simpler' . . . 'between' birth and death will break down,» BT 425–426; SZ 373–374), he characterizes the ordinary interpretation of the connectedness of life. In the two paragraphs after that («Dasein does not fill up . . . *ontological* understanding of *historicality*,» BT 426–427; SZ 374–375), he presents his concept that «Dasein *is stretched along and stretches itself along*» (BT 427; «*erstrecktes Sicherstrecken,*» SZ 375) as the proper approach to the problem of the connectedness of life. He then continues toward the formulation of his thesis that Dasein «*exists historically and can so exist only because it is temporal in the very basis of its Being {im Grunde seines Seins}*» (BT 428; SZ 376), and outlines what is to follow. The sections 72–77, and especially the first four paragraphs of section 72, are replete with references to inauthentic Dasein and authentic Dasein and to «Dasein's authentic potentiality-for-Being-a-whole» («das eigentliche Ganzseinkönnen des Daseins»), «its authentically *Being-a-whole*» («seines eigentlichen *Ganzseins*»), or «Dasein's totality» («Daseinsganzheit,» «Ganzheit des Daseins»). Moreover, Heidegger uses «ursprünglich» («primordial») several times.

«Ursprünglich» is an adjective to the noun «Ursprung» (origin) (whose abstract noun, «Ursprünglichkeit,» as Hildegard Feick rightly says in her *Index to Being and Time*, «runs through» the entire book[4]). It has been pointed out often enough that Heidegger understands Dasein neither as a substance nor as a subject, each of which has being independent of its activities and relations to others. Rather, Dasein is a set of structured activities, or motions, that already include the Being-with-others. For that reason, many interpreters claim that *Being and Time* is not a philosophy of origin; a claim that depends entirely on how one defines such a philosophy. I agree with those who maintain that from Division Two on (BT 274ff.; SZ 231ff.), if not already earlier, the discourse on Dasein's activities gets overdetermined by what one cannot help calling a kind of philosophy of origin, along the lines of a Neoplatonist or, for that matter, Christian discourse on the relation of the One and the many.

Heidegger uses «ursprünglich» («primordial»), or its comparative form «ursprünglicher,» in reference to his project, that is, his interpretation of Dasein as well as in reference to the object of his interpretation. An interpretation is the more «ursprünglich» the more «ursprünglich» its object is (SZ 231ff.; BT 274ff.). Concerning the claim that *Being and Time* is not a philosophy of origin, it is often pointed out that «Ursprung» or «ursprünglich» has a new meaning in Heidegger completely different from the traditional one. Ursprung is no longer a primary being essentially at rest and out of which other beings originate. Rather, Ursprung is the original leap, the first leap, as an activity that no longer depends on an Ursprung in the traditional sense. Consider, however, the following passage: «If, therefore, we demonstrate that the 'time' which is accessible to Dasein's common sense is *not* primordial, but arises rather from authentic temporality {*nicht* ursprünglich und vielmehr entspringend aus der eigentlichen Zeitlichkeit}, then, in accordance with the principle, "*a potiori fit denominatio*", we are justified in designating as "*primordial time*" {*ursprüngliche Zeit*} the *temporality* which we have now laid bare» (BT 377; SZ 329). As the reference to a sentence developed within metaphysical ordo-thinking already indicates, this statement assumes a hierarchical structure. Here the Ursprung as a leap is the emergence of the time that is accessible to Dasein's common sense. This leap, however, presupposes something out of or from which it emerges and without which it could not emerge, namely, authentic temporality. Because of this ranking, Heidegger labels authentic temporality «ursprüngliche Zeit,» that is, primary, primordial time, the first, or origin out of which other beings or structures and activities «entspringen» (arise).

To be sure, this first principle, or origin, is not a substance at rest. Rather, it is the structure of the basic activity by means of which Dasein is open to other beings, the basic act of transcendence; it is this structure and this activity itself. Furthermore, this «ursprüngliche Zeit» temporalizes itself in the «equiprimordiality» (BT 378; «Gleichursprünglichkeit,» SZ 329) of the three ecstases past, present, and future. However, all this, as is well-known from Neoplatonism and Christian philosophy, can easily go hand in hand with ordo, with a hierarchy of several entities that, in this or that way, entspringen (arise) from the first origin. One finds in Heidegger also the ambivalence concerning what entspringt from the first origin in this kind of philosophy of origin. On the one hand, what entspringt is the manifestation of the origin itself. It is the origin's way to realize itself and to rule over its manifestations.[5] On the other hand, what entspringt from the origin removes itself, or deviates, from the origin. As the power of the origin weakens, the origin loses its ruling power until finally what ist entsprungen, has jumped out of/from the origin comes close to being nothing or even covers up its relation to the origin and that origin itself. *Being and Time* is rich in sentences about this double aspect of what ist entsprungen from the origin.

Heidegger may have chosen «entspringen» because of the ambiguity inherent in the verb itself. It denotes the aspect of manifestation, of strength and ruling of the origin over its manifestations, just as water entspringt (from) its source and is thus the manifestation of this source or is this origin itself. For pointing to the water flowing out of its source one also says, «The source entspringt»; that is, the flowing water is the source itself in its process of manifestation. At the same time, however, what entspringt (ent-leaps, ent-jumps), leaps out of and leaves the dominion of the origin just as a rivulet silts up as soon as the source has exhausted itself and vanished. This is the other aspect of entspringen, namely, a separation from the origin. The German prefix «ent» often indicates an act of separation. In section A of chapter 1, I already mentioned the acts of separation inherent in an Entscheidung (Ent-separation, decision, Ent-parting) and in Entschlossenheit (resoluteness).

There are many German words consisting of the prefix «ent-» and a verb indicating movement; generally they refer to a separation or loss and emphasize that, at least from the vantage point of the origin, of what is left behind, the separation is involuntary or illegitimate. Something «ent-gleitet (ent-glides, ent-slides, ent-slips, escapes) meinen Händen,» that is, it «slips from my hands.» Some inconsiderate remark «ent-gleitet,» or «ent-fährt (ent-drives, escapes) meinem Mund, meinen Lippen,» that is, «slips from my mouth, my lips.» Some fact «ent-zieht (ent-draws, ent-pulls, ent-tucks, escapes) sich meiner Kenntnis (knowledge),» that is, «it is unknown to me.» Or something «ent-schwindet (ent-dwindles, ent-wanes) meinem Blick,» that is, «vanishes from my sight.» Or, using the perfect participle of «entspringen,» namely, «entsprungen,» one might say, «However, the flea ist mir wieder entsprungen» as the ending of a story about the unsuccessful hunt for a flea in which I had already grasped the critter between my fingers, but it managed to jump away. Similarly, prisoners who have escaped from jail are referred to as «die entsprungenen Häftlinge.» Of course, these prisoners do not want to be seen again by the origin, the place they came from and its agents. They want to hide themselves and their relation to the origin from the origin itself, from other Daseine, and from themselves as well insofar as by their flight from prison they maintain that this origin has no claim on them. In this regard, one might also point to the composite of «ent-» and the root of the verb discussed in section A of chapter I above, namely, «ent-laufen» (ent-run). Dogs, slaves, teenagers, and prisoners «entlaufen ihrem Herrn, ihren Eltern, dem Gefängnis,» that is, «run away from their master, their parents, the prison» and thus «ent-ziehen (ent-draw, ent-pull, ent-tug, ent-haul, escape) sich deren Herrschaft,» that is, «put themselves out of their control, domination.» The prisoner's jailbreak is referred to as «sie sind dem Gefängnis entsprungen» or «sie sind aus dem Gefängnis entlaufen.» (they have jumped out of prison, have escaped prison). On the news you might hear that «die entsprungenen Häftlinge sind immer noch auf der Flucht,» or «die entsprungenen Häftlinge sind immer noch flüchtig» (The escaped prisoners are still on the run).

In section 68, in the subsection entitled "The Temporality of Falling {des Verfallens}" (BT 396; SZ 346), Heidegger uses these terms to characterize the temporality of the ordinary and inauthentic mode of curiosity, and he puts «entspringen» in quotation marks (rendered in the translation as single quotation marks) to indicate the sense of the forbidden leaping away. I will quote only some of the several occurrences of «entspringen» with quotation marks in this context: «The Present 'arises or leaps away' {"entspringt"} from the awaiting which belongs to it, and it does so in the sense of running away from it, as we have just emphasized {in dem betonten Sinne des Entlaufens}. . . . This 'leaping away' {Das "Entspringen"} is rather an ecstatical modification of awaiting, and of such a kind that the awaiting *leaps after* {*nachspringt*} the making-present» (BT 397–398; SZ 347).[6]

This «*nachspringt*» means that curiosity cannot catch, cannot keep up with, what it wants to catch. Thus, what curiosity wants to catch entspringt curiosity; that is, it backs out of curiosity's grasp and its memory: «In the 'leaping away' {Im "Entspringen"} of the Present, one also forgets increasingly» (BT 398; SZ 347). Going back to the entsprungene or entlaufene (escaped) prisoners, one might say that if they manage to escape the police, they have managed «sich dem Blick der Polizei zu entziehen» (to hide from the police's sight). As to death, authentic Dasein, as already quoted, «will go right under the eyes of Death» (BT 434; SZ 382). Ordinary and inauthentic Daseine, however, behave like these escaped prisoners: «As a mode of temporalizing, the 'leaping-away' {"Entspringens"} of the Present is grounded in the essence of temporality, which is *finite*. Having been thrown into Being-towards-death, Dasein flees—proximally and for the most part—in the face of this thrownness, which has been more or less explicitly revealed {flieht . . . vor . . . dieser . . . Geworfenheit}» (BT 399; SZ 348).[7] Thus, it flees its «Ursprung»: «The Present leaps away from {entspringt} its authentic future and from its authentic having been, so that it lets Dasein come to its authentic existence only by taking a detour through that Present. The 'leaping-away' of the Present—that is, the falling into lostness—has its source in that primordial authentic temporality itself which makes possible thrown Being-towards-death {Der Ursprung des "Entspringens" der Gegenwart . . . ist die ursprüngliche, eigentliche Zeitlichkeit selbst}» (BT 399; SZ 348).[8]

The tone of this passage is highly derogatory. In my brief digression on the several uses of «ent-,» I left open whether the prisoners might manage to escape the police. Heidegger, however, presents the actions of curiosity as very clumsy and not promising of a successful outcome. At the same time, the last sentence quoted shows that Heidegger, as Guignon rightly points out, works with the old model of a «*mythos* of pristine beginnings, a time of "falling," and a final recovery of origins» (HC 141).[9] Heidegger could have used a different vocabulary, for instance, «sich entwickeln aus,» «entstehen aus,» «sich konkretisieren als,» «sich ableiten von,» «sich darstellen als,» or something similar. However, that terminology would not have allowed him to phrase his project rhetorically in terms of basic motifs of metaphysical thinking; that is, in terms of an origin that is left behind or forgotten in an illegitimate act, so to speak, and that demands obedience, punishes the leap away from it, and brings Dasein back to its origin. To summarize, what entspringt (arises) from something as from its origin is a manifestation of the origin, or even the origin itself. At the same time, however, it is a weak manifestation of, a desertion or apostasy from, and a distortion of the origin. It covers up its relation to the origin and pretends to be something in its own right. It is this double aspect of what entspringt combined with what is also familiar from Neoplatonism and Christian philosophy, namely, the demand to represent in thought and in one's conscience the relation to one's origin in an undistorted manner that taints the sphere of ordinary Dasein's historizing with that twilight that is critical and calls for a decision. Ordinary Dasein is living in the twilight of arising from and depending on a past that, at the same time, this ordinary Dasein denies. Thus, the origin, the past, calls upon ordinary Dasein to no longer deny its origin but to acknowledge it in present Daseine, in the sphere of the «they,» and to struggle for its revitalization in the sphere of Being-with-others.

Heidegger was no Platonist or Neoplatonist. Neither was he a believer in the official God of the Catholic Church. When he wrote *Being and Time,* he had already sich entzogen dem (withdrawn from) Catholicism (Entziehungskur = detoxification treatment).[10] Being is essentially temporal. There is no eternity, no being beyond time. This, however, does not prevent Heidegger from, so to speak, temporalizing the basic structures of metaphysics. As I have already suggested in chapter I and as I will elaborate also in this and the following chapters, the One Heidegger assumes is the Volksgemeinschaft, which is within time and whose sempiternity is in danger. A similar usage of temporalized metaphysics can be found in his treatment of Ganzheit (being a whole). In his discussion of death in sections 46–53, Heidegger refers to the metaphysical concept of Ganzheit of temporal beings as it was developed based on the distinction between eternity (beyond time) and time or temporal beings. A temporal being has achieved Ganzheit if it has realized all the characters it is capable of realizing or has to realize due to its nature. However, it does not do this prior to its death. In and after death, however, as Heidegger rightly points out, this being no longer exists, at least those who do not believe in the immortality of the soul say that it no longer exists. Thus, one might expect Heidegger to give up Ganzheit (so to speak, to leap out of metaphysics into postmodern fragmentation) or to develop a concept of Dasein that allows for Dasein's continuous striving for Ganzheit but that does not require that this Ganzheit of Dasein, as the primordial existentiale, already preexists Dasein's endeavor to achieve it. However, Heidegger temporalizes Ganzheit, which in this case means that Ganzheit is always already present within Dasein's being, to the effect that achieving Ganzheit does not mean to produce something new but rather to get in touch with something already given.

Ordinary or inauthentic Dasein covers up its origin, death, and thus does not achieve Ganzheit, whereas authentic Dasein does achieve it by bringing itself into the proper relation to its origin, to death, which is then no longer covered up. By doing so and by relating itself to its «real» origin, that is, to «heritage» and «destiny» (BT 435f.; SZ 383f.), Dasein enters the state of «Eigentlichkeit» («authenticity») or «eigentliche Existenz» («authentic existence») in which it no longer vacillates. All those who maintain that, as «Ursprünglichkeit» in general, «Eigentlichkeit» in particular does not mean primarily a state but rather an activity, namely, Dasein's activity of appropriating the structures at work in its existence, can hardly claim that Heidegger has chosen his terms carefully. For, as I already discussed in section A of chapter I with regard to «Entschlossenheit» («resoluteness»), the German suffix «-keit,» or «-heit,» indicates a state or condition. For instance, «Beweglichkeit» (mobility, the condition of being able to be moved [by oneself], movableness; also used metaphorically) is that state—or in Aristotelian terms, ἕξις—that enables one to move oneself or be moved by others easily. Looking at German translations of Plato or Aristotle from any period shows that words with the suffix «-keit,» or «-heit,» (Gerechtigkeit, Schönheit, Tapferkeit, etc.) are used as translations of Plato's ideas or, in terms of Aristotle's *Categories*, as translations of instances of secondary substances or of one of the other nine categories whenever Aristotle abstracts from their being present within a primary substance. Heidegger could have used other expressions. He could have said, «die Tätigkeit des sich zu Eigen Machens» (the activity of appropriation), «das Sich-zu-eigen-machen» (ditto), «die Aneignung» (the appropriation) or something similar, or he could have commented on Eigentlichkeit in terms of these phrases. Thus, if he had wanted to focus on an activity, his terminology is completely misleading. It is thus more likely that «Eigentlichkeit» refers primarily to a state or habit and only secondarily to the activities necessary to achieve this state or those concomitant with it.[11]

## B. Anschwellender Bocksgesang

At the beginning of section 73 Heidegger points to an ambiguity in the term «history» («this term may mean the 'historical actuality' {"geschichtliche Wirklichkeit"} as well as the possible science of it»), stating that «we shall provisionally eliminate the signification of 'history' in the sense of a "science of history" (historiology)» (BT 430; SZ 378). That is, in sections 73–75 Heidegger is talking about Dasein's historical actuality, and only in sections 76–77 does he discuss the science of this historical actuality. If Dasein's authentic historicality is characterized by the act of repetition, we might expect that inauthentic Dasein does not repeat. This is implied in section 74 and is explicitly stated in the penultimate paragraph of section 75 («In inauthentic historicality, . . . the "they" evades choice. Blind for possibilities, it cannot repeat what has been, . . . it seeks the modern. But when historicality is authentic, it understands history as the 'recurrence' of the possible, and knows that a {die} possibility will recur only if existence is open for it fatefully, in a moment of vision, in resolute repetition» [BT 443f.; SZ 391f.]).[12] If «repetition» and «the modern» make up a clear contrast, we might say that to perform a «repetition» and to seek the «modern» are the outcome of the crisis that is potentially present within ordinary Dasein's historizing. Heidegger likes metaphors of vertical movement («Fallen, fall,» «Absturz, downward plunge»), and in terms of spatial imagery, he would see authentic Dasein moving upward, inauthentic Dasein moving downward. We move upward only if we have to bridge a distance to a higher level. Thus, ordinary Dasein has already fallen and is still falling. However, it does so in a different way than inauthentic Dasein. In a horizontal image, authentic Dasein would move backward while inauthentic Dasein proceeds forward along the time line. Heidegger's vertical image might be inappropriate because it is too reminiscent of the metaphysical framework of time and eternity and of the efforts of metaphysical philosophers to transcend time and to return to, or assimilate themselves to, the One, or God. The horizontal image isn't appropriate either because even for the Heidegger of sections 72–77 «time goes by,» and no

Dasein can physically move backward in time. However, we can remove the flaw from the horizontal image and, at the same time, integrate the temporalized vertical image, that is, its temporalized hierarchical structure, if we assume that the return to the past is not a physical but rather a mental step— one toward the past as present in the present time and which will lead to the past being rerealized in the future.

However, I would like to briefly touch upon two additional points before discussing sections 72–77. In section 73 Heidegger says that a particular «*world* is no longer» (BT 432; SZ 380), and in section 74 he characterizes the «possibilities of existence which 'circulate' in the 'average' public way of interpreting Dasein today» in the following way: «These possibilities have mostly been made unrecognizable by ambiguity; yet they are well known to us» (BT 435; SZ 383).[13] By «world» («Welt»), Heidegger means the third of the four senses of the word developed in sections 14ff. The first two refer to entities that are not Daseine and to their being (BT 93; SZ 64). In the third meaning, the term signifies «that '*wherein*' a factical Dasein as such can be said to 'live'. "World" has here a pre-ontological existentiell signification. Here again there are different possibilities: "world" may stand for the 'public' we-world, or one's 'own' closest (domestic) environment {Umwelt}» (BT 93; SZ 65). A world in this sense is not something present-at-hand or ready-to-hand. Rather, it is the result of all those practices of Dasein, or of a group of Daseine, that enable them in their average everydayness to encounter other beings within a framework or within a horizon that relates all these beings to each other and to the Dasein and provides them with significance for the Dasein or for a group of Daseine. Or a world is that entity, or Being, that determines how Daseine can encounter other beings. As he says a few pages later, «the world itself is not an entity within-the world; and yet it is so determinative for such entities that only in so far as 'there is' a world can they be encountered and show themselves, in their Being, as entities which have been discovered» (BT 102; SZ 72). These worlds can and, in fact, do change. However, according to Heidegger, all these worlds share some basic structures that make a world as such possible. For this, Heidegger uses the term «worldhood» («Weltlichkeit»), the fourth meaning of «"world",» namely: «the ontologico-existential concept of *worldhood*. Worldhood itself may have as its modes whatever structural wholes any special 'worlds' may have at the time; but it embraces in itself the *a priori* character of worldhood in general» (BT 93; SZ 65).

In the remaining chapters of Division One, Heidegger elaborates the existentiales that make a world possible.[14] With reference to situations such as a craftsman hammering in his workshop or a writer writing books at his desk, Heidegger develops the existentiale «involvement and significance» (BT 114ff.; «Bewandtnis und Bedeutsamkeit,» SZ 83ff.). As to the second point— the «possibilities of existence which 'circulate' in the 'average' public way of interpreting Dasein today»—in chapter 4 (BT 149ff.; SZ 113ff.) he emphasizes that Dasein is not a subject existing independently of others but rather that «Dasein in itself is essentially Being-with» (BT 156; SZ 120). To be sure, in his analysis of the mode of the «they» (BT 163ff.; SZ 126ff.) Heidegger is not necessarily contemptuous of that mode. Each group of Daseine needs the mode of «they» as the «who» of Dasein. Heidegger acknowledges this, for instance, in his analysis of the craftsman. There is nothing wrong with the craftsman living in the mode of the «they,» and there might not be anything wrong with Heidegger's analysis except that Heidegger's description leaves out the average everydayness of the work of workers. However, already in his analysis of the «they,» a tone of crisis can be heard, of some unstable and critical situation, that the «they» covers up. Consider the following: «Overnight, everything that is primordial {Alles Ursprüngliche} gets glossed over as something that has long been well known. . . . The "they" is there alongside everywhere [ist überall dabei], but in such a manner that it has always stolen away whenever Dasein presses for a decision {wo das Dasein auf Entscheidung drängt}» (BT 165; SZ 127).

At the same time, Heidegger hints at a *«eigentliche* Verbundenheit»* (SZ 122; to «become *authentically* bound together,» BT 159) in contrast to the everyday modes of being. His tone becomes more urgent in chapter 5, section B. Here, Heidegger elaborates on the existentiales of section A as they are present in average everydayness, that is, he elucidates «the everyday kind of Being of discourse, sight, and interpretation» (BT 210; SZ 167). In the entire section B, and especially in section 37, entitled "Ambiguity" ("Die Zweideutigkeit"), one can hear what a German writer, drawing on Heidegger, recently has chosen as the title of an essay in which he announced his turn to the political right, namely, "Anschwellender Bocksgesang."[15] There is a buzzing sound in the air announcing something else, something new. Several times, Heidegger speaks of «what "they" have surmised and scented» concerning possible «deeds» (BT 218; «was *man* ahnte und spürte . . . Tat,» SZ 173). However, by «disguise or distortion» (BT 219; «Verstellung und Verdrehung,» SZ 175), «the publicness of the "they"» (BT 210; SZ 167) performs a double operation. It neutralizes possibilities for the Dasein, notably those of «taking action and carrying something through» (BT 218; SZ 174) by stamping them «as something merely subsequent and unimportant» (BT 218; SZ 174). Thus, in effect, it «becomes impossible to decide what is disclosed in a genuine {echtem} understanding, and what is not» (BT 217; SZ 173). At the same time, however, the publicness of the «they» disguises this difference itself or, more important, presents as «genuine» or authentic what is not, and presents as inauthentic what is genuine, or authentic: «Everything looks as if it were genuinely {echt} understood, genuinely taken hold of, genuinely spoken, though at bottom {im Grunde} it is not; or else it does not look so, and yet at bottom it is» (BT 217; SZ 173). Furthermore, «It {curiosity} seeks novelty only in order to leap from it {abzuspringen (which is, so to speak, the comparative to the negative side of entspringen, J. F.)} anew to another novelty. In this kind of seeing, that which is an issue for care does not lie in grasping something and being knowingly in the truth. . . . *not tarrying* alongside what is closest. . . . {It} seeks restlessness and the excitement of continual novelty and changing encounters» (BT 216; SZ 172).

All this is more than, so to speak, the regular fallenness of everydayness in the workshop of the carpenter, and thus Heidegger labels it «Verfallen» (SZ 175; «"falling",» BT 219 with the note referring to two other notes on the difference between «Fallen» and «Verfallen») and sees it as a *«"downward plunge"* [Absturz]» and «turbulence [Wirbel]» (BT 223; SZ 178).[16] Regarding the cause of this intensification of «fallen» into «verfallen,» Heidegger merely says that this is «a primordial kind {ursprüngliche Seinsart} of Being of Dasein» (BT 210; SZ 167). Anyway, on the most ursprünglich level of historicality, it turns out that those possibilities of deeds for authentic Dasein that the «they» scents and covers up can be found only in the past. Since in these passages Heidegger identifies the past with a vanished world, one might summarize this by saying that up to $t_1$ a world $w_1$ was present. After $t_1$, $w_1$ begins to vanish, and at $t_2$, it has already almost completely vanished. It is at this point $t_2$ that Heidegger situates ordinary Dasein's historizing, and historicality. To be sure, according to Heidegger's concept of Dasein and world, no Dasein can live without this or that world. Thus, one might say that from $t_1$ on, a different world, $w_2$, has begun to emerge that is more or less fully developed at $t_2$, and in which ordinary Dasein is living. Living in $w_2$, ordinary Dasein looks back to the time before $t_2$.

Heidegger finds four «significations {Bedeutungen}» (BT 431; SZ 379) in the ordinary understanding of history. His aim in presenting these four significations is to point out that «'the past' has a remarkable double meaning» (BT 430; SZ 378) and «the remarkably privileged position of the 'past' in the concept of history» (BT 431; SZ 379). The first signification «may well be the pre-eminent usage» (BT 430; SZ 378). Something is regarded to be history in the sense of «something *past*» when we say «that something or other "already belongs to history"». Here 'past' means "no longer present-at-hand", or even "still present-at-hand indeed, but without having any 'effect' on the 'Present'"» (BT 430; SZ 378). However, the saying, «"One cannot get away from history"» (BT 430; SZ 378), indicates the opposite, namely, that the past has some claim and effect on us. Thus, Heidegger finds a «remarkable double meaning»:

We have in view that which is past, but which nevertheless is still having effects. Howsoever, the historical, as that which is past, is understood to be related to the 'Present' in the sense of what is actual 'now' and 'today', and to be related to it, either positively or privatively, in such a way as to have effects upon it. Thus, 'the past' has a remarkable double meaning; the past belongs irretrievably to an earlier time; it belonged to the events of that time; and in spite of that, it can still be present-at-hand 'now'—for instance, the remains of a Greek temple. With the temple, a 'bit of the past' is still 'in the present'. (BT 430; SZ 378)

The second meaning of «history» as past is «*derivation [Herkunft]* from such a past» (BT 430; SZ 378), the third focuses on the difference between history and nature (BT 430f.; SZ 379), and the fourth is «whatever has been handed down to us {das Überlieferte als solches} . . . , whether it is something which we know historiologically {historisch erkannt}, or something that has been taken over as self-evident, with its derivation hidden» (BT 431; SZ 379).

Heidegger summarizes these four meanings by saying «that history is that specific historizing of existent Dasein which comes to pass in time, so that the historizing which is 'past' in our Being-with-one-another, and which at the same time has been 'handed down to us' and is continuingly effective, is regarded as "history" in the sense that gets emphasized» (BT 431; SZ 379). Ordinary Dasein, however, is not capable of realizing the specific way in which the past is past as well as present within ordinary Dasein's present time. Characterizing «what is *primarily* historical . . . Dasein» and «*secondarily* historical . . . equipment ready-to-hand . . . but also the environing *Nature* as 'the very soil of history'» (BT 433; SZ 381), Heidegger says that one can show «that the ordinary conception of 'world-history' arises precisely from our orientation to what is thus secondarily historical» (BT 433; SZ 381). Ordinary Dasein treats past Dasein as present-at-hand of which it maintains that it no longer exists and that, as present-at-hand, it is no longer of any significance for ordinary Dasein's present. Against this reduction of the past to a vanished past without any significance for the present, Heidegger utilizes his concept of «world»:

> What is 'past'? Nothing else than that *world* within which they {items of equipment} belonged to a context of equipment and were encountered as ready-to-hand and used by a concernful Dasein who was-in-the-world. That *world* is no longer. But what was formerly *within-the-world* with respect to that world is still present-at-hand. As equipment belonging to a world, that which is *now* still present-at-hand can belong nevertheless to the 'past'. But what do we signify by saying of a world that it is no longer? A world *is* only in the manner of *existing* Dasein, which *factically* is as Being-in-the-world. (BT 432; SZ 380)

And he refers back to his concepts «*da-gewesen*» or «*Gewesenheit,*» which he has developed in section 65:

> However, can Dasein be *past* at all, if we define 'past' as 'now *no longer either present-at-hand or ready-to-hand*'? Manifestly, Dasein can *never* be past, not because Dasein is non-transient, but because it essentially can never be *present-at-hand*. Rather, if it is, it *exists*. A Dasein which no longer exists, however, is not past, in the ontologically strict sense; it is rather "*having-been-there*"

[*da-gewesen*]. . . . It may be shown further that when one designates a time as 'the past', the meaning of this is not unequivocal; but 'the past' is manifestly distinct from *one's-having-been* {*Gewesenheit*}, with which we have become acquainted as something constitutive for the ecstatical unity of Dasein's temporality. This, however, only makes the enigma ultimately more acute; why is it that the historical is determined *predominantly* by the 'past', or, to speak more appropriately, by the character of having-been, when that character is one that temporalizes itself equiprimordially with the Present and the future? (BT 432f.; SZ 380f.)

Heidegger solves this enigma in section 74. However, he does so not by showing that gewesenes Dasein, the past, does not determine the present at all, but rather by showing that gewesenes Dasein is present in, and determines, ordinary Dasein's present in a much stronger way than ordinary Dasein is able or willing to admit. It is not necessary to see in Heidegger's «dagewesen» his ironic appropriation of Hegel's «"gewesen"»[17] and of Hegel's insistence that the Wesen has to realize itself to understand this point. Whatever merits Heidegger's analysis of death and birth might have—on the level of historicality death and birth obviously have the function of guaranteeing that the past is not only, in this or that way, ontically present within ordinary Dasein's present but rather co-present as the ontological origin of ordinary Dasein's present. Heidegger writes:

Understood existentially, birth is not and never is something past in the sense of something no longer present-at-hand; and death is just as far from having the kind of Being of something still outstanding, not yet present-at-hand but coming along. Factical Dasein exists as born; and, as born, it is already dying, in the sense of Being-towards-death. As long as Dasein factically exists, both the 'ends' and their 'between' *are*, and they *are* in the only way which is possible on the basis of Dasein's Being as *care*. Throwness and that Being towards death in which one either flees it or anticipates it, form a unity; and in this unity birth and death are 'connected' in a manner characteristic of Dasein {In der Einheit von Geworfenheit und flüchtigem, bzw. vorlaufendem Sein zum Tode "hängen" Geburt und Tod daseinsmäßig zusammen}. As care, Dasein *is* the 'between'. (BT 426f.; SZ 374)

Ordinary Dasein does not acknowledge the presence of the past, or of what-has-been-there (Gewesenheit), in ordinary Dasein's present. Or, it scents the presence of what-has-been-there and the latter's call for a deed, but it works on all these ways of the past's presence only in order to neutralize them and to keep them reduced to something present-at-hand, that is, to something that has no significance for Dasein. In this way, it renders them unrecognizable, insignificant for only as long as it is able to do so can ordinary Dasein continue in its way of life. This is the critical situation that calls for a decision. Some Daseine will break through ordinary Dasein's work of ambiguity, will recognize the possibilities covered up by ordinary Dasein as the authentic ones, and will turn them against ordinary Dasein. These Daseine become authentic. Other Daseine, however, will continue to try to get rid of the past, of what-has-been-there, and its presence in ordinary Dasein's present, and thus they will become inauthentic.

## C. The Crisis

It is important to note that the movement of authentic Dasein starts not from a point somewhere beyond and independent of ordinary Dasein but rather from within ordinary Dasein's world. As discussed above, in section 74 Heidegger begins with «vorlaufende Entschlossenheit» (SZ 382; «anticipatory resoluteness,» BT 434). He points out that the act of resolutely running forward into death guarantees «only the totality and authenticity of one's resoluteness» and that the possibilities of authentic existence cannot be gathered from death (BT 434; SZ 383). However, these very possibilities are present in the very same world in which ordinary Dasein lived before it resolutely ran forward into death. Resolutely running forward does not disclose a new world. Rather, it simply enables authentic Dasein to see the same world with new eyes, to see through and no longer go along with the work of ambiguity ordinary Dasein has performed. As Heidegger explains:

As thrown, Dasein has indeed been delivered over to itself and to its potentiality-for-Being, *but as Being-in-the-world.* As thrown, it has been submitted to a 'world', and exists factically with Others. Proximally and for the most part the Self is lost in the "they". It understands itself in terms of those possibilities of existence {Es versteht sich aus den Existenzmöglichkeiten} which 'circulate' in the 'average' public way of interpreting Dasein today. These possibilities have mostly been made unrecognizable by ambiguity {durch die Zweideutigkeit unkenntlich gemacht}; yet they are well known to us. The authentic existentiell understanding is so far from extricating itself from the way of interpreting Dasein which has come down to us, that in each case it is in terms of this interpretation {aus ihr}, against it {gegen sie}, and yet again for it {für sie}, that any possibility one has chosen is seized upon in one's resolution. {Das eigentliche existentielle Verstehen entzieht sich der überkommenen Ausgelegtheit so wenig, daß es je aus ihr und gegen sie und doch wieder für sie die gewählte Möglichkeit im Entschluß ergreift.} (BT 435; SZ 383)

These sentences mark the beginning of the crisis at the end of which authentic Dasein will subjugate itself to the past («erwidert»), and will cancel the sphere of ordinary and inauthentic Dasein («Widerruf»). Thus, in this opening movement with its three steps «aus,» «against,» and «for» the sphere of inauthentic Dasein, the second and third steps anticipate the sentences on erwidert and Widerruf. By choosing its hero, Dasein turns «against» the sphere of ordinary Dasein and destroys the world of ordinary Dasein that, for authentic Dasein, has become inauthentic after Dasein has resolutely run forward into death. That authentic Dasein does so «for» inauthentic Dasein is the conservatives' and rightists' understanding of their «Berufung» (vocation), another noun containing «Ruf»; the implication was that the right-minded Daseine will save the «they» by destroying the world of the «they» and by replacing it with one that is ensouled by the properly present origin. Thus, «against» and «for» seem to be clear. However, «aus» and, correspondingly, the phrase «the way of interpreting Dasein which has come down to us {überkommenen Ausgelegtheit}» (to which «this interpretation {aus ihr}» refers) are ambiguous. «Aus» has several meanings. It can mean «out of» in the sense of «to get out of this place»—I go «aus dem Haus,» that is, I leave the house. Thus, Heidegger's «aus» may mean the place or the possibilities authentic Dasein will leave. In this case, the phrase «the way of interpreting Dasein which has come down to us» refers only to a subset of all possibilities present within the world of ordinary Dasein, namely, only to those ordinary Dasein practices as its own positive possibilities. I'll call these «inauthentic possibilities.» However, these are not the only possibilities available to Dasein. Rather, there are all the possibilities that have been «made unrecognizable» by ordinary Dasein and that, therefore, ordinary Dasein doesn't recognize as significant possibilities anymore. Instead ordinary Dasein distances itself from those «unrecognizable» possibilities by keeping them reduced to something present-at-hand. Since these are the possibilities authentic Dasein will seize, I'll call them «authentic possibilities.»[18] A second meaning of «aus» is «out of» or «from.» I take an apple aus, that is, out of, a basket. In this sense, the phrase «way of interpreting Dasein which has come down to us» would define, so to speak, a pool containing the inauthentic as well as the authentic possibilities, and the «aus» would indicate that authentic Dasein takes from this pool its possibility or heroes. This too, fits the sequence «aus,» «against,» and «for.» Authentic Dasein selects «aus (from)» the pool containing authentic as well as inauthentic possibilities. Authentic Dasein acts «against» either the inauthentic possibilities or against the entire pool as this strange mixture within which the authentic possibilities as part of the pool have been made unrecognizable by ordinary Dasein (or it acts «against» the way in which the authentic possibilities are present for ordinary Dasein, that is, it cancels the work of ambiguity performed by ordinary and inauthentic Dasein). Authentic Dasein acts «for» the inauthentic possibilities in the sense mentioned above, and/or for the authentic possibilities. Or, authentic Dasein acts «for» the entire pool since it acts for the sake of the present world. In any case, it also and mainly acts for the past since authentic Dasein is struggling for the sake of the authentic possibilities and the past's rebirth. In all these renderings, the world in which ordinary Daseine live and which they try to keep unambiguous is in fact freighted with possibilities, the resolute grasping of which leads to the destruction of ordinary Dasein's world. Both meanings of «aus» are meanings of the Greek ἐκ, ἐξ, as well, and the second meaning of «aus,» «from,» already comes close to a third meaning of aus as the main meaning of the Greek ἐκ, ἐξ. By definition, a principle is that aus (out of, from) which the other beings come, while it itself doesn't come out of/from anything else as Aristotle says in *Physics* I:5, 187 a 27–28, and it is that aus which something consists (ibid., I:7, 190 b 17–20).

This polysemous particle «aus» renders the entire section 74 difficult. However, before discussing this in detail, I would like to remind readers that, as the second of the long quotes from Guignon I presented close to the beginning of chapter 1, section B, already shows, Guignon and I agree that Heidegger's concept of historicality contains a move against the present. Both Guignon and I regard this to be the content of the sentence about disavowal (Widerruf). For me and maybe also for Guignon, this move against the present is also indicated by the «against» («gegen») of the sentence discussed from the beginning of this section on. Consider the following passage in section 74 shortly after the one quoted at the beginning of this section:

> Only by the anticipation of death is every accidental and 'provisional' {"vorläufige"} possibility driven out. Only Being-free *for* death, gives Dasein its goal outright and pushes existence into its finitude. Once one has grasped the finitude of one's existence, it snatches one back from {reißt aus} the endless multiplicity of possibilities which offer themselves as closest to one—those of comfortableness, shirking, and taking things lightly {Behagens, Leichtnehmens, Sichdrückens}—and brings Dasein into the simplicity of its *fate* [*Schicksals*]. This is how we designate Dasein's primordial historizing, which lies in authentic resoluteness and in which Dasein *hands* itself *down* to itself, free for death, in a possibility which it has inherited and yet has chosen {Damit bezeichnen wir das in der eigentlichen Entschlossenheit liegende ursprüngliche Geschehen des Daseins, in dem es sich frei für den Tod ihm selbst in einer ererbten, aber gleichwohl gewählten Möglichkeit *überliefert*}. (BT 435; SZ 384)

(Note in passing that the German expression «sich drücken» especially is extremely derogatory.) One might wonder whether authentic Dasein can go back to the possibilities characterized by «comfortableness, shirking, and taking things lightly.» One might imagine that some person experiences some event and behaves in such a way that Heidegger might call this proper resoluteness. After this experience, however, he goes on as usual. Nonetheless, his attitude toward his possibilities has changed. He will no longer grumble about his fellow citizens or himself, but he will be thankful to God, destiny, or whomever that he is still alive, and he will appreciate and enjoy life. Thus, he will see his ordinary life, though nothing has changed externally, «with new eyes.» Or, consider many philosophers, especially in late antiquity (if they may count as authentic Daseine). They maintained to know better than the many; they knew that the gods, or God, were not what public opinion considered them to be. Those philosophers nevertheless followed the public practices with the private caveat that, philosophically, they didn't agree with these possibilities. Or, the phenomenon of camp might point to the possibility that one indulges in exactly the same things and activities as inauthentic Dasein; however, through a special «kick» one has given one's attitude, one signals one's distance and authenticity. However, the tone of the quoted sentence as well as the sequence of «aus,» «gegen,» and «für» and the passage on disavowal show that, according to Heidegger, authentic Dasein will not return to the possibilities ordinary and inauthentic Dasein have chosen; on this Guignon and I agree. (Thus, the «aus» in «snatches one back from . . . » indicates, as the tone of this sentence already suggests, not a provisional but rather a final «out of this place» with no possibility of return.)

«Überkommene Ausgelegtheit» («the way of interpreting Dasein which has come down to us») is the first of a series of four concepts in section 74. It is followed by «Erbe» («heritage»), «Schicksals» («fate»), and finally by «Geschick» («destiny,» which is explained in terms of «Gemeinschaft, des Volkes,» «community, of {the} people»). In sections B and D of chapter 1, I mentioned Birmingham's interpretation of the sentences on erwidert and Widerruf. According to her, authentic Dasein does nothing but negate or distance itself from possibilities offered by the past and does not identify itself with any possibility proposed by the past. From the perspective of this interpretation of «erwidert» and «Widerruf,» one might feel tempted to interpret the sequence from «überkommene Ausgelegtheit» to «Geschick» in the same way, all the more so since obviously right from its beginning this passage is pervaded by a strong sense of «aus» as «out of this place,» «out of this possibility.» She quotes completely from Macquarrie and Robinson's translation the passage beginning with «But if fateful Dasein,» containing the sentence, «destiny is not something that puts itself together out of individual fates,» and ending with «Only in communicating and in struggling does the power of destiny become free» (BT 436; SZ 384), and comments on it as follows:

> Two points must be noted. First, when Heidegger writes, "our fates have been guided in advance," he means no more and no less than that *Dasein* is always already implicated, immersed in historical happenings and events. Second, the event of destiny emerges *only* in the shared (*Mitgeschehen*) realm of speech and action. The event of destiny is situated in the *Augenblick,* which we have seen is an historical conjunction of traditions, discourses, and practices. The taking over of destiny is located, *taking place* only by acting with and upon the actions and discourses of others through communication and struggle: "But if fateful *Dasein,* as being-in-the-world, exists essentially in being-with-others, its historizing is a co-historizing and is determinative for it as *destiny* (Geschick). This is how we designate the historizing of the community, of a people [Volk]" (SZ, 384/436). This passage calls into question any interpretation of the "we"

(*Mitgeschehen*) as the "we" of a homogeneous totality. Indeed, this passage suggests that Heidegger thinks *Volk* only in terms of *Mitgeschehen*: the heterogeneity of historical actors who constitute the event of destiny through their critical, *agonal* response to historical possibilities.

There is here a clear distinction between destiny and tradition. The critical response (*Erwidert*) to shared historical possibilities frees the historical space of destiny to be something *different* from what has been. (TP 30; after this she quotes the passage on erwidert and Widerruf and comments on it as quoted above in section B of chapter 1.)

Her usage of «fate» seems unclear. Either she means by it all those traditions in which each Dasein is always already implicated and with which authentic Dasein breaks since authentic Dasein has an «*agonal* response to historical possibilities» (TP 30) and «disrupts identity and continuity . . . refuting the notion of history as a continuum» (TP 31). Or she means that fate is the critical response itself to the tradition in which each Dasein is implicated. Similarly, Birmingham's use of «destiny» («Geschick») isn't quite clear. It is either the event that, constituted by the Daseine, turns against tradition (and fate) and excludes it, or it is tradition (and fate) itself in its moment of being overruled by the struggles of different Daseine.

However, even prior to a discussion of possible differences between the terms, native speakers of German would intuitively say that both Schicksal and Geschick designate something that cannot be overruled by a Dasein. These terms do not name something that by definition gets overruled or is the event of overruling itself. Though some Dasein might manage to avoid its fate for some time, its fate will ultimately «es einholen,» catch or get hold of it. Furthermore, speakers of German would also say that it is not the Dasein—nor a group of Daseine—that constitute destiny or fate but rather the other way round: destiny and fate determine the Dasein. There is not the slightest hint in the entire passage indicating that Heidegger uses the notions of destiny and fate ironically, or that he uses them in a meaning different from their meaning in everyday language and in philosophical language. Instead, he uses them precisely the way they were used by conservatives and right-wingers at the time (see chapter 3). Thus, he did not mean that Dasein overrules destiny and fate or that destiny is the break with any tradition. (If he had wanted to advance an argument like the one Birmingham reads into this passage, he might have used his term «co-historizing,» but then he would not have commented on this in terms of «und bestimmt als *Geschick.*») Furthermore, in ordinary language «wird frei» (becomes free) refers to something that exists prior to this becoming free and that remains free after becoming free. Again, Heidegger would not have used this phrase (or would have used it only with a further comment) if he had wanted to describe an event that is constituted by several Daseine in such a way that it takes place just to disappear again or to eliminate tradition and fate. Furthermore, Birmingham does not explain in what way her statement «historical actors who constitute the event of destiny» can be seen as not contradicting one of Heidegger's sentences she herself quotes, namely, «Destiny is not something that puts itself together out of individual fates» (BT 436; «Das Geschick setzt sich nicht aus einzelnen Schicksalen zusammen,» SZ 384). One might pass over these flaws in her interpretation of this passage, or perhaps Birmingham might justify them in some way. However, as I will show in this section, the idea that «destiny» in Heidegger is an event disrupting any identity and continuity can be maintained only with utter disregard for the context of this passage.[19]

Guignon is more moderate insofar as, according to him, authentic Dasein ultimately identifies itself with possibilities offered by the past, or tradition— though, in the end, the difference may not count for much, since Guignon believes that what Dasein chooses is determined not by some offer of the past but by the utopian ideal of the choosing Dasein. He also does not distinguish among the four terms in Heidegger's series of «überkommene Ausgelegtheit» and «*fate,*» « heritage,» «*destiny,*» which is explained as «community, of {the} people»; to him they all seem to be merely different names for the one pool from which authentic Dasein can draw its choice. Consider, for example, the following passage contained in the second of the long quotes presented close to the beginning of section B of chapter 1: «The present can be seen as deformed or defective only in contrast to an understanding of the potential built into our heritage and the truest aims definitive of our destiny» (HC 138). Here, «heritage» seems to be equivalent to «überkommene Ausgelegtheit.» Turning back to «überkommene Ausgelegtheit,» authentic Dasein recognizes that among other possibilities there is something—in Guignon's words, built into this «überkommene Ausgelegtheit»—that authentic Dasein, in contrast to the inauthentic one, will choose. Thus, «heritage» is the «überkommene Ausgelegtheit» itself viewed from the perspective of authentic Dasein, which regards it as the pool from which it can draw its choices, whereas ordinary and inauthentic Daseine don't realize the different possibilities within the «überkommene Ausgelegtheit» since they don't turn back and don't look at it in the light of some utopian ideal, or they do so but decide to stick to their possibilities. Or consider a passage prior to this:

> As thrown, Heidegger reiterates, Dasein "understands itself in terms of those possibilities which 'circulate' in the 'average' public away {*sic!*} of interpreting Dasein today" (*BT,* 435). There is no exit from the understanding of things deposited in the public language and embodied in the practices of our current world. But, in the context of this discussion of historicity, Heidegger points to a different manner in which we might encounter those public possibilities. As authentic, he says, one can encounter them as a "heritage" (*Erbe*). Dasein's resoluteness "discloses current possibilities as *from the heritage* which resoluteness, as thrown, *takes over*" (*BT,* 435). (HC 135)

This seems to be the same idea as in the earlier quote with «built in.» «Heritage» is the same as «überkommene Ausgelegtheit,» the only difference being that authentic Dasein regards «überkommene Ausgelegtheit» as the pool, and thus as heritage, from which it can and must make its choice, whereas inauthentic Dasein does not turn back to the pool and does not make a choice. Yet, even if Guignon distinguishes between «überkommene Ausgelegtheit» and the other concepts, he regards—as I explained in section B of chapter 1—the past as the pool that contains several possibilities, none of them binding in itself but each receiving its meaning only in the light of a utopian ideal.

However, there is a big difference between «the way of interpreting Dasein which has come down to us» on the one hand and «heritage,» «fate,» and «destiny» on the other.[20] Maybe already «heritage» but certainly «destiny» is no longer identical with «überkommene Ausgelegtheit,» but is rather that possibility that authentic Dasein catches, or by which it is caught, and that Dasein in the next step turns against the «überkommene Ausgelegtheit,» that is, against the world of ordinary Dasein. In other words, «überkommene Ausgelegtheit» contains the inauthentic possibilities as well as the authentic ones. Destiny, however, is no longer this pool containing both kinds of possibilities. Rather, it comprises only the authentic possibilities, the specific choices authentic Daseine have selected from the pool and in the name of which they will turn «against» ordinary Dasein and its mode of interpreting and being in the world, that is, against «überkommene Ausgelegtheit.» Thus, destiny is no longer some neutral pool, filled with a plurality of possibilities, but a reality that imposes itself onto Dasein and does not leave Dasein any choice; it does not allow Dasein to distance itself from it. Not to see this difference between überkommene Ausgelegtheit on the one hand and destiny on the other might indeed turn Heidegger's concept of historicality into a politically neutral one or, perhaps, even into a philosophy of Riß, as Birmingham puts it (TP 37). However, to see the distinction Heidegger made here is to realize that, as I will show in chapters 3 and 4, Heidegger used «destiny» the way it was used by the political Right.

I said, «but certainly destiny» because there is some ambiguity about «heritage,» or at least the impression of ambiguity since Heidegger seems to use the preposition «aus» («in terms of the heritage {aus dem Erbe} which that resoluteness, as thrown, takes over» [BT 435; SZ 383]) in the same meaning he uses «aus» in the sentence on «überkommene Ausgelegtheit.» However, «aus» in the phrase with «heritage» acquires a new meaning due to the different character of the container of possibilities to choose from. Those who can listen to language as Heidegger does already expect the new meaning once they read the word «heritage» as the new word for the container to choose from, especially since Heidegger says in the same sentence that authentic Dasein «discloses» (BT 435; «erschließt,» SZ 383) the relevant possibilities.[21] Those who are not that good at listening to language realize the new meaning at the latest after reading the entire paragraph beginning with the sentence on heritage. To put it differently, similarly to his punning on «Wieder,» «erwidert,» and «Widerruf,» in the entire passage with its several «aus» Heidegger is punning on the different meanings of «aus» which are the same as the different meanings of the Greek word ἐκ. He does so because in this way the master of listening to language is again able to situate his project within the different meanings of a prominent preposition in the Greek language; the language that is «along with German . . . (in regard to its possibilities for thought) at once the most powerful and most spiritual of all languages» (IM 57; EM 43). In the passage beginning with «in terms . . . , against it, and yet again for it,» these different meanings enable him to switch from «aus» as «from which,» or «out of which,» to «aus» in the sense of «that out of which something consists» so as to establish heritage, destiny, and fate as that entity to which authentic Dasein has to subjugate itself since the former is its origin, is what provides Dasein with its identity and stability.[22]

Heidegger writes: «The resoluteness in which Dasein comes back to itself, discloses current factical possibilities of authentic existing, and discloses them in *terms of the heritage* which that resoluteness, as thrown, *takes over* {aus dem Erbe, das sie als geworfene übernimmt}» (BT 435; SZ 383). In chapter 1, I already pointed out the contrast between Guignon's interpretation and mine. Guignon understands the past here as something whose seeming unity is dissolved by the different Daseine interpreting it in the light of their various utopian ideals. As I will elaborate in chapter 4, when Guignon applies his interpretation to political choices, the conclusion is that different Daseine choose different heroes who oppose each other and who struggle against each other. One Dasein chooses a communist hero, another a liberal, and so on. Needless to say, in the realm of politics every one is everyone else's opponent or foe. Thus, according to Guignon, «heritage,» or «community, of {the} people,» is in itself not a determining factor. Rather, resoluteness reveals that heritage in itself entails several contradictory possibilities, and different authentic Daseine will choose different heroes from those possibilities. These choices are not determined by the heritage but by the different utopian ideals.

In contrast, my interpretation is that «heritage» and «community, of {the} people» present a strongly unified entity that imposes itself onto the authentic Dasein. This unity leaves room for, and requires, several different ways of being in it—in Heidegger's terms, different Schicksale (fates). However, these different Schicksale, or the different Helden, do not oppose each other or struggle against each other but are united by the common heritage or Volk (and thereupon fight against ordinary and inauthentic Daseine). The power of the origin is that it allows and requires several different members who do not oppose each other but are united by and within the unity of the origin. That this idea of past and heritage is at work in section 74 and not Guignon's is shown already by the passage under discussion. To be sure, the phrase «*aus dem Erbe»* looks like the phrase «aus den Existenzmöglichkeiten» or «aus ihr.» Furthermore, in both cases the «aus» designates some sort of pool from which authentic Dasein can make its choice. However, the pool is no longer the same. This is clearly indicated by the formulation as well as by the steps following it. It is indicated by the formulation itself insofar as the «aus» designates exclusively something from which authentic Dasein chooses, whereas in the context of «überkommene Ausgelegtheit» the «aus» has the double meaning of «from which (one chooses)» and «(the place) out of which (one gets by the choice) and against which (one turns one's choice).»

The same is shown by the following sentence on «everything 'good'» and «'goodness'.» Heidegger writes: «Wenn alles "Gute" Erbschaft ist und der Character der "Güte" in der Ermöglichung eigentlicher Existenz liegt, dann konstituiert sich in der Entschlossenheit je das Überliefern eines Erbes» (SZ 383f.). Macquarrie and Robinson translate: «If everything 'good' is a heritage {Erbschaft}, and the character of 'goodness' lies in making authentic existence possible, then the handing down of a heritage {Erbe} constitutes itself in resoluteness» (BT 435). The translation is inaccurate or at least misleading in three ways. Today it might require some effort to recognize the meaning of Heidegger's sentence. However, at Heidegger's time probably no one familiar with the political discourse of the conservatives and right-wingers would have had much difficulty. First, in the first part of the subordinate clause the translation has an indefinite article in front of «heritage» while the German «Erbschaft» has neither a definite nor an indefinite one. Second, the translators use the same word, namely «heritage,» as in the sentence with *«in terms of {aus} the heritage {Erbe}.»* However, while in the sentence with *«in terms of {aus} the heritage»* Heidegger uses «Erbe,» in the subordinate clause with «everything 'good'» he uses «Erbschaft.» The usage of «Erbe» and «Erbschaft» in German is somewhat intriguing. Both notions can be used interchangeably. If both occur in the same sentence or context as they do here in Heidegger, the speaker most of the time wants to make a distinction between two perspectives. An individual or group *A* inherits some *X* from *B*. Since in *Being and Time* «heritage» is used for the German «Erbe» as well as «Erbschaft,» I avoid in what follows the notion of heritage and call *X* «estate.» The estate is handed down by *B* to *A*. In German, *B* is said to «hinterlassen eine Erbschaft,» to bequeath an Erbschaft, to *A*, and *A* is said to «ein Erbe zu empfangen,» to inherit an Erbe, from *B*. That is, from the perspective of *B* the estate is called an Erbschaft while from the perspective of *A* the estate is called an Erbe. However, the notions are also used the other way round. To elaborate the second usage, by definition a proletarian leaves nothing behind besides his or her children. Other people leave an Erbe, an estate, to their children. Each of the children «macht/bekommt/erhält/tritt an eine Erbschaft,» inherits his or her, as I translate, «inheritance,» that is, his or her share in the estate. Thus, a property is labeled an Erbe, an estate, when one focuses on the identity of an estate over several generations or when one looks upon the act of handing down from the perspective of its respective owner, while the same property and Erbe is called Erbschaft when one looks upon the act of handing down from the perspective of the heirs of an estate.

Heidegger employs the notions in the second way. Resoluteness discloses current factical possibilities of authentic existence «*in terms of the heritage {aus dem Erbe}*» (BT 435; SZ 383). This Erbe contains «the possibilities that have come down to one» (BT 435; SZ 383), of which Heidegger speaks in the next sentence. That is, the Erbe comes from the past and contains possibilities that come down to us from the past. Coming from the past, the Erbe is an estate and can be taken over by authentic Daseine. Heidegger introduces this latter perspective in the relative clause: «*in terms of the heritage {aus dem Erbe}* which that resoluteness, as thrown, takes over {übernimmt}*» (BT 435; SZ 383). Since, from the perspective of the Daseine that take it over, the Erbe can be called an «Erbschaft,» Heidegger uses «Erbschaft» in the sentence beginning with «If everything 'good' is a heritage {Erbschaft}» (BT 435; SZ 383). This step from «Erbe,» estate, to «Erbschaft,» inheritance, is reasonable, for after introducing the estate as well as the one who takes it over it is useful, if not even necessary, to focus on the relation of the heirs to the estate they inherit. The passage is a good instance of the power of a principle, be it Plato's ideal state, an Aristotelian form, a conservative Gemeinschaft, a right-wing Volksgemeinschaft, or «the proletariat.» It is one and the same Erbe that provides for different slots, different Erbschaften. The different heirs to one and the same estate know that they owe their property to the same estate, and they don't fight against each other but work for the preservation and benefit of the estate and of the group owning the estate. This is the conservative idea of Erbe, and Erbe functions that way as long as family values and a good sense of the value of traditions are still in place. As I will discuss in chapter 3, in the passage on destiny and fate Heidegger rephrases the same relation of the one to the many in terms of destiny and fate. Destiny is the Erbe that provides for and requires several individual slots, fates, in order for it to be faithfully transmitted and actualized by several Daseine. The Daseine know themselves to be united in their common destiny and committed to preserve and actualize their destiny. This requires that they are willing to fight against a common enemy of their Erbe. In order to express the common relation of the different Erbschaften («Wenn alles "Gute" Erbschaft ist,» SZ 383) and their commitment to one and the same Erbe, Heidegger gathers the different Erbschaften under the short title «alles 'Gute'» (SZ 383; «everything 'good',» BT 435) and subsumes them under the singular «Erbschaft» without any article.[23] The English translation, however, definitely contributes to Guignon's interpretation of section 74. For by translating both «Erbe» and «Erbschaft» with the same word, «heritage,» and by adding an indefinite article before «Erbschaft» Heidegger's «Erbe» can be equated with the «überkommenen Ausgelegtheit» (SZ 383; «the way of inter-preting Dasein which has come down to us,» BT 435). Both are the same, the only difference being that, in contrast to inauthentic Dasein, authentic Dasein looks upon «the way of interpreting Dasein which has come down to us» as a pool containing several possibilities for its choice. On this account, each of these possibilities can indeed be labeled «a heritage» (BT 435), one estate among many different estates. In this way, the unity of the estate in Heidegger is dissolved into a multiplicity of different and opposed small estates, as it were. In fact, none of them is even an estate any longer. For, according to Guignon, none of them is in itself binding for authentic Dasein as the latter's choice depends on its utopian ideal. By using «Erbe» in the singular and by reducing «everything 'good'» to «Erbschaft» in the singular, however, Heidegger emphasizes the unity of the estate and the obligation for the heirs to take it over. This becomes more clear if one considers the other aspects of the sentence in question.

In the subordinate clause, Heidegger makes a clear distinction, de-cision, or separation. He makes a statement on «everything 'good',» namely, that «everything 'good' is heritage {Erbschaft}.» From the sentence that every-thing «good» is Erbschaft it follows logically that nothing that is not Erb-schaft or that has no Erbschaft is good. In addition, the sentence that every-thing «good» is Erbschaft does not allow the inference that the Erbe only contains good possibilities. However, the second part of the subordinate clause—the phrase «and the character of 'goodness' {Güte} lies in making authentic existence possible» (BT 435; SZ 383)—is obviously meant to estab-lish by definition, or by listening to language, that the Erbe exclusively con-tains good possibilities.[24] Quite obviously, Heidegger makes a distinction between what is good and what is not good, and he makes this distinction in terms of the notion of Erbe. The notion of Erbe qualifies some possibilities as good—all those that are inherited, are Erbschaft, since they are a share in the Erbe—and disqualifies others as not good, namely, all those that don't partake in the Erbe. In addition, this distinction corresponds to the distinction between authentic Dasein on one side and ordinary and inauthentic Dasein on the other. The good possibilities are chosen by authentic Dasein, and the bad ones are those in which ordinary and inauthentic Daseine live. One has to take over the Erbe, since this is the only way of acquiring something good and thus of being good. Furthermore, the distinction quite obviously takes up the distinction with regard to «the way of interpreting Dasein which has come down to us» (BT 435; SZ 383), namely, that this way contains the inauthen-tic possibilities as well as the authentic ones. Ordinary Dasein has no access to the Erbe and is therefore not good. Or rather it prevents itself, or is pre-vented by the «they,» from access to the Erbe since the «they» covers up by the work of ambiguity the authentic possibilities; the ones in which the Erbe is present. It is only upon becoming authentic that Dasein has access to the

Erbe and becomes good. Thus, the notion of «the way of interpreting Dasein which has come down to us» (BT 435; SZ 383) and the notion of «heritage» in «*in terms of {aus} the heritage{Erbe}*» (BT 435; SZ 383) are not identical. The former contains all the available possibilities, namely, the inauthentic as well as the authentic ones. The latter, however, contains only the authentic possibilities. By drawing on the authentic possibilities, authentic Dasein will act «against» (BT 435; «gegen,» SZ 383) «the way of interpreting Dasein which has come down to us» (BT 435; SZ 383); that is, authentic Dasein will replace the possibilities or the world of ordinary and inauthentic Dasein with authentic ones, with the authentic world.

The difference between «the way of interpreting Dasein which has come down to us» and the «*heritage{Erbe}*» (BT 435; SZ 383) is further elaborated in the second part of the subordinate clause, namely, the phrase «and the character of 'goodness' {Güte} lies in making authentic existence possible» (BT 435; SZ 383). «Goodness» sounds like the abstract noun for «good.» In Platonic terms, something is good because it partakes in goodness. According to my experience, English readers tend to assume that Heidegger has in mind here something like an idea of the good, derived from Plato or another philosophical tradition; an idea that serves as a criterion for evaluating political constitutions and the empirical political life in a given society. Though Guignon doesn't discuss this sentence, he might have had it in mind. Authentic Dasein has its specific utopian ideal, because authentic Dasein assumes this ideal is the best, fits best the idea of the good (or is itself the good). With the idea of the good and its utopian ideal in mind, authentic Dasein turns back and realizes that «the way of interpreting Dasein which has come down to us» (BT 435; SZ 383) is the «Erbe» that contains several possibilities (BT 435; SZ 383). It screens all these possibilities in order to pick out the one that fits its utopian ideal and thus the idea of the good best. It chooses this possibility and rejects all the others. In this way, Guignon might have found textual support for his distinction between an utopian ideal and the various possibilities included in the «Erbe»; a distinction that at the same time makes readers identify the «Erbe» authentic Dasein takes over (BT 435; SZ 383) with «the way of interpreting Dasein which has come down to us» (BT 435; SZ 383). However, Heidegger does not make such a distinction between a pool containing various possibilities and a universal criterion enabling authentic Dasein to screen the pool and to reject all but one possibility. The German word «Güte» normally doesn't denote a universal criterion for ethical and political choices. (It can be said, for instance, that the «Güte» of an action consists in realizing a «Gut,» a good, a value; in that case, however, the criterion is the Gut, and the action has Güte only because it conforms to that criterion.) Rather, «Güte» often denotes a certain property that only things that are an Erbschaft have and that things that are not Erbschaft lack.[25] Thus, in the second part of the subordinate clause Heidegger further elaborates on the notion of Erbe and its obligatory character and does not make a distinction between Erbe and a criterion in the light of which the Erbe loses its obligatory power.

As was said, the entire sentence reads: «If everything 'good' is a heritage {Erbschaft}, and the character of 'goodness' {Güte} lies in making authentic existence possible, then the handing down of a heritage {Erbe} constitutes itself in resoluteness {dann konstituiert sich in der Entschlossenheit je das Überliefern eines Erbes}» (BT 435; SZ 383f.). Note that in the main clause Heidegger returns to the word «Erbe» (estate). In resoluteness the handing down of the Erbe constitutes itself. Only authentic Dasein has access to the Erbe. By obeying the call to turn back to the Erbe, Dasein no longer covers up the Erbe. Instead, it acknowledges its Erbschaft, that is, its share in the Erbe, and becomes authentic and good, whereas all those ordinary Daseine that don't listen to the call become inauthentic Daseine and remain deprived of any good. (Perhaps it can be said that ordinary Daseine are deprived of any good, while inauthentic Daseine are evil.) In this way, the handing down of the Erbe constitutes itself. Note that Heidegger does not say that heritage constitutes itself, but that «the handing down of» the Erbe «constitutes itself.»[26] This is a further indication that Heidegger quite self-evidently assumes that Erbe, destiny, and fate exist prior to the one who receives, or takes over, the Erbe, destiny, or fate. As I will show in chapters 3, 4 and 5, this is the common understanding of these notions in everyday language as well as in philosophical texts. For conservatives and rightists, destiny or fate governed history, while liberals and leftists maintained that destiny and fate were notions without reference, and that, instead, reason or the means of production governed history. According to Heidegger, Dasein becomes authentic only through receiving the Erbe as its Erbschaft. Furthermore, in resoluteness the handing down of the Erbe constitutes itself. If Heidegger had left out the first claim and if, instead of the second one, he had said that in resoluteness the Erbe or an Erbe constitutes itself, one might have thought that he talks about an act in which someone establishes out of the blue, as it were, a new tradition for the following generation. However, since Heidegger says that only an Erbschaft makes authentic Dasein possible and that in resoluteness the handing down of the Erbe constitutes itself, Erbe exists prior to authentic Dasein and prior to the moment in which the handing down of the Erbe constitutes itself, as is already implied in the notion of Erbe. According to Birmingham, in section 74 authentic Dasein breaks with each and any tradition. If Heidegger had wanted to say this, he would certainly not say that only an Erbschaft makes authentic Dasein possible. He would also not say that authentic Dasein is about the handing down of the Erbe. Finally, he would not use a sentence whose grammatical subject is not authentic Dasein but rather the handing down of the Erbe. «Konstituieren» means «to set up, to establish, to form, to compose.» Not only Heidegger would say that, quite literally, it means—like the Latin verb constituere, con-statuere—«to place at some location, to put together, to put together/to join several things at some location.» Thus, «sich konstituieren» means «to put oneself together, to place and join one's parts at some location.»

One can hear on the news a sentence such as: «Heute hat sich in Bonn der neue Bundestag konstituiert» (Today, the newly elected parliament has constituted itself in Bonn); or, «Heute trat in Bonn der neue Bundestag zu seiner konstituierenden Sitzung zusammen» (Today, the newly elected parliament assembled for the session in which it constituted itself). (Note that the second sentence even contains two formulas of «putting itself together.») Three points are important about such usages of «sich konstituieren.» First, the new parliament doesn't come out of the blue. Rather, its members only gather because they have been elected and thus have the right and the duty to work for the new parliament. They do not break with any tradition but rather continue a tradition, for the new parliament succeeds the preceding parliament and was elected according to the rules of the old parliament. (Even if, after a revolution, a «verfassungsgebende Versammlung sich konstituiert» [a constitutional assembly constitutes itself], it does so only because it was preceded by deliberations and decisions to constitute a verfassungsgebende Versammlung.) Second, though the individual members represent their electorate, they must not work for the private advantage of themselves or their electorate but rather for the well-being of the state and the German people. Third, in light of the first two points the phrase «sich konstituieren» means that an entity that exists prior to its constitution but does so in such a way that it cannot yet fully act comes out into full existence in order, to put it somewhat sloppily, to step out and «get the job done,» as Patrick Ewing and his colleagues used to say. (They say so not because they gather spontaneously but rather because their employer makes the team put itself together, actualize itself, at a certain time to play the Chicago Bulls. The Bundestag exists prior to its constitution as the new Bundestag; according to Aristotle, the productive power included in the male seed, the form, exists prior to the moment in which it begins to work, that is, to inform female menstruation; the explosive power in a bomb exists prior to the moment the bomb explodes; the bomb couldn't explode without the material capable of exploding, and the material is present in order to be capable of exploding at the requested time; several recently developed bombs explode upon contact between two or more materials in the bombshell; that is, the bomb puts its parts together, as the new Bundestag does when its members assemble in Bonn. For an Aristotelean the species puts its parts, a male being and a female being, together to come out again as a newborn individual of the same species. In other words, the phrase «konstituiert sich» (constitutes itself) borrows its intelligibility mainly from the traditional metaphysical logic of potentiality and actuality. The new Bundestag is the «actualization» of the Bundestag, the latter being an entity that has «potential existence,» and this potential existence in turn presupposes a prior actual Bundestag or a verfassungsgebende Versamm-lung. However, the new Bundestag exists only because the Bundestag intends its actualization as the new Bundestag, as each entity existing in potentiality «strives for» actuality. Something that exists in potentiality is not nothing; rather your capacity to practice medicine exists in you and it «strives for» being actualized or actualizing itself, that is, you strive to work as a physician.) In cases such as the Bundestag its individual members have the duty to make it happen that the Bundestag comes out of its potential existence so as to work in actuality.[27]

Incidentally, what Heidegger means can best be explained by a phrase Reiner Schürmann uses in the acknowledgment of his 1987 book *Heidegger: On Being and Acting—From Principles to Anarchy:* «While working on the original French edition {published in 1982} of this study, I published several sections in the English language. These pieces not only suffered from being taken out of their systematic context, but all of them were also preliminary versions, later reworked. Nevertheless I wish to thank the directors of the following publishing houses and journals for their permission to resettle in its native habitat material first printed in diaspora.»[28] Indeed, the publication of *Heidegger: On Being and Acting* establishes a new tradition of Heideggerian scholarship and thinking. However, it doesn't come out of the blue. Rather, the new tradition established by the publication of the English book has already existed prior to its establishment through the publication. For it has existed as the French original, *Le Principe d'anarchie: Heidegger et la question de l'agir,* and as some papers published here and there in English journals. In addition, it has already existed even in Heidegger's writings, since Schürmann's book is an interpretation of Heidegger's writings. Thus, no new Erbe or tradition is established through the publication of the English book. Rather something that has already existed prior to the publication of the English book enters a context in which it has previously been absent, and it begins to have an influence in that context. Or it was already present in that context but only as the few papers here and there in various English journals behind which only those who already knew the French original could recognize the whole project. In the publication of the English version the whole project, so to speak, puts itself together, gathers itself, constitutes itself, out of its fragmentary existence scattered into the various papers living in the diaspora. It is similar in Heidegger. By definition, the Erbe exists prior to its heirs. As long as the prospective authentic Dasein has not yet made the choice, the Erbe exists only in a scattered way, namely, in some possibilities hard to recognize. For ordinary Dasein has covered up by the work of ambiguity all the ways in which the Erbe is present in the world of the «they.» In authentic Dasein's choice, the Erbe constitutes itself; that is, it puts itself together out of its dismembered parts, and enters a context in which it has been previously absent or in which it has been present only in a scattered way.

According to postmodernists, modernists would say that Schürmann wanted to replace the discourse on Heidegger prior to 1987 with his book, while postmodernists themselves would say that Schürmann wanted to «enrich» the existing discourse on Heidegger. Be this as it may in Schürmann's case—the phrase «gegen» (SZ 383; «against,» BT 435) already indicates that in Heidegger the Erbe is polemical against the world of the «they.» As I already elaborated in chapter 1, at the end of the drama authentic Dasein even cancels the world of the «they» in order to rerealize the past or the Erbe.

Why does Schürmann say that the English papers were printed in the diaspora, and that the publication of the English translation resettles them in their native habitat? I don't know whether, for Schürmann, missionaries live in a diaspora or not. However, even if they do, after successful conversions the missionaries and their church don't resettle themselves in their native habitat. Rather, the missionaries have «conquered» new land—in Schürmann's case, the English readers—for their church in addition to the native habitat of their church and its members—in Schürmann's case, the French original of his book and the French audience. According to the strict notion of diaspora, the original habitat was indeed lost, because one was driven out of it by an enemy that has taken over the native habitat. In that case, Schürmann would present the expansion of the original territory as an act in which one regains the lost original territory, and prior to which one had no territory at all, since the original territory was lost. Why does Schürmann present his missionaries from French territory into the English language as though their native habitat, the French site, had been destroyed and taken over by an enemy? Only on this assumption can the English papers be said to be resettled in their native habitat through the publication of the English book. Schürmann's Heidegger in *Heidegger: On Being and Acting* is, so to speak, a very «cool,» a very Foucauldian Heidegger. Still, in *Heidegger: On Being and Acting* as well as in his posthumously published work[29] Schürmann remains faithful to the basic tenet of Heidegger's philosophies from the thirties on; the fascination of «the Greeks» shared by many German intellectuals since Winckelmann. In the pre-Socratics, Being was present in the primordial way. With the beginning of metaphysics, Being withdraws. From that moment on, Being as well as the humans are, so to speak, in the diaspora, and only a few individuals, Meister Eckhart or Hölderlin, have an experience of Being in its primordial way. However, their writings are covered up by the work of ambiguity. At the end of metaphysics, primordial Being raises its voice, and it is possible and necessary to repeat the primordial experience of Being in the pre-Socratics. Schürmann's commitment to this crucial feature in Heidegger is obviously the reason for his peculiar attitude toward the fortune of his book on its way into the English language. However, the same motif is already present in *Being and Time,* though with different actors. As was mentioned above, in the drama of the entire book *Being and Time* at the end of Division

One, in large parts of Division Two, and at the beginning of section 74 ordinary Dasein has fallen away from its original world and is living in a new world. In addition, the constant strife for something new, for the modern, plus the forgetting of what was left behind are the mark of curiosity practiced by ordinary and inauthentic Daseine. Ordinary Dasein looks forward without looking backward and without taking over the Erbe. At the end of chapter 3, it will be clear that ordinary Dasein has fallen away from Gemeinschaft (community) and is living in Gesellschaft (society). At some point in the downward plunge away from community, community, the Erbe neglected by ordinary Dasein, raises its voice and demands to be recognized. Prior to this moment, the Erbe has remained, so to speak, in the background or in the diaspora; it has been present only as the possibilities covered up by ordinary Dasein's work of ambiguity. Thus, the Erbe exists prior to all ordinary Daseine, those that become authentic as well as those that become inauthentic. In addition, the Erbe is not identical with «the way of interpreting Dasein which has come down to us» (BT 435; SZ 383). Rather it is the estate «*in terms of* {*aus*}» (BT 345; SZ 383), or from which, authentic Dasein receives its appropriate share, inheritance, and which is only one set of all the possibilities in the pool of «the way of interpreting Dasein which has come down to us» (BT 435; SZ 383), namely, all those possibilities that ordinary Dasein covers up to go on living in its fallen world, in Gesellschaft, and in the possibilities coming along with Gesellschaft. The Erbe provides authentic Daseine with identity and thus enables them to «become *authentically* bound together» (BT 159; «*eigentliche* Verbundenheit,» SZ 122) or to have «primordial Being-with-one-another» (BT 219; «das ursprüngliche Miteinandersein,» SZ 174). Being authentically bound together through their common origin, the Erbe, the authentic Daseine don't fight «against» (BT 435; SZ 383) the Erbe or each other. Rather they fight «against» (BT 435; SZ 383) ordinary Daseine and inauthentic Daseine; that is, against all the Daseine that live in «deficient modes of solicitude» (BT 158; SZ 120).[30] The being-with-one-another of the «they» is the opposite of «[being] *authentically* bound together» (BT 159; SZ 122): «Being-with-one-another in the "they" is by no means an indifferent side-by-side-ness in which everything has been settled, but rather an intent, ambiguous watching of one another, a secret and reciprocal listening-in. Under the mask of "for-one-another" {Füreinander}, an "against-one-another" {ein Gegeneinander} is in play» (BT 219; SZ 175).[31] Being authentically bound together, the authentic Daseine fight «against» (BT 435; SZ 383) the ordinary and inauthentic Daseine and the world in which the ordinary and inauthentic Daseine live; that is, the authentic Daseine fight against «the way of interpreting Dasein which has come down to us» (BT 435; SZ 383) in order to replace that world with one in which the Erbe is properly rerealized. The authentic Daseine do so «for» (BT 435; SZ 383) «the way of interpreting Dasein which has come down to us» (BT 435; SZ 383) since through the repetition of the Erbe not only the Erbe but also the ordinary and inauthentic Daseine are resettled in the native habitat, in world $w_1$ as I called it above, since world $w_2$ is a diaspora from the viewpoint of $w_1$. Thus, the sentence that in authentic Dasein's choice «the handing down» of the Erbe «constitutes itself,» means that the Erbe has existed prior to all the ordinary Daseine; that it «puts itself together» out of its scattered existence as fragments covered up by the work of ambiguity; that it enters a context in which it has previously not been present, or in which it has been present only as scattered and inactive fragments; and that it begins to be active in that context as a unified force and power. The Erbe doesn't enter the scene without authentic Daseine taking it over. However, by being called upon and by uniting themselves and subduing themselves to the Erbe the authentic Daseine become the means, or the missionaries, of the Erbe. Appropriately, they are no longer the subject of Heidegger's sentence. Instead, they are just the site on which and through which «the handing down of» the Erbe «constitutes itself» (BT 435; SZ 383). That the handing down of the Erbe puts itself together means that the Erbe enters the scene and becomes active. Thus, the ultimate subject is the Erbe, as it becomes even more clear in the following sentences.[32]

As I already pointed out, in the following paragraphs Heidegger determines the Erbe as destiny and fate. In the passage on the Erbe he says that authentic Dasein acts «against» (BT 435; SZ 383) «the way of interpreting Dasein which has come down to us» (BT 435; SZ 383). In the penultimate sentence of the passage on destiny and fate, Heidegger adduces the appropriate noun. He says that «only in communicating and in struggling {im Kampf} does the power of destiny become free {wird frei}» (BT 436; SZ 384). As I already pointed out, the phrase «wird frei» («becomes free») does not mean that something is created anew but rather that something previously in bonds, so to speak, becomes free. In terms of the prisoners I talked about in section A of this chapter, ordinary Dasein has run «aus» («out of» in the sense of «illegitimate flight») Gemeinschaft, $w_1$. In the new world of ordinary Dasein, in $w_2$, the ordinary Daseine have imprisoned the remnants of $w_1$ or all the missionaries of $w_1$ occurring at the time of the Bocksgesang preceding the end of $w_2$. Some ordinary Daseine, however, listen to the call of the imprisoned Daseine and of destiny speaking through them. These Daseine and the prisoners are the authentic Daseine; those who understand themselves «*in terms of* {aus} *the heritage*» (BT 435; SZ 383) the «aus» in this case indicating the source of their identity and strength. Through the heritage, the prisoners and the Daseine that have liberated them become authentically bound together, and they take up the fight «against» the «they,» against Gesellschaft, which has imprisoned the messengers of destiny. They do so not for the sake of selfish interests but as missionaries of the Erbe.[33]

Even Guignon might admit that, at this point, «heritage» is not just «überkommene Ausgelegtheit» («the way of interpreting Dasein which has come down to us,» BT 435; ST 383) viewed from the perspective of authentic Dasein but only the authentic possibilities that thereafter are turned against «überkommene Ausgelegtheit.» However, this passage cannot be reconciled with his assumption that authentic Dasein maintains distance to the past so that it can reject some possibilities and choose others. Note that already here the subject has changed. Like the passage on repetition I discussed in section C of chapter 1, the first sentence of this paragraph has, if not a Dasein, then at least a resoluteness (of a Dasein) as its subject («The resoluteness {Die Entschlossenheit} in which Dasein comes back to itself, discloses . . . ,» BT 435; SZ 383). In the sentence, «If everything 'good' . . . the handing down of a heritage constitutes itself in resoluteness,» however, the «handing down of a heritage,» and by this, «heritage» is the active subject that imposes itself onto authentic Dasein. Thus, by this point, the Dasein that at the beginning seemed to be highly active since it ran forward becomes passive in the sense I explained in regard to the notion of Entschlossenheit in section A of chapter 1. As a result of this change, in the following sentences one cannot find anything indicating Dasein's sovereign ability to reject some offers of the past, much as one might like to. Heidegger insists that heritage brings Dasein «into the simplicity of its *fate*» (BT 435; ST 384), that heritage enables or even forces Dasein to unequivocality by which «every accidental and 'provisional' {«vorläufige»} possibility {is} driven out»[34] (BT 435; ST 384) and that in all this Dasein gets its «Ziel schlechthin» («goal outright») (BT 435; ST 384). All this, of course, in this paragraph as well as in many others in *Being and Time*, is intended as the opposite of ordinary and inauthentic Dasein, which chooses now this, now that, and indulges in «comfortableness, shirking, and taking things lightly» (BT 435; SZ 384). Furthermore, death, and heritage, «pushes {stößt}» and «snatches» authentic Dasein «back from {reißt aus . . . zurück}» (BT 435; ST 384) the possibilities ordinary Dasein indulges in. All this rules out the idea that authentic Dasein has a conversation with the past in which it rejects several offers and adopts others. Thus, what Heidegger says is the opposite: authentic Dasein has no choice, so to speak, to deliberate with heritage. Rather, heritage catches Dasein and puts it under heritage's command.

Thus, what authentic Dasein does is execute the act of separation. Dasein, or heritage, κρίνει, de-cides, separates. In the twilight of ordinary Dasein there are inauthentic possibilities, and there are authentic possibilities the latter being covered up by ambiguity. Authentic Dasein draws on the latter. It chooses «aus (from)» all the possibilities in the twilight those that have been made unrecognizable by ordinary Dasein, and it does so in order to get «aus (out of)» ordinary Dasein and its world and to then turn its choice «gegen (against)» ordinary Dasein and its world. This ambiguity of «aus» in the passage on «überkommene Ausgelegtheit» is, as I have discussed, resolved in the first passage on «heritage» insofar as Heidegger there uses «aus» exclusively in the sense of that from which authentic Dasein draws its choice without leaving this place it has reached in its decision and choice. Correspondingly, the «aus» in the passage on «Being-free for death» snatching «one back from {aus}» the endless possibilities of comfortableness, shirking, and taking things lightly (BT 435; SZ 384) exclusively means «to get out of» those possibilities without ever returning to them. Heritage is that place «aus (from)» which the authentic possibilities are derived that ordinary Dasein covers up. As such heritage is the site that provides authentic Dasein with identity and the strength to turn the authentic possibilities «against» ordinary Dasein's world. This site, heritage, imposes itself onto authentic Dasein and enables authentic Dasein to resolve the twilight of ordinary Dasein into the opposition between authentic Dasein living in heritage and inauthentic Dasein living outside the realm of heritage.

The last sentence of that paragraph also shows that it is heritage that catches Dasein and not the other way around. That sentence explains the notion «the simplicity of its *fate*» and summarizes the entire paragraph. It reads: «Damit bezeichnen wir das in der eigentlichen Entschlossenheit liegende ursprüngliche Geschehen des Daseins, in dem es sich frei für den Tod ihm selbst in einer ererbten, aber gleichwohl gewählten Möglichkeit *überliefert*» (SZ 384). Macquarrie and Robinson have translated this as: «This is how we designate Dasein's primordial historizing, which lies in authentic resoluteness and in which Dasein *hands* itself *down* to itself, free for death, in a possibility which it has inherited and yet has chosen» (BT 435). The relative clause at the end, «in dem . . . *überliefert*» («and in which . . . yet has chosen»), is rather cryptic. German speakers know that it can be difficult to find the antecedent a personal pronoun or reflexive pronoun refers to if several nouns of the same gender as the pronoun occur in the context. Usually only minor measures are required to avoid such inconveniences for the readers. The personal pronoun «ihm» in «ihm selbst» («to itself») is the dative masculine and neuter personal pronoun. «Dasein» («Dasein's»), «Tod» («death»), and «dem» (the «which» in «in which,» referring to the neuter «das . . . Geschehen des Daseins») are all masculine or neuter (that is, none are feminine in which case the dative personal pronoun would be «ihr»). Thus, the dative object «ihm» in «ihm selbst» («to itself») can refer to «dem» (which refers to «Geschehen,» that is, «primordial historizing»), or to «es» («itself») (which refers to «Daseins»), or to «Tod» («death») as well. Heidegger could easily have avoided this inconvenience for the reader. He could have just replaced «ihm selbst» with «dem Tod,» «diesem selbst,» or «diesem,» «dem Dasein selbst,» «sich selbst (to Dasein itself),» or «dem Geschehen selbst,» if he had wanted the dative object of handing down to be clear and unambiguously refer to «death,» «Dasein,» or to «primordial historizing.» However, he chose the enigmatic «ihm.» The translators have chosen to refer «ihm selbst» to the Dasein (the «to itself» in «in which Dasein *hands* itself *down* to itself, free for death»). Guignon, I suppose, read the sentence in the light of later ones in section 74, which I discussed in chapter 1, particularly the one with «*kann, sich selbst die ererbte Möglichkeit überliefernd*» (SZ 385; «*by handing down to itself the possibility it has inherited,*» BT 437) as well as in the light of his interpretation of the sentence with «*erwidert*» (SZ 386; «*reciprocative rejoinder,*» BT 438). If Dasein hands something down to itself, that is, if Dasein is the active subject as well as the recipient of this handing down, Dasein is active and regards everything from its own vantage point. Thus, Guignon reads the relative clause as an anticipation of Dasein's capacity to freely choose out of the several possibilities offered by the past the one that fits its particular utopian ideal. In fact, up to and around the middle of the nineteenth century, one could have said, «Dasein überliefert sich ihm selbst,» if one wanted to refer the dative personal pronoun to «Dasein.» However, in such cases Heidegger seems to use the current «sich,» as a sentence at the beginning of the paragraph in question shows («Die Entschlossenheit, in der das Dasein auf sich selbst zurückkommt,» SZ 383; «The resoluteness in which Dasein comes back to itself,» BT 435). Since, therefore, Heidegger did not write «dem Dasein selbst,» nor «sich selbst,» the phrase «ihm selbst» cannot refer to Dasein. Since death doesn't provide Dasein with authentic possibilities (BT 434; SZ 383), one can rule out the case that Heidegger wanted to say that Dasein hands itself down to death. Therefore, one is left with «primordial historizing» and thus with «fate» and «heritage» to which Dasein hands itself down. Clearly, then, this sentence and indeed the entire paragraph anticipates what is later on explained in terms of repetition, including the switch to «sich überliefern» as subjugation, which I discussed in section C of chapter 1.

However, perhaps Heidegger intentionally left the sentence open to several interpretations. In this case, one would have not only Guignon's notion of the choosing Dasein. Within the context of the entire section 74, the sentence would still anticipate the step concerning Dasein's subjugation to the past. Or perhaps Heidegger wanted to express within his syntax and grammar that Geschehen he is talking about. In this case, the «ihm selbst» would be, so to speak, the Whitsuntide of heritage, fate, death, and Dasein. However, even based on this assumption, one cannot find anything in this paragraph that indicates Dasein's autonomy and independence toward the heritage in Guignon's sense, much as one would like to. In fact, this aspect that, theologically, might be designated as Whitsuntide is operating implicitly in the entire sentence whether one relates «ihm selbst» to one of the three nouns or to some, so to speak, grammatical supersubject resulting from the movement described in the entire paragraph and its last sentence. Despite the objections regarding Heidegger's usage of «sich,» one might reasonably refer «ihm selbst» to «es» (= «des Daseins»). However, this Dasein is then no longer the choosing Dasein at the beginning of its choice. Rather, it is the Dasein as transformed by the choice, or, in Heidegger's terms, it is the «ursprüngliche, unverlorene ... Erstrecktheit der ganzen Existenz» (SZ 390; «the whole of existence stretched along . . . in a way which is primordial and not lost» BT 442) that has to be grasped and achieved by the empirical Dasein in order for the latter to become authentic. As was mentioned, Heidegger could have written «sich selbst» to refer to Dasein. (In order to avoid a possible inconvenience for the readers in regard to the dative object and the accusative object, he might have rearranged the words, and he might have used an «an» with the accusative: «in dem es, frei für den Tod, sich an sich selbst in einer ererbten, aber gleichwohl gewählten Möglichkeit überliefert.») However, this would not have sufficiently emphasized that he is talking here about three different aspects of Dasein or about three different Daseine in one and the same Dasein. The «Dasein» («es»), the subject of the relative cause, is Dasein on its way to authenticity. On this way, it hands «itself» («sich»), the accusative object, down; the «itself» refers to Dasein as ordinary Dasein or to Dasein as the Dasein that, as each Dasein, is open for both authenticity and inauthenticity (BT 68; SZ 42f.). It hands itself down «to itself» («ihm selbst,» the dative object); as to itself in the sense of «the whole of existence stretched along . . . in a way which is primordial and not lost» (BT 442; SZ 390). The expression «ihm selbst» is a somewhat pathetic formula indicating the radical difference between Dasein prior to its choice and Dasein after the choice. Dasein can achieve authenticity or «the whole of existence stretched along . . . in a way which is primordial and not lost» (BT 442; SZ 390) only by being snatched «back from» (BT 435; «aus . . . zurück,» SZ 384) the «they» and by being brought «into the simplicity of its *fate*» (BT 435; SZ 384).[35] Thus, Dasein hands itself down to fate and what fate entails, namely, heritage, which makes fate possible. The phrase «ihm selbst» designates the slot destiny has allotted to a given Dasein, and which that Dasein has to take over in order to become authentic. As the terminology already indicates, there is an aspect of violence in this; however, it is a purifying violence. «To have fate,» as Heidegger puts it in the following paragraphs, is a good state, and it was a desirable state for all those young people in the Youth Movement whom I mentioned in section A of chapter 1 and to whom I will refer again in chapter 3. Anyway, what on the level of «being-towards death» (BT 279ff.; SZ 235ff.) was «coming back to itself» as nullity reveals itself on the more «ursprüngliche» level of historicality as identification with and subjugation to a fate representing heritage and all the richness contained in it. In the entire section 74, Heidegger is not talking about a free choice, that is, a choice in which the subject chooses freely and remains free and autonomous during and after the choice, as the bourgeois subject claims to be in his acting and choices since the subject is subject only to reason but not to tradition, destiny, or fate. Rather, Heidegger talks about a choice that transforms Dasein. He clearly indicated this also by the «gleichwohl» («yet») in «yet has chosen» (BT 435; ST 384). Though freedom of individual choice is no longer an issue in authentic Dasein, the choice has been Dasein's free choice since, after all, the Dasein ran forward into death. As I will explain in more detail in chapter 3, in these passages Heidegger calls upon the bourgeois subject to replace its framework of reason, subjectivity, individuality, and autonomy with that of fate and community. However, this replacement has to be an act of bourgeois autonomy itself, otherwise authentic Dasein would be haunted by a bad conscience. In other words, the resignation of the autonomous subject must be an act of the autonomous subject himself, otherwise it would be too «they»-like, too ordinary, and too proletarian. This act of subjugation to heritage and, as it turns out, to Volk, however, is—in its structure—nothing other than the notion of sacrifice demanded by the extreme Right or fascism.

Authentic Dasein does not leave the world of ordinary Dasein, and it does not criticize the world of ordinary Dasein from a vantage point beyond ordinary Dasein's world. Rather, authentic Dasein turns around, or reevaluates, ordinary Dasein's world from within this world. Or it turns ordinary Dasein's world upside down. Authentic Dasein recognizes that the possibilities that «have mostly been made unrecognizable by ambiguity» (BT 435; SZ 383) are, once the work of ordinary Dasein is seen for what it is, the authentic possibilities that bring authentic Dasein into the proper relation to its origin, to heritage, destiny, and Volksgemeinschaft. With this activity authentic Dasein produces a separation between the Daseine. In the next paragraph Heidegger clarifies this difference in terms of that between the Daseine that have fate (the authentic Daseine) and those that do not (the inauthentic Daseine):

> Dasein can be reached by the blows of fate only because in the depths of its Being Dasein *is* fate in the sense we have described {weil es im Grunde seines Seins in dem gekennzeichneten Sinne Schicksal *ist*}. Existing fatefully in the resoluteness which hands itself down {Schicksalhaft in der sich überliefernden Entschlossenheit existierend}, Dasein has been disclosed as Being-in-the world both for the 'fortunate' circumstances which 'come its way' and for the cruelty of accidents. Fate does not first arise from the clashing together of events and circumstances. Even one who is irresolute gets driven about by these—more so than one who has chosen; and yet he can 'have' no fate {Durch das Zusammenstoßen von Umständen und Begebenheiten entsteht nicht erst das Schicksal. Auch der Unentschlossene wird von ihnen und mehr noch als der, der gewählt hat, umgetrieben und kann gleichwohl kein Schicksal "haben"}. (BT 436; SZ 384)[36]

Several points are noteworthy here. First, far from being something a Dasein creates or changes or breaks, «fate» exists prior to the Dasein and demands the latter's subjugation. The point is not how to create or break fate. Rather, the problem is whether a Dasein accepts, opens itself for, hands itself down to, subjugates itself to, or sacrifices itself to fate—which is what authentic Dasein does—or whether a Dasein denies fate and continues trying to evade it—which is what ordinary, and therefore inauthentic, Dasein does. Second, this passage shows that fate, and thus heritage, is all-pervasive. Even the inauthentic Dasein that believes itself to be outside of the realm of fate has to acknowledge that it is «im Grunde seines Seins» («in the depths of its Being») fate and heritage. In the passage following this, Heidegger, in his peculiar way, makes clear what is implied already here, namely, that ordinary Dasein's world is dependent on heritage and Volksgemeinschaft, that is, that the way from $w_1$ to $w_2$, as I called it before, is by no means one in which $w_1$ and its origin, i.e., Volksgemeinschaft, is completely annihilated; rather, «in the depth of» (BT 436; SZ 384) world $w_2$ the origin of $w_1$ remains present or, at any rate, begins to represence itself in the Bocksgesang. Ordinary Dasein has not left behind heritage and Volksgemeinschaft, it has merely fallen away from them and has made unrecognizable all those ways in which the «real» origin remains present within the verfallene world of ordinary Dasein. Thus, there is only one world. Ordinary Dasein's world is not a new world but just a verfallene version of a world in which the origin is properly present. Authentic Dasein understands this and reestablishes the origin in an undistorted way so that as a result authentic Dasein «so erst der *Gewesenheit* ihren eigentümlichen Vorrang verleiht» (SZ 386; «for the first time imparts to *having-been* its peculiarly privileged position,» BT 438). Thus, we have an asymmetrical situation. Ordinary Dasein claims that its world is independent of the one vanished in the past. Authentic Dasein, however, claims that this is not at all the case. Rather, according to authentic Dasein, ordinary Dasein's world is just a verfallene version of the world of the past and has to be canceled to make room for the reestablishment of that past world.[37] Third, there is an ambiguity in the sentence «und kann gleichwohl kein Schicksal "haben"» (SZ 384; «and yet he can 'have' no fate,» BT 436). This sentence may mean that it is impossible for inauthentic Dasein to have fate. It may also mean that inauthentic Dasein is not capable of having fate. And it can mean that it is possible that inauthentic Dasein does not have fate, since it evades fate. It has no fate, but it should have one, since «in the depths of its Being» (BT 436; SZ 384) it is fate. Thus, one might infer that what Heidegger means is that inauthentic Dasein can be forced to have fate, that is, in the struggle for the rerealization of the past authentic Dasein can force inauthentic Dasein into its fate, which inauthentic Dasein by itself cannot, or does not want to, reach. This is in line with my interpretation of «Widerruf» and of the «gegen» and «für» as an activity of authentic Dasein in which it replaces inauthentic Dasein's world for the sake of the latter. In the paragraphs on conscience, this motif is anticipated in the sentence: «Das entschlossene Dasein kann zum "Gewissen" der Anderen werden» (SZ 298; «When Dasein is resolute, it can become the 'conscience' of Others,» BT 344).

As this shows, the separation that authentic Dasein carries out, namely, that between authentic Dasein and ordinary Dasein—which in this separation becomes inauthentic Dasein—is a situation that calls for what is termed «Kampf» («struggle») in the subsequent passage. In this part, I have discussed the emergence and the unfolding of the crisis. In the twilight there emerges the anschwellende Bocksgesang that calls for the separation. In contrast to ordinary Dasein and inauthentic Dasein, authentic Dasein sees the present in the light of «Heute» («"today"»), realizes that there is a dangerous situation, and relates itself to the «heritage.» In so doing, it produces the separation between the Daseine that have fate and those that do not, i.e., the inauthentic Daseine. In the next step authentic Dasein realizes that its heritage and destiny is the Volksgemeinschaft, which calls it into struggle. I will discuss this step in chapter 3. After this, authentic Dasein hands itself down to the Volksgemeinschaft and recognizes what is at stake in the struggle. This is the passage on repetition I discussed already in chapter 1. Finally, authentic Dasein reaffirms its subjugation to the past and to the Volksgemeinschaft and begins the struggle, that is, the cancellation of the world of inauthentic Dasein. This is the passage on erwidert and Widerruf I discussed in chapter 1. There, the phrase «was im Heute sich als "Vergangenheit" auswirkt» (SZ 386; «that which in the "today", is working itself out as the 'past',» BT 438) refers to «überkommenen Ausgelegtheit» (SZ 383; «the way of interpreting Dasein which has come down to us,» BT 435) as follows: «that which in the "today", is working itself out as the 'past'» is the remnant of «the way of interpreting Dasein which has come down to us» after authentic Dasein has made the separation. By seeing the Volksgemeinschaft as the suppressed origin in and of the possibilities that ordinary Dasein has made unrecognizable in its work of ambiguity, authentic Dasein realizes that it has to cancel the world of inauthentic Dasein, that is, «that which in the "today", is working itself out as the 'past'» (BT 438; SZ 386) in order to make possible the rebirth of a Gemeinschaft, community, in which its origin, the Volk, is properly present.

By the end of chapter 3, it will be clear that what authentic Dasein destroys in the name of Volksgemeinschaft is the Gesellschaft, that is, liberal society and the political institutions coming with it. As I will show in the following chapter, for Scheler at the beginning of World War I «our German fate took its stand before us,» and he heard «just one single answer resounding from all German souls» (PPS 11). Heidegger demands that authentic Dasein «erwidert» (SZ 386) the call of the past. Scheler urges us to «hear God's call for a turning back» (PPS 646). What Heidegger labels «that which in the "today", is working itself out as the "past"» (BT 438; SZ 386) is called by Scheler «rubbish {Abfall, literally "fall-down-and-away-from"}» (RE 166; UW 140). In the kairos of World War I and the Weimar Republic, «we» recognize that our Gesellschaft is rubbish, a fall-down-and-away-from Gemeinschaft. What Heidegger calls «a disavowal» (BT 438; SZ 386) occurs in Scheler as the demand that Europe «expels from its blood like a foreign poison» (PPS 153) Gesellschaft. «We» have to destroy Gesellschaft in order to rerealize Gemeinschaft.

# 3

# Fate, Community,
# and Society

## A. Fate, Community, and Society

All political concepts, images, and terms have a polemical meaning {einen *polemischen* Sinn}. They are focused on a specific conflict and are bound to a concrete situation; the result (which manifests itself in war or revolution) is a friend-enemy grouping, and they turn into empty and ghostlike abstractions when this situation disappears. Words such as state, republic, society {Gesellschaft}, class, as well as sovereignty, constitutional state, absolutism, dictatorship, economic planning, neutral or total state, and so on, are incomprehensible if one does not know exactly who is to be affected, combated, refuted, or negated by such a term.[1]

These sentences in Carl Schmitt's *The Concept of the Political,* published in 1927, by no means mark an extravagant insight, difficult to come by, and peculiar to Schmitt. Rather, he explicitly formulated and generalized a common practice and self-understanding of many authors of his time. In this chapter of the book, I will deal with a cluster of notions, one of which occurs on Schmitt's list of examples, namely, Gesellschaft, society. Already by the end of the eighteenth century, the notion of society and the one Heidegger uses in section 74 of *Being and Time,* namely, that of Gemeinschaft, community (BT 436; SZ 384) had entered a constellation that became more and more polemical. From the perspective of right-wing authors, society was a realm, or a form of a synthesis of individuals, in which isolated persons act for the sake of their selfish interests. In this view, the only bond between individuals in society is the common assumption that each individual acts on behalf of his or her selfish interests, while regarding other individuals exclusively as a means in the pursuit of his or her interests. Thus, this bond is not a «real» bond, since the individuals are connected only in a superficial or—as it has often been put—in a mechanical way and are therefore not really united at all. Right-wing authors at Heidegger's time maintained that liberal parties, left parties, and labor unions do not transcend the realm of selfishness, but are merely means to pursue selfish ends more efficiently. In contrast to society, community and the different communities—family, the village or small town, the Volk, the nation, for some also the state—provide individuals with a stable identity through traditions, customs (Sitte), and feelings uniting individuals on the «deep» level of «positive» emotions. These feelings and attitudes enable the individual to transcend selfishness and to regard himself or herself as part of a larger whole that is not mechanically put together but, like an organism, has a life of its own, exists «prior» to the individuals, and enables them to display «positive» emotions—trust, love, care, awe—both toward the community as well as toward the other members of the community.[2] Related to the notion of Gemeinschaft is that of Volk, people. In section 74 of *Being and Time,* Heidegger identifies «Gemeinschaft,» «community,» and «Volk,» «people», which are designated by the concept of Geschick, to which that of Schicksal is related:

> But if fateful {schicksalhafte} Dasein, as Being-in-the-World, exists essentially in Being-with-Others, its historizing is a co-historizing and is determinative for it as {bestimmt als} *destiny [Geschick].* This is how we designate the historizing of the community {Gemeinschaft}, of {the} people {des Volkes}. Destiny is not something that puts itself together out of individual fates {Schicksalen}, any more than Being-with-one-another can be conceived as the occurring together of several Subjects. Our fates have already been guided in advance, in our Being with one another in the same world and in our resoluteness for definite possibilities. Only in communicating and in struggling does the power of destiny become free. (BT 436; SZ 384)[3]

In right-wing discourse, the notion of Vorsehung (providence) is related to Schicksal (fate) and Geschick (destiny). Gesellschaft, Gemeinschaft, Volk, Volksgemeinschaft, Geschick, Schicksal, Vorsehung—each of these concepts has its specific history in which it acquired different meanings and polemical functions. However, in the 1910s and 1920s a peculiar constellation of these notions emerged that was exclusively used by authors on the political Right. For my purposes, I can proceed, so to speak, according to the German saying, «Rechts ist, wo der Daumen links ist» (the right side is [that hand] where the thumb is [on the] left [side of the hand]). In the first two decades of this century, authors were «politically Right» if they explicitly argued against (classical) liberals and if, at the same time, they also argued against leftist authors. «Liberals» were all those authors who advocated a liberal society, in other words, those who—relying on Adam Smith's «invisible hand»—proposed a free capitalist economy, in which the state did not interfere, and who also argued for parliamentary democracy. All those authors who maintained that the capitalist economy and society had to be transformed, either by a peaceful evolutionary process or by a revolution, into a socialist economy and society, whose major feature was the absence of private property of the means of production, were «leftists.» (In between liberals and leftists were those who wanted to keep the capitalist economy and society but also wanted to integrate the institutions of social welfare, etc. into it. Early in the century, many people maintained that the actual politics of the social democrats clearly showed that this was their intention.) In arguing against liberals and leftists, rightists made the following assumptions: (1) It is not reason or the development of the means of production that «governs» or «rules» history, but rather Geschick, Schicksal, or Vorsehung; (2) One must break with liberal society, because liberal society is either not «good» in itself or it is not «good» because, sooner or later, it will lead to a socialist society; (3) Liberal society is an aberration from, or has done away with, the «real» forms of life, with Gemeinschaften or with Gemeinschaft; (4) The Gemeinschaft can be rerealized through a destruction of liberal society.

As the song of the Social Democrats ("Brüder, zur Sonne, zur Freiheit!" [Brothers, onward to the sun, onward to freedom!]) already indicated, for social democrats as well as for liberals the development of society—the enormous advance of the means of production in capitalist economy and the progress of parliamentary democracy—was a step upward and forward. For right-wingers, however, this advance was actually a fall, even a downward plunge, that had to be «corrected» by canceling society and by rerealizing community. To cancel society meant to eliminate parliamentary democracy, but for many rightist authors it did not mean to exclude but rather to keep private possession of the means of production, that is, a capitalist economy. Canceling society, as far as its economy was concerned, meant purifying the Gesinnungen, the mentality, attitudes, and sentiments of all individuals involved in the capitalist economy of their alleged selfishness, since it was only this Gesinnung that was harmful and produced crises. Once that Gesinnung is removed, it will be clear that private property and modern technology are not a hindrance but rather the best means for promoting the development of the community. While some right-wing authors, among them the nostalgic, or conservative, romantics wanted a return to a pretechnological community, those I am interested in here adhered to the scheme outlined above. I will illustrate these assumptions with reference to two authors, Adolf Hitler and Max Scheler, who explicitly and in public declared themselves politically on the Right. However, authors who did not explicitly argue against liberals and leftists also must be considered rightists if they shared the above-mentioned premises that enabled rightist authors to condemn the liberals and leftists and if one finds in their works no premises or passages that could identify them as advocates for liberals, social democracy, or communism or from which one might be led to either of the latter positions. It is along these lines that I will infer from the fact that Heidegger's notion of historicality is identical with the positions of Scheler and Hitler that Heidegger's concept of historicality is also politically on the Right. In chapter 4, I will present leftist notions of decision in order to illustrate more concretely both concepts of decision, that of the Right and that of the Left.

Adolf Hitler's *Mein Kampf* consists of two volumes. The first, published in 1925, has 406 pages and includes his autobiography from his youth to the first successes of the Nationalsozialistische Deutsche Arbeiterpartei in Munich in 1920. In the second volume, published in 1927 and 376 pages long, Hitler explicates the program of the party in the context of his interpretation of history in general and of political history in particular, especially from the Kaiserreich up to November 1926. He presented the main points of the second volume already in the first one since he believed one had to repeat the main points again and again to hammer them home. In both volumes, it is Schicksal (fate), Vorsehung (providence), and God that govern history. In the first volume, fate is present from the first sentence on. He thanks fate for having allocated to him Braunau on the Inn as his birthplace:

> Als glückliche Bestimmung gilt es mir heute, daß das Schicksal mir zum Geburtsort gerade Braunau am Inn zuwies. Liegt doch dieses Städtchen an der Grenze jener zwei deutschen Staaten, deren Wiedervereinigung mindestens uns Jüngeren als eine mit allen Mitteln durchzuführende Lebensaufgabe erscheint! (MK 1)

> Today it seems to me providential that Fate should have chosen Braunau on the Inn as my birthplace. For this little town lies on the boundary between two German states which we of the younger generation at least have made it our life work to reunite by every means at our disposal. (MKe 3)

Reading the English translation, one could get the impression that Hitler by himself made up as his life's work the reunification of Germany and Austria and that fate comes into play only as a power placing the individual into circumstances that are either favorable or not favorable for the individual's realization of the lifework he has set for himself. In the first case, he will deplore fate, in the latter, however, he will thank fate, as Hitler does here. At that time, however, German readers would have read those two sentences differently. They would have taken for granted that fate, in the first place, has given Hitler his life's work, and that Hitler thanks fate for having placed him into circumstances that made it relatively easy for him to recognize what task fate has given him.[4] Still, to become aware of such an extraordinary mission as his is not easy, and he had to go to some lengths before he was able to recognize his fate.[5] The young Hitler wanted to become a painter and later on an architect. However, as he realized in November 1918, it was his fate to become a politician. He had been wounded at the western front in France in World War I and had been brought to a hospital in Pommern, East Prussia, where he heard of the revolution in Germany:

> In the days that followed, my own fate became known to me {wurde mir auch mein Schicksal bewußt}. I could not help but laugh at the thought of my own future which only a short time before had given me such bitter concern. Was it not ridiculous to expect to build houses on such ground? At last it became clear to me that what had happened was what I had so often feared but had never been able to believe with my emotions.
>
> Kaiser William II was the first German Emperor to hold out a conciliatory hand to the leaders of Marxism, without suspecting that scoundrels have no honor. While they still held the imperial hand in theirs, their other hand was reaching for the dagger.
>
> There is no making pacts with Jews; there can only be the hard: either—or.
>
> I, for my part, decided to go into politics {Ich aber beschloß, Politiker zu werden}. (MKe 206; MK 225)[6]

It is not quite clear whether his suspicion or fear, now vindicated, refers to Kaiser William II, the revolution, or his decision, or to two or all three of them. If it refers to his decision too, the passage also testifies that his fate is hard, but that it is only a great «person» («Person») that can have a great fate because the tenets of Marxism and liberalism to the contrary notwithstanding, history is made by the great person and the great race (e.g., MKe 382ff.; MK 419ff.). At any rate, this passage is one of the shorter examples among many statements in which he expounds upon what he considers crucial in his life and his understanding of world history. His decision to become a politician does not come about as the culmination of a process in which, independent of anything or anyone else, the individual has freely imagined and considered several possibilities for his life and then, for this or that reason, adopted one of the options. Rather, here the individual simply becomes aware of his fate, which is not produced by him, or the individual—to use a formula of Heidegger's in regard to Plato—«only responded {entsprach} to what addressed itself to him {was sich ihm zusprach}» and what the individual himself «did not bring about» (BW 299; VA 21). The individual does not create his fate. Instead, his fate exists prior to him and, at some point, explicitly raises its voice. It is in this moment that the individual becomes conscious of his fate and has the choice to obey, take on, and realize his fate or not to do so. This choice, however, is not an arbitrary one. The individual does not express his personal freedom by deliberating on his own whether or not he should take on his fate. On the contrary, he proves his freedom by obeying the compelling call of fate, for it is his «*sacred duty {heilige Pflicht} to act in this way*» (MKe 640; MK 725).

There is no choice, for I can't not do what is my duty. This in no way diminishes the greatness of the individual—quite the contrary. Obeying the call proves the greatness of the person who is capable of recognizing the enormous duty to save the Germans and the entire world. Only a coward, or an inauthentic Dasein, shies away from the task fate has ordered him to carry out. Obeying the call, however, is also already the first step toward the rerealization of the Aryan race, for the strong sense of duty and the willingness to sacrifice oneself for the community of the people and the race are both indications and effects of the superiority of the Aryan race, whose political domination over the entire world has to be reestablished (e.g., MKe 296ff.; MK 325ff.). The «Jew» is the opposite of the «Aryan.» While the Aryan's blood was originally pure but later became contaminated, the Jew kept his blood pure and contaminated the blood of other people. While the Aryan has the strongest sense of self-sacrifice for the sake of the Volksgemeinschaft, the Jew has the strongest sense of individual self-preservation, and he always acts for the sake of his selfish interests (MKe 300ff.; MK 329ff.). In liberalism and parliamentary democracy, it has become manifest that the Jew has spoiled the blood of the Aryan. Social democracy and Marxism are just means for the Jew to achieve dominion over the entire world. One of the leitmotifs of Hitler's book is the often repeated assumption that, no longer guided by the common good but rather by their selfish private interests, the bourgeois individuals and their parties—the liberals as well as the conservatives—compromise and «bargain» with the political enemy to the extent that they are no longer capable of seeing the enemy as enemy, just as in the passage quoted above, their emperor was no longer able to do. Hitler characterizes this as «*the steadily increasing habit of doing things by halves {Halbheit in allem und jedem}*,» no «sense of joy in responsibility {Verantwortungsfreudigkeit},» no «will,» no «force of decision {Entschlußkraft}» (MKe 236f; MK 258). Caring only about themselves and having only one God, namely, «money» (MKe 406; MK 449), these bourgeois people want to avoid any clear either-or; they don't want to have fate for fate in decisive moments does not operate like merchants and moneymakers. The bourgeois and the social democrats in their internationalism try «to deny the entire past . . . , to make it bad or worthless, which shows either inferiority or even an evil intention,» since the meaning and the purpose of revolutions does not lie in the destruction of the works of the past but in the effort «to remove what is bad or unsuitable and to continue building on the sound spot that has been laid bare» (MKe 261; MK 286).[7] Having no sense for and actively denying the only source of a meaningful future, that is, the past, and lacking force of decision, the bourgeois certainly has no sense for the future (e.g., MKe 29, 398; MK 29, 440).[8]

The second and crucial chapter of the first volume is entitled "Years of Study and Suffering in Vienna" (MKe 19; "Wiener Lehr- und Leidensjahre," MK 18). The title is an allusion to Goethe's famous novels *Wilhelm Meisters Lehrjahre* and *Wilhelm Meisters Wanderjahre*. In fact, the first volume follows the pattern of a Bildungsroman, a novel about a character's intellectual or spiritual development, in style, organization, and also in Hitler's efforts to imitate the language of such novels. In other words, here too the individual leaves his place of birth, goes out into the world to experience all the Mächte des sittlichen Lebens, powers of the ethical life, to which he has to establish a relationship. The ideal of the bourgeois Bildungsroman was, as Hegel put it in a formulation that is as polemical and ironic as characteristic of his entire philosophy, the «Einbildung» («building of . . . into»).[9] The free individual bildet sich, forms or molds himself by, so to speak, molding, or merging, himself into the powers of the ethical life. In this process, the individual transcends his particularity and abstract freedom and becomes general or universal. By the same token, the powers of the ethical life bilden the individual by bilden themselves ein into the individual, that is, by molding themselves into the individual. In this way, the powers of the ethical life realize and affirm their actuality in the free individuals. Hitler rejected this model of the Bildungsroman. For he did not acknowledge the powers of the ethical life prevalent during his time. However, he also rejected the second type of the Bildungsroman, namely, that the individual, either triumphantly or in resignation, does not recognize himself in the powers of the ethical life, withdraws from them, and leaves them as they are. For Hitler was serious about the demand that individuals have the right to recognize themselves in the powers of the ethical life as well as about the demand that the powers of the ethical life must be proper manifestations of the ideal common good. In his view, none of the powers of the ethical life in existence at that time could live up to these standards. Thus, all of them had to be thoroughly transformed or pushed aside. Therefore, the title of the first volume is utterly un-bourgeois, namely, "A Reckoning" (MKe 1; "Eine Abrechnung," MK n.p.). In the course of his Bildung, Hitler encountered all the powers of the ethical life prevalent in the literature on community and society, and he encountered them in the order in which they are discussed there. Hitler begins with the small-scale communities of the family and the villages or small towns, in his case Braunau. He was privileged by fate to be able already there to encounter the large-scale communities, especially the people, for he experienced the Slavic people and the threat they posed to Germany. He then moves on to society, the big city, in his case Vienna. Here he encountered capitalist society and the associations related to it, such as the unions and the political parties. In Vienna he also got to know more thoroughly the large-scale communities, namely, the nation, the people, the race, and the state. Later on in the book, he also discusses the issue of the different German Stämme, tribes.[10] However, in none of these societies and communities can he find the common good realized. Society is the realm of selfish interests, more or less openly in the hands of the Jews. The large-scale communities have fallen prey to the modus operandi of society. For because of their inability to make decisions and their creeping liberalism the bourgeois and the social democrats in their internationalism have fallen prey to the Jews who use them to pursue their dominion of the world. Thus, all these groups have to be canceled or thoroughly transformed in order to make room for the rebirth of the proper community, namely, the Volksgemeinschaft, the community of the people, of the Germans, acting as the proxy of the Aryans whose dominion over the world has to be reestablished.

Duplicating the pattern of the literature on Gesellschaft and Gemeinschaft, however, Hitler's position in it is a distinguished one not only because he makes a case for something not all of the literature advocated, namely, the Volksgemeinschaft, but also because, in contrast to most of the literature on Gemeinschaft, Hitler depicts the small-scale Gemeinschaften not so much as a stable realm threatened only by society. Rather, according to him, they are threatened and about to dissolve first and foremost because of the Slavic people and their blood, who are in the process of taking over the Hapsburg monarchy. This is the epistemological and emotional advantage fate gave him so as to facilitate his task of becoming conscious of his enormous fate. For, outside the Kaiserreich and having lived under the threat of the Slavic blood already as a child, Hitler could learn a lesson that, being busy with making colonies and building up a navy, the Germans of the Kaiserreich were in a position to learn only after World War I, namely, «what it means to be forced to fight for one's nationality {für sein Volkstum kämpfen zu müssen}» (MKe 11; MK 9). Already as a kid he «became a nationalist.» And, in addition, already as a kid he «learned to understand and grasp the meaning of history {Geschichte ihrem Sinne nach verstehen und begreifen}» (MKe 10; MK 8). Throughout his political career, he would unpack the notion of history he had learned from Dr. Leopold Pötsch:

> Even today I think back with gentle emotion on this gray-haired man who, by the fire of his narratives, sometimes made us forget the present; who, as if by enchantment, carried us into past times and, out of the millennial veils of mist, molded dry historical memories into living reality. On such occasions we sat there, often aflame with enthusiasm, and sometimes even moved to tears. (MKe 14; MK 12f.)[11]

The way back into the past is not such that it can lead one to forget the present. Rather, Dr. Leopold Pötsch taught his students the relevance of the past for the present, and that transformed Hitler into a revolutionary:

> What made our good fortune all the greater was that this teacher knew how to illuminate the past by examples from the present, and how from the past to draw inferences for the present. As a result he had more understanding than

anyone else for all the daily problems which then held us breathless. He used our budding nationalistic fanaticism as a means of educating us, frequently appealing to our sense of national honor. . . . And indeed, though he had no such intention, it was then that I became a little revolutionary. (MKe 14f.; MK 12f.)

To be a fervent nationalist already as a little kid was the gift of a fate that ensured that Hitler on his way through life would not fall prey to Gesellschaft. After the death of his mother, Hitler could not live on his orphan pension. Thus, he moved to Vienna to earn a living. Fate itself sent him there. Already prior to his settling in Vienna, fate removed one obstacle on his way to recognize his fate, for he had already failed to receive admission to the art school. Thus, the first sentence of the second chapter reads: «When my mother died, Fate, at least in one respect, had already made its decision {Als die Mutter starb, hatte das Schicksal in einer Hinsicht bereits seine Entscheidung getroffen}» (MKe 19; MK 18). It was a hard time in Vienna, «five years of hardship and misery» (MKe21; MK 20), with «hunger» as the only «faithful bodyguard» (MKe 21; MK 20). However,

> what then seemed to be the harshness of Fate {Härte des Schicksals}, I praise today as wisdom of Providence {Weisheit der Vorsehung}. While the Goddess of Suffering took me in her arms, often threatening to crush me, my will to resistance {Wille zum Widerstand} grew, and in the end this will was victorious.
>
> I owe it to that period that I grew hard and am still capable of being hard. And even more, I exalt it for tearing me away from the hollowness of comfortable life; for drawing the mother's darling out of his soft downy bed and giving him 'Dame Care' {Frau Sorge} for a new mother; for hurling me, despite all resistance, into a world of misery and poverty, thus making me acquainted with those for whom I was later to fight. (MKe 21; MK 20)

As the context and the other quotations in this section show, with «my will to resistance grew,» Hitler does not at all mean that his will to resist fate grew. Quite the opposite. Fate puts to the test the one it has chosen for higher ends in order to bring to the fore his ability to live up to his fate and to harden him for the mission before him. As one says in German, «sich seines Schicksals würdig erweisen» (to prove oneself worthy of one's fate), or «sich einer Aufgabe würdig erweisen» (to prove oneself worthy of a task) is what persons of character or what «Kämpfer» (MK 10; «fighters,» MKe 12) do, while only cowards or «die Lauen» (MK 10; «the lukewarm,» MKe 12) lose heart in face of the odds fate confronts them with.[12] Thus, his «will to resistance» and the hardness he has achieved are the will to resist the odds fate tests him with and also the will to resist the future odds he will have to overcome to carry out his life's work fate will reveal to him. The will to resistance is part of the training of his capacity to listen to and to comply with fate so as to prove himself worthy of fate when fate will reveal his life's work to him. He came to know those for whom he would fight later on, namely, the betrayed German workers, and he came to know their enemies, whom he would fight against, for he got to know «Marxism and Jewry» (MKe 21; «Marxismus und Judentum,» MK 20). Hitler maintains that on his arrival in Vienna he was unbiased toward society and the powers of ethical life related to it. He even enjoyed the struggle of the social democrats for the general right of the secret vote, as this seemed to contribute to the breakdown of the Austrian state. He also appreciated the social democrats' and the unions' pretension to work for the improvement of working conditions (MKe 37f., 46f.; MK 39f., 48f.). As for the Jews, he had adopted the attitude of his father, who in the course of his life «had arrived at more or less cosmopolitan views . . . , despite his pronounced national sentiments» (MKe 51; MK 54). He did not even recognize Jews as Jews (MKe 52; MK 54), and at the beginning of his time in Vienna the tone of the Viennese anti-Semitic press still seemed to him «unworthy of the cultural tradition of a great nation» (MKe 52; MK 56). Moreover, he had «a certain admiration» for the English parliament as «the most sublime form of self-government of a people» (MKe 76; MK 82). Thus, «it required the fist of fate {Faust des Schicksals} to open my eyes to {all the} betrayal of the peoples» (MKe 38; MK 40). Or, as he put it, in Vienna «fate itself became my instructor» (MKe 46; MK 48). As to parliamentarism, he felt he had to «be more than thankful to Fate for laying this question before me while I was in Vienna.» For if he had first encountered «this absurd institution known as 'parliament' in Berlin,» he might just have become a regular follower of the emperor (MKe 79; MK 85). All this is supposed to convey the idea that it was truth itself that forced him to cleanse his soul of the prevalent misjudgments and attitudes and to develop into the gift of fate and divine providence. Fate enabled him to see the truth. In the third book, he summarizes his political experiences and thinking of his time in Vienna. The penultimate paragraph reads:

> I do not know what my attitude toward the Jews, Social Democracy, or rather Marxism as a whole, the social question {soziale Frage}, etc., would be today if at such an early time the pressure of destiny {Druck des Schicksals}—and my own study—had not built up a basic stock of personal opinions within me. (MKe 125; MK 137)

Even prior to the first chapter, readers are informed that Hitler's philosophy of history is one of a «wieder» («re-»), of the return of a vanished past. In his "Dedication," he lists the names of all those who fell «on November 9, 1923, at 12.30 in the afternoon, in front of the Feldherrnhalle» (that is, during the unsuccessful putsch through which Hitler and his party wanted to take over the rule of Bavaria). They did so «with loyal faith in the resurrection of their people» (MKe n.p.; «im treuen Glauben an die Wiederauferstehung ihres

Volkes,» MK n.p.). Probably, there is no other book with as many occurrences of «wieder» («re-»). Just consider this example, representative of numerous similar passages:

> Through his physical strength and dexterity, he must recover {wiedergewinnen} his faith in the invincibility of his whole people. For what formerly {einst} led the German army to victory was the sum of the confidence which each individual had in himself and all together in their leadership. What will raise the German people up again {wieder emporrichten} is confidence in the possibility of regaining {Wiedererringung} its freedom. (MKe 411f.; MK 456f.)

The pervasive terminology of bodily infection, from which the Volkskörper, the body of the people, has to be cured drives home the same point. The body had been healthy, but then it fell ill. The sickness must be removed to restore the body to its healthy state. Sickness is a fall from health, and this fall must be reversed. At the very beginning of the chapter "Causes of the Collapse" (MKe 225ff.; "Ursachen des Zusammenbruchs," MK 245ff.), in which Hitler examines the causes of the defeat of Germany and Austria in World War I, he writes:

> The extent of the fall of a body is always measured by the distance between its momentary position and the one originally occupied. The same is true of nations {Völker} and states. A decisive significance must be ascribed to their previous position or rather elevation {Höhe}. . . . This is what makes the collapse of the Reich so hard and terrible for every thinking and feeling man, since it brought a crash from heights which today, in view of the depths of our present degradation, are scarcely conceivable. . . .
> So deep is the downfall of the Reich and the German people, . . . so blinded by the sublime {of the former Reich} {are the people} that they forget to look for the omens of the gigantic collapse which must after all have been somehow present.
> Of course, this applies only to those for whom Germany was more than a mere stop-over for making and spending money, since they alone can feel the present condition as a collapse, while to the others it is the long-desired fulfillment of their hitherto unsatisfied desires. . . .
> The cure of a sickness can only be achieved if its cause is known, and the same is true of curing political evils. (MKe 225f.; MK 245f.)

For many conservatives, the «re-» of history was about the reestablishment of the Kaiserreich. However, for Hitler the very fact that it had lost the war is sufficient indication that fate has something different in mind.[13] At the end of the chapter, he repeats that the «deepest and ultimate cause» was the «failure to recognize the racial problem and its importance for the historical development of peoples» (MKe 283; MK 310). This is the myth of the original purity of the Aryan race and its dominion over the world. This past has to be rerealized. For when the Aryan race conquered other people, its blood no longer remained pure but became mixed with inferior blood. This is the infection that has dragged mankind into the fall. Liberalism and parliamentary democracy are its latest steps in the downward progression. However, the fall is by no means already at its end. Rather,

the Western democracy of today is the forerunner of Marxism which without it would not be thinkable. It {Western democracy} provides this world plague with the culture in which its germs can spread. In its most extreme form, parliamentarianism, it created {In ihrer äußeren Ausdrucksform, dem Parlamentarismus, schuf sie sich noch} a 'monstrosity of excrement and fire' {quote from Goethe's *Faust,* part I, v. 5356}, in which, however, sad to say, the 'fire' seems to me at the moment to be burned out. (MKe 78; MK 85. Instead of «In its . . . created,» it should read «In its {democracy's} outer manifestation, namely parliamentarianism, it {democracy} even/at the end created. . . . »)

Marxism, in turn, culminates in bolshevism. Both are the means for the Jews to dominate the world, and bolshevism is the most advanced of the two (e.g., MKe 621ff; MK 700ff; Marx wrote *Capital* to provide the practice of the Jews with a theory, e.g., MKe 215; MK 234; even the social democrats are already lead by Jews, MKe 60; MK 64). Once bolshevism has taken over Europe entirely, everything will be lost.

However, prior to the end of the downward plunge—at a time when it is still possible to reverse its course—fate, arranged by God, interferes. Or it changes its mode of guiding history and adds thunderstorms and the call to reverse the downward plunge to its constant silent presence in history. For many, World War I was such an occasion. Prior to 1914 Hitler had felt that the entire world was becoming «one big department store» with the English as merchants, the Germans as the administrative officials, and the Jews as owners (MKe 157; MK 172). The fact that he was born into this period and not a hundred years earlier, at the time of the Wars of Liberation against the French, the fact that his «earthly pilgrimage . . . had begun too late,» in a «period 'of law and order',» he regarded as «a mean and undeserved trick of Fate» (MKe 158; «eine unverdiente Niedertracht des Schicksals,» MK 173). In this situation, the Boer War was «like a summer lightning,» and the Russo-Japanese War found him «considerably more mature» (MKe 158; MK 173). Still, fate, or rather Heaven, had decided to take some years to clean the air and to provide the Germans with an opportunity to get rid of the mentality of department stores and of their supposed owners:

Since then many years have passed, and what as a boy had seemed to me a lingering disease, I now felt to be the quiet before the storm. As early as my Vienna period, the Balkans were immersed in that livid sultriness which customarily announces the hurricane, and from time to time a beam of brighter light flared up, only to vanish again in the spectral darkness. But then came the

Balkan War and with it the first gust of wind swept across a Europe grown nervous. The time which now followed lay on the chests of men like a heavy nightmare, sultry as feverish tropic heat, so that due to constant anxiety the sense of approaching catastrophe turned at last to longing: let heaven at last give free rein to the fate which could no longer be thwarted {der Himmel möge endlich dem Schicksal, das nicht mehr zu hemmen war, den freien Lauf gewähren}. And then the first mighty lightning flash struck the earth; the storm was unleashed and with the thunder of Heaven there mingled the roar of the World War batteries. (MKe 158; MK 173)[14]

However, the war was lost. World War I and its outcome could not merely be the deplorable end of the Kaiserreich. It had to have a deeper meaning. Hitler maintains that fate brought about World War I and its consequences so as to make the disease visible and thus warn the Germans while there was still time for them to cure themselves and the world:

For the German people it must almost be considered a great good fortune that its period of creeping sickness was suddenly cut short by so terrible a catastrophe, for otherwise the nation would have gone to the dogs more slowly perhaps, but all the more certainly. The disease would have become chronic, while in the acute form of the collapse it at least became clearly and distinctly recognizable to a considerable number of people. (MKe 232; MK 253)

«Man» was able to master the plague because it comes in terrible waves. «Man» was not able to master tuberculosis because it comes along slowly and stealthily (MKe 232; MK 253).

Exactly the same is true of diseases of national bodies. If they do not take the form of a catastrophe, man slowly begins to get accustomed to them and at length, though it may take some time, perishes all the more certainly of them. And so it is a good fortune—though a bitter one, to be sure—when Fate resolves to take a hand in this slow process of putrefaction {wenn das Schicksal sich entschließt, in diesen langsamen Fäulnisprozeß einzugreifen} and with a sudden blow makes the victim visualize the end of his disease. For more than once, that is what such a catastrophe amounts to. Then it can easily become the cause of a recovery beginning with the utmost determination {Ursache einer nun mit äußerster Entschlossenheit einsetzenden Heilung werden}. (MKe 232f.; MK 254)

He continues:

But even in such a case, the prerequisite is again the recognition of the inner grounds which cause the disease in question.
Here, too, the most important thing remains the distinction between the causes and the conditions they call forth. This will be all the more difficult, the longer the toxins remain in the national body {Volkskörper} and the more they become

an ingredient of it which is taken for granted. For it is easily possible that after a certain time unquestionably harmful poisons will be regarded as an ingredient of one's own nation or at best will be tolerated as a necessary evil, so that a search for the alien virus is no longer regarded as necessary. (MKe 233; MK 254)

In the mixing of blood, that of the German people did not retain a unified racial nucleus and did not achieve another unity, even a lower one. This is a disadvantage, as it has prevented the Germans from confronting the common enemy in the moment of danger as a «solid front of a unified herd» (MKe 396; «geschlossene Front einer einheitlichen Herde,» MK 437).[15] However, this was, so to speak, the cunning of fate, as it is this very fact itself that makes the recovery possible:

> Today our people are still suffering from this inner division; but what brought us misfortune in the past and present can be our blessing for the future. For detrimental as it was on the one hand that a complete blending of our original racial components did not take place, and that the formation of a unified national body was thus prevented, it was equally fortunate on the other hand that in this way at least a part of our best blood was preserved pure and escaped racial degeneration. (MKe 397; MK 438f.)

In contrast to the widespread ignorance, especially in the era of liberalism, and the commonly held assumption that all human beings are of equal value («in völliger Gleichwertung»),

> today we know that a complete intermixture of the components of our people might, in consequence of the unity thus produced, have given us outward power, but that the highest goal of mankind would have been unattainable, since the sole bearer, whom Fate had clearly chosen for this completion {den das Schicksal ersichtlich zu dieser Vollendung ausersehen hat}, would have perished in the general racial porridge of the unified people.
> But what, through none of our doing, a kind Fate {ein gütiges Schicksal} prevented, we must today examine and evaluate from the standpoint of the knowledge we have now acquired. (MKe 397; MK 439)

The «highest goal of mankind» is «a peace . . . based on the victorious sword of a master people, putting the world into the service of a higher culture» (MKe 396; MK 438).

Once upon a time, the Aryans had been pure. Fate allowed for or even arranged for their fall. At a certain point in their fall—when it was still possible to restore purity and the lost supremacy—fate interfered in order to allow the Germans to become aware of the fallenness. For fate has chosen the Germans as the saviors of mankind. At the same time, fate has provided them with the means to restore their purity. Fate has brought about World War I and the Weimar Republic in Germany for the purpose of creating a crisis or a «great turning point» (MKe 406; «große Zeitenwende,» MK 450). Now it is possible to «halt the chariot of doom {Wagen des Verhängnisses} at the eleventh hour» (MKe 373; MK 409). Or, as Hitler put it regarding himself and his fellow Nazis, «today we are a reef; in a few years Fate may raise us up as a dam against which the general stream will break, and flow into a new bed» (MKe 667; MK 758). It is, as he says of the beginning of World War I, the site «where all playing is at an end and the inexorable hand of the Goddess of Destiny {die unerbittliche Hand der Schicksalsgöttin} begins to weigh peoples and men according to the truth and steadfastness of their convictions {Gesinnung}» (MKe 163; MK 178). It is the moment of the either-or: «*And assuredly this world is moving toward a great revolution. The question can only be whether it will redound to the benefit of Aryan humanity or to the profit of the eternal Jew*» (MKe 427; 475). Or, as he puts it close to the end of the book, «*Germany will either be a world power or there will be no Germany*» (MKe 654; MK 742).

Indeed, at this point what individuals do really matters. It depends on their reactions whether fate will be realized or not. The fate of the German people, Russia, and, ultimately, the entire world, is in their hands. In this sense, the individuals or people become fate, or agents, on whose behavior the «fate» of all people depends. Many don't want to hear the call of fate, as, for instance, in spring 1923: «With the occupation of the Ruhr, Fate once again held out a hand to help the German people rise again. . . . When the Frenchman carried out his threats, . . . a great decisive hour of destiny had struck for Germany {eine große, entscheidende Schicksalsstunde geschlagen}» (MKe 675–677; MK 767–769). For no one in Europe had an interest in a stronger France and would have opposed if the Germans had fought back. However, the parliamentarians missed the opportunity of resolute resistance and of building up military power (Mke 677ff.; MK 769ff.). Those who listen to the call realize that it will take centuries to restore the purity of blood and race (MKe 562; MK 629). However, it needs only six years of resolute National Socialist education and gymnastics to ready the Germans for war (MKe 633; MK 716). This is important, since the Germans need land and should take it from Russia, as Hitler explains at length in the last two chapters. «Here Fate itself seems desirous of giving us a sign» (MKe 654; MK 742), for the Russian revolution, lead by «the Jew,» has done away with the «intelligentsia {Intelligenz}» that built the Russian state. This intelligentsia, however, goes back, not to the Slavs, but rather to the Germans (MKe 654f.; MK 742f.). Indeed, in the «great turning point» (MKe 406; «große Zeitenwende,» MK 450) the «hand of the world clock . . . is loudly striking the hour in which the destiny of our nation must be decided in one way or another {in der unseres Volkes Schicksal so oder so entschieden werden muß}» (MKe 663; MK 752).

The fate of the Germans, and thus, of the world, depends on the individual Germans. Indeed, the «great turning point» brings freedom, action, and responsibility for the individuals. As it has become clear, however, the freedom of the individual does not consist in freely choosing among possibilities he has created by himself. Nor does it consist in freely choosing among several possibilities that the past, having become multiplied under the eyes of authentic Dasein and its utopian ideal, offers to authentic Dasein. And it does not consist in authentic Dasein breaking with the past or with all the possibilities in the past. Rather, in the «great turning point» all the different possibilities in which Dasein has lived so far become null and void in relation to the one fate imposes on the Daseine. Their freedom is the freedom of either not listening to fate or doing so, that is, submitting to fate, and realizing the command fate reveals. The first means that the chariot of history will irrevocably go down the drain, the second might lead it back to former heights, which fate has revealed in the «turning point.»[16] It has already become clear that the logical structure of Hitler's concept of history and the «turning point» is identical to that of Heidegger's concept of historicality. Thus, in Hitler one finds numerous sentences showing the same logic as Heidegger's sentence on erwidert and disavowal (BT 438; SZ 386). For Heidegger, in the moment of crisis authentic Dasein erwidert, responds to, the call for help of fate and of a past world which is being pushed aside but which demands to be repeated. Authentic Dasein hears the message that, in order to repeat the past world, it has to push aside what is now pushing the past aside or has already done so, that is, authentic Dasein must cancel, or widerrufen, Gesellschaft. Consider, for example, just the following two quotes: «If we understand that the resurrection {Wiedererhebung} of the German nation represents a question of regaining {Wiedergewinnung} our political will for self-preservation, it is also clear that this cannot be done by winning elements which in point of will at least are already national, but only by the nationalization of the consciously anti-national masses» (MKe 333; MK 366). The antinationalism of the masses (and the indecisiveness of the bourgeois parties) has pushed aside the German nation. Authentic Dasein erwidert the call for the Wiederholung of the German nation. Hearing the call, authentic Dasein realizes that it cannot wiederholen the German nation without a Widerruf of that mentality, that mode of the «they,» that has pushed aside the German nation. The «wider-» of the Widerruf cancels the «wider-,» that is, the «anti-» of the antinationalism of the masses or, in general, of the alleged hostile stance of society against community. Or, as Hitler put it on the next page:

Historically it is just not conceivable that the German people could recover {noch einmal einnehmen} its former position without settling accounts with those who were the cause and occasion of the unprecedented collapse which struck our state. For before the judgment seat of posterity November, 1918, will be evaluated, not as high treason, but as treason against the fatherland {Landesverrat}.

Thus, any possibility of regaining {Wiedergewinnung} outward German independence is bound up first and foremost with the recovery {Wiedergewinnung} of the inner unity of our people's will. (MKe 334; MK 367f.)

The reestablishment of the inner unity of the people's will is achieved by a Widerruf of the mentality of those who have destroyed it or—in terms of Hitler's architectural metaphor quoted above—by the demolition of what they have built in order to lay bare the sound foundations for the rebuilding of the National Socialist state.

As to the political aspect of Gesellschaft, it has already become clear from the few passages I have quoted here that Hitler develops an antiparliamentary and thoroughly illiberal domestic policy and an imperialistic foreign policy agenda that foreshadows the policy put to work in 1933. Of course, nothing else can be expected from someone who constantly stresses that peoples as well as individuals belonging to one and the same people are unequal and of different value, as for instance in the following passage:

In the state the folkish philosophy {völkische Weltanschauung} sees on principle only a means to an end and construes its end as the preservation of the racial existence of man. Thus, it by no means believes in an equality of the races, but along with their difference it recognizes their higher or lesser value and feels itself obligated, through this knowledge, to promote the victory of the better and stronger, and demand the subordination of the inferior and weaker in accordance with the eternal will that dominates this universe. Thus, in principle, it serves the basic aristocratic idea of nature and believes in the validity of this law down to the last individual. It sees not only the different value {den verschiedenen Wert} of the races, but also the different values of individuals. From the mass it extracts the importance of the individual personality, and, thus, in contrast to disorganizing Marxism, it has an organizing effect. But it cannot ... for in a bastardized and niggerized world. ... Anyone who dares to lay hands on the highest image of the Lord {i.e. the Aryan race, the Germans, and their leader} commits sacrilege against the benevolent creator of this miracle and contributes to the expulsion from paradise. (MKe 383; MK 421; see also MKe 442ff.; MK 492ff. and passim)

Moreover, a person who maintains that already in August 1914 it was the duty of the German government to «exterminate mercilessly» (MKe 169; «unbarmherzig auszurotten,» MK 185) the leaders of the Social Democratic Party and the Jews, was probably ready and willing to use violence, even to the point of physical annihilation, against all those who refused to exchange their mentality for that of National Socialism or who had been declared the eternal racial foe of the Germans.

As to the economic aspect of Gesellschaft, Hitler's diagnosis is that, indeed,

in proportion as the economic life grew to be the dominant mistress of the state, money became the god whom all had to serve and to whom each man had to bow down. More and more, the gods of heaven were put into the corner as obsolete and outmoded, and in their stead incense was burned to the idol Mammon. A truly malignant degeneration {Entartung} set in; what made it most malignant was that it began at a time {in the Kaiserreich} when the nation, in a presumably menacing and critical hour, needed the highest heroic attitude {heldische Gesinnung}. (MKe 234; MK 256)

However, this is not a result of private property and capitalism. Rather, it is a result of the fact that through international finance and stock exchange capital, the Jews have taken over the German economy and initiated class-struggle (MKe 313; MK 344f. and passim). One has to distinguish between capital itself and the Jewish international capital. This distinction «offered the possibility of opposing the internationalization of the German economy without at the same time menacing the foundations of an independent national self-maintenance by a struggle against all capital» (MKe 213; MK 233). In fact, private property and competition is the best means to promote the Volksgemeinschaft and the Aryan race since it is in accordance with the general law of nature, namely «Kampf» («struggle») as «Auslese» («selection») of the strongest and best (MKe 245; MK 267 and passim). To put the economy into the service of the Volksgemeinschaft will renationalize capital by a Widerruf of its denationalization, and it will restore the sense of duty and sacrifice in the capitalists as well in the workers by a Widerruf of their deheroification. In this way, private property and competition will contribute strongly to the flourishing of the Volksgemeinschaft (MKe 596; MK 670ff.).

I have mentioned several ways in which fate becomes active in the moment of crisis. There is, however, one more. The last paragraph of the third chapter, following the one with «the pressure of destiny» as quoted above, reads:

For if the misery of the fatherland can stimulate thousands and thousands of men to thought on the inner reasons for this collapse, this can never lead to that thoroughness and deep insight which are disclosed to the man who has himself mastered Fate only after years of struggle {der selber erst nach jahrelangem Ringen Herr des Schicksals wurde}. (MKe 125; MK 137; the phrase «der selber . . . Herr des Schicksals wurde» is literally «who has himself become master of Fate»)

Just as the phrase «the will to resistance» does not mean «the will to resist his fate,» the phrase «Herr des Schicksals» or master of fate does not mean that he has successfully resisted fate and even has become its master in the sense that it is now he who rules over and determines fate. In its brevity,

«Herr des Schicksals sein oder werden» (to be or become master of fate), the phrase is somewhat unusual. The phrase, «Er ist sein eigener Herr» (he is his own master) refers to a person mature enough to take care of himself or if used ironically, to a stubborn person. The phrase «Er ist seines eigenen Schicksals Herr» (he is the master of his own fate) is used—though not very frequently anymore—to refer to a mature, independent, and autonomous person. As the insistence on «own» shows, probably this expression goes back to atheist liberals, just like the saying «Jeder ist seines eigenen Glückes Schmied» (everyone is the smith of his own fortune = everyone is the architect of his own fortune). However, «Er ist (wurde) seines Schicksals Herr» (he is [became] master of his fate) describes someone who managed not to break down under «the pressure of his fate» but endured in dignity and thus realized his fate properly. Similarly, «Er wurde der Aufgabe Herr» (he mastered/became master of the task) means that someone managed to properly carry out a task given to him. It is with a view to these latter usages that Hitler says of himself that he became «master of fate.» Only cowards and the lukewarm break down under the test of fate and don't want to, or are not able to, take over their fate. For English readers, it might perhaps be surprising that Hitler uses a word of mastery and domination to describe what is actually a being subsumed by fate. However, he is not alone in the usage of expressions of mastery for acts of submission. It is one of the strategies of the right wing to polemically redefine for its purposes the liberal vocabulary of autonomy and freedom.[17]

In this case two additional ideas made it very easy and expedient for Hitler to use this formulation. By proving worthy of his fate and by anticipating the accomplishment of the task fate has given him, Hitler has become the master of the fate of Germany and the world. By listening to fate, he is going to reverse the downward course of Germany and the world and thus be their fate in the sense mentioned above. This leads to the idea that he is the «master of fate» in the sense that he is the «master» of Germany and the world, sent by fate to save them. It is precisely the brevity of the phrase «master of Fate» that allows it to take on the sense of «the master whom Fate has sent» («Eine gute Gabe Gottes» = a good gift of God = a good gift God has given). Hitler is fate's Geschenk or its Gabe, fate's gift, to the world in the moment of crisis, and to him the world must submit. Hitler explicitly says so more than once. In the chapter "The Strong Man is Mightiest Alone" (MKe 508; "Der Starke ist am mächstigsten allein," MK 568, a quote from Schiller's play *Wilhelm Tell*, act 1, scene 3), he writes:

Yes, it can come about that centuries wish and yearn for the solution of a certain question, because they are sighing beneath the intolerable burden of an existing condition and the fulfillment of this general longing does not materialize. Nations {Völker} which no longer find any heroic solution {heroische

Lösung} for such distress can be designated as *impotent* while we see the vitality of a people, and the predestination for life guaranteed by this vitality {die Lebenskraft eines Volkes und die durch sie noch verbürgte Bestimmung zum Leben}, most strikingly demonstrated when, for a people's liberation from a great oppression, or for the elimination of a bitter distress, or for the satisfaction of its soul, restless because it has grown insecure—Fate some day bestows upon it the man endowed for this purpose, who finally brings the long yearned-for fulfillment {wenn ihm . . . vom Schicksal eines Tages der dafür begnadete Mann geschenkt wird, der endlich die lang ersehnte Erfüllung bringt}. (MKe 510; MK 570; see also MKe 116, 581, 606; MK 126f, 651, 682)

## B. Scheler in War

Scheler was one of the very few contemporary philosophers whom Heidegger appreciated. In fact, «Max Scheler was, aside from the sheer scale and quality of his productivity, the strongest philosophical force in modern Germany, nay, in contemporary Europe and even in contemporary philosophy as such,»[18] as Heidegger said when he interrupted his lecture course, *The Metaphysical Foundations of Logic,* in summer 1928 to give an obituary on Scheler shortly after the latter's death. In 1915 Scheler published a book entitled *Der Genius des Krieges und der Deutsche Krieg* (The genius of war and the German war) (in PPS). Before the end of 1915 a second edition came out, followed by a third edition only one year later. The book's dedication reads, «Meinen Freunden im Felde» («For my friends in combat»), and its motto is a verse by Friedrich Schiller: «Aber der Krieg hat auch seine Ehre,/der Beweger des Menschengeschicks» («War also has its honor/the mover of the Geschick of humans»).

In World War I several German philosophers and intellectuals wrote for the cause of the Germans. Some of them perhaps felt some sort of social pressure to do so. However, to have finished a book of 443 pages (in its editions in the 1910s) as early as «the first half of November 1914» (PPS 10; the date of the preface), that is, three months after the beginning of the war, was more than, so to speak, even the German Emperor could have asked for. I will discuss only the three features of Scheler's hymn on the war and the Germans that are pertinent to my purposes here, namely, the contrast between Gesellschaft and Gemeinschaft, the step out of Gesellschaft into Gemeinschaft, and the status of Schicksal.

Scheler has two visions. The first is «the most horrible imagination can depict» (PPS 153). There are three empires, the Japanese regime in Asia, the Russian empire that has expanded to the West, and a «more or less mechanized America» (PPS 153). England is the servant of Russia. Germany, France, and Italy have been pressed down to the level of Spain (PPS 153). In his second vision, Scheler conceives the victory of Germany and Austria (PPS 153)—like

Hitler—with a metaphor of bodily disease caused by a virus from outside that has entered the body: «A Europe that expels from its blood like a foreign poison Anglo-American capitalism and the concomitant Calvinistic-puritanistic devastation of Christianity, and at the same time turns the expansion from east to west back into an expansion from west to east» (PPS 153; «ein Europa, das englisch-amerikanischen Kapitalismus und dazugehörige calvinistisch-puritanische Verödung der Christlichkeit aus seinem Blute wie ein fremdes Gift ausscheidet und gleichzeitig die ost-westliche Expansionsbewegung in eine west-östliche wieder zurückverwandelt»). This Europe will «keep forever the spiritual leadership of the world» (PPS 217)—«under Germany's military leadership against the East» (PPS 216f.). For Scheler, England is the main enemy in World War I since it has been the vanguard of capitalism—a mentality he calls «English cant.»[19] Liberalism, Enlightenment, and «English cant» are all the same. In addition, social democracy, Marxism, and socialism by no means represent a mentality that has overcome «English cant.» Rather, it is the same mentality developed further, and it is the «truth» behind Enlightenment and «English cant.»

Let me begin with a passage that includes all three relevant aspects. Scheler has pursued his reflections to a point where he can reveal «the core of the great ethical paradox of war» (PPS 76). Those who argue against the war—the «moderns and liberals» (PPS 76)—do so «in the name of "universal love for mankind," in the name of "humanity"» (PPS 76; «Im Namen einer "allgemeinen Menschenliebe," im Namen der "Humanität"»). In Scheler's view, however, by doing so the moderns and liberals «abuse the noble name of "love"» (PPS 76; «mißbraucht man den edlen Namen der "Liebe"»). Indeed, they use the notion of love for what has been the modern project of liberal capitalist society, namely, for the «clever dovetailing of private interests such that the promotion of each of their parts also promotes the other parts» (PPS 76; «solche kluge Verzahnung der Privatinteressen, daß die Förderung jedes ihrer Teile die anderen Teile mitfördert») to the effect that this system «economically "saves," puts aside, what is divine in man, namely, love, sacrifice, duty, even spirit itself to the point that all spirit becomes superfluous» (PPS 76; «was die edelste Kraft im Menschen, das Göttliche in ihm, was Liebe, Opfer, Pflicht, ja am Ende Geist überhaupt so lange ökonomisch "spart", bis aller Geist überflüssig wird.» «Saves» here in the sense of, as it were, «to take money out of circulation, to put it into a savings account, and thereupon to forget about the existence of this savings account,» or «to maximize profit by downsizing,» that is,—in Heideggerian terms—to de-cide, to sort out, to eliminate love, etc.). The moderns and liberals reduce man to what he has in common with animals. They deny love, sacrifice, duty, highest values, religion, art, philosophy, Sittlichkeit, state, right, and essence. In brief, they deny that the idea of man «represents itself only in a multitude of characteristically different national units and units of Volk» (PPS 76f.). The attempt to isolate and universalize any one specific and personal value amounts to a blindness concerning the totality of highest spiritual values and reduces all values to the lowest level of values, the one of sensual pleasure and pain (PPS 77). Thus, here we have the paradox of war, which is a paradox only for moderns and liberals, for true love of mankind and humanity one finds «not prior to the war, neither after the war, but precisely only in war itself» (PPS 77). Thus, according to this reversal of the relation between peace and war, Scheler maintains that if in history there is progress in regard to the «soulfulness and depth of the unity of mankind,» it is due to «not peace of the world, but rather to war and the everlasting moral effects on the human soul that accumulate and flow out of war's traditions and deep memories» (PPS 77). It is not peace but war that is «the constructive force of this uniting process» (PPS 77).

Scheler continues in this vein, but I will quote only three more sentences from this context. The fact «that war counteracts the forces that separate the minds and disintegrate Gemeinschaft and that are at work in the civilization and Gesellschaft of peacetime only {die gemüterscheidenden und gemein-schaftszersetzenden Kräfte, die in bloßer Friedenszivilisation und -gesellschaft wirksam sind}, can be regarded as the vehicle of ethical progress» (PPS 77). The pacifists forget that the nations as we know them are the results of war. They forget «that the nations have been welded together by wars, and that the common memory of war is at the core of their community of fate {Kern ihrer Schicksalsgemeinschaft}» (PPS 77). To be sure, peace also develops unions. However, except for matrimony, family, and some sects, all these unions «are always only *associations for* particular ends and *interests,* organized according to laws and contracts, but not *communities of life united by love* {durch Recht und Vertrag geordnete Zweck- und *Interessengesellschaften,* nicht aber durch irgendeine Art der *Liebe zusammengefaßte Lebensgemeinschaften*}» (PPS 77).

Another passage concerns the issue of a «just war» between England and Germany. Again Scheler points out that the war did not occur as a result of intrigues or mistakes by some diplomats. Rather, England's colonial politics and imperialism and the building up of the German navy all were «a necessity» (PPS 121). «We» rightfully no longer adhere to Fichte's and Bismarck's politics, and «we» began a politics with regard to colonies that was meant to provide «us» with that «"place in the sun"» («"Platz an der Sonne"») that is demanded «peremptorily» («gebieterisch») «already by the rapid growth of our population and by the lack of space for expansion in our own country» (PPS 121).

In doing so, we have followed the call of a fate that is as unshakable and as firmly built into the entire German history up to now as England's fate is into England's history! The fates of both people *had* to clash! They can be decided ultimately only in an all-out war. {Da sind wir dem Rufe eines Schicksals gefolgt, das genau so ehern und festgefügt ist in der ganzen bisherigen deutschen Geschichte wie das Schicksal Englands! Diese Schicksale beider Völker *mußten* zusammenstoßen! Sie können nur in einem radikalen Kriege entschieden werden.} If the current war does not decide them, it will be another war, or an entire series of such wars. (PPS 121)

An individual, or a group, does not create its fate. Rather, its fate exists already prior to it and calls upon the individual and the group in a situation in which the individuals, the moderns and liberals, want to forget about fate. The pacifists, moderns, and liberals want not to have fate. Scheler goes on:

In a letter to Gerhart Hauptmann, Mister Romain Rolland wrote: "The French man doesn't believe in fate. Fate is the excuse of the weak ones." In this sentence he unknowingly uncovered the principle of the impudent and unholy arbitrariness that has governed French history from the French revolution on, when it became classical. The opposite is true: Only the strong and great man has a true "fate." Similarly, only that Volk has a true fate that is strong and great and that has deep respect for the inner necessities of its history and follows the profound orders of its inner makeup beyond all transient opportunistic ends and the possible arbitrariness of its government and its diplomats. (PPS 121; Wie nur der starke und große Mensch ein echtes "Schicksal" hat, so auch gerade das starke, große vor den inneren Notwendigkeiten seiner Geschichte ehrfürchtige, und den tiefen Weisungen seiner inneren Konstitution über alle momentanen Opportunitätszwecke, etwaige Regierungs- und Diplomatenwillkür hinaus folgende Volk.)

This is what justifies the war and makes it a «just war»: «Precisely the fact that the war between England and Germany is ordained by fate {Schicksalsmäßigkeit} makes this war a "just" war» (PPS 121).

For Plato, Aristotle, and the philosophers of the Middle Ages the basic axiom of causality was that the cause of an effect must be at least as great as the effect. Modern physics has challenged this axiom and its metaphysical presuppositions. Thus, modern philosophers joke about small causes having great effects—the notorious fly that in the morning harasses the king who at noon declares war on this or that country. Scheler follows the medieval way in his thinking: «What is boundless requires a source that is boundless» (PPS 99).[20] This war is a great and sublime event; indeed, the «most sublime {erhabensten} event since the French revolution» (PPS 9), and therefore, its cause must be great and sublime as well. With this notion he rules out chance, mistakes, or intrigues on the part of this or that government or its diplomats as well as the usual suspect adduced by the Marxists (PPS 106ff. and often elsewhere). Thus, what remains as the only possible cause of war and what definitely is the cause, is fate. He quotes Dostoyevsky who spoke concerning the Russians of the

necessity of remaining steadfast on the problem of the Orient {that is, to conquer Constantinople in order to control access to the Black Sea and to gain access to the Adriatic Sea} and of pursuing with determination this politics, which our entire history has set before us as our duty {die uns unsere ganze Geschichte zur Pflicht gemacht hat}.... In this question lies our definitive clash... with Europe.... {To conquer Constantinople} is almost our entire fate {unser ganzes Schicksal} for the future.... Is it possible that Europe already understands the significance for our entire life, ordained for us by fate, that lies in the resolution of this question {diese ganze, uns vom Schicksal bestimmte Lebensbedeutung, die für uns in der Entscheidung dieser Frage liegt}? (PPS 108f.)

Two pages later, Scheler summarizes: «As great and as all-encompassing for all the spheres of Russia's life the push {Drang} toward Constantinople is, so great and all-encompassing is also the power of fate that pushes us {Germans} to resist it» (PPS 110; «die Schicksalskraft, die uns zum Widerstande dagegen treibt!»). In fact, Scheler uses the concept of fate throughout, beginning with the very first line of his introduction. I quote only the following passage as a summary. The introduction begins with this sentence:

When, at the beginning of the month of August, our German fate {unser deutsches Schicksal} took its stand before us like a single immense dark question {wie eine einzige ungeheure dunkle Frage} and shook each individual to the core—the same fate that only a few weeks ago lay before us like a straight and well-built path and that simply embraced us without being noticed {unempfunden} and with the insouciance and self-evidence of the space around us— it was just one single answer that echoed from all German souls {nur eine Antwort, die aus allen deutschen Seelen zurücktönte}, one raised arm {ein einziger erhobener Arm}: Forward to sword and to victory! {Zu Schwert und zum Siege!} (PPS 11)

Making its demand, fate does away with all the previous disagreements and separations. Scheler continues:

In the holy demand of the hour {In der heiligen Forderung der Stunde} along with all the quarreling of the parties {Parteiengezänk} the greatest differences between our worldviews have also been drowned. With the amazement of a generation for whom the state of peace had gone as unnoticed as the atmosphere, we all saw and felt that the call for serious deeds {Forderung ernster Tat} unifies anything and anyone formerly separated by their opinion on war and the interest in war and peace. (PPS 11)

Fate leaves the individual no choice and does not allow any «bargaining.» Scheler continues:

{We all saw and felt}, clear as daylight and without any ambiguity, how a conscience confronted with a deed can and must answer {ein vor die Tat gestelltes Gewissen antworten kann und muß} in a situation where only a moment before the thoughts on war in general and the avoidability of this war in particular differed widely and were worlds apart. (PPS 11)[21]

In these hours, we realize that it is fate that has brought about everything, and that determines each individual. Scheler continues:

> The fact that in these hours we actually perceived that a specific national fate reaches down into the core of each individual, of the lowliest and the grandest, and that by this fate it is preordained and codetermined what each of us is and what the value of each of us is, and what will become of each and his life's work—this fact was the most public and universal and at the same time the most intimate {das Heimlichste} and the most individual of what these generations of peace could experience. (PPS 11)

We are no longer alone, we are no longer isolated bourgeois subjects; as Scheler puts it in the following sentence:

> All of a sudden, the wide and great path of the world and the most intimate aspiration of each soul saw each other tied together and in a miraculous way interdependent in their development. We were no longer what we had been for so long: alone {Allein}! All of a sudden, the living connection between the individual, the Volk, the nation, the world, and God, which had been torn asunder, was reestablished, and the powers {of the individuals, the Volk, the nation, the world, and God} swing to and fro {between the individuals, the Volk, the nation, the world, and God} more powerfully than previously any poetry, any philosophy, any prayer, and any cult could evoke. However, . . . this miracle best remains unspoken and in the heart alone. (PPS 11)[22]

With this tactful remark, Scheler concludes this passage and introduces the «paradox» (PPS 13) he will solve in the 438 pages to come.

## C. Scheler's *Formalism in Ethics*

For liberals, World War I was the breakdown of everything they believed in and fought for.[23] For Scheler, however, World War I is the proof that his ethical theories as already developed prior to World War I are true. In modernity, «English cant» has taken over. For Scheler, World War I proves that things cannot go on that way and that the «real» forces in history are the powers of Schicksal, Gemeinschaft, and love as they have reemerged in World War I. In the preface of *Der Genius des Krieges,* he points out that he often refers to his other writings to allow readers to inform themselves about the «basic notions and axioms» («Grundbegriffe und Grundsätze») he uses in *Der Genius des Krieges* (PPS 10). In 1915 Scheler published a collection of essays, *Abhandlungen und Aufsätze,* in the preface to which he emphasizes that all the essays were written prior to World War I (UW 7) and comments as follows: «In what way the enormous event in the moral world occasioned by the war, which now overshadows and shapes the new thoughts of the time, seems to powerfully pull the European forms of Dasein precisely into the direction of development that prior to the war these essays {in *Abhandlungen und Aufsätze*} have conveyed the author has recently shown in his book *Der Genius des Krieges und der Deutsche Krieg»* (UW 8).[24] Similarly, in the preface to the first edition of *The Formalism in Ethics,* published in 1916, Scheler stresses that its first part was already published in 1913 and that the second part was already finished in manuscript form in the same year (FEe xvii; FE 9). Even in the preface to the second edition of *The Formalism in Ethics,* written in 1921, Scheler simply states without further comment: «Concrete application of my principles of general ethics to a number of specific problems and to questions concerning our own time will be found in my books *Vom Umsturz der Werte* (2d ed. of *Abhandlungen und Aufsätze*) and *Genius des Krieges,* in my essay *Ursachen des Deutschenhasses,* and in my forthcoming book *Schriften zur Soziologie und Weltanschauungslehre»* (FEe xxii; FE 14).

Thus, Scheler maintains that what he wrote prior to World War I was proven true by the war. World War I and his argument in *Der Genius des Krieges* are the desired and logical consequences of his philosophy. In the preface to *Der Genius des Krieges,* Scheler makes use of Plato's simile of the cave:

> While the first part {of *Der Genius des Krieges,* "The Genius of War," the part on war in general} proceeds in such a way that what appears is only the shadow of the war that surrounds us, the shadow the war projects by virtue of the light from the eternal world of ideas, onto the wall of Being; the second part {"The German War"} shows the very same ideas completely immersed into concrete life, into action {Tat} and dictates of the hour {Forderung der Stunde}. (PPS 9)

This is a convenient metaphor for the relationship of his prewar writings to *Der Genius des Krieges.* The prewar writings deduce the «necessity» of war and anticipate its occurrence, the first part of *Der Genius des Krieges* gives a fuller picture of the deduced idea of war, and the second part shows the realization of the idea. The metaphor is analogous to the sentences with «*erwidert»* and «*Widerruf»* (SZ 386; BT 438) in Heidegger's *Being and Time.* Prior to the war, liberals stare at their phantasms of liberal society on the walls of their caves. A shadow falls onto those walls and phantasms, but liberals are unable, or unwilling, to recognize what is heralded by this shadow and instead try to cover up the shadow by the work of ambiguity in order to keep those liberal phantasms alive. However, the authentic Daseine see through this work of ambiguity. They erwidern the call of the ideas, which announces itself in the shadow, and they widerrufen the phantasms of liberal society. They extinguish those phantasms and replace them with a proper realization of the ideas that have announced themselves in the shadow and that now take over the place formerly occupied by those liberal phantasms, or as the war approached, by the twilight of those liberal phantasms and the shadow of war. The realization of these ideas is a rerealization. Actually, what is at stake, as Scheler puts it in the preface to the second edition of *Abhandlungen und Aufsätze,* is the «resurrection of the eternal order of the human heart, which has been toppled by the bourgeois-capitalist spirit {Wiederaufrichtung der durch den bürgerlich-kapitalistischen Geist umgestürzten ewigen Ordnung des Menschenherzens}» (UW 9).

For Scheler there is no question that modernity is a turning away, or falling away, from the realm of objective values, to which the communities and Christian philosophy in early Christianity as well as in the Middle Ages had been properly related. In the unfinished essay "Christliche Demokratie" (Christian democracy), written in 1919 (PPS 698), Scheler uses a gesture one could call the foundational gesture of metaphysics proper and which allows one to dismiss entire epochs with one fell swoop. Distinguishing between two kinds of «democratism of sentiment» («Gesinnungsdemokratismus»), which in itself has nothing to do with political freedom and equality (PPS 679), he writes:

> The first {kind of Gesinnungsdemokratismus} is present in the combination of the Christian idea of love with the theory of objective ranks of values and— corresponding to this theory of objective ranks of values—with the theory of estates {Stand} and professions formulated by Christian philosophy and teaching ("ordo amoris"). The second {kind of} democratism of sentiment has been, in my mind, the root of all those humanitarian movements that pit the love of humankind and the love of God against each other and the love of humankind against that of the fatherland; this second kind of democratism of sentiment wants to promote the welfare of human beings by *renouncing the acknowledgment of an objective world of values and truth* {unter *Verzicht auf die Anerkennung einer objektiven Güter- und Wahrheitswelt*} that has to be recognized and actualized within the human realm, that is, {in contrast to early Christianity up to the Middle Ages, modernity maintains that} no longer is the salvation of a person to be placed above his or her spiritual education and morality, and no longer do these two values have to be ranked above health, strength, and welfare, or the vital values above utility and pleasure; rather, {in modernity} the material happiness of the greatest number (Bentham) replaces the objective world of values. (PPS 680)

As is known, in *Formalism in Ethics* Scheler presents a realm of values that exists independently of human beings. Unlike the Marburg Neo-Kantians, Scheler maintains that human beings don't produce the values but only partake in them; in other words, human beings are only the «bearers of values» (FEe 85; «Wertträger,» FE 103). Values do not exist in their realm in an undifferentiated conglomeration. Rather, they are placed in a clear hierarchic order: «In the *totality* of the realm of values there exists a singular order, an *"order of ranks"* {*"Rangordnung"*} that all values possess among themselves. It is because of this that a value is *"higher"* or *"lower"* than another one. This order lies in the *essence* of values themselves, as does the difference between "positive" and "negative" values. It does not belong simply to "values known" by us» (FEe 86f.; FE 104). We actualize the differences with regard to the level of the values in a specific act; Scheler calls this «*preferring*» (FEe 87; «*"Vorziehen"*,» FE 105), and this must not be confused with «conating, choosing, and willing» (FE 87; «Streben, Wählen, Wollen,» FE 105). The fact that the «being higher» is given «in» our preferring must not lead us to infer that «being higher» means «to be preferred.» For «if the height of a value is given "in" preferring, this height is nevertheless a relation in the *essence* of the values concerned. Therefore, the *"ordered ranks of values"* {*"Rangordnung der Werte"*} are absolutely *invariable*, whereas the "rules of preferring" {"Vorzugsregeln"} are, in principle, variable throughout history (a variation which is still very different from the apprehension of new values)» (FEe 88; FE 105f.).

Different values are grouped according to what Scheler calls systems of «value-modalities» and their «a priori relations of rank» (FEe 104ff.; «apriorische Rangbeziehungen zwischen den Wertmodalitäten,» FE 122ff.). Scheler develops four such modalities. The lowest system are the values «ranging from *the agreeable* to the *disagreeable*» (FEe 105; «*Angenehmen* und *Unangenehmen*,» FE 122). The second lowest are the values of «*vital feeling*» (FEe 106; FE 123). Above them are the «*spiritual values*» (FEe 107; FE 124), and at the top of the hierarchy are the values of the «holy» and «unholy»:

> 4. Values of the last modality are those of the *holy* and the *unholy* {des *Heiligen* und *Unheiligen*}. This modality differs sharply from the above modalities. It forms a unit of value-qualities not subject to further definition. . . . "Faith" and "lack of faith," "awe," "adoration," and analogous attitudes are specific reactions in this modality. However, the act through which we *originally* apprehend the value of the holy is an act of a specific kind of *love*. . . . The order is this: the modality of vital values is *higher* than that of the agreeable and the disagreeable; the modality of spiritual values is *higher* than that of vital values; the modality of the holy is *higher* than that of spiritual values. A more detailed attempt to found {nähere Begründung} these propositions cannot be undertaken at this point. (FEe 108–110; FE 125f.)

One can easily see what, according to Scheler, has happened in modernity. But first let me add further distinctions in Scheler's *Formalism in Ethics*, which are also important for his use of the terms Gemeinschaft and Gesellschaft. After distinguishing between several kinds of values, he adduces the distinction between

> g. Individual Values and Collective Values. . . . If one turns to values of oneself, such values may be individual values or collective values proper to one as a "member" {"Mitglied"} or "representative" of a "social rank," "profession," or "class"; or they may be values of one's own individuality. This holds also for values of the other.[74] . . . {In the case of the individual values} we have differences among

bearers of values that lie in the whole of an experienced *"community,"* { *"Gemein-schaft"* } by which we mean only a *whole experienced* by all its "members" { "Gliedern" }. Such a life-community is not a factually existing (more or less) artificial unit of mere elements which act among each other objectively and conceive their unit as a unit. We shall call this latter unit of human beings a *society* { *"Gesellschaft"* }. Now, all "collective values" are *"values of society."* Their bearers form not experienced "wholes" but majorities of a conceptualized class. Life-communities { "Gemeinschaften" }, however, may also function as *"individual"* vis-à-vis "collectives," e.g. an individual marriage, a family, a community, a people { Volk }, etc., as opposed to the totality of marriages or families or communities of a country or the totality of peoples, etc. (FEe 102f.; «only» in «we mean only» has the force of «exclusively»; instead of «life-community» and «life-communities» read «community» and «communities»; FE 119f.)

The accompanying note 74 reads:

> Thus love (in the Christian sense) is always *individual love,* both as *self*-love and love of the *other,* which is also called love of one's neighbor, but not as love for one who is a *member* of the class of workers, for example, or a "representative" of a collective group. The "social consciousness" of the working class { für den Arbeiterstand } has nothing to do with "love of one's neighbor." The latter pertains to the worker, but only as a human *individual.* (FEe 102, n. 74; FE 119f., n. 1)

As so often in Scheler, these sentences also lack a «more detailed attempt to found» them, which is to say there is no attempt to give them a foundation. In fact, in these passages Scheler has hardly given any reasons for any of his propositions, and in German the formulation, «A nähere Begründung of these propositions cannot be undertaken at this point» (FEe 110; FE 126), is most often used as a euphemism for cases in which the author hasn't made the slightest attempt to present arguments for his statements. As often in the literature on Gesellschaft and Gemeinschaft, such sentences represent the crossroads between the political Right and Left. For right-wingers, the realm of society is no longer an object of erotic and reasonable interests. Rather, «marriage, a family, a community, a people» have become the exclusive object of love, and society is experienced as a threat to family, community, and people. As will become even clearer in what follows, Scheler's statements amount to two theses. The first is that the material circumstances of the proletarians are not the top priority for those believing in authentic Christian love of one's neighbor. The second thesis is that the individuals engaged in the parties of the working class—at the time mainly social democrats who had fought for and won minimal social security, voting rights, and education for the workers—by no means transcend their selfish interests and move toward love for their neighbors or other higher values but are just as selfish and concerned about the lowest values as the liberal bourgeois subjects. Scheler's claims are simply a more abstract formulation of a thesis he still maintained in his writings after the war, for instance, in the essay "Christlicher Sozialismus als Antikapitalismus" (Christian socialism as anticapitalism), written in 1919:

> Thus, we have to state as a matter of principle {grundsätzlich}: In none of its variants does the Marxist socialism of the fourth estate represent a true opposition against capitalism, against capital and its root, namely, the capitalist spirit. Instead, it merely represents the material interests of its class within the capitalist society, the interests of the manual laborers, and these only insofar as those laborers are ensouled by the same capitalist spirit as the entrepreneurs and the bourgeois. (PPS 634f.)[25]

At the end of the chapter on value-modalities, Scheler poses the question

> how one can obtain from {the four kinds of value-modalities} . . . the *pure types of communal forms of togetherness* {*die reinen Typen der Gemeinschaftsarten*}, such as the community of love {Liebesgemeinschaft} (plus its technical form, the church), the community of law {Rechtsgemeinschaft}, the community of culture {Kulturgemeinschaft}, and the life-community {Lebensgemeinschaft} (plus its technical form, the state), and the mere forms of so-called society {der sog. "Gesellschaft"}. (FEe 109f.; FE 126)[26]

Scheler gives an answer in the chapter entitled "The Person in Ethical Contexts" (FEe 476ff.; FE 469ff). In it, Scheler distinguishes between four kinds of social units. The «lowest» one is the «*mass*» (FEe 526; FE 515 «"*Masse*"»). With regard to the other three units, he follows a scheme familiar in its general outlines since Hegel (who did not use it for rightist purposes). There are the small Gemeinschaften, in the first place, as in Hegel, families. Furthermore, there are, so to speak, large-scale Gemeinschaften, the state, people, nation, and the church, and there is Gesellschaft. The second social unit after the mass is the «*life-community*» («"*Lebensgemeinschaft*"») (FEe 526–528; FE 515–517). Following that is the Gesellschaft. Scheler defines it negatively as that unity in which, in contrast to «*life-community,*» there is no primordial «"living-with-one-another"»:

> 3. The social unit of the *society* {*Gesellschaft*} is basically different from the essential unit of the life-community. First, the society, as opposed to the *natural* {*natürlichen*} unit of the life-community, is to be defined as an *artificial* {*künstliche*} unit of individuals having *no* original "living-with-one-another" {"Miteinandererleben"} in the sense described above. (FEe 528; FE 517)

Instead, in society each individual is the center of his or her experience, and the individual's relationships to others are contractual:

> Rather, *all* relations among individuals are established by *specific conscious* acts that are experienced by each as coming from his *individual* ego, which is

experientially given *first in this case,* as directed to someone else as "another."
. . . Moreover, common cognition, enjoyment, etc., presuppose some *criteria* of
the true and the false, the beautiful and the ugly, which have been agreed upon
beforehand. Every kind of willing together and doing together presupposes the
*actus* of *promising* and the phenomenon [*Sachgebilde*] of the *contract* that is constituted in mutual promising—the basic phenomenon of all private law. (FEe
528f.; FE 517f.)

Due to the nature of synthesis in society, trust, for instance, is not possible:
«Just as boundless *trust* in one another is the basic attitude in the life-
community, unfathomable and primary *distrust* of all in all is the basic attitude in society» (FEe 529; FE 518). Finally, at the top of the hierarchy is the
«love-community,» which has been preferred for the first time in history in
early Christianity:

> 4. From the essential types of social unity thus far mentioned, namely, mass, soci-
> ety, and life-community, we must distinguish the highest essential type of social
> unity, with whose characteristics we began this chapter: *the unity of independ-
> ent, spiritual, and individual single persons "in" an independent, spiritual, and
> individual collective person {Die Einheit selbständiger, geistiger, individueller
> Einzelpersonen "in" einer selbständigen, geistigen, individuellen Gesamtper-
> son}.* We assert that this unity, and it alone, is the *nucleus* and total *novelty* of
> the true and ancient Christian idea of community, and that this Christian idea rep-
> resents, so to speak, the historical discovery of this unity. In quite a peculiar
> manner, this idea of community unites the being and indestructible self-value of
> the individual "soul" (conceived in terms of creation) and the person (contrary
> to the ancient theory of corporation and the Jewish idea of "people") by means
> of the idea of the salvational solidarity of all in the *corpus christianum,* which is
> founded on the Christian idea of love (and which is contrary to the mere ethos of
> "society," which denies moral solidarity). (FEe 533; FE 522)

As this passage already shows, the love-community—though not a result of
the life-communities and society but having priority over them—preserves
the main features of both life-community and society. In life-community, each
individual has coresponsibility for the whole, and its self-responsibility is
based on that coresponsibility because in this kind of community the individual is not yet valued in its own right (FEe 529f.; FE 518f.). In society,
however, all responsibility is based on self-responsibility, and there is no
longer any coresponsibility (FEe 526ff.; FE 515ff.). The love-community
gathers together several collective persons (Gemeinschaften, so to speak,
above society), and here we find both individual persons and responsibility
for the whole:

> If one takes a look at the *relation* of this idea of the highest form of social
> unity—as the idea of a solidary realm of love of individual, independent spir-

itual persons in a plurality of collective persons of the same character (this unity of collective persons among themselves, as well as the unity of the individual person and the collective person, is possible in God alone)—to the ideas of *life-community* and *society,* one can see that life-community and society as essential forms of social unity are *subordinated* to this highest essential social form, and that they are determined to serve it and to make it appear, but, to be sure, in different manners {ways}. Although the idea of the highest form of social unity is not a "synthesis" of life-community and society, essential characteristics of *both* are nevertheless co-given in it: the independent, individual person, as in society; and solidarity and real collective unity, as in community. (FEe 538f,; FE 527)

In the realm of values the lowest values, those of the agreeable and the useful, are relegated to the level of society. The values of the noble and vulgar, the spiritual values, etc., belong to the domain of various small-scale and large-scale communities, while the values of the holy and unholy have their place in the highest community, the love-community, which is, however, also concerned with all values, as the lower social units are subordinated to the highest unit and serve the latter (FEe 551ff, FE 539ff.).

Scheler writes: «As a whole, the essential social unit of society is not a special reality outside or above individuals. It is simply an indivisible {unsichtbares} fabric of *relations* that represent "conventions,"[181] "usage," or "contracts," depending on whether they are more explicit or more tacit» (FEe 529; FE 518; read «invisible» instead of «indivisible»; the accompanying note 181 reads: «Hence conventions {Konvention} and mores {Sitte resp. Brauch}, like fashions {Mode} and costumes {Tracht}, must be sharply distinguished. Conventions and fashions belong entirely to society; mores and costumes, to the life-community.»). This is the crucial difference between society and the small-scale Gemeinschaften and the large-scale Gemeinschaften, as communities of both types do indeed have a reality above and beyond the individual (FEe 523, 527, 544; FE 513, 517, 532). This is another expression for the basic assumption that in society there is no solidarity and no responsibility except for oneself (FEe 529; FE 518). At the same time, this statement supports the thesis that, empirically, there is no society without community whereas communities can exist without a society:

> Yet there are interconnections of a quite determinate character *between* society and life-community {Gemeinschaft} (as essential structures of social unity). The basic nexus is this: there can be *no society without life-community* (though there can be life-community without society). All *possible* society is therefore *founded* through community. (FEe 531; instead of all three occurrences of «life-community» read «community»; FE 520)

Scheler illustrates his thesis by maintaining that the duty to keep a contract «does *not* have its source in *another* contract to keep contracts. It has its

source in the *solidary* obligation of the members of the community to realize the contents that ought to be for the members. A so-called contract *without* this foundation would be nothing but a fiction» (FEe 531; FE 520). The
thesis that a society is impossible without being grounded in communities is
not new. However, what is distinctive about the way rightist authors use this
thesis is their distorted notion of society. In modern times at any rate, the
concept of society has been closely connected to that of reason, Vernunft.
The universality of reason as posited in Enlightenment thinking and in Kant
allowed for the procedures and processes of Bildung, education, formation,
of one's will and person so that one transcends the limits of the self and can
see oneself from the viewpoint of others and see each other individual not
only as a means but also as an end in himself or herself. Classical liberalism
assumed that the pursuit of one's own self-interest would simultaneously promote the interests of the others and that this was the best way to promote the
common good. After the waning of classical liberalism, the assumption of the
universality of reason still served as the imperative to realize consciously
what, as Adam Smith called it, the invisible hand by itself could not realize,
that is, reason grounded classical liberalism as well as later liberalism and
social democratic politics.

Like many others who would like to rerealize the «original spirit» of Christianity, Scheler downplays the role of reason. In fact, the concept of reason as
developed by Kant is his main target from the outset. Unlike Kant, Scheler
maintains that human reason is by no means synthetic and productive. Moreover, according to him, the other faculties and activities—to will, to love, to
hate—do not become ethical only by virtue of being determined by reason (FEe
63ff.; FE 82ff.). Thus, in Scheler reason is no longer a faculty that determines
others but only accompanies their activities. Certainly to regard reason as fruit-
ful and indispensable in the realm of politics does not require subscribing to a
strong concept of reason. Scheler, however, rejects both the «strong» as well
as the «weak» concept of reason. As he points out regarding Kant, Hume,
Spencer, and Comte, one misses the «peculiar nature of community as an *essential kind* of social unity,» if one refers to the idea of contract in order «to explain
the origin . . . of all social structures of the spirit . . .; and in order to have a
*standard* by which to assess the legal order and the degree of the development
of any extant social structure» (FEe 539; FE 527). Or, some pages earlier: «We
must reject the theory of a contract in any of its three possible forms: as a
genetic theory, as a theory of origin, or as a theoretical standard (according to
which only the type of order of a community is to be assessed against the idea
of a contract)» (FEe 524; FE 513f.).

It is only this step of ruling out reason as a relevant faculty that allows
Scheler to dismiss classical liberalism as well as social democracy and to
maintain that both are identical to or further developments of what he calls

«English cant,» which in Scheler's view is nothing more than a theory of the selfish individual, regarding himself or herself as free of any responsibility for others and looking upon others as mere means to his own ends. With this step, Scheler participates in the process of—in Carl Schmitt's terms—intensifying a tension or an opposition by destroying any possibility of mediation between the opposites. Anticipating the scenario Schmitt develops in the last part of the *Political Theology*, Scheler writes on reason in the essay "Soziologische Neuorientierung und die Aufgabe der deutschen Katholiken nach dem Krieg" (Sociological reorientation and the task of the German Catholics after the war):

> {Reason} only has the choice between a subordination to that meaning {Sinn} which the whole of religious revelation {religiöse Gesamtoffenbarung} gives to life and thus to reason itself—a subordination that is *free* and that results from reason's insight into its own dependency and limits—*or* an enslavement, slowly progressing and compulsory, to the life of the instincts and drives {Triebleben}, which darkens and sultries the light of reason more and more. (PPS 409)

As was already indicated, Scheler's overall project, which places him on the political Right, is the revitalization of the proper «order of the human heart,» that is, of the original Christian community by means of the destruction of «English cant,» that is, of society, which has taken over in modernity and which therefore has to be destroyed or to be expelled «from {Europe's} blood like a foreign poison» (PPS 153) to make room for the revitalization of the Christian community. This is the same gesture as in section 74 of *Being and Time*. Both «Schelerians» and Heideggerian authentic Daseine repeat something—original Christianity or Volksgemeinschaft—by redeeming it from its state of fallenness, of being impure or destroyed; that is, both perform an Erwiderung. Both Schelerians and Heideggerian authentic Daseine do so by canceling society, as society has toppled original Christianity or Gemeinschaft. In other words, both perform a Widerruf. This is a de-cision in Heidegger's sense. In order to separate the two opposites the mixture must be purified through a purification of both opposites. In order to be reduced to its supposed original and pure state the «good» opposite, Christianity, must be cleansed of any of its later developments. The «bad» opposite, society, is purged of any reason and is reduced to, as Scheler puts it, «English cant» (PPS 218ff. and often). These two purifications «expel» any possibility of mediation between the opposites, and they also expel any dialectical tension within one opposite—as, for example, the dialectical mediation between universality and individuality in classic liberalism—that makes possible a process of self-reflection resulting in such institutions as social welfare.[27] The two reductions provide the ground for the cancellation of the «bad» opposite in order to rerealize the «good» opposite as the last and crucial step in the decision. In Scheler this motif represents his general political agenda and also forms the heart of his book, *Formalism in Ethics*. Scheler quite literally reifies the thinking, prevalent at his time, in terms of the methodological device of ideal types, Idealtypen. He reifies the ideal types insofar as they become the ideal social units existing independently of human beings in the realm of values.[28] The social units, then, are used in order to reduce each empirical phenomenon, such as a political movement, to just one principle. Liberalism and social democracy can have only one principle, just as Christianity can have only one principle, and this one principle has to be cleansed of any impurities it has acquired over the years. In these reductions, Scheler is partial. In his criticism of Nietzsche in *Ressentiment*, Scheler admits that in its history Christianity was often an expression of ressentiment (RE 67, 71, 99; UW 57, 61, 84). However, in the realm of values and also in the first instance when it was preferred in history, Christianity, though only for a short time, was the proper and unadulterated realization of the highest values. Thus, in Scheler Christianity is «upgraded.» Liberalism and social democracy, however, are «downgraded» even though from the outset active reason was part of them. This move is already a decision, and it alone allows for the final decision between Christianity on the one hand or liberalism and social democracy on the other, for the purification of Christianity from any liberal or social democratic elements, for the purification of liberalism and social democracy from any reason, and for the cancellation of society in order to revitalize Christianity. However, as Tillich emphasized in 1933, each individual as well as each political group lives—prior to the fact that each of them partakes in several social units and prior to the problems of compromises and alliances in everyday politics—in tension between several principles or demands. In other words, each principle is never simply one principle. As Hegel realized when he turned away from his aspirations to revitalize «the Greeks» or early Christianity and, finally, developed a «theological» as well as a «reasonable» justification of bourgeois society, it is theoretically wrong and morally unjust to reduce a phenomenon to one principle whose purity one has established by a decisive reduction. In this way, Tillich deploys principles in a way one could label post-metaphysical; in contrast, the authors on the Right reinvent a reductive metaphysics of a primordial state, a falling, and a return and apply it and all its reductions to the realm of human politics.

Scheler completely instrumentalizes reason. However, the Christian community preserves the «individual person, as in society» (FEe 539; FE 527). Thus, a liberal might assume that in Scheler's idea of a love-community there is nothing that speaks against liberal purposes. As long as the individual person is preserved in the love-community, any addition to Gesellschaft might simply be welcomed. Furthermore, historically freedom and equality of the individual has been an achievement of modern reason. However, it may not be necessary to ground these two values in reason. Given Scheler's sloppy standards of providing evidence and arguments for his statements and the complete absence of any reasoning at crucial points, another philosopher might have assumed, just for the sake of the argument, a realm of values independent of human beings and might have easily found freedom and equality not only among those values but indeed at the pinnacle of the hierarchy of values. However, Scheler does not even see equality as one of the values. In Scheler, equality is not a value but a criterion that God and «we» use when «we» assess individuals and peoples or nations in their acts of preferring values. Scheler's notion of a person not only allows for but indeed explicitly demands that persons are unequal as far as the higher values are concerned. He begins with a more factual statement: «Every man is, as we saw, an *individual* and therefore a unique being, distinct from all others to the *same* degree that he is a *pure* person. And, similarly, his value is a unique value» (FEe 508; FE 499). According to Scheler, this holds true also for people: «This, of course, also pertains to both the individual person and the collective person, e.g., the Greek or Roman people» (FEe 508; FE 499). At the latest, postmodern sensibility would recommend resisting any effort of ranking individuals and people in their respective values. However, for the metaphysician and premodern Scheler the sheer fact of differences implies different ranks and inequality: «Hence all *ultimate* bearers of moral value, to the degree that they are conceived as *pure* persons, are *different and unequal* not only in their being but also in their value» (FEe 509; FE 499). This is simply true, independent of our capacities to recognize the persons and peoples in their different values: «It remains to be seen how and to what extent the extant differences and differences in value among persons can be shown as given or even be "established." If this were not possible, such differences would in any case be present before the idea of an all-loving and all-knowing God» (FEe 509; FE 500; note that Scheler means that it remains to be seen whether we individuals down here on earth can recognize the different values of different empirical persons and peoples). For it is a misunderstanding to assume that before God we are all equal: «Persons and their individual values must be considered different precisely "before God." We must not assume any so-called equality of souls before God, which some interpret to be the teaching of historical Christianity—though, we believe, without justification[147]» (FEe 509; FE 500; the accompanying note 147 reads: «Such a doctrine could be explained as a distortion produced by Stoic philosophy,» ibid.).

This principle has important implications. The values the state is concerned with are higher than those of society. Thus, Scheler demands that the state must no longer remain liberal with respect to the economy. Rather, from the a priori relationships between value-modalities it follows that the person as social person and as «*subject of private law*» as well as the person as «*economic subject*» must be «*subordinated*» to the person as citizen «because the state achieves the highest meaning of its existence in the rational regulation of the will to live and the reasonable distribution of the goods of life (of a community, of a people {einer Volksgemeinschaft})» (FEe 511; FE 501f.).

In this generality, social democrats would agree with Scheler. However, liberals and social democrats would not link this thesis to the assumed inequality and to the notion of Volksgemeinschaft. In particular, they would strongly disagree with Scheler's second formulation of this thought. He maintains that with regard to the lowest level the tasks and goods «*ought* to become more equal for men. They ought to become more equal, for *precisely because of this*, men's differences do not remain concealed and hidden with regard to *absolute* or less relative values of being and with regard to the higher goods and tasks connected with faculties of *higher* value» (FEe 510; FE 500).[29] In the accompanying note, Scheler explains that he «cannot develop the many important applications of this principle to theories of society, politics, and law» (FEe 510, n. 148; FE 500, n. 1).

However, already here it becomes clear that these applications are illiberal as well as anti–social democratic, that is, that they are rightist. Scheler states that philosophers during the Enlightenment said precisely the opposite. For,

> men and their values are to be regarded all the *more* equal, the *more* their being approaches the *absolute* level of being (as "rational entity") and the *more* their values are compared to values of the *highest* rank (salvation and spiritual values); and they and their values should (or at least may) appear all the more *unequal*, too, the more their being approaches sensible states of the lived body and the more their values are compared to values of the *lowest* rank. (FEe 510; FE 501)

This assumption is the «exact *opposite*» of Scheler's, and it has its philosophical basis «in the premise of *one* so-called supra-individual transcendental reason» (FEe 510; FE 501). Liberal theory has assumed the equality of all human beings, and it has assumed that the participation of all human beings as equals in the political realm, as in parliamentary democracy, would provide them with the possibility to discuss freely and rationally all the political and social problems, including existing inequalities in the economic sphere. Scheler rejects the presupposition, namely, the unity of reason in all human beings, and he rejects political equality as well. At a later point, in a discussion of the task of the state with regard to culture, he writes that

> the state will do a *better* job in its task, which belongs essentially to it, of *realizing* culture, the *less* it claims autonomous guidance and leadership in cultural

activities, the *less* it claims to inspire this activity, the *less* it follows a direct cultural policy (instead of a policy of power) toward other states, and the *less* it orders the relations of power among people living in its life-communities according to cultural points of view (propagation of education) rather than the point of view of justice. (FEe 553; in German «rather than the point of view of justice» is in parentheses; FE 541)

The occurrence of the word «justice» in parentheses is remarkable, for in Scheler's entire book of no less than 659 pages, the word itself hardly shows up more than a handful of times. It is an amazing phenomenon that in an extremely long and systematic book on ethics the author makes not the slightest effort to develop at least a basis for a theory of justice, not to mention a theory of justice itself. It is all the more amazing since, in this book as well as in his other writings, the author addresses social and political questions, and since, due to the full emergence of capitalism («the social question»), social and political problems have developed into a form previously unknown. The only theoretical statements on justice occur in passing during his discussion of reprisal and punishment, in which he argues mainly against Kant: «Therefore "reprisal" does not follow as a consequence from the demand that justice ought to be. Justice orders and governs only the impulse of reprisal by *adding* the idea of proportion, like for like, to the demand for reprisal (in some more determinate way)» (FEe 361; FE 361). Two pages later, he says that one «falls victim to another basic misconception of the essence of the idea of reprisal and the idea of punishment when one attempts to derive them from *purely* moral values and demands, especially the demand for "justice"» (FEe 363; FE 363). For «insofar as the pure essence of justice is understood, justice does not require the repayment of evil with evil. Only from that part of the essential core of justice according to which it is good and proper that under the *same value conditions* the *same behavior* of willing persons should occur does it follow that—if there is to be retaliation—this retaliation must be the same for deeds of equal value. However, the demand for "retaliation" as such does not follow from justice.»[30]

As to the old distinction between arithmetical justice and proportional justice, in the first of the three quotes Scheler seems to use the terms «justice» and «like» either as «proportional justice» or in such a way that they cover both arithmetical and proportional justice. In the third quote, he says that arithmetical justice is demanded by only one part of the essence of justice. This statement allows for and even requires a continuation such that in all the other parts of the essence of justice, proportional justice is required. Stated in this way, arithmetical justice has always been a special case of proportional justice. According to proportional justice, persons of different values (e.g., a slave and a freeman) are punished differently for equal wrongdoings, that is, in inverse proportion to their values, or political honors and rights are distributed in proportion to the different values of the individuals and groups (with the result that, for instance, slaves don't have any political honors and rights). This entails that persons of equal values (e.g., two free citizens) are punished for equal wrongdoings equally, and that persons of equal value have equal political honors and rights. Scheler seems to assume proportional justice as the essence of justice. According to Scheler, arithmetical justice is appropriate with regard to the low values. Equality with regard to the low values even enhances the process of manifestation of inequality of different persons with regard to higher values. Political values are higher values. Liberalism has always stood staunchly behind the tenet that all persons are free and equal, that is to say, all persons have to be treated according to arithmetical justice. Scheler revokes this. In fact, in the note to the sentence on state and culture quoted above Scheler explains: « I.e., the state must give life-communities equal or unequal {political} rights {gleiche, resp. ungleiche politische Rechte} according to their degree of significance with respect to the whole of the state» (FEe 553, n. 222; FE 541, n. 1). This sentence clearly presupposes proportional justice with regard to the political, as the phrase «equal or unequal {political} rights» can only mean «equal rights to groups of equal value, and unequal rights to groups of unequal value,» if this distribution is supposed to be just. Again, one might wonder why in a huge book on ethics at the beginning of the twentieth century an author refers to such an important issue only in a dismissive way. However, one might also say that Scheler need not expound further on this issue. Once one assumes that a realm of values exists independently of human beings, that there are a priori relations between the values such that there are higher and lower ranks of values, that the sphere of the political embraces relatively high values, that persons and peoples are not only different but of different value and are themselves ranked according to the rank of the values, that not only God, but humans too are in a position to recognize the different values of persons and peoples, and that in our social and political organizations we have to «mirror» the ranking of the different persons and peoples, then it follows that we have to abandon arithmetical justice in the realm of the political. Scheler makes all the above-mentioned assumptions. Thus, it is only logical that he abandons arithmetical justice in politics. Probably the above quoted note immediately refers to the topic, much debated at the time, of the rights of the churches in the educational system. However, the statement is a general statement. In 1919, that is, during and after the establishment of the Weimar Republic, Scheler fervently attacked parliamentary democracy, as I will show in the following section.

## D. Scheler on the Genesis and Future of Capitalism

A history of the «historical variability and differences in moral value-estimation among different peoples and races {volks- und rassenmäßige Verschiedenheit}» (FEe 295; FE 300) in the spirit of Scheler's project does not primarily investigate the different notions of, say, «love and justice» at different times in different peoples and races. Rather, the crucial dimension for Scheler's project are changes taking place in peoples' and races' empirical acts of preferring in regard to the ranking of the values themselves. Thus, a history of ethics will investigate «the great *typical forms of ethos itself,* i.e., the experiential structure of values and their immanent rules of preferring, which lie *behind* both the morality and the ethics of a people (primarily those of the large racial groups) ... {it will investigate} the rules by which such *values themselves* were preferred or placed after» (FEe 302; FE 306). Such a history does not succumb to relativism. It is just the opposite. According to Scheler, the assumption of the realm of values existing independently of human beings combined with the assumption of individuals, peoples, and races of different values, who realize these values down here on earth, is the only theory that can avoid relativism. Scheler compares the moral history of the different peoples and races to a huge canvas. All other theories can see in it only a «palette daubed with paint.» His theory, however, enables one to look at it «from a correct distance and with proper understanding» such that one sees «the interconnection of sense of a grandiose painting, or at least of the fragments of one. And in this painting, one will be able to see mankind, mixed as it is {so bunt gegliedert sie (= die Menschheit) ist}, beginning to take possession, through love, feeling, and action, of a realm of objective values and their objective order, a realm that is independent of mankind as well as of its own manifestations; and one will be able to see mankind draw this realm into its existence, as happened in the history of knowledge, e.g. the knowledge of the heavens» (FEe 297; FE 301).[31]

This history is the «inner history of the *ethos itself,* i.e., the central history *in* all history» (FEe 305; FE 309), which is to say—as he develops in the book *Formalism* mainly with regard to liberalism, and as he develops with regard to Marxism, social democracy, and liberalism as well in his other writings—that, with respect to its causes, it cannot be explained by the means offered by liberalism, Enlightenment, or Marxism, but only in terms of peoples, races, and their different blood. According to Scheler, a history of «the central history *in* all history» has to take into account «five strata,» of which I mention only the first and the second:

> First, there are variations in *feeling* (i.e., "cognizing") values themselves, as well as in the *structure of preferring* values and *loving* and *hating.* Let us take the liberty of calling these variations as a whole variations in the *"ethos."*
>
> Second, there are variations which occur in the sphere of *judgment* and the sphere of rules of the *assessment* of values and value-ranks given in these functions and acts. These are variations in "ethics" (in the broadest sense of the term). (FEe 299; FE 303)

(The variations in the first stratum make up «the great *typical forms of ethos itself*» mentioned in a passage quoted close to the beginning of this section;

they «lie *behind* both the morality and the ethics of the world of the peoples,» that is, they determine, most of the time unconsciously, the contents occurring in the strata 2 through 5, though it might happen that conscious assumptions on the level of stratum 2 are not in accordance with the preferences on the level of stratum 1; a discrepancy between stratum 1 and stratum 2 that will become crucial in his theory of disavowing capitalism, or capitalistic mentality.) There is a hierarchy of values, which are preferred and ranked by human beings in their acts of realizing them down here on earth. Thus, according to an authoritarian and belligerent Christian, Platonist, and foe of modernity like Scheler, there are two basic possibilities with regard to changes in the ethos. A new ethos, or a new state of the same ethos, either provides an empirical image of the ranking in the realm of values itself that is more proper than the ethos it supersedes, or it provides a worse image. The first can happen either as an adjustment of existing preferences or as the discovery of values ranked higher than the ones preferred so far. A discovery of higher values «occurs in the movement of *love*,» and «it is to the *moral-religious genius* that the realm of values opens up,» Jesus' Sermon on the Mount being the most grandiose example (FEe 305; FE 309). If the resulting image is worse than the former, the ethos is one of «*deceptions*,» «*falsifications*,» and «*overthrows*»:

> There are also in history all those forms of value-*deceptions* {*Täuschungen*} and *deceptions* in preferring, as well as *falsifications* {*Fälschungen*} and over-*throws* {*Umstürze*} which are founded on *such* deceptions and which pertain to {durch *sie* begründeter *Fälschungen* und *Umstürze* von} earlier forms of ethical assessment and standards that had {already} conformed to the objective rank of values. I discovered one such deception in my study of *ressentiment*. (FEe 306; note that the German text is more clear and direct than the English translation might sound: value-deceptions in preferring cause acts in which we falsify—or even alter fraudulently—and overthrow earlier forms, etc.; FE 310)

Hitler's notion of history combines two motifs. On the one hand, there is Kampf as the basic phenomenon of life and as the way in which selection is at work. His notion of Kampf is the modern notion of progress cleansed of any implications connected with the modern notion of reason. On the other hand, there are the axioms concerning race. There is a pure race that is the highest race, the Aryan race. In addition, there are other races, less high or noble. At the bottom is the Jewish race. According to Aristotelianism and most medieval philosophers, under normal circumstances each cause produces something similar to itself, that is, no cause can produce something ontologically «higher» than itself. Similarly in Hitler, the pure race reproduces itself as a pure race. Each of the lower races, left to itself—just as every other cause—just reproduces itself. That is to say, it is incapable of producing by itself something higher than itself, or it is incapable of developing itself into something higher. Thus, progress—or decadence—occurs through mixture, the mixture of races. The highest race loses its purity and its highest state by mixing, or being mixed, with lower races. The lower race gains a higher place, not by reproducing itself, but by mixing with a higher race. In this way, it «partakes in» the higher qualities contained in the higher race, and, at the same time, it drags down the higher race, as now the higher race contains in itself elements of the lower one. In this way, the hierarchy of beings and the axioms concerning causality in medieval thinking are made to serve a modern notion of progress gone astray, and the modern notion of progress deprived of reason is put in the service of medieval thinking; together this amounts to a materialistic Platonism with a perverted idea of the good. The Jews are demonized prime matter. They strive for participation, drag down what they participate in, and at the same time remain in all their activities unaffected by their participation. It is part of the perfidy of the Jews that they don't mix with other races. They don't allow their women to marry non-Jews. However, the male Jews spoil the blood of the other races. Thus, they themselves remain pure while they make impure and drag down the other races (MKe 386ff., 661f. and frequently; MK 425ff., 751f.). The pure is more efficient and «stronger» than the impure. Since only the lowest race has remained pure, it will gain dominion over the entire world. Fortunately, however, God and his hand, fate, interfere and call upon some chosen Daseine to reverse the process and to «halt the chariot of doom {Wagen des Verhängnisses} at the eleventh hour» (MKe 373; MK 409); or, as is said not only by soldiers of almost any sort of rescue mission, «den Karren aus dem Dreck ziehen» (to pull the cart out of the muck, to clear up the mess). Fortunately, God does so at a time when the rescue mission is still possible. Though impure, the Germans are still such that six years of gym will enable them to conquer Russia. Also, there are pure remnants of the pure race, and one can spot them and stop the Jews from spoiling the German blood. It is the combination of these two elements—a certain version of the modern notion of progress, stripped of reason by being reread in terms of the struggle of races, and the Aristotelian and medieval notion of causality reread in terms of the struggle of races— that turns both elements of the mixture—the notion of progress as well as Aristotelianism—into utter violence.

The same logic found in Hitler is also at work in Scheler's writings. There are the highest values, and they were once realized in the proper way, namely in early Christianity up to the Middle Ages. Individuals and peoples full of resentment—due to their race or, in consequence of mixtures, due to infection—act like the Jews. They partake in the higher values by undermining the order of values. In this way, they spoil the higher values and drag them into the muck and do not transform themselves at all through their activities since they use, or instrumentalize, everything as a means in the service of

their low values and do not enjoy the higher values in order to bilden, to educate and transform themselves. I have already pointed to what is perhaps the
most obvious and most stunning manifestation of the medieval aspect of
Scheler's thinking, namely, his version of Descartes's proof of God's existence.[32] Also, I have already shown how the theoretical framework in
Scheler's major work, *Formalism in Ethics,* is tailored to and possibly—in
its entirety—hardly allows for anything else but a thinking in terms of
dragging-down, of mixture, and the reversal, the de-cision; a thinking of an
objective order, which has been properly realized, but thereafter gets spoiled
and overthrown by, as he puts it, «English cant,» and which has to be rerealized by expelling the «English cant» out of one's blood «like a foreign poison.» For Scheler, as for Hitler, war is «the constructive force» (PPS 77) of
history. As in Hitler, this is due to the expulsion of reason from the notion
of development and progress. A distinctive achievement of the modern age
was a concept of progress according to which, in contrast to the Aristotelian
and medieval notion of causality, the end does not preexist its own beginning. In cosmology as well as in history and morality, this allowed for the
assumption, culminating in Freud's notion of sublimation, that an entity, or
drive, of «low» value, sexuality or selfishness, can transform itself into a state
of «higher» value. Scheler points to the modern notion of development only
to dismiss it as utterly wrong (RE 114ff.; UW 99ff. and passim) and to reduce
the activity of modernity to acts of overthrowing and deception. According
to Scheler, resentment is the result of two opposing factors. On the one hand,
there is the incapacity to realize the higher values and the impulse of revenge,
hate, and envy toward those who have successfully preferred them. On the
other, there is the experience of powerlessness, of the lack of power to immediately take revenge and do away with the «higher» values and their bearers.
This tension results in a repreferring of the values. The virtues of premoder-
nity, so resentment says, are bad, one's own mediocre values are good. Resentment also results in a suppression of one's feelings of revenge, etc. Resent-
ful persons prove their resentfulness precisely because in their understanding
of themselves they harbor no resentment (RE 68–72; UW 59–63, and prior).
This allows for the logic of suspicion and «revealing.» A person's own statement about the issue and reasons for a judgment do not matter. According to
Scheler,

> it goes without saying that genuine moral value judgments are never based on
> *ressentiment.* This {Nietzsche's} criticism only applies to false judgments
> founded on *value delusions* and the corresponding ways of living and acting.
> Nietzsche is wrong in thinking that genuine morality springs from *ressentiment.*
> It rests on an eternal *hierarchy of values,* and its rules of preference are *fully
> as objective and clearly "evident"* as mathematical truth. There does exist an
> *ordre du coeur* and a *logique du coeur* (in Pascal's words) which the moral
> genius gradually uncovers in history, and it is eternal—only its apprehension

and acquisition is «historical.» *Ressentiment* helps to subvert this eternal order in man's consciousness, to falsify its recognition, and to deflect its actualization. (RE 72f.; UW 63)

In his essay on resentment, Scheler kills three birds with one stone. He refutes Nietzsche's thesis on Christianity; he refutes Marx concerning the causes of capitalism, and in the process he prepares the ground for his thesis that private property is an important feature of an authentic community. Concerning his criticism of Nietzsche, I just mention in passing two things. Though Scheler cannot but acknowledge that already in Luke (RE 99; UW 84) and also in one sentence in St. Paul (RE 71; UW 61)—not to mention Tertullian (RE 67; UW 57)—resentment takes over, the original idea of Christian love has its roots in a completely different site. Scheler sees the original Christian idea of love as a gesture of self-expression, a spontaneous overflow, which is by no means directed toward the other as its end. This allows for the dismissal of those Christians who allied themselves with the social democrats (RE 83–113; UW 70–93). Modernity is nothing but deception and overthrow. By implication, what preceded the modern era was good. Scheler explains this by means of a simplistic and violent theory of epochs that serves as a means to, and is constituted by the same gesture as, his philosophy of values and modernity, namely, the gesture of producing unity and purity by expelling «the other.» Though, as he stresses, ethics in antiquity differed from Christian ethics, and though Aristotle got it wrong with regard to the value of persons (FEe 524; FE 514), Aristotle can serve as an authority if he fits Scheler's reactionary bill. Everyone knows that Aristotle maintained that some human beings by their nature are slaves and others by their nature are free. Everyone also knows that, making his case, Aristotle argued against those who had denied the thesis (*Politics* I:3, 1253 b 14ff.). Thus, when it comes to this issue Scheler adds the qualifier «true» («echte») to «antiquity.» It is not the case that in antiquity some maintained *a* and others maintained non-*a*. Rather, the «true antiquity» maintained *a* (RE 128; UW 108), and who maintained non-*a* was simply not part of «true antiquity.» Thereafter, he explicates Aristotle's opinion on slavery in order to then even forget his gesture of exclusion by saying:

> For the ancients {Der antike Mensch} it is axiomatic that equal rights are in any case unjust. Only opportunism can bring them about, and they always conceal a "just" inequality of rightful claims by the different groups. It is true that Christianity destroys this point of view, but only by making an even greater qualitative distinction between men, which penetrates much more deeply into the ontological depths of the person. (RE 128; UW 108)

The idea of equality of human beings (equal reason, equal claims for salvation, equal abilities, equal innate ideas) «was added to Christian ideology at an early date, but has not grown from its living roots» (RE 129; UW 109). Indeed, this idea and the idea of a «reasonable sphere» below the sphere of grace gained full victory in Thomas Aquinas. However, these conceptualizations «represent the first incursion of the young bourgeois ideals into the ideological system of the Christian Church» (RE 188 n. 28; UW 109 n. 1).[33] This is the same gesture of de-cision as found in Hitler and Heidegger. Instead of prudently balancing demands, promises, and possibilities that have been there from the beginning or have arisen in history, Scheler purifies the mixture by reestablishing the supposed pure entity and by «downgrading» the «value» of the others or completely abandoning them. There are several different phenomena in the modern age. However, those that don't fit into his picture are left out, and all the others are reduced to resentment. Aspirations, intrinsically boundless, and desire for progress («*Grenzenlosigkeit* des Strebens,» «"Fortschrittsstreben"») as a perversion of means and ends (RE 56; UW 48), «*modern universal love of man*» (RE 114; «*moderne allgemeine Menschenliebe*» UW 96), «value of things self-earned and self-acquired» (RE 138; «Der Wert des Selbsterarbeiteten und -erworbenen,» UW 115) as opposed to what one has by nature, race, and tradition, «subjectivization of values» (RE 144; «Die Subjektivierung der Werte,» UW 122) as the denial of the objective realm of values and their hierarchy, «elevation of the value of utility above the value of life» (RE 149; «Erhebung des Nützlichkeitswertes über den Lebenswert,» UW 126) and related phenomena—they all go back to resentment. Before the modern era, in the vertical hierarchy of offices, every individual—«from the king down to the hangman and the prostitute»—was aware that his or her office was fate, that is, assigned to him or her by God and nature, and that to meet the requirements of it was his or her duty. Each individual compared himself or herself only to individuals of the same rank, and each individual was «"noble" in the sense that he considers himself irreplaceable» in his or her office (RE 56; UW 48). In the modern era, all this was overthrown and replaced with limitless motions forward, in which mere means become ends, and in which objective ranking among values in themselves as well as among the empirical human beings is denied. Indeed, as Scheler summarizes right at the end,

> the spirit of modern civilization does not constitute "progress" (as Spencer thought), but a *decline* {*Niedergang*} in the evolution of mankind. It represents the rule of the weak over the strong, of the intelligent over the noble, the rule of mere quantity over quality. It is a phenomenon of decadence, as is proved by the fact that everywhere it implies a *weakening of man's central, guiding forces* as against the anarchy of his automatic impulses. The mere means are developed and the goals are forgotten. And that precisely is decadence! (RE 174; UW 147)

Since it is not necessary for my purpose, and since he does not give reasons but just appeals to intuitive evidence when it comes to his thesis that all this goes back to resentment, I won't go into the details, but just present a passage close to the end in which Scheler summarizes several of his themes with the concepts of community and society. In modern times, «the principle of summation» is at work, according to which the whole is nothing but the sum of its parts and is subordinate to them. In the realm of values, the whole is prior to its parts and allots each of them its place:

Thus the principle of summation is in contradiction with the principle of {Christian, not socialist} solidarity. Both in idea and feeling, it entails a fundamentally different relation between the individual and the community {Gemeinschaft}. Under the sway of the principle of {Christian} solidarity, everyone knows and feels that the community as a *whole* is inherent in him—he feels that his blood is the blood which circulates in the community, that his values are part of the values which permeate the community. Here all values are *based* on solidarity of feeling and willing. The individual is the community's organ and at the same time its representative, its honor is his honor. This material inherence in the community is now replaced by the notion that the community is only the product of the *interaction* between the individuals. The communal values are supposedly created by adding up the values invested in the individuals. The individual values circulate merely through conscious communication and instruction, or by conscious recognition and "agreement." To put it more simply: The "community" {"Gemeinschaft"} and its structure is replaced by "society" {"Gesellschaft"}, in which men are arbitrarily and artificially united by promise and contract.

In fact, "society" is not the inclusive concept, designating all the "communities" which are united by blood, tradition, and history. On the contrary, it is only the *remnant,* the *rubbish* {Abfall, literally "fall-away-from"} left by the inner *decomposition* of communities. Whenever the unity of communal life can no longer prevail, whenever it becomes unable to assimilate the individuals and develop them into its living organs, we get a "society"—a unity based on mere contractual agreement. When the "contract" and its validity ceases to exist, the result is the completely unorganized "mass" {"Masse"}, unified by nothing more than momentary sensory stimuli and mutual contagion. Modern morality is essentially a *"societal morality"* {*"Gesellschaftsmoral"*}, and most of its theories are built on this basic notion. . . . negation of all primary *"co-responsibility."* . . . The state, language, and custom are inventions. . . .

Here again, the feelings and ideas of those elements the old "community" had cast aside (its pariahs) have determined the general image of man and his associations. Even marriage and family . . . were artificially more and more degraded to a matter of civil contract.

Wherever a "community" existed, we find that the *fundamental forms* of communal life were endowed with a value far *superior* to all individual interests, to all subjective opinions and intentions. . . . Thus marriage . . . is a "sacrament." Wherever there is a real community, the *forms* of life have an intrinsic value on which individual interests, joys, and sufferings have no bearing. This valuation disappears with the rise of "society"! . . . Instead of *respecting* them, one feels free to change them *arbitrarily*.

Another consequence of this basic attitude is the predominance of the principle of majority in politics and the state. In the communities, the will of the *whole* is manifested and revealed in the will of those who are the "noblest" by birth and tradition. Now, however, the will of the majority supposedly constitutes the will of the state.

· All this shows the *victory of ressentiment in morality*. . . . Such a postulate can only be established by those who feel that they are worthless and who want to pull the others down to their level. Even if a man is *nothing* at all, he is still "one"! (RE 165–168; UW 139–142)

Resentment is a psychological habit. From the thirteenth century on, it has been at work continuously and in silence in order to eruptively burst out in the French Revolution, «the greatest achievement of *ressentiment* in the modern era» (RE 196 n. 54; UW 145 n. 2). Due to their nature and social position, some groups, for instance women, are very prone to resentment (RE 60ff.; UW 51ff.), whereas «the *soldier* is least subject to *ressentiment*» (RE 65; UW 56). What was it that brought about resentment on a large scale such that resentment could topple the right order? It must have been a change of natures and cannot have been the usual suspect adduced by the Marxists; a change of natures that goes back to an infection. At the time, many German sociologists, philosophers, and intellectuals had already devoted a remarkable amount of intellectual energy to refuting Marx. In *Der Bourgeois,* Scheler sides with Sombart:

> Sombart traces the "bourgeois spirit" ultimately to a *bio-psychic type {biopsychischen Typus}*, which can be explained only as a result of blood mixture {der nur auf Grund der Blutmischung verstanden werden kann}. It is precisely at this most dangerous place in his work—where it is most open for the attack of those who regard "true" and "demonstrable" as identical—that we must fundamentally agree with him. Those who—being familiar with many basic types of humankind and having a firm and clear mental picture of them—have seen and felt the spiritual unity of this very type {i.e., the bourgeois type} in all of its manifestations will not let themselves be talked into buying the notion that this type is a product of the "milieu," of "education," of adaptation and habit. Still, even Sombart himself will admit that he hasn't given a strict "proof" of his thesis. (UW 356)[34]

Such is Scheler's theory on the genesis of capitalism. Capitalism has emerged because the Jews infected the body of the people and spoiled its blood. Scheler's theory of the genesis of capitalism is mirrored in his theory of the future of capitalism. Some readers might be wondering how Scheler can argue against liberals as well as leftists and at the same time demand that Europe «expel out of its blood like a foreign poison Anglo-American capitalism and the Calvinist-puritanistic obliteration of Christianity» (PPS 153). It has already become clear, however, that the emphasis is on «blood,» «Anglo-American,» and the «Calvinistic-puritanistic obliteration of Christianity,» and not on «capitalism.» Scheler distinguishes between «'capitalist' spirit» and «industrialism» («Industrialismus»). The latter has nothing to do with the former, and it is only from the former and not the latter, that we have to liberate our minds, souls, and hearts (PPS 194f.). If Marx is wrong and Sombart right, «capitalism» is not a matter of the property structures in production, but a matter of spirit or ethos, as Scheler already said in *Formalism in Ethics*. The values and also their realization here on earth are largely independent of goods and also of relations between individuals mediated by the possession of goods. In fact, once the bourgeois spirit is expelled from our blood, private property of the means of production itself is beneficial to and necessary for the community. In the essay on resentment, Scheler criticizes Locke, Smith, and Ricardo. In their theories, private property becomes a matter of functional expediency. Scheler, however, maintains, again without giving any reason: «But just as all moral activity takes place within the framework of moral *existence* {*Seins*}, all labor on objects *presupposes* their ownership {Eigentum}» (RE 140; UW 118; quite obviously, he is so preoccupied with private property that he does not even notice that the sentence as it stands might equally well serve the workers as a slogan to expropriate the owners of private property). In the manuscript, "Christlicher Sozialismus als Antikapitalismus" (Christian Socialism as Anti-Capitalism), written in 1919 (PPS 697), Scheler maintains that, as a matter of principle, the Christian notion of property forbids socialization of the means of production. Only if certain ends cannot be achieved by private property is socialization allowed. Especially the private property of the middle class has to be preserved (PPS 663ff.). As to the problem of the replacement of the bourgeois ethos with a communitarian ethos, he maintains that private property of the means of production does not exclude social ethos and production for actual needs. Psychologically and sociologically, the entrepreneurial spirit of initiative and free responsibility is independent of egoism and selfishness. It can have other motives such as honor, respect in the community, and «enjoyment of being capable» («Könnensfreude») (PPS 672ff.). One might also assume that, once the Gesinnungen are cleansed of «English cant,» the institution of private property provides individuals with the necessary means to display the different rankings of their values. In this way, private property follows from the aristocratic principle, which he constantly stresses, and which liberalism, in his view, has perverted:

> Even the last remnants of a social hierarchy—as a meaningful selection of the best and an image of the aristocracy that pervades all living nature—are cast overboard, and society is atomized in order to free the forces required for doing better business. The "estate" {"Stand"}—a concept in which noble blood and tradition determine the unity of the group—is replaced by the mere "class"

{"Klasse"}, a group unified by property, certain external customs ruled by fashion, and "culture." (RE 159; UW 135)

Still, one has to expel the bourgeois ethos. Scheler's model of the genesis of capitalism out of a mixture of blood and infection and the general framework of his theory of history also determine his thoughts on how to expel it. Though the pure has been overthrown, something of it has remained. For «the core of Christian theory and practice remained *free* from those phenomena. . . Christian philosophy as well remained basically free from the "dualism" of soul and body» (RE 135; UW 114). Also at the bottom of the hierarchy nothing essential has changed. In all its activities, resentment has not gebildet and transformed itself, and by definition it cannot do so. Rather, it has remained what it was from the beginning. Scheler acknowledges that things have become more complicated than at the time of the emergence of capitalism (RE 172; UW 145). He also insists that one has to distinguish between genetic causes and causes related to the maintenance of the already existing entity (UW 347). However, the former thought is not developed at all, and the latter is adduced only because it fits into Scheler's refutation of Marx. At the beginning of "Die Zukunft des Kapitalismus" (The future of capitalism), written in February 1914 (UW 385), Scheler quotes in Latin a further axiom of medieval thinking on causality that was used especially in the theory of creation and motion and was overthrown by modern physics. By doing so he indicates that, not only concerning the genesis but also the future of capitalism, he adheres to the same reductionism he has practiced with regard to the genesis of capitalism. It is not a matter of prudently working on individual aspects of capitalism in order to somehow overcome its shortcomings. Rather, one has to focus on the one and only cause. This approach allows him to exclude leftist, liberal, as well as conventional conservative politics, and to develop a right-wing position that, in its spirit, is more strongly antileftist and antiliberal than other parties on the Right. In fact, it provides the rationale for a militant anti-Semitism. Since the passage also shows a certain resolute antibourgeois tone typical of antibourgeois bourgeois intellectuals like Scheler (though other passages do so much better), I will quote the entire beginning of the essay:

Capitalism is, in the first place, *not* an economic system of distribution of property, but rather an entire *system of life and culture*. This system originated from the objectives and value-preferences of a certain *biopsychic type of man*, namely, the bourgeois, and it is sustained by the tradition of these preferences. If this assumption is right, which we share with Sombart, then we can—according to the axiom: *cessante causa cessat effectus* {If the cause disappears, the effect will also disappear}, and to the equally valid one that a change (decrease) of the effect can be expected only from a change (decrease) of the cause—hope for a decline of capitalism only if, and to the extent that, precisely this *type of man* loses his power, either because he carries the seeds of his extinction in his own nature and its immanent developmental tendencies or because his ethos at least will lose its power to the ethos of a different type of man. (UW 382)

It is already this «result of the research into the causes of the genesis of capitalism» that excludes the expectation of capitalism's disappearance «from any change, of any kind, of the existing order of property, production, and distribution of the economic goods (as all the socialist parties demand and hope for)» (UW 382). Proletarians and their parties as well as liberals have been deprived of reason by Scheler. Therefore, they cannot bilden, educate, refine, themselves. Thus, they remain selfish. In consequence, the disappearance of capitalism is not to be expected «by a mere increase in number of the proletariat as an economic class and by a corresponding increase of its political power and rights» (UW 382f.).

For the same reason, not even a «lowering» of the capitalist ethos can be expected from social welfare run by the state (UW 383f.). If, by reduction, the proletarians as well as the liberal entrepreneurs are just selfish, one cannot hope for an overthrow of capitalism by allying oneself with them. All that is left is that one might hope for precapitalist residues among the bourgeoisie. Scheler has formulated the ontological presupposition of this in *Formalism in Ethics:*

> Principles of value-judgment in an age, in the sense of a dominant or acknowledged *"ethics,"* {assumptions on the level of stratum 2} can rest on such deceptions {in stratum 1}; and they can be overtaken {nachgeredet} and judged accordingly {nachgeurteilt} by those whose *ethos* {that is, stratum 1} did *not* fall victim to such deceptions. (FEe 306; FE 310)

The conservatives are «the only groups whose bio-psychic type and historical traditional values can still be expected to put up a resolute fight *against* capitalism» (UW 385). However, they too have fallen prey to the capitalist ethos (UW 384f.).[35] At this point, Scheler steps out of the realm of ordinary conservatism, as it were, and opens up the space for an anti-Semitic politics of de-cision and expulsion. He develops the latter along two lines. First, Sombart is praised for having pointed to the «only possible final solution {die einzig mögliche endgültige Lösung}» of the question, namely, the «*problem of population {Bevölkerungsproblem}*» (UW 387). However, in Scheler's view, Sombart didn't pose the problem correctly, for it is not just a matter of the quantity of the population, but rather its «qualitative» aspect (UW 387f.). The proletarians and conservatives don't present the active core of the bourgeois ethos, though they have been so thoroughly infected by it that their politics remain completely in its domain. At the core of the bourgeois ethos, in its active bearers, Scheler discovers its decline. For, it is

> an inner law of the bourgeois type itself that, to the degree of their presence, precisely those properties that enable him to succeed as entrepreneur, trader,

etc., in the capitalist order, carry along as their consequence his diminished procreation and, by this, a diminution of the transmission of those characterolog-
ical *hereditary values* that make up the aptitude for the capitalist spirit. . . . In
consequence of precisely this *attitude of calculating* {*Rechenhaftigkeit*} follow
at the same time economic prosperity *and* the diminished will for procreation,
that is, the decrease of numbers of children of the calculating elements. According to what was said previously, beyond any doubt the *aptitude* to this attitude
of calculating itself is a *hereditary value* and is bound to a vital type of lower
value. (UW 388)

If, according to what was said previously, the «good old world» was free
of capitalism, and if capitalism came about as the result of a mixture of blood,
the German liberal entrepreneurs are not the ultimate cause. Rather, their
hereditary values themselves are the result of the mixture of blood, which
brought about capitalism, and which was initiated by someone else, who
smuggled into them the bad genes. The ultimate cause are the Jews, and they
should, and will, die out. One can hardly avoid getting the impression that
this latter thought silently underlies Scheler's thinking, or that those interested in such a way of reasoning might assume it to be the underlying thought,
when Scheler adds to the passage just mentioned: «There is an index, widely
visible, of the slow dying out of the bourgeois type, namely, the fact of the
*dying out of the German Jew,* as established recently by F. A. Teilhaber, in
proportion to their gaining leading positions in capitalism and, at the same
time, stepping out of the mysterious protective sphere of the Jewish tradition
of family» (UW 389). As also in other passages, here the «type» is clearly
grounded in what one calls «race,» and the view of the Jews is that they should
die out. In the next sentence, Scheler adds that they will be the first to die
out, and he reminds his readers of Zionism:

It is with regard to this Jewish type—today, with the inner right of the worthi-
ness of being preserved of this great, gifted people the courageous and noble
Zionism brusquely confronts it {= this Jewish type} with a different type and
presses him deeply down into his honor and his conscience; often bloody and
yet justly—that in time first and on a small scale the *tragique destiny* {das
*tragische Geschick*} executes itself, which will execute itself with the bourgeois type in general; namely, that in the midst of the increasing gaining of
capitalist power it {= the bourgeois type} will perish with all of its hereditary
faculties, and it will fall prey to the increasing elimination {Ausschaltung} from
history. (UW 389)

Certainly, by maintaining that war is «the constructive force» (PPS 77) of
history, Scheler is virtually disempowering other elements in his theory, which
might prevent those interested in such a way of thinking from speeding up
«the increasing elimination» of the Jews «from history» by supporting Zionism or, if the Jews don't want to leave voluntarily, by throwing them out of

Germany. The second line, complementary to the first, relates to «one of the most important tendencies governing the entire world-historical development of this system of culture» (UW 385), and it pertains also to the political aspect of the bourgeois ethos, namely democracy—or, as he puts it, «*"democratistic" value-preferences ("demokratistischen" Wertschätzungen)*» (UW 385). According to him, democracy is no longer the preference of the majority. Rather, it has become the preference of the ruling minority. This follows from his theories in *Formalism in Ethics* and the essay on resentment. For, if democracy were still the preference of the majority, one could not speak of democracy as «a slave insurrection.» However, by Scheler's definition democracy is a slave insurrection. Thus, democracy must be the preference of a minority, which somehow for some time managed to give the semblance of representing the majority:

> If these democratistic morals had remained the morals of the ruled "large number" and would not have become precisely the morals of the *ruling* "small number," one would *never* be entitled to talk of a slave insurrection in morals, that is, of an uprising of the inferior *systems of value-preferences* above the superior systems of value-preferences. For, always and ever it is the necessarily "small number" of the ruling individuals that determines *which* systems of value-preferences become the ruling ones. It is only the fact that the ethically and biologically inferior systems of value-preferences become the ones of the *ruling* minority that renders "revolution" something like a constant feature in the course of the modern development of states. (UW 387)

Only in a state of affairs where by means of democratism the vital type of inferior value has taken over, as in the modern era, does there exist a right of revolution (UW 387). Thus, one must not walk into the trap of taking the actors' words at face value. Rather, one has to hear that they are actually saying precisely the opposite of what they explicitly proclaim, and what they actually say is precisely what follows from Scheler's theoretical construction. Doing so, one hears that the cry for a revolution calls for precisely the opposite of what it explicitly demands. For, actually it calls for a cancellation of the democratic values: «The *deepest soul* of these movements is not the cry for "freedom and equality," which just lies on the surface; rather, it is the search for a *minority which is worthy of ruling* {over the members of the movements and the entire Gemeinschaft}» (UW 386).

The various voices are not taken with all their ambiguities and contradictions. Rather, they are reduced to the prejudice of the philosopher. In the movements outside of the economic realm, Scheler sees in the German youth, as well as in the French youth, the emergence of the new that is precisely the reemergence of the vital type that was toppled by the modern era: «In {these movements} a *new type of man* raises its head—still somewhat diffident—*that* type that has been suppressed by the epoch of capitalism» (UW 390).

Scheler points to the phenomena of the Youth movement: one turns away from the socioeconomic opposition between «"poor and rich"» and focuses on the questions of «*vitality,* and psychic and physical *health* of the Volk and the race» (UW 391). There is a «new *love* of nature and sport» and other phenomena (UW 391). In the first place, however, there is the concern about «*questions regarding the choice of one's partner.* . . . Historically, one of the roots of capitalism was the indiscriminate mixing of the noble vital type with the base type, whether for reasons of utility or for the sheer thrill of it» (UW 392). This is the second aspect of possible discrepancies between preferences in stratum 1 and preferences in stratum 2. According to Scheler, the young people have already realized that they did not mean equality, freedom, and the social question when they talked about democracy, and they have already replaced the old liberal or social democratic judgments in stratum 2 with the ones that conform to their antibourgeois preferences in stratum 1 and that present properly the reemergence of the old vital type, pushed aside by capitalism and now reemerging in stratum 1.

Scheler dwells on this theme for the rest of the essay (UW 390–395) and links it to «the best» in the countries in Asia. Despite all the noise about the universalization of capitalism, they know that in its center, in Western Europe, the bourgeois ethos «is already in the process of slowly *dying out.* . . . The time is not far off when {the story of progress in science} is believed only by Australian niggers» (UW 394f.). (Scheler claims of the Youth movement that those changes permeate «*all* classes with their new spirit» [UW 391]. Certainly it is more accurate to say that the Youth movement was mostly, if not exclusively, a bourgeois phenomenon. However, for the structure of his reasoning this doesn't matter.) Scheler maintains that «each ethical and political orientation concerning the ought, which might speed up the process of the disappearance of the capitalist ethos, can have its meaning only within the frame of this process {= the dying out of the Jews and the active bearers of the bourgeois ethos}, which is *necessary,* and which is not a matter of our conscious will» (UW 390).

Each political relation to the individuals who are supposed to be the promoters of the bourgeois ethos has to be based on the supposed biological fact that they will die out. The individuals are addressed not with regard to their logos, but with regard to their biology, which makes them die out, and they are not considered as individuals but only in reductive terms of biology and race. Only in some passages does Scheler distinguish linguistically between the ethos and the individuals as bearers of an ethos, though even here the distinction is more implicit (if present at all, for he talks not about the proletarians, but about the proletariat «qua "proletariat"» [UW 383]). However, when the «old world,» the world of capitalism, is toppled by the «new world,» which is the reemergence of the world capitalism had toppled, proletarians qua proletarians, liberals qua liberals, and conservatives qua conservatives have to disappear anyway. If one considers the entire course of Scheler's essay, one sees immediately that it is the same as in section 74 of Heidegger's *Being and Time*. Ordinary Daseine live in the mode of the «they»; they live their lives as proletarians, liberals, or conservatives. In the stifling atmosphere of the late Kaiserreich and in the busy noise of the Weimar Republic something else announces itself, and something new arises. Still, ordinary Dasein covers this up and sticks to the «they»-like mode of life. However, a situation arises, for instance, with the beginning of World War I, that definitely calls for a decision. Some evade the call of fate and remain in their «they»-like modes. They become inauthentic. Others see through the work of covering up and obey the call. They become authentic. They realize that they are called upon to leave behind the «they»-like mode of parliamentarism and democracy. They are called into the Kampf, in which they recognize the real agent and the real foe. They realize that they are called upon to rerealize Gemeinschaft, that is, to erwidern its call for help, and they realize that they can do so only by expelling that which has pushed aside Gemeinschaft; that is, they are called upon to make a Widerruf of Gesellschaft.

I have already pointed out that for Scheler to expel capitalism does not mean to expel private property. Rather, if properly put in the service of the Gemeinschaft, private property of the means of production is a vital feature of it. As is already clear, for Scheler parliamentarism and democracy are not a feature of Gemeinschaft. Rather, they have to be expelled. Already in his book *Formalism,* Scheler indicated this in several passages, some of which I have already mentioned. After the passage on deceptions, falsifications, and overthrows as quoted above, Scheler gives an example of the ramifications of his theory:

> Norms that come from vital values alone undoubtedly require in principle {prinzipiell, here a shorthand for «in accordance with the relations between values in the hierarchy of values as they exist independently of human beings»} an aristocratic structure of society, i.e., a structure in which noble blood {das edle Blut} and character-values of heredity belonging to such noble blood possess political prerogatives. But norms coming from values of utility dictate an equalization of biological value-differences among groups. Values of utility taken by themselves at least tend toward political democracy. (FEe 306f., FE 310f.)

Here too, Scheler gives no argument for his thesis. After the war, Scheler takes up this idea, for instance, in the essay "Christliche Demokratie" (Christian democracy) of 1919. I have already quoted a major passage that shows that the logic of de-cision is also at work in this essay. Modern democracy is the result of the denial of the objective realm of values and, thus, has to be replaced with a revitalized Christian democracy. Christian democracy means that pace their differences in race, etc., human beings are equal before God, but only insofar as they are all children of the same father and thus brothers in the same family of God. This equality does not exclude inequalities in the realm of values and down here on earth. God has offered each human being grace—«though in accordance with the individuality of the soul a different measure of grace to each» (PPS 680f.). The ruler and the ruled have to conceive of their roles as a service to God (PPS 681). The paradigm of Christian democracy is the Catholic Church as the proper realization of the hierarchy of values. Power runs from above downward, not the other way around. It is democratic insofar as no one is excluded from being considered worthy of entering the ladder and moving upward (PPS 681ff.). Modern democracy has perverted the order of values. It regards freedom rather than the realization of the eternal order to be the end of history. It regards all forms in which human beings live together as produced by themselves and, thus, human beings can also dissolve them. This too runs counter to the eternal order. In modern democracy, the order of values is freedom, equality, and brotherliness. In Christian democracy, it is different. First comes truth, second goodness, and third brotherliness. Only then follow freedom and equality. Freedom goes before equality because of the notion of justice as already mentioned (PPS 683). This is in line with Scheler's interpretation of autonomy in *Formalism in Ethics,* one crucial aspect of which is the following:

> But morally valuable obedience {Gehorsam} exists whenever, despite the *lack* of insight into the moral value of a commanded state of affairs which characterizes obedience as obedience, the insight into the moral goodness of willing and willing persons (or their "office") is evidentially given, the goodness becoming manifest in the making of the commandments or (*in concreto*) in the ordering of the orders. In this case there is autonomous and immediate insight into the moral value of commanding, heteronomous and mediate insight into the value of the commanded value-complex, and at the same time complete autonomy of willing in rendering obedience. (FEe 500; FE 491)

The paradigm of this concept of autonomy is obedience to God (FEe 500; FE 491). Of the numerous passages in which Scheler praises the sense of sacrifice suppressed by Gesellschaft, I quote only one from the essay on resentment:

> We do believe that life itself can be sacrificed for values higher than life, but this does not mean that all sacrifice runs counter to life and its advancement. . . . *We have an urge to sacrifice* before we ever know why, for what, and for whom! {*Es drängt uns, zu opfern*—ehe wir wissen, warum und wofür und für wen!} (RE 89; UW 75f.)[36]

This was written shortly before World War I. Scheler had hoped that World War I was the rerealization of the Gemeinschaft, which had been toppled by modern society and parliamentarism. However, World War I turned out to be disillusioning.[37] In addition, it was lost, and consequently a full-blown modern democratic constitution took over. In February of 1919, the National Assembly released a provisional constitution and elected as president the Social Democrat Friedrich Ebert. In July 1919, the Weimar Republic was inaugurated with a Social Democratic president and the Social Democrats as the strongest party. In the speech, "Christlicher Sozialismus als Antikapitalismus" (Christian socialism as anticapitalism) in April 1919 (PPS 697f.), Scheler summarizes his criticism of Marx and his own theory on capitalism and history (PPS 624f.) and elaborates on the issue in eight points. At the end of the third, he formulates the opposition between Hegel, Marx, and the social democrats on the one hand and himself on the other, again employing metaphors identical to those Hitler used: «Not progress, but development and falling-down-and-away-from and re-naissance» (PPS 628; «Nicht Fortschritt, sondern Entwicklung und Dekadenz und Wiedergeburt»). «Progress» was the catchword of liberals as well as—according to Scheler—of Hegel, Marx, and social democracy. The progressive development of Gesellschaft would realize freedom, for liberals within a liberal, for social democrats within a socialist, and for Marxists within a communist society. For Scheler, this project of liberals and leftists is a falling-down-and-away-from, a de-cadence, which must be countered by a renaissance of the proper order of the human heart, which has to overthrow the capitalism that has toppled it. The «lower» entities are devoid of reason, and too thoroughly infected by «English cant.» They themselves cannot achieve «higher» values. Thus, we are in need of, in Scheler's terms, a new «moral-religious genius.» It is a very moving as well as very frightening passage:

All history of religion and church has its main phases—its soul—in new religious men: Benedict, St. Bernard, St. Francis, Ignatius, Luther, Calvin, etc. History of religion is the soul of history. The soul of history of religion in turn is the history of the souls of the saints. . . . We can only wait and hope, prepare the way and believe that God is gracious and will one day send us such a soul. Again, here one can "do" {"machen"} nothing; very unpleasant for the new-German belief in deed and power, but unfortunately unchangeable. However, as a matter of fact, we see that at the beginning was not the deed, as Kantians and Fichtians believe, but rather the Logos and love; however, not the impersonal Logos, as Hegel believed, but rather the person capable of spirit and love, namely, the man, whom one believes—without reasons; believing first and foremost in his being and the specific nearness of this being to God; the man, who— as we Christians believe—would know to reproduce {reproduzieren} the Savior {Heiland} anew; however, not externally copying him, but rather from within; from the depths of his divine mind and character. We know one thing:

he would have to combine, like no other, and concentrate within himself the entire uncurable illness and sin of this time—just as, on the cross, the Savior "was completely sin." Thus, we definitely will not find him (1.) among the healthy ones, (2.) among politicians, (3.) among the correct bourgeois individuals. In all his utmost concentration of sin in his heart, he must, however, at the same time carry in his heart an equally strong will for salvation {zum Heile} and for recovery—not only for himself, but for all—in the extreme exertion of co-responsibility—such that he only just—I say only just—looked beyond sin; the one who would objectify sin as sin and, by this, would become its free lord and master. Everything else he might be is only his concern, not ours. How could we be in a position to prescribe how he is supposed to be? How could we do so as, indeed, we hope to experience from him what we have to be and do? For the time being, as we have not the slightest idea of such a thing, we Christians believe only one thing, namely, that he would be a Christ {ein Christ} according to the broad and noble definition our faith gives to this word. (PPS 645f.)

## E. Heidegger's *Being and Time*, Section 74

After the last passage quoted, Scheler goes on to say that in order for us to recognize the new savior's arrival when he comes, we must hear the «great preach of recent history with the inner ears of our faith and our love»; we must hear not only the words «but rather the call of God to turn back {diesen Umkehrruf Gottes} in the things, in history itself. Everyone has to try to turn himself, every human being, every family, every group. It is only in a total loyalty {Gesamttreue} that this evil gaze onto the world, which has led to the dominion of mammon, can melt» (PPS 646).

In the context of a concept of history as development, falling-down-and-away-from, and renaissance, one can take all the metaphors literally. People move along with the development of society. Many believe that it will lead upward toward the sun, to a liberal society or to socialism. However, for right-wingers the road leads away from the sun, down into a desert of ice. As in Scheler's formulation of 1915—we have to expel Anglo-American capitalism «from {our} blood like a foreign poison» (PPS 153)—and as in Heidegger's sentence on Widerruf (BT 438; SZ 386), society must be canceled. The political structure of society will simply be expelled when the new Christ comes. As for the economic structure of society, leftists would say of Scheler's proposal that that structure remains unchanged since Scheler does not want the institution of private property to be sublated. For, according to Scheler, capitalism is not a matter of private property. Thus, the expulsion concerns the capitalist Gesinnung or mentality that has to be replaced with a communitarian Gesinnung. «Everyone» (PPS 646) has to be prepared so he does not miss this event. Everyone can prepare himself by listening to the «call of God to turn back» in the things, and in history itself, a call the liberals and leftists don't want to hear. Umkehren is «to turn back.» I move forward on the road, and then I kehre um, that is, I turn around and move back into the direction I came from. For a Christian, it is at the same time a move upward, toward God. Listening to the call, we realize that we are moving down into a desert of ice, that the promised land is where we came from, what we have fallen away from, and that we have to make an «authentic repetition of a possibility of existence that has been» (BT 437; SZ 385). Since we are already in the icy desert, the repetition is not a simple one but rather an Erwiderung that, as such, is a Widerruf of society (BT 438; SZ 386). In the section on conscience, Heidegger writes:

> In calling forth to something, the "whence" of the calling {das Woher des Rufens} is the "whither" to which we are called back {das Wohin des Zurückrufens}. When the call gives us a potentiality-for-Being to understand, it does not give us one which is ideal and universal; it discloses it as that which has been currently individualized and which belongs to that particular Dasein. We have not fully determined the character of the call as disclosure until we understand it as one which calls us back in calling us forth {als vorrufender Rückruf}. (BT 325f.; SZ 280)

We are engaged in some project and move forward on the timeline toward the future. In our project, we happily enjoy, or at least have given in, «to be subsumed under the idea of a business procedure that can be regulated» (BT 340; «Idee eines regelbaren Geschäftsganges,» SZ 294; one of Heidegger's terms for Gesellschaft). The call doesn't stop our forward movement on the timeline, for it does not physically kill us. It does call us back, however, from the project we are engaged in. Calling us back, it calls us «vor auf das Schuldig*sein*» (SZ 291; «forth to *Being*-guilty,» BT 337), and by this it opens up «the very *possibility of taking action*» (BT 340; «*die Möglichkeit zu handeln,*» ST 294) for us. Heidegger need not add «authentically.» His emphasis, the entire sentence, and the entire paragraph make sufficiently clear that he is talking about Daseine who, as he says in the last sentence of the paragraph, «*hear it authentically*» (BT 341; «im *eigentlich hörenden* Anrufverstehen,» SZ 294). As Scheler's metaphors, Heidegger's can be taken quite literally. The call calls us forth, that is, calls upon us to step out of the crowd that plods forward on the road called downward plunge. Understanding the call, authentic Daseine realize that it calls them back to the site of the call itself, from where the call calls. As one can see already in these passages, Heidegger's notion of the call of conscience is directed against an interpretation of conscience in terms of universal reason. It is also directed against the concept of just exchange, which in the modern era is closely related to that of reason. In fact, what Heidegger criticizes as inauthentic interpretation of conscience, and what he calls upon us to leave behind, is Gesellschaft and a thinking in terms of Gesellschaft. The other aspect of Gesellschaft, the public sphere, Berlin, Weimar, and the mass media, Heidegger criticizes in the section B entitled "The Everyday Being of the 'There', and the Falling {Verfallen} of Dasein," as «idle talk,» «curiosity,» «ambiguity» (BT 210ff.; SZ 166ff.). In society, we are in the *downward plunge* and *turbulence* (BT 223; «*Absturz*» and «*Wirbel,*» ST 178). We have fallen into Gesellschaft out of the world of the craftsmen, the world of the πράγματα, where we encounter beings as «equipment» (BT 96; SZ 68). In some ways, Heidegger's *Being and Time* has the same structure as all the literature on Gemeinschaft and Gesellschaft. We begin in Gemeinschaft and somehow we end up in Gesellschaft. In Gesellschaft, we are lonely, either not caring about others or even antagonistic to them: «Dasein maintains itself proximally and for the most part in the deficient modes of solicitude. Being for, against, or without one another, passing one another by, not "mattering" to one another—these are possible ways of solicitude. And it is precisely these last-named deficient and Indifferent modes that characterize everyday, average Being-with-one-another» (BT 158; SZ 121). However, as was already mentioned,[38] the downward plunge is not yet over. For, somehow, the deficient mode of solicitude turns into a positive mode of solicitude, namely, socialism or social democracy as the «truth» of Gesellschaft. In it, the subjects lose the kind of fake freedom and autonomy they enjoy in the liberal Gesellschaft. «The Other» becomes the object of social welfare work, in which «the Other can become one who is dominated and dependent, even if this domination is a tacit one and remains hidden from him» (BT 158; SZ 122). It is at this point, under the threat of socialism, that it becomes possible to turn around the downward plunge. For, there is another positive mode of solicitude, one Heidegger only hints at darkly after his description of Gesellschaft:

> A Being-with-one-another which arises [entspringt] from one's doing the same thing as someone else, not only keeps for the most part within the outer limits, but enters the mode of distance and reserve. The Being-with-one-another of those who are hired for the same affair often thrives only on mistrust. On the other hand, when they devote themselves to the same affair in common, their doing so is determined by the manner in which their Dasein, each in its own way, has been taken hold of. They thus become *authentically* bound together, and this makes possible the right kind of objectivity [die rechte Sachlichkeit], which frees the other in his freedom for himself. (BT 159; SZ 122)[39]

Though I would disagree, one might say that in the section on conscience Heidegger still leaves open whether the step out of Gesellschaft leads to the political Right or the political Left.[40] Even if, however, the section on historicality stood alone and were not preceded by the sections on falling and on conscience and solicitude, one sees easily that Heidegger's concept of historicality is identical to Hitler's and Scheler's ideas of history and, thus, politically on the Right. Before I summarize Heidegger's notion and present some concluding remarks, I would like to address the two general problems of the political Right I mentioned in chapters 1 and 2.

As is already clear from my discussion of Hitler's and Scheler's works, one problem of the political Right was which of the different pasts one had to repeat. Should people just go back to the Kaiserreich and rerealize it? Or, via the Renaissance in Italy—the «country where the lemons grow,» as Goethe had said—could it turn out that the Germans too had the great personalities whom Nietzsche admired so much? Should the world of the knights with their Minnesang, minnesong be repeated? Maybe, however, what ought to be rerealized is the hierarchy supposedly developed by Thomas Aquinas, who had been declared the official theologian of the Roman Catholic Church as recently as 1879. Or perhaps one needs to go back even farther and rerealize the German people of early history when they were still living in the dark forests. Or are the Greeks to be included among the real Germans and Aryans, as Hitler also acknowledged?[41] The other problem was whether the past to be rerealized should be rerealized the way it was lived out when it was present, or whether its rerealization should incorporate the major achievements of modern times, namely, private property of the means of production on a large scale and modern technology? From the viewpoint of Hitler, Scheler had given an answer that was doubly naive. First, Scheler wanted to rerealize the early Christian love community. Second, he wanted the rerealization of this very community he distinguished so sharply from Protestant ethics and even from Luke to incorporate modern technology. For Scheler maintained that the Germans should be prepared for an entire series of wars against England (PPS 121). However, he also has another reason for this. The basic principle of his philosophy is that «for value-personalism, all history {alle Gemeinschaft und Geschichte} has its goal in the *being and activity of persons*» (FEe 505; FE 496; read «all community and history»). Another sentence seems to be incompatible with this basic principle, however: «in the course of history the driving forces behind historical change were to shift more and more from persons to the masses» (FEe 505; FE 496). However, these sentences don't contradict each other, according to Scheler, but the second one even supports the basic principle (FEe 505; FE 496). This «singular nexus» allows for another principle:

All positive values that *can* be realized by *extra*personal and *extra*spiritual powers *ought* to be so realized. Or, more briefly, everything that can be mechanized *ought* to be mechanized. Needless to say, this proposition does not coincide with the orientation of thinking in positivistic ethics, e.g., the ethics of H. Spencer, which sees in the progressive exclusion of love, sacrifice, conscience, duty {Liebe, Opfer, Gewissen, Pflichtzwang}—and finally the person and spirit in general—a growing "progress" in history. But this proposition does establish a clear boundary between all truly ethical personalism and idealism and their truly reactionary and "romantic" copies {Scheinformen}, which would artificially maintain and fix the personal principle *at the expense* of a *possible* mechanism, e.g., love and sacrifice at the expense of a possible solidarity of interests, spiritual personal activity at the expense of a possible collective organization and mechanism. These copies do not serve to liberate the personal in men; on the contrary, they serve to maintain the servitude of the personal. Here we will not elaborate on the range of applicability of this principle but will only point out that it is valid for all forms of personal spirit, not only singular but also collective forms, for instance, for nations in relation to the international mechanism of civilization. Increasing mechanization in actualizing values that are *at all* mechanizable lifts the *peculiarity* and *self-value* of personal forms of spirit to ever purer heights; it does not destroy them, as both positivism and false personalism assume, though with opposing assessments. (FEe 506; FE 496f.)

Hitler has only contempt for those who promote «romantic copies.» He polemicizes against those who sport «flowing beards and primeval Teutonic gestures» (MKe 462; MK 517), and praises the Prussian state for having «adapted to the modern world and put into organized form» the «German army's instinct of self-preservation and self-defense» (MKe 647; MK 734). Also, «our» politics must not just repeat old ways. Adherence to the «alliance with the Hapsburg state cadaver» out of «sentimentality for the fantastic conception of the Nibelungen» has been «the ruin of Germany» (MKe 630; MK 712). In Heidegger's terms, such efforts mix up the third meaning of «world» («that *'wherein'* a factical Dasein as such can be said to 'live'») with the first meaning of «world» («the totality of those entities which can be present-at-hand within the world») (BT 93; SZ 64f.).[42] After the past has been overthrown by Gesellschaft worldwide, or at least in Europe, one cannot just repeat the past in Germany the way it supposedly was at this or that time. The rerealization of the past world in the sense of «that *'wherein'* a factical Dasein as such can be said to 'live'» must abstract from its former realization on the level designated by the first meaning of «world.» Only then is the rerealization strong enough to incorporate modern technology as an achievement of, but by no means identical with, the Gesellschaft that has to be disavowed in order for the past Gemeinschaft to be rerealized. Hitler labels the «romantic copies» a «mechanical restoration of the past» and claims that «with the founding of the NSDAP, for the first time a movement had appeared whose goal did not, like that of the bourgeois parties, consist in a mechanical restoration {mechanischen Restauration} of the past, but in the effort to erect an organic folkish state in place of the present senseless state mechanism» (MKe 534; MK 598; see also MKe 649ff; MK 735ff. and passim).

These thoughts also guide the choice of the flag. One must avoid any allusion to a specific historical state, for this would promote the misunderstanding of reducing the Aryan race to just one, already more or less fallen, historical state. It also would fill people's minds with the concrete modes of that past world, and thus prevent them from being modern and able to cope with the French and the Britons and to conquer Russia. For that reason, the flag of the National Socialists must not be the flag of the Kaiserreich or of some of the individual German states, whether present or past. On the other hand, the flag must contain the colors of the flag of the Kaiserreich, black, red, and white, as they are the German colors and thus are the proper protest against the colors of the flag of the Weimar Republic, black, red, and gold. The spirit of the past, in the sense of the third meaning of «world» in Heidegger, has to be cleansed of any of its former concrete realizations, for each of them would just prevent the rerealization of the past from incorporating the achievements of the modern era. Only if there is no reference to any concrete past, can the rerealization of the past incorporate modern technology and the necessary attitudes. Also, only then is the past sufficiently present in the present time, which has overthrown it, and is sufficiently omnipresent so that it becomes impossible to ridicule it by pointing to, for instance, the «flowing beards» of the old Germans or the mustaches of the officials of the Kaiserreich (MKe 492ff; MK 551ff.). In this way the swastika was chosen: «In *red* we see the social idea of the movement, in *white* the nationalistic idea, in the *swastika* the mission of the struggle for the victory of the Aryan man, and, by the same token, the victory of the idea of creative work, which as such has always been and always will be anti-Semitic» (MKe 497; MK 557).[43]

It has often been said that Division Two of *Being and Time* in general and the section on historicality in particular is not well argued and rather unclear. One can say so only if one isolates Heidegger's text from its historical context and fails to recognize, in Carl Schmitt's terms, its polemical situation; both of these moves are an invitation to, and already a part of, deconstructive interpretations such as Birmingham's. Rather, one should acknowledge that section 74 of *Being and Time* is a brilliant text and also very clear. In just five pages, Heidegger here concisely summarizes the common motif uniting the parties on the revolutionary political Right in their fight against romantic right-wingers, liberals, and leftists. In the mid-1920s, many Germans were no longer enthusiastic about war, but had «fallen» into the Gesellschaft of a democratic republic. It is here that the Daseine are called upon by the Volksgemeinschaft. They have to get out of Gesellschaft. They cannot do so by relating positively to the Other in the way social democrats transcend Gesellschaft. For the right-wingers know that this leads only deeper into Gesellschaft. In addition, any direct collective effort to get out of Gesellschaft would just be too proletarian and heteronomous. The decision must not result from a debate with social democrats, who finally convince people. Rather, it must be the autonomous and eigenste act of the bourgeois subject, alone with himself and with his authentic Dasein. Only then will people not fall prey to the social democratic society, but will reestablish the true community. Heidegger cannot refer to models such as Augustine's conversion. As he himself would be the first to point out, not everyone on the Right considered himself a Christian and thus not everyone would appreciate this allusion to our Christian values and humanistic traditions. In addition, systematically such references to Christianity don't serve the purpose. Augustine, as well as most Christians, insisted that Christians leave earthly political matters as they are and explicitly forbade themselves to turn back and to widerrufen the respective societies in order to realize heaven here on earth. Furthermore, Augustine's weibisches Geschluchze, womanish sobbing, in the garden in Milan and also his talkativeness is anachronistic and does not allow for the «reticence» (BT 318; «Verschwiegenheit,» SZ 273) and the «hardness of the will»[44] required for the struggle to widerrufen society. Each eigentlicher philosopher has called upon us to distance and detach ourselves from worldly matters, to cleanse our minds of the worldly forms, which shape us in our everyday life. In addition, one of the few motifs Hegel adhered to in the transition from the «young Hegel» to the «late Hegel» was that death—the threat of death, which the soldier takes upon himself—is an appropriate means to de-form oneself.[45] Furthermore, having lost so much property in the war, in inflations and economic crises, people should realize that, indeed, death is the only property no one can take away from a given Dasein.[46] It is not through some collectivity, but rather through what is our ownmost that the turn has to be brought about. Finally, World War I and the remembrance of it was a common cause of all right-wingers, whether they were fighting for the Kaiserreich or for the rerealization of some other community. At the same time, an allusion to World War I already hints at the reward we will finally get for our courageous act of giving up everything and facing what is our ownmost. Thus, Heidegger evokes the «Helden von Langemarck» as the telos of the step out of society: «Resoluteness gains its authenticity {Eigentlichkeit} as *anticipatory* resoluteness {*vorlaufende* Entschlossenheit}. In this, Dasein understands itself with regard to its potentiality-for-Being, and it does so in such a manner that it will go right under the eyes of Death in order thus to take over in its thrownness that entity which it is itself, and to take it over wholly» (BT 434; SZ 382).

World War I and the Weimar Republic were experienced by many, if not all, rightists as, in Hitler's terms, the «great turning point» (MKe 406; MK 450). In the preface to the third edition of *Formalism in Ethics,* Scheler labeled the «great turning point» the «*kairos,* i.e., the call of the *hour of our* human and historical being and life» (FEe xxxi; FE 23); the decisive moment in the course of a sickness, at which alone it is possible for the physician to interfere and to restore the body to its healthy state before it is definitely too late. I have discussed passages in Hitler and Scheler that testify to the peculiar feeling that existed at the beginning of World War I, namely, that something new had raised its voice and was calling upon people to make a decision. Already prior to that, something strange, uncanny, had cast its shadow over people's ordinary way of living, and they have somehow felt that there was something in the air heralding something new. Rightists claimed that people should realize that there was something wrong with the way of life and assumptions they had taken over from their parents and fellow citizens and had been repeating in their ordinary way of Dasein according to the «they.» According to rightists, «we» somehow feel that behind the forms of ordinary Dasein's life, behind Gesellschaft, something else is emerging that is covered up by them. In Scheler's terms,[47] «we» become aware that under our ethos on stratum 2 a new ethos on stratum 1 is emerging, or has always already been there, and that both do not conform to each other; that underneath our explicit judgments and ways of life of our ordinary Dasein something else begins to raise its voice, our eigentliches ethos. The call of the new tells us that «we» have to cancel our ordinary Dasein and replace it with an ethos 2 that conforms to our eigentliches ethos. «We» should do so because it benefits not only ourselves but all of us to get rid of Gesellschaft, even though those who adhere to Gesellschaft claim the opposite and want us to assume not only that our ordinary Dasein is better than our eigentliches ethos but also that there is no eigentliches ethos behind our ordinary Dasein, and that the conflict between our ethos and our eigentliches ethos is reactionary propaganda. Our ethos has become antagonistic. Some ordinary Daseine want to cover up the new emergence of what-has-been-there. They become inauthentic. Authentic Daseine have to realize the new against the inauthentic Daseine. Heidegger encapsulates this in the paragraph on the work of ambiguity ending with the formula: «The authentic existentiell understanding is so far from extricating itself from the way of interpreting Dasein which has come down to us, that in each case it is in terms of {aus} this interpretation, against {gegen} it, and yet again for {für} it, that any possibility one has chosen is seized upon in one's resolution» (BT 435; SZ 383). Authentic Daseine take the eigentliches ethos «from {aus}» «the way of interpreting Dasein which has come down to us,» because the eigentliche ethos is contained in the latter, though covered up by the ordinary Daseine. Authentic Daseine turn the eigentliches ethos «against» «the way of interpreting Dasein which has come down to us,» because they cancel the latter, that is, Gesellschaft. Authentic Daseine do so «for» «the way of interpreting Dasein which has come down to us,» because they bring ordinary Daseine back to their origin, that is, Gemeinschaft.[48]

Starting in our ethos 2, our ordinary Dasein, and obeying the call of our eigentliches ethos, «we» begin to see that our ordinary Dasein is a forgetting. We realize that our ordinary Dasein is a falling-down-and-away from a past and that at the same time it has forgotten about the fall and even interprets it as progress. We also realize that our eigentliches ethos draws its identity and strength from the forgotten past. This is the paragraph in which Heidegger states: «If everything 'good' is a heritage, and the character of 'goodness' lies in making authentic existence possible, then the handing down of a heritage constitutes itself in resoluteness» (BT 435; SZ 383). Relating itself to the past, or being taken over by the past, authentic Dasein can step out of ordinary Dasein and the latter's vain possibilities, and can realize that it owes its eigentliches ethos and identity to the past, which was brought down. Thus, it gets snatched back from «the endless multiplicity of possibilities» in society into what it recognizes as «the simplicity of its *fate*» (BT 435; SZ 384). It recognizes its fate. It recognizes that its autonomy and its pride in what it believed to have acquired and achieved in society by itself are a vain pretension, and that it instead depends on powers and circumstances it has not produced and these determine its life, that is, they are its fate. Its fate is simple, because in contrast to the «endless multiplicity of possibilities» in society, Volk, being an organic entity, does not allow for all the detractions and all the Firlefanz, gewgaws, gimcrackery, of society, and because it calls the Dasein into a situation of a clear either-or and a clear distinction between the foe and the völkische. In this moment, the antagonism becomes an antagonism between all those who recognize their fate, obey the call, and submit to their fate, and those who don't want to do so. The latter don't submit to their fate and don't take it over. They miss the opportunity to become, in Hitler's terms, «master of their fate,» and, thus, they are tossed around and pushed into irrelevance like the liberals at the beginning of World War I. Thus, this part ends with the sentence: «Even one who is irresolute gets driven about by these—more so than one who has chosen; and yet he can 'have' no fate» (BT 436; SZ 384).[49]

Recognizing its fate, authentic Dasein understands that the past, to which it owes its eigentliches ethos and identity, is an entity that was pushed aside by Gesellschaft, and that the past allows for positive relations to the Other in contrast to the loneliness and instrumental relations to the Other in Gesellschaft, that is, in contrast to solicitude in its deficient mode as well as in the first of its positive modes. Regardless of the differences between them, all rightists have used as the term for the past and the real power in Gesellschaft and history the notion of Gemeinschaft. Thus, Heidegger writes: «But if fateful Dasein, as Being-in-the-world, exists essentially in Being-with-Others, its historizing is a co-historizing and is determinative for it as *destiny* (*Geschick*). This is how we designate the historizing of the community, of {the} people» (BT 436; SZ 384).[50] Heidegger need not develop the notion of Volksgemeinschaft. In the polemical and kairos situation of the twenties it is clear that it functions as polemical to Gesellschaft and reason as employed by liberals and leftists as principles of history. One can give a description of Volk that contrasts it to Gesellschaft and reason, and one can even, as Scheler did, give an account of a realm of values and social units that contains the Volksgemeinschaft. However, one cannot «rationalize» a Volk. In fact, it is part of the rightist polemics against reason and understanding as the principles of «English cant,» Enlightenment, and subjectivity to point out that such entities like Volk cannot be understood by the means employed by subjectivistic thinking or by finite individuals who are part of the embracing entity Volk in its mysterious life. Furthermore, for the same reason Heidegger need not mention the name of the social unit to which Gemeinschaft is polemical, and which, as Gemeinschaft calls upon us to do, «we» have to overthrow, since it earlier ousted Gemeinschaft. For even those who have not read Scheler have learned about this polemical opposition somehow, perhaps from the books of Jünger or Hitler, or just from the atmosphere of the kairos. In addition, in the following sentence Heidegger himself elaborates on both concepts, Gesellschaft as well as Gemeinschaft, in a way that can be found in all books on the topic. According to Scheler, the «principle of summation» guides liberalism and all thinking in terms of Gesellschaft. Liberalism assumes that a social unit is a whole that is not more than the sum of its parts, that is, that the social units are constituted, or «put together» («zusammengesetzt»), by the autonomous subjects so that they can pursue their selfish interests. In reality, however, a Gemeinschaft has priority over the individuals. Again according to Scheler, along with the «principle of summation» goes the assumption that the autonomous subject makes his life by himself, relies only on what he achieves by himself, and does not allow any authority over and above reason to determine his life. In reality, however, it is Gemeinschaft that determines the life course of the individual. Heidegger formulates these two thoughts in the sentences immediately following the sentence on the Volksgemeinschaft:

> Destiny is not something that puts itself together out of individual fates {setzt sich nicht aus einzelnen Schicksalen zusammen}, any more than Being-with-one-another can be conceived as the occurring together of several Subjects. Our fates have already been guided in advance, in our Being with one another in the same world and in our resoluteness for definite possibilities. (BT 436; SZ 384)[51]

In the kairos, right-wingers experience that the time of the ordinary way of Dasein—«English cant» in Scheler, «endless discussion» in Schmitt, «'business'» (BT 336; SZ 289), as the ordinary interpretation of conscience, or the era of «reckoning up claims and *balancing* them off» (BT 328; «im Sinne des *ausgleich*enden Verrechnens von Ansprüchen,» SZ 283; italics mine, J. F.),[52] as Heidegger correctly summarizes a major principle of parliamentary democracy—is over. As for Scheler at the beginning of World War I, and as for Hitler in the kairos of the Weimar Republic, fate, or destiny, itself has brought about a situation in which «we» have to replace liberalism with a communitarian ethos in order to rerealize Gemeinschaft, as in the same moment fate has called upon us to do. Up to that point, fate has been silent, either withdrawn or present, but covered up by the liberals' work of ambiguity. Now, it raises its voice to call upon us to expel liberalism and to rerealize Gemeinschaft. It comes to the fore and demands this realization in a resolute fight. Heidegger goes on: «Only in communicating and in struggling {im Kampf} does the power of destiny become free» (BT 436; SZ 384).[53] Obeying the call of fate, «we» become the agents of fate, which in this way steps out of the background, where it has been covered up by the work of ambiguity, and enters the scene explicitly. The task allotted to us by fate, the repetition of the past, is not a simple repetition of the past. A simple repetition of some past is what ordinary Dasein does all the time by just taking over and repeating the assumptions and attitudes «which 'circulate' in the 'average' public way of interpreting Dasein today» (BT 435; BT 383). Also, a «romantic copy» of the past would be a simple repetition, because it does not take into account the changed circumstances in which the eigentliche past, that is, its spirit, or the past in the third sense of «world,» has to be repeated. Thus, Heidegger explains: «The repeating of that which is possible does not bring again [Wiederbringen] something that is 'past', nor does it bind the 'Present' back to that which has already been 'outstripped'. Arising, as it does, from a resolute projection of oneself, repetition does not let itself be persuaded of something by what is 'past', just in order that this, as something which was formerly actual, may recur» (BT 437f.; SZ 385f.).[54] For authentic Dasein repeats the past in a situation in which the past has been overthrown, or is about to be overthrown, and authentic Dasein knows that it must not make a «romantic copy» of the past. Dasein listens to the call for help and defends, rescues, and rerealizes the past against what has already overthrown it, or is in the process of doing so. Thus, authentic Dasein does not repeat, but rather «erwidert the possibility of that existence which has-been-there» (BT 438; SZ 386). As it realizes in the kairos, in the moment of danger and decision, it can rerealize the past only if it makes a «disavowal» (BT 438; SZ 386) of what has overthrown Gemeinschaft; it disavows, cancels, Gesellschaft, the world in which it has lived as ordinary Dasein and in which inauthentic Daseine still live.[55] As I have already mentioned, the «"today"» («Heute») in the sentence, «disavowal of that which in the "today", is working itself out as the 'past' {sich als "Vergangenheit" auswirkt}» (BT 438; SZ 386) is the present as seen by authentic Dasein.[56] In the kairos, authentic Dasein realizes that life is a mixture that has to be purified, that what it has constantly repeated as ordinary Dasein is not the «real» life, and that it is called to enter the struggle for cleansing. In the kairos, authentic Dasein realizes that its ordinary way of existence, liberalism, which has developed since the thirteenth century, is a past, but not the real past. Thus, Heidegger puts «past» into quotation marks. The ordinary mode of Dasein, liberalism, goes back to a principle or is a world. Thus, authentic Dasein cancels not the entire present, but rather its principle or its world, that is, «that which in the "today", is working itself out as the 'past' {sich als "Vergangenheit" auswirkt}» (BT 438; SZ 386), in Schelerian terms, the bourgeois ethos, which has to be expelled out of Europe's blood like a foreign poison in order to make the rerealization of Gemeinschaft possible. Thus, «we» are entitled to take over into the rerealization of Gemeinschaft all we regard as indifferent toward Gemeinschaft and Gesellschaft, or all we regard to be necessary for the rerealization, for instance, private property of the means of production and modern technology. The Erwiderung that is at the same time a disavowal calls us back from our march forward on the road of Gesellschaft and progress and affirms the primacy of the past—or, in Heideggerian terms, of what-has-been-there—pitted by rightist authors against the «denigration» and «falsification» of the past in Enlightenment, liberalism, and on the political Left. Thus, it is only this Erwiderung that «for the first time imparts to *having-been* {*Gewesenheit*} its peculiarly privileged position in the historical» (BT 438; SZ 386).[57] Since only such a repetition will be successful in contrast to a «romantic copy,» at the end of section 75 Heidegger can summarize the result of the de-cision between inauthentic and authentic Daseine just by using the term «Wiederkehr» («recurrence») without any qualifications. Inauthentic Dasein, liberals and social democrats, live in a false past, the ethos of Gesellschaft, and by projecting it onto the past they misinterpret and neglect the «real» past. As in Scheler, authentic Dasein knows of this and keeps itself open for the advent of the «real» past. Even if Heidegger had not extensively used the vocabulary of falling throughout the book, his notion of history is identical with the one in Hitler and Scheler and with formulations in Scheler such as «Not progress, but development and falling-down-and-away-from and renaissance» (PPS 628):

> When, however, one's existence is inauthentically historical, it is loaded down with the legacy of a 'past' which has become unrecognizable, and it seeks the modern. But when historicality is authentic, it understands history as the 'recurrence' {"Wiederkehr"} of the possible, and knows that a possibility will recur {wiederkehrt} only if existence is open {offen} for it fatefully, in a moment of vision, in resolute repetition {in der entschlossenen Wiederholung}. (BT 444; SZ 391f.)[58]

It has often been said that, working in his Hütte, the Denker and Gelehrte Heidegger was aloof from politics and didn't know what he was doing when he stumbled into Nazism. According to my interpretation, Heidegger's notion of historicality is identical with the notions of history and politics as developed by the revolutionary rightists and as exemplified here in regard to Hitler's and Scheler's works. It is hard to imagine that this is coincidental. Heidegger's text is just too excellent a summary of the revolutionary rightist notion to be the result of a somnambulistic thinking whose author didn't know what the significance of his writings would be in the world outside his Hütte and outside his book.[59] In addition, it is not fate—«fate» in the «truly German» sense as I have «repeated» it here by «disavowing» the misinterpretation of the notion in Heidegger under the spell of the spirit of the American self-made man—that drove Heidegger into Nazism. As Scheler observed, at the beginning of World War I the majority of German intellectuals were liberals opposed to the war (PPS 12), and in the twenties Scheler himself changed his politics dramatically and became a liberal after the end of classic liberalism or even a social democrat.[60] The rightists had enough foes—liberals, social democrats, and Communists—among intellectuals. In addition, as the differences between Hitler and Scheler show, there were strong disagreements among the revolutionary rightists themselves in regard to the question of which community had to be repeated. In light of these disagreements, Heidegger's formula of «the community, of {the} people» (BT 436; SZ 384) is truly remarkable, as I will show in the remainder of this section.

Certainly, Heidegger knew Scheler's book *Formalism in Ethics* and, thus, Scheler's discussion of the four types of social units, that is, Masse (mass, herd), Lebensgemeinschaft (life-community), Gesellschaft (society), and Liebesgemeinschaft (love-community). When it comes to the different large-scale communities, Scheler—as many of the other authors on this topic—takes great pains to explain what he regards as the proper hierarchy. It is at this point that Heidegger builds a very specific option into his excellent summary of the revolutionary rightist notion of history and politics. As to the hierarchy among the various large-scale communities, Scheler uses four criteria. One is the ranking of the value each large-scale community is concerned with (FEe 541; FE 529 and passim). Another is the number of human beings it is concerned with. Furthermore, it matters whether a community is a «collective *person*» (FEe 543; FE 531; see also FEe 520ff.; FE 510ff. and passim) and the degree to which it comes more or less close to this. Finally, it is crucial whether a community acknowledges the individual as a person in his own right independent of his functional contribution to the Gemeinschaft, and the degree to which it comes close to this (FEe 524f.; FE 513f.). With respect to all criteria, the love-community and its earthly organization, the church, is unambiguously at the top of the hierarchy. It is with regard to the love-community and the church that Scheler reestablishes the universalism he denied to reason as developed by Enlightenment and «English cant.» He also ascribes to the love-community another capacity he denied reason, namely, to realize its universal ends in a variety of different empirical churches, that is, to abstract from and at the same time acknowledge the differences and to realize its value within the various churches without negating their differences. The church is concerned with the highest value (FEe 554f.; FE 541f.). It cares not only for all living human beings, but also for all dead and future ones and for all finite individual persons (FEe 547f.; FE 535). It regards the individual not as a member of a family, tribe, or Volk, but rather as a *«purely spiritual individual person»* (FEe 547; FE 535); or, as already mentioned, the individual person as in Gesellschaft is preserved in the love-community. Scheler develops his understanding of the Last Judgment: «Suppose that we find ourselves in a world court. No one *alone* would be tried by its highest judge; all would have to answer to him in the unity of *one* act, and all taken together would have to listen to this judge in *one* act. He would not sentence anyone until he had heard, understood, and valued *all* others *with* this one. In *each* he would cosentence the *whole* no less than the whole in each» (FEe 535; FE 523). Postmoderns and deconstructionists will probably not acknowledge this court as the institutionalized site of, as it is said, the recognition of «the Other as Other,» and they might be right. The author of *Formalism in Ethics* definitely belongs to the revolutionary Right, and only those who lack any sense of the «spirit» and the letter of different philosophies mistake Scheler and «Schelerians» for Habermas's theory of communicative action. However, the mentality giving rise to the notion of the court in Scheler definitely enabled him to distance himself from the advocates of the Volksgemeinschaft.

It would take readers too far beyond the scope of this book to go into the details of Scheler's reasoning. At any rate, for him the order below the love-community is that «the state is, in ranks of values, *above* the people {Volk} but *below* the nation» (FEe 547; FE 534f.; the «nation» being the Kulturgemeinschaft, community of culture, which embraces several peoples, as for instance, western Europe forms a Kulturgemeinschaft). That is, the ranking is the following: at the top is the love-community; next is the community of culture followed by the state; at the bottom of the hierarchy is the Volksgemeinschaft. The «people» concerns the smallest number of individuals (and, thus, excludes the largest number of other individuals), and it is not concerned about the individual as a value in himself (FEe 546; FE 534). Since all the lower communities and society as well are in the service of the highest community, it follows from this reasoning that the church has a right of intervention in regard to the lower Gemeinschaften. The church does not positively interfere by prescribing specific norms. However, again Scheler ascribes to the church a universalistic function in regard to the community of culture (and—since the community of culture is higher than the community of the people—in regard to the state and the community of the people), something he had denied reason: «First, there is the essentially *negative* task of immediately controlling all cultural activity and its works in order to see that the ethos of this activity and the guiding structure of the preferring of the values of the domain in question (style in the arts, the methodological structure of science) *do not conflict* with the conditions of a possible collective *salvation* and, if necessary, of issuing an authoritative declaration on the matter» (FEe 551; FE 539).

In the twenties, Scheler became a social democrat and liberal. At that point, as a social democrat, city-dweller, and notorious frequenter of bars and brothels, Max Scheler would definitely not have joined the National Socialists. However, the author of *Formalism in Ethics* and of the essay on resentment would probably also not have done so. Though, as I have shown, his theories in *Formalism* and related writings present a paternalistic and hierarchical view of the different nations and states that ascribes to the Germans as the proxy of the Liebesgemeinschaft and the Kulturgemeinschaft the task of an imperialistic and militaristic politics of dominion over the world, the internationalism of the Church (which he was to stress in his writings from 1916 onward), the insistence on the individual person as a value in himself, and other elements in his theory, such as the emphasis on the «intimate person» (FEe 561ff.; FE 518ff.) and, so to speak, dialectical thoughts such as the one on mechanization and person would have served as a strong means of critique of a movement that places the Volksgemeinschaft at the top, instrumentalizes all the other communities as a means to pursue the interests of the Volk, and explicitly denies that individual persons have value independent of their functionalistic contribution to the politics of the Volksgemeinschaft. From the viewpoint of Scheler's theory, Hitler's preference for the Volksgemeinschaft looks like an overthrow in the realm of the large-scale communities similar to the overthrow of all communities by Gesellschaft. In fact, in the twenties, due to his Catholicism, Scheler identified the real foe, namely, the National Socialists, recognized that rightist politics gravitated toward them, and saw that they would become the strongest force on the Right. As a consequence, Scheler gave up any rightist politics of history as the rerealization of some overthrown community, reviewed his basic notions, and turned toward the center.

In contrast to Scheler, Heidegger joined the National Socialists, and he did so with great enthusiasm. In light of this, in the light of Scheler's theory of the large-scale communities, and also in light of Scheler's later abandonment of any rightist politics, Heidegger's formula of «of the community, of {the} people» (BT 436; SZ 384) is telling. I have mentioned Guignon's assumption that each authentic Dasein can choose the past that fits his respective utopian ideal. Regarding politics, this means for Guignon that Heidegger's

notion of historicality and politics is neutral and does not exclude any political options, whether liberalism, conservatism, social democracy, or communism (see chapter 4, section A). I have criticized his notion of the relation of
authentic Dasein to the past. In addition, I have shown that Heidegger's notion
of historicality is pro-revolutionary rightist politics and antiliberal and antileftist. One might say, within Heidegger's option for revolutionary rightist politics Guignon's notion emerges. For Heidegger gives a summary of the notion
of history and politics of all the revolutionary rightists, and thus, he does not
yet exclude any specific option. He does not yet exclude the friends of the
Kaiser, the German Renaissance, or the Christian love-community, or the
Vikings, provided that they don't want to rerealize a «romantic copy,» but
rather present an updated version of the respective past they want to rerealize. In fact, Heidegger would not have excluded anyone of the revolutionary
rightists if he had just written «of a community.» For «community» was the
catchword among those on the Right, and this would have left open the possibility that this individual opts for the Kaiserreich, another for the love-
community, etc. However, he adds «of the people» («of the community, of
{the} people,» BT 436; «der Gemeinschaft, des Volkes,» SZ 384). This is a
very conscious choice by which he also performs the second step in the debates
of the rightists. By developing the common motive of all the revolutionary
rightists, he establishes community as the «real» principle in history. In the
second step, he adds his option in the debates, or struggles, among the rightists as to which community has the priority. From the viewpoint of Scheler's
theory, this is a clear decision against Scheler's option and for the politics of
the extreme right, the National Socialists, in the name of the Volksgemeinschaft. (One might add that by proceeding philosophically in the correct
way—step by step, first the general notion and then its specification—he at
the same time avoids the word Volksgemeinschaft itself, since this might have
sounded too blunt in the ears of many of his conservative colleagues or students.) Again, Heidegger must have been aware of the significance of his
choice. Even if he had not read any of the many writings of Scheler's on politics, the political applications of Scheler's *Formalism* are all too obvious and
intended by Scheler, and even prior to the emergence of the National Socialist Party, in the preface of the second edition of *Formalism* in 1921, Scheler
distinguished his theory not only from the Left, but also from developments
on the Right (FEe xxiiif.; FE 15). One might say, the addition of the qualifi-
cation «of the people» is voluntaristic in the sense that the text doesn't provide any argument allowing for this step. In some sense, this doesn't make
things better. Why should one add an unwarranted specification, unless one
has a strong interest in it? This interest then might inspire one to bridge the
gap, and to concreticize theoretically the general option for rightist revolutionary politics such that it becomes an option for National Socialism. In fact,

however, in some sense he had no need to bridge the gap. His way of criticizing subjectivity and universality of reason placed his thinking on the right side of the political spectrum. It is not only the absence in *Being and Time* of anything analogous to Scheler's theory of values and social units that removed the possible resistance of, so to speak, regular and extreme conservatives on the Right against National Socialism. Rather, Heidegger explicitly criticizes the theoretical framework that enabled someone like Scheler to keep his distance to National Socialism and finally turn against any rightist politics (e.g., BT 131ff.; SZ 98ff.). As to the other parts of *Being and Time,* one cannot see anything that might enable its author to resist and criticize National Socialism (which is, of course, not to say that all of Division One and the other parts of Division Two are downright national socialistic). In this sense, one has to regard the addition of the specification «of {the} people» as the author's explicit affirmation that *Being and Time* and the notion of historicality allow for, and even invite, the extreme party on the side of the revolutionary Right and do not enable one to criticize National Socialism. If he did not want to convey this, he would have left out the phrase «of {the} people,» or he would have developed specifications that would have drawn a line between the National Socialists and other rightists with sympathy for the Volksgemeinschaft as the primary community. However, *Being and Time* as it stands does not allow for such specifications, and Heidegger even explicitly criticizes possible rightist means to criticize National Socialism. In light of this, one can hardly imagine a philosophical work that leads into National Socialism more directly than Heidegger's *Being and Time.* Therefore, one should not be surprised that, six years later, on May 1, 1933, Heidegger joined the Nationalsozialistische Deutsche Arbeiterpartei,[61] and that twenty-six days later—on May 27, 1933—he gave his, as Jonas called it, «infamous» (MH 200) rectorate address.

At no point do Scheler and Heidegger feel any need to explain what they mean by «Schicksal.» Indeed, they do not need to explain the notion, for their use of it is completely in line with the everyday one. Schicksal is not something an individual or a group creates in this or that way. Rather, this Schicksal precedes the individual or the group whose fate it is. The question is not as to the need and the way of inventing one's fate, but rather as to whether one—to use one of the later Heidegger's pet words—«fügt sich in,» complies with, one's fate, or whether one tries to ignore or even to fight against it. According to common understanding as well as in Scheler's and Heidegger's views of the matter, only unwise or inauthentic people try the second path. The only difference between Scheler and Heidegger is that Heidegger replaces «unser deutsches Schicksal» or «ein eigentümlich nationales Schicksal» (PPS 1; «our German fate,» «a peculiar national fate») with «Geschick» (SZ 384; «destiny,» BT 436) in order to maintain a terminological distinction between the all embracing Geschick and the different individual slots allotted by Geschick to each individual, «the lowliest as well as the greatest» (PPS 11).[62] Still, fate does not realize itself automatically. The rerealization of Gemeinschaft depends on Dasein's proper listening and successful fighting. It can no longer be assumed that what is supposed to happen according to fate will happen anyway. Rather, without Dasein's compliance with fate and Dasein's active struggle for its realization, that fate would not be realized. The fate of fate requires that those whose fate it is properly realize it[63] and thus properly rerealize Gemeinschaft. In 1934/35, in his lecture course on two hymns by Hölderlin, Heidegger said that the notion of fate in this sense is «an essentially German notion» (HH 173), and he denounced the «traditional» notion of fate as the «Asian notion of fate» (HH 173), according to which what fate ordains will happen anyway, no matter whether one actively subjugates oneself to it and fights for its realization or doesn't care to do so.

This redefinition, however, required as it is in the moment of crisis, does not do away with the basic meaning of fate as something we do not choose but have to comply with. Indeed, the redefinition even strengthens this basic meaning insofar as we ourselves would not even survive if we did not listen to the call and act accordingly. Also, it makes explicit the normative aspect in the everyday usage of the word fate. Thus, neither Scheler nor Heidegger need to elaborate on the notion, because both of them could rely on everyone understanding what they meant. The redefinition itself, however, might have been a further reason for Heidegger in the passage in *Being and Time* to use the word «Erwiderung,» as erwidern is often used for answering someone's call for help. Fate calls upon us and demands us to help it. Without our help, fate could not realize itself, but rather would, so to speak, be drowned and disappear. The implication that we ourselves would be drowned if we don't help fate, is evident in the abundant usage of metaphors of falling and downward plunge in the works of Hitler, Scheler, and also Heidegger. Accordingly, in my view the label «empty decionism» for Heidegger's notion of decision is only half of the story. Authentic Dasein is empty insofar as it has to empty itself from the forms of ordinary and inauthentic Dasein. Becoming empty in this sense, however, is already part of the process of facing a decision that is an either-or such that Dasein must obey the call and must not fail to listen to it.[64]

I have identified Heidegger's section 74 of *Being and Time* as politically rightist on the grounds that it shares with other works unambiguously on the Right the premises of their reasoning against leftists and liberals. In addition, as I will show in more detail in chapter 4, Heidegger's reasoning lacks any of the premises used by leftist authors. One might object that this procedure is unfair and unreliable. However, even those agreeing with this objection will probably admit that Heidegger's case is a special one. For not only did he some years later join the most extreme of the rightist parties, the National Socialists, but he also said in 1936 that the section on historicality in *Being and Time* was the basis for his engagement with National Socialism.[65] True, an author's words about his works do not necessarily have to be taken at face value. However, unless there is substantial evidence that the author's assessment of his works is wrong, his statements have to be respected. At the beginning of my book, I mentioned the «Helden von Langemarck» and the «Helden von Verdun.» Scheler's writings provide a good example of the hopes several rightist authors associated with World War I. As the following quote shows, quite obviously in 1914 the same hopes were present in Heidegger, and he saw in the Machtübernahme of the National Socialists in 1933 a «new beginning,» a new opportunity to realize the hopes of 1914 that had then been betrayed by the outcome of the war and by the Weimar Republic. As Jaspers tells in a pretty macabre story, in Heidelberg on June 30, 1933, Heidegger gave a talk entitled "The University in the new Reich":

> As to its form, it was a masterly talk, as to its content it was a program for the National Socialist renewal of the universities. . . . Our conversations after the talk were, as far as I was concerned, not frank. I told him that one had expected him to stand up for our university and its great tradition. No answer. I talked about the Jewish question, about the vicious nonsense of the 'Wise Men of Zion,' to which he replied: "As you know, there is a dangerous international connection {Verbindung} among Jews." During dinner, he said in a somewhat furious tone that it was nonsense to have that many philosophy professors in Germany; only two or three should be retained. "Which ones?" I asked. No answer. "How can such an uneducated man like Hitler govern Germany?"— "Education {Bildung} doesn't matter at all," he replied. "Just look at his wonderful hands! {sehen Sie nur seine wunderbaren Hände an!}"
>
> Heidegger himself seemed to have changed. Already on his arrival a distancing mood had begun to develop. National Socialism had intoxicated the population. I went up to Heidegger's room to welcome him. "It is like 1914," I began, and I wanted to continue, "again the same delusive mass ecstasy." However, faced with a Heidegger who agreed with my first words and beamed, the words stuck in my throat. This radical break left me extremely troubled. With no one else had I experienced something like this. It was all the more provoking since Heidegger seemed not to notice it at all.[66]

## F. Scheler "im Weltalter des Ausgleichs"

Quite certainly, Heidegger saw in Hitler «the man» (PPS 646) Scheler had been waiting for after the outcome of World War I and the establishment of the Weimar Republic had disappointed the latter's hope for a rerealization of his version of a Christian love-community through World War I. In the twenties, however, Scheler changed his mind on the task of politics dramatically, and he did so precisely at the time when Heidegger was writing and publishing *Being and Time*. If, according to the old theory of opposites, in ethics and politics the state in the middle is the eigentliche extreme to each of the extremes, he became the eigentliche extremist. For Scheler became a post-classic liberal or some sort of social democrat. For an inspired philosopher like Scheler, this turn, or Kehre, perhaps did not exclude a belief in a hierarchy of values independent of human beings. But it certainly did exclude the theory of social units and their hierarchy as developed in *Formalism in Ethics*. I will not discuss this question nor the development of his change. Rather, I will only present a speech he gave in the Deutsche Hochschule für Politik in Berlin in November 1927, less than one year before his death. To be sure, in this speech also the author sometimes rhetorically underscores the obvious fact that he is by no means, so to speak, counting peanuts. Rather, as one says in German ironically, «er geht aufs Ganze.» All of his great topics are present in a speech of not more than twenty-five pages; God, religion, metaphysics, capitalism, socialism, Europe, England, Russia, Japan, China, India, the genius, fate, blood and its mixtures, and «man» being «a direction of the *movement of the universe* itself, indeed, of its ground» (WA 151). However, all are treated from a point of view that is the exact opposite of the one in the writings I have discussed so far and that is already announced in the title of the talk, namely, "Der Mensch im Weltalter des Ausgleichs" (Man in the age of conciliation). Ausgleich is «balance, adjustment, conciliation, equalization, settlement» and thus the opposite of the politics of de-cision he had proposed in his writings discussed in the preceding sections. To be sure, the meaning of fate remains the same, for the process of Ausgleich is «*inescapable*» (WA 152), that is, it is «*fate*—not choice» (WA 165), and one who wants to oppose fate will, with an allusion to Don Quixote, «in die Luft stoßen» («thrust into the air») (WA 152). However, the task fate imposes on us is precisely the opposite of its gift[67] in the years around World War I. For the cluster of notions I have presented as the hallmark of the rightist notion of history is dissolved. The notion of Gemeinschaft is not even mentioned once. It is not used, because what is at stake is the defense of Gesellschaft, of parliamentary democracy. In his phase of de-cision, Scheler considered class struggle and the various oppositions between Gesellschaft and Gemeinschaften a result of the value-falsifying process through which liberalism and Gesellschaft had taken over not only the entrepreneurs but also the workers, but now democracy just «*unveils*» these oppositions but «does not produce them» (WA 145). What matters is «the free democratic discussion and formation of will in parliament» (WA 146). He says that «in the dangerous crisis, in which today parliamentary democracy . . . finds itself almost all over the world, in its hard struggle, not as in former times against this or that kind of conservative monarchism (today, this opposition is almost dead), but rather against the dictatorial tendencies from the Right and from the Left, parliamentary democracy will assert itself only if» (WA 145) his—or rather fate's—recommendations for this struggle are followed. The text is paragraph by paragraph a revocation of his politics of de-cision. The theme of the genius, leader, or saint is taken up as the quest for an elite in democracy. However, the elite is not regarded as the vanguard in the upward movement of authentic value-realiziation but rather as an effort «to beat the foes of parliamentary democracy at their own game» (WA 145). Scheler's statement that «the development of human mind and of its forms of activities has become *autonomous* and *independent of its bodily organisation*» (WA 148) dismisses all the variants of thinking in terms of biology or in terms of an opposition between the mind and the «deeper» forces of soul, race, etc. (WA 146–150). Distancing himself from the rightist authors, Scheler at the same time comes closer to Marx. To be sure, pace Marx the religious ideas cannot be reduced to economic factors. However, pace the de-cisionistic Scheler they are not independent of them either, for: «still, an inner bond ties them together, an ultimate conception and attitude toward Being, shared by both, even though this bond is hard to perceive and to investigate» (WA 168). The materialism of Marxism is a reaction against the idealistic ideologies, including Christianity, of the ruling classes (WA 167f.). «Man» is different from what the rightists maintain who reduce him to a pre-given identity, from which the moderns have fallen away: «Man is a being whose essence itself is the decision, still open, of what this being wants to be and to become. . . . *Thus, allow for man and his movement, infinite by his essence! No fixation on an "exemplary state," on a certain form, taken from either natural history or world history*» (WA 150f.).[68] Clearly it is impossible «to try to renew again {wieder erneuern zu wollen} the "pagan" man, the "early Christian" man, the "Gothic" man,» etc. (WA 152). In contrast to his de-cisionistic assessment of the League of Nations as a means of Anglo-American economic world domination (PPS 382f., 665), here Scheler defends it (WA 166). Certain groups in the Catholic Church are reprimanded for their claim that basic features of the constitution of the Weimar Republic contradict the teaching of the Church (WA 169). Instead of the renovations by de-cision, the name of the new world age is «*Ausgleich*» (WA 152), Ausgleich in all relevant areas, races, cultures, sexes, etc. (WA 152f.). While in his de-cisionistic phase mixture was the cause of the downward plunge and the movement up again entailed the reemergence of the pure type, now it is mixture that moves forward and upward. In his de-cisionistic phase the supposed causes of mixture of blood were relegated to Israel. Now, the one who wants to expel them out of Germany and the world ought to leave the country: «Without fail, the Ausgleich of races, the mixture of blood, will progress. . . . All those who expect the Heil of the world from the preservation of a "pure" race, in his view the "noble-race" . . . should retreat with his fellow race-nobles to an island and despair» (WA 153). In Scheler's de-cisionistic phase, already by 1913 Germany has «moved with full sails into the first phases of the socialist state . . . hostile to freedom» (UW 383f.). Also back then he regarded Spencer's assumption that the development of capitalism would cure the damage it initially inflicted as the «basic error» (RE 173; UW 146). Now, Scheler takes recourse to the dialectical formula of progress: «To be sure, {spirit} inflicts wounds. However, it also heals them» (WA 150). The same capitalism that has devastated the environment in the eighteenth century has already developed the means to protect organic natural life, and it will do so better and better (WA 150). The ideal of the nineteenth century, the sovereign national state, is doomed to disappear. The Ausgleich of the different nations, the development of international strata between them, will not do away with their specific identities. Rather, it will produce tolerance, and their spiritual and cultural autonomy will flourish (WA 164f.). In his de-cisionistic phase, he regarded the internationalization in society as a threat against the Gemeinschaften. Now, it is hailed as the vanguard of diversity through Ausgleich and mixture (WA 154). In the new economic politics from 1924 on, Russia has already adopted capitalist elements. The capitalist states, in turn, will maintain private property and, nonetheless, adopt more and more socialist elements to the effect «that, more and more, the *realities* on both sides will bridge the oppositions of the names and concepts» (WA 166). «Bridging of . . . oppositions» is now the key phrase, a bridging that takes place by processes of mixture, of adaptation of opposing elements.These processes are by no means benign, and the only end of politics is to facilitate them (WA 152f.). Now, politics is about precisely the opposite from what it was in his de-cisionistic phase.

Quite obviously, the causes for Scheler's turn were not the leftists and bolshevism. For the rationale for his de-cisionistic politics had been the liberals and the Social Democrats as the outcome and consummation of liberalism. Also, still in his de-cisionistic phase, in 1919, Scheler had maintained that bolshevism would not last long (PPS 651), and—in his search for precapitalist mentalities—he even recommended a cooperation between Germany and bolshevist Russia against England and the United States in order to prepare for the overthrow of capitalism (PPS 658). The cause of his turn was the emergence of National Socialism. He realized that the National Socialists represented, as it were, the «truth» of the politics of de-cision, one version of which he himself had pursued around World War I, and that they would take over the politics of the Right. This recognition made him completely turn away from any version of rightist politics and instead join his former foes, the liberals and the Social Democrats.

Especially in light of the thesis, again promoted recently in Germany by Ernst Nolte, that knowing that the Weimar Republic would not be able to do anything against bolshevism, National Socialism was an understandable, if not necessary, reaction against the threat of bolshevism,[69] Scheler's philosophical and political career is remarkable. His way led in the opposite direction. Scheler was, to use a sloppy expression, a Sozialistenfresser[70] only as long as there was not yet any bolshevism and as long as he faced only liberals and social democrats, of whom many said that they had already lost sight of the notorious «expropriation of the expropriators.» When, in the twenties, bolshevism as well as National Socialism emerged, Scheler realized that neither social democracy nor bolshevism was the foe but rather National Socialism. This recognition disabused him of the viewpoint of the rightists and enabled him to reevaluate liberalism after the end of classic liberalism and social democracy and to join the fight of the parliamentary Center against National Socialism.

At the beginning of section B, I have mentioned Heidegger's high praise for Scheler in his obituary on Scheler. Heidegger doesn't talk directly about politics. However, he says of Scheler that, «standing in the midst of the whole of beings, he had an unusual sensitivity for all the new possibilities and forces opening up.»[71] Two things are clear in his obituary. Heidegger highly appreciated the book *Formalism in Ethics.* His first point after his praise of Scheler is that Scheler «clearly perceived the new possibilities of phenomenology»; he took up phenomenology not «superficially,» but he «furthered it essentially and unified it directly with central problems of philosophy. In particular, his critique of ethical formalism bears witness to this.»[72] However, the Scheler after *Formalism in Ethics* is not appreciated that much by Heidegger. Heidegger refers to Scheler's Catholicism and his thoughts on man as «God's co-worker,» in order thereupon to pose an incisive question one would not expect after the great praise in the beginning of the obituary. Heidegger asks: «Were his changing views a sign of a lack of substance, of inner emptiness?»[73] His answer is devastating. Logically one is strongly invited to or even has no other choice but add between the question and Heidegger's own comment on it something like «Yes, indeed!» For Heidegger does not answer the question explicitly. However, he comments on Scheler in a way that sounds like an excuse for Scheler's supposed lack of substance:

> But one recognizes here—something which of course only a few could directly experience in day-and-night-long conversations and arguments with him—an obsession with philosophy, which he himself was unable to master and after which he had to follow, something which in the brokenness of contemporary existence often drove him to powerlessness and despair. But this obsession was his substance. And with every change he remained loyal to his inner direction of his nature in always new approaches and endeavors. And this loyalty must have been the source from which sprang the childlike kindness he showed on occasion.[74]

Thereupon, Heidegger summarizes Scheler's «greatness» again with recourse to a formula of the early, the de-cisionistic, Scheler. It lies in «an encounter with mankind that allows for no appeasement {beschwichtigen} and leveling through a sterile humanism.» He then concludes: «Max Scheler is dead. We bow before his fate {Wir beugen uns vor seinem Schicksal}.»[75] Especially in the light of Heidegger's question, one might refer the last sentence not only to Scheler's physical death in 1928, but also, or even mainly, to his development. «Beschwichtigung» («appeasement») belongs to the same semantic field as «Ausgleich.» What Heidegger says here about Scheler's way is somewhat ironic, if not even a severe distortion by omission. In the preface to the third edition of *Formalism,* Scheler says that he does «not wish to see the bond with *Kairos,* i.e., the call of the *hour of our* human and historical being and life, severed as completely as it is in Hartmann's work» (FEe xxxi; FE 23). In the manuscript, this is followed by the sentence: «Ultimately ethics is a 'damned bloody affair' {eine "verdammt blutige Sache"}, and if it can give me no directives concerning how 'I' 'should' live now in this social and historical context, then what is it?» (FEe xxxi, n. 14; FE 591).

The later Scheler completely abandoned the political advice given in his book dating from his de-cisionistic phase, and he identified himself with precisely those politics his book had advised people to expel out of the blood. Heidegger either neglects this or even denounces it with his question and his answer. «Sich beugen vor jemandes Schicksal» means «to recognize and accept his fate.» At the same time, however, it often implies also that «it is not our fate; he could not but go his way, and we couldn't prevent him from doing so; however, our way is different.» Though Heidegger always regarded thinking in terms of values as what amounts in his framework, so to speak, to the original sin of philosophizing, namely, as a reduction of Dasein and being to a Vorhandenes, he highly appreciated *Formalism in Ethics,* certainly because of Scheler's criticism of the modern subject and probably also because of its logic and politics of de-cision which, in its most radical version, Heidegger was about to renew precisely at the time when Scheler abandoned it on account of its devastating political implications. Most certainly, Heidegger's allusion to the «lack of substance» refers to Scheler's Catholicism. Already in *Formalism,* the internationalism of Catholicism prevented Scheler from identifying his politics with a politics of Blut und Boden, and, some years later, enabled him to identify the foe, to break with his politics of de-cision and to realize that the promise entailed in Catholicism is preserved by those against whom his former politics of de-cisionism was directed, namely, by the liberals and social democrats.

In the speech "Der Mensch im Weltalter des Ausgleichs," Scheler describes rightist thinking and leftist thinking in a series of several «either-or»-combinations. In one of the pairs, he uses the notion of Angst so prominent in Heidegger:

> The praise of the "good old time," combined with Angst of the future, *or* the directedness toward some utopian ideal, in eschatological hope and expectation,

combined with a fierce critique of the past; . . . *both* of them are not founded in the things themselves. Both are logical categories, *ideologies,* that one-sidedly are caused by class myths and that bear witness to the power of interests over reason {Vernunft}. Anyone who, politically, wants to see clearly, has to take off *both.* (WA 166f.)

In this passage, Scheler gives a clear account of the basic difference of the notion of history and politics on the Right and on the Left. Whether out of Angst or not, the rightists saw the progress of Gesellschaft as the chariot of doom, whose course had to be stopped in order to rerealize the past, this or that Gemeinschaft, which had been overthrown by Gesellschaft. The leftists, however, maintained that it was good that the progress of Gesellschaft liberated us from the different Gemeinschaften in the past. It is in this alternative that in Scheler Vernunft resurfaces, as a faculty of mediation between the two opposites. Politically, Scheler addressed post-classic liberals and the Social Democrats to defend the project of Vernunft against the Right. Five years after Scheler's speech in Berlin, the Social Democrats suffered huge losses, and the extreme Right was about to become the strongest party. In this situation Scheler's successor to his chair in Frankfurt, Paul Tillich, carried Scheler's suggestion of reason as Ausgleich further, and he developed the thesis that the Social Democrats and the Left are the legitimate heirs of the promises entailed in Christianity as well as in liberalism (see section B of chapter 4).

# 4

# Being and Time
# and Leftist Concepts
# of History and Decision

## A. Lukács's *History and Class Consciousness*

As mentioned in section E of chapter 3, in the section on conscience Heidegger characterizes the call as «vorrufenden Rückruf» (SZ 280; «one which calls us back in calling us forth,» BT 326). After the discussions in chapters 1–3 it is now clear that this means: Ordinary and inauthentic Daseine are engaged in the project of Gesellschaft, and the authentic Daseine step out of Gesellschaft. In section 74 it turns out that what calls them back and out of Gesellschaft is Geschick, and Geschick is the Volksgemeinschaft. The Volksgemeinschaft calls each Dasein back into its Schicksal, and authentic Daseine listen to, and erwidern, the call whereas only inauthentic Daseine try not to listen to and not to erwidern the call. Dasein's Schicksal is to disavow Gesellschaft in order to rerealize Gemeinschaft. It is clear against whom Heidegger is arguing in these passages. He argues against liberals and leftists, that is, against all those who are engaged in the project of Gesellschaft; and who maintain that we have to go on in our project of developing Gesellschaft, that is, to develop a capitalist society and its accompanying political structures, parliamentarism and also labor unions.

In the preceding chapters, I have compared my interpretation with Guignon's and Birmingham's interpretations. I wanted to show that Heidegger's notion of repetition is not, as Birmingham has it, about the anarchistic break with each and every tradition. As to Guignon, I pointed out that according to his interpretation, under the gaze of authentic Dasein the monolithic bloc of the present and the past dissolves. Upon becoming authentic, Dasein realizes that there are many possibilities in the past that have been covered

149

up by ordinary Dasein, by the «they.» Those who have become authentic realize that in the past there are Socrates, Galileo, and many other heroes who
have established a profession, or a certain way of practicing a profession and
who might be taken up and repeated by the authentic Dasein. By virtue of its
utopian ideal, authentic Dasein has a distance to each of them, and it can
screen the heroes of the past to choose and «creatively reinterpret» (HC 138)
the one who fits his or her utopian ideal best. In *Being and Time,* Heidegger
merely presents this general structure, and he does not make any specific suggestions as to who should choose which hero. I wanted to show that this interpretation also turns the relation of the present to the past, or to what-has-been-
there, upside down. According to Guignon, Heidegger's notion of historicality
also encompasses the explicitly political choices of different Daseine. On that
level, his thesis means that *Being and Time* is politically neutral.

At the beginning of his essay, Guignon refers to the meeting between Karl
Löwith and Heidegger in Rome in 1936 and says his essay «should help to
clarify why Heidegger said that "his concept of historicity was the basis for
his political engagement" with the Nazis in the thirties. But I hope to show
also that this connection between *Being and Time* and Heidegger's actions
does not entail that this early work is inherently fascist or proto-Nazi» (HC
131). After the passages on authentic historicality which I quoted at length
in section B of chapter 1, Guignon discusses Heidegger's concept of «situation» and then turns back to the question of the beginning in order to conclude his essay with the following sentences:

> My own view is that Heidegger's accounts of historicity and authenticity do not
> point to any particular political orientation, and that his actions in the thirties
> resulted solely from his own deeply held conservative beliefs. The early concepts
> of history and authentic action seem consistent with diverse political views
> because of their highly formal nature. Heidegger's ontology of human existence
> identifies a tripartite temporal structure according to which Dasein's "happening"
> springs from a projection onto future possibilities, draws on what is embodied in
> the past, and thereby acts in the present. The authentic mode of this temporal exis-
> tence involves encountering a future as a "destiny," the past as a "heritage," and
> the present context as a "world-historical Situation." The clear-sighted recog-
> nition that we are always implicated in the undertakings of the shared "co-
> happening of a community" gives one some guidance in making choices. But it
> should be evident that this formalistic image of "temporalizing" and historicity
> *by itself* gives us no guidance as to which political stance we should adopt.
>
>   In fact, it appears that this picture of historical unfolding—this "metanarra-
> tive" or "narrative framework"—can be made to accommodate almost any polit-
> ical position. With its *mythos* of pristine beginnings, a time of "falling," and a
> final recovery of origins, it recapitulates the traditional Christian model of cre-
> ation, sinfulness, and redemption. It is this soteriological model which also
> underlies the Marxist story-line of human species-beings currently deformed by
> capitalism but promised fulfillment in world communism. And it can be made

to fit the liberal story of humans who are born to be free but now languish in the chains of ignorance and superstition, or the conservative story of a return to community after wandering in the wilderness of extreme individualism.

Heidegger's account of authentic historicity demanded that he take a stand on the situation in Germany in the thirties. This explains his comment to Löwith that "the concept of historicity was the basis for his political engagement." What we do know is that, faced with what most Germans at the time saw as the need for a decision between Bolshevism and Nazism, Heidegger sided with the Nazis. Yet ultimately it seems to be only a mix of opportunism and personal preference that directed his decision, not anything built into his fundamental ontology. (HC 141–142)

There are several remarkable points in this passage. It is not quite clear how this passage with its emphasis on the «*mythos* of pristine beginnings, a time of "falling," and a final recovery of origins» relates to the passage on «authentic historiography» with the latter's claim «that it is only on the basis of utopian ideals together with a sense of alternative ways of living discovered by antiquarian preservation that we can have a standpoint for criticizing calcified forms of life of the present» (HC 138). In addition, Guignon wants to show that *Being and Time* is politically neutral, and that it was «not anything built into {Heidegger's} fundamental ontology» that directed Heidegger's commitment to Nazism. In light of this, it is amazing that he uses formulations such as «can be made to accommodate almost any political position» and «can be made to fit» without any further comment. Finally, it is truly amazing that he assumes that the short paragraph on Christians, Marxists, and liberals is all that needs to be said on the different political movements of that time.[1]

However, it is simply untrue that, as Guignon maintains, everyone at the time employed a notion of history as a «*mythos* of pristine beginnings, a time of "falling," and a final recovery of origins» (HC 141). Neither liberals nor the political party Guignon does not mention, namely, the Social Democrats, adhered to Guignon's model. In hindsight, in the eleventh of his *Theses on the Philosophy of History*, written in 1940, Benjamin said:

> The conformism which has been part and parcel of Social Democracy from the beginning attaches not only to its political tactics but to its economic views as well. It is one reason for its later breakdown. Nothing has corrupted the German working class so much as the notion that it was moving with the current. It regarded technological developments as the fall of the stream with which it thought it was moving {das Gefälle des Stroms, mit dem sie zu schwimmen meinte}.[2]

The twelfth thesis reads:

> Not man or men but the struggling, oppressed class itself is the depository of historical knowledge. In Marx it appears as the last enslaved class, as the avenger

that completes the task of liberation in the name of generations of the downtrodden. This conviction, which had a brief resurgence in the Spartacist group, has always been objectionable to Social Democrats. Within three decades they managed virtually to erase the name of Blanqui, though it had been the rallying sound that had reverberated through the preceding century. Social Democracy thought fit to assign to the working class the role of the redeemer of future generations, in this way cutting the sinews of its greatest strength. This training made the working class forget both its hatred and its spirit of sacrifice, for both are nourished by the image of enslaved ancestors rather than that of liberated grandchildren.[3]

To move «with the current,» to move with «the fall of the stream,» or in Heidegger's and Hitler's terms «to move with the downward plunge» without looking back is exactly the stance against which, in order to discontinue it, Heidegger and other rightist authors developed their notion of history, one that demands that «we» widerrufen, cancel, the current of society and that gives «*having been* its peculiarly privileged position in the historical» (BT 438; SZ 386). «Moving with the current» of Gesellschaft, of capitalist society and parliamentarism, toward the future is what liberals and Social Democrats had in common. The difference between them was that liberals did so for the sake of the liberal individuals, Social Democrats for the sake of future socialism. Both employed a notion of progress according to which, step by step, we leave behind the ignorance and imperfection of the past and the present. We move with the current precisely in order to liberate ourselves from the imperfections of the past and the present, not in order to rerealize this or that past. According to Heidegger and other rightist authors, however, this is precisely our downward plunge. Thus, we have to cancel this move, have to perform a «*Widerruf*» (SZ 386; BT 438); or, as Scheler put it, we have to «expel Anglo-American capitalism from {Europe's} blood like a foreign poison» (PPS 153) in order to rerealize community. If, however, some liberals or social democrats at the time did in fact, as Guignon maintains, use the «*mythos* of pristine beginnings, a time of "falling," and a final recovery of origins» (HC 141), they did so in a way contrary to how it was used by rightist authors. According to rightist authors, we rerealize the past by canceling Gesellschaft, since the development of Gesellschaft leads us only deeper into the abyss of the downward plunge, which Gesellschaft itself is, without ever leading us back to the lost origin. Those liberals, social democrats, and communists, however, who used the «*mythos* of pristine beginnings, a time of "falling," and a final recovery of origins» (HC 141) restored the lost origin— freedom or «primordial communism»—only at the end of the full development of Gesellschaft. We must not cancel our gradual progress toward that development, but rather must move forward, because only in this way can we restore the lost origin. Philosophically, this is the difference between Heidegger's notion of «*Widerruf*» (SZ 386; «*disavowal*,» BT 438) of Gesellschaft, or of Scheler's act of expulsion of Gesellschaft, and a dialectical

Aufhebung, sublation, of bourgeois Gesellschaft.[4] Politically, the pronounced difference between a Widerruf and an Aufhebung was the reason that allowed liberals and Social Democrats to join forces against conservative bourgeois parties. In this sense, Heidegger's notion of historicality is tailored polemically against the notion of history in liberalism and social democracy. In what follows, I will not refer to texts by liberals or social democrats. Rather, I turn to two authors of the twenties—Lukács's book *History and Class Consciousness,* published in 1923, and Paul Tillich's *The Socialist Decision,* published in 1933—who saw the difference between the social democrats and liberals on the one hand and rightist authors on the other as clearly as Hitler and Scheler did, and who regarded themselves as leftists without relying on the social democratic, or liberal, concept of history. In the course of the discussion of their views, it will become clear that Heidegger's concept of historicality was opposed not only to liberals and social democrats but also to their views, and that they themselves regarded their ideas as also directed against concepts of history such as Heidegger's.[5]

In myth, a human being can turn into a pig and back again into a human being (Homer, *Odyssey* X, vv. 235ff.). In some way, the Geist, the spirit, of this remains present in some pre-Socratic philosophers, especially in those whom Plato, appropriately, calls the «more tightly strained of the Muses.»[6] Metaphysics of substance does away with such a notion of change and motion and all its remnants in philosophy. An idea does not admit, and does not change into, its opposite. However, not only an idea, but also an idea «in us» does not change into its opposite. Rather, if it can no longer resist its approaching opposite, it will leave the scene instead of transforming itself into its opposite. In accidental change, an accident does not change itself into its opposite either. Rather, it has to leave its subject. Only in this way can the new accident arrive at, or be realized within, the substance. A substance changes only accidentally. In order for a substance to allow the emergence of a different substance from it, the substance and its substantial form have to disappear and its matter has to be emptied of forms, or de-formed, down to the level of the four elements and simple bodies. Only if the, so to speak, «higher» substantial form has disappeared, is matter in a position to receive a new «higher» substantial form.

Unorthodox teaching on the eucharistic host and alchemy fully acknowledge this model. The substance of bread is not transubstantiated into the substance of Jesus Christ. Rather, the substance of bread is annihilated by God, or its matter is emptied of forms down to the level of prime matter or the four elements before Jesus Christ becomes present. One cannot produce the body of all bodies, gold, by informing existing substances. Rather, one has to expel the forms, that is, to deform their matter, until one has arrived at pure prime matter. Only at that point can the form of gold be introduced. Each form within matter prevents it from, closes it against, receiving the form of gold. Matter is open, entschlossen, for the new form, only if it has been cleansed of any other form. The arrival of the new presupposes the expulsion of the old, and does not allow for the possibility that the old forms work on themselves and transform themselves according to their tendencies and needs.

In his theory on authentic Dasein, Heidegger follows the metaphysical model of substances and their changes. We do not achieve authenticity by building upon all the states, the forms we have due to our living in the mode of the «they.» Rather, we achieve authenticity, are entschlossen for the new form that authenticity is, only after deforming ourselves, only after having been cleansed of the forms of ordinary Dasein. This happens in Angst, in anxiety (BT 225ff.; SZ 180). If we manage to endure it and do not shrink away from it, anxiety rewards us by cleansing us of all the forms of ordinary everydayness, and thus makes us entschlossen for the new state of authenticity. In Heidegger, there is no intrinsic relation between ordinary Dasein and Angst. At least, he does not develop any. Ordinary Dasein tends to shy away from Angst, and Angst is not the intrinsic result of a tendency built into the forms by which ordinary Dasein is shaped.[7] One implication of this model is that there is nothing intrinsic to the forms of ordinary Dasein that makes them worth preserving in the new state of authenticity. Of course, it might happen that some, or even many, features of ordinary Dasein are preserved in authenticity, for instance, as Hitler and Scheler argued, private property of the means of production and modern technology. However, this is purely accidental, a matter, so to speak, of the «grace» of authenticity.

The substance of bread has been annihilated. Its accidents remain. However, they are neither the end nor a necessary means of the Eucharist. Rather, God does not want to trigger our disgust for cannibalism and thus allows the accidents of the bread to cover up the raw flesh of Jesus Christ's body. Heidegger has chosen the proper expression. For, as was mentioned in section D of chapter 1, an act of «*Widerruf*» (SZ 386; «*disavowal,*» BT 438) is indeed a cancellation, a destruction, in which something is negated completely and must never recur. In contrast, in Hegelian dialectics the transition into a new sphere also proceeds by way of deformation. However, that deformation is brought about, not by the cancellation of the determinations, but rather by the process of the self-determination of the determinations and of the subject, which never exists independent of its process of determining itself and which thus never relapses into pure matter.

Accordingly, dialectic negation is not a Widerruf. Being negated or negating themselves, the determinations are not destroyed, annihilated, or canceled, but rather aufgehoben, sublated. They still are, and they are in their truth, for they are moments of a new and larger structure into which they have sublated themselves. Politically speaking, the difference between a dialectical Aufhebung and a Heideggerian Widerruf—a thoroughly metaphysical presencing of the renewal via the destruction of the old—also accounts for the difference between the end of rightist struggle and leftist class struggle. In dialectics, nothing is abandoned. Instead, everything and everyone will be redeemed. The end of the class struggle is the sublation of the sway of classes and thus the production of equal and free individuals no longer confined by class distinctions. The rightist struggle, however, is about the rerealization of ranks, orders, and distinctions that supposedly were leveled by liberalism and Social Democracy. The rerealization requires that Gesellschaft is expelled, and that its members are either expelled or integrated into one or the other of the lower ranks of Gemeinschaft.

According to Lukács, the establishment of a socialist society presupposes a fully developed capitalist society and, if it happens at all, is brought about by the proletarians who are, as he puts it by quoting Marx, «the dissolution {Auflösung} of the existing social order {Weltordnung}» (HI 3; GK 15).[8] In a fully developed capitalist society, all those individuals who are not capitalists have to offer their skills as commodities on the job market; they have become commodities. However, it is only proletarians who can distance themselves from, that is, cleanse themselves of, all the bourgeois forms and can recognize the ultimate bourgeois form, namely, that of being a commodity, as the one they have to, and can, liberate themselves from by transforming the capitalist society into a socialist one. Though all individuals have become a commodity, that is not all they are. Those who are not part of the proletariat can use these other forms to cover up, so to speak, the blunt fact that they have to offer their skills as commodities. You might deplore the fact that Geist, spirit and mind, has become a commodity. Still, if you can satisfy your vocation to geistige Führung, spiritual leadership, or your interest in studying philosophical texts, only by selling your Geist to a newspaper or a university, you might do so, and you might always maintain, as it were, in a metaphysical fashion that Geist is different from, irreducible to, and higher than, flesh and money. A proletarian, however, cannot do so:

> For his work as he experiences it directly possesses the naked and abstract form of the commodity, while in other forms of work this is hidden behind the façade of 'mental labour', of 'responsibility', etc. (and sometimes it even lies concealed behind 'patriarchal' forms). The more deeply reification penetrates into the soul of the man who sells his achievement as a commodity the more deceptive appearances are (as in the case of journalism). (HI 172, GK 188)

Informed by the notion of responsibility, etc., the non-proletarian individual feels no need to distance himself from being a commodity and, thus, becomes more and more reified in all his faculties. To be a commodity permeates all his other forms and capacities. However, the proletarian cannot cover up being a commodity. Thus, he recognizes it as the form from which he has to distance himself. In the preface to the 1968 edition, Lukács said that, in *History and Class Consciousness,* he has analyzed the emergence of revolutionary praxis as though it were a «sheer miracle.»[9] In a passage that is almost a miracle in German since one immediately gets his point though the relations of grammar, logic, and meaning are nonetheless enigmatic, Lukács continues:

> Corresponding to the objective concealment of the commodity form, there is the subjective element. This is the fact that while the process by which the worker is reified and becomes a commodity dehumanises him and cripples and atrophies his 'soul'—as long as he does not consciously rebel against it—it remains true that precisely his humanity and his soul are not changed into commodities. He is able therefore to objectify himself completely against his existence while the man reified in the bureaucracy, for instance, is turned into a commodity, mechanised and reified in the only faculties that might enable him to rebel against reification. Even his thoughts and feelings become reified. As Hegel says: "It is much harder to bring movement into fixed ideas than into sensuous existence." (HI 172, GK 188f.)

In addition, in contrast to proletarians, who, as Marx and Engels said, «have nothing to lose but their chains,»[10] bourgeois individuals have something to lose. And if they don't have anything to lose, they at least have a lot to gain:

> The worker experiences his place in the production process as ultimate but at the same time it has all the characteristics of the commodity (the uncertainties of day-to-day-movements of the market, etc.). This stands in contrast to other groups which have both the appearance of stability (the routine of duty, pension, etc.) and also the—abstract—possibility of an *individual's* elevating himself into the ruling class. By such means a 'status-consciousness' is created that is calculated {geeignet ist} to inhibit effectively the growth of a class consciousness. (HI 172; GK 189; note that Lukács's formulation «geeignet ist» does not imply any intention of any individual or group; thus instead of «is calculated» read «is fit» or even «happens.»)

The form of being a commodity has not only permeated all other forms, but it has also emptied the proletarians of any substance. A proletarian cannot justify his job in terms of responsibility, etc., and his job itself has become an unstable affair. In addition, he is no longer able to interpret his activities on the job as a means to a reasonable end (HI 87ff; GK 98ff.). It is only in the state of deformation of all other forms that human beings can recognize that they have been made into a commodity and can distance themselves from this form and thus from all history. Lukács goes on:

> Thus the purely abstract negativity in the life of the worker is objectively the most typical manifestation of reification, it is the constitutive type of capitalist

socialisation. But for this very reason it is also *subjectively* the point at which this structure is {werden kann} raised to consciousness and can be breached in practice. As Marx says: "Labour . . . is no longer grown together with the individual into one particular determination." (HI 172; instead of «is raised» it should read «can be raised»; GK 189)

In former societies this process of becoming conscious was not possible. The economy was not yet autonomous (HI 238ff.; GK 244ff.). Political forms of domination were part of the economy and provided a framework of forms people could identify with and from which it was not necessary to abstract. This is no longer true for the «free» worker in a capitalist society. In addition, individuals and goods were not yet commodities in earlier societies. To be a commodity, however, requires a constant dividing of oneself and distancing of oneself from oneself (HI 90ff., 165ff.; GK 102, 182ff.). In addition, one might add, former processes of distancing, in stoic, Christian, and bourgeois philosophy all intended to make conscious, to lead to, and to strengthen, the reality of the form of human beingness that informs each individual human being and in regard to which all humans are equal. However, one can no longer rely on the way this form was realized in bourgeois society, since its realization has resulted in the inhuman conditions of modern capitalist society. The proletarians have been distanced from, deformed of, all traditional forms under the pressure of the commodity form. They can become aware of the power of distancing at work in commodities since due to the inner dynamics of capitalism, they themselves have become sheer commodities. Only because they have become pure commodities can they turn the power of distancing against commodities and distance themselves from the commodity form in order to realize by way of sublation the universalism inherent in bourgeois universalism. Thus, Lukács calls the consciousness of the proletarians «*the self-consciousness of the commodity*» (HI 168; GK 185).

For a communist, the average everydayness and the world of ordinary Dasein is certainly the economy and one's place in it. In line with Hegel's dialectics and in contrast to Heidegger, the de-formation that is the precondition to authenticity—to be a communist and finally a socialist society—is a result of the inner tendency at work in ordinary Dasein itself. Still, one must not overlook the «can» in Lukács's statements on becoming conscious. To become a commodity, to become aware of it, and to finally realize a socialist society is made possible, and indeed in some way intended, by the inner tendency active in ordinary Dasein in its average everydayness. However, it is only in becoming a commodity that the necessary and unavoidable outcome of this inner tendency is realized. To become aware of having become a commodity and to follow this through to the realization of socialism, however, is by no means a necessary outcome of this inner tendency even though it remains its intention. This is the difference, in Lukács's view, between social democrats and communists, and it compels Lukács, as he maintains, to defend Marx against the social democratic revisionists.

Having become a commodity, a proletarian might realize a number of things, first, that the antagonism between the forces of production and the relations of production is the driving power in history, at least in the modern era (HI 10; GK 23). Second, he also begins to understand what Marx and Lukács call reification. In capitalist society, the relations between human beings have become relations between things, and these relations between things produce their own system, the capitalist economy, which determines all the other realms. The system follows its own self-generated laws (HI 83ff.; GK 94ff.) and produces a specific type of rationality—specific forms of thinking and acting—for all individuals working in it. The structure of these forms of thinking and acting differs from that of the system itself and its laws, though the former is necessary for the working of the system. Bourgeois thinking interprets the system in terms of the structure of thinking produced by the system and thus misinterprets the latter. As a consequence, bourgeois thinking misses the historical character of capitalism and takes capitalism for eternal and «natural» (HI 181ff.; GK 198ff.). Third, proletarian thinking recognizes that the relations between things are relations between human beings and at the same time that the system can function only when individuals misinterpret the laws of the system. The proletarians comprehend that the system of capitalist economy is by no means eternal but rather historical, for the inner contradictions inherent in it push it beyond liberal capitalist economy, though by no means necessarily into socialism and communism. In particular, a proletarian who is philosophically educated realizes that in modern philosophy the general conditions of reification are tacitly presupposed, in particular in German idealism, and that for that reason modern philosophy cannot solve the problems it itself raises (HI 110ff.; GK 122ff.). Concerning all these points one might find in *Being and Time* or in the later Heidegger an analogous claim, and it might be useful to compare them, if only because some might find Lukács's analysis of what Heidegger called «Vorhandenheit,» or Lukács's version of a thinking in terms of process as opposed to a thinking in terms of things and facts, more interesting and useful than Heidegger's analysis. However, this is not relevant to my purpose here.

Recognizing the antagonism between the forces of production and the relations of production as the driving power in history, proletarians can look through former theories on history as ideology in the Marxist sense. Lukács makes this point several times, twice only in a short comment. In a passage recapitulating Rousseau and Schiller, he adds in parentheses the proper Marxist terms: «culture and civilisation (i.e., capitalism and reification)» (HI 136; GK 150). Or, in a passage on the theory of history in Rickert he adds in parentheses his Marxist comment to a quote from Rickert: «However, this does no more than enthrone as the measure and the index of objectivity, the "cultural values" *actually* "prevailing in his community {Gemeinschaft}" (i.e., in his class)» (HI 151; GK 166). Lukács's replacement of «Gemeinschaft» with «class» in the quote from Rickert is typical of leftist authors; they insist that class and class struggle are the relevant parameters in history and that the traditional Gemeinschaften will be replaced with a rational Gesellschaft. Thus, history is precisely not a return of some past. On the contrary, to them, using this or that Gemeinschaft as the relevant parameter and primary entity in history is a sign that the author either wrote at a time of not yet fully developed capitalism or is trying, more or less consciously, to «save» capitalist society against the threat from the Left. As I have shown in regard to Hitler, Scheler, and Heidegger, after the emergence of liberalism and socialism rightist authors want to replace the conceptual framework of society, class, and class struggle with that of Gemeinschaft in the minds of the proletarians. In this sense, Heidegger's use of «Gemeinschaft» in *Being and Time* by itself already indicates strongly that the author proposes a rightist theory of history, even if Guignon's claim that everyone at that time employed a «*mythos* of pristine beginnings, a time of "falling," and a final recovery of origins» (HC 141) were correct.

However, liberals, social democrats, and communists did not use such a model. Having become «the self-consciousness of the commodity» (HI 168; GK 185) and managing to make the first steps toward a proper class consciousness (which will be achieved only in a difficult process, HI 173ff.; GK 189ff.), the proletarians realize that bourgeois individuals will not leave behind their reified consciousness. However, they also realize that many of their fellow proletarians either don't reach the point of self-consciousness or, if they have done so, are not capable of maintaining this achievement. Instead of distancing themselves from the forms of reified thinking and action and instead of replacing them with the proper dialectical ones, they stay in, or relapse into, bourgeois ways of thinking and acting. The bourgeois forms of consciousness are strong and, as Hegel observed, adhere to the law of inertia more than physical bodies. For Lukács, the Social Democratic party is where bourgeois consciousness has the strongest hold on proletarians.

Social Democrats, and also to some extent Rosa Luxemburg, adhere to a model of history Lukács describes as «*the organic character* of the course of history» (HI 277; «des *organischen Charakters* der gesellschaftlichen Entwicklung,» GK 281), or «economic fatalism» (HI 305; «ökonomistischen Fatalismus,» GK 308). The three basic assumptions of this model are first, that the development of the forces of production will automatically bring about a socialist economy (HI 277; GK 281); second, proletarian consciousness is always in tune with the economic development (HI 305; GK 308); and third, the task of the working class is merely to adjust the political and social superstructure to the level of economic development realized at the respective time. Parliamentary democracy provides a forum for achieving this without violence. It is this reliance on economic development Benjamin called the assumption of «moving with the current.» Lukács labels it «fatalism,» because, according to this model, it is fate, or necessity, that brings about socialism, and individuals simply can go along with fate. Fate is not determined by individuals. People only have to follow fate, that is, just remove any remaining obstacles. This is in line with the general meaning of Schicksal as some process or entity that determines our life in advance and thus is our fate. We have to comply with fate and must not try to resist it. Lukács can label it «organic» because, in this way of thinking, the socialist society will come about almost as naturally as biological growth; every stage of economic development always finds its proper expression in the proletarian consciousness and thus proceeds in as organic and holistic a fashion as growth in plants or animals where all the different parts always develop in tune with each other.

Lukács himself considers his and the communist concept of history a «non-fatalistic, non-'economistic' theory» (HI 305; GK 308), because, first, in his view it is by no means the case that the forces of production will bring about a socialist economy automatically. Though there is necessity within history, and though the agent of the necessity is economic development, this necessity or inevitability prevails only up to the moment of crisis:

> For capitalism, then, expedients can certainly be thought of in and for themselves. Whether they can be put into practice *depends, however, on the proletariat.* The proletariat, the actions of the proletariat, block capitalism's way out of the crisis. Admittedly, the fact that the proletariat obtains power *at that moment* is due to the 'natural laws' governing the economic process. But these 'natural laws' only determine the crisis itself, giving it dimensions which frustrate the 'peaceful' advance of capitalism. However, if left to develop (along capitalist lines) they would not lead to the simple downfall of capitalism or to a smooth transition to socialism. They would lead over a long period of crises, civil wars and imperialist world wars on an ever-increasing scale to "the mutual destruction of the opposing classes" and to a new barbarism.
>
> Moreover, these forces, swept along by their own 'natural' impetus have brought into being a proletariat whose physical and economic strength leaves capitalism very little scope to enforce a purely economic solution along the lines of those which put an end to previous crises in which the proletariat figured only as the *object* of an economic process. The new-found strength of the proletariat is the product of objective economic 'laws'. The problem, however, of converting this potential power into a real one and of enabling the proletariat (which today really is the mere object of the economic process and only potentially and latently its co-determining subject) to emerge as its subject in reality, is no longer determined by these 'laws' in any fatalistic and automatic way. (HI 306; GK 309f.)

Throughout his book, Lukács formulates this thesis in terms of the «tendency» or «objective possibilities» inherent in the economic development, and I will give some examples of this. For Lukács, the different theories of history lead to a crucial difference between communists and social democrats in their concrete politics, namely, their attitudes toward violence. First, relying on the fatalism, or inevitability, of economic development, social democrats deny that violence is necessary to bring about socialism. Lukács and other communists, however, insist that violence has always been an economic power and is necessary for the realization of socialism (HI 239ff; GK 246ff). Second, there is no organic relationship between economic development and the consciousness of the proletariat. Rather, due to the inertia, the consciousness of many proletarians lags behind the economic development (HI 304; GK 307). This situation is extremely serious. As early as in *The Communist Manifesto* Marx and Engels formulated the issue of Gemeinschaft and Gesellschaft, of the destructive forces unleashed by the modern age, in an unsurpassed way, and already at that point they reduced the issue to its economic basis:

> The bourgeoisie cannot exist without constantly revolutionizing the instruments of production, and thereby the relations of production, and with them the whole relations of society. Conservation of the old modes of production in unaltered form, was, on the contrary, the first condition of existence for all earlier industrial classes. Constant revolutionizing of production, uninterrupted disturbance of all social conditions, everlasting uncertainty and agitation distinguish the bourgeois epoch from all earlier ones. All fixed, fast-frozen relations, with their train of ancient and venerable prejudices and opinions are swept away, all new-formed ones become antiquated before they can ossify. All that is solid melts into air, all that is holy is profaned.[11]

Looking back from the present into the past, one thus realizes how often and quickly, at least in modern times, forms of consciousness had already become anachronistic before they were finally swept away by history. However, the same applies to the present as well. Perhaps one's own consciousness too is already outdated, especially since capitalism is the institutionalized constant revolution of all relations due to the basic structure of private ownership of the means of production. In precapitalist societies this gap between consciousness and economic basis is absent, since the instruments of production didn't change that much. In addition, in precapitalist societies the available means for working on nature and society were much more limited. In the light of this, social democrats are naive and lack any sense for the peculiar character of the modern age. Relying on the organic relationship between economic development and consciousness, a social democrat infers from the absence of a clear and common will to revolution in the proletariat that, indeed, no revolutionary situation exists (HI 305; GK 308). A communist, however, might infer that the proletariat is just not up to its task. This gap between consciousness and economic development allows Lukács to describe the behavior of the social democratic parties and of the unions in a way that is similar to how Heidegger characterizes the behavior of ordinary and inauthentic Dasein, which covers up the authentic possibilities of authentic action. The tactical theses of the Third Congress very rightly emphasize that every mass strike tends to transform itself into a civil war and a direct struggle for power. However, as Lukács emphasizes, «it only tends to do so.» Though the economic and social preconditions were often fulfilled, this tendency has not yet become reality. This *«precisely is the ideological crisis of the proletariat»* (HI 310; GK 312). The social democratic parties and the unions prevent the proletarians from developing the proper class consciousness, and they do so in a division of labor. The unions «take on the task of atomising and de-politicising the movement and concealing its relation to the totality,» while the social democratic parties «perform the task of establishing the reification in the consciousness of the proletariat both ideologically and on the level of organisation» (HI 310; GK 312f.). Thus, as the inauthentic Daseine in Heidegger, the social democrats and the unions prevent the proletarians from resolving the crisis *«by the free action {freie Tat} of the proletariat»* (HI 311; GK 313).[12]

In contrast to social democrats and liberals, Heidegger and Lukács share the assumption of the critical character of the moment, the kairos, the crisis brought about by history. History does not realize the new state after bourgeois society—socialism or Volksgemeinschaft—in the way that trees produce fruits but leads to a crisis, in which both the authentic Daseine in Heidegger's sense and the proletarians believe to realize that the current state of society is transitory and will disappear. Both also maintain that the «real» logic of history differs from what individuals have considered it to be before becoming authentic or self-conscious. Moreover, both maintain that history can now develop in two directions and that it is up to the individuals which way history will go. Finally, both regard themselves as called upon by history to guide it in one direction and to prevent it from going the other way. Because of these similarities, one finds the rhetoric of crisis, decision, and call also in Lukács. In fact, at one point Lukács uses the concept of Schicksal in the same way the rightist authors did. According to Lukács, Rosa Luxemburg overlooked the limitation of possible choices «which fate forced upon the proletarian revolution right from the start» (HI 276; «die vom Schicksal aufgezwungene Wahl zwischen,» GK 280; note, however, that fate here does not call for a repetition). One must listen to and obey fate, otherwise one will fail. Rosa Luxemburg did not listen to fate. Thus, her criticism «has been refuted . . . by history itself» (HI 276; GK 280). In his strictly theoretical passages, Lukács uses not Schicksal but rather Geschichte, history, and according to him the communist theory is «non-fatalistic.» For he wants to oppose the social democrats already on the level of terminology, and in the eyes of leftists the fact alone that rightists use the term «fate» already reveals the latter's «irrational» view of history. Thus, as in the case of the replacement of «Gemeinschaft» with «class,» leftist authors do not use «fate» as a basic term. They use it only polemically to indicate that other parties pretending to be leftists have in fact fallen prey to bourgeois ideology, as Lukács does regarding the social democrats. Otherwise, however, the structure and the vocabulary are the same as Heidegger's. Consider, for instance, the following sentence: «The proletariat "has no ideals to realize." When its consciousness is put into practice it can only breathe life into the things which the dialectics of history have forced to a crisis {nur das von der geschichtlichen Dialektik zur Entscheidung Gedrängte ins Leben rufen}; it can never 'in practice' ignore the course of history, forcing on it what are no more than its own desires or knowledge» (HI 177f; GK 194).[13] Or, on the next page Lukács comments on the issue of force: «For this is the point where the 'eternal laws' of capitalist economics fail and become dialectical and are thus compelled to yield up the decisions regarding the fate of history to the conscious actions of men {dem bewußten Handeln der Menschen die Entscheidung über das Schicksal der Entwicklung zu überlassen gezwungen ist}» (HI 178; GK 195). As the last quotation shows, Lukács also uses the concept of fate in the derivative sense in that the actions of someone can become the fate of someone else in the future. However, as in the authors on the Right, this is a derivative sense, insofar as the individuals or groups are morally not free to realize whatever they wish. Rather, they are bound, called upon, by history to realize this—on the Right Volksgemeinschaft and on the Left socialism—and to avoid that—on the Right socialism and on the Left Volksgemeinschaft. For this obligation history places on the proletariat Lukács uses the word Beruf, mission:

> Only the consciousness of the proletariat can point to the way that leads out of the impasse of capitalism. As long as this consciousness is lacking, the crisis remains permanent. . . . But the proletariat is not given any choice. {Das Proletariat hat aber hier keine Wahl.}. . . . But the proletariat cannot abdicate its mission. {Denn das Proletariat kann sich seinem Beruf nicht entziehen.} The only question at issue is how much it has to suffer before it achieves ideological maturity, before it acquires a true understanding of its class situation and a true class consciousness. (HI 76; GK 88f.)

Or he speaks of «the universal mission {weltgeschichtliche Sendung} of the proletariat» (HI 325; GK 327).[14] However, strong as these similarities between Heidegger and Lukács might be—in the decisive point Lukács's theory on history is the total opposite of Heidegger's. For the proletarians are called to a decision whose structure with regard to temporality is just the opposite of decision in Heidegger. Lukács often talks of the «new,» or «the radically new character of a consciously ordered society {Gesellschaft}» (HI 252; GK 258). This is not a mere phrase. History is not about the repetition of some vanished past but about the production of something essentially new that has never existed before, as the following features of Lukács's concept of history clearly show.

The moment of crisis is decisive for the future of the world, and it is decisive for Lukács's entire theory on dialectics and history. In nature there is no critical dialectics between subject and object. Thus, dialectics and historical materialism do not apply to nature but only to the history of humanity (HI 1ff.; GK 15ff.). Since in precapitalist societies there is no reification and no critical dialectics either, dialectics and historical materialism apply to them, if at all, only in a modified and restricted way, one that still has to be determined by future theoretical work (HI 238ff.; GK 244ff.). In socialism, there will no longer be reification and critical dialectics between subject and object. Marx has shown that, pace Hegel, the categories of reflection are not «eternal» but rather valid only for bourgeois society (HI 177; GK 194). At the time of *History and Class Consciousness,* dialectics and Marxism in Lukács is, as he put it self-critically in 1968, not a universal ontology, but rather a «theory of society,» a «social philosophy» (HI xvi),[15] indeed, a theory of Gesellschaft that pertains only to a very small portion of the history of all societies. Still, in *History and Class Consciousness* Lukács makes two claims for history in general. First, he speaks of «the world-historical mission of the process of civilisation that culminates in capitalism {weltgeschichtliche Sendung des im Kapitalismus gipfelnden Zivilisationsprozesses},» and this mission is «to achieve control over *nature*» (HI 233; GK 239). The laws of reified capitalist society «have the task {Funktion} of subordinating the categories of nature to the process of socialisation {Vergesellschaftung}. In the course of history they have performed this function» (HI 233; GK 239). Certainly, this mission of capitalism is sublated and preserved in socialism. Insofar as no society prior to the modern capitalist ones ever achieved full domination over nature, this criterion excludes any repetition of a vanished past as the end of history. Indeed, in the context of these reflections Lukács does not speak of any repetition of a vanished past within socialism. Even if certain features of this or that precapitalist society recurred in a socialist society, this would be accidental, or they would recur as something instrumental to the functioning of a socialist society and its complete domination of nature. As rightist authors see it, however, it is just the other way around, and if any achievements of Gesellschaft are preserved at all in the revitalization of Gemeinschaft, it will be those that are instrumental to the life of the revitalized Gemeinschaft.

The second claim is the 'identical subject-object' that history intends to bring about. Again, in the systematic parts of this discussion Lukács does not even mention the problem of a «re.» As in the case of the first criterion either the second criterion also allows no room for a reoccurrence of a vanished past, or if so, the reoccurrence is accidental to the realization of the 'identical subject-object.' Lukács maintains that the central problem of German idealism was overcoming the separations characteristic of the modern age and resulting from the split between subject and object due to reification. The greatness of

German idealism lies in the fact that it did not deny but instead faced the separations and contradictions of the modern age, that is, of capitalism; it searched
for ways to overcome them, and finally Hegel pointed the way out of those contradictions. The tragedy of German idealism lies in the fact that in its day the
agent that alone was capable of overcoming bourgeois Gesellschaft and reification did not yet exist. Thus, German idealism wound up in mythologies. History is the result of an agent, of the subject who acts and who acts on something, the object; and history is about the realization of the subject's freedom.
The subject will be free only if the object it acts on is not alien to the subject
and if the subject is not acted upon by an alien object. An alien object is one
that is different and independent from the subject and was not produced by the
latter, or having been produced by the subject, it has a life of its own that determines the subject. The science of history has to show that over time what seems
to be alien to the subject turns out to be indeed the subject itself, which will
overcome its own determination by what is alien to it; the subject dirempts itself
into itself as subject and its own object. Thus, the science of history shows that
the latent identity of subject and object becomes manifest in history. German
idealism could develop the abstract logic of this motif. However, in its time,
the real subject-object in history did not yet exist. Thus, in Lukács's view,
Hegel's philosophy was driven into mythology by a methodological necessity.
Being unable to identify the real subject-object in history, Hegel made history
itself dependent on something transcendent, and he introduced as the real agent
in history the notorious World Spirit and its concrete incarnations, the Volksgeister, the spirits of the individual peoples (HI 141–149; GK 156–164). With
the emergence of the proletarians German idealism faces a crisis as well. If one
adheres to the «idealism» in Hegel, one will lose the vitality of dialectics. One
will be left only with the antinomies and their increasingly mythological solu-
tions. This is what German idealism «bequeath{es} to succeeding (bourgeois)
generations» (HI 148; the German text has «Erbschaft,» GK 164). If an adherent of German idealism wants to remain faithful to its intention, he has to abandon Hegel's material theories, has to isolate their method, dialectics, and has
to transplant dialectics into a context completely unfamiliar to philosophers,
namely, into history as the history of production:

> The continuation of that course which at least in method started to point the
> way beyond these limits, namely the dialectical method as the true historical
> method was reserved for the class which was able to discover within itself on
> the basis of its life-experience the identical subject-object, the subject of action;
> the 'we' of the genesis: namely the proletariat. (HI 148f.; GK 164)[16]

Only by a radical transformation of itself can German idealism remain faithful to its intention; if it remains the same and unchanged, it becomes unfaith-
ful to its intentions and turns reactionary. In this sense Lukács approvingly

quotes Engels's sentence on «the 'German workers' movement' as the 'heir {Erbin} to classical German philosophy'» (HI xlv; GK 9). Quite soberly, Lukács acknowledges that later ages always use «the historical heritage {historische Erbschaft}» by «bending it to their own purposes» (HI 111; GK 123). Followers of the Volksgemeinschaft or other Gemeinschaften use Hegel selectively and abandon his dialectics and his liberalism in order to defend an illiberal bourgeois society against the threat of liberalism and leftist politics. Proletarians save Hegelian dialectics by radically transforming it, and they do so, according to Lukács, to save the intentions of German idealism. These three are the only occurrences of the word «Erbschaft» or «Erbe» in *History and Class Consciousness*. For Heidegger, nothing in modern Gesellschaft is intrinsically worth preserving in the state of authenticity (see chapter 2, section C). Reacting to the dynamics of the modern era, Heidegger transforms Erbschaft into a false god that demands obedience and subordination. Erbschaft or Erbe is intrinsically completely good, and it demands of the heirs that they rerealize it through their cancellation of modern Gesellschaft. Lukács acknowledges that, at least in the modern era, an Erbe is often contested and is always in danger. Whether it will be beneficial or not depends on how the heirs use it, on whether their use is attentive to the inner tensions and possibilities in the Erbe itself as well as to its context. Lukács uses this motif only in the context of philosophical knowledge, and not in the context of the different historical Gemeinschaften that have been pushed aside or are threatened by modern Gesellschaft. Tillich later claimed that to have missed the latter was the crucial political mistake of all liberals and leftists.

As to the identical subject-object, capitalism plays a crucial role. Prior to capitalism, the technologies of human beings were too limited not to be determined by nature and natural circumstances that humans could not control because they are different from them and not produced by them. Lukács does not tire of emphasizing that capitalism does away with this limitation. He speaks of a «'receding of natural limits'» (HI 237; «"Zurückweichen der Naturschranke",» GK 243) through capitalism. Or he puts it as follows: «The uniqueness of capitalism is to be seen precisely in its abolition of all 'natural barriers' {alle "Naturschranken" aufhebt} and its transformation of all relations between human beings into purely social relations {rein gesellschaftliche}» (HI 176; GK 193). One might object that, unless Lukács explains in more detail what he means, a receding of natural limits does not necessarily mean that the natural limits completely disappear, which seems to be what he implies in this as well as in several other passages (though one has to acknowledge that the German «aufhebt» sounds definitely more subtle than the English translation «abolition»). However, assuming purely social relations prepares the ground for the production of the identical subject-object. Lukács maintains that bourgeois thought necessarily «trails behind the objective development» (HI 176; GK 193), because it remains enmeshed in the abstract categories of reification and treats the categories of capitalist economy as eternal, and he continues:

> The proletariat, however, stands at the focal point of this socialising process {Vergesellschaftung}. On the one hand, this transformation of labour into a commodity removes every 'human' element from the immediate existence of the proletariat, on the other hand the same development progressively eliminates everything 'organic', every direct link with nature from the forms of society so that socialised man can stand revealed in an objectivity remote from or even opposed to humanity. It is just in this objectification, in this rationalisation and reification of all social forms that we see clearly for the first time how society is constructed from the relations of men with each other. (HI 176; GK 193)[17]

If the relationships in capitalism were not purely social, the proletarians would not be capable of reflecting on their situation and of recognizing that the alien objectivity is social, that is, produced by them and thus in itself identical to them. They would not be able to establish themselves as the identical subject-object, because human society would still be determined by something not made by human beings. According to Lukács, the capitalist objectivity is «remote from or even opposed to humanity,» not «remote from or even opposed to nature.» Alienation from and return to nature or a natural state of humankind by retreat from, Widerruf of, or Aufhebung of, Gesellschaft—a great theme in philosophy from the eighteenth century on—is not Lukács's concern. Rather, emancipation from all natural barriers as achieved in capitalism and thereafter sublation of the reified objectivity of capitalism are the necessary steps toward the production of the identical subject-object of history. It is obvious that this concept of history leaves no room for a return to or a revitalization of a past Gemeinschaft that was pushed aside by capitalism, for previous Gemeinschaften simply do not meet the two criteria, namely, full domination over nature and the realization of the identical subject-object. Features of former Gemeinschaften recur in the consciously ordered society only accidentally.

The proletarians are the object of history, insofar as they are the result of history. The proletariat has to become its subject by becoming self-aware and by sublating the reified objectivity of capitalism. Having established a consciously ordered society the proletariat will have established a society in which human beings are no longer determined by something alien. The proletarians act on behalf of all human beings because they remove reification, and they realize the purpose of history:

> The self-understanding of the proletariat is therefore simultaneously the objective understanding of the nature of society. When the proletariat furthers its own class-aims it simultaneously achieves the conscious realisation of the—objective—aims of society, aims which would inevitably remain abstract

possibilities and objective frontiers but for this conscious intervention. (HI 149; GK 165)

It is only the relationships in capitalism that are dialectical. In connection with the proletariat, Lukács discusses two features of dialectics, mediation and the category of totality (HI 1ff., 149ff.; GK 13ff.; 165ff). The proletarians must not remain in the immediacy of their everyday experiences. Rather, they have to learn to conceive their situation as a result of historical processes. By doing so, they can relate themselves to the processes of history as a totality. Since only the relations in capitalism are dialectical and since the purpose of history is the production of the identical subject-object, the issue of a past returning is not even mentioned in this book. Rather, by becoming conscious of themselves the proletarians discover the immanent tendencies in the present and their task to consciously push these tendencies further. For Lukács, this effort does not imply that these tendencies in the present are related to some past to be rerealized. Consider, for instance, the following passage:

> The methodology of the natural sciences which forms the methodological ideal of every fetishistic science and every kind of Revisionism rejects the idea of contradiction and antagonism in its subject matter. . . . But we maintain that in the case of social reality these contradictions are not a sign of the imperfect understanding of society; on the contrary, they belong to *the nature of reality itself and to the nature of capitalism.* When the totality is known they will not be transcended and *cease* to be contradictions. Quite the reverse, they will be seen to be necessary contradictions arising out of the antagonisms of this system of production. When theory (as the knowledge of the whole) opens up the way to resolving these contradictions it does so by revealing the *real tendencies* of social evolution. For these are destined to effect a *real* resolution of the contradictions that have emerged in the course of history. (HI 10; GK 23)

Or consider a passage in which Lukács summarizes this motif in terms of the three modes of time:

> Becoming is also the mediation between past and future. But it is the mediation between the concrete, i.e. historical past, and the equally concrete, i.e. historical future. When the concrete here and now dissolves into a process it is no longer a continuous, intangible moment, immediacy slipping away; it is the focus of the deepest and most widely ramified mediation, the focus of decision and of the birth of the new. As long as man concentrates his interest contemplatively upon the past *or* future, both ossify into an alien existence. . . . Man must be able to comprehend the present as a becoming. He can do this by seeing in it the tendencies out of whose dialectical opposition he can *make* the future. Only when he does this will the present be a process of becoming, that belongs to *him*. Only he who is willing and whose mission it is {berufen} to create the future can see the present in its concrete truth. . . . But when the truth

of becoming is the future that is to be created but has not yet been born, when it is the new that resides in the tendencies that (with our conscious aid) will be realised, then the question whether thought is a reflection {Abbildlichkeit des Denkens} appears quite senseless. (HI 203f.; GK 223)

Indeed, this is a further description of the kairos, the crisis. Heidegger develops the dramatics of a move forward and away from the past, back to the past, and again forward with the past, a maneuver in which the past, or having-been, raises its voice and claims «its peculiarly privileged position in the historical» (BT 438; SZ 386). One finds nothing of this in Lukács. The proletariat does not retrieve a past. Rather, understanding itself as the result of a process, it sees that there are tendencies at work in the present that enable, indeed force, the proletariat to transform capitalist Gesellschaft into something radically new, namely, a socialist Gesellschaft which as such is not a repetition of a past. According to Heidegger and Scheler, in the crisis authentic Dasein understands that it draws its identity from something other than Gesellschaft, namely, from a Gemeinschaft it has to rerealize. The authentic Dasein becomes, as it were, the self-consciousness or conscience of Geschick and Gemeinschaft when it comprehends that Gemeinschaft has been pushed aside by Gesellschaft and when Gemeinschaft raises its voice demanding to be rerealized. In liberalism, individuals are the self-consciousness of reason. In Lukács, the proletarians draw their identity and strength only from the inner tendencies of Gesellschaft itself. To indicate that there is nothing beyond Gesellschaft and that the proletarians only rely on the emancipating power of the commodity form, Lukács defines the revolutionary proletarians neither in terms of Gemeinschaft nor in terms of reason, but rather as «*the self-consciousness of the commodity*» (HI 168; GK 185).[18]

Lukács takes up the issue of a «re»—a repetition of or a return to the past— three times. In the first part of the long essay "Reification and the Consciousness of the Proletariat," he explores the phenomenon of reification as it occurs in capitalist economy and other areas of modern society, in particular bureaucracy. The second part begins with the thesis, «Modern critical philosophy springs from the reified structure of consciousness» (HI 110f.; GK 122). In the first two sections, he discusses this with reference to Kant and Fichte. In the third, he turns back to the eighteenth century and presents briefly what he regards as the central antinomy with which its philosophers dealt and which goes back to reification. The antinomy renders the concept of nature, for instance, ambivalent. «Nature» means the «"aggregate of systems of the laws" governing what happens.» «Nature» also functions as a «*value concept*» (HI 136; GK 150). However, there is a third meaning «quite different» from, and «wholly incompatible with,» the other ones. This notion of nature is related to «the feeling that social institutions (reification) strip man of his human essence and that the more culture and civilisation (i.e. capitalism and reification) take possession of him, the less able he is to be a human being» (HI 136; GK 150). Nature becomes «the repository» of all tendencies opposing «mechanisation, dehumanisation and reification.» In this context, Lukács refers to Rousseau and Schiller: «But, at the same time, it can be understood as that aspect of human inwardness which has remained natural, or at least tends or longs to become natural once more {die Tendenz, die Sehnsucht hat, wieder Natur zu werden}. "They are what we once were," says Schiller of the forms of nature, "they are what we should once more become" {"sie sind, was wir wieder werden sollen"}» (HI 136; GK 150f.). Schiller's aesthetic-pedagogical writings, however, are excellent examples of a thinking in terms of Aufhebung as opposed to a thinking in terms of Widerruf.[19] Thus, even if Lukács were to endorse Schiller's view, he would still be opposed to the rightist program. However, Lukács criticizes the proposal of an overcoming of capitalist reification through aesthetics (HI 137ff.; GK 151ff.). The second occurrence of the rhetorics of a «re» is at the beginning of the following section in which Lukács presents Hegel's philosophy, which definitely comes closer to the relevant point than an aesthetic overcoming because Hegel considers history to be the relevant realm: «The reconstitution {Wiederherstellung} of the unity of the subject, the intellectual restoration {Rettung} of man has consciously to take its path through the realm of disintegration and fragmentation» (HI 141; GK 156). Again, if Lukács followed Hegel, the resulting model would still be one of Aufhebung of Gesellschaft and not of its Widerruf. In addition, particularly regarding Hegel's theory of Gesellschaft, the motif of a return of a past is indeed accidental to Hegelian dialectics.[20] However, again one need not elaborate this point, for, as mentioned, Lukács criticizes Hegel's turn to mythology. What is relevant in Hegel is not the world spirit or the Volksgeister, but only the dialectical method (HI 141–149; GK 156–164). As indicated earlier, the dialectical method in Lukács operates independently of any assumption of the return of the past pushed aside by capitalist Gesellschaft. This is confirmed by the third occurrence of the «re.» In the essay "The Changing Function of Historical Materialism," Lukács argues that with capitalism the «umbilical cord between man and nature» has been cut and that the past becomes transparent only when the present can practice self-criticism in an appropriate manner, and consequently, precapitalist societies can be understood only after historical materialism has proved that capitalist society is not a natural and eternal, but rather a historical phenomenon (HI 237; GK 243f.). In fact, Lukács continues: «For only now, with the prospect opening up of reestablishing {Wiedererlangung} non-reified relations between man and man and between man and nature, could those factors in primitive, pre-capitalist formations be discovered in which these (non-reified) forms were present—albeit in the service of quite different functions» (HI 237f.; GK 244). Lukács then points out that though

historical materialism in its classic form can be applied to the nineteenth century it can be applied to old societies only with «much greater caution» than
the revisionists assumed (HI 238f; GK 244). This passage shows that the
dialectical theory of revolution does not, and—due to the imperfect state of
Marxist research of precapitalist societies—must not, depend on specific theories about precapitalist societies and the possible discovery of societies with
so-called primitive communism. Rather, it is the other way around. Only if the
dialectical theory of capitalist society can show the inner tendencies at work in
capitalist society to overcome reification, can Marxist research of precapitalist
societies look for nonreified relationships in them. In addition, the absence of
reification is only one criterion among others, and it is common knowledge
among Marxists that the absence of reification in precapitalist societies served
conditions that should not be rerealized. Lukács's metaphor of the «umbilical
cord between man and nature» (HI 237; GK 244) clearly indicates that his theory is not about the repetition of a past or—in Heidegger's terms—a world that
has-been-there. Probably no one wants to repeat a state in which one is as helpless and as dependent on something or someone else as a newborn child is.
Umbilical cords are cut to bring the child on his way to independence and not
to be reestablished at a later point. If the newborn child has features that also
occur in the adult, these features and the world they were part of are by no
means the end for the sake of which a communist society is established.[21]

One might say that Guignon's notion of repetition applies to Lukács's relationship to Hegel. The revisionists have no proper understanding of Hegelian
dialectics in Marx. Thus, Lukács takes the authentic Hegel as his hero whom
he repeats. However, Lukács as well as Heidegger in section 74 talk about
history and not about the theory of history, and Lukács's repetition of Hegel
serves his concept of history that does not allow for a repetition of a past. In
addition, though I will not go into detail here, Lukács's concept of repetition
of Hegel is certainly much more interesting than Guignon's. Lukács has
always been very sensitive to the phenomenon that in the course of history a
theory, either as unchanged or in different phases of its development, can be
placed «in the service of quite different functions.» While at the time of its
formulation Hegelianism was progressive because of its articulation of problems and the means it offered for their solution, Hegelianism became reactionary as soon as it let the moment slip past unused when it had to thoroughly transform itself in order to realize its intentions. Besides missing the
distinction between a Widerruf and an Aufhebung of the present, Guignon's
concept of repetition also does not address this idea of saving a past from
itself by virtue of its thorough transformation.

Though one might argue that under the impact of Lukács's theory of the
Communist Party one has often underestimated the limitations of dialectics in
Lukács, from a Heideggerian perspective Lukács's concept of history clearly
presents inauthentic historicality. The later Heidegger would certainly have

regarded it as part of the last phase of metaphysics. Lukács adheres to the idea of a «collective plan» (HI 247; «Gesamtplan,» GK 254) for society, and he assumes that the purpose of history is for human beings to do away with any determination of human history by something other than human beings themselves. Whether Heidegger read *History and Class Consciousness* or not, from the perspective of *Being and Time* Lukács just offers another formulation of precisely the process Heidegger criticizes as a downward plunge, a falling-down-and-away-from the origin, from Gemeinschaft, the process targeted by Heidegger's criticism of the idea of a «business procedure that can be regulated» (BT 340; «Idee eines regelbaren Geschäftsganges,» SZ 294). There has always been a certain Platonism in Heidegger, namely, the assumption that human beings are authentic, or realize their essence, only if they no longer deny that they are essentially related to, and dependent on, something that is «higher» than and independent from their understanding or reason and their other faculties. In the essay "The Question Concerning Technology," Heidegger writes that, today, «the illusion comes to prevail that everything man encounters exists only insofar as it is his construct {Gemächte}. This illusion gives rise in turn to one final delusion: it seems as though man everywhere and always encounters only himself» (BW 308; VA 31).[22] He adds: «*In truth, however, precisely nowhere does man today any longer encounter himself, i.e., his essence. Man . . .* fails in every way to hear {überhört} in what respect he eksists, from out of his essence {aus seinem Wesen her}, in the realm of an exhortation or address {Zuspruch}, so that he *can never* encounter only himself» (BW 308f.; VA 31). Again, it is the same story as in *Being and Time*. In *Being and Time,* Gemeinschaft stands for the entity whose «Zuspruch» the inauthentic Daseine fail to hear, and maybe already in the unwritten «second half» (BT 17; SZ n.p.) of *Being and Time* Heidegger would have located Gemeinschaft in the larger picture of Being. Liberals, social democrats, and communists alike take pride in the certainty that the ideal Gesellschaft we have to realize is the result of our rational contracts and planning and that in it human beings have emancipated themselves from all human follies and all nonhuman entities that determined their lives in the Gemeinschaften. From the perspective of *Being and Time* as well as that of Hitler and Scheler (prior to his Kehre), Lukács is just a social democrat with more advanced methods, and thus he is nothing more than an advanced liberal. Lukács opposes what he regards to be the social democrats' naiveté concerning how a socialist society can be brought about, and for this purpose he presents his conceptual framework. However, the end is the same, namely, to establish a Gesellschaft and to do so by leaving behind any past. That my interpretation of Lukács is not, so to speak, a deconstructive one, but rather represents the way he was read by other leftists at the time is confirmed by Tillich's analysis in 1933. Tillich maintains that not to have looked back to the past was precisely the decisive political mistake of liberals, social democrats, and communists alike, and—in much the same way in which

Lukács regards it to be necessary for Hegelian dialectics to transform itself if it wants to remain faithful to its intentions—he presents the offer to the rightists to transform themselves and their traditions in order to save themselves from themselves and to realize their intentions.

## B. Tillich's *The Socialist Decision*

The moment of decision arises out of a situation. The situation is the historical reality that has reached the crisis stage and calls for a decision. Historical reality develops into a crisis when the historical agents—individuals, groups, parties, and classes—no longer rely on the basic tenets of their social and political life, that is, when at least one agent no longer acknowledges the work of the other as its own. One party renounces the social contract—whether it had been an explicit or an implicit one—and reality begins to deteriorate into a struggle between different parties, none of which acknowledges the claim of the other to realize the common good. Each party, or at least one of them, acts in the name of the common good by separating itself from the others and by claiming that the others are the foe and must be destroyed if need be. To strengthen and promote the conflicting tendencies that are inherent in reality and thus to destroy the common good may be the path to glory for those who believe in this or that sort of necessity in history, whether they call it fate, destiny, or by some other name. In the terms of *Being and Time,* a person following this path is a Held, since he responds to and fulfills destiny rather than evading it; that is, he submits to the sort of necessity he assumes to be at work in history. Carl Schmitt is often believed to have done so on the political right. According to him, there are no common norms, values, or third parties to intervene when one of two or several other parties have defined the other as the foe one must be willing to kill in order to preserve «one's own form {die eigene, seinsmäßige Art} of existence.»[23] Schmitt became famous for these theories, for in taking the radical step he fulfilled fate and destiny and thus became what «Germans» mean by Held, which is different from the American understanding of authenticity (see chapter 5, section C). Submitting to destiny required rightists to step out of the bounds of the Weimar constitution, the sphere of mediation, and to consider it and politics in general from the viewpoint of the warrior who has distanced himself from the other whom he has defined as the foe to be killed if need be.

However, is there really only one way of understanding decision, Entscheidung? Is Entscheidung necessarily always a de-cision, a separation, a Scheidung, divorce, and the subsequent struggle? Adorno, Heidegger's great antipode in the 1960s in Germany, who, like Benjamin, took the temporality of beings much more seriously than Heidegger did and who therefore did not look for an origin of history in or beyond history, permitted himself once to indulge in an etymological speculation. Notwendigkeit, Necessity, means, as he said, «die Not wenden,» to turn around, against, necessity, to set one's face against and break fate, destiny, and necessity—in other words, not subjugation to necessity, but breaking necessity. Along the lines of this remarkable piece of etymology, one might also listen more closely to the word Entscheidung, and what one might hear is that Ent-Scheidung is the End' of Scheidung, the end of separation or divorce. Combined with Notwendigkeit in Adorno's sense of the turn against destiny, Entscheidung as the end of divorce is the call for alliance, for the covenant, in the moment of danger, of crisis. For all those who think in terms of fate and necessity and who thus favor the clarity of the «one» voice, this may have seemed futile and idealistic and indicative of a lack of the Härte des Willens, hardness of the will that Heidegger and his ilk held in such high esteem.[24] But who knows whether the destiny and necessity they claim «we» have to subjugate ourselves to is not just their own self-fulfilling demagogy. To look for the covenant, alliance, in the moment of crisis is the opposite of what Heidegger and the other rightists understand by decision. It is not to divorce oneself from the other, expelling him out of oneself, so as to be prepared to kill the other, and it is also not simply recognizing the other as other, as some people have interpreted Heidegger's concept of authenticity. Looking for the covenant involves the recognition of the other in his own right as well as of the other in oneself and of oneself as the other. At the same time it also implies accepting that the other, in fact, all human beings, have a claim on one. It is the recognition of the reciprocal χάρις, grace, potlatch between me and the other and respect for our human rights. Looking for the covenant aims at ending the gesture of divorcing the other and one's own «part maudit» from oneself. Maybe, Carl Schmitt also meant something like this when after World War II he gave a short and enigmatic interpretation of his concept of the foe: «The foe is our own question as Gestalt.»[25] In terms of philosophy and politics in the twenties, to recognize one's «part maudit» was to make an alliance with the Jews and the Jew in oneself—or, rather, with the Jewish prophet in oneself—and not, as in right-wingers, to deny and expel the Jews and the Jewish prophet in oneself.

In a section entitled "The Break with the Myth of Origin {Ursprungsmythos} in the Enlightenment and the Romantic Reaction,"[26] Tillich maintains: «The powers of the myth of origin, to be sure, have been broken by the Enlightenment; their symbols and forms of expression have been destroyed; but they have not been eradicated as powers, neither as psychological nor as social powers» (SD 24f.; SE 33). In a section entitled "The Struggle Concerning Tradition," he states:

A weariness with autonomy {Daß man der Autonomie müde geworden ist} can be discerned in all groups and levels of society. This is one of the most significant mood-determining elements in the background {einer der wichtigsten stimmungsmäßigen Hintergründe} of contemporary political events. It is also a root {Wurzel} of the antiparliamentary tendency of the younger generation. (SD 169, n. 21; SE 41, n. 1)

In his analysis of "The leading Groups and the Limits of the Bourgeois Principle {bürgerlichen Prinzips}," he points to certain developments among the bourgeois parties and argues that they testify to «a true consciousness of the limits of the bourgeois principle and the impossibility of its standing alone without a supportive pre-bourgeois substance» (SD 56; SE 55). These three passages outline the common ground of a rightist analysis and Tillich's analysis of the political situation of that time. Tillich and the rightists, however, interpret these assumptions differently, and they also draw completely different conclusions.

In the table of contents of Tillich's book, there are the following entries: "Introduction: The Two Roots {Wurzeln} of Political Thought," "1. Mythical Powers of Origin {Ursprungsmythische Mächte}," "Part Two: The Principle of Bourgeois Society {Das Prinzip der bürgerlichen Gesellschaft} and the inner Conflict of Socialism," and "5. Eros and Purpose in the Life of the Community {im Leben der Gemeinschaft}" (SD vff.; SE 5f.). Looking at these titles and the few passages quoted above, one would not necessarily expect the author to be on the left part of the political spectrum. Rather, his vocabulary («roots,» «principles,» «origin,» «Gemeinschaft») sounds more conservative. In part, the vocabulary results from his Christian beliefs and his conceptualization of those beliefs. More important, however, is Tillich's use of these terms, which distinguishes his position from both the Right and the Left. Concerning the Right, Tillich attempts to meet «the others» on their own ground and to convince them that, for their own sake, they should consider using the rightist way of thinking and vocabulary not in the name of a philosophy of origins but in order to oppose a philosophy of origins, for only in opposition to such a philosophy can the rightists realize their intentions as well as that of the origin. Concerning the Left, Tillich is convinced that the Left was wrong in neglecting the claims of all the Gemeinschaften.

For Tillich political behavior and thought have two roots. He introduces one of them with reference to Heidegger:

> Human beings find themselves in existence {Der Mensch findet sich vor}; they find themselves as they find their environment, and as this latter finds them and itself. But to find oneself means that one does not originate from oneself; it means to have an origin that is not oneself, or—in the pregnant phrase of Martin Heidegger—to be "thrown" into the world. The human question concerning the "Whence" of existence {die menschliche Frage nach dem "Woher"} arises out of this situation. Only later does it appear as a philosophical question. But it has always been a question; and its first and permanently normative answer is enshrined in myth.

The origin is creative {Der Ursprung läßt entspringen}. Something new springs into being, something that did not previously exist and now is something with its own character over against the origin. We experience ourselves as posited, yet also as independent. Our life proceeds in a tension between dependence on the origin and independence. For the origin does not let us go; it is not something that was and is no longer, once we become independent selves. Rather, we are continually dependent on the origin; it bears us, it creates us anew at every moment, and thereby holds us fast. The origin brings us forth as something new and singular; but it takes us, as such, back to the origin again. Just in being born we become involved in having to die. "It is necessary that things should pass away into that from which they are born," declares the first saying handed down to us in Western philosophy {the fragment of Anaximander}. Our life runs its course in terms of birth, development and death. No living thing can transcend the limits set by its birth; development is the growing and passing away of what comes from the origin and returns to it. This has been expressed in myth in infinitely diverse ways, according to the things and events in which a particular group envisages its origin. In all mythology, however, there resounds the cyclical law of birth and death. Every myth is a myth of origin, that is, an answer to the question about the "Whence" of existence and an expression of dependence on the origin and on its power. *The consciousness oriented to the myth of origin is the root of all conservative and romantic thought in politics.* (SD 3f.; SE 18)

The other root raises the opposite question:

But human beings not only find themselves in existence; they not only know themselves to be posited and withdrawn in the cycle of birth and death, like all living things. They experience a demand {eine Forderung} that frees them from being simply bound to what is given, and which compels them to add to the question "Whence?" [*Woher*] the question "Whither?" [*Wozu*]. With this question the cycle is broken in principle and humankind is elevated beyond the sphere of merely living things. For the demand calls for {Die Forderung fordert} something that does not yet exist but should exist, should come to fulfillment. A being that experiences a demand is no longer simply bound to the origin. Human life involves more than a mere development of what already is. Through the demand, humanity is directed to what ought to be. And what ought to be does not emerge with the unfolding of what is; if it did, it would be something that is, rather than something that ought to be. This means, however, that the demand that confronts humanity is an unconditional demand {unbedingte Forderung}. The question "Whither?" is not contained within the limits of the question "Whence?" It is something unconditionally new {ein unbedingt Neues} that transcends what is new and what is old within the sphere of mere development. Through human beings, something unconditionally new is to be realized; this is the meaning of the demand that they experience, and which they are able to experience because in them being is twofold. For the human person is not only an individual, a self, but also has knowledge about himself or herself, and thereby the possibility of transcending what is found within the self and around the self. This is human freedom, not that one has a so-called "free will," but that as a human being one is not bound to what one finds in existence, that one is subject to a demand that something unconditionally new should be realized through oneself. Thus the cycle of birth and death is broken; the existence and the actions of human beings are not confined within a mere development of their origin. Wherever this consciousness prevails, the tie to the origin has been dissolved in principle and the myth of origin has been broken in principle. *The breaking of the myth of origin by the unconditional demand is the root of liberal, democratic, and socialist thought in politics.* (SD 4f.; SE 18f.)

However, as Tillich explains «we cannot stop with a simple opposition between these two aspects of human existence» (SD 5; SE 19). For, as he argues throughout the entire book, the «unconditional demand» must not ignore and simply push aside the powers of origin, nor must the powers of the origin exclude the demand. Thus, from the beginning Tillich's key motif is just the opposite of Heidegger's. If one reads Heidegger's concept of historicality along the lines of Birmingham or Guignon, one will probably expect Heidegger to be mentioned in connection with Tillich's second «root.» However, I hope to have shown that, indeed, Tillich is right in connecting Heidegger with the first root. For all the emphasis on futurality in Heidegger, in the moment of becoming authentic Dasein realizes the «peculiarly privileged position in the historical» of «*having-been*» (BT 438; SZ 386), and the resulting futurality of authentic Dasein consists in its work of canceling Gesellschaft and of rerealizing «*having-been*,» the Gemeinschaft.

To be sure, as happens so often in situations of crisis, Tillich, too, develops a «grand narrative.» However, Heideggerians are the last to deny that a more or less «grand» narrative is needed to illuminate our concrete situation. In addition, Tillich's version differs from the others I have presented so far in two respects. First, he develops it in order to meet the rightists on their own ground. Second, it enables him to present an interpretation of Germany's political history from the nineteenth century on that, like no other book written by a professional philosopher in the 1910s and 1920s, illuminates the concrete tensions of the different political movements and parties. Explaining this second aspect in concrete detail would go beyond the scope of this book, and the same is true for a detailed presentation of Tillich's interpretation of Jewish and Christian religions and their relationship to politics. Thus, the following presentation of the motifs found in Tillich that are relevant to my purpose here is somewhat abstract and sketchy and does not capture the richness and concreteness of his original text.

In his foreword, Tillich explains that the

political events of recent years have been decisive in providing the impulse to begin and complete this book: the decline of the political influence of the Social

Democrats, the apparently final split in the proletarian working class {between the Social Democrats and the communists}, the triumphal advance of National Socialism, the consolidation of the late-capitalistic powers on a military basis, the increasingly perilous situation in foreign affairs. (SD xxxiii; SE 12)

In his framework, this means that the first root of political thinking is about to exclude the second one and its representatives, liberalism, Social Democrats and communists. At the same time, this sentence indicates the Left's political failure in not having been able to offer forms in which the adherents of rightist movements and parties or all the vacillating Daseine can recognize themselves and their needs.

The first root thinks in terms of origin. An origin is always a particular origin, a particular «*soil,*» a particular «*blood,*» or a particular «*social group*» that provides its members with identity and claims their allegiance while punishing their departure from it. It is the holiness of Being that, in religious terms, is sanctified by the priests who consecrate a particular site, blood, or group as origin. Though each origin is particular, there is a tendency to enlarge its dominion. Thinking in terms of origin is a spatial thinking, since it excludes the new, and justice is not relevant to it (SD 13ff., 18ff.; SE 24ff., 27ff.). Tillich uses the notion of «principle» («Prinzip») in order to denote a dynamis, a power of a historical reality, that accounts for the emergence of new and unexpected realizations of an origin or root (SD 9f.; SE 22f.). The first root is meant to account for mythology, for strands in Greek philosophy, and also attitudes and mentalities in modern societies as they are manifest in psychological and social phenomena and in movements such as the Youth Movement. Indeed, it is part of the anthropology Marxism must not lack (SD 164, n. 3; SE 16, n. 3). The first root is the opposite of the second whose first realization Tillich sees in Jewish prophecy:

It is the significance of *Jewish prophetism* to have fought explicitly against the myth of origin and the attachment to space and to have conquered them. On the basis of a powerful social myth of origin, Jewish prophetism radicalized the social imperative to the point of freeing itself from the bond of origin. God is free from the soil, the sacred land, not because he has conquered foreign lands, but precisely because he has led foreign conquerors into his own land in order to punish the "people of his inheritance" and to subject them to an unconditional demand. The bond of origin between God and his people is broken if the bond of the law is broken by the people. Thus the myth of origin is shattered— and this is the world-historical mission of Jewish prophetism. With the breaking of the tie to the soil, the other forms of the myth of origin also lose their power. The sacred aristocracy, including the monarchy, is rejected for the sake of righteousness. The claim of belonging to the people avails nothing in face of the unconditional demand, on account of which the alien can be held in equal, indeed, in higher esteem. The priestly tradition is not abolished but is judged

by the demand of righteousness, and its cultic aspects are devalued. The breaking of the myth of origin becomes evident, finally, in the prophet's opposition
to the priests. (SD 20; SE 29)

Christianity has adopted «the spirit of Judaism.» However, the myth of the
origin has made its way into Christianity (SD 21; SE 30):

> Over against {the fact that the myth of origin has made its way into Christian-
> ity} it remains the *function of the Jewish spirit* to raise the prophetic protest,
> both in Judaism and in Christianity, against every new attempt to revive such
> bondage to the myth of origin, and to help time, the unconditional demand, and
> the "Wither" to be victorious over space, mere being, and the "Whence." The
> spirit of Judaism is therefore the necessary and eternal enemy of political roman-
> ticism. Anti-Semitism is an essential element in political romanticism. Chris-
> tianity, however, by virtue of its principle, belongs radically and unambigu-
> ously on the side of Judaism in this conflict. Any wavering on this issue is
> apostasy from itself, involving compromise and denial of the shattering—man-
> ifest in the cross—of all holiness of being, even the highest religious being. A
> Christianity that abandons its prophetic foundation by allying itself with polit-
> ical romanticism has lost its own identity.
>
> Of course, prophetism and Judaism cannot simply be equated. Old Testa-
> ment prophetism is the persistent struggle of the "spirit of Judaism" with the
> *realities of Jewish national life.* For the actual life of the Jewish nation, like
> the actual life of every nation, is by nature pagan. Hence, we see the foolish-
> ness of certain nationalistic demands that the Old Testament be dismissed as
> an expression of an alien nationality. In fact, the Old Testament writings are
> a continuous testimony to the struggle of prophetic Judaism against pagan,
> national Judaism. For this reason, and solely for this reason, the Old Testament
> is a book for humanity—because in it the particular, the bondage to space and
> blood and nationalism, are seen as things to be fought against.
>
> Now it is the tragedy of Judaism that its historical fate not only broke the
> hegemony of the powers of origin, but also frequently dissolved them alto-
> gether, insofar as no new ties to the soil were created in their place (though this
> did come to pass in east-European Judaism). This negative element, the criti-
> cal dissolution of the myth of origin instead of its prophetic transformation,
> gives to anti-Semitism and political romanticism an apparent justification for
> resisting this tendency. But this justification is invalid, because such resistance,
> instead of strengthening the prophetic element in Judaism against the dissolv-
> ing tendency, fights against the prophetic element itself and thereby weakens
> its power, even within Judaism. (SD 21f.; SE 30f.)

The basic attitude is «Erwartung,» Erwartung of the unconditioned new.
Erwartung, expectation, is the opposite of Ursprungsbindung, tie to the origin,
and the political Right. Erwartung is not passive but rather entails action (SD
100ff.; SE 85ff.). The second root is also present in the modern era. In fact, the
modern age is the presence of the second root in world history. Autonomy as

well as «objectification» («Verdinglichung») and «analysis» («In every origin there is an element of the unconditioned. The wholly conditioned, that which has become merely a thing, no longer bears any marks of the origin» [SD 48; SE 49].) carry out the principle of bourgeois society, namely, to radically break and do away with any bondage to the origin and its powers (SD 23ff., 47ff.; SE 31ff., 49ff.).

The political Right is a reaction against the developed bourgeois society and against the latter's principles and procedures. Tillich labels the political right «political romanticism» (SD 27ff.; SE 34ff.), distinguishes between two forms—a conservative and a revolutionary form—and argues that the

> two forms of political romanticism, despite the differences in their concept of the goal, are united in their desire to return to the origin—not in a general way, but to the particular powers of origin from which prophetism and bourgeois society have broken away. All their political demands are basically to be understood in terms of this return to origin.
> The *return to the soil* {*Boden*}. . . .
> Blood and race {Blut und Rasse}. . . .
> The *return to the social group* is expressed in the appeal for "community" {Gemeinschaft} which is so common to all forms of political romanticism. . . . It presents the demand, so to speak, for the son to create the mother and to call the father into being out of nothing. (SD 29–32; SE 36–38)

Tillich then develops this motif in regard to several aspects, among them tradition:

> Between the origin and the present stands tradition. It is therefore of decisive importance in every respect for political romanticism to be able to relate itself to prebourgeois traditions.
> The fact that there has been an almost two-hundred-year-old *break with traditions* in most sectors of life cannot, however, be wished away. Political romanticism, in the face of this, has only two possibilities: either to defend such islands of tradition as remain, even though they have become meaningless in the total structure of existence, or to attempt to revive the old, lost traditions. But a tradition that has been broken is really no longer a tradition, but a literary remembrance. The attempt to make tradition out of literary remembrances is the true mark of romanticism, on account of which it is called romanticism; and this is also the clearest expression of its inner contradiction. . . . In every case, tradition has two connotations: descent from an origin and subordination to the authority of the origin, i.e., of a special realm and its structure. Small as the practical value of these ideas may seem at the present time, their ideological power is strong, and thus their value as weapons against existing forms {Kampfwert gegen bestehende Gestaltungen}. Their attack is directed against {gegen} universal humanistic education, against the leveling of moral standards {Sitten, that is, customs and the ethical standards embodied in them} and philosophies of life as a result of the uniform framework of social interchange; against the intellectual auton-

omy of the individual and the lack of inwardly authoritative criteria; against the openness of the professions to everyone and the lack of established social rankings; against the equalizing tendencies of the metropolis, in which many realms of life interpenetrate one another, and whose influences, through technical means such as radio and cinema, draw even the rural areas into this single unit. Finally, and chiefly, it is directed against the political autonomy of the individual, detached from all special traditions. Positively, the myth of tradition concentrates on the national tradition. It finds its climax in the demand to maintain this tradition, to strengthen it through the creation of a national historical legend, and to free it from international traditions. Political romanticism demands such a myth of tradition and sets about creating it. (SD 33f.; SE 39)

This passage can be regarded as an excellent summary and critique of the intentions of the political Right. Concerning Heidegger, what I wanted to show in this book is that section 74 of *Being and Time* in its logical structure as well as its contents is a brilliant summary of the revolutionary Right. What in Tillich is «subordination to the authority of the origin,» is in Heidegger «*erwidert* vielmehr» (SZ 386; BT 438). What in Tillich is «their attack is directed against {gegen},» is in Heidegger the «*disavowal {Widerruf}* of that which in the "today", is working itself out as the 'past'» (BT 438; SZ 386), this disavowal already being anticipated in the sentence that authentic Dasein acts «against {gegen}» «the way of interpreting Dasein which has come down to us» (BT 435; SZ 383; see above, chapter 2, section C). Since the subordination to the origin occurs in a situation in which the origin is seen as endangered or even as already pushed aside by «that which in the "today", is working itself out as the 'past'» (BT 438; SZ 386), Heidegger labels the subordination an Erwiderung («*erwidert* vielmehr,» SZ 386; BT 438) in the sense of «I erwidere, respond, to a call for help.» I respond to the call for help by destroying («*Widerruf*») what threatens or has pushed aside the origin. Since the past calls upon me to rerealize it against «that which in the "today", is working itself out as the 'past'» (BT 438; SZ 386), my repeating of the past does not just simply «bring again [Wiederbringen] something that is 'past'» (BT 437; SZ 385; the last sentence belongs to the passage through which Heidegger makes clear that he is summarizing not just rightist politics, but the politics of the revolutionary rightists; by adding «of {the} people» [BT 436; SZ 384], he turns his summary into an option for National Socialism; see chapter 3, section E). In fact, in Tillich's analysis of political romanticism one finds several sentences with the same structure found in Heidegger's passage on Erwiderung and Widerruf (SZ 386; BT 438). Consider, for instance: «The leading groups, especially of revolutionary romanticism, seek to counter the threat of their complete loss of power {Entmächtigung} by depriving the rising proletariat of its power {Wider-entmächtigung}» (SD 43, hyphen mine, J. F.; SE 46); or: «The way from being to consciousness, from origin to structure, cannot be reversed {rückwärts gehen} without the destruction of the society that has undergone this development {Vernichtung der Gesellschaft, die ihn gegangen ist}» (SD 56; SE 55f.). Or, consider his definition of political romanticism:

> Out of the convergence of all these forces {that is, eros, fate, and death}, political romanticism arises. It is an attempt to restore {wieder herzustellen} the broken myth of origin, both spiritually and socially.
> *Political romanticism is, thus, the countermovement to {Gegenbewegung gegen} prophetism and the Enlightenment on the basis of a spiritual and social situation that is determined by prophetism and the Enlightenment.* (SD 25f.; SE 33f.)

The first part in each quote corresponds to the sentence on Erwiderung, and the second corresponds to the sentence on Widerruf in Heidegger.[27]

Tillich's criticism of the social democrats and the communists does not soften the basic distinction between the Right and the Left as to temporality. On the contrary, his definition of political romanticism captures the intention of the political Right to turn back to the past so as to replace the basic features of the present, Gesellschaft, with those of the revitalized past, Gemeinschaft. Socialism, however, is not oriented toward the past, but rather toward the unconditioned new in the future, as is all prophecy: *«The socialist principle, so far as its substance is concerned, is prophetic.* Socialism is a prophetic movement, but it exists in a context in which the myth of origin has been broken and the bourgeois principle has become dominant. *Socialism is prophetism on the soil of an autonomous, self-sufficient world»* (SD 101; SE 86). As the first sentence already indicates, however, Tillich differs from the leftist theories I have discussed in his attitude to the Gemeinschaften of the past. For to most Leftists the Gemeinschaften were of no positive significance. In Heidegger's terms, social democrats were engaged in inauthentic futurality, that is, a temporality that does not impart «to *having-been* its peculiarly privileged position in the historical» (BT 438; SZ 386). For social democrats, as Benjamin put it (see section A), «thought fit to assign to the working class the role of the redeemer of future generations.» According to Benjamin (see section A), Blanqui and the members of the Spartacist groups acted out of «hatred» toward the past. According to them, the various Gemeinschaften in the past «enslaved» their «ancestors.» Heidegger would probably regard this as an even more intense form of inauthentic futurality than the one practiced by the social democrats. For Lukács, the process of the proletariat becoming conscious was the first manifestation of the identical subject-object as the purpose of history. All these leftists regarded relics of former Gemeinschaften as obstacles to joining the Left. Tillich, however, maintains that it was the decisive mistake of the socialist theoreticians to insist on the complete reification of the proletarians (SD 99; SE 84). According to him, the proletarians oppose the bourgeois society for the same reasons the political romantics do:

> *That which reacts in the proletarian is the same as that which political romanticism makes the sole principle of human nature and of society—the origin.* Here is the point where they stand together in opposition to the bourgeois principle. They differ only in that, presupposing this relation to the origin, political romanticism seeks to reject {zurücknehmen} the bourgeois principle, while socialism seeks to incorporate it {aufnehmen}. In this light we can understand that in spite of their common point of departure, namely, the elevation of humanity as opposed to the dehumanizing bourgeois principle, political romanticism attacks socialism so forcefully. The bourgeoisie from its inception has guarded itself, both psychologically and socially, against a complete severance of its connection with the origin. It has never consistently carried through its own principle. The proletariat, by contrast, was forced into such consistency by its situation. . . . *There remains an element of proletarian being which has not been reduced to the status of a thing, and from this element there emerges the struggle against the bourgeois principle.* (SD 98f.; SE 83f.)

Again, a comparison to section 74 of *Being and Time* reveals the same differences. The political Right erwidert the call of the origin for help and widerruft (zurücknehmen as in the last quote: something has moved forward on the road; I nehme, catch it and pull it zurück, back to cancel or destroy) the bourgeois principle. Liberals as well as the leftists do not listen to the call and proceed on the road of Gesellschaft (aufnehmen as in the last quote: I pick it up and carry it forward in order to save it from those who want to zurücknehmen it) toward a future society no longer marked by the political suppression characteristic of former Gemeinschaften. According to Tillich, the proletarians erwidern the call of the different Gemeinschaften. In this, they behave like rightists and not like liberals and not in the way socialist theoreticians have so far believed them to behave. However, they don't cancel Gesellschaft, but like liberals and leftists, they rely on it. Socialism adheres to the bourgeois principle of breaking the power of origin and of subjecting everyone to the unconditional demand (SD 100ff., 109ff.; SE 85ff., 92ff.). However, socialism can no longer adhere to the bourgeois belief in harmony. For reification and economic crises have proven the liberal realization of the bourgeois principle wrong, or at least one-sided. The laws of capitalist economy do not lead to equality, freedom, and harmony but to their opposites. Thus, socialism has to assume that the bourgeois principle can be realized only in a socialist society (SD 57ff.; SE 56ff.). The bourgeois society must be overcome and be replaced with a different economy if its ideals are to be realized. Tillich describes this relationship between proletarians and bourgeois Gesellschaft and the bourgeois principle in formulations such as that socialism is «*the fulfillment* {*Vollendung*} *of the bourgeois principle*» and at the same time «*the expression of its destruction*» (SD 61; SE

59). Clearly, he is talking about a dialectical Aufhebung and not a Widerruf of Gesellschaft. Socialism is the expression of the destruction of the bourgeois principle also for the reason that, according to Tillich, socialism has to draw on the powers and needs of the origin and take them seriously. His thesis is that the powers of the origin are not a hindrance to socialism, but rather the very drives without which there would be no realization of socialism. The need for Boden, Blut, and Gemeinschaft cannot be satisfied immediately, that is, in precapitalist communities, for this leads to the struggle of different origins. It has to be translated into the terms of the second root. However, this need cannot be realized within bourgeois society either, for this leads to imperialism, poverty, and abstract autonomy. Socialism does realize the needs of the Gemeinschaften and of autonomy by transferring them to a different sphere. Tillich uses for this the expression that socialism has to be able «at once to break {brechen} and to confirm {bestätigen}» (SE 123; the English translation has «to judge and to support,» SD 151) the needs of the first root. The National Socialists are «false prophets,» and false prophets are not those «whose predictions don't come true,» but rather those who preach «"'peace, peace,' {Heil}, when there is no peace {Heil}," for example in an origin-related group that expects to achieve stability and power by avoiding the demand for justice» (SD 173f., n. 4; SE 89 n.). The end of the last longer quotation above already contains Tillich's theory on why, so far, socialism has failed to take into account the needs of the powers of origin. Stripped of the details of Tillich's conceptual framework and his rich references to German history, his theory reads as follows. In the nineteenth century the bourgeoisie entered into alliances with the prebourgeois origins of Blut, Boden, and Gemeinschaft to strengthen its dominion. In the process, the prebourgeois groups were integrated, and the needs of the origins were more or less satisfied. In this situation, emerging socialism had no other choice but to side with the radical bourgeoisie, the liberals and thus realize the bourgeois principle better than the bourgeoisie itself, because otherwise society could not reach the point at which socialist changes would become possible. Thus, socialism ended up in pronounced opposition to all groups and needs that belong to the first root (SD 66ff.; SE 62ff.). However, this situation has changed because of the World War:

> The new and pivotal factor in the present situation is that the origin-related groups have assumed, to a large extent, a stance of opposition to bourgeois society. It is a function of National Socialism to have accomplished this revolution by means that corresponded to the origin-related character of these groups. Prerequisite to this success was, to be sure, the shattering of the mutually supportive relationship of the bourgeois and the prebourgeois forces through which they maintained the system of class domination at the expense of the proletariat. The World War, the inflation, and the international economic crisis forced the bourgeoisie to impose the cost of dominion upon the middle classes, too. They were sucked into

the crisis of capitalism, not only as individuals but also as groups. For a time, capitalism had held out advantages for them: the possibility of appointment and promotion as clerks and middle-level officials in the bureaucracy; strong safeguards against unemployment; the management of, and payment of interest on, savings; the heavy demand especially for products created by advanced agricultural methods. But all this perished in the war, the inflation, and the economic crisis. Thereby a new situation was created for socialism. It is not mere demagoguery for the revolutionary movement of the middle classes to call itself socialist {the NSDAP}. It has a real "expectation." The symbolic term *the Third Reich,* for example, refers not only to the concept of a third German empire; it also, by virtue of the magic number three, conjures up the ancient expectations of a third age. The content of this expectation is simply the unbroken origin, reflecting the inner contradiction of political romanticism in general. Thus the movement is in constant danger of being absorbed by the conservative form of political romanticism and of being led back into the service of class rule. This danger is all the greater since the movement's *Führer* appears to be working for this end. If this should happen, the realization of socialism in Germany would be impossible, unless new movements should arise out of economic or political catastrophes. (SD 129f.; SE 106)

When the book was published in 1933, the National Socialists had already come to power, Tillich had to leave Germany, and Heidegger was about to give his rectorate address in which he would continue to use motifs that were also used by Christians in a pagan sense. At least from 1929 on, it was pretty obvious that the National Socialists and «big business» had become allies. In contrast to the National Socialist Heidegger, Scheler and Tillich had sufficient judgment to anticipate that the alliance of German capitalists, conservative bourgeoisie, and National Socialism would be disastrous. One might call Tillich's suggestion a dialectical approach. In doing so, however, one should not forget two things. First, there is no dialectical development in Tillich. His notion of socialism is an act of balance at the last minute, an effort to save Europe from a «return to barbarism {Rückkehr in die Barbarei}» (SD 161; SE 130), and it is an offer to the rightists:

> But a socialist decision is demanded also of the enemies of socialism. Above all, those groups that today carry the word *socialism* in their names must be brought to a real socialist decision. . . . These groups are not to become a part of the proletariat but rather are to be drawn to its side, so that by a common socialist decision the fate of death now facing the people of Europe can be averted {damit in gemeinsamer sozialistischer Entscheidung das Todesschicksal der europäischen Völker gewendet werde}. Only the socialist decision can avert this fate. It is for this reason that we are summoned to it. (SD xxxif.; SE 11)[28]

Second, Tillich's book is a very concrete piece of party politics with regard to the major topics.[29] One can surely say that Tillich's suggestion is in line with and is in fact a further development of the late Scheler's suggestion of a politics of «Ausgleich.» However, my purpose here is not a discussion of the concept of socialism at the time, but only the difference between Heidegger's idea of historicality and the liberal and leftist concepts of history. Clearly, Tillich's suggestion is based on the difference between the Right and the Left that I have elucidated from the writings of Hitler, Heidegger, Scheler, and Lukács. Tillich's own suggestion does not blur the distinction but rather emphasizes it even more, insofar as he insists that, indeed, the needs of the origin, of the past, have a right to be fulfilled; however, they cannot be fulfilled by canceling Gesellschaft and by rerealizing or returning to a Gemeinschaft, but only by sublating bourgeois Gesellschaft into a socialist Gesellschaft, which is not the repetition of some past but rather something unconditionally new even though it can be brought about only with the powers of the origin. As Tillich puts it:

> The actual origin {the one conjured up by the rightists} is not the origin in truth. It is not the fulfillment of what is intended for humanity from the origin. The fulfillment of the origin lies rather in what confronts us as a demand, as an ought. The "Whence" of humanity finds its fulfillment in the "Whither." The actual origin is contradicted by the true origin, not absolutely and in every respect, for the actual origin—in order to be actual at all—must participate in the true origin; it expresses it, but at the same time both obscures it and distorts it. The mentality oriented solely to the myth of origin knows nothing of this ambiguity of the origin. Therefore it clings to the origin and feels that it is a sacrilege to go beyond it. The ambiguity of the origin is first revealed to it when the experience of the unconditional demand frees this consciousness from bondage to the origin. (SD 5f.; SE 19)

Tillich continues:

> The demand is directed towards the fulfillment of the true origin. Now a person experiences an unconditional demand only from another person. The demand becomes concrete in the "I-Thou" encounter. The content of the demand is therefore that the "thou" be accorded the same dignity as the "I"; this is the dignity of being free, of being the bearer of the fulfillment implied in the origin. This recognition of the equal dignity of the "Thou" and the "I" is justice. *The demand that separates from the ambiguous origin is the demand of justice.* From the unbroken origin proceed powers that are in tension with one another; they seek dominion and destroy each other. From the unbroken origin there comes the power of being, the rising and perishing of forces that "pay one another the penalty and compensation for their injustice according to the ordinance of time," as is asserted in the already quoted first statement of Greek philosophy {Anaximander's fragment}. The unconditional demand transcends this tragic cycle of existence. It confronts the power and impotence of being with justice, arising from the demand. And yet, the contrast is not absolute, for the ought is the fulfillment of the is. *Justice is the true power of being.* In it the intention of the origin is fulfilled.

The result is that the two elements of human being and the two roots of political thought are related in such a way that the demand is superior to mere origin and justice is superior to the mere power of being. The question "Whither?" is of higher rank than the question "Whence?" *Only when the myth of origin is broken and its ambiguity disclosed may it enter into political thinking.* (SD 6; SE 19f.)

Neither Heidegger in *Being and Time* nor Tillich talk about the choices of an individual with regard to his or her private life but about decisions in the realm of the political. Sentences such as Tillich's on the I and the Thou and on justice do not exist anywhere in Heidegger. Already before Heidegger announced the return to his version of the pre-Socratics in public, Tillich had realized that in the political romanticism of the time—and that included Heidegger—the Greek myth of the origin was at work. He saw that it would be disastrous to renew this type of thinking in the context of a fully developed capitalist society and at the risk of excluding the Jewish-Christian tradition. Today, many American Heideggerians or post-Heideggerians talk about the «JewGreek,» after Derrida did so.[30] Often, it seems as though one can become a «JewGreek» only via carefully studying Heidegger in all his maneuvers, achievements, and for some interpreters also his failures. Tillich identified the «pure Greek» much earlier, and he put the «JewGreek» to work with regard to the political situation of his days in an admirably concrete manner.[31] Perhaps, some will say the demand of justice with which he confronted the «Greeks» interferes with the other in a metaphysical fashion. However, in hindsight one will agree that his diagnosis of the other was right. Besides, to let the other be the other is much more risky than—and therefore can never simply mean—just letting the other be the other.

# 5

# Heidegger after
# the Machtergreifung

## A. Geschlecht, Gemächte,
## and Technology in Heidegger

Heidegger's concept of politics as it is presented in *Being and Time* is not politically neutral. Rather, it is a brilliant summary of the politics of the revolutionary Right and as such is directed against the conservative Right, liberals, social democrats, communists, and socialists like Paul Tillich. Leaving aside the issue of repetition and construed according to the formula of the political used a lot nowadays, that is, in terms of «the other,» the different concepts of decision can be summarized as: decision or Ent-scheidung as Ausscheidung, the excretion of the other and the other within oneself, accompanied by the destructive turn against the other as in Heidegger; decision as the intensification of the antagonistic relationship to the other so that finally, in a classless society, the polemical relationship to the other can be overcome, as in Lukács's model; finally, as in Tillich, decision as the end of separation that allows one to make a covenant, an alliance, with the other, a covenant that acknowledges the other and the other within oneself and thus prevents oneself and the other from drifting apart, which would result in an Aus-scheidung of the other. The act of Ausscheidung of the other presupposes the Ausscheidung of one's own ordinary or inauthentic Dasein, the Ausscheidung of oneself as «they» and of Gesellschaft, in order to reconstitute oneself as a healthy and pure Gemeinschaft. For some this act was painful. However, the political Right managed to make many people think that they would eventually be rewarded for the act of Ausscheidung with the blessings of the revitalized Gemeinschaft.

The concept of fate or destiny, used by philosophers and politicians on the Right, drew its impact and power from its polemical character in regard to the Center and the Left. As long as there was the common enemy, that is, the liberals and the leftists, many people on the political Right felt no need to consider their actual and possible alliances with other groups on the political Right. Many rightists did not join the National Socialist Party. However, Heidegger had built into his brilliant summary of revolutionary rightist politics in *Being and Time* an option for the National Socialists, and there was nothing in *Being and Time* on which he could have based a critique of National Socialism. Heidegger joined the National Socialist Party in 1933—notably, on May 1, prior to 1933 the national holiday honoring the working class, an achievement of the Left.

Conservatives as well as National Socialists used the term «Opfer,» sacrifice, for the Ausscheidung. In the sections on Hitler and Scheler, I have already mentioned some occurrences of Opfer. In a speech, "The University in the National Socialist State," delivered on November 30, 1933, in Tübingen, Heidegger said:

> We of today are in the process of fighting to bring about the new reality. We are merely a transition, a willing sacrifice. As the warriors in this struggle we must be a hard race {ein hartes Geschlecht}, that cares for nothing of its own, that rests firmly on the foundation of the people and the nation {auf den Grund des Volkes}. The struggle is not about individuals and colleagues, nor about empty tokens and general measures. All genuine struggle bears some permanent mark of the image of the combatants and their work. Struggle alone reveals the true laws whereby things are brought into being. The struggle we seek is one in which we stand shoulder to shoulder, man to man.[1]

«Geschlecht» can be used in several ways. As Derrida remarks, depending on its contexts it can be translated by «sex, race, family, generation, lineage, species, genre/genus»[2] or «sex, race, species, genus, gender, stock, family, generation or genealogy, community.»[3] Nowadays the word «Geschlecht» is used in bureaucratic and administrative forms and documents, in science, and in words like «Geschlechtskrankheit» (venereal disease) or «Geschlechtsverkehr» (sexual intercourse). In these contexts, it is used as a descriptive term without any emotional connotations. Nevertheless, in other contexts it can be given dramatic flavor, as in the passage Derrida quotes from Fichte,[4] in the quote from Heidegger above, or in the statement a somewhat old-fashioned Heideggerian today might make, namely, that our Geschlecht is living in the closure of metaphysics. In this last sense all human beings alive in the present are the current Geschlecht. The term can also have emphatic connotations when used in the sense of lineage, family, dynasty as the Geschlechter in aristocratic societies («Agamemnon belongs to/is of the Geschlecht of the Atrides»). The emphasis is on the nobility of the Geschlecht whose members are noble because of the nobility of their blood. Of course, it can also mean race or Volk as, for instance, in the quote from Heidegger. Again, the emphasis is on the nobility and purity of the race or the Volk. «Hart» is «hard,» «hart wie Krupp-Stahl,» «as hard as steel made by Krupp,» as the Führer wanted German soldiers to be.

«Geschlecht» in the sense of race or Volk implies that there are several Geschlechter here on earth, and for right-wingers only some are noble and pure. Drawing upon this sense of Geschlecht, Heidegger could easily indicate in one word the imperialistic mission of the German Volk to act as the proxy of mankind. Empirically, the German Volk is one among several Geschlechter; because of its nobility, however, it can and must act «for» (BT 435; SZ 383) all the Geschlechter, that is, for the entire generation, for the human Geschlecht, that is, for all human beings. The passage wiederholt, repeats, section 74 of *Being and Time* and in particular the sentences on Erwiderung and Widerruf. The call in *Being and Time* demands that authentic Dasein erwidert the call of the Volk, that is, that Dasein hands itself down to the Volk in order to regain a stable identity in the face of the vacillations of ordinary and inauthentic Dasein. In the same way, in Heidegger's speech, Dasein is called upon to rest firmly on the Grund, foundation, of the people, for only the people provides Dasein with a stable identity. Already in *Being and Time* this requires that Dasein widerruft, scheidet aus, cancels, eliminates itself as the ordinary Dasein it has been so far. Thus in the speech Dasein no longer cares for anything «of its own,» that is, it sacrifices all what is its own. («Eigenem» [«its own»] is not «eigentlich,» «authentic,» as in «authentic» and «inauthentic,» but rather is that which belongs exclusively to oneself, one's individuality or, as in Eigentum,[5] one's private property one has to give up; that is, it is what belongs to inauthentic Dasein; authentic Dasein has to give up its individuality.) In *Being and Time,* having sacrificed its ordinary Dasein and having found its Grund in the Volk, Dasein is called upon to properly realize the Grund, the Volksgemeinschaft; that is, it is called upon to carry out the Widerruf of the Gesellschaft. Thus, in his speech, Heidegger says: «We of today are in the process of fighting to bring about the new reality.» In *Being and Time,* the realization of the Volksgemeinschaft is a rerealization of Gemeinschaft or of destiny. Destiny is not produced by the authentic Daseine. Rather, «only . . . in struggling {im Kampf} does the power of destiny become free» (BT 436; SZ 384). Similarly, in the speech struggle does not create the law of the new reality. Rather, «struggle alone *reveals* the true laws whereby things are brought into being» (italics mine, J. F.).[6] The struggle for the new reality requires the sacrifice of «us» as Gesellschaft as well as of those whom we ausscheiden, expel, from the Gemeinschaft. In the first step we expel our Jewish, liberal, or social democratic colleagues out of the university,[7] then out of Germany, «und morgen die ganze Welt» («and tomorrow we conquer the entire world,» as the song of the

National Socialists had it). We as well as those whom we ausscheiden might die in this battle. Thus, «we are but a transition, a sacrifice.» However, this sacrifice of our colleagues and maybe also of ourselves is a rightful claim the Volk has on all of us. For, «the battle is not about persons or colleagues.» Therefore persons and colleagues must be sacrificed if need be. Furthermore, we gain something, we gain on a large scale what bourgeois subjects enjoyed only in a fallen version in the privacy of their chambres séparees, that is, the public intimacy of «heart to heart, man to man» as the fulfillment of the promise of Gemeinschaft.

The speech, "The University in the National Socialist State," was Heidegger's last public speech outside of Freiburg under the National Socialist regime.[8] At the time, he was already somewhat at odds with the empirical realities of National Socialism, though he remained a National Socialist and faithful to Hitler (MH 158). After the war, Heidegger came to regard politics and action as practiced in the kairos of the twenties and the thirties as metaphysical. He considered the cause he fought for as well as its consequences—namely, Auschwitz—as sent by Geschick and Gestell, destiny and enframing, for which individuals are not responsible,[9] and promoted a post-metaphysical notion of praxis, namely, Gelassenheit. In several of his texts of that time, he used another word with the notorious prefix «ge-» whose meanings overlap with those of the word «Geschlecht.» Concerning sex and gender, the word «Geschlecht» often means specifically the male or female sex organ, the vagina or the penis.[10] Another word for the male Geschlecht, the male sex organ, is das Gemächte, nowadays an old-fashioned term. Nonetheless, even in 1970 Marg renders «μήδεα» in lines 180 and 188 of Hesiod's *Theogony*—that is, the genitals of Ouranos, which his son, Chronos, cuts off and throws into the sea, out of the foam of which Aphrodite emerges—as «Gemächte.»[11] In 1939, in his essay on Aristotle's notion of nature, Heidegger uses «das Gemächte» as a technical term and as his translation of the Greek word ποιούμενον. He comments on Aristotle's *Physics*, 192 b 16–20:

> In opposition to beings like "plants," animals, earth, and air, Aristotle now sets beings like bedsteads, robes, shields, wagons, ships, and houses. The former are "growing things" ["*Gewächse*"] in the same broad sense that we use in speaking of a "field under growth." The latter are "artifacts" (ποιούμενα), in German, *Gemächte,* although this last term must be stripped of any derogatory connotations.[12]

Probably Heidegger arrived at this term in three steps. He begins, so to speak, here on earth, within «a 'here' and a 'yonder'» to which each «'there' {Da}» points (BT 171; SZ 132f.). Thereupon, several individual cases of these «'here'» and «'yonder'» allow for some, so to speak, floating generality. In the third step, Heidegger claims that, as death in *Being and Time,* something else «*enters into*» (BT 292; «*in dieses hereinsteht,*» SZ 248; literally «stands into») this floating generality. The verb «machen» (to make, to do, to produce, to fix, to manage, to arrange, to perform, to finish) is a word of everyday language used especially when the action performed does not need to be specified. I have ordered a chair at a carpenter's shop, or I have taken a jacket to a tailor for mending. When I go to pick it up, however, the person says: «I have es not yet fertig gemacht, finished it.» Or, the person might say, «It is still in der Mache, in the making.»[13] In an art gallery someone admires a canvas. Proudly, I point to myself and say: «I have gemacht it.» Accused of having produced this or that mess, I point to someone else and to the mess and exclaim: «Der da hat das (da) gemacht!» (That da [-sein over there] has done this [mess over there]!). Or, babies or children «machen Pipi,» or «machen sich in die Hose,» that is, urinate or defecate into their pants. As one can already see from these examples, the word—or at least the noun, das Gemachte, or das Machwerk—has a flavor of craftsmanship. It belongs, as it were, to the ordinary world «in the mode of its genuineness» (BT 189; «im Modus seiner Echtheit,» SZ 148), the world of «preparing, putting to rights, repairing, improving, rounding-out» (BT 189; SZ 148) where we see things «as a table, a door, a carriage, or a bridge» (BT 189; SZ 149); it belongs to our human-all-too-human everyday affairs in which we proudly present or tenderly cover up «das nackte Vorhandene» (SZ 150; «some naked thing,» BT 190), or try to blame someone else for it. Still, as the most general term it can be used in almost any situation to point to the cause of something. In this sense Heidegger says in "The Question Concerning Technology": «The fact that the real has been showing itself in the light of Ideas ever since the time of Plato, Plato did not bring about {hat nicht Platon gemacht}. The thinker only *responded* to what *addressed* itself to him {Der Denker hat nur dem *entsprochen,* was sich ihm *zusprach*}» (BW 299; VA 21, italics mine, J. F.).[14]

Machen is a verb («I mache something»), gemacht is the perfect participle, used both in the active and passive voice: «I have gemacht it,» and «The table is gemacht.» The participle can be made into a noun: «The table is a Gemachtes.» Or, as Hegel says, the constitution of a state should not be regarded as «ein Gemachtes.»[15] Thus, we have a general noun that can be used for everything produced by human beings, for the corresponding comportment of human beings, and maybe also for what brings about this comportment. However, Heidegger could not leave it at das Gemachte, for as a general term in the theory of epochs of Being the word is just too naked and sober. If it has a flavor, it is by no means the entsprechende for the philosopher of destining history of Being. Also, it might have affirmed the illusion that we are the author of what brings about the comportment in which we treat everything as a Gemachte or as raw material for a Zu-Machendes. Thus, Heidegger crowned das Gemachte with diacritical marks (Umlaut) and asks us to abstract from its derogatory usage. «Das Gemächte» is indeed a very old and by now outdated expression for what a person or nature has produced or for what God has created. Crowned by the Umlaut, in Heidegger Gemächte is supposed to acquire some sort of Güte.[16] Heidegger uses the term «Gemächte» for all products of human beings from Plato and Aristotle onward up to the present day and, at the same time, points out a decisive difference between modern products and Gemächte in Aristotle.

There is a remarkable shift in his basic vocabulary from the essay on Aristotle to "The Question Concerning Technology." In the essay on Aristotle, Heidegger uses as the common term for natural products and technical products—that is, as the common term for «Gemächte» and «Gewächse» (see the quote above)—«Herstellung» or «Herstellen.» Physis is «das Sich—aus sich her, auf sich zu—Herstellen» (WM 367; «production of itself from out of itself unto itself»).[17] This allows for the term «Gestellung.» In quite an unusual maneuver, Heidegger translates Aristotle's μορφή with «Gestellung in das Aussehen» and comments:

> By translating μορφή as placing into the appearance {Gestellung in das Aussehen}, we mean to express chiefly two things which are equal in the Greek word but thoroughly lacking in our word "form." First, placing into the appearance is a mode of becoming present, οὐσία. Μορφή is not an *ontic* property present in matter, but a mode of *Being*. Secondly, "placing into the appearance" is being-moved, κίνησις, which "moment" is radically lacking in the concept of form.[18]

Thus, a «Gewächs» is the result of a «Herstellung» as a «Gestellung.» However, a «Gemächte» is the result of a «Herstellung» as a «Machen.» Still, according to Heidegger, there is a difference between human products at Aristotle's time and in modernity. Heidegger maintains that Aristotle wrote lines 192 b 23–27 «in order to avoid misunderstanding φύσις as a kind of *self-producing* and the φύσει ὄντα merely as a special kind of artifact {eine besondere Art von Gemächten}.»[19] In a rather unusual interpretation of these lines Heidegger maintains that, according to Aristotle, «τέχνη can only cooperate with φύσις, can more or less expedite the cure; but as τέχνη it can never replace φύσις and in its stead become itself the ἀρχή of *health* as such.»[20] The latter, however, is the notion of technic in modernity: «That could only happen if life as such were to become a "technically" producible artifact {"technisch" herstellbaren Gemächte} . . . Sometimes it seems as if modern man rushes headlong towards this goal of *producing himself technologically.*»[21]

From this perspective of modern man, the «Gewächse» in ancient Greece are misinterpreted. For, as Heidegger argues, «the idea of "organism" and of the "organic" is a purely modern, mechanistic-technological concept according to which "growing things" are interpreted as artifacts that make themselves {sich selbst machendes Gemächte}.»[22] In "The Question Concerning Technology," however, Heidegger calls production in nature and technology no

longer «Herstellung,» but rather «Hervorbringen.» Physis is the «Her-vor-
bringen» («bringing-forth») that has the «Aufbruch des Her-vor-bringens»
(«bursting open belonging to bringing-forth») in itself, whereas technology is
the «Hervorbringen» which does not have the «Aufbruch seines Hervorbrin-
gens» in itself (VA 15; BW 293). Surprisingly enough, however, both terms
for physis in the essay on Aristotle, «Herstellung» as well as «Gestellung,» are
used in "The Question Concerning Technology" for technology. «Her-stellen»
or «Darstellen» («producing and presenting») is used for the Greek poiesis (VA
24; BW 303). «Gestellung,» however, is stripped of its suffix «-ung» and
becomes the technical term for modern technology, «Ge-stell» («enframing»)
(VA 23; 301). Thus, «Gemächte» is no longer a term for artifacts in Aristotle
nor for the products of modern technology. Consequently, «das Gemächte» is
used only three times, and always in the negative.[23]

One reason for these changes is probably that «Her-stellen» and «be-
stellen» («Bestand,» «Gestell») allowed Heidegger to distinguish between
Greek poiesis and modern technology also in his terminology. Furthermore,
Hiroshima, Dresden, and Auschwitz happened after he wrote the essay on
nature in Aristotle. Since in "The Question Concerning Technology" he talks
in an oblique way about the «skeleton{s}» (BW 301; «Knochengerippe,» VA
23) in Auschwitz, and how to forget about them,[24] it would be somewhat inde-
cent to use a word for the male sex organ too frequently. In the section on historicality in *Being and Time,* Heidegger characterized authentic Dasein as the
Dasein that—in contrast to inauthentic Dasein—is able to relate itself properly
to its death as well to its birth and thus to the Volksgemeinschaft of the Germans. "The Question Concerning Technology" was delivered as a speech in
Munich in 1953 and published in *Vorträge und Aufsätze* in 1954. It might have
embarrassed some listeners and readers if the two cornerstones of *Being and
Time,* death and birth, had recurred in that speech as the skeletons in Auschwitz
together with the frequent usage of a word for the male sex organ.

As far as I know, studies of Heidegger's use of terms for sex organs have
not yet addressed the passages I have discussed here. Those who maintain
that Western metaphysics is phallocentric might find further support in Heidegger's use of the noun «Gemächte.» Furthermore, the passage on the «harte
Geschlecht» seems to indicate that crucial motifs of the Heidegger of *Being
and Time* have remained the same in his thinking after the Machtergreifung,
as I will explain in the next section.

## B. Heidegger's *An Introduction to Metaphysics*

Besides Rilke and Nietzsche, Hölderlin was the author whose poems and
writings educated German soldiers in World War I, and also later in World
War II, carried with them in their «Tornister» (knapsack) when they went to
war. In his *Mein Kampf,* Hitler had left no doubt that, as to foreign affairs,

his top priority or Lebensaufgabe was to conquer Russia by war (MKe 641ff.; MK 726ff.), and he had maintained that only six years of National Socialist rule would suffice to make the German Volk ready for war (MKe 633; MK 716). In the year after the Machtergreifung, in the winter semester of 1934–35, Heidegger gave a lecture course on Hölderlin's hymns "Germanien" (the German word for the Latin word for Germany, Germania) and "Der Rhein" (The [river] Rhine), in which he also interpreted two lines of an unfinished poem by Hölderlin,

> Seit ein Gespräch wir sind
> Und hören können voneinander. (HH 71)

It is a subclause and runs, literally translated: «Since we have become a conversation and are able to hear from (of) each other.»[25] In Heideggerian terms, one might say that, in 1933, Being took over. Verfallen, taken in by the beings, the ordinary and inauthentic Daseine ignored or covered up Being and stuck to their Gesellschaft. However, Being, Gemeinschaft, raised its voice and demanded that Gesellschaft be canceled so that Being, Gemeinschaft, could be properly manifested. In 1933 Being was successful. Heidegger adds to Hölderlin's subclause what he thinks was the main clause Hölderlin intended and then comments on the two lines as follows:

> Since we are a conversation, we are placed into and at the mercy of the being as it reveals itself {ausgesetzt in das sich eröffnende Seiende}; it is only since then that the Being {Sein} of the being as such can encounter and determine us {uns begegnen und bestimmen}. (HH 72)[26]

The inauthentic Daseine wanted to deny and cover up Being in order to avoid being taken over and determined by Being. Now Being reveals itself as it is in reality, no longer covered up and distorted by the inauthentic Daseine. In this moment, we realize that it is not we who determine ourselves. Rather, we give up the pretense of autonomy and expose ourselves to, open ourselves for, or submit ourselves to, the Being of the beings as such, which catches hold of us and determines us. We realize that only now can we relate to the other authentically. Heidegger goes on:

> The fact, however, that the being as to its Being {das Seiende . . . in seinem Sein} is unconcealed in advance for each of us, is the presupposition for being able to hear from the other something, that is, something about some being, whether this being is what we are not—that is, nature—or whether it is what we ourselves are—that is, history. (HH 72)

Being in Heidegger has priority over the beings that Being gives. The proponents of Gemeinschaft maintained that, prior to being in Gesellschaft, human beings had been in Gemeinschaft and that the individuals in Gesellschaft regarded the latter as a mere means to pursue their selfish interests and, for that very reason, were not really happy, even if they accumulated a fortune. For, in reality Gemeinschaft founded the individuals, and it was only Gemeinschaft that gave them identity and rewarding feelings about themselves, the others, and the Gemeinschaft. Heidegger continues:

> The ability to hear by no means produces the relation of the one to the other, that is, the Gemeinschaft. Rather, the ability to hear presupposes the Gemeinschaft. This primordial {ursprüngliche} Gemeinschaft by no means originates through entering into a relationship; that is how Gesellschaft originates. Rather, Gemeinschaft *is* because of the preceding bond, a bond that binds *each individual* to that which keeps bound and determines each individual in a superelevating manner {das, was jeden Einzelnen überhöhend bindet und bestimmt}. (HH 72)[27]

Authentic belonging-to-one-another results neither from the Aristotelian natural inclination toward society nor from contracts, as, for instance, in liberalism. Heidegger considered it convenient to give an example. For German right-wingers after World War I, the paradigmatic Gemeinschaft were the heroes of Langemarck. As I've pointed out in the sections on Hitler and Scheler, right-wingers thought the war would surely be lost if it was approached with the attitudes of Gesellschaft. When faced with war, Gesellschaft evaporates, and Gemeinschaft raises its voice. War is the ultimate rationale, the Grund or ground, of Gemeinschaft. Fully in line with that sort of reasoning, Heidegger continues:

> That which neither the individual by itself nor the Gemeinschaft as such is, that must become manifest. The comradeship of the frontline soldiers was grounded neither in the fact that they had to gather together with other humans because they needed them and could find them only at other places {daß man sich zusammenfinden mußte, weil andere Menschen, denen man fern war, fehlten}, nor in agreeing upon a shared enthusiasm {daß man sich auf eine gemeinsame Begeisterung erst verabredete}. Rather, at bottom it is grounded only in the fact that the nearness of death as a sacrifice placed each one in advance into the same nullity, so that this latter became the source of the unconditional belonging-to-each-other. (HH 72f.)

It is not the bargaining of social democrats and liberals in labor unions and in parliament that leads to authentic belonging-to-each-other. This is, according to Heidegger, what the Philistines have to learn:

> It is precisely death—the death each human being has to die for himself and which singularizes each individual to the utmost extent—it is precisely death and the willingness of its sacrifice {= the willingness to offer one's own death as a sacrifice} that first and foremost and beforehand creates the site of Gemeinschaft, from which comradeship emerges {entspringt}. Thus, does comradeship grow {entspringt} out of Angst? No and yes. No, if one, like the Philistine, understands

by Angst only the helpless quivering of a panicky cowardice. Yes, if Angst is understood as a metaphysical nearness to the unconditional, a nearness that is given as a gift only to the highest self-sufficiency and readiness. If we do not compel powers into our Dasein that, like death as a free sacrifice, bind and singularize unconditionally—that is, powers that catch hold of {angreifen} each individual at the root of its Dasein and that, like death as a free sacrifice, stand deeply and wholly in an authentic knowing—then no 'comradeship' will emerge. In that case, the result will at best be a modified form of Gesellschaft. (HH 73)[28]

One sees that it is, so to speak, «the same old story» as in *Being and Time*. In 1926, Heidegger shied away from calling the actors by their proper names. He left out the name of the foe, and he wrote «der Gemeinschaft, des Volkes» (SZ 384; «of the community, of {the} people,» BT 436). The latter phrase allowed him to use as well as to avoid the blunt word «Volksgemeinschaft» and at the same time be understood by philosophers, that is, by people who are not Denker, but just Verstandesdenker, and who proceed from the genus to the species. After 1933, Heidegger could use the proper names, for everyone knew what he was talking about anyway, and he could leave out the Volk of the Volksgemeinschaft. Indeed, the German Volksgemeinschaft was not just one species among several others; it was the proper manifestation and agent of Being, which would clean up the remaining Gesellschaften in Europe and, as the song had it, «tomorrow {in} the entire world.» Heidegger's last two sentences in the above-quoted passage are a warning. No one must have recourse to «the endless multiplicity of possibilities . . . of comfortableness, shirking, and taking things lightly» (BT 435; «Behagens, Leichtnehmens, Sichdrückens,» SZ 384), for «each individual» is in charge. However, at the same time Heidegger's sentences might express some doubts as to whether «we» were fast enough or even whether «we» were still «mit beiden Beinen,» with both legs, on the authentic track.

The lecture course on Hölderlin took place in winter 1934–35. In the next semester, in the summer of 1935, Heidegger gave the lecture course *An Introduction to Metaphysics*. Having read the passage on erwidert in *Being and Time,* the readers might recall the following passage:

It is absolutely correct and proper to say that "You can't do anything with philosophy." It is only wrong to suppose that this is the last word in philosophy. For the rejoinder imposes itself: granted that we cannot do anything with philosophy, might not philosophy, if we concern ourselves with it, do something *with us*? So much for what philosophy is not. (IM 12; EM 9)

This is an unambiguous instance of what in chapter 1, sections B and D, I referred to as an Erwiderung in the dative, namely, someone proposes something, and I contradict, or object to him. Thus, the English reader might expect that the translator has rendered the German word «Erwiderung» through the English term «rejoinder.» However, the reader might also become suspicious, since this rejoinder is very impressive, or at least says something, whereas the rejoinder in *Being and Time* didn't say anything at all. The reader would be right, for the German text has, not «Erwiderung,» but rather «Gegenfrage» («Es kommt nämlich noch ein kleiner Nachtrag in der Gestalt einer Gegenfrage,» EM 9). The corresponding verb to «Gegenfrage,» or «Entgegnung,» is «entgegnen.» «Gegenfrage,» «Entgegnung,» and «entgegnen» are unambiguous formulations of what I referred to as «erwidern» in the dative, and they can also serve as «erwidern» in the accusative in the sense of fighting back. Thus, instead of the ambiguous «erwidert» Heidegger could have used «entgegnen» if he had wanted to indicate a reciprocative rejoinder in Guignon's, the translators', or Birmingham's sense. Furthermore, as mentioned, «erwidert» in the dative and also, to some degree, «erwidert» in the sense of «fighting back» would have required Heidegger to tell the readers what the authentic Dasein erwidert.[29] As was indicated above, he could have also used «Auseinandersetzung» or «auseinandersetzen» or «Widerspruch» or «widersprechen» if he had wanted to say what Guignon and Birmingham take him to say.[30] Since he did not use any of these expressions, he must have meant his «erwidert» as subjugation.[31] In the same context as the first passage quoted above, Heidegger writes:

> Philosophy is essentially untimely because it is one of those few things that can never find an immediate echo {Widerklang} in the present *and that must never find such an echo* {und auch nie finden zu dürfen}. When such an echo {solches} seems to occur, when a philosophy becomes fashionable, either it is no real philosophy or it has been misinterpreted and misused for ephemeral and extraneous purposes. . . . But what is useless can still, *and even more than ever* {und erst recht}, be a force, perhaps the only real force. What has no immediate echo {Widerklang} in everyday life can be intimately bound up {im innigsten Einklang stehen} with a nation's {eines Volkes} profound {eigentlichen} historical development, and can even anticipate it {dessen Vorklang}. What is untimely will have its own times. This is true of philosophy. (IM 8; EM 6f.; the words in italics have been left out in the English translation, J. F.)

The phrase «is one of those few things that» is a somewhat colorless translation of Heidegger's phrase «sie zu jenen wenigen Dingen gehört, deren Schicksal es bleibt» («belongs to those very few things whose fate it remains»). «Echo,» «intimately bound up,» and «anticipate» are translations of Heidegger's sequence of «Widerklang,» «Anklang,» and «Vorklang»:

> Die Philosophie ist wesenhaft unzeitgemäß, weil sie zu jenen wenigen Dingen gehört, deren Schicksal es bleibt, nie einen unmittelbaren *Wider-klang* {echo} in ihrem jeweiligen Heute finden zu können und auch nie finden zu dürfen. Wo solches scheinbar eintritt, wo eine Philosophie Mode wird, da ist entweder keine

wirkliche Philosophie oder diese wird mißdeutet und nach irgendwelchen ihr fremden Absichten für Tagesbedürfnisse vernutzt. ... Aber, was nutzlos ist, kann doch und erst recht eine Macht sein. Was den unmittelbaren *Wider-klang* {*echo*} in der Alltäglichkeit nicht kennt, kann mit dem eigentlichen Geschehen in der Geschichte eines Volkes *im innigsten Ein-klang* stehen {*intimately bound up*}. Es kann sogar dessen *Vor-klang* {*anticipate*} sein. (EM 6f.; italics and hyphens mine, J. F.)

This sequence of «Widerklang,» «Einklang,» and «Vorklang» is brilliant. All three nouns have as their root the noun «Klang,» sound. «Wider» in «Widerklang» is, pace Birmingham, not «in opposition to,» but rather, as in «I erwidere/return a favor,» «back,» or «re-»; that is, «Widerklang» is «resonance» or, as the translator rightly puts it, «echo.» «Ein» in «Einklang» is «in accord with»; thus, «Einklang» is «unison,» «accord,» or «harmony.» «Vor» in «Vorklang» has a temporal sense; thus, «Vorklang» is an anticipation in the sense that there is some so far unknown event in the future that makes itself felt somehow in the present for those who are open to perceive this, that is, philosophy, or exclusively Heidegger himself who thus becomes the «Vorklang» of this futural event. In German, one expects words like these in two kinds of situations. One uses them in descriptions of very subtle, often erotic, situations in which one communicates indirectly.[32] Or, imagine someone sitting pensively, melancholic, or in pangs of love on some hill not too far away from a village, and the bells of the church begin to ring. He listens to them and, duplicating or echoing, erwidernd in the accusative, their Klang, he opens himself to them, and his thoughts and feelings follow the sounds. (He might refer to his state after the bells have actually stopped ringing by using another compound noun with «Klang»: «Even several hours later, I felt the Nachklang, echo, of the bells in me.») In Heidegger, however, these words receive a slightly tragic as well as defiant tone. As one knows, the lecture course *An Introduction to Metaphysics* was delivered in 1935, that is, shortly after Heidegger had resigned from the rectorate, and after he had declared in a speech broadcast on radio why he would not go to Berlin but rather stay in the provinces.[33]

In 1935 Heidegger still believed in Hitler and National Socialism as the notorious sentence claiming «the inner truth and greatness of this movement» (IM 199; EM 152) in *An Introduction* shows.[34] However, the truth of National Socialism has become an «inner» one; that is, it seems the empirical reality of National Socialism no longer counts as a proper realization of the Volk and National Socialism. In 1926 and subsequent years, the philosopher had thought that the «fate» allotted by «destiny» to philosophy was to bring about, or to help to bring about, the practical comeback of the Volk. However, something must have gone wrong. Thus, through the mouth of its only incarnation philosophy declares that all those who thought that philosophy had become practical had simply misunderstood philosophy, and philosophy also declares that it is its fate never to find an immediate echo. Nevertheless, the philosopher remains the one with privileged access to the authentic historizing of the Volk, and he is the only one, except perhaps for the Führer. Thus, the expressionistic and actionistic vocabulary of «Kampf,» «hörig,»[35] «erwidern,» and «Widerruf» of *Being and Time* is replaced with the bucolic Innerlichkeit, inwardness, of «Anklang,» «Einklang,» and «Vorklang» (in which the «Vorklang» no longer insists on the possibility of immediate realization and thus, as in contrast to «Vorlaufen zum Tode,» can be properly translated as «anticipate»).

Something else, however, has not changed. Imagine if Heidegger had published section 74 of *Being and Time* in a journal and had written an abstract. It might have looked like the following:

> **Heritage** in section 74 stands in the closest connection with *krinein,* to separate, in the sense of de-cide in collecting toward the **authentic historizing of the German Volk.** Erwiderung and Widerruf are the foundation and proof of the pursuit of **the Volk as authentic community** and the battle against **liberal and democratic Gesellschaft.** The meaning of *krinein* includes to pick out, to favor, to set a measure that will determine rank.

Replace the phrases in bold type with «*logos,*» «the collectedness of being {Sein},» «Selection,» «being,» and «appearance,» respectively, and you have Heidegger's summary of his interpretation of Parmenides in *An Introduction to Metaphysics:*

> *Logos* here stands in the closest connection with *krinein,* to separate [Scheiden] in the sense of de-cide [Ent-scheiden] in collecting toward the collectedness of being. Selection [das *auslesende* "Lesen"] is the foundation and proof of the pursuit of being and the battle against appearance. The meaning of *krinein* includes to pick out {auslesen}, to favor, to set a measure that will determine rank. (IM 174; EM 133; as in the next quotation italics with «auslesende» mine, J. F.)

This sentence reads in German: «Λόγος steht hier im engsten Verband mit κρίνειν, dem Scheiden als Ent-scheiden im Vollzug der Sammlung auf die Gesammeltheit des Seins. Das *auslesende* "Lesen" begründet und trägt den Verfolg des Seins und die Abwehr des Scheins. In der Bedeutung des κρίνειν schwingt mit: auslesen, abheben, die rangbestimmende Maßgabe» (EM 133).[36]

In this summarizing passage key terms of *Being and Time,* «Ent-scheiden» («de-cision»), «Entschlossenheit,» («resoluteness») occur alongside items from the National Socialist vocabulary, such as «Auslese» («selection» or «pick out» as in «rassische Auslese,» «racial selection»). At the same time, in the text Heidegger forcefully promotes Sammlung, sammeln (gathering, to gather) to a key term of his later philosophy. The passage precisely «repeats» the passage on erwidert and Widerruf in *Being and Time,* section 74. We live in a fallen state of mixture. The call of the Volksgemeinschaft calls us back («erwidern») and calls upon us to purify the mixture, that is, to throw out the impure and alien elements and to restore the pure Gemeinschaft («erwidern» and «Widerruf»). In the passage from *An Introduction to Metaphysics,* it is especially the phrase «das auslesende "Lesen"» («selection») that carries the required restoration of the pure Gemeinschaft by throwing out the alien elements. The phrase «das auslesende "Lesen"» («selection») specifies the phrases «de-cide» («Ent-scheiden») and «collecting» («Sammlung»). By this, «gathering» in Heidegger follows the same logic as «gathering» in National Socialism. Within National Socialism, the inconspicuous everyday word «sammeln» all of a sudden gained a prominent place in the political vocabulary in precisely the sense in which Heidegger uses it in the above-quoted passage from *An Introduction to Metaphysics.* To be sure, the notions Versammlungen, Sammlungen, and Sammlungsbewegungen, meetings and merger movements (of political parties or religious groups), were used already before the emergence of National Socialism. However, from 1933 on the word «sammeln» acquired a new sense.

The history of the Sammlungsbewegung National Socialism prior to its final defeat consisted of three stages. First, the members of the party sammelten sich selbst, assembled by leaving the city, the Weimar Republic, to congregate outside of it or by forming their own city within the city. This is «to separate in the sense of de-cide in collecting toward the collectedness of being» (IM 174; EM 133). In doing so, they cleanse themselves of the unhealthy mixtures and corruption they believed to be prevalent in the city. They cleanse themselves of any trace of Gesellschaft, liberalism, social democracy, and Jewishness in themselves. From their vantage point, the city was afflicted with alien elements from which it had to be purged so that its purity might be restored. In other words, the city was in a state of unhealthy mixtures of Being and Non-Being, and the philosophical term for this usually is «Schein» (EM 133; «appearance,» IM 174). That first act was an Auslese, a separation, a selection, a de-cision, and the party members were the subjects as well as the objects of this act. They de-cided themselves from the city by leaving it and forming their party. The authentic Daseine are «followers {Hörige}» (IM 129; EM 99)[37] of Being. They only collect themselves because they listen to Being's commands. Thus the first act is the moment in which Being collects itself («in collecting toward the collectedness of being»). The phrase «in collecting toward the collectedness of being» corresponds to the phrase «the handing down of a heritage constitutes itself in resoluteness» (BT 435; SZ 383f.), which I discussed in section C of chapter 2. In the first act, the authentic Daseine erwidern the call of Being; Being is no longer covered up; rather it begins to be active and to be the main actor in the second and third act in which the authentic Daseine widerrufen, cancel, Gesellschaft. In the second act the party members took over the city, the so-called Machtübernahme. In the third act, they realized the program they had developed in the first act, namely, the removal of those whom they have declared to be the alien, unhealthy elements from which the city had to be cleansed. They remove the alien elements and their world, Gesellschaft, to restore a pure Gemeinschaft. Especially this third act is a selection, a de-cision. The party members remain the subjects of this decision; however, the object has changed. The objects of this decision are now those whom the party members have designated as the foe of the Volk and who must be ausgelesen, selected, and eliminated.

One might say not only the first sentence in the passage on logos in *An Introduction,* but also the second and the third sentences—the ones with «selection» and «to pick out»—are analogous at most to what I described as the first step of the history of National Socialism. To be sure, it might not be completely impossible for an ingenious exegete of Heidegger to refer the second and the third sentences to the first step. In this way, he might reduce all three sentences to the first step and leave out the Machtübernahme and the disavowal of Gesellschaft and of the alien elements. However, there is nothing that can prevent one from referring the second and third sentences to the second and the third step. In fact, if one looks at the German expressions Heidegger uses, one is strongly moved and encouraged—if not in fact forced—to refer them to the third step. Heidegger employed a widely used and well-known expression that was also part of the official vocabulary of the National Socialists. What is translated by «selection,» reads in German: «auslesende "Lesen".» While in relation to texts and writing lesen means «to read,» in the context of agriculture and cooking, for instance, «Lese» and «lesen» refer to the gathering of crops and beans. In this process, «lesend,» one stands «in» the «"Lese[n]"» (EM 133; «Selection,» IM 174), or «in der Sammlung,» as Heidegger put it on the preceding page («Der Mensch ist als der im Logos, in der Sammlung, Stehende und Tätige: der Sammler,» EM 131f.; «Standing and active in logos, which is ingathering, man is the gatherer,» IM 172). Harvesting, however, entails that one will «die Spreu vom Weizen trennen» («separate the chaff from the wheat»), as a well-known saying puts it. Applied to the sorting of beans, the Bohnen-Lese, this saying became «die schlechten ins Kröpfchen, die guten ins Töpfchen,» i.e., the good beans are gathered in the cooking pot («Töpfchen») and the bad ones are «ausgelesen,» «aussortiert,» sorted out and thrown into the trash («Kröpfchen»).[38] Thus, by adding «auslesende» to «"Lese",» Heidegger just makes what is implied in «Lese» explicit. This amounts to no less than the supposed Einklang (unison) between everyday discourse, especially the one of the peasants, and that of the National Socialist Party. Since sammeln, to gather, is «auslesende "Lese",» «auslesende» simply expresses what is clearly implied in the very act of gathering, namely, a sorting out and elimination. Once the party members leave the city and regain their purity, they come back, take over the city, and purify the mixtures; that is, they redeem and restore the originally pure ones by pushing the aliens out of the city. From 1933 on, all human beings, first in Germany and later in all of Europe, became the object of this auslesende Lese, of this gathering and sorting.

From the very beginning of their reign, the National Socialists set up sites where aliens were gathered. One did not use the German «sammeln» to designate these sites but rather a related word of Latin derivation, namely, «konzentrieren,» «Konzentrationslager» (concentrate, focus, «concentration camps»), konzentrieren being the most intense form of sammeln. The German word «sammeln» was used from the beginning of the mass deportations. «Sammelstelle,» «Sammelplatz,» or «Sammellager» («collecting point, collecting camp») designated the sites in the villages and cities where the Jews had «sich einzufinden» (the bureaucratic word for «to appear, to assemble at a certain time and a certain place») in order then to be pushed into the trains to Auschwitz and the other concentration camps. As objects of the Lese, they were forced to move from the village to the Sammelplatz at the brink of the village, that is, they were forced to move to and gather at the railway station, made to enter the trains, and to move along the tracks until the final gathering on the Verlade-Brücke in Auschwitz.[39]

Heidegger's interpretation of logos in *An Introduction to Metaphysics* is identical with the activities called for in the sentences with «erwidert» and «Widerruf» in *Being and Time*. Thus it might be that eigentlich, in truth, Heidegger's pre-Socratics and his history of Being are the characters of *Being and Time*, sections 72–77, transposed under new names onto the broader stage of the history of Being. They are, so to speak, the Führer's «new clothes.» Though it is not possible to pursue this in more detail in this book and though there are many, more or less different, Heideggers after the Kehre, I want to address at least briefly one later Heidegger, the one Caputo developed in his *Heidegger and Aquinas*, published in 1982, before he began his project of *Demythologizing Heidegger* in the second half of the eighties.

The carpenter in his workshop in Division One of *Being and Time* (BT 95ff.; SZ 66ff.) is not yet in the «downward plunge,» for he is in the ordinary world «in the mode of its genuineness» (BT 189; SZ 148). However, he is already on the road «Falling,» which will lead into the downward plunge. Similarly, we peregrinatores, as Augustine has called us—Heidegger might say that the language of the «they» translates this with «tourists»—are, to use one of Heidegger's pet expressions, immer schon, always already, on the road that leads into the excess of idle talk, curiosity, and ambiguity of the ordinary and inauthentic Daseine (BT 210ff.; SZ 167ff.). As is known, Thomas Aquinas struggled so hard to reconcile all the different paths on the broad road «Falling.» Ordinary Dasein is not aware that it is no longer at the beginning. It takes its falling or downward plunge as given traditions, and doesn't reflect on the fact that they are a fallen-away version of the real beginning that nonetheless is somehow responsible for the falling and the downward plunge and, thus, holds the Daseine even as they are moving away from it. Similarly, Thomas Aquinas «does not put the tradition itself into question; . . . He thinks within the tradition without thinking the tradition as precisely what is to be thought, that is, as a Being-process in which Being is withdrawn precisely insofar as it gives itself.»[40] Thus, as ordinary Dasein does not recognize that it is caught up on the road «Falling,» Thomas Aquinas «is caught up in the historical sweep of the "it gives" without experiencing the giving itself which is at work in Scholasticism, without experiencing Scholasticism as a constellation of meaning which itself has been made possible on deeper—alethiological—grounds. Thomas stands within the clearing without thinking the clearing as such.»[41]

Impatient Daseine on the road and a

follower of St. Thomas might object at this point that not every age of Being is equally an oblivion, not every period of thought is equally an "epoch" of withdrawal. For even though the "It" which gives remained behind, Being as presence was bestowed upon the early Greek thinkers with a primal and undistorted originality. And if such a gift has been granted to the early Greeks, who were no more historically minded than St. Thomas, why not for Thomas too? Why cannot Thomas have a status somewhat like Parmenides who thought Being in its truth as presencing, even though the "It" which "gives" was concealed from him?[42]

However, first of all, Dasein on the road is quite obviously not at the beginning. In other words, there are «important differences between the primal bestowal of Being as presence in the early Greeks and the metaphysics of *esse.*»[43] Second, the time is not yet ripe, the Bocksgesang has not yet arisen to break out of Gesellschaft, or «to break the spell of metaphysics.»[44] Thus, Thomas Aquinas «stands at neither end (terminus, ἔσχατον) of the tradition, but precisely, as a "medieval," in the middle.»[45]

The authentic Dasein realizes that Volk is not to be reified. In the beginning, Volk is a fluid something, and later on Volk is somehow responsible for the move away from itself that nonetheless remains within itself. Authentic Dasein begins from within ordinary Dasein and sees through the activities by means of which ordinary Dasein forgets that it is in the downward plunge as a forgetfulness of the origin. Thus, authentic Dasein looks through the forgetting of a forgetting. Similarly, there is a double Vergessenheit, «oblivion *simpliciter* or the oblivion of that oblivion, concealment *simpliciter* or the concealment of that concealment.»[46] The latter is Gesellschaft, or «metaphysics, and metaphysics can be overcome»[47] only at the end of the downward plunge where either everything falls apart and into chaos, socialism or anarchy, or the origin as such reenters the stage. It is only here that the Bocksgesang arises and the crisis begins. In this crisis, the Daseine become responsible for their becoming authentic or inauthentic and for the future of the world. Those capable of listening will become authentic. Thus, one can

determine where the element of human "responsibility" enters into Heidegger's thought. It has not always been possible to overcome metaphysics, to spot the withdrawal *as* a withdrawal. For as long as thought was caught up within the sweep of the tradition and what it passed along, *in medias res*, the thinker was inevitably drawn along with it. But now, in these days, we live *in extremis*, in the extreme radicalization of this withdrawal, at the "end" of philosophy, when the tradition of withdrawal and concealment has reached its deepest and most ominous stage. Now, in this very moment of extreme danger, the saving is most palpable for those who would submit themselves to the discipline of "thought" and who would lay aside the pretension of rationality.[18] Awakening from oblivion in this sense can be carried out. If men would be thought-ful enough, attentive enough to the movement of withdrawal whose vibrations we all can feel, whose soft reverberations we all can hear if we lend an ear, then the awakening from oblivion to oblivion would take place. The primal withdrawal of Being itself is something over which no man has any influence, for which he has no responsibility. But the oblivion of this concealment can be escaped. It lies within the pale of man's responsibility, that is, of his responsive-ness, to awaken to the movement of this withdrawal and to think this withdrawal as a withdrawal. If we make the turn into the *Ereignis* (*Einkehren in das Ereignis*), the withdrawal of the *Ereignis* is not removed; we come rather to stand in it, to attend to it. And this is a possibility for thought itself.[48]

Authentic Dasein cancels Gesellschaft to rerealize the origin. Similarly, in the later Heidegger «a new beginning will become possible. . . . and we shall be granted an experience of Being comparable to that of the early Greek thinkers. Then we too shall be the recipients of the gift and grace of presencing in its primal splendor.»[49] For these Greek thinkers «whom philosophy considers to be semi-philosophical and still encumbered by the old myths, are in fact non-metaphysical thinkers who were not yet victimized by Western *ratio*. Their thinking is still close to the source, primal, freshly bestowed upon Western man, like the new-fallen snow outside the cabin in Todtnauberg.»[50]

Having been called upon and facing heritage to repeat it, authentic Dasein realizes that the repetition is not a simple repetition. Similarly, «we today live in the eschatology, in the ending of the first great beginning, in the ever-growing night which is the evening-land called the "West" (*Abendland*). We seek not literally to repeat the first beginning, which would be "vain and absurd" (Weg.[2] 369/210), but»—and this might be a dose of Guignon's interpretation of *Being and Time* in the later Heidegger—«to find in what the early Greeks thought a renewal of our own history in a way which is uniquely proper to us.»[51] However, it is, if at all, only a dose. For, as Heidegger in section 75 (BT 444; SZ 391f.), Caputo returns to a return *simpliciter:* «Hence, this early Greek experience must come again, at the end of the present history of Being, and thereby set free a new dispensation, a new beginning, precisely at the point at which the old dispensation takes its leave.»[52]

He doesn't elaborate this delicate point. But who would blame him for this? After all, Heidegger himself hasn't done so. At least, he did not offer much beyond the formula of logos I discussed above. In Anaximander, justice still managed to «subdue the stubbornness of that which wants to persist inordinately.»[53] After Parmenides, however, something has happened. In *Being and Time* Heidegger doesn't talk about a single Dasein that becomes authentic individually by distancing itself from any tradition or by freely exploiting any tradition, but about Daseine that, called upon by heritage, break out of Gesellschaft in order to rerealize, against Gesellschaft, the denied origin Volk, Volksgemeinschaft, they are called upon to identify with. Similarly, what is at stake in the later Heidegger is the entire Westen and thus by implication the entire world.

At least Caputo's later Heidegger shows that the basic framework in his late writings remains the same as in *Being and Time*. Thus, it might be possible that, in contrast to many interpreters, the later Heidegger was right when, especially in *Brief über den "Humanismus"* (*Letter on Humanism*), he stressed the continuity between *Being and Time* and his later writings. In addition, in an ambiguous sentence in the *Letter on Humanism,* Heidegger invites us to regard the analysis of the «they» in *Being and Time* as I took it, namely, as an analysis of Gesellschaft. For, the analysis of the «they» is a «sociology.» And what, after Weber, was sociology about if not about—as the German title of Weber's famous book from 1922 reads—*Wirtschaft und Gesellschaft,* economy and society? However, at the same time Heidegger's analysis of the «they» is much more than a contribution to sociology. After talking about «the dictatorship of the public realm {Diktatur der Öffentlichkeit}» (BW 197; WM 149), he continues: «Was in "Sein und Zeit" (1927), ## 27 und 35 über das "man" gesagt ist, soll keineswegs nur einen beiläufigen Beitrag zur Soziologie liefern» (WM 149). This means that «what is said in *Being and Time* (1927), sections 27 and 35, about the "they" is by no means supposed to furnish a merely incidental contribution to sociology.» That is, what is said in those sections about the «they» is indeed a contribution to sociology, but it is also much more than that. (The English translator has misunderstood the German phrase «keineswegs nur» and has mistranslated the sentence: «What is said in *Being and Time* [1927], sections 27 and 35, about the "they" in no way means to furnish an incidental contribution to sociology,» BW 197.) It is a contribution to sociology, and it is much more than an incidental contribution, because it is undertaken from the viewpoint of fundamental ontology, and it is offered on the way to the true origin of Gesellschaft, on the way to Gemeinschaft. (Given Heidegger's remarks on the relation of his fundamental ontology to «subordinated» sciences [BT 28ff.; SZ 8ff.]—remarks that are certainly authoritarian as no other First Philosophy has ever been—one is entitled to say that the phrase «incidental contribution» is of ironic modesty; from his point of view, a sociology that is not undertaken under the auspices of his fundamental ontology is simply not a science.) Heidegger goes on:

> Just as little does the "they" mean merely the opposite, understood in an ethical-existentiell way, of the selfhood of persons. Rather, what is said there contains a reference, thought in terms of the question of the truth of Being, to the word's primordial belongingness to Being. This relation remains concealed beneath the dominance of subjectivity that presents itself as the public realm. (BW 197f.; WM 149)

One might read these sentences as Heidegger's veto against interpretations of section 74 such as Guignon's and Birmingham's. For in one way or another, both miss the peculiar pull of the Gemeinschaft, or of Being, to which Gesellschaft, subjectivity, and the ordinary Daseine are subject. One must not resist the pull or ignore the call. In other words, both Guignon and Birmingham miss the peculiar figure of handing oneself over, or sacrificing oneself to, that origin Volk, hidden up to now, whose agents the authentic Daseine become. In this sense, section 74 may have been in fact already «this turning [*Kehre*]» (BW 208; WM 159), or the threshold to it, in which «everything is reversed» (BW 208; WM 159).[54]

## C. Heidegger in the USA

Moving from the 1930s in Germany more than half a century ahead and halfway around the world, it has to be noted that—at least, as far as I know—in the German literature concerning politics in *Being and Time* no interpretation with a claim as strong as mine can be found. However, one also does not find there an interpretation such as Birmingham's. Perhaps that is because, prior to any detailed analysis, German readers generally sense intuitively that Heidegger's language is so thoroughly impregnated with conservative figures of speech as to make the idea that he could have proposed Birmingham's anarchistic notion of politics unlikely. American readers perhaps do not share this background understanding to the same extent and so enjoy greater freedom in their interpretations. However, interpretations such as Birmingham's are also based on the fundamental self-understanding of the individual in the USA; a self-understanding that was either completely absent among many Germans of Heidegger's time or was precisely the kind that conservatives argued and fought against. It is, Scheler would say, «English cant» (PPS 218) and its sociological and cultural ramifications that make possible interpretations such as Birmingham's. The «German» Held and the «German» notion of fate are indeed foreign to the average person, to the «they,» so to speak, in the United States.

At the beginning of chapter 4, I presented Guignon's reasoning that *Being and Time* is by no means «inherently fascist or proto-Nazi» (HC 131). His interpretation is directed in particular against Wolin's claim that

> Heidegger's involvement with National Socialism—which was of the order of deep-seated, existential commitment—was far from being an adventitious, merely biographical episode. Instead, it was *rooted in the innermost tendencies of his thought*. This claim in no way entails the assumption that Nazism is somehow a necessary and inevitable outgrowth of the philosophy of *Being and Time*. It does suggest, however, that the politics of the Nazi movement emphatically satisfied the desiderata of authentic historical commitment adumbrated in that work. (PB 66)

As mentioned at the beginning of chapter 1, section B, Guignon begins his essay by quoting Wolin's statement that «*Existenzphilosophie* in its Heideggerian variant tends to be inherently destructive of tradition» (PB 32) (HC 130), a statement that might lead us to expect that Wolin interprets the sentences on erwidert and Widerruf as acts of simple negations—like Birmingham. But Wolin does not comment on these sentences;[55] however, amazingly, Guignon would probably accept all of Wolin's statements about destiny and fate, but give them a slight twist, and add his own interpretation of Heidegger's sentence on erwidert so as to present *Being and Time* as politically neutral. This is an interesting hermeneutical situation. Wolin's statements on Heideggerian philosophy's inherent tendency to destroy all tradition occur in the general introduction to his interpretation of *Being and Time* ("The 'Historicity' of *Being and Time*," PB 22–35); he also adds there, however, a note that a «full exposition and justification of this claim will have to wait until our analysis of Heidegger's concept of "resolve" (*Entschlossenheit*) below» (PB 32, n. 45). Accordingly, his interpretative statements refer not so much to Heidegger's concept of historicality as to that of resoluteness; in fact, they function as interpretation of historicality only with a stipulation that Guignon does not mention. After his interpretation of "Authenticity and Decision" (PB 35–40) and of "The Call of Conscience" (PB 40–46), Wolin interprets Entschlossenheit under the heading "A Self-Canceling Social Ontology; The Aporias of 'Decisiveness'" (PB 46–53). He focuses on the problem of «criterionlessness» (PB 52), and summarizes his analysis as follows:

> For when {Heidegger's concept of decisiveness, or decisionism in general} is devoid of any and every normative orientation, "decision" can only be *blind* and *uninformed*—ultimately, it becomes a leap into the void. Without any *material criteria* for decision, it becomes impossible to distinguish an *authentic* from an *inauthentic* decision, *responsible* from *irresponsible* action—let alone on

what grounds an individual would even prefer one course of action to another. Indeed, at times, Heidegger seems to openly glorify the irrationalist basis of decision. (PB 52)

However, Guignon's reference to Wolin does not lead us to expect that in "'Destiny' or The Incorporation of Dasein Within A Historical Community" (PB 53–66), Wolin, in a sense, interprets «historicality» from pretty much the same point of view as Guignon himself, namely, arguing that, according to Heidegger, the past is meant to provide decision with those meanings that decision in itself lacks: «Historicity is a mode of *authentic, past-directed temporalization:* Dasein situates itself in relation to a meaningful historical continuum, and this act endows its projection toward the future with content and direction» (PB 60). However, in contrast to Guignon, Wolin discusses the past, as I did in chapters 1 and 2, using the singular, and he characterizes Dasein's relation to it, as I did, in terms of subjugation:

> The discussion of "authentic temporality," in which the concept of "destiny" figures so prominently, is specifically intended to solve the problem of the self-referentiality of resolve in its preliminary version. In effect, the indeterminacy of resolve is answered by the demand that the individual subordinate *him or herself* to a common destiny. (PB 57)

Wolin finds this sense of subjugation, subordination, or, as he puts it, «fatalism» (PB 62), in section 74 in the passages preceding the sentence on «repetition» (BT 434–437; SZ 382–385), and this leads Wolin to posit an opposition between voluntarism and fatalism:

> The opposition between voluntarism and fatalism in *Being and Time* is never reconciled. Heidegger tries to have it both ways and fails: "destiny" is meant to provide the existentiell basis for the empty self-referentiality of authentic decision, thereby furnishing a measure of content for an otherwise ungrounded, free-floating will. However, the "fatalistic" implications of this category subsequently undermine the autonomy of authentic resolve, an autonomy that was so painstakingly wrested (via the Angst of Being-towards-death) from the inauthentic *Existenzialien* of everydayness. Since this manner of reconciling the opposition is unpalatable, Heidegger at times lurches to the opposite extreme, suggesting that destiny itself can be "chosen" or "willed." But with this move, we have essentially relapsed into the same decisionistic arbitrariness that the concept of destiny was intended to counteract in the first place. (PB 62f.)

According to Wolin, the concept of destiny is grounded in that of repetition. He quotes the sentence on repetition («But when one has, . . .» BT 437; SZ 385) (PB 63) to address the problem of mere reproduction of the past, but he focuses not on the passage about Erwiderung and Widerruf (BT 438; SZ 386) but rather on the sentence about the choice of the hero (BT 437; SZ 385). Based on this, he launches the same criticism as above and reiterates the same aporia:

> To repeat an authentic possibility derived from the past means that "Dasein may *choose its hero*," . . . But the question remains: on what basis is the hero to be chosen? How is one to recognize an *authentic* hero from an icon with feet of clay? Unless some criteria of selection are provided, we run the risk once more of relapsing into the vertiginous arbitrariness of pure decisionism. The only answer Heidegger provides to this question is characteristically unsatisfying. When we inquire as to the *basis* on which authentic repetition is to proceed and in terms of which true heroes might be distinguished from charlatans . . . we are told that repetition itself is "grounded existentially in anticipatory resolve." {BT 437; SZ 385} Thus, resolve is grounded in repetition (e.g., the choice of a proper hero), and repetition itself is grounded in resolve. Once again, circular reasoning replaces cogent insight and sheer assertion substitutes for compelling argumentation. (PB 63f.)

Note that in this passage Wolin switches from the singular «destiny» to the plural of several possibilities, the «true heroes» and «charlatans.» Already here Guignon can step in and reevaluate Wolin's entire argument. However, Wolin goes a step further. Since Heidegger's concept of decision lacks any content, Dasein is not only not capable of any reasonable decision but also has no way to resist any preexisting decision. Thus,

> not only is decisionism thoroughly "unprincipled"; it is also on this account *nakedly opportunistic*. And all voluntaristic bluster about "will," "choice," etc., notwithstanding, opportunism in the end reveals itself often enough as a base and simple conformism. Thus, because it lacks any and every *inherent* basis for choice, decisionism is forced to grasp at random existing opportunities for self-actualization. And as we saw earlier, an authentic resolve that shunned self-actualization would be a contradiction in terms. As innately destitute of inner substance, resolve has no choice but to conform to whatever options are historically available. (PB 64f.)

Thus, if one combines the inherent opportunism with the «sufficiently formal and abstract» (PB 76) character of the existential analysis of *Being and Time,* «one could virtually imagine the philosopher opting for a *Bolshevist* instead of a *Nationalist* revolutionary course» (PB 76). Since from the beginning Wolin has made it clear beyond any doubt that, for him, Heidegger belonged to the conservatives who opposed the Weimar Republic as well as bolshevism, this second step of his interpretation introduces some ambiguity into his summary, either intentionally or by accident. Wolin continues:

> The consequences of this decisionistic "ethical vacuum," coupled with the prejudicial nature of Heidegger's conservative revolutionary degradation of the modern life-world, suggest an undeniable theoretical cogency behind Heideg-

ger's ignominious life-choice of 1933. In its rejection of "moral convention"—which *qua* convention, proves inimical to acts of heroic bravado—decisionism shows itself to be distinctly nihilistic vis-à-vis the totality of inherited ethical paradigms. For this reason, the implicit political theory of *Being and Time*—and in this respect, it proves a classical instance of the German conservative-authoritarian mentality of the period—remains devoid of fundamental "liberal convictions" that might have served as an ethicopolitical bulwark against the enticement of fascism. Freed of such bourgeois qualms, the National Socialist movement presented itself as a plausible material "filling" for the empty vessel of authentic decision and its categorical demand for existentiell-historical content. The summons toward an "authentic historical destiny" enunciated in *Being and Time* was thus provided with an ominously appropriate response by Germany's National Revolution. The latter, in effect, was viewed by Heidegger as the ontic fulfillment of the categorical demands of "historicity": it was Heidegger's own choice of a "hero," a "destiny," and a "community." (PB 65)

Thus, one might ask, Was the Heidegger of *Being and Time* a Nazi? Or was he just a conservative who unfortunately wrote a book that took any weapons against National Socialism out of his hands? Did he write a book against the alleged conformism of the «they» without realizing that he himself did nothing but reestablish this conformism on the noble level of authentic Dasein? Would Heidegger have become a communist if the communists, in some way or another, had seized power? These are embarrassing conclusions. To be sure, Georges Sorel changed from a Leninist into an admirer of Mussolini; in the latter years of the Weimar Republic, some Social Democrats or communists changed over to National Socialism; in 1933, many people who had formerly been neutral—or lukewarm—became National Socialists. And perhaps even in politics, the French proverb that the extremes touch each other contains some truth. However, German professors at that time insisted on the difference between the Right and the Left, and according to Wolin, so did Heidegger. Should we assume that all this notwithstanding, Heidegger wrote a book in which he blurred these differences? Not in his prephilosophical opinions but rather in his masterpiece, the great philosopher maneuvers himself into the position of the double-headed mortals who vacillate between the Right and the Left and consequently conform to whatever decisions are forced upon them. At this point, Guignon can see not only the possibility but, so to speak, the necessity to intervene. And he can do so very smoothly.

Wolin already anticipated the result of his interpretation early on in his argument concerning historicality, namely, in the note accompanying his quotation of the sentences «The resoluteness in which Dasein comes back to itself, . . . but not necessarily *as* having thus come down» (BT 435; SZ 383):

> The concluding phrase to this citation is of great interest insofar as it indicates a profound decisionistic residue in the entire discussion of historicity. It implies

that the taking up of historically extant possibilities is never something unal-
terable and merely given, but in the last analysis something codetermined by
the autonomous decision of Dasein itself. (PB 60, n. 107)

For Wolin, this autonomy of the Dasein vis-à-vis the past is the unwanted outcome of Heidegger's analysis. Heidegger wanted a past, or destiny, that subjugated the Daseine. Because of his concept of resoluteness, however, these
Daseine turn out to be those «Helden» who care only about their glorious self-
affirmation and thus negate the past and its offers. However, Heidegger did not
explicitly state that he wanted to develop a concept of a subjugating past that
left no room for Dasein's objection against the past's exaction. Therefore, one
can regard Dasein's autonomy, if properly understood—that is, in terms of, as
Guignon says with reference to Taylor, «situated freedom» (HC 131)—to be
not the unwanted outcome but rather exactly the aim Heidegger was reaching
for. On this basis, one can see *Being and Time* in its political import as a book
of fundamental, and in themselves neutral, politics rather than as a proto-
fascist or at least very confused book. Guignon might even concede that in the
passage preceding the sentences on repetition and the choice of one's hero, Heidegger allows some demanding aspect in heritage, destiny, and past. However,
beginning with the sentence «But when one has, by repetition, handed down
to oneself a possibility that has been, . . .» (BT 437; SZ 385), Heidegger might
introduce Dasein's relative independence vis-à-vis the past and the present; this
independence is not the same as Wolin's glorious acts of self-affirmation or
nihilism in regard to the past; rather, it is made possible by Dasein's utopian
ideal, and it enables Dasein to consider the various possibilities offered by the
past, to choose what fits its utopian ideal, and to distance itself from the others
as well as from the present, as, according to Guignon, Heidegger states in the
sentences on erwidert and Widerruf (BT 438; SZ 386).[56]

Wolin sees an unresolved tension in Heidegger's theory. On the one hand,
there is fate as a tradition demanding obedience. On the other, Dasein is only
concerned with its self-affirmation and is intrinsically nihilistic vis-à-vis the
past.[57] Regarding the nihilistic Dasein, it seems to me that—when reading
Heidegger, at least—Wolin has not sufficiently distanced himself from a
specifically North American notion of authenticity. As an advertisement for
the aftershave lotion «eXcesS» puts it, «an overstepping of bounds»—this is
what Americans have to do to be noticed socially. The attitude of overstepping bounds, of being creative, of making a difference, of breaking with the
tradition and initiating something new, and of distancing oneself from all others as the norm of life is probably related to the admirable figures of cow-
boys, dishwashers, and self-made men. Each of them had left behind the suf-
focating traditions of the «Old World»; each of them was concerned with
making his own life and fate.[58] The self-made man, however, is actually the

opposite of a German «Held» and of the «Helden» (SZ 385; «hero,» BT 437) in *Being and Time*. A German Held is not someone who distances himself from tradition so as to realize himself in his individuality; rather, he is someone capable of forgetting himself, of putting his entire being into the service of the common good, and of «sacrificing» himself for it. Or—more precisely and in terms of the logic of transfiguration[59] —a Held even finds his self-fulfillment in self-sacrifice for the common good.[60] Still, especially under the sway of deconstructive theory, which fits nicely into, as Heidegger would say, the American «they,» a large majority of American commentators project the self-made man onto Heidegger's Held and authentic Dasein, and even project the aspect of distancing onto the notion of fate. Fate becomes something created by the authentic Dasein itself, or it becomes the site of resistance to and breaking with any tradition.

Guignon probably intends his emphasis on utopian ideals as a means to avoid Wolin's criticism of circularity.[61] In his book *Heidegger: Thought and Historicity*, Fynsk finds nothing wrong in circularities like these, once we come to think of the circular movement not «in a linear fashion,» but «on the contrary, as a simultaneous, open-ended movement in two opposing directions—not in terms of a circle but in terms of a paradoxical structure of simultaneous approach and withdrawal, of a casting forth that casts back.»[62] In some sense, this anticipates his interpretation of section 74. Fynsk warns against an interpretation in which we lose sight of «the possibility of thinking the political import of Heidegger's thought.»[63] Thus, by his «largely immanent readings of Heidegger's texts,»[64] Fynsk wants to illuminate «those points where the text marks its relation to something that exceeds it and that provokes its movement.»[65] Yet, in his interpretation of *Being and Time*, in the chapter "The Self and its Witness,"[66] he doesn't talk about politics, at least not in the sense of Wolin and Guignon. It is «the other» and «the more primordial experience that is an originary encounter with alterity»[67] that ignites the paradoxical structure of simultaneous approach and withdrawal. Choosing one's hero is this act of approaching and following. However, as the sentences on erwidert and Widerruf show, «choosing as affirming and following is not a form of passive reception; insofar as it involves interpretation, it is also a struggle»;[68] a struggle whose purpose is to distance Dasein from its hero. The way from *Being and Time* does not lead to the Nazis but to Heidegger's lectures on Nietzsche:

> Therefore, if the "following" that is made possible by such an existentiell choice is a fateful necessity, then it might be said that, by writing *Being and Time*, Heidegger had to write *Nietzsche*—at least, insofar as a fate must be written.
> *Nietzsche*, we might say, represents Heidegger's effort to *lose* Nietzsche. The engagement with that possibility of existence (or of thought) that is Nietzsche's—a repetition of the engagement marked in *Being and Time*—is

. . undertaken for the purposes of disengagement and the demarcation of a new historical position.[69]

I leave open whether Fynsk's interpretation is closer to Birmingham or to Guignon, or whether it marks a genuine stand within the field demarcated by «erwidert» as conversation with, and negation of, the past. In my view it is a further example of the devastating effects of Heidegger's «playful» punning with «wieder» and «wider,» and with the dative and accusative.

Guignon developed an interpretation according to which authentic Dasein distances itself from the present and the past and yet identifies itself with some past. However, as I pointed out in section B of chapter 1, this would have required the dative with «erwidert.» Yet, there is even a sense of «erwidern» in the accusative according to which it might mean an act of distancing even stronger than in Guignon. As Guignon and also Fynsk, Birmingham too might have admitted a strong demand in the passages on heritage, destiny, and repetition in order then to make the act of negation that, according to her, authentic Dasein performs in the sentences on erwidern and Widerruf even more dramatic. In section B of chapter 1 I presented Birmingham's interpretation of the passage on erwidert and Widerruf, and in section C of chapter 2 I summarized her interpretation of the passage on «destiny.» Birmingham wants to show that «Heidegger does not articulate a philosophy of history at all, but instead opens the way for rethinking political judgment» (TP 25), and that Lacoue-Labarthe is wrong in his claim that Heidegger's engagement in National Socialism was «permitted» by «an unexamined theory of mimetic identification» (TP 44).[70] Following her interpretation of «erwidert» and «Widerruf» she states in a bluntly metaphysical way that there are entities with a clear definition, that Heidegger knew of this, and that, in the passage in question, he wrote about these entities:

> Events, by definition, are occurrences that interrupt routine processes, and Heidegger clearly understands this when he writes of the *event* of destiny as that which allows for the disavowal of the past and possibility of something unexpected and unpredictable. . . . In still other words, *Dasein*'s critical response dissolves any authorization of repeatable historical possibilities based on a myth of beginnings. (TP 31)

By this, she smuggles into the text a term of the later Heidegger, «Ereignis,» which Heidegger does not use at all as a technical term in *Being and Time*. (Note that she translates «Geschehen» with «historizing,» or «historicity»; thus, «event» must be the translation of the term «Ereignis» in Heidegger's later writings.) She regards her projection of her specific interpretation of the later Heidegger's concept of event onto the two passages in *Being and Time* in section 74 as sufficient to refute Lacoue-Labarthe's analysis of the *Rectorate Address* and of *Being and Time*. After these two points, she tries to show that this project of *Being and Time,* namely, to develop a philosophy of Riß, of antitotalitarian politics, is central in Heidegger's lectures on Nietzsche between 1936 and 1940 (TP 33ff.).[71] Thus, if Lacoue-Labarthe is wrong, what else was it that «permitted» Heidegger's engagement in National Socialism? Her answer is brief: «in certain crucial texts in the 1930s, namely, the Rectorial Address and in some passages of *Introduction to Metaphysics,* Heidegger forgot the *sublime* moment which calls for *Dasein's* resolute judgment» (TP 44). He forgot. Thus, according to Birmingham, having been engaged since at least the early 1920s until, at least, the end of the 1930s in a philosophy of antitotalitarian politics, the greatest philosopher simply forgot his entire philosophy though it was tailored precisely as a theoretical and practical critique of situations like his and Hitler's Machtübernahme in 1933.[72]

# 6

# Epilogue

## A. Keep silent! Or, Heidegger's Machtergreifung

Birmingham's and Guignon's interpretations to the contrary notwithstanding, *Being and Time* is neither anarchist nor politically neutral. Rather, it is a brilliant summary of the politics of the revolutionary Right. But is it «inherently fascist or proto-Nazi» (HC 131)? There is no need for long speculations, for Heidegger himself has given a clear answer to the question. As was mentioned above,[1] Guignon refers to the meeting between Heidegger and the Jew Karl Löwith in Rome 1936. Heidegger wore the swastika during his entire stay in Rome, even during an excursion to Frascati and Tusculum with his wife, his sons, and Löwith. They talked about this and that until Löwith brought up the controversy in the *Neue Zürcher Zeitung* of January 1936 between Hans Barth and Emil Staiger (see MH 241–248) and said that he agreed neither with Barth nor with Staiger, «insofar as I was of the opinion that his partisanship for National Socialism lay in the essence of his philosophy {daß seine Parteinahme für den Nationalsozialismus im Wesen seiner Philosophie läge}.»[2]

If Birmingham were right, Heidegger's answer probably would have been very short: *«Being and Time?* Historicality? Never heard of it!»* According to Wolin, he would have shaken his head slowly and pensively, and would have finally said: «Well, Mr. Löwith! You know, I was just a regular conservative, and with Volk and all that kind of stuff; I wanted to ground these ideas in a theory of autonomy and decision. Unfortunately, it turned out that I lost any criteria. So, I couldn't help but become a conformist. Thus, in 1933 I couldn't resist. If the communists had achieved power, I would have become a hard-working communist instead.» According to Guignon's interpretation, one would have expected a statement like the following: «Mr. Löwith, you are wrong. My partisanship for National Socialism is by no means inherent in the essence of *Being and Time*. I would not even call *Being and Time* the basis of my political engagement. However, if you like to think of it that way, you must keep in mind that it is the basis only in a very, very weak sense. For, first, as I say at the beginning of section 74, "In the existential analysis we cannot, in principle, discuss what Dasein *factically* resolves in any particular case. Our investigation excludes even the existential projection of the factical possibilities of existence" (BT 434; SZ 383). Thus, whatever one might read out of section 74, it doesn't affect *Being and Time* itself. Second, in my concept of historicality in sections 74–77, I merely explain the general structure of the situation in which, at that time, each person had to make his decision. From this analysis of the general structure one cannot infer anything about my own decision. Thus, third, even if one reads into section 74 a decision for National Socialism, one has to keep in mind that it is just one example of the possible decisions and could easily have been replaced with an example of the decision of a communist.»

However, as is known, «Heidegger agreed with me without reservation and added that his concept of "historicity" was the basis {die Grundlage} of his political "engagement" ("Einsatz"). He also left no doubt about his belief in Hitler.»[3] Guignon misreads the notion of «basis {die Grundlage}»[4] and he doesn't realize that «erwidert» in section 74 does not mean some deliberating conversation with the past, or some other act of distancing oneself from the past, but rather indicates compliance with the call of the past. According to my interpretation, in section 74 Heidegger presented a brilliant summary of the motif common to all revolutionary rightist authors. In his peculiar way, however, he inserted the notion of Volksgemeinschaft into his summary. In preceding parts of *Being and Time,* he explicitly criticized basic assumptions of Scheler's theory. In addition, there is no discussion in *Being and Time* that is analogous to Scheler's discussion of the different Gemeinschaften and that thus might have enabled Heidegger to criticize National Socialism. In light of these facts, his addition of the Volksgemeinschaft has to be read as an option for National Socialism. At the same time, the theory of history and politics is formulated in such an abstract way that philosophical readers could easily mistake it for a neutral fundamental ontology or at least could easily leave aside the impression that it was much more specific. The general motif of downward plunge and recovery in *Being and Time* as a whole and in its section 74 in particular could certainly not be missed, and it might be the case that in the eyes of many readers this motif could pass as fundamental ontology. Heidegger's option for National Socialism, however, was not so obvious. In order to recognize it one had to revert the sequence of «der Gemeinschaft» (SZ 394; «of the community,» BT 436) and «des Volkes» (SZ 384;

«of {the} people,» BT 436) and had to connect the resulting Volksgemein-schaft not only with Heidegger's criticism of the subject but also with his criticism of Scheler's notion of value and of the basis of Scheler's entire ontol-ogy, namely, the latter's distinction between a temporal realm and a realm of eternal entities. Still, even more was necessary, namely, to relate these find-ings to the presence of an absence, the absence of any discussion compara-ble to Scheler's theory of the different Gemeinschaften. In this way, Hei-degger's option could easily be overlooked or ignored. No one reading a book on fundamental ontology by the «most famous» philosopher would normally be prepared for the possiblity that its author was making a case for the most radical party on the revolutionary Right.

The presentation in section 74 has been carefully prepared, not only from the beginning of section 74 and of section 72, but already from the end of Division One on, if not almost from the beginning of the entire book. It is certainly true that nothing in *Being and Time* allows for the step from Gemein-schaft in general to the Volksgemeinschaft in particular. However, it is equally true that there is nothing in *Being and Time* that might have prevented its author from making this specification. Like Scheler prior to his Kehre, Hei-degger «deconstructs» liberalism and leftism and thus paves the way for an alignment with the Right. In contrast to Scheler, however, Heidegger also explicitly and implicitly «deconstructs» positions on the right, such as Scheler's, that allow their authors to distance themselves from and criticize Nazism. It is in this sense that, indeed, *Being and Time* leads directly into Nazism. Thus, one should not be surprised that Heidegger adds the specific difference «Volk» to the genus «Gemeinschaft» (BT 436; SZ 384) and thus sides with Hitler's «Volksgemeinschaft.» One also should not be surprised that, five years later, he joined the Nationalsozialistische Deutsche Arbeiter-partei on May 1, 1933, and that twenty six days after that, on May 27, he gave his, as Jonas said, «infamous» (MH 200) rectorate address. All this underpins the assessment of Hans-Georg Gadamer, who himself has never been a detractor of Heidegger and his philosophy: «Sometimes, in admira-tion for the great thinker, Heidegger's defenders declared that his political error had nothing to do with his philosophy. That they could pacify them-selves with such an argument! They did not notice how insulting such a defense of such an important thinker was» (MH 142).[5]

*Being and Time* is a miraculous work, and its section 74 is perhaps some sort of picture-puzzle, one of those Gestalt-switch figures used in psychol-ogy, for Heidegger's students at the time at least.[6] You see something, and then, all of the sudden, after the Gestalt-switch, or after the leap, you see something else, and even if you try hard, you can no longer go back and see what you had first seen. You see in *Being and Time* the terrifying face of the old witch of the loneliness of the isolated bourgeois subjects, or the un-erotic groupings in their Gesellschaft, and you see the desire for a leap out of

Gesellschaft. Explicitly from 1929 on, the philosopher produces in you the mood to make the leap, and he gives you the clear direction for the leap. Maybe a critic steeped in deconstructive theory might say that you rearrange the words in «der Gemeinschaft, des Volkes» (SZ 384; «of the community, of {the} people,» BT 436), and thus, you open up the female receptivity of «die Gemeinschaft» to become impregnated by the sober, male, or neuter force of «das Volk.» In this process, you incorporate and make «frei» (SZ 38; «free,» BT 436) the real origin, and you eroticize it. Thus, you see the beautiful woman of the «Volksgemeinschaft,» as Heidegger says in the *Rectorate Address* (SB 15; MH 10), in all the radiance of her spiritual and technical armament. Another picture-puzzle is placed by Heidegger at the end of his *Rectorate Address*. Heidegger develops the same motif of identification I discussed with reference to *Being and Time*. As in *Being and Time,* the origin is present in an extremely endangered situation, and you have to listen to its call to grasp it in order to regain stable identity, authenticity, or your own true essence, and in order to fulfill the demand of the origin to be faithfully rerealized: «But neither will anyone ask us whether we will it or do not will it when the sprirtual strength of the West fails and the West starts to come apart at the seams {in seinen Fugen kracht}, when this moribund pseudo civilization {abgelebte Scheinkultur} collapses into itself, pulling all forces into confusion and allowing them to suffocate in madness.»[7]

Everyone understands the very colloquial metaphor, «in den Fugen krachen» (to creak in the joints, to split, come apart, at the seams). For instance, a shaky chair «kracht in den Fugen» if one sits down on it, for its joints no longer keep the different parts firmly together. This expression is sometimes accompanied by some sort of enjoyment of or satisfaction with the shakiness, similar to the peculiar sadism children display from time to time. At this point in Heidegger's speech, it is the triumphant gesture indicating that meanwhile, the anschwellender Bocksgesang has become such a Krach (very loud noise) that no one can any longer miss it or cover it up with the work of ambiguity, and that those whose victory has been forecast in the sentences on erwidert and Widerruf have in fact taken over the city. The countermovement to this downward plunge of collapse and suffocation is performed in the next paragraph, although he has already presented it several times before, and at one place in terms of Fuge. For about three pages prior to the sentence with «moribund pseudo civilization» he says that to realize the «primordial and full essence of science» requires that «we *submit ourselves* to the command decreed from long ago by the beginning of our spiritual-historical existence {wir *uns* in die ferne Verfügung des Anfangs unseres geistig-geschichtlichen Daseins *fügen*}» (SB 16; italics mine, J. F.).[8] The Fuge (joint) keeps something in the proper order. «In den Fugen krachen» is one state within the process of falling apart that can be counteracted only if one turns back and listens to the call of the Fuge to which the corresponding, or echoing, verb is «sich fügen.» «Sich fügen» is «to fit oneself (back) into the proper order,» and is often used with the implication that one has tried hard to avoid fitting in but can no longer resist and thus gives in. «Sich in sein Schicksal fügen» means to accept one's fate and no longer try to resist it. To accept one's fate is what authentic Dasein does since it realizes that by this it gains fullness and authenticity of life. Only inauthentic Dasein does not sich fügen into its fate. Pace Birmingham, Guignon, and Caputo, fate is neither made by the individual nor can it be evaded by the individual. Often, «sich fügen» means simply to surrender, «sich überliefern dem»;[9] correspondingly, that into which Dasein sich fügt, is the Fuge, Fügung, or Gefügtheit. Heidegger doesn't use Schicksal or Fügung. Rather, he prefers the noun «Verfügung.» For the latter is a bureaucratic, legal and military term and often means a command given in a very serious situation. Furthermore, the Verfügung is fate, namely, fate as it raises its voice and delivers a command. A command has to be heard. In *Being and Time,* (in contrast to inauthentic Dasein, which doesn't listen to the call) authentic Dasein erwidert the call of the Volk. In the *Rectorate Address,* «we» «fügen» ourselves into the call, that is, the «Verfügung.» The «Verfügung,» however, verfügt, commands, that the city—the universities and Germany— has to be cleaned up from all the «moribund pseudo civilization» in order to make room for the proper realization of Volk and Führer, just as the call in *Being and Time* verfügte that Gesellschaft had to be destroyed in order to make room for the proper rerealization of Gemeinschaft.

To return to the end of the *Rectorate Address,* after the paragraph with «in seinen Fugen kracht» Heidegger goes on:

> Whether such a thing occurs or does not occur, this depends solely on whether we as a historical-spiritual Volk will ourselves, still and again {noch und wieder}, or whether we will ourselves no longer. Each individual *has a part* in deciding this {entscheidet darüber *mit*}, even if, and precisely if, he seeks to evade this decision.[10]

As opposed to the situation in 1927, in 1933 the origin is already «free» in several empirical Daseine and has already taken over. Thus, one has to identify oneself with these authentic Daseine since they are the truth of oneself. In an ugly parody of Kant's fact of freedom, and as an example of the phenomenon that, as it was called in *Being and Time,* some Dasein can be the «'conscience' of Others» (BT 344; SZ 298),[11] Heidegger goes on:

> But it is our will that our Volk fulfill its historical mission. We will ourselves. For the young and youngest elements of the Volk, which are already reaching beyond us, *have* already *decided* this. {Aber wir wollen, daß unser Volk seinen geschichtlichen Auftrag erfüllt. Wir wollen uns selbst. Denn die junge und jüngste Kraft des Volkes, die über uns schon hinweggreift, *hat* darüber bereits *entschieden*.}[12]

He then moves on with one of his characteristic «aber» («however»): «We can only fully understand the glory and greatness of this new beginning, however,

{Die Herrlichkeit aber und die Größe dieses Aufbruchs} if we carry within ourselves that deep and broad thoughtfulness upon which the ancient wisdom of the Greeks drew in uttering the words:»[13] in order to conclude with a quote from Plato: «ta . . . megala panta episphale . . . ("All that is great stands in the storm . . . ") {"Alles Große steht im Sturm"} (Platon, Republic, 497d, 9).»[14]

The sentence with «however» is well placed. The proverbial German «zerstreute Professor» (absentminded professor) might have been somewhat embarrassed by the format and tone of Heidegger's address. Now he can lean back relieved: Heidegger remains one of ours, concerned with Plato and serious study. Non-absentminded professors and all the «verblendeten jungen Leute» (deluded young people),[15] however, could see in the last sentences the appropriate expression of the sublime event, and for them the particle «however» amounted to a «now, finally.» However, just as at the forked road where we negate the obligations contained in the institutions of χάρις,[16] there is more than one way. Those who already had a more specific agenda than the one of the non-absentminded professors and of the deluded young people will have heard, and read, the end differently. For them, the particle «however» introduced a warning to all the absentminded and non-absentminded professors: «Ihr werdet euch noch wundern!» (or: «Ihr werdet noch euer blaues Wunder erleben!» You will get the shock of your life!). The name of the most disgusting journal of the extreme Right in the Weimar Republic was Der Stürmer, a magazine full of the most horrifying anti-Semitic propaganda. The noun «Stürmer» is grammatically, in Aristotelean terms, paronymous, and a «Stürmer» is, psychologically and christologically, a figure of, with Heideggerian hyphens, In-Spiration and redemption. As «the grammarian gets his name from grammar,»[17] a Stürmer, stormer, gets his name from Sturm, storm. As the grammarian is able to practice grammar in virtue of the grammar in him, the Stürmer stürmt, storms, in virtue of the storm in him, which is the primary agent in the storming of the Stürmer: «The Stürmer stürmt. This individual storms in virtue of the storm that has ergriffen, captured, him, or that has sich in ihm niedergelassen, settled itself in this individual; therefore, this individual stands in the storm and is a stormer.» Stürmer was another name for those soldiers who—as in Langemarck and Verdun—ran out of their trenches in order to erstürmen, to take by storm, the lines of the enemy. Of course, the editors and readers of Der Stürmer used this name to indicate where they came from, and where they wanted to go to, namely, from the battlefield against the external enemy of World War I back into the city, in order to erstürmen, take by storm, the city and throw out whomever they regarded as the city's internal enemies, notably, the Jews, social democrats, liberals, communists, Asphalt-Literaten, and homosexuals, and to establish their sway. To be sure, no one can reasonably maintain that Heidegger found his anti-Semitism represented, or erwidert, echoed, in Der Stürmer, or that Heidegger wiederholte or erwiderte the anti-Semitism of Der Stürmer. Yet, Der Stürmer and its readers formed a remarkable and vociferous group of those in whose leader Heidegger still believed in 1936. However, even without the existence of *Der Stürmer,* the people listening to Heidegger's speech could not but be reminded of the heroes of Langemarck and Verdun. Most of the educated readers at that time had read Ernst Jünger's diary of *his* World War I, published for the first time in 1920 under the title *In Stahlgewittern* (In the thunderstorms of steel). In this book one could read about the dangers, excitements, and pleasures of warriors that were unattainable within bourgeois Gesellschaft, and about true comradeship brought about by the war; or, rather, made «free» (BT 436; SZ 384) by the war; the war that makes manifest whether in one's own true self one is really a comrade or not. In Jünger, this was literature and for the most part free of what bourgeois readers might have regarded to be the vulgarities of many of the other novels on World War I. Even without Jünger's text, however, everyone was familiar with the vocabulary of Sturm, in which Sturm, or the command «Auf zum Sturm!,» «Sturmangriff!,» («Attack! Assault!») governs—as a substance or health in an Aristotelean πρὸς ἕν[18] —all the activities, persons, and materials necessary for an assault, as, for instance, with Heideggerian hyphens, «Sturm-Gepäck,» «Sturm-Gewehr,» «Sturm-Führer,» «Sturm-Abteilung,» and so on. Jünger's title is ambivalent. On the one hand, it refers, of course, to all the munition exploding on the battlefields. On the other hand, it refers to the alleged process whereby the war makes «free» one's true self, and that the war forms, informs, that is, «steels» the individual, as the Führer used to say that the German soldier had to be «hart wie Krupp-Stahl» («as hard as steel manufactured by Krupp»). Jünger can indicate these multiple meanings already in the title of his novel because he can quite naturally rely on the use of the German preposition and prefix «in-» (in) in metaphors of In-Spiration. «Seid einig im Geiste!» («Be united in spirit!») is a formula used in church at several occasions in order to indicate that we open the hardened houses of our selfish egos to surrender the interior of our houses to God and to let the Geist enter, to let the Geist be the primary agent in all our deeds, and to be «authentically» united with the others im Geiste, in our spirits, because we are united in God's spirit in which we are because it is in us.[19] In 1934 the artist Ernst Barlach, who had hoped for a short time that the National Socialists would officially acknowledge his art as «German art,» made a sculpture entitled with a variation on the last words of the *Rectorate Address,* namely, "Wanderer im Wind" (Wanderer in the wind), today on display in the Ernst Barlach Museum in Hamburg. As the face of the upright person shows, it is a piece of inner emigration. This is probably the reason why Barlach preferred «wind» over «storm.» For «im Sturm» can of course be used, say, as the title of a painting showing a shipwreck or sailors trying to avoid one. However, its use as a metaphor of «heroic» enthusiasm and inspiration is common. A Wind can carry and inspire me as well, and it can also «blow into my face.» However, a Wind is by definition less strong than a Sturm, and it can even be very light. Furthermore, in contrast to «Sturm» the word «Wind» can invite a certain pensiveness and even melan-choly.[20] Thus Barlach's figure is not a «Stürmer» but a «Wanderer,» who does not have a specific agenda to realize or a target to «take by storm.» Still, he walks «in» the wind. The hair of the wanderer is moved by the wind. Either the wind is erwidert, in all its different meanings (including resistance to it), by an inner movement of the wanderer, or there is no exterior wind, and the face as well as the hair is the exterior expression of an inner wind. Or it is both ways at the same time.

Again, all these possibilities of this sculpture are covered in a completely appropriate way by the «im» of the title since, especially when faced with the accusation of resistance against the Sturm, Barlach can always refer to, and rely on, the uses of «in» in different inspirations depending on what it is that is in me and inspires me, as grammatically, according to Aristotle, the grammar is «ἐν,» «in,»[21] me and enables me to practice it, to be realized grammar, and, thus, to be called a grammarian.

Educated in ancient literature as he was, Heidegger could have used another Greek quote, especially if he had wanted to calm the enthusiasm about the National Socialist «new beginning» down in some way, or to indicate, in whatever manner, inner reservations toward National Socialism. However, he chose the one which, by virtue of its context in Plato[22] as well as in Heidegger's speech, was, like no other, pertinent to support die Sache des, the cause of the, New National Socialist State as well as die Sache des Denkens, the issue of thinking. Or he could have given the entire sentence as it appears in the widely used translation by Schleiermacher: «Denn alles Große ist auch bedenklich und, wie man sagt, das Schöne in der Tat schwer» («For, all that is great is also grave, and, as they say, the beautiful is difficult, indeed»). Since «bedenklich» often means «dubious,» this might have been read even as some sort of mental reservation toward National Socialism by those inter-ested in that. If he had wanted to avoid any possibility of being understood as having reservations toward National Socialism, he could have replaced «bedenklich» with several other words, the best of which, in this situation, would probably have been «erhaben» (sublime). However, he left aside the second part of Plato's sentence, and he translated its first part extremely will-fully. If one assumes that Heidegger maintained, as do all the translators I know of, that Plato's «ἐπισφαλῆ» was supposed to mean something like «pre-carious,» «risky,» or «grave,» he deliberately turned Plato's intention into the opposite. By this, he produced a stirring metaphor of inspiration for all, so to speak, normal National Socialists, and for all not yet decided. At the same time, however, he turned the «*Military Service [Wehrdienst]*» (MH 10; SB 15ff.), about which he had talked before, into explicit aggression. In addition, he did not distance himself from the readers and producers of *Der Stürmer*. Rather, he invited them to add their «Angriff» (attack) to his «im Sturm»; all those Stürmer who already at that time wanted the war, or at least, as a relative of mine (not a reader of *Der Stürmer*) put it, a «small war» to conquer the Soviet Union and to make good for the «shame of Versailles.»

However, things are much simpler. As to *Being and Time,* one might wonder whether for its students at the time it was a picture-puzzle or straightforward national socialistic. The last line of the *Rectorate Address,* however, is definitely too blunt to be a picture-puzzle. For—to assume the impossible—even if none of the listeners to the *Rectorate Address* had ever heard of *Der Stürmer,* Jünger, or World War I, the presence of the SA with their swastika flags at the *Rectorate Address* was all too obvious, and—«um das Maß voll zu machen» (to fill the cup to the brim)—Heidegger had ordained that, at the end of the entire procedure, all attendants had to sing the so-called "Horst-Wessel-Lied."[23] During the Weimar Republic the SA, the Sturm Abteilung, had been the illegal army of Hitler's party, and the "Horst-Wessel-Lied" was their Kampflied (and, under the National Socialists, «the other» German national anthem). The members of the SA had erstürmt the meetings of their political foes and had beaten up and killed a lot of people. Thus, also the last sentence of Heidegger's speech is an open command to überliefern oneself to the new state. The military term «Sturm Abteilung» meant the leading group, the vanguard, in a Sturm-Angriff. Of course, being the vanguard of the National Socialists, the SA and the editors of *Der Stürmer* used these names to call upon a political and military Wiederholung—Wiederholung in Heidegger's sense, namely, under new circumstances, that is, this time victorious—of the Sturm-Angriffe of the brave German soldiers in World War I. Thus, let's zoom in one last time on the heroes of Langemarck and Verdun in order, then, to disappear into the German or non-German forests and to leave for other shores.[24]

## B. Events under Trees and Stars

Hans Castorp was no dandy, nor an environmentalist. He wasn't a Held either, neither a «Held von Verdun» nor some other Held. And he was no Heros. Without knowing how, he stumbled into World War I as it burst into the last four pages of Thomas Mann's novel *The Magic Mountain.* Nonetheless, like the «Helden von Verdun,» Hans Castorp too ran forward, he too listened to some call of the Volk, and he too gave voice to the call he was hearing. But he was not singing the German national anthem. Rather, he sang some love song, a song of Heimat, homeland, and love, "Der Lindenbaum" ("The Lime Tree"):

> Up he gets, and staggers on, limping on his earth-bound feet, all unconsciously singing:
>
> > "Its waving branches whi—ispered
> > A mess—age in my ear—"
>
> and thus, in the tumult, in the rain, in the dusk, vanishes out of our sight.[25]

He wasn't in the first line, and he didn't seem to be very enthusiastic, or skill-ful. For, he didn't have the German Volk, or some of its blonde women in mind. Rather, he had fallen in love with the foe, with Madame Chauchat, Clavdia Chauchat, the Russian with a French husband; with her peculiarly gliding step, her broad cheek-bones, and her Kirghiz eyes that went through him «like a knife»[26] when he passed her by in the dining room. We don't know what happened to Hans Castorp. The author, son of the haute bour-geoisie in the open-minded Lübeck, for one moment feels tempted «to press a finger delicately to our eyes at the thought that we shall see you no more, hear you no more for ever.»[27] However, he immediately er-mann-t sich (pulls himself together), and even confesses that it is without great concern that he leaves Castorp's fortunes open.

"The Lime Tree" is part of the collection of poems "Winter Journey" ("Winter Reise"), written by the disappointed and persecuted democrat Wil-helm Müller, and set to music by Franz Schubert. Without its fifth angry and political stanza, it became very popular, a Volkslied. Heinrich Heine, a Jew, also wrote a poem that became a Volkslied, "Die Loreley." During National Socialism, in anthologies of folk songs, Heinrich Heine's name as the author was replaced with «author unknown,» or simply «Volkslied.» I don't know whether Heidegger liked "The Lime Tree." Maybe it doesn't particularly fit areas like the Black Forest, or the Harz about which Heine wrote his *Die Harzreise*. Nor does it seem to fit, or to respond, to erwidern, Heidegger's specific melancholia. Probably, there are folk songs about fir trees that he would have liked more.[28] To be sure, trees show up not only in Germany. After all, there is the Porphyrean tree in logic and ontology, and it was under a tree, notably, a fig tree, the Geschlecht of the mother, that Saint Augustine was converted:

> So I stood up and left him where we had been sitting, utterly bewildered. Some-how I flung myself down beneath a fig tree and gave way to the tears which now streamed from my eyes, the sacrifice that is acceptable to you. . . . I was asking myself these questions, weeping all the while with the most bitter sorrow in my heart, when all at once I heard the sing-song voice of a child in a nearby house. Whether it was the voice of a boy or a girl I cannot say, but again and again it repeated the refrain 'Take it and read, take it and read' {tolle lege, tolle lege}.[29]

Nonetheless, there might be something special to the Deutsche Wald, even for those who have no sense for the German Soldier. Even in Benjamin, at a crucial point, namely, in his explication of aura, a tree shows up.[30] One might read as an implicit criticism of the theological abuse of the tree in Augustine the aphorism,

> Commentary and translation stand in the same relation to the text as style and mimesis to nature: the same phenomenon considered from different aspects. On

the tree of the sacred text both are only the eternally rustling leaves; on that of the profane, the seasonally falling fruits.[31]

The same might hold true of a short piece in the context of aura not translated into English:

> I climbed up a slope and lay down under a tree. The tree was a poplar or an alder. You ask why I have forgotten its species? I did so because, as I looked into the foliage and followed its movements with my eyes, language in me was absorbed by it so that, in my presence, language at that moment consummated again the very old marriage with the tree. The branches and the top swayed in consideration or bent in refusal. The branches presented themselves as inclined or as high-handed. The foliage fought against a rough draft of wind, shuddering before it or complying with it. The trunk had its good ground to stand on. And the leaves cast their shadows upon each other. A soft wind played for the wedding and soon took away the children, quickly sprouted from this bed, carried them into the world as an image-language.[32]

Maybe, these sentences show that, sometimes, even Benjamin could write somewhat kitschig. Nonetheless, they also show a little bit of Benjamin's tender nominalism as in contrast to the call in Augustine and Heidegger. Notably, they bear witness to Benjamin's concern with nature. After all, already in 1928, in *One-Way Street,* Benjamin wrote, «If society has so degenerated through necessity and greed that it can now receive the gifts of nature only rapaciously, that it snatches the fruit unripe from the trees in order to sell it most profitably, and is compelled to empty each dish in its determination to have enough, the earth will be impoverished and the land yield bad harvests.»[33] Thus, Benjamin was the first environmentalist, not Heidegger! «I'm just kidding,» as one often hears in this country after some joke, even after not very good ones of which, as I frankly admit, my book might contain some. Anyway, I started with the «Helden von Langemarck,» and I referred to Max Scheler's hymn on the war. Most probably, Heidegger had also read Ernst Jünger's *In Stahlgewittern,* and, immediately after its publication, he studied carefully Jünger's *Der Arbeiter* (SB 24f.; MH 17f.). Let me finish by just quoting the last, and pretty strange, piece, "To the Planetarium," of Benjamin's *One-Way Street:*

> If one had to expound the doctrine of antiquity with utmost brevity while standing on one leg, as did Hillel that of the Jews, it could only be in this sentence: "They alone shall possess the earth who live from the powers of the cosmos." Nothing distinguishes the ancient from the modern man so much as the former's absorption in a cosmic experience scarcely known to later periods. Its waning is marked by the flowering of astronomy at the beginning of the modern age. Kepler, Copernicus, and Tycho Brahe were certainly not driven by sci-

entific impulses alone. All the same, the exclusive emphasis on an optical connection to the universe, to which astronomy very quickly led, contained a portent of what was to come. The ancients' intercourse with the cosmos had been different: the ecstatic trance. For it is in this experience alone that we gain certain knowledge of what is nearest to us and what is remotest to us, and never of one without the other. This means, however, that man can be in ecstatic contact with the cosmos only communally. It is the dangerous error of modern men to regard this experience as unimportant and avoidable, and to consign it to the individual as the poetic rapture of starry nights. It is not; its hour strikes again and again, and then neither nations nor generations can escape it, as was made terribly clear by the last war, which was an attempt at a new and unprecedented commingling with the cosmic powers. Human multitudes, gases, electrical forces were hurled into the open country, high-frequency currents coursed through the landscape, new constellations rose in the sky, aerial space and ocean depths thundered with propellers, and everywhere sacrificial shafts were dug in Mother Earth. This immense wooing of the cosmos was enacted for the first time on a planetary scale, that is, in the spirit of technology. But because the lust for profit of the ruling classes sought satisfaction through it, technology betrayed man and turned the bridal bed into a bloodbath. The mastery of nature, so the imperialists teach, is the purpose of all technology. But who would trust a cane wielder who proclaimed the mastery of children by adults to be the purpose of education? Is not education above all the indispensable ordering of the relationship between generations and therefore mastery, if we are to use this term, of that relationship and not of children? And likewise technology is not the mastery of nature but of the relation between nature and man. Men as a species completed their development thousands of years ago; but mankind as a species is just beginning his. In technology a *physis* is being organized through which mankind's contact with the cosmos takes a new and different form from that which it had in nations and families. One need recall only the experience of velocities by virtue of which mankind is now preparing to embark on incalculable journeys into the interior of time, to encounter there rhythms from which the sick shall draw strength as they did earlier on high mountains or at Southern seas. The "Lunaparks" are a prefiguration of sanatoria. The paroxysm of genuine cosmic experience is not tied to that tiny fragment of nature that we are accustomed to call "Nature." In the nights of annihilation of the last war the frame of mankind was shaken by a feeling that resembled the bliss of the epileptic. And the revolts that followed it were the first attempt of mankind to bring the new body under its control. The power of the proletariat is the measure of its convalescence. If it is not gripped to the very marrow by the discipline of this power, no pacifist polemics will save it. Living substance conquers the frenzy of destruction only in the ecstasy of procreation.[34]

After this, one might turn back a few pages and compare to Heidegger the notions of decision and resoluteness in "Madame Ariane—Second Courtyard on the Left."[35] Isn't that more interesting and much better written as well?

After all, it is you, dear readers, who are *called upon* to make up your minds, to make a *decision,* and «to have the last word»! Anyway, don't forget the end of "Madame Ariane—Second Courtyard on the Left":

> Each morning the day lies like a fresh shirt on our bed; this incomparably fine, incomparably tightly woven tissue of pure prediction fits us perfectly. The happiness of the next twenty-four hours depends on our ability, on waking, to pick it up.

# Notes

### Preface

1. Richard Rorty, *Essays on Heidegger and Others: Philosophical Papers* (Cambridge and New York: Cambridge University Press, 1991), 193.

2. Jim Miller, *The Passion of Michel Foucault* (New York: Simon & Schuster, 1993).

3. Victor Farías, *Heidegger and Nazism*, trans. P. Burrell and G. R. Ricci (Philadelphia: Temple University Press, 1989); *Heidegger et le nazisme* (Lagrasse: Éditions Verdier, 1987); *Heidegger und der Nationalsozialismus*, trans. K. Laermann (Frankfurt: Fischer, 1989); Hugo Ott, *Martin Heidegger: A Political Life*, trans. A. Blunden (New York: Basic Books, 1993); *Martin Heidegger: Unterwegs zu seiner Biographie* (Frankfurt and New York: Campus, 1988). For the literature up to the beginning of 1991 see Pierre Adler, "A Chronological Bibliography of Heidegger and the Political," in *The Graduate Faculty Philosophy Journal* 14, no. 2–15 no. 1 (1991): 581–611. The issue is a special issue entitled "Heidegger and the Political," edited by Marcus Brainard with David Jacobs and Rick Lee.

4. A revised version (Paris: Les Éditions de Minuit, 1988) was translated into English: *The Political Ontology of Martin Heidegger*, trans. P. Collier (Stanford, CA: Stanford University Press, 1991); Alexander Schwan, *Politische Philosophie im Denken Martin Heideggers* (Köln and Opladen: Westdeutscher Verlag, 1965; exp. ed. 1989).

5. Jacques Derrida, *Of Spirit: Heidegger and the Question*, trans. G. Bennington and R. Bowlby (Chicago and London: University of Chicago Press, 1991). See also Philippe Lacoue-Labarthe, *Heidegger, Art, and Politics*, trans. Ch. Turner (Oxford: Basil Blackwell, 1990) (*La fiction du politique* [Paris: Christian Bourgois, 1987]); Jean-François Lyotard, *Heidegger and "the Jews,"* trans. A. Michael and M. Roberts (Minneapolis: University of Minnesota Press, 1990) (*Heidegger et "les juifs"* [Paris:

Éditions Galilée, 1988]). Tom Rockmore wrote a book on the history of Heidegger's presence in France: *Heidegger and French Philosophy* (London: Routledge, 1995).

6. David Wood edited a volume of papers on Derrida's book. Krell's is the first, and it begins as follows: «Will a more important book on Heidegger than Jacques Derrida's *De l'esprit* appear in our time? No, not unless Derrida continues to think and write in his spirit. Let there be no mistake: this is not merely a brilliant book on Heidegger, it is thinking in the grand style, wholly in the spirit of Heidegger but also spiriting him across borders into strange territories» (David Farrell Krell, "Spiriting Heidegger," in D. Wood, ed., *Of Derrida, Heidegger, and Spirit* [Evanston: Northwestern University Press, 1993], 11).

7. In his "Preface to the MIT Press Edition" of Richard Wolin, ed., *The Heidegger Controversy: A Critical Reader* (Cambridge and London: MIT Press, 1993), xvii.

8. Ibid., xii.

9. Tom Rockmore, *On Heidegger's Nazism and Philosophy* (Berkeley: University of California Press, 1992), 5.

10. John D. Caputo, *Demythologizing Heidegger* (Bloomington: Indiana University Press, 1993).

11. See, for instance, James F. Ward, *Heidegger's Political Thinking* (Amherst: University of Massachusetts Press, 1995) and Dana R. Villa, *Arendt and Heidegger: The Fate of the Political* (Princeton: Princeton University Press, 1996).

12. Fred R. Dallmayr, *The Other Heidegger* (Ithaca: Cornell University Press, 1993), 5.

13. Rockmore, *On Heidegger's Nazism and Philosophy*, 47. If not indicated otherwise, throughout the text, both «historicality» as well as «historicity» are translations of Heidegger's «Geschichtlichkeit» (SZ 372ff.; «Historicality,» BT 424ff.).

Up to now, the English secondary literature on Heidegger was based on Macquarrie and Robinson's translation *Being and Time* (BT). In 1996 Joan Stambaugh's translation was published under the title *Being and Time: A Translation of Sein und Zeit* (Albany: State University of New York Press, 1996). I discuss her translation of the key passage in section 74 in chapter 5, n. 72.

As is known, Heidegger introduced a new term for individual human beings, namely «Dasein» (SZ 7ff., 11ff.; «Dasein,» BT 27ff., 32ff.). One of the reasons for his choice of the term is its polemical aspect. «Da» is a deictic particle always pointing to an individual in a specific site and situation (BT 171; SZ 132). As such it corresponds to Hegel's usage of the demonstrative pronoun «diese» («this») in "Die sinnliche Gewißheit" ("Sense-Certainty"), the first section of the *Phänomenologie des Geistes* (*Phänomenologie des Geistes*, ed. J. Hoffmeister [Hamburg: Felix Meiner, 1952], 79ff.; *Phenomenology of Spirit*, trans. A. V. Miller [Oxford: Oxford University Press, 1977], 58ff.) the difference being that Hegel applies «diese» also to beings other than humans. In the course of Hegel's *Phenomenology of Spirit* the «this» disappears, or is sublated, into the pointer of—as is said in the penultimate line of the book—«this realm of spirits» («dieses Geisterreiches») on «the Calvary of absolute Spirit» («die Schädelstätte des absoluten Geistes») (*Phenomenology of Spirit*, 493; German edition, 564). According to Heidegger, Hegel, Kant, and Neokantians subsume the individual human beings under general and universal notions that, so to speak, cheat the individuals out of their individualities. Thus, he uses the term «Dasein,» and he uses it throughout the book. Heidegger, too, elaborates structures that are supposed to hold true for each Dasein and to enable it to have, and to be in, a world. However, these structures are meant to account for Heidegger's assumption that, in the very Being of an individual Dasein, «that Being is an *issue* for» (BT 32; SZ 12) the individual Dasein. In light of Heidegger's emphasis on the individual Dasein, it might be surprising that he very often uses impersonal constructions where he could have easily used personal ones. English readers cannot recognize this, since Macquarrie and Robinson frequently made «Heidegger less Heideggerian» and used personal constructions «where Heidegger has avoided them» (BT 15). Heidegger's usage of impersonal constructions has several aspects two of which I mention here in passing. It contributes to what to my knowledge hasn't been examined yet; namely, that Heidegger executes in philosophy what Max Weber has analyzed as bureaucratization in modernity. The other strands in Heidegger's language are certainly the expressionistic gestures and the tone of the Youth Movement with their polemics against the routines as well as insecurities of modern life. In addition, there is a strong flavor of a wretched Protestantism. All these different languages and discourses are hard to combine, and it is part of Heidegger's ingenuity to have managed to do so. Probably, with any one of them missing Heidegger would have been much less fascinating than he was at his time. The second aspect concerns the topic of my book more directly. For, his usage of impersonal constructions is the grammatical equivalent to the motif he elaborates in section 74; namely, that individual Dasein hands its own individuality over to a community, the community of the people.

Individual human beings are either masculine or feminine, and also a hermaphrodite is not considered neuter. In English, nouns like «person,» etc., are all gendered. Grammatically, the German noun «Dasein» is neuter and thus requires the neuter article «das» and the neuter personal pronoun «es,» it. Heidegger uses «das Dasein» and «es» both in the context of his inquiries of Dasein «with regard to its Being» (BT 27; SZ 7) and when he refers to activities of individual Daseine.

In German, the latter use sounds as strange, as «it» in reference to an individual human being probably sounds in English for anyone who is not completely taken in by Heidegger. Several existentiales in Heidegger are grammatically feminine, most notably, Sorge ("Die Sorge als Sein des Daseins," SZ 180ff; "Care as the Being of Dasein," BT 225ff.). In addition, Heidegger is often said to be so concerned about the individual as individual. Furthermore, sometimes it is not quite clear whether he uses «Dasein» and «es» in reference to Dasein «with regard to its Being» or in reference to an individual as individual. In light of these facts, one can easily imagine that he could have introduced a convention allowing him to speak of individuals as individuals in terms of gendered expressions, or he could have used expressions such as «ein Individuum da/dort,» in the sense of «an individual over there (and not somewhere else) and thrown into the world.» The translators for the most part preserved Heidegger's use, and this is certainly a good choice. I have used «Dasein» and «it» whenever I talk about Heidegger's text and the problems discussed in it.

14. Since both groups on the political Right strive for the resurrection of a vanished past, Tillich uses the term «romantics» as the common denominator and distinguishes between «conservative romantics» (by and large my «conservative rightists») and «revolutionary romantics» (my «revolutionary rightists») (see chapter 4, section B). I will use both Tillich's and my own terms and may also refer to the former group occasionally as «nostalgic romantics.»

15. «Feldwege» are field-paths. The singular (der Feldweg) was used by Heidegger as the title of a short text published in a private edition in 1949 that appeared in the bookshops in 1953 (Frankfurt: Klostermann, 1953). On this, see my paper "On Brinks and Bridges in Heidegger" (*Graduate Faculty Philosophy Journal* 18, no. 1 [1995]: 111–186, esp. 151–154).

16. As Foucault remarked, Derrida offers a pedagogy that «gives to the master's voice the limitless sovereignty which allows it to restate the text indefinitely» (quoted in Richard Wolin, "Afterword: Derrida on Marx, or the Perils of Left Heideggerianism," in his *Labyrinths: Explorations in the Critical History of Ideas* [Amherst: University of Massachusetts Press, 1995], 232). When Derrida in *Of Spirit* compares Heidegger to Husserl, he gets most of it «wrong; in fact, terribly and horrendously wrong» (Wolin, *The Heidegger Controversy*, xvi).

17. Reiner Schürmann, *Heidegger On Being and Acting: From Principles to Anarchy* (Bloomington: Indiana University Press, 1987), 3.

18. «Holz» is wood. In 1950 Heidegger published a collection of essays entitled *Holzwege* (Frankfurt: Klostermann, 1950). As he explains in the beginning of that book, «Holz» is also an old word for a small forest or wood. «Holzwege» are paths in the wood that often end abruptly and do not seem to lead anywhere. As Heidegger points out, the foresters and woodcutters know those paths, and they know what it means to be «on a Holzweg» (ibid., n.p.).

### Chapter 1

1. Johann Gottlieb Fichte, *Foundations of the Entire Science of Knowledge*, in *Science and Knowledge*, ed. and trans. P. Heath and J. Lachs (New York: Appleton-Century-Crofts, 1970), 123. German: «Das Ich setzt sich, als bestimmt durch das Nicht-Ich» (*Grundlage der gesammten Wissenschaftslehre, Fichtes Werke*, vol. 1, ed. I. H. Fichte [Berlin, 1845; reprint Berlin: De Gruyter, 1971], 127).

2. Fichte, *Foundations*, 130 («*Thätigkeit*,» *Grundlage*, 134).

3. *Grundlage*, 134.

4. «One could wish that the word suffering {Leiden} had fewer connotations. It scarcely needs saying that we are not to think of painful feelings here» (*Grundlage*, 134f.). One might say that this sentence reads a little bit strangely, since «painful feeling» is not a connotation but one of the core meanings of «Leiden.» Obviously, Heath and Lachs had this sentence in mind when they chose to translate Fichte's «Leiden» with «passivity.» Thus, their translation reads: «One could wish that the word passivity had fewer associated meanings. It scarcely needs saying that we are not to think of painful feeling here» (*Foundations*, 130). This sentence too, one might say, looks a little bit strange, but not for the same reason as Fichte's. «Passivity» (as the German abstract noun «Passivität») is much more general than «painful feeling.» Thus, «painful feeling» is not a meaning of «passivity» at all, but rather is related to «passivity» as species is to genus, or it would be a connotation of some species of «passivity.»

5. If «to anticipate» is used in connection with physical motion, as for instance, in the phrase «the basketball player anticipated the pass,» it refers less to the run itself and more to the preceding mental activity in the sense of «he anticipated the pass and thus ran forward and intercepted the ball.» Moreover, the broader connotations of the verb «to run» are preserved at both the level of mental and that of physical motion.

Thus, I can say that I «ran into a strange sentence in a book,» or just as easily that I «ran into a friend on the street» and thus had a conversation.

In German, in a description as short as the English «He anticipated the pass,» one uses neither «(vor)laufen» nor «antizipieren» (or «vorwegnehmen, vorhersehen») but rather «abfangen» («He fing the pass ab»). In a longer narrative, one says, as in English, «He antizipierte the pass (or: sah the pass voraus), lief vor (or dazwischen), and fing the pass ab.» At a conference on Lacan at the Collège International de Philosophie in Paris in June 1990, Derrida talked about the different occasions when he had met Lacan. One time, they were sitting on a plane to Baltimore. As Derrida told it, what came to their minds was la mort, death. If Heidegger had been sitting next to them or between them and had counted this as an instance of authentic «Vorlaufen,» he would have been the only one to apply «vorlaufen» to a mental activity.

6. On Heidegger's notions of «Bestand» and «Ge-stell» (enframing) and their relation to Auschwitz see my paper "On Brinks and Bridges in Heidegger," 130–142.

7. After World War I, the «Helden von Verdun» and their «Vorlaufen in den Tod» definitely were—to use the vocabulary of the late seventies when conservative philosophy professors and other intellectuals in Germany began what they called a «semantischen Kampf» (semantic battle) against Habermas and other leftists— «besetzt» (occupied, claimed, or possessed) by the political Right. Certainly, whatever Heidegger meant by «Vorlaufen zum Tod,» it would have indicated slightly more than «anticipate,» as employed in the phrase «I anticipate that it will rain tonight, therefore, I will bring my umbrella.» Furthermore, Heidegger's «anticipation of death» would have required him to minimalize the time interval between the anticipation and the situation anticipated, so as to make the ultimate possibility of death and its attendant threat strikingly present. For it is only inauthentic Dasein that, as it were, remains inside the walls and treats death as some remote future possibility that it needs not be concerned about for the present. Was it necessary to express the dramatic surplus value of «anticipation of death» over «anticipation of a rainfall» by means of «vorlaufen»? As mentioned, in contrast to the English «anticipate,» the German «antizipieren» is used only for mental activities, each of which entails a time interval. Precisely for this reason, one might say, Heidegger was forced to use «vorlaufen.» To be sure, even without its association with the Helden von Langemarck, «vorlaufen» provides the required dramatic flavor.

However, a lot of other words would have done just as well. Heidegger could have used phrases such as «sich konfrontieren mit» (to confront oneself with), «konfrontiert werden mit» (to be confronted with), «sich einer Gefahr oder dem Tode aussetzen» (to expose oneself to a danger or to death), «einer Gefahr ausgesetzt werden» (to be exposed to a danger), or something like «dem Tode ins Angesicht schauen» (to look into the face of death). (In section 74, he in fact says «go right under the eyes of Death,» BT 434; «dem Tod unter die Augen geht,» SZ 382.) The corresponding nouns «Konfrontation mit dem Tode,» «das Sich dem Tode Aussetzen,» or «das dem Tode ins Angesicht Schauen» would have looked like most other Heideggerian nouns, neither better nor worse. All these expressions would have been fully sufficient for academic discourse. In fact, they would have been preferable since academic discourse usually requires both a degree of abstraction and emotional neutrality. Quite clearly, anyone who wanted to avoid any possible associations between his theory of death and World War I and its attendant politics would not have used the phrase «vorlaufen in den Tod.» Furthermore, as shown above, there would have been no difficulty finding other terms. Consequently, Heidegger's use of «vorlaufen» is itself an «Übersetzung,» a transgression—indeed, a transgression of the very limits of academic discourse itself.

Of course, this transgression is in line with Heidegger's criticism of the universities of his time from the beginning of his career on, namely, that they did not address the concerns of factical existence. Because of the several peculiarities concerning the «vorlaufen in den Tod» I have pointed out, from the beginning of Division Two on one should be aware of the possibility that Heidegger did not mean his theory of historicality and politics to be (a) a-political (that is, about the exclusively personal decisions of an individual), (b) politically neutral, or (c) a theory of antitotalitarian, that is, anti-National Socialist politics.

8. Parmenides, *Fragments,* trans. David Gallop (Toronto: University of Toronto Press, 1984), 60 (fr. 6, l. 5).

9. See «Die Zueignung des Verstandenen, aber noch Eingehüllten vollzieht die Enthüllung» (SZ 150); «When something is understood but is still veiled, it becomes unveiled by» (BT 191). See the translators' remark (BT 15).

10. In German, the adjective «entschlossen» is used far more often than the abstract noun «Entschlossenheit.» (One might say, «I admire his Entschlossenheit,» or one might say «Im Zustand der, i.e. in the state of, Entschlossenheit.») However, one never says «in der Entschlossenheit sein» (to be in the Entschlossenheit). In section 74, Heidegger writes «Schicksalhaft in der sich überliefernden Entschlossenheit existierend» (SZ 384; «Existing fatefully in the resoluteness which hands itself down,» BT 436). Especially in the thirties, the preposition «in» in Heidegger has often, so to speak, enthusiastic connotations (see chapter 6, section A). In the state of Entschlossenheit Dasein no longer vacillates and is no longer in the dark, so to speak. Rather, in the state of Entschlossenheit Dasein itself, other Daseine, and matters in general have become entschlossen, i.e., unlocked in the sense of «offenbar» (SZ 386; «manifest,» BT 438), or they have become ent-hüllt in the sense of «durchsichtig» (SZ 122; «transparent,» BT 159). Therefore, in the state of resoluteness, Dasein is «hellsichtig» (SZ 384; «to have a clear vision,» BT 436). Thus, the «enthusiasm» of the state of resoluteness reminded Heidegger of the potential of «enthusiasm» in the preposition «in,» and he formulated the unusual phrase «in der . . . Entschlossenheit existierend.» For a further aspect of the prefix «ent-» and its function in Heidegger see chapter 2, section A.

In a note, the translators give the German text of the entire sentence with «to have a clear vision» and comment on it: «It should perhaps be pointed out that 'Ohnmacht' can also mean a 'faint' or a 'swoon', and that 'Hellsichtigkeit' is the regular term for 'clairvoyance'. Thus the German reader might easily read into this passage a suggestion of the seer's mystical trance» (BT 436, n. 2). This explanation is somewhat misleading. I have never met anyone who thought of a faint when reading the sentence with «*Übermacht*» («*superior power*») and «*Ohnmacht*» («*powerlessness*») (SZ 384; BT 436). It might be the case that when going «right under the eyes of Death» (BT 434; SZ 382), some inauthentic Dasein faints. However, authentic Dasein most certainly does not do so, and in the sentence on Übermacht and Ohnmacht Heidegger is definitely talking about authentic Dasein. Furthermore, the adjective «hellsichtig» is used in the sense of «clear-sighted» or «keen-minded,» and less often in the sense of «clairvoyant.» The regular German adjective equivalent to the English «clairvoyant» is «hellseherisch.» The related abstract noun, «Hellsichtigkeit,» is used in the sense of «clear-sightedness» or «keen-mindedness,» and only secondarily in the sense of «clairvoyance.» Even the German noun and verb for «(to be) clairvoyant,» that is, «Hellseher» and «hellsehen,» mean not only «clairvoyant» and «to be clairvoyant,» but often «someone who sees clearly» or «to have a keen mind.» The abstract noun related to those two words when they refer to clairvoyance is «Hellsehen» (clairvoyance) or «Hellseherei» («During periods of what one calls Enlightenment it is not that easy to make one's living by Hellseherei»). I have never encountered any native speakers of German who read into this passage «a suggestion of the seer's mystical trance,» nor do I recall having come across such an interpretation in the German literature on *Sein und Zeit.*

11. «Running into» sentences such as «Only by the anticipation of death is every accidental and 'provisional' possibility driven out» (BT 435; SZ 384), or «What if it is only in the *anticipation* of death that all the factical '*anticipatoriness*' of resolving would be authentically understood—in other words, that it would be *caught up with* in an existentiell way» (BT 350; SZ 302), one should keep in mind that, as the translators note (BT 350, n. 1), with «'provisional' possibility» they have translated Heidegger's «"vorläufige" Möglichkeit» (SZ 384), and with «'*anticipatoriness*'» Heidegger's «"*Vorläufigkeit*"» (SZ 302). «Läufig» is the adjective of «laufen» (to run). It is applied almost exclusively to animals: «die läufige Hündin» is «a bitch in heat.» When it is applied to human beings, it sounds as vulgar as the adjective to «heat» in similar phrases in English. (Heidegger's «vulgär» is translated by Macquarrie and Robinson not as «vulgar» but as «ordinary» [see, for instance, "of the Ordinary {vulgären} Conception of Time," BT 456; SZ 404].) «Vorläufig» (and its abstract noun «Vorläufigkeit»), however, is used only in the sense of «preliminary,» «provisional,» «temporary,» or «interim,» and does not sound vulgar at all. The English word «streetwalker» is obviously tailored as a non-discriminatory word for people of that profession of which the above mentioned English translation of «Hündin» is a discriminatory expression. Perhaps, it was coined because «to walk» is precisely what streetwalkers do not do. Either they «hang around,» or, in a case of danger, they run, rush, or hurry. «Streetwalker» has no direct German equivalent. One does not say «Straßengeherin» or «Straßengeher.» However, not the noun but rather the verb «gehen» (to walk, to go) is used that way in phrases like «Ich gehe zur Universität» (I go to a university = I am a student at a graduate school), or «Ich gehe täglich ins Museum» (I go to the museum every day). Thus, as others go to a university, streetwalkers «gehen auf den Strich» (walk on[to] the line). As is evident from this, in sentences like these, «gehen» can be used with various prepositions followed by the dative or the accusative. As for the streetwalkers, it is used with «auf» in the accusative («auf den,» not «auf dem»). This might be surprising since «Strich» (line) probably refers to the edge of the sidewalk along which streetwalkers walk. Thus, one might expect the German language to say «sie gehen am Strich (entlang)» or «sie gehen auf dem Strich (hin und her or entlang).» However, one might think, they «gehen auf den Strich (zu)» is meant in the sense of «Sie gehen zum Strich» (they go to[ward] the line) as a shorthand for «Sie gehen auf den Strich zu und dann an ihm entlang» (they go toward the line, turn onto it, and walk along the line). Thus, most probably the expression «auf den Strich gehen» is syntactically similar to sentences such as «Ich gehe auf die Wiese» or «Ich gehe auf's Eis (des Flusses),» that is, I approach a certain area, a

meadow or a frozen river, and then I move around in that area (see *Deutsches Wörter-buch von Jacob und Wilhelm Grimm*, vol. 19 [Stob–Strollen] [Leipzig: Hirzel Verlag, 1957; reprint Munich: Deutscher Taschenbuchverlag, 1984], 1529f., 1561). From the viewpoint of ordinary Dasein, the streetwalkers have «immer schon» (always already) transgressed the edge. Thus, «gefallene Mädchen» (fallen girls) is another name for streetwalkers. Most of the time, «gefallene Mädchen» is somewhat derogatory though it can connote some sympathy or mercy. However, there is hardly any sympathy implied when «fallen» is combined with the prefix «ver-» (Heidegger's «verfallen,» «Verfallenheit» is translated with «fallen,» or «deteriorate,» «fallenness» ; see «ver-fallen» in the glossary of BT, 519). One says, some person is « einer Droge, einem Menschen, einer sexuellen Perversion, einer Ideologie, etc. verfallen» (addicted to a drug, a person, a sexual perversion, an ideology, etc.) if one highly disapproves of this behavior, if one thinks the person will ruin his or her life, and if one sees no chance for that person to liberate himself or herself from the addiction. Probably for ordinary Dasein in the twenties in Germany, Prof. Unrat in Heinrich Mann's novel *Professor Unrat* (adapted for the screen as *Der Blaue Engel* [*The Blue Angel*] star-ring Marlene Dietrich and Emil Jannings) was the paradigm of a person who is «jeman-dem verfallen.» («Unrat» means «rubbish,» or «filth» ; in his novel Heinrich Mann often has the word sound as though the character's name were «Professor Un-Rat,» that is, «Professor without-Counsel» or «without Way out» or «Professor With-the-Wrong-Advice.») As in these examples, the verb «verfallen» is used in the perfect participle form in the passive voice. Thus, an ordinary Dasein might have said or thought, «Die gefallenen Mädchen sind dem Strich verfallen» (the fallen girls are addicted to the edge of the sidewalk) in the sense of «the fallen girls have fallen down the edge of the sidewalk,» that is, «sie liegen in der Gosse» (they are lying in the gut-ter) with no hope of reversing their fallenness. At that point another meaning of «ver-fallen» comes to mind. Their lives are verfallen (have expired). Thus, during fascism they were, along with others, put into concentration camps.

On a walk toward a brink and along the brink to the point, or area, of fall in Hei-degger with further remarks on the use of prepositions such as «am,» «an den,» «zum,» «auf den» in connection with verbs like «gehen» see my paper "On Brinks and Bridges in Heidegger," 116–124.

12. Heidegger uses the notion of call in both the chapters on conscience (sections 54 through 60, BT 312–348; SZ 267–301) and on anticipatory resoluteness (sections 61 through 66, BT 349–382; SZ 301–333) but not in the section on historicality. How-ever, in section 72 he says that in the chapter on historicality «we come back in our investigation to the problem which we touched upon immediately before exposing temporality to view—the question of the constancy of the Self, which we defined as the "who" of Dasein,» and in the accompanying note he refers to section 64 (BT 427; SZ 375; see also the reference to section 63, BT 428; SZ 375). As was already men-tioned, at the beginning of section 74 Heidegger returns to the notion of anticipatory resoluteness and refers to sections 60 and 62 and a passage in section 58 (BT 434; SZ 382f.). In addition, in the same section he says that «only if death, guilt, con-science, freedom, and finitude reside together equiprimordially in the Being of an entity as they do in care, can that entity exist in the mode of fate» (BT 437; SZ 385). In the chapters on conscience and on anticipatory resoluteness, Heidegger shows how the call calls Dasein forth into anticipatory resoluteness, and he already characterizes

the call as «one which calls us back in calling us forth» (BT 326; «vorrufenden Rück-ruf,» SZ 280). However, it is only in the chapter on historicality that Heidegger elaborates the «horizon» (BT 434; SZ 383) of possibilities from which Dasein, having run forward into death, can choose. In other words, in the chapters on conscience and anticipatory resoluteness Heidegger elaborates the notion of death. In the chapter on historicality, however, he complements this analysis with that of birth, heritage, destiny, and fate. The analysis of conscience and anticipatory resoluteness would, so to speak, stand only on one leg without the chapter on historicality, and the former finds its completion only in the latter.

In the course of this book, I will to some degree discuss the relation between Division One of *Being and Time*, the chapters on conscience and anticipatory resoluteness, and the chapter on historicality. For more on this issue, however, see my book *Society, Community, Fate, and Decision: From Kant to Benjamin* (in progress). In addition, it will become clear that the key terms in section 74 take up and echo the ones in the chapters on conscience and anticipatory resoluteness.

13. Jürgen Habermas, *The Philosophical Discourse of Modernity: Twelve Lectures,* trans. F. Lawrence (Cambridge, MA: MIT Press, 1987), 141.

14. As the beginning of her comment shows, she interprets Macquarrie and Robinson already according to the model of counterattack and regards Heidegger's «erwidert» to be an even stronger distancing than a counterattack would be. Since my main point is that any interpretation of «erwidert» as some sort of distancing is false, I can leave open what precisely she means by «resistance and displacement» (TP 31) and whether the translators would regard Birmingham's or my «Guignonian» account of them as more faithful to their intentions. Birmingham obviously doesn't distinguish between «erwidert» and «Widerruf» («disavowal»). As her quote from *Being and Time* and her comments show, Birmingham always adds «(*Erwidert*)» to «*reciprocative rejoinder*» and its equivalents, but she never adds Heidegger's German word «Widerruf» to the English «disavowal.» Since for Birmingham both sentences, the one with «erwidert» as well as the one with «Widerruf,» refer to the same gesture of displacement, she seems to assume that one can therefore regard the verb «erwidert» as, so to speak, the verbalization of the preposition and prefix «wider» in «Widerruf.» Grammatically, only the «wider» in «Widerruf» is a preposition, or rather a prefix, whereas the «wider» in «erwidert» is the root of a verb that can be connected with several different prefixes, for instance, «er-» in «erwidern,» or «an-» in «anwidern.»

15. See Aristotle's summary: «For it is by proportionate requital (τῷ ἀντιποιεῖν ἀνάλογον) that the city holds together. Men seek to return either evil for evil—and if they cannot do so, think their position mere slavery—or good for good—and if they cannot do so there is no exchange (μετάδοσις), but it is by exchange that they hold together. This is why they give a prominent place to the temple of the Graces (Χαρίτων ἱερὸν)—to promote the requital of services (ἀνταπόδοσις); for this is characteristic of grace (ἴδιον χάριτος)—we should serve in return (ἀνθυπηρετῆσαι) one who has shown grace to us (χαρισαμένῳ), and should another time take the initiative in showing it» (*Nicomachean Ethics,* V, 8, 1132b: 33–1133a: 5)

In the classical book on the issue of gifts, Marcel Mauss writes, for instance: "Les dons échangés et l'obligation de les rendre" (M. Mauss, *Essai sur le don: Forme et raison de l'échange dans les sociétés archaïques,* in *Sociologie et anthropologie* [Paris: Presses Universitaires de France, 1973], 154), and «*L'obligation de rendre est tout le potlatch,* dans la mesure où il ne consiste pas en pure destruction. . . . L'obligation de rendre dignement est impérative. On perd la "face" à jamais si on ne rend pas, ou si on ne détruit pas les valeurs équivalentes» (ibid., 212). Moldenhauer in her translation uses «Erwiderung,» «Erwidern,» and «erwidern» in the accusative: "Die Gaben und die Pflicht, sie zu erwidern" (*Die Gabe: Form und Funktion des Austauschs in archaischen Gesellschaften,* trans. Eva Moldenhauer [Frankfurt: Suhrkamp, 1968], 27) and «*Die Pflicht des Erwiderns.* Soweit er nicht in reiner Zerstörung besteht, macht die Pflicht des Erwiderns das Wesen des Potlatsch aus. . . . Außerdem muß die Erwiderung in würdevoller Form geschehen. Man verliert für immer sein "Gesicht", wenn man ihn nicht erwidert oder die entsprechenden Werte nicht zerstört» (ibid., 100f.). Her translation comes to the mind of every translator immediately and without any thinking. Any other translation—even one with «(be)antworten» or «zurückerstatten» —would require some time to come up with and would sound more or less awkward, if only in comparison to her translation. An English translation reads: "Gifts and the Obligation to return Gifts" (*The Gift: Forms and Functions of Exchange in Archaic Societies,* trans. Jan Cunnison [New York: Norton, 1967], 6) and «*The Obligation to Repay.* Outside of pure destruction the obligation to repay is the essence of potlatch. . . . The obligation of worthy return is imperative. Face is lost for ever if it is not made or if equivalent value is not destroyed» (ibid., 40f.). I might note in advance that, in my interpretation, Heidegger's use of «*erwidert*» does not coincide with an Erwiderung in the sense of the potlatch since it lacks the symmetrical reciprocity, the to and fro, of expectations and obligations of the potlatch. However, in contrast to the other forms of Erwiderung, Heidegger's concept of it has in common with the potlatch that one meets an expectation, or fulfills a request, whereas in an Erwiderung in the dative («No, I won't leave the room!») as well as in an Erwiderung in the accusative in the sense of a successful defense or counterattack one does just the opposite of what one's opponent commands, hopes, or expects one to do. For in the latter cases one does not, so to speak, give in or obey, but rather resists.

16. See the «telephone receiver» (BT 141; SZ 107). For the «appeal» of a phone call that called upon one in one of these huge and quiet Berlin apartments of the haute bourgeoisie, see Walter Benjamin's "Das Telephon" in his *Berliner Kindheit um Neunzehnhundert* (*Gesammelte Schriften,* vol. IV.1 [Frankfurt: Suhrkamp, 1972], 242–243).

17. In Heidegger's text Volk is accompanied by the definite article and not, as in the English translation, by the indefinite one («das Geschehen der Gemeinschaft, des Volkes,» SZ 384). It might be hard to imagine for English readers, but the definite article makes a big difference. If Heidegger had used the indefinite one, he would have written—at that point, at least—in the attitude of Weberian Wertfreiheit, value neutrality; or he would have talked about different people the way Herder talked about them, namely, as so many different flowers in the huge garden of mankind. In other words, he would have used «Volk» as a descriptive category that doesn't exclude any empirical member of the respective Volk. However, at Heidegger's time «Volk» with the definite article was most of the time used as a polemical notion in Carl Schmitt's sense, that is, as an excluding category. By using «Volk» with the definite article in texts on history and politics an author most of the time polemicized against liberals and leftists and thus excluded some empirical members of the Volk from the Volk (see chapters 3 and 4), especially since, at Heidegger's time even the phrase with the indefinite article could serve polemical purposes.

In the last years of his life, Hermann Cohen spent all his energy on a book on religion, Judaism, and reason without being able to complete it fully. In 1919, one year after his death, it was published under the title *Die Religion der Vernunft aus den Quellen des Judentums* (The religion of reason from the sources of Judaism). It had to be edited in great haste. In its second, revised edition in 1929 the definite article before «religion» was left out since in two letters to the Gesellschaft zur Förderung der Wissenschaft des Judentums from July and December 1917 Cohen had said that he wanted the title without the definite article (see the afterword of the editor, Bruno Strauß, to the second edition, Hermann Cohen, *Religion der Vernunft aus den Quellen der Judentums* [Frankfurt: J. Kauffmann; photomechanical reprint Darmstadt: Joseph Melzer, 1966], 625). In his 1930 review of the second edition, Franz Rosenzweig describes the circumstances surrounding the first edition and comments on the change of the title as follows: «In the first nine years of its existence, the book even came along under a wrong title. It was entitled: "Die Religion der Vernunft aus den Quellen des Judentums." It's true title is: "Religion der Vernunft aus den Quellen des Judentums"—without the aggressive and intolerant definite—in this case really all too definite—article. Of course, the opposite is not meant either, namely, the indefinite article, which in this case would certainly be too indefinite. Rather, as far from haughty exclusiveness as from lazy "anything goes," Cohen focuses on that share in the one and universal religion of reason that is passed on to him by the sources of Judaism he has inherited» (Franz Rosenzweig, "Vertauschte Fronten," *Der Morgen,* 6. Jahrgang, April 1930, 1. Heft, 85f.). While Rosenzweig's comment in regard to the article is certainly always possible, and while from a narrow logical point of view one might even say that it is not necessarily cogent, it was certainly appropriate in, and facilitated by, the polemical usage in the twenties of the definite article on the Right («das Volk») and, for that matter, on the Left as well («das Proletariat,» «die Kapitalistenklasse»). In all my subsequent quotations of Heidegger's sentence with «der Gemeinschaft, des Volkes» I will quote the English translation in the following way: «the community, of {the} people» (BT 436; SZ 384).

One can witness the increase of the polemical politics of de-cision and exclusion by comparing the prefaces Hermann Cohen's widow, Martha Cohen, wrote for the two editions of the book. Especially the preface to the second edition is a very moving document. In addition, she points out a geographical fact that illuminates Cohen's effort. Having quoted a non-Jewish theologian's praise of the first edition, she continues: «How much consolation, how much hope is given by such a sincere and heartfelt understanding {of the Jew Cohen's book by a Christian theologian} in these times of great conflicts! How strongly does {the sincere and heartfelt understanding of the Jew Cohen's book by a Christian theologian} confirm the unifying influence of the great personality of Hermann Cohen! Indeed, it might seem not without deeper significance that his town of birth, Coswig, is situated between the town of Luther, Wittenberg, and the home of Moses Mendelssohn» (*Religion der Vernunft aus den Quellen der Judentums,* n.p.). It is the same politics of Ausgleich pursued by the late Scheler after his Kehre (see chapter 3, section F) and taken up by Tillich (see chapter 4, section B) in order to overcome the polemical politics of decision.

18. Walter Benjamin, "The Storyteller: Reflections on the Works of Nikolai Leskov," in *Illuminations: Essays and Reflections,* ed. Hannah Arendt, trans. Harry Zohn (New York: Schocken Books, 1969), 83f. Benjamin says «Stellungskrieg.» Thus, one might replace «tactical warfare» with «trench warfare.»

19. Walter Benjamin, "Erfahrung und Armut," *Gesammelte Schriften,* vol. II.1 (Frankfurt: Suhrkamp, 1977), 214.

20. Ibid., 218. Mickey Mouse shows up also, not in the second, but in the first version of Benjamin's *The Work of Art in the Age of Mechanical Reproduction, Gesammelte Schriften,* vol. I.2 (Frankfurt: Suhrkamp, 1974), 462.

21. See on this my book *Society, Community, Fate, and Decision: From Kant to Benjamin* (in progress).

22. In *Deutsches Wörterbuch von Jacob und Wilhelm Grimm,* vol. 23 (Stuttgart: Hirzel Verlag, 1936; reprint Munich: Deutscher Taschenbuchverlag, 1984), cc. 396f., one finds for «überliefern» a first group of meanings with examples like «to deliver a letter» or «he handed over the flock of sheep to his master» and a second group summarized by the formula «to *ausliefern/preisgeben* (hand over/surrender) someone to the enemy, the court, the devil, etc.» with both German words belonging to the strongest ones available for such events. «Ausliefern/Auslieferung» is still today the official term for «to extradite, extradition.» It is also used with regard to private relationships. Person A is treated extremely badly by A's lover, B. However, for some reason A is not able to leave B, as much as A would like to, and A doesn't know why A cannot leave B. Thus, if asked why he or she doesn't leave B, A can give only that type of answer that, in a way, is no answer, and this answer is formulated with the perfect passive participle of «ausliefern» («I am ihr/ihm ausgeliefert») or of «verfallen» («I am ihm/ihr verfallen») (see above, n. 11). «To be completely (or, auf Gedeih und Verderben) ausgeliefert to someone» is used to convey that one is completely at someone else's mercy.

23. A literal translation would read: «for it is in resoluteness that first and foremost the choice is chosen which makes free for the fighting emulation and loyalty for what-can-be-repeated.» The phrase «emulation» («Nachfolge») might be an allusion to the Christian Imitation of Christ. As will become clear in the course of the book, however, Heidegger's notion of historicality is independent of the Christian theory of history. There are certainly similarities between some Christians and people on the Right, and some people on the Right used those similarities to make their position attractive for Christians. However, neither genetically nor systematically did extreme rightist politics at Heidegger's time derive from the Christian theory of history. In my book, Tillich and Scheler are two cases in point. Tillich strongly opposed the Christian notion of history as he understood it to any rightist one (see section B of chapter 4), and so did Scheler after for some time deriving from his understanding of Christian politics a notion of revolutionary rightist politics that was incompatible with National Socialist politics (see chapter 3). In addition, if one wants to see the Christian motif of original sin and recovery at work in rightist politics at the time, one should keep in mind that rightist politics has forgotten about the theological veto upon the realization of recovery here on earth as a human achievement. Much more important is the notion of «loyalty» (Treue). The «emulation» is fighting «kämpfende» . If there is a fight («Kampf» as in «Only in communicating and in struggling {In der Mitteilung und im Kampf} does the power of destiny become free,» BT 436; SZ 384), there might be casualties. Off the top of my head, I would say that with the exception of Rockmore (*On Heidegger's Nazism and Philosophy,* 48), critics have not considered the possibility that in choosing its hero, authentic Dasein might run the risk of getting killed in the fights consequent upon this choice (though on the lists of possible heroes to choose from several individuals are named who

suffered a violent death: Socrates, Martin Luther King, and Sitting Bull, see above p. 8). (As I realized after finishing the chapters on Heidegger, it might well be the case that my book is just an elaboration of pp. 47 and 48 of Rockmore's book.) The reason for this omission in the American interpretations of Heidegger will become obvious in chapter 5, section C. As I have already shown with reference to Guignon, and as will become clearer in section C of chapter 5, there is a certain instrumentalization of the hero at work in the usual American understanding of the hero and his or her function for the authentic Dasein that has chosen the hero. For the hero is not chosen for his own sake. Rather, he is chosen for the sake of the utopian ideal of the choosing Dasein and thus for the sake of the choosing Dasein itself. The self-understanding of the choosing Dasein, however, does not necessarily imply a reference to something, or someone, else which is, as it were, «higher» than the choosing Dasein itself. The same holds true if it is not one Dasein alone but rather a group of Daseine that chooses. If the chosen hero is not chosen for his own sake, but rather for the sake of the choosing Dasein, the latter might have second thoughts about its choice, if it turns out that in consequence of this choice the Dasein might get killed. It might abandon its hero, or it might, as Guignon says, «creatively reinterpret» (HC 138) the hero in order to avoid its own death. However, such an instrumentalization of the hero or of what can be repeated, that is, the past, is the opposite of what was understood by «Treue zum Wiederholbaren.» Conservatives and right-wingers of Heidegger's time would have felt insulted by such a Zumutung, imposition. To be sure, conservatives and right-wingers are also familiar with and prone to all the «kleinen Treuen und Untreuen,» fidelities and infidelities. But these are matters of everyday life or of a Dasein more or less close to the bottom of its downward plunge, or—if one is an authentic Dasein—they are the exceptions from the norms of the ethical life a true conservative or rightist in some way always maintains to have a right to. When conservatives or rightists speak of Treue in contexts where it matters, that is, in the context of historicality, destiny, fate, and Kampf, they mean the Treue for which «we Germans» are well-known, which has always waited behind the everyday Treue and Untreue for the call and its hour, and which some of the rightists—not all!—call «Nibelungentreue,» the Treue of the Nibelungs. Such a Treue designates a loyalty to the past, common cause, or good, that is willing to go «bis in den Tod,» into death; that is, people showing this Treue are willing to sacrifice their lives if that is required by the pursuit of the repetition of the past or the common good. Right at the beginning of Hitler's *Mein Kampf*—nay, even prior to its beginning, namely, in the dedication—Hitler has a sentence that sounds similar to Heidegger's sentence as quoted above. He lists the names of, and dedicates the first volume to, all those who died «on November 9, 1923, at 12.30 in the afternoon, in front of the Feldherrnhalle» (that is, during the unsuccessful putsch in which Hitler and his party wanted to take over the rule of Bavaria). They did so «with loyal faith in the resurrection of their people» (MKe n.p.; «im treuen Glauben an die Wiederauferstehung ihres Volkes,» MK n.p.). By quoting this sentence of Hitler's, I don't maintain that Heidegger's sentence is National Socialist. Taken by itself, it might not even necessarily be conservative or rightist. As will become clear, however, its context, if nothing else, makes Heidegger's sentence an expression of right-wing politics.

Treue is the capacity to abandon, overcome, transcend one's egoistic concerns and to dedicate oneself wholeheartedly and continuously to the cause of something else, an individual, a group, or the Volksgemeinschaft. Right-wingers of Heidegger's time maintained that only right-wingers are capable of Treue whereas liberals and leftists indulge in their egoistic interests and are not capable nor willing to transcend them (see chapter 3). However, for the sake of the argument the right-wingers might allow Treue to be present also in liberals and leftists. Even in that case, however, they themselves as well as leftists and liberals would insist on the difference between the Right on one hand and all others. For, as I will show in chapters 3 and 4, right-wingers as well as leftists and liberals were aware of the fact that right-wingers are loyal to a repeatable past, whereas liberals and leftists are loyal to the present and the future as being different from the past and only secondarily, if at all, loyal to the past.

24. One might think that the expression «hands itself down» in the subordinate clause, «The resoluteness which comes back to itself and hands itself down» (BT 437; SZ 385), means an act in which resoluteness establishes a tradition for future generations. However, this is excluded by the main clause of the sentence, by the preceding passage on heritage, destiny, and fate (see chapter 2) as well as by the sentences, immediately following, on repetition and on the choice of the hero and Treue. Thus, one cannot read the expression as «hands itself down [to/for the future generations]» but only as «hands itself down [to the possibility it has inherited].»

25. In German this passage reads as follows: «Das wiederholende Sichüberliefern einer gewesenen Möglichkeit erschließt jedoch das dagewesene Dasein nicht, um es abermals zu verwirklichen. Die Wiederholung des Möglichen ist weder ein Wiederbringen des "Vergangenen", noch ein Zurückbinden der "Gegenwart" an das "Überholte". Die Wiederholung läßt sich, einem entschlossenen Sichentwerfen entspringend, nicht vom "Vergangenen" überreden, um es als das vormals Wirkliche nur wiederkehren zu lassen» (SZ 385f.). None of the thirteen sentences of the entire paragraph has as its grammatical subject a «Dasein,» but rather each of them has «resoluteness,» «*repetition*,» and the like. See the translators' remark (BT 15). To be sure, nouns ending in «-ung,» «-keit,» or «-heit» can shorten the text significantly. However, at the same time, in this case it is part of the strategy to reveal basic passivities as the purpose of Dasein's activities.

26. «If you are not willing, I use violence» (Johann Wolfgang von Goethe, "Erlkönig").

27. Birmingham sets off the passage beginning with «The repeating of that which . . . » (BT 437; SZ 385) and ending with the sentence with «Widerruf» (BT 438; SZ 386), and she quotes the sentence with «Widerruf» as follows: «But when such a rejoinder is made to this possibility in a resolution, it is made in a *moment of vision; and as such* it is at the same time a *disavowal* of that which in the 'today' is working itself out as the "past" (SZ, 385–386/437–438)» (TP 31). Thus, readers familiar with Macquarrie and Robinson's usage of quotation marks will expect the same German text as above. For they will assume that the single quotation marks with «today» represent Heidegger's quotation marks, and that the double quotation marks with «past» are one of those added by the translators. Readers not familiar with the translators' usage of quotation marks will wonder about the single quotation marks with «today,» will consult Macquarrie and Robinson's translation, and will finally realize that Birmingham treated the quotation marks in *Being and Time* as though she had run in the quote and not set it off as a block quotation.

28. See above, n. 14.

29. As the title of a short text by Freud already indicates ("Erinnern, Wiederholen und Durcharbeiten," "Recollecting, Repeating, and Working Through"), the psycho-

analytic notion of repetition refers to a person retrieving and repeating his or her past. However, the purpose of this repetition is to liberate oneself from this past by «disempowering» it. This notion of origins and one's relation to them is in line with the modern notion of Enlightenment and of reflection. Birmingham interprets «fate» as the moment in which tradition is displaced and disempowered, that is, destroyed (see above pp. 46ff.). She could have made her interpretation more dramatic if she had interpreted «Schicksal» as I do. Fate, destiny, or Volk raises its voice and demands our subjugation. However, in the sentences on Erwiderung and Widerruf, authentic Dasein disrupts continuity and refuses to subjugate itself. Alternately, one might say that in the sentence on Erwiderung authentic Dasein tentatively subjugates itself in order thereupon, however,—that is, in the sentence on Widerruf—to fight back and to distance itself from the past (see on this possibility section C of chapter 5). However, the fact that the objects of the Erwiderung and the Widerruf differ excludes both variants of this interpretation.

30. This is already shown by a passage in which Heidegger uses «Heute» with regard to inauthentic Dasein and thus puts it in quotation marks since inauthentic Dasein is not capable of seeing the Gegenwart (present) as «Heute» («today»): «In inauthentic historicality, on the other hand, the way in which fate has been primordially stretched along has been hidden. With the inconstancy of the they-self Dasein makes present its 'today' {sein "Heute"}» (BT 443; SZ 391). It is also supported by the sentence in question itself. For the Erwiderung «is made *in a moment of vision*» (BT 438; in the German text, the words in italics modify «Erwiderung» : «Die Erwiderung . . . *als augenblickliche* der *Widerruf,*» SZ 386), and Heidegger explains «*Augenblick*» («*moment of vision*») as the present that is present for authentic Dasein, i.e., as «*eigentliche Gegenwart*» («*Present . . . authentic*») in contradistinction to «*Gegenwärtigen*» («*making present*») as the present as it exists for inauthentic Daseine (SZ 338; BT 387f.). In the context of this passage as well as in section 74, Heidegger uses the concept of «Situation» («situation»). The best commentary on his usage seems to be his own comment in the so-called Natorp-Bericht: «In contrast to *location* [Lage], the *situation* [*Situation*] of factical life denotes life's taking-a-stance which is made transparent as falling and which is *apprehended* in the given concrete worry as in the possible counter-movement to falling care {verfallenden Sorge}» ("Phenomenological Interpretations with Respect to Aristotle: Indication of the Hermeneutical Situation," trans. Michael Baur, *Man and World* 25 [1992], 364; "Phänomenologische Interpretationen zu Aristoteles: Anzeige der hermeneutischen Situation," *Dilthey-Jahrbuch* 6 [1989], 243).

31. As in English, quotation marks in German indicate that one is quoting, talking about a term and its meaning or that one is distancing oneself from what one refers to. Derrida wrote an entire book on the use of quotation marks with «Geist» in *Being and Time* and their absence with the same word in the *Rectorate Address* (*Of Spirit: Heidegger and the Question*). So as not to have to comment on all quotation marks or the lack of them, I note here that, of course, not all quotation marks in *Sein und Zeit* are meant to indicate distance. The fact that many quotation marks are not distancing or disparaging makes those that are all the more disparaging.

32. See on this my book *Society, Community, Fate, and Decision: From Kant to Benjamin.*

33. The mountains cannot but repeat what is called out to them. The only other possibility left to them is not to answer at all, that is, not to listen to the call. In English,

one can say that a performance or a speech had a «good echo» or that it had a «bad echo.» Thus, in contrast to the mountains, those who produce the echo are in a position to contradict. In German, «Echo» in this sense is used only seldom and only as «good echo,» as a confirmation. One doesn't say a speech received a «schlechtes Echo» (bad echo). That is, in German an echo is almost by definition something that cannot contradict the original sound. The English «bad echo» is usually translated as «schlechten Anklang,» Anklang being somewhat similar to but not the same as Echo. However, in contrast to English, in German «Echo» is not used as a verb. In an article about the new conservatism among many young people in Spain, Alan Riding writes that the new leader of the People's Party, Mr. José María Aznar, «is still just 40 and, while anything but a charismatic campaigner, he has found himself being acclaimed in universities by young people for whom attacks on the Government echo their own growing frustration with the Spain spawned by a decade of Socialist rule» ("Spanish Students Rebelling against the Left," *The New York Times*, Friday, June 4, 1993, 59). Hannah Arendt would surely have liked sentences such as this one. For in situations like these some people «echo» others who in turn, so to speak, «re-echo» the former and so on. This is how power is generated that is then turned against the status quo and its inherent violence. As to Heidegger's notorious sentence on the German and Greek languages as «the most powerful and most spiritual of all languages» (IM 57; EM 43), in this case he is right at least with regard to the similarities between both languages. For, the Greek verb ἠχέω, or ἀχέω, seems to have been used in the sense of «to sound,» «to ring,» or «to peal,» but not in the sense of the quote. Even if, however, it was also used that way, most of the Greek philosophers didn't like motions as formless as power in Hannah Arendt's sense.

Note that, at least for the person who receives it, an echo is most of the time a wonderful or miraculous event. An echo always entails more than, so to speak, echo simple, more than just the physical process of literally repeating what was said. The surplus over echo simple is what makes an echo an echo, and this surplus is present in the sentence «Die Berge erwidern meinen Ruf.» One must not mix that sentence up with the German saying «Wie man in den Wald hineinruft, so schallt es heraus» (As you call into the forest, so does the sound return to you). One uses the latter in the sense of «you get as much as you give» and in cases of echo simple, if one is annoyed with, or angry about, someone who agrees to anything, and who doesn't show any initiative. Thus, Heidegger might say that it is said by someone who finds forests pretty boring, and who thus isn't a «real German.» A «real German» would use this sentence only ironically (to hide his anger) since the person lacking any initiative, or enthusiasm, would display the caricature of the relationship between a «real German» and the «deutsche Wald» (the German Forest). For the «deutsche Wald» animates and inspires a «real German.» The «German forest,» as it were, «echoes» the «real German,» or rather, the «real German» «echoes» the «German forest.» As to suggestions or commands, the person receiving a command must not just respond by means of echo simple. For such a response always gives rise to the suspicion that the person has mental and emotional reservations about the command. Rather, he must display the proper surplus over echo simple that shows that he obeys and realizes the command wholeheartedly and enthusiastically (see, for instance, the fourth and fifth of the National Socialist «laws of life» of the German student, chapter 3, n. 17; see also «to stand in the storm» in section A of chapter 6). Note that, if one applies this to authentic Dasein, one no longer talks exclusively in terms of mere subjugation. The enthusiasm accompanying subjugation enables one to realize the call, that is, to cancel the world of inauthentic Dasein. See also chapters 2 and 3.

I have gathered the «German experience» of the «German forest» by listening to the call or whisper of the «German soul» or by just echoing—like the echo simple or «idle talk» —an old stereotype. However, here are some pieces of a speech by Heidegger on Albert Leo Schlageter. Schlageter was one of the top «Helden» of the Nazis. He belonged to the «Freikorps,» illegal armed groups that performed acts of sabotage in Poland, East Prussia, and in the «occupied» Rheinland and that attacked the Polish people, Communists, Social Democrats and other «enemies of the people.» Sabotaging a railroad track in the Rheinland, Schlageter was captured, sentenced to death, and executed according to martial law on the twenty-sixth of May 1923 (see Farías, *Heidegger and Nazism,* 87ff.; *Heidegger und der Nationalsozialismus,* 142ff.; Jay W. Baird, *To Die for Germany: Heroes in the Nazi Pantheon* [Bloomington: Indiana University Press, 1990], 26ff.). In Baden, each year a ceremony commemorating Schlageter was held on the anniversary of his execution. On this occasion in 1933, that is, shortly after the Machtergreifung, in his speech on the front steps of the main entrance to the university Heidegger said: «Whence this *hardness of will {Härte des Willens},* which allowed him to endure the most severe ordeal {das Schwerste durchzustehen}? Whence this *clarity of heart,* which allowed him to envision what was greatest and most remote {*Klarheit des Herzens,* das Größte und Fernste sich vor die Seele zu stellen}? Student of Freiburg! German student! When on your hikes and marches you set foot in the mountains, forests, and valleys of this Black Forest, the home of this hero {die Heimat dieses Helden}, experience this and know: the mountains among which the young farmer's son grew up are of primitive stone, of granite! They have long been at work hardening the will {Sie schaffen seit langem an der Härte des Willens}. The autumn sun of the Black Forest bathes the mountain ranges and forests in the most glorious clear light. It has long nourished clarity of the heart {Sie nährt seit langem die Klarheit des Herzens}» (Farías, *Heidegger und der Nationalsozialismus,* 146; this is my own translation; see Farías, *Heidegger and Nazism,* 91; Wolin, ed., *The Heidegger Controversy,* 41). Another passage reads: «With a hard will and a clear heart, Albert Leo Schlageter died his death, the most difficult and the greatest of all. Student of Freiburg, let the strength of this hero's native mountains flow into your will {in deinen Willen strömen}! Student of Freiburg, let the strength of the autumn sun of this hero's native valley shine into your heart! Preserve both within you and carry them, hardness of will and clarity of heart, to your comrades at the German university» (Wolin, ed., *The Heidegger Controversy,* 41; see Farías, *Heidegger and Nazism,* 92; German edition, 147). I will also quote the next passage, for as I will discuss in chapters 2, 3, and 5, several scholars regard «fate» («Schicksal») in section 74 of *Sein und Zeit* to be a power with which authentic Dasein breaks. Or, alternatively, they maintain that fate is produced by the Dasein in the sense that once Dasein has become authentic, it can freely—no longer determined by the «they» or someone else—create its own fate. I will show that it is just the other way around, namely, that an individual's fate preexists and determines the individual, and that authenticity consists in complying with one's fate, whereas inauthentic Daseine try to avoid or to «shirk» it. At the same time, the passage shows also that Heidegger used «Held» in the sense prevalent at that time, namely, in line with the paradigmatic case of the «Helden von Langemarck»: «Schlageter walked these grounds as a student. But Freiburg could not hold him for long. He was compelled to go to the Baltic; he was compelled to go to Upper Silesia; he was compelled to go to the Ruhr. He was not permitted to escape his destiny so that he could die the most difficult and greatest of all deaths with a hard will and a clear heart {Er durfte seinem Schicksal nicht ausweichen, um den schwersten und größten Tod harten Willens und klaren Herzens zu sterben}. We honor the hero {den Helden} and raise our arms in silent greeting» (Wolin, ed., *The Heidegger Controversy*, 42; see Farías, *Heidegger and Nazism*, 93; German edition, 148). Since I began this part with the «Helden von Langemarck,» let me mention that—one feels tempted to say, of course—Heidegger began his speech on Leo Schlageter with a reference to the German soldiers in World War I (see Farías, *Heidegger and Nazism*, 89f.; German edition, 144f.; Wolin, ed., *The Heidegger Controversy*, 40; instead of the sentence «He alone must convey to the soul of the people the image of their future awakening to honor and greatness, in order to die in faith» in Farías [*Heidegger and Nazism*, 90] read with Wolin: «Alone, drawing on his own inner strength, he had to place before his soul an image of the future awakening of the Volk to honor and greatness so that he could die believing in this future» [*The Heidegger Controversy*, 40f.]; see Farías, *Heidegger und der Nationalsozialismus*, 145).

Note that the second of the four quotes provides a good example of the double aspect of Entschlossenheit I mentioned in section A of this chapter. Heidegger calls upon the listeners to make an Entscheidung, that is, to no longer vacillate between several voices but rather to listen to the one voice, the voice of the people. In doing so, one ent-schließt sich, opens oneself and becomes a passive vessel so that «the power of the mountains of this hero's home» can «stream in your will.» Filled with «the power of the mountains of this hero's home,» one acquires «*hardness of will*» that enables one to be verschlossen für (closed against) the other voices and that empowers one to work for the realization of the task fate has ordained and to endure the consequences of this labor.

I will elaborate the «German» notion of fate in chapters 2 and 3. However, let me already here point out a passage in Hitler's *Mein Kampf*. The very first sentences of the book read as follows: «Als glückliche Bestimmung gilt es mir heute, daß das Schicksal mir zum Geburtsort gerade Braunau am Inn zuwies. Liegt doch dieses Städtchen an der Grenze jener zwei deutschen Staaten, deren Wiedervereinigung mindestens uns Jüngeren als eine mit allen Mitteln durchzuführende Lebensaufgabe erscheint» (MK 1). «Schicksal weist mir zu» means that fate allots something to me; that fate «gives,» «assigns,» something as its «gift» to me. Its gift is often a task I must perceive and carry out. «Aufgabe» is «task;» «Lebensaufgabe» is a task one has to pursue throughout one's entire life and which is one's main or only mission in life to which everything else has to be subordinated. Thus, the entire passage can be translated as follows: «Today it seems to me providential that Fate chose Braunau on the Inn as my birthplace. For this little town lies on the boundary between two German states the reunification of which seems at least to us of the younger generation as the mission of our life, which we have to pursue by every means at our disposal.» The expression «das scheint/erscheint mir gut (zu tun)» (this seems to me good [to do]) is often used in the sense of «I have decided to do this,» namely, as a shorthand of the longer sentence «this seems to me good to do and thus I have decided to do it.» However, one has to keep two things in mind. First, grammatically my «life work» or the thing to be done by me occurs as the subject of the sentence, and the verb «erscheinen» is sometimes used in a very emphatic sense. Christians speak of «Marienerscheinungen» (apparitions of Mary), «Wundererscheinungen» (apparitions of miracles = miracles). «Heute ist mir der Herr erschienen» (Today, the Lord appeared to me = I had a vision of the Lord)—this sentence might be used by someone who had such an experience. In fact, Heidegger uses «erscheinen» in his definition of the authentic experience of Being in the pre-Socratics: «But for the Greeks standing-in-itself {Insichstehen} was nothing other than standing-there, standing-in-the-light {Im-Licht-Stehen}. Being means appearing {Sein heißt Erscheinen}. Appearing is not something subsequent that sometimes happens to being. Appearing is the very essence of being {Sein west als Erscheinen}. . . . The essence of being is *physis*. Appearing is the power that emerges, unconcealment, alētheia» (IM 101–102; EM 77). In a passage on historical man as the breach (see chapter 2, n. 32), Heidegger takes advantage of the possibility that a Erscheinung can be sudden and overpowering. In light of such uses of «erscheinen,» it is quite possible that the thing to be done, so to speak, appears to me, approaches me, and claims to be done by me, to be recognized as my «life work» I have to take over. (Note that grammatically in both cases the concerned subject—the one who has a vision of the Lord as well as the one who decides to do something— occurs as the dative object of the sentence.) This is important for the second point one has to keep in mind. For even if the expression «es/etwas erscheint mir» (it/something seems/appears to me) is used in the sense of «I decide/have decided to do,» it is most of the time not meant in the sense of «I have arbitrarily decided to do» but rather in the sense of «the issue itself—die Sache selbst, as Hegel would say—suggests that the best thing to do, or the only thing to do, is. . . .» Throughout his book, Hitler leaves no doubt that he hasn't come to his «life work» by his own arbitrary choice but rather that it was fate that assigned his «life work» to him, and he makes extensive use of the «German» notion of fate according to which fate exists prior to «us» and «gives» «us» our «life work» (see section A of chapter 3). With all this in mind, Heidegger might have even translated the relative clause, «the reunification of which seems . . . means at our disposal» with «the reunification of which has unconcealed itself at least to us of the younger generation as the task of our life, which we have to pursue by every means at our disposal.»

In light of these facts as well as in light of the politics and rhetorics of the National Socialists, German readers quite naturally and without hesitation would have connected «Lebensaufgabe» (life work) and «Schicksal» (fate). Listening to our fate, we realize that it gives us our «Lebensaufgabe.» Or our «Lebensaufgabe» as allotted to us by fate becomes clear, or reveals itself, to us if we are capable of listening to fate. That is, by no means do we come up with our «Lebensaufgabe» by ourselves. Instead, fate «gives» us our «Lebensaufgabe,» as Schlageter did not freely choose, or come up with, his «Lebensaufgabe»; rather, he «was compelled to go to the Baltic; he was compelled to go to Upper Silesia; he was compelled to go to the Ruhr. He was not permitted to escape his destiny so that he could die the most difficult and greatest of all deaths with a hard will and a clear heart» (Wolin, ed., *The Heidegger Controversy*, 42; see Farías, *Heidegger and Nazism*, 93; German edition, 148). Inauthentic Dasein wants to evade the task fate has in store for it. Authentic Dasein, however, obeys and tries to realize its «Lebensaufgabe.»

Manheim in his English translation has replaced the structure, «it seems to us» with one in which «we» is the active subject («Today it seems to me providential that

Fate have chosen Braunau on the Inn as my birth place. For this little town lies on the boundary between two German states which we of the younger generation at least have made it our life work to reunite by every means at our disposal,» [MKe 3]). For readers not familiar with the «German» notion of fate Manheim's alteration might change the meaning of the passage. Fate has given us something, for instance, our place of birth. Our «life work,» however, we create by ourselves without fate giving it to us. Or each authentic Dasein has created its «life work» by itself without being subject to any command. Some authentic Daseine have «good luck» («good fate»), others have «bad luck» («bad fate») because for some, fate—that is, life in all the aspects that authentic Dasein cannot change—is such that authentic Dasein can carry through its life work. For others, however, life is not such that Dasein can succeed in its life work. In this sense, Manheim's translation is even prone to completely reverse the meaning of the sentence: «We» have made up our «life work» by ourselves; it is only at this point (i.e., after the decision) that fate—as being favorable to our life work—steps in to provide us with a place advantageous for the pursuit of our life work or, if it is unfavorable to our life work, prevents us from carrying it out successfully. In German, however, the sentence reads the other way around: Fate has assigned our «Lebensaufgabe» to us, and it has put us in a place where «we» can easily and early on recognize the «Lebensaufgabe» we have been given. The «glückliche Bestimmung» («Today, it seems to me providential») is not that fate provides us with useful means or a favorable environment to realize our life work created by ourselves independent of fate, but rather that fate has its «Lebensaufgabe» for us and that at the same time it has placed us in such a position that we do not need long and painful journeys to perceive our «Lebensaufgabe.» The «glückliche Bestimmung» —or «Gunst des Schicksals» (favor of fate)—consists in that, as Hitler acknowledges in 1925, he was put by fate in a position where he could recognize his «Lebensaufgabe» assigned to him by fate very early on in his life. This is in contrast to a bourgeois Bildungsroman, where the readers learn, or are confirmed in their belief, that it takes some time, and often diverse—as the title of one of Fontane's novels says—*Irrungen und Wirrungen* (or dialectical movements as in the Bildung of spirit in Hegel's *Phenomenology of Spirit*), to recognize or accomplish one's life work or to realize that one has failed to do so. By the way, Heidegger might say that already the word «Lebensaufgabe» itself tells us all this. For, as was said above, «Lebensaufgabe» consists of «Leben» and «Aufgabe.» «Aufgabe» in turn consists of the noun «Gabe» and the prefix «auf-.» «Gabe» is «gift.» The prefix «auf» marks the gift as a task, and the addition of «Lebens-» emphasizes that the task is a very special task, namely, one that demands that one puts all of one's energies into its service. One doesn't produce a gift to oneself. Instead, one accepts a gift from someone else. This is certainly true of the relationship of Being and Daseine in the writings of the later Heidegger. For a given way of unconcealment is not produced by the Daseine or, as he often says, by «man» («der Mensch»). Rather, it is Being that gives it to the Daseine. As I will show, the same relation holds for destiny/fate and authentic Dasein in *Being and Time*. Of course, Hitler's listening to the call and his task—to reunite Germany and Austria as the precondition of conquests of other countries (MKe 3; MK 1)—entailed a lot of «disavowal[s]» (BT 438; SZ 386). In his book, he adduces as the first disavowal the «Vernichtung» (MK 14; «destruction,» MK 16) of the Austrian state.

In *Mein Kampf,* the second proper name of a human being to occur is «Leo Schlageter.» The first name is «Johannes Palm.» During the Napoleonic War, as Hitler tells his readers, Palm practiced resistance against the French troops. However, he was betrayed by an Austrian official, but he didn't disclose anything or anyone to the French. After this, Hitler just says: «In this he resembled Leo Schlageter» (MKe 4; in German the sentence is shorter: «Also wie Leo Schlageter,» MK 2) in order, thereupon, to make a new point. He could take for granted that to all his readers Schlageter was very well known. It is only after Palm and Schlageter that Hitler's parents are mentioned; they are not referred to by their names but only as «der Vater» («the father») and «die Mutter» («the mother»). On page 6 of the German edition, Hitler refers to himself via the voice of his political enemies: «dieser 'Hitler'» (MK 6; «this 'Hitler',» MKe 8). Only after he has narrated the life of his father up to the latter's death does the fourth proper name occur: «Professor Dr. Leopold Pötsch,» his teacher of history in elementary school who taught him the understanding of history that would remain with him for life (MK 12; MKe 14). Only the «Helden» of National Socialism deserve a name. By saying just «der Vater» and «die Mutter,» he can kill two birds with one stone. (Such speaks the English language; the German language isn't better, or is even worse, on this issue; translated word-by-word, it says that you «beat {in the sense of «kill» } two flies with one stroke.») By saying «die Mutter,» he can present his beloved mother as the proper incarnation of and representative of the Sitte (custom) of the Heimat (homeland); by saying «der Vater,» he can maintain the same with regard to the powers represented by the male and at the same time hide his dislike for his father. In fact, Hitler really killed three birds with one stone. For by simply saying «der Vater» he need not tell the story of his father's name, that is, that his father was the illegitimate child of a Miss Schickelgruber and thus was named Alois Schickelgruber. Later on, Alois's mother married a Mr. Hitler. It was only several years after his mother's death and with the help of the testimony of three illiterate witnesses that Alois Schickelgruber claimed to be the legitimate child of Mr. Hitler and was registered in the parish register as Mr. Alois Hitler. For various reasons, as the last name of someone who propagates the purity and superiority of the Aryan race the name «Schickelgruber» sounded pretty ridiculous. (His political enemies would have referred to him as «der Schickelgruber.»)

For all that was said about the «German forest» in this note, «echo» is of course too nice and delicate an expression. For what is required from the listeners is just plain subjugation to the call of the Black Forest, Heidegger, Hitler, and Schlageter. At the same time, the experience of the «German Forest,» at least in it's Heideggerian version, excludes the experience of otherness that several interpreters consider to be Heidegger's central theme in section 74; the experience of otherness as in a passage in Henry David Thoreau's *Walden:* «There came to me in this case a melody which the air had strained, and which had conversed with every leaf and needle of the wood, that portion of the sound which the elements had taken up and modulated and echoed from vale to vale. The echo is, to some extent, an original sound, and therein is the magic and charm of it. It is not merely a repetition of what was worth repeating in the bell, but partly the voice of the wood; the same trivial words and notes sung by a wood-nymph.» This passage is quoted in a book on Heidegger, the title of which refers to what this note is about, namely, in John Sallis' *Echoes: After Heidegger*

(Bloomington and Indianapolis: Indiana University Press, 1990), 4. Sallis has not echoed the different echoes on the story of Echo he tells in the first chapter, "'Ηχώ" (ibid., 1–14) with an account of the possible echoes of Heidegger's sentences on erwidert and Widerruf in Heidegger's interpreters, and he doesn't refer to these sentences at a later point either.

34. In German, one would say, «in the following beiläufigen situation.» «Beiläufig» is another instance of a composite of a prefix («bei-») and «läufig,» «läufig» being the adjective to the verb «laufen» (to run, to walk) (see above, n. 11). In the case of «beiläufig,» «bei» is an abbreviation of «vorbei,» which means «past» primarily in the spatial sense. Thus, «an einem Kino vorbeilaufen» is «to walk past a movie theater» in the sense of «to pass by a movie theater.» «Beiläufig erwähnen» is «to mention in passing.»

35. The third stanza of Baudelaire's poem "A une passante" reads: «Un éclair . . . puis la nuit!—Fugitive beauté/Dont le regard m'a fait soudainement renaître,/Ne te verrai-je plus que dans l'éternité?» What is the «éclair»? Is it the look of the «femme» who «passa,» as introduced in the first stanza and whose eyes are mentioned in the second stanza? Is it the shock of the I (the «Moi, je» of the second stanza) when he sees the femme? Is it the shock of the I when he sees that the femme returns his gaze? Is it the passing of the femme? Or is it the passing femme? Or all together? In any case, the «Dont» refers to the «Fugitive beauté.» However, the «Dont» might be either the genitivus subjectivus or the genitivus objectivus of «regard.» In the first case, the «regard» is that of the femme who looks at the I. In the second case, the «dont» would be the object of the look of the I who looks at the femme. In this case, it would be left open whether the femme looks back or not. In "On some Motifs in Baudelaire," Benjamin is certain that, as in contrast to the I in a poem by Stefan George, «Baudelaire leaves no doubt that *he* looked deep into the eyes of the passer-by» (*Illuminations: Essays and Reflections,* 196, n. 3). However, he translates the third stanza and the entire poem in such a way that one is inclined to assume that the femme did not return the gaze of the I, and he uses a word, «leihen,» that can be used as an equivalent to «erwidern» in the accusative in the sense of «to return» : «Ein Blitz, dann Nacht! Die Flüchtige, nicht leiht / Sie sich dem Werdenden an ihrem Schimmer./ Seh ich dich nur noch in der Ewigkeit?» (*Gesammelte Schriften,* IV.1, 41). I mention this in order to point out that Benjamin comments on «Aura» in terms of, or even defines «Aura» as, the return of a gaze and that, in this context, he uses «erwidern» in the accusative: «Since the camera records our likeness without *returning* our gaze {ohne ihm dessen Blick *zurückzugeben*}. But looking at someone carries the implicit expectation that our look will be *returned* {Dem Blick wohnt aber die Erwartung inne, von dem *erwidert* zu werden, dem er sich schenkt; the relative clause is left out in the English translation; it reads something like: «the look will be returned by the one to whom the look gives itself» }. Where this expectation is *met* {Wo diese Erwartung *erwidert* wird} . . . , there is an experience of the aura to the fullest extent. . . . The person we look at, or who feels he is being looked at, looks at us in turn. To perceive the aura of an object we look at means to invest it with the ability to look at us in return» ("On Some Motifs in Baudelaire," 188; *Gesammelte Schriften,* I.2, 646f.; italics mine, J. F.). As in the case of the echo (see above n. 33), not every physical look in return is an Erwiderung in this sense. For this, see also Benjamin's remarks on eyes in Baudelaire's poems (*Illuminations,* 189) and his comment on a sentence in Baude-

laire on eyes «sad and translucent like blackish swamps,» or having «the oily inert-
ness of tropical seas» : «When such eyes come alive, it is with the self-protective
wariness of a wild animal hunting for prey. (Thus the eye of the prostitute scrutinizing the passers-by is at the same time on its guard against the police. . . .) That the
eye of the city dweller is overburdened with protective functions is obvious» (ibid.,
190f.). See also the subsequent quote from Georg Simmel on another aspect of hearing and seeing in the modern cities and in public conveyances (ibid., 191). Anyway,
as one might gather from this note and from my examples of «erwidern,» in a theoretical text every instance of «erwidern» requires a careful, contextual, or explicit comment or calls for an «Erwiderung» in the accusative in which it is determined or
explained or in which it can, so to speak, develop into this or that narrative. One might
regret that Heidegger did not comment at all on his short sentence with «erwidert»
aside from the sentence on «Widerruf» about which I will say more in chapters 2 and
3—in fact, one might even rebuke him for it. However, one must not forget that the
grammatical structure and the semantics unambiguously allow only for my interpretation and not for Guignon's or Birmingham's.

As mentioned above, in the quote from "On Some Motifs in Baudelaire," the relative clause «dem er sich schenkt» has been left untranslated. «Schenken» is «to give
a gift» ; «sich jemandem schenken» is «to give oneself (as a gift) to someone.» Quite
literally, the entire sentence reads: «But inherent to the gaze is the expectation to be
returned by the one to whom the gaze has given itself (as a gift).» One might say, the
I in Baudelaire's poem «schenkt sich» to the femme, and hopes that the gaze of
the femme «leiht sich ihm» in return. On the level of historicality in *Being and Time,*
the gaze that schenkt sich to the femme (or the eye of the prostitute scrutinizing the
passersby) is the command delivered by destiny, fate, and the community of the people (see chapters 2 and 3), and the gaze of the femme who, if she erwidert the gaze
of the I, sich leiht to the I (or the passerby who erwidert the gaze of the prostitute)
is Heidegger's «sich {einer überkommenen Existenzmöglichkeit} überliefernde Entschlossenheit» (SZ 385; «The resoluteness which . . . hands itself down {to the possibility of existence that has come down to us},» BT 437).

36. As one sees with regard to the last sentence, «erwidern» in the dative and
«erwidern» in the accusative in the sense of «to fight back» amount to a Wider-rede,
or Wider-spruch, both being expressions for «to contradict.» In contrast to «erwidern»
and «Erwiderung,» both «Widerrede» and «Widerspruch» are used only as negations
and cannot be used the way «erwidern» is used in the sense of «to comply with a
request.» Thus, if Heidegger had wanted to say what Guignon and Birmingham assume
he does, he could have written, for instance, «Die Wiederholung widerspricht vielmehr
der (or, spricht/redet vielmehr gegen die) Möglichkeit der dagewesenen Existenz. Die
Widerrede/Der Widerspruch gegen die Möglichkeit im Entschluß ist aber/sogar zugleich. . . . »

The words «Widerrede» and «Widerspruch/widersprechen» show that there might
be something about Birmingham's suggestion that the verb «erwidern» is, so to speak,
the verbalization of the prefix «wider» in «Widerruf » (see above, n. 14). However,
the reasons presented in this chapter and in the following ones show that Heidegger
uses «erwidern» in the sense of «to comply with,» and not in the sense of a
«Widerrede» or in the sense of «to fight back.» In addition, contrary to Birmingham
(TP 31) the prefix «wider-» is by no means used exclusively in the sense of «contrary

to or against» (see chapter 5, n. 70). On my interpretation, the prefix «wider-» in Widerruf in fact means «contrary to» or «against,» for a Widerruf is a disavowal or revocation. However, if one wants to regard Heidegger's use of «erwidern» as a verbalization of a prefix, it would not be the prefix «wider-» but rather the prefix «wieder-» (re-, back, again), or the prefix «wider» in the sense of «wieder» (see chapter 5, n. 70). This is appropriate, and perhaps even consciously intended by Heidegger, since his erwidern/Erwiderung is meant as a peculiar Wiederholung (repetition) whose features I will spell out in more detail in the following chapters.

Erwidern as Widerrede or Widerspruch shows that «erwidern» in the dative and «erwidern» in the sense of «to fight back» have, so to speak, one foot in the vocabulary of speaking and calling. However, the same holds true for «erwidern» in the sense of «to comply with a demand,» as my examples and «erwidern» in the sense of «to echo» show. In addition, the noun «Widerruf» (disavowal, revocation) contains the noun «Ruf,» call. Thus, erwidern, Erwiderung, and Widerruf all, so to speak, echo the language of the sections on the call of conscience. In section 58 Heidegger says of authentic Dasein: «When Dasein understandingly lets itself be called forth to this possibility, this includes its becoming free for the call—its readiness for the potentiality of getting appealed to. In understanding the call, Dasein is in thrall to [hörig] its ownmost possibility of existence» (BT 334; SZ 287). The German adjective «hörig» contains the root «hören» (to hear, to listen). Readers should keep in mind that, at Heidegger's time as well as today, «hörig» is only used in one of two ways: either as a sociological term in the sense of «thrall» with regard to slaves or peasants in feudal societies (and in this sense in Germany at Heidegger's time no one was any longer hörig to anyone else), or as a synonym for «verfallen» (see above, n. 11). Instead of saying, «A ist verfallen (addicted to) B, a drug, or a sexual habit,» one might as well say that A «ist hörig B, etc.» The sentence with erwidern in section 74 echoes precisely the sentence with hörig in section 58. Quite certainly, Heidegger used the adjective «hörig» in order to have the strongest expression for «obligation» and «submission.» The sentence with hörig and the entire chapter on conscience show that neither the chapter on conscience nor, by inclusion, section 74 talks about a conversation with the past or the peculiar act of disavowal Birmingham finds in it.

The sentence with hörig at the same time testifies to the two aspects of Entschlossenheit mentioned in section A above, namely, an activity of Dasein that results in an act of submission to the call. (Though Dasein is passive from the beginning and becomes active only in order to comply with the call. The call, however, demands obedience. It is one's duty to comply with the call, and a duty is what cannot not be done.) In doing so, authentic Dasein opens itself for the voice of the Volk and locks up, or seals off, itself from the many other voices. Those Daseine that become inauthentic, however, are not capable of doing so since they are verfallen to the many voices of idle talk and curiosity.

In his 1935 lecture, An Introduction to Metaphysics, Heidegger finds his notion of Hörigkeit in Heraclitus's fragment 34: «Correspondingly, the hearing that is a following [Hörig-sein] is contrasted with mere hearing. Mere hearing scatters and diffuses itself in what is commonly believed and said, in hearsay, in doxa, appearance. True hearing has nothing to do with ear and mouth, but means: to follow the logos and what it is, namely, the collectedness of the essent itself. We can hear truly {das echte Hörigsein} only if we are followers {Hörige}. But this {Hörigkeit aber} has nothing to do with the lobes of our ears. The man who is no follower {Wer kein Höriger ist} is removed and excluded from the *logos* from the start, regardless of whether he has heard with his ears or not yet heard» (IM 129; EM 99; see also the continuation of the quote). On the formula «the collectedness of the essent itself» see section B of chapter 5. The people who merely hear or who, so to speak, hear only with their ear lobes are the people engaged in idle talk, etc., or those who listen to the call such a way that «causes get pleaded» and the call «becomes perverted in its tendency to disclose» (BT 319; SZ 274); that is, people who don't listen to the call or who—what amounts to the same thing—answer to the call with an Erwiderung in the dative or an Erwiderung in the sense of «to fight back.» The distinction between one who «has heard with his ears» and one who has «not yet heard» corresponds to the distinction between inauthentic Daseine and ordinary Daseine. The distinction between authentic, or höriges, Dasein and those who are «removed and excluded from the logos» corresponds to the distinction in section 74 of *Being and Time* between those Daseine that have fate—the authentic Daseine—and those that don't have fate—the inauthentic Daseine (see section C of chapter 2). After World War II and after his engagement with National Socialism, Heidegger felt that his language was somewhat rough. For, in "The Question Concerning Technology," published in 1954, he writes: «Always the unconcealment of that which is goes upon a way of revealing. Always the destining of revealing holds complete sway over men. But that destining is never a fate that compels {das Verhängnis eines Zwanges}. For man becomes truly free only insofar as he belongs to the realm of destining {des Geschickes} and so becomes one who listens, though not one who simply obeys {nicht aber ein Höriger}» (BW 306; VA 28). One might infer from this passage that his notion of hörig sein in *Being and Time* and, by inclusion, his notion of erwidern in section 74 indeed mean «to simply obey,» in contradistinction to inauthentic Dasein, which does not obey. On Geschick, Gemüt, Gebirg, Gestell, and Gewährendes in "The Question Concerning Technology" see my paper "On Brinks and Bridges in Heidegger," esp. 130–135.

## Chapter 2

1. Rockmore, *On Heidegger's Nazism and Philosophy*, 47.

2. Ibid., 48.

3. This aspect as well as the sections at the beginning of Division Two require a more detailed treatment. See my book *Society, Community, Fate, and Decision: From Kant to Benjamin*.

4. Hildegard Feick, *Index zu Heideggers "Sein und Zeit"* (Tübingen: Max Niemeyer, 1991), 94.

5. In this—according to the standards of Heideggerians, deeply metaphysical—sense Heidegger adduces the notion of Ursprung, origin, in one of his lectures on Hölderlin:

> The pure origin {Der reine Ursprung} is not one that just simply releases something out of it {entläßt} and leaves it to itself {überläßt}; rather, it is that beginning whose power constantly leaps over {überspringt} that-which-has-arisen from it {das Entsprungene}; it is that beginning that leaps ahead of {vor-springend}, and outlasts, that-which-has-arisen {from it}; in this way, the pure origin is present in the foundation of what-endures {des Bleibenden}, present not as some aftereffect of former times but rather as what leaps

ahead {das Vorausspringende}; thus, as the beginning {Anfang} the pure origin is in reality at the same time the determining end, that is, the goal {Ziel}. (HH 241; for «das rein Entsprungene» see, for instance, ibid., 254).

6. Probably the phrase «in dem betonten Sinne des Entlaufens» does not mean «in the sense of running away from it, as we have just emphasized» but rather «in the emphatic sense of running away from it.»

7. Or, consider «What is the motive for this 'fugitive' {"flüchtige"} way of saying "I"? It is motivated by Dasein's falling; for as falling, it *flees* in the face of itself into the "they" {Durch das Verfallen des Daseins, als welches es vor sich selbst *flieht* in das Man}» (BT 368; SZ 322). Note that in everyday language one uses «flüchtig» in the sense of «on the run» as predicate adjective («The escaped prisoners are still flüchtig [on the run].») but only rarely as a modifying adjective. The meaning of the modifying adjective is most often «transitory» or «short-lived» («der flüchtige Augenblick»). The insertion of «"flüchtige"» does not contribute anything to the passage with the exception that in this way Heidegger characterizes the «I,» and thus Kant and the Enlightenment, as short-lived. This is one of Heidegger's peculiar etymologies of which «vorläufig» is another (see above, chapter 1, note 11).

8. As in these quotes concerning all the «"entspringen",» in the quote I gave from BT 377 (see p. 32), Heidegger puts «"Zeit"» into quotation marks to indicate that «the 'time' which is accessible to Dasein's common sense,» the later so-called ordinary concept of time, pretends to be the «real» time but, according to Heidegger, is by no means the «real» time.

9. On the difference between this motif in Guignon's and in my interpretation, see below and chapters 3 and 4.

10. See his letter to Engelbert Krebs, 9 January 1919, as in Hugo Ott's biography of Heidegger, *Martin Heidegger: A Political Life,* 106f.; German edition, 106f.

11. For instance, look at the entries for «Eigentlichkeit» in Hildegard Feick's *Index zu Heideggers "Sein und Zeit"* (*Index zu Heideggers "Sein und Zeit,"* 16f.). One cannot but read them as pointing to a state, a habit, and only secondarily to the activities accompanying that state or leading to it. Heidegger approved this index and, obviously, had helped her to some degree (ibid., ix).

Among the suggestions of terms Heidegger might have used if he had wanted to focus on an activity I included «Tätigkeit,» which Fichte uses (see above, n. 2 of chapter 1). It is the abstract noun of the verb «tun,» or «tätig sein,» which itself designates an activity. All other possible nouns without the ending «-keit» or «-heit» would have been too weak. Thus, «Tätigkeit» is an exception that confirms the rule. In the case of the verb «leiden,» however, Fichte could employ the articular infinitive, «Leiden,» and thus avoid any possible association to a state. Though there is the word «Wehleidigkeit,» probably no one has ever used «Leidheit» or «Leidigkeit» as the abstract noun to «leiden.»

12. On the indefinite article in the English translation instead of the definite one in Heidegger see chapter 1, n. 17. To use in both occurrences the definite article certainly contributes to a sense of urgency and weakens the attitude of a detached observer.

13. In German, it reads: «Meist sind sie durch die Zweideutigkeit unkenntlich gemacht, aber doch bekannt» (SZ 383). This is probably an allusion to the famous sentence in the preface of Hegel's *Phenomenology of Spirit,* namely, «Das Bekannte über-

haupt ist darum, weil es *bekannt* ist, nicht *erkannt*» (*Phänomenologie des Geistes,* 28); English: «Quite generally, the familiar, just because it is *familiar,* is not *cognitively understood*» (*Phenomenology of Spirit,* 18). Note that Heidegger says not «are unrecognized,» but rather «have been made unrecognizable.» To anticipate my conclusions, the origin is present even though ordinary Dasein has fallen away from or leapt out of it. However, by the work of ambiguity, ordinary Dasein makes the ways in which the origin is present unrecognizable. Authentic Dasein sees through ordinary Dasein's work. Thus, authentic Dasein recognizes that what is covered up by ordinary Dasein's work of ambiguity are in fact the authentic possibilities, which it thereupon turns against ordinary Dasein. Thus, authentic Dasein erkennt what, due to ordinary Dasein's work of ambiguity, has been up to that point only bekannt. «Unkenntlich» is an adjective to «Unkenntnis,» which in turn is the negation of «Erkenntnis.» Thus, ordinary Dasein, so to speak, strikes through the «Er-» in Erkenntnis (~~Er~~kenntnis) and thus falls into Unkenntnis. However, even as stricken through, the origin remains present, and bekannt. This enables authentic Dasein to strike through the «Un-» in Unkenntnis (~~Un~~kenntnis) and thus to restore the «Er-» in Erkenntnis that ordinary Dasein has unsuccessfully tried to strike out.

14. At the end of Division One, Heidegger gathers all these structures into that of care in order to reinterpret them in Division Two from the more «ursprünglich» level of temporality. In Division Two, chapter 5, he understands these structures «noch ursprünglicher» (SZ 372; «more primordial,» BT 424; it should read «still more primordial»), namely, from the vantage point of historicality. There is no level that is «noch ursprünglicher» than historicality, that is, historicality is the ultimate primordial level.

15. Botho Strauß, "Anschwellender Bocksgesang," in the weekly *Der Spiegel,* no. 6, 1993, 202ff. Botho Strauß has always had a high reputation for being especially delicate and subtle. In its editorial, *Der Spiegel* discreetly reminds its readers that the word der Dichter has chosen, Bocksgesang, is the literal translation of the Greek τραγῳδία, tragedy, namely, song of the he-goats (ibid., 203). Concerning the anschwellen, there is no need of explanation. Jubilation in a theater, or in a political meeting, if it increases, or an erecting penis, «schwillt an,» as does some strange buzzing in the air one cannot really locate. For a long time, Strauß had been regarded as a kind of leftist. Now he has realized: «How strange it is that one can call oneself 'leftist!' For from ancient times, left has been looked upon as synonym for what goes wrong {Fehlgehende}. Thus, one attaches to oneself a sign of what is bewitched and perverse {Verkehrten}. For full of enlightenment-haughtiness, one grounds one's politics on the alleged proof of the powerlessness of magical notions of order» (p. 203f.). His vocabulary and his motifs are quite obviously very close to the language of Heidegger, Spengler, and Scheler, though Strauß opts for some sort of elitarian arcane politics, or withdraws from politics, as did, for example, the George-Kreis. Has Botho Strauß undergone some transformation similar to St. Paul? Some people suspect that he always was a kind of conservative. In this latter case, it is the political situation in Germany that makes his fate «erst frei» (SZ 384; «free,» BT 436). One might also say that, so far, he was only bekannt. If one continued the last sentence along the lines suggested by Luther's German translation of the Holy Scripture, one would indeed «den Holzwegen der deutschen Sprache auf den Leim gegangen sein» (have fallen prey to the seductive force of the Holzwege of the German language) and one might

have apologized: «Wann ich so schwerz bin, schuld ist nicht mein ~~allein~~.» Nonetheless, some readers might have exclaimed, «Zu spät bekannt,» which might be translated as, «~~It is~~ too late ~~that you have~~ confessed.» Quite surely, Heidegger generated the horizontal lines in his later texts by his fountain-pen guided by his hand, whereas most of the authors today will use the respective commands in the menu of their computer programs. What would he say if he had seen all the authors with their desk- and laptops? If the "real" Heidegger was the one criticized in Adorno's *Jargon of Authenticity* and *Negative Dialectics,* he certainly would have said: «Gott bewahre!» If Heidegger had been Derrida, he would have written a strong and eloquent «*reciprocative rejoinder*» (BT 438); or, he would have begun an Auseinandersetzung with Adorno. «Auseinandersetzung» is a word Heidegger might have used instead of «erwidert,» if he had wanted to say what Guignon and Birmingham think he said. However, Heidegger kept silent. But this was long ago. It was in the fifties and sixties when the paradigmatic German menu was still a fatty and thoroughly nourishing Eisbein mit Sauerkraut («Eine Kalorienbombe!») and not yet McDonald's with mousse au chocolat. Would Heidegger—who, after all, maintained that only a God can save us (MH 57)—have approved of the bio-technological revolutionary guerrilla war on the internet as advocated by Derrida: «Today, the general strike does not need to demobilize or mobilize a spectacular number of people: it is enough to cut the electricity in a few privileged places, for example the services, public and private, of postal service and telecommunications, or to introduce a few efficient viruses into a well-chosen computer network or, by analogy, to introduce the equivalent of AIDS into the organs of transmission, into the hermeneutic *Gespräch*» (Derrida, "The Force of Law: The 'Mystical Foundation of Authority'," in Drucilla Cornell et al., eds., *Deconstruction and the Possibility of Justice* [New York: Routledge, 1992], 37f.)?

16. On «verfallen» see above, n. 11 of chapter 1. In ordinary language, mainly airplanes (of which all were military up to the twenties) «stürzen ab.» However, also other sorts of Abstürze, for instance the Abstürze of mountaineers, are often deadly. That Joseph Beuys survived his plane crash during World War II is the exception that confirms the rule. Some say, Beuys is a «very German artist,» and his art is his way of making good for his experiences in World War II. If that's the case, it differs completely from the way in which Heidegger's *Being and Time* «makes good» for World War I. Beuys's art focuses on the resolute and tender gestures of rubbing the fragile human body, of wrapping it in fat and pelt to keep it alive. And it reaches out to the animals, the coyotes and the rabbits, he saw in the Russian steppe after the Kirghiz people helped him open his eyes anew after thirty days in a coma. It reaches out for all the creatures here on the ground without tying them up to a supposed Bodenständigkeit (rootedness-in-the-soil) of each Dasein and being. Heidegger's making up for World War I, however, consists in the appeal to enter the war plane again and, like the heroes of Verdun, to transgress the line to and in war again.

17. G. W. F. Hegel, *Wissenschaft der Logik, Zweiter Teil,* ed. G. Lasson (Hamburg: Felix Meiner, 1969), 3. «The German language has preserved essence in the past participle [*gewesen*] of the verb *to be;* for essence is past—but timelessly past— being» (*Hegel's Science of Logic,* trans. A. V. Miller [Atlantic Highlands, NJ: Humanities Press, 1993], 389).

18. Here and in all of what follows, I present ordinary Dasein as being involved in two different activities. It positively relies on and lives in certain possibilities pro-

vided by the «they,» the inauthentic possibilities. At the same time, like the «they,» it covers up certain other possibilities, the authentic ones. One might object that this misrepresents the passage beginning with «Proximally and for the most part» and ending with «in one's resolution» (BT 435; SZ 383). For Heidegger might say here that the «they» relates to all possibilities in the same way, namely, it has made each of them «unrecognizable by ambiguity» (BT 435; SZ 383). I see ordinary Dasein involved in two kinds of activities because of the passages on ordinary Dasein I discussed in the preceding section on the anschwellender Bocksgesang. In addition, Heidegger says «mostly» (BT 435; SZ 383) and not «always,» and other expressions in the passage seem to indicate that he thinks of the two activities I mentioned. However, for two reasons I need not elaborate this issue. First, even if one assumes that the «they» has made all possibilities unrecognizable, the result is the same. For once authentic Dasein has begun to undo the work of ambiguity with regard to some or all of the possibilities, ordinary Dasein sees that another Dasein, authentic Dasein, interprets a given possibility differently than ordinary Dasein itself does. From that moment on, a possibility, or even every possibility, is split up into two different ones. Ordinary Dasein sticks to its interpretation and is told by authentic Dasein that ordinary Dasein's interpretation is inauthentic and should be replaced with the authentic interpretation of the possibility. Thus, it might be the case that prior to the anschwellender Bocksgesang ordinary Dasein was engaged only in one type of activity. However, with the beginning of the anschwellender Bocksgesang, or at the latest with the beginning of the crisis, ordinary Dasein is engaged in two kinds of activities. Second, it will become clear in chapter 3 that the problem of whether prior to the beginning of the anschwellender Bocksgesang ordinary Dasein is engaged in only one activity or in two was indeed an interesting question for conservatives and right-wingers but that they didn't need to discuss it in detail. The brevity of Heidegger's passage on the issue in section 74 reflects this fact.

19. On destiny and fate see also chapter 3. In part, her misunderstanding of the passage might go back to the fact that the sentence on fateful Dasein that she quotes is falsely translated (see below, chapter 3, n. 3).

20. One can be sure that Guignon does not distinguish between «überkommene Ausgelegtheit» and «*heritage*» (or, rather, the only distinction he makes is that from the viewpoint of authentic Dasein what was labeled «überkommene Ausgelegtheit» becomes a source of choices and as such might be called «heritage»). For if he had made a distinction, he would have noted this in some way since it is the decisive point for the entire passage. Not distinguishing between the notions is a practice with a long history in English interpretations of *Being and Time*. In fact, I have not found any interpretations that distinguish between them.

21. Ordinary Dasein «understands itself in terms of» (BT 435; SZ 383) possibilities, but it doesn't «disclose» (BT 435; SZ 383) them. Rather, it lives quite as a matter of course in the possibilities its parents, peer group, etc. have instilled into it, and it has «made unrecognizable by ambiguity» (BT 435; SZ 383) the authentic possibilities by reducing them to something present at hand, that is, to something without any significance for Dasein. As to the authentic possibilities, ordinary Dasein, so to speak, «verschließt» (locks up) them. Authentic Dasein undoes this operation. The best expression for authentic Dasein's operation is indeed that it «erschließt» (SZ 383; «discloses,» BT 435) these possibilities, that is, unlocks them. Thus, authentic Dasein's

operation is concerned only with a subset of all possibilities contained in the «way of interpreting Dasein which has come down to us» (BT 435; SZ 383). Heidegger introduces as the term for this subset the notion of heritage.

22. Heidegger can pun on «wieder» and «wider» (BT 438, n. 1) because he runs no risk of being misunderstood. For, as I have shown in chapter 1, his usage of erwidern is familiar to German speakers. In addition, because of the phrases, «But . . . at the same time» («aber zugleich») and «that which in the "today", is working itself out as the 'past'» («was im Heute sich als "Vergangenheit" auswirkt») (BT 438; SZ 386) native speakers of German recognize immediately (or after some thought) that the objects of erwidern and Widerruf are not the same. It is similar in the case of Heidegger's usage of the preposition «aus.» Those who know German are familiar with the different meanings of «aus» as for instance in «Ich renne aus dem brennenden Haus» (I run out of the burning house) versus «Er kommt/ist aus dem Hause Windsor» (He comes/is from the house Windsor = he is a member of the Windsor family) or «Das besteht/ist gemacht aus Stahl» (This consists/is made out of steel).

23. When a soccer player normally not known for outstanding skills performs a brilliant move, one says, «Das war (schlicht und einfach) Glück/Zufall» (That was [simply] a matter of luck/chance). However, if the same move is made by a famous player, one might exclaim, «Das ist Können/Genialität/Professionalität!» (That is skill/the genius/professionalism!). When faced with a sad or tragic event that happened to oneself or someone else, one might exclaim, «Das war Schicksal!» (That was fate.) In all these sentences one points out the «real» cause and thus rejects other factors that could be adduced as causes of the event to be explained. The soccer player shouldn't pretend that he is capable of producing such moves by himself. It was not your fault that your friend was hit by a car after you had invited him or her for dinner and several drinks. It was fate. For those who believe in fate the word «fate» denotes God or some other overall power guiding affairs in this world. Those who don't believe in fate use the sentence «das war Schicksal» as a shorthand way of saying that the event happened due to a combination of factors that one could not be expected to foresee. The fact that in such sentences in such situations one always implicitly rejects other possible causes is probably the reason why one doesn't use any article with «Schicksal.» The indefinite or definite article would, so to speak, be «the breach into which» (IM 163; EM 124) not, as Heidegger says there, «the preponderant power of being {Sein}» (IM 163; EM 124) but the «power» of questioning and dialectics «bursts» (IM 163; EM 124) to challenge one's claim and to require one to explain why God or that entity called «fate» wanted to kill your friend and how it made the car do so. Thus, to leave out any article as Heidegger does with regard to «Erbschaft» rhetorically immunizes the sentence against possible criticism. As these examples show, the absence of any article can be used to serve the polemical function of the definite article (see above chapter 1, n. 17). In the case of a surprising and pleasant event, one uses the indefinite article with «Wunder» : «Das ist/war ein Wunder!» (That is/was a miracle.). The reason for the difference is probably that «Schicksal» always denotes an agent acting continuously and over time or a web of intertwined causes acting over time, while a miracle is by definition a sudden break with such webs. The definite article with «Erbe» («aus dem Erbe,» SZ 383; «in terms of the heritage,» BT 435) is as polemical as the definite article with «Volk» (SZ 384; «people,» BT 435) (see chapter 1. n. 17) since two paragraphs after the one with the

Erbe, Heidegger explains the Erbe as «community, of {the} people» (see chapter 3), and authentic Dasein will finally cancel the world of the «they» (see already chapter 1).

24. See below, note 25.

25. The assumption that Heidegger uses «"Güte"» (SZ 383; «'goodness',» BT 435) in the sense of a universal criterion is incompatible with the sentence in which the expression occurs. For it doesn't follow logically from an idea of the good that everything good is a heritage. In addition, it should not follow if one wants to develop the goodness as a criterion for criticism of a given form of life. Even if one assumes for the sake of the argument that it might follow, one would be curious to see an argument for this and not just the statement. However, Heidegger doesn't refer to something like an idea of the good as a criterion for criticism. Rather, the sentence is an example of his method of listening to language. Within that framework, the entire sentence makes sense, doesn't refer to some universal idea of the good, and doesn't imply a long argument either. If within a philosophical text «'goodness'» in the first instance seems to be the abstract noun for «'good'» (BT 435) and seems to point into the direction of a universally applicable standard or criterion, «'goodness'» is not a fortunate translation of Heidegger's German word «"Güte".» In everyday language as well as in philosophical language the abstract noun for «gut» (good) is usually not «Güte» but «das Gute» or «das Gut» (see, for instance in the index of Scheler, FE 620f.; FEe 613). Heidegger regarded philosophy of values as trapped in the ontology of beings as present-at-hand (BT 132; SZ 99; see IM 196ff, EM 149ff.). The word «Güte» is used in two ways. It can mean «quality,» the quality of products, for instance. In comparison to «Qualität» («this product is of the highest quality») or simple expressions such as «sehr gut» («this product is very good»), «Güte» («this product is of the highest Güte») sounds slightly old-fashioned or hypocritical, at least for all those who have a rather sober attitude toward current techniques of advertisement. For those who use «Güte» in that way try to take advantage of the second use of «Güte» and its sociological and economic implications. In what follows, I use «Güte» only in the second meaning, according to which at Heidegger's time «Güte» was a polemical notion, which it still is even today though probably to a lesser degree and though it has become somewhat old-fashioned. «Güte» denotes an inner core that manifests itself in a kind of atmosphere—Benjamin might say aura—that some things have and others do not. For instance, a well-crafted piece of furniture, an old piece of jewelry inherited from one's ancestors, or fruits produced by the farmer in the proper traditional way have Güte. Pieces manufactured by a craftsman have Güte, whereas things from the assembly line or the results of modern farming techniques with all their chemicals don't have Güte. The word most often implies that products of Güte are based on tradition and are for that reason better than products from the assembly line. Therefore, conservatives like to use the word Güte whereas most others get a little bit nervous when they hear it since the use of this word most of the time implies an appreciation of tradition and a denigration of what is new (that is, of what is there and is developed without presenting a long history and tradition), or of «das Moderne» (SZ 391; «the modern,» BT 444). Thus, Heidegger listens to the conservative use of the word Güte according to which exclusively things incorporating a tradition or being an Erbschaft have Güte whereas no modern thing has Güte, and from this he infers the etymology of the German adjective gut and the abstract noun Gut. For a conservative

and right-winger like Heidegger, «gut» and «Gut» do not go back to «das Gute» but rather to «Güte» for there is no highest value «das Gute.» For a conservative and right-winger like Scheler, «gut» and «Gut» go back to «das Gute» but «das Gute» in turn goes back to «Güte» for «das Gut» has been properly realized only in precapitalist times with their Güte, whereas capitalism represents an overturning of values and has no Güte (see below, chapter 3, sections B, C, and D). All those who live in stable traditions are «good» because they partake in the «good» that keeps this tradition alive. Being the core of tradition, «das Gute» is transmitted from one generation to the next as estate. Only something that partakes in «das Gute» is good. According to Heidegger, there is no such thing «das Gute.» However, there is «Güte.» Something can be «gut» and have «Güte» only if it partakes in an estate. For nothing can be good independent of an estate. Partaking in an estate, something good is (a part of the) inheritance, or it is someone who is the heir of (a part of) an estate. Thus, Heidegger says that «everything 'good' {alles "Gute"} is a heritage {Erbschaft}» (BT 435; SZ 383) and that «the character of 'goodness' {"Güte"} lies in making authentic existence possible» (BT 435; SZ 383). Heidegger might add that estate and everything partaking in estate has Güte in the sense of «grace, generosity,» since the estate provides Daseine with their identity, gives it to them as a gift, whereas the moderns don't have such a source of identity; a source that is gütig, kind-hearted, benevolent, generous to them. In this sense, Heidegger would say the subordinate clause is justified. The «if» indicates that he cannot give any other reason for this equation of «good» and «heritage.»

Given this use of the word «Güte» and given the conclusions Heidegger draws from it, an association comes to one's mind he would probably not have objected to. Leave away the «e» in «Gute» («everything 'good'»), that is, take «Gut,» and add an «r» to «"Güte"» («'goodness'»), then we have «Gut» and «Güter,» the singular and the plural of «estate,» «farm,» that is, what aristocrats and, on a smaller scale, farmers have, namely, the land they cultivate. The farmers and aristocrats have a stable identity because the land they have inherited from their ancestors provides them with that identity. (Today, in German supermarkets one can find liverwurst, Sauerkraut, and other food advertised as having been produced «nach Gutsherrenart» [according to the way it was produced on the Güter of a gentleman farmer], which is supposed to convey that the respective product is much better than others of its kind.) The proletarians, however, by definition have nothing inherited and after their death they leave behind only their children without handing anything down to them. The farmers and aristocrats can lose their land; the proletarians, however, «have nothing to lose but their chains,» as Marx and Engels wrote at the end of the *Communist Manifesto* (Karl Marx and Friedrich Engels, *The Communist Manifesto,* trans. S. Moore [London: Penguin Books, 1985], 121). Thus, the struggle between the Right and the Left over the proletarians. The Left offered the promise that by further developing the contradictions within Gesellschaft one can transform bourgeois Gesellschaft into a socialist Gesellschaft and thus get rid of Gemeinschaft (see chapter 4). The Right promised that by canceling Gesellschaft, that is, by ending the class struggle, canceling the realm of the public and political, and by identifying themselves with the Volksgemeinschaft, the proletarians would get something. Every proletarian would get his or her «fate,» that is, his or her share in «destiny» and Volk, that miraculous entity that has Güte for all of its members provided that they submit to its call (see chapter 3).

Idle talk in Europe says that the United States is the country «without history and tradition,» and many U.S. citizens are proud of their «dynamism» and «creative attitude.» Still, sometimes some miss something. Thus, they like to go to Heidelberg, Rome, Tuscany, and all the other places with Güte. As is known, European companies try to cash in on this need for Güte. On the inner side of the back cover of *The New Yorker*, November 10, 1997, the Swiss watch company Patek Philippe placed an advertisement for its new watch, «Men's Neptune.» The advertisement shows a photo of a father and his son in winter coats playing chess in a park. The text reads: «You never actually own a Patek Philippe. You merely take care of it for the next generation.» It also says that the men's Neptune is «self-winding» and «hand-crafted in 18-karat solid gold.» Since Americans don't have traditions and since the average reader of *The New Yorker* is not a proletarian, the line under the photo of the men's Neptune reads: «Begin your *own* tradition.» On page 3 of the same issue of *The New Yorker*, a company for electronic goods, Sony, advertises its new «VAIO Notebook.» The advertisement suggests connecting Sony's portable data projector, its digital handycam camcorder, etc., lists other advantages, and concludes: «Then take a break and sneak off to your favorite hideaway for some intel-powered video gaming. Hey, who says you can't mix business with pleasure?» Sony would never advertise its notebook the way Patek Phillipe advertises its men's Neptune. Everyone knows that notebooks after some time look unsightly or somewhat dirty, that technically they are outdated after two years or so, and that they stop working after a few years anyway. In contrast to the men's Neptune, the VAIO notebook has no Güte. Still, it is a product of high quality. In Germany as in all other countries in Europe, industrialization and capitalism emerged in a country with old traditions and many products of Güte, and this was often experienced as a brutal offense and threat to the traditional ways of life, not only because of the economic crises coming along with capitalism. For an example of a piece of Güte see the baptismal font in Thomas Mann's novel *The Magic Mountain* (trans. H. T. Lowe-Porter [New York: Knopf, 1975], 30ff.). As was mentioned, a piece of Güte does not need to consist of gold. In his analysis of "The Worldhood of the World" (BT 91ff; SZ 63ff), Heidegger refers to the world of a craftsman and the world in a village or small town. He points out that, in that world, Dasein «does not 'devour the kilometres'» (BT 140; «es "frißt nicht Kilometer",» SZ 106). Also, Dasein's suit is «cut to his figure {auf den Leib zugeschnitten}» in contrast to suits and other goods «produced by the dozen {Dutzendware}» (BT 100; SZ 70f.). Cars and other products from the assembly line have no Güte.

26. At that point, Heidegger uses the indefinite article with Erbe («the handing down of a heritage {eines Erbes} constitutes itself» [BT 435; SZ 435]). One might say that he should have said, «des Erbes» (of the heritage). However, the indefinite article is by no means a slip of the pen or imprecise. Rather, in this sentence he generalizes his model of the polemical aspect of the Erbe (see chapter 1, n. 17). In the German text, this is underscored by the word «je» (in each occurrence of such an happening or, as Staumbaugh has it, «always» [*Being and Time: A Translation of* Sein und Zeit, 351]), which Macquarrie and Robinson have left untranslated.

27. On athletes in Heidegger see below, chapter 6, n. 24. Heidegger's phrase «konstituiert sich» is the Latin word for the German word «sich zusammensetzen,» which he uses in the negative two paragraphs later in regard to destiny («Destiny is not something

that puts itself together {setzt sich nicht . . . zusammen} out of individual fates» [BT 436; SZ 384]). See also below, this chapter n. 32, chapter 3, n. 51, and chapter 6, n. 24.

28. Schürmann, *Heidegger: On Being and Acting—From Principles to Anarchy*, n. p.

29. Reiner Schürmann, *Des hégémonies brisées* (Mauvezin: Trans-Europ-Repress, 1996). Readers of the book will hope that in a few years time it will be discussed as what it is, namely, by far the most powerful response (or «reciprocative rejoinder» [BT 438]) by Heideggerians to Hans Blumenberg's *The Legitimacy of the Modern Age*. An English translation with Indiana University Press is under way. Several messengers into the English language have already arrived: "Neoplatonic Henology as an Overcoming of Metaphysics: On a Strategy in the History of Philosophy," *Research in Phenomenology* 13 (1983), 25–41; "The Law of Nature and Pure Nature: A Thought-Experience in Meister Eckhart," *Krisis* 5–6 (1986–87), 148–169; "Tragic Differing: The Law of the One and the Law of Contraries in Parmenides," *Graduate Faculty Philosophy Journal* 13:1 (1988), 3–20; "Ultimate Double Binds," *Graduate Faculty Philosophy Journal* 14:2–15:1 (1991), 213–236; "Riveted to A Monstrous Site," Joseph Margolis and Tom Rockmore, eds., *The Heidegger Case: On Philosophy and Politics* (Philadelphia: Temple University Press, 1992), 313–330; "A Brutal Awakening to the Tragic Condition of Being: On Heidegger's *Beiträge zur Philosophie*," Karsten Harries and Christopher Jamme, eds., *Martin Heidegger: Art, Politics, and Technology* (New York: Holmes and Meier Publishers, 1994), 89–105. A bibliography of Schürmann's writings can be found in *Graduate Faculty Philosophy Journal* 19:2–20:1 (1997), 73–78; the issue is a special issue "In Memoriam Reiner Schürmann." It should be noted that Schürmann regarded French as his native habitat.

30. On the different modes of solicitude in Heidegger see chapter 3, n. 25.

31. As Heidegger goes on, the «they» would of course not agree with his interpretation. However, it «would be a misunderstanding if we were to seek to have the explication of these phenomena confirmed by looking to the "they" for agreement» (BT 219; SZ 175).

32. It is the activity of the Erbe that constitutes the act in which it delivers itself into the present in order from now on to be active in the present. It demands of the Daseine to passively überliefern sich selbst, to hand themselves over, to the Erbe (see pp. 16ff. and what follows above in this section). In *An Introduction to Metaphysics*, Heidegger uses a military term for the same motif. Being breaks into the present like a group of soldiers breaking through the lines of the enemy: «The overpowering as such, in order to appear in its power, *requires* a place, a scene of disclosure. The essence of being-human opens up to us only when understood through this need compelled by being itself {das Sein selbst}. The being-there of historical man means: to be posited as the breach {Bresche} into which the preponderant power of being bursts in its appearing {in die die Übergewalt des Seins erscheinend hereinbricht}. . . . Thus the being-there of the historical man is the breach through which the being embodied in the essent can open. As such it is an *in-cident* [Zwischen-fall, a fall-between], the incident in which suddenly the unbound powers of being come forth and are accomplished as history» (IM 163f.).

The German text of the sentence with the second occurrence of «breach» reads as follows: «Als die Bresche für die Eröffnung des ins Werk gesetzten Seins im Seienden ist das Dasein des geschichtlichen Menschen ein *Zwischen-fall,* der Zwischenfall, in dem plötzlich die Gewalten der losgebundenen Übergewalt des Seins aufgehen und ins Werk als Geschichte eingehen» (EM 125). Literally translated, it reads: «Being the breach for the opening/manifestation/revelation of Being having been put to work in the realm of the essents, the Dasein of the historical man is an *in-cident*; that incident in which suddenly the powers of the unbound superior power of Being come forth and enter into/become the work as history.» «Being» («Sein») corresponds to «heritage» («Erbe»). «To have been put to work (by itself),» «to become the work,» and «to be unbound (by itself)» correspond to «Überlieferung» («handing down»), and «opening/manifestation/revelation» corresponds to «constitutes itself» («konstituiert sich»). It might also be the case that «to have been put to work (by itself),» «to become the work,» and «to be unbound (by itself)» correspond to «constitutes itself» («konstituiert sich»), and «opening/manifestation/revelation» corresponds to «Überlieferung» («handing down»). Since this question is immaterial for my purposes, I don't discuss it. The entire happening is the coming forth of the powers of the unbound superior powers of Being for which the humans are just the site and incident. «Manifestation,» «to have been put to work (by itself)» and «to be unbound» (either by itself or by someone else) also correspond to «become free» (BT 436; SZ 384). In each of these cases, that which has been put to work, etc., exists prior to the moment in which it is put to work, etc., as for instance, in the explosion of a nuclear plant the atomic energy slumbering in the reactor is all of a sudden «unbound.» In *Being and Time,* the sentence on handing down of the Erbe constituting itself is the beginning of the crisis the resolution of which consists in authentic Dasein bringing the Daseine out of their diaspora back to their native habitat through the repetition of the Erbe, that is, the Volksgemeinschaft (see chapter 3). In *An Introduction to Metaphysics,* being breaks into the breach in order for the essence of being-human to be «carried back to its ground» (IM 163f; EM 124f.).

Macquarrie and Robinson did not change the grammatical structure of the sentence with the handing down of the heritage. Stambaugh seems to have overlooked the reflexive pronoun «sich» in «konstituiert sich» (SZ 383; «constitutes itself,» BT 435). By this failure, she turns the sentence upside down and presents the happening in which the Erbe takes over the Daseine as though the handing down of the Erbe were passively grounded in authentic Dasein, which in this way remains the basic entity: «If everything "good" is a matter of heritage and if the character of "goodness" lies in making authentic existence possible, then handing down a heritage is always constituted in resoluteness» (*Being and Time: A Translation of* Sein und Zeit, 351). Probably it is also a matter of different philosophical and cultural traditions that make it difficult for Americans to understand such sentences in Heidegger. In Anglo-American philosophy, the empiricist and pragmatic strands are dominant, and American culture is about the self-invention of individuals (see section C of chapter 5), while in Germany entities like reason, Geist, tradition, and community have always been rather strong.

33. As I pointed out, in the sentence with «the way of interpreting Dasein which has come down to us» (BT 435; SZ 383) the preposition «aus» has several meanings. However, the same preposition in the sentence with «*in terms of {aus} the heritage {Erbe}*» has only one meaning, namely the same as in the sentences from Aristotle's *Physics* mentioned above. Heritage claims that each Dasein recognizes that Dasein can acquire identity and stability, that is, that Dasein can become «good» only if it gives up its ordinary way of life and submits itself to the Erbe and one of its slots. In

the time of his engagement with National Socialism, Heidegger liked to use «aus» in the sense of the principle or origin to which one has to submit, because only in this way can one become «good.» I already mentioned Leo Schlageter, who was imprisoned and sentenced to death, and I already quoted some passages of Heidegger's speech on him in May 1933 (see chapter 1, n. 33). The first sentence of the speech was the following: «Wir wollen zu seiner Ehrung diesen Tod einen Augenblick bedenken, um aus diesem Tod unser Leben zu verstehen» (Farías, *Heidegger und der Nationalsozialismus*, 144). In both Farías, *Heidegger and Nazism* (89) and Wolin, ed., *The Heidegger Controversy* (40), the preposition «aus» is left out. To carry over its force one might translate: «We wish to honor him by reflecting, for a moment of vision, upon his death, in order to understand our own lives from out of {aus} this death.» At a later point in section 74 Heidegger talks about Dasein choosing its hero (BT 437; SZ 385). Schlageter was one of those possibilities covered up by ordinary Dasein. The preposition «aus» («from out of») designates one of the slots contained in the Erbe that, as the other quotes from Heidegger's speech show (see chapter 1, n. 33), «we» have to submit to as to «our» principle in order thereupon to cleanse ourselves of our ordinary way of life and to become authentic. As I already pointed out in chapter 1, the repetition of what-has-been-there does not mean that «we» repeat the past the way it has been present in the past. For the past recurs under changed circumstances. In addition, it is not necessary that we literally repeat the deeds of Schlageter. We need not go to Silesia. Rather, destiny and Schlageter himself, if properly understood, tell us that our place to repeat Schlageter is the Freiburg University. Authentic Dasein «*übernimmt*» (SZ 383; «*takes over,*» BT 435) the Erbe and its appropriate share in it. It realizes that the Erbe demands to take over the institutions of ordinary Dasein in order to drive out the spirit of the «they» and the bearers of that spirit and to reestablish the institutions in the right spirit of the Erbe. The first sentence of Heidegger's *Rectorate Address* reads: «The assumption of {Die Übernahme} the rectorate is the commitment to the *spiritual* {*geistige*} leadership of this institution of higher learning» (MH 5; see Wolin, ed., *The Heidegger Controversy,* 29; SB 9). The commitment has its principle in the Erbe. Thus, in the second sentence Heidegger refers to the principle by means of the preposition «aus» : «The following of teachers and students only awakens and strengthens through a true and common rootedness in the essence of the German university {aus der wahrhaften und gemeinsamen Verwurzelung im Wesen der deutschen Universität}» (MH 5; see Wolin, ed., *The Heidegger Controversy,* 29; SB 9). We have to re-submit to, and regain, the principle, the beginning of Greek philosophy. «All science remains bound to that beginning of philosophy and draws from it {Aus ihm schöpft sie} the strength of its essence» (Wolin, ed., *The Heidegger Controversy,* 31; see MH 7; SB 11). Right at the end of the rectorate address, Heidegger says: «We can only fully understand the glory and greatness of this new beginning, however, if we carry within ourselves that deep and broad thoughtfulness upon which the ancient wisdom of the Greeks drew in uttering the words {aus der die alte griechische Weisheit das Wort gesprochen}: *ta . . . megala panta episphale . . .* "All that is great stands in the storm . . ." (Plato, *Republic,* 497d, 9)» (Wolin, ed., *The Heidegger Controversy,* 39; see MH 13; SB 9). (See on the last quote section A of chapter 6.) As was mentioned, the beginning—community in *Being and Time* and the pre-Socratics in the later Heidegger—has disappeared; however, having disappeared it continues to exist; we have to regain and repeat it, and we can do so only because it hasn't disappeared after its disappearance. It is by no means my intention to ridicule such an assumption. To the contrary, with regard to community Tillich maintains that it was precisely the basic flaw of all the leftists to have neglected the presence of community after its disappearance, and he himself wanted to develop a politics that pays attention to that fact and that fulfills the needs embodied in communities (see section B of chapter 4). However, Heidegger refers to the assumed fact of the existence of the Greek beginning after its disappearance in an extremely reifying and violent way. See the long passage with the short sentence, «The beginning *exists* still» (Wolin, ed., *The Heidegger Controversy,* 32; see MH 8; «Der Anfang *ist* noch,» SB 12). On a similar sentence with «ist» see my paper "On Brinks and Bridges in Heidegger," 148ff.

34. For Heidegger's «'provisional'» («"vorläufige"») see above, n. 11 of chapter 1. Heidegger puts his «"vorläufig"» into quotation marks because he wants us to hear in vorläufig in the sense of «provisional» ordinary Dasein's running forward on the time-line (and the other way round). Ordinary Dasein is engaged in all its vulgar possibilities. The call calls it back from them. Thus, ordinary Dasein's vorlaufende possibilities are vorläufig, that is, provisional.

35. «So if it wants to come to itself {zu ihm selbst}, it must first pull itself {sich} together from {aus} the dispersion and disconnectedness of the very things that have 'come to pass'» (BT 441f.; SZ 390). In this sentence, too, Heidegger could have written «sich selbst» instead of «ihm selbst.» However, for him «sich selbst» would not have carried sufficiently the soteriological aspect, so to speak, of the happening he is talking about. For by becoming authentic, Dasein hands itself down to the Volksgemeinschaft and is relieved from the burden of autonomy of the bourgeois subject and from isolation from others in bourgeois society (see chapter 3 and section C of chapter 5). The fact that the English translators don't bring out the difference between «sich selbst» and «ihm selbst» (and probably cannot do so without commentary) contributes to the «American» understanding of the passage and the entire section 74 according to which the individual Dasein does not give up its individuality but remains the focal point of historicality (see section C of chapter 5).

As I show in this chapter at least to some degree, the motif of repetition in section 74—that in authenticity the Daseine are called upon to cancel the present world in order to repeat a world that has-been-there—doesn't break into *Being and Time* out of the blue. Rather, it is well prepared in the course of the book up to that section. In regard to this and sentences such as the one quoted at the beginning of this note, Heidegger's use of notions like «dispersion» and especially his use of the preposition «zurück» («back») require a detailed treatment. They contribute to the atmosphere of the Bocksgesang—that we must go back and repeat—especially when they don't contribute directly anything to the thought he presents in the respective paragraph. I mentioned Schürmann's acknowledgment in his book on Heidegger, where he presents an expansion of territory as the regaining of lost territory. Of course, in a framework of history as the repetition of a lost world the problem becomes urgent why ordinary Dasein left this world to begin with. It is interesting that this problem caused something like a Freudian slip of the tongue in *Being and Time*. In section 75 Heidegger says that the question concerning the connectedness of life asks «in which of its own kinds of Being Dasein loses itself in such a manner {verliert es sich so} that it must, as it were, only subsequently pull itself together out of its dispersal {sich . . . aus der Zerstreuung zusammenholen}, and think up for itself a unity in which that "together" is embraced» (BT 442; SZ 390). This is the question of why ordinary Dasein left the original world. However, as also the following sentences show, the question is raised just in passing and as instrumental to the main question, namely, how subsequently to pull oneself together out of dispersion. The translators remark that the older editions have «verliert es sich nicht so» instead of «verliert es sich so» (BT 442, n. 1). That is, in the older editions the question was «in which of its own kinds of Being Dasein does not lose itself in such a manner.» This question gives a sharper edge to the instrumental question of the later editions and even asks for the conditions rendering the main question of the later editions superfluous: Under which conditions would Dasein not have fallen into dispersion? It would have been better, if it hadn't done so. If it hadn't fallen into dispersion, we would not have to deal with the main question of the later editions, namely, how to pull oneself together out of dispersion. (To «pull itself together» is required of Dasein in the moment when the handing down of the heritage pulls itself together or «constitutes itself» [BT 435; SZ 383].) Right at the beginning of the sections on conscience, Heidegger talks about «Dasein's lostness in the "they"» (BT 312; SZ 268) and writes: «So Dasein makes no choices, gets carried along by the nobody, and thus ensnares itself in inauthenticity. This process can be reversed {rückgängig gemacht werden} only if Dasein specifically brings itself back to itself {zurückholt zu ihm selbst} from its lostness in the "they". But this bringing-back {Dieses Zurückholen} must have that kind of Being *by the neglect of which* Dasein has lost itself in inauthenticity. When Dasein thus brings itself back [Das Sichzurückholen] from the "they", the they-self is modified in an existentiell manner so that it becomes *authentic* Being-one's-Self. This must be accomplished by *making up for not choosing [Nachholen einer Wahl]*. But "making up" for not choosing signifies *choosing to make this choice {Wählen dieser Wahl}*—deciding for a potentiality-for-Being, and making this decision from one's own Self» (BT 312f.; SZ 268). Here, too, Heidegger could have said «zu sich selbst,» but for the reason mentioned above preferred to say «zu ihm selbst.» Contrary to Birmingham, to become authentic does not mean to break with each and every past. Contrary to Guignon, it does not mean either to screen the different possibilities offered by the past and choose the one that fits one's utopian ideal best. Rather, to become authentic means to repeat the possibility that Dasein has been before it lost that possibility by losing that possibility and itself in the «they.» To become authentic is a «Wieder-holung» (SZ 385; hyphen mine, J. F.; «repetition,» BT 437). Authentic Dasein brings (holen) back (wieder) Dasein's own past, which has disappeared since Dasein has lost itself in the «they.» Authentic Dasein does so by bringing (holen) up again for reconsideration, or re-decision, (nach) a choice that it failed to make. This choice (against the «they») would have prevented Dasein from loosing itself in the «they.» Since Dasein failed to make the choice, the past has disappeared and the «they» have taken over. Thus, authentic Dasein's «choosing to make this choice» (BT 313; SZ 268) chooses against the world of the «they» in order to repeat the past, which has disappeared since Dasein failed to choose against the «they» and to keep the past alive. In section 74 the past, which has been pushed aside by the «they,» raises its voice as heritage and «constitutes itself» (BT 435; SZ 383) by calling upon Dasein to choose to make the choice, that is, to cancel the «they,» society, in order to rerealize heritage, or community, which has been pushed aside by society. In this sense, one is entitled to read the phrase «ursprüngliche» («primordial») in «the whole of existence stretched along . . . in a way which is primordial and not lost» (BT 442; SZ 390) in a temporal sense, as this is, by the way, the sense in which «ursprünglich» is used in everyday language most of the time.

It is interesting that the change of the negation into an affirmation on page 390 of *Sein und Zeit* (BT 442) didn't require any changes in the following sentences. It is also interesting that the question of the older editions (as well as the instrumental question of the later editions) is raised just to disappear, and that Heidegger doesn't give any reason for his claim that authentic Dasein's choice is «choosing to make this choice [Wählen dieser Wahl]» (BT 313; SZ 268). For right-wingers didn't like to go into the issue. It is simply destiny or fate. The only more detailed answer was Hitler's, which not everyone wanted to subscribe to, though Scheler did so for some time (see below, chapter 3, sections A and D). «Destiny» and «fate» were polemical notions gaining their strength and appeal from their denial of leftist theories (see chapter 3; see also this chapter, n. 23)

The edition of *Sein und Zeit* as volume 2 of the Gesamtausgabe (Frankfurt: Klostermann, 1977) is a reprint of the seventh edition and contains Heidegger's notes in the margins of his «Hüttenexemplar,» that is, the copy he used in his hut. However, it doesn't contain the changes Heidegger made from the second edition onward. (Upon Heidegger's request, the editor, Friedrich-Wilhelm Herrmann, even made changes of the text of the seventh edition without indicating them as such; see ibid., 579.) Independent of the Gesamtausgabe and its publishing house, Rainer A. Bast and Heinrich P. Delfosse have produced the *Handbuch zum Textstudium von Martin Heideggers 'Sein und Zeit,'* vol. 1: *Stellenindizes: Philologisch-kritischer Apparat* (Stuttgart-Bad Canstatt: Frommann-Holzboog, 1979). It contains a word index based on the fourteenth edition, «examples» (ibid., 388) of the changes in the second edition, an index of the changes in the seventh edition, an index of the misprints, the list of misprints included in *Sein und Zeit* from the first to the sixth edition, and several other indices and material. In none of the indices is the change from the negative to the affirmative form on page 390 listed. Klaus Heinrich, chair of the Institut für Religionswissenschaften (located in the Paul Tillich-Haus) at the Freie Universität Berlin, in one of his lectures in the mid-seventies talked about page 390 of *Sein und Zeit*. His occasional comments on Heidegger (for instance, *tertium datur: Eine religionsphilosophische Einführung in die Logik* [Frankfurt: Stroemfeld/Roter Stern, 1981], 65ff.; vol. 1 of Klaus Heinrich, *Dahlemer Vorlesungen*) are invaluable, and so were all his lectures.

36. Note that, as in «Die . . . sich überliefernde Entschlossenheit» (SZ 385; BT 437; see above, pp. 16ff.), here too one has an instance of a missing dative object. The context, however, makes it unavoidable to add as the dative object «fate» and «heritage» of the preceding paragraph. Thus, this sentence confirms, or makes explicit, that «ihm selbst» in the preceding paragraph ultimately refers to «fate» and «heritage.»

37. I pointed out Schürmann's attitude toward the English translation of his French book on Heidegger and Heidegger's assumption that even after its disappearance the origin still exists (see n. 33 of this chapter). I also pointed out the Freudian slip of the tongue in Heidegger and the fact that the change of the negative into an affirmative expression didn't require any changes in the subsequent text (see n. 35 of this chapter). One can see all these problems also in regard to the passage I discussed in this section: «As thrown, it has been submitted to a 'world', and exists factically with Others.

Proximally and for the most part the Self is lost in the "they." It understands itself in terms of {aus} those possibilities of existence which 'circulate' in the 'average' public way of interpreting Dasein today. These possibilities have mostly been made unrecognizable by ambiguity; yet they are well known to us. The authentic existentiell understanding is so far from extricating itself from the way of interpreting Dasein which has come down to us, that in each case it is in terms of this interpretation {aus ihr}, against it, and yet again for it, that any possibility one has chosen is seized upon in one's resolution» (BT 435; SZ 383). The passage allows for two interpretations. The phrase, «those possibilities of existence which 'circulate' in the 'average' public way of interpreting Dasein today» might refer to the possibilities of the original world $w_1$; in that case, the phrase, «These possibilities . . . known to us,» means that living in $w_2$ ordinary Dasein has, so to speak, perverted the possibilities of the original world $w_1$. However, the phrase, «those possibilities of existence which 'circulate' in the 'average' public way of interpreting Dasein today» might also refer to the possibilities in $w_2$. In that case, the phrase, «These possibilities . . . known to us,» means that living in $w_2$ ordinary Dasein covers up by ambiguity all those possibilities, or all those aspects of all of its possibilities, in which $w_1$ has always been present or in which it raises its voice once the Bocksgesang begins. (According to the second interpretation, both occurrences of «aus» have the ambiguity I pointed out; in the first interpretation, only the second one has it, while the first «aus» is used the way it is used in the sentences on the Erbe.) However, this doesn't mean that Heidegger speaks unclearly or imprecisely. For from the viewpoint of authentic Dasein both interpretations amount to the same. Or in the first interpretation the issue is formulated more from the perspective of the estate, $w_1$, and in the second interpretation it is formulated from the perspective of the heirs of $w_1$ (see this chapter, n. 25). Both issues are the same problem, for the estate demands of its heirs to be rerealized. In addition, the problem and its aspects are familiar to conservatives and right-wingers (see in this chapter, nn. 25 and 35).

### Chapter 3

1. Carl Schmitt, *The Concept of the Political,* trans. George Schwab (New Brunswick, NJ: Rutgers University Press, 1976), 30f.; *Der Begriff des Politischen* (Berlin: Duncker & Humblot, 1972), 31.

2. This tension has given rise to a huge amount of literature on Gemeinschaft and Gesellschaft by sociologists, political scientists, and philosophers. For an excellent survey see Manfred Riedel, "Gesellschaft, Gemeinschaft," in: O. Brunner, W. Konze, R. Koselleck (eds.), *Geschichtliche Grundbegriffe: Historisches Lexikon zur politisch-sozialen Sprache in Deutschland,* vol. 2 (E—G) (Stuttgart: Klett, 1975), 801–862.

3. Several English commentators maintain that an individual authentic Dasein produces its fate or destiny by itself. (According to Guignon authentic Dasein does so insofar as its utopian ideal determines which hero it chooses [see above, chapter 1, section B]; for Birmingham see above, chapter 2, section C; see also below, chapter 5, section C.) Macquarrie and Robinson's phrase, «is determinative for it as *destiny*,» might contribute to this misinterpretation. For in their translation Heidegger seems to say that fateful Dasein is destiny and as such determines co-historizing. However, Stambaugh is certainly right in translating «ist . . . bestimmt als *Geschick*» (SZ 384) with «is determined as *destiny*» (*Being and Time: A Translation of* Sein und Zeit,

352). That is, «*destiny*» is introduced as a technical term for fateful Dasein's historizing as a co-historizing. It is certainly the case that the one determines the other, and one might find this indicated by the phrase «ist . . . bestimmt als *Geschick.*» However, it is destiny that determines Dasein, and not the other way around. For «fateful Dasein» designates Dasein that has subjugated itself to heritage in the moment in which heritage constitutes itself. Dasein as fateful Dasein has given up its autonomy and has become the missionary of heritage (see above, chapter 2, section C). The term «Geschick» («destiny») replaces or further determines the term «heritage,» after heritage has constituted itself. In other words, in the moment in which heritage constitutes itself, it reveals itself as the primary entity in history, and as such it reveals itself as «destiny.» Thus, heritage as destiny is the primary actor and entity in history, and authentic or fateful Daseine are its means or organs. Heidegger makes this point in two ways. First, in the next sentence he says that the notion of destiny designates the Volksgemeinschaft («the community, of {the} people,» BT 436; SZ 384), and everyone familiar with the literature on community and society knew that the advocates of Gemeinschaft maintained that a Gemeinschaft existed prior to the individuals and had ontological priority over them (see above, this chapter). Second, in the sentence after the one on Volksgemeinschaft Heidegger himself states explicitly that destiny determines the Daseine. For he writes, «Destiny is not something that puts itself together out of individual fates, anymore than Being-with-one-another can be conceived as the occurring together of several Subjects. Our fates have already been guided in advance, in our Being with one another in the same world and in our resoluteness for definite possibilities» (BT 436; SZ 384); that is, destiny precedes the Daseine and determines their fates, and not the other way round.

4. See above, chapter 1, n. 33.

5. It is the difference between what the individual thinks of himself, and what, as he will recognize later, fate has allotted to him that, in hindsight, allows for facetious formulations such as the last sentence of the first chapter: «I, too, hoped to wrest from Fate {dem Schicksal abzujagen} what my father had accomplished fifty years before; I, too, wanted to become 'something'—but on no account a civil servant {Beamter}» (MKe 18; MK 17).

6. In Hitler's German text the Jews occur in the singular and with the definite article («mit dem Juden»). See on the definite article above, chapter 1, n. 17.

7. As has already become clear in chapters 1 and 2 and will become clearer in this chapter, one of the main theoretical problems of rightist authors was the question of how the vanished past was nonetheless still alive. The architect Hitler gives an answer that makes one forget that there was ever a problem: The past has never disappeared; the foundation of a building precedes and survives the shaky walls erected by the architects of society.

8. Because of the deplorable state of the bourgeoisie (which by opposing in the «most immoral way» even completely justified demands of the workers drove them into the arms of the social democrats, MKe 45; MK 47), Hitler has given up on them (which did not prevent him from making a strong case in his book for private property and capitalism and which, in 1929, did not prevent him and big business in Germany from forming an alliance). His targets are the workers who have fallen prey to internationalism and big business as well as the peasants. Still, the door has to be kept open for as many other Germans as possible. Both churches are treated with respect

and are given political advice. The Catholic Church is even praised for its «amazing youthfulness . . . , its spiritual suppleness and iron will-power» (MKe 432; MK 481). The friends of the ancient Greeks are also invited: «Especially in historical instruction we must not be deterred from the study of antiquity. Roman history correctly conceived in extremely broad outlines is and remains the best mentor, not only for today, but probably for all time. The Hellenic ideal of culture should also remain preserved for us in its exemplary beauty. We must not allow the greater racial community {die größere Rassengemeinschaft} to be torn asunder by the differences of the individual peoples. The struggle that rages today is for very great aims. A culture combining millenniums and embracing Hellenism and Germanism is fighting for its existence» (MKe 423; MK 470).

9. G. W. F. Hegel, *The Philosophy of Right,* trans. T. M. Knox (Chicago, London, Toronto: William Benton, 1952), 86 (section 270). The notion is polemical since it is an ironic appropriation of the Romantics' Einbildungskraft, faculty of imagination. «Bilden» is «to educate» as well as «to form, to mold.» «Sich bilden» is «to educate oneself.» «Sich einbilden» is «to fancy, to fantasize, to hallucinate, to flatter oneself with the belief.» According to Hegel, the Romantics used Einbildungskraft precisely to avoid to bilden themselves. Hegel uses the term «Romantics» here in reference to the ironic romantics, that is, those who through Einbildungskraft, imagination, and reflection distance themselves from any possible content with which they might identify themselves. I use the term in my book in the other meaning (see above, preface, n. 14).

10. Hitler uses the words Gemeinschaft and Gesellschaft as they were used in the literature on the subject and in everyday language. As representative of numerous passages, I quote the continuation of the passage on the Greeks and the Romans: «A sharp difference should exist between general education and specialized knowledge. As particularly today the latter threatens more and more to sink into the service of pure Mammon, general education, at least in its more ideal attitude, must be retained as a counterweight. Here, too, we must incessantly inculcate the principle *that industry, technology, and commerce can thrive only as long as an idealistic national community {Volksgemeinschaft} offers the necessary preconditions. And these do not lie in material egoism, but in a spirit of sacrifice and joyful renunciation {in verzichtfreudiger Opferbereitschaft}*» (MKe 423; MK 470). Here one has the typical opposition between the supposed material egoism of Gesellschaft and the values of Gemeinschaft. Thus, in the next paragraph Hitler comments on the saying «The young man must some day become a useful member of society {Gesellschaft}» that such a sentence does not lead to the proper national enthusiasm (MKe 424; MK 470). «Kampfgemeinschaft» («combat group») is used especially when he talks about his Kampfgefährten and the SA, the civil war army of the Nazis, illegal in the Weimar Republic (MKe 490; MK 550).

11. See on Dr. Leopold Pötsch above, chapter 1, n. 33.

12. Note that, already grammatically, Schicksal functions like an Aufgabe, a task; the task it itself has given. This is the background of Heidegger's assumption throughout his career that in contrast to a Vergangenheit (past) Gewesenheit (what-has-been-there) approaches us from the future.

13. He does not apply this logic to the supposed event that the originally pure Aryan race became impure by the admixture of inferior blood. The state of purity of the Aryan blood corresponds to the state in paradise prior to original sin, and the admixture of impure blood causing the first ecstasis out of purity is analogous to Eve

and the snake in paradise. But in Christianity the fall is a single and sudden event, whereas in the case of the admixture of inferior blood it is more a kind of gradual decline. In contrast to the regaining of paradise in Christianity, which according to orthodox teaching, cannot be achieved by humans, in Hitler human beings, that is, the Germans can restore the state of purity if the one who is elected by fate to do so properly listens to fate's commands. Because of this inherent difference as well as for other reasons, Christian politics is never structurally totalitarian.

14. In the face of the fact that «the greatest friend of the Slavs had fallen beneath the bullets of Slavic fanatics,» «a light shudder began to run through me at this vengeance of inscrutable Destiny {Rache des unerforschlichen Schicksals}» (MKe 159; MK 174). Now, «a stone had been set rolling whose course could no longer be arrested» (MKe 159; MK 174). The war was necessary and unavoidable. If Austria had waited longer, its position would have become worse and worse. The «guilt of the German government» was that in its efforts to keep peace it had already missed several opportunities to launch the war; a war that was desired by the whole people (MKe 159ff.; MK 174ff.). «To me those hours seemed like a release from the painful feelings of my youth. Even today I am not ashamed to say that, overpowered by stormy enthusiasm {stürmischer Begeisterung}, I fell down on my knees and thanked Heaven from an overflowing heart for granting me the good fortune of being permitted to live at this time» (MKe 161; MK 177).

15. Certainly this sentence marks one of the differences between Hitler and the German philosophers and sociologists of his time concerning theories of human beings as a Masse, mass, or Herde, herd. Perhaps with the exception of Benjamin, none of those scholars was taken in by the kind of phenomena to which Hitler refers. They more or less feared them and saw in them the threat of chaos and anarchy, for instance, in demonstrations of workers, or they explained them away with «idealistic» interpretations, as in the case of the Helden von Langemarck.

16. Due to this situation, one finds in Hitler's book sentences characterizing someone as the fate of someone else, for instance: «The danger of secret organizations today lies . . . in the fact that . . . the opinion arises that the fate of a people {Schicksal eines Volkes} really might suddenly be decided {entschieden} in a favorable sense by a single act of murder» (MKe 543; MK 609). Even if a person «decides the fate» of some people or the world in this sense, the individual nevertheless does not freely create the fate of the people, for he or she acts either in compliance to a call of fate or not. In the latter case the individual will fail.

17. In his report on his life in Germany, Karl Löwith quotes the National Socialist "laws of life" of the students, printed as an introduction in the guidebook to the Marburg University in 1939–40. There are ten laws:

(1) German student, it is not necessary that you live, but rather that you fulfill your duty to your *Volk* {deine Pflicht gegenüber deinem Volk erfüllst}! Whatever becomes of you, act as a German. (2) Honour is the highest law and greatest dignity for the German man. An offence against one's honour can be avenged only by blood. Your honour is loyalty to your Volk and to yourself. (3) To be a German means that you have character. You too are called upon {mitberufen} to fight for the freedom of the German spirit. Seek for the inherent truths resolved upon by your *Volk* {die in deinem Volk beschlossen liegen}. (4) Licentiousness and a lack of ties do not represent freedom. There is more freedom in serving than in following your own commands. The future of Germany is dependent on your faith, your enthusiasm and your preparedness to fight. (5) Those who lack the imag-

ination to conceive of anything will achieve nothing, and you cannot light anything if you do not have a flame kindled within yourself. Have the courage for admiration and reverence. (6) One is born to be a National Socialist, even more one is brought up to become one, but most of all one educates oneself to be one. (7) If there is some thing mightier than fate, it is your courage to bear it without wavering {Wenn etwas ist, gewaltiger als das Schicksal, dann ist es dein Mut, der es unerschütterlich trägt}. What does not kill you makes you stronger still {Was dich nicht umbringt, macht dich nur stärker}. Praised be what hardens you {Gelobt sei, was hart macht}. (8) Learn to live in an orderly manner. Training and discipline are the foundations {unerläßlichen Grundlagen} of any community {jeder Gemeinschaft} and the beginning of all education. (9) As a leader, be rigid in your own fulfillment of duty, resolute {entschlossen} in representing what is necessary, helpful and good, never petty in the assessment of human weaknesses, magnanimous in recognizing others' necessaries of life and modest with your own. (10) Be a comrade {Sei Kamerad}! Be chivalrous and modest! Be a model in your personal life! The measure of your moral maturity will be seen in your relations with people. Be at one in thought and action. Model your life on the *Führer*'s. (K. Löwith, *My Life in Germany Before and After 1933: A Report*, trans. E. King [Urbana and Chicago: University of Illinois Press, 1994], 105f.; *Mein Leben in Deutschland vor und nach 1933: Ein Bericht* [Stuttgart: Metzlersche Verlagsbuchhandlung, 1986], 100f.; the last sentence in the third law should be translated as «Seek the truths enshrined in your Volk!»).

Though otherwise the language of these laws is quite blunt, the authors preferred the comparative («more freedom») for what in fact means: there is freedom only in serving, and there is no freedom in following your own commands. You are something by birth and race. This is your fate. You have to consciously realize your fate, and to submit yourself to the commands ordained by your fate. You are not free to make up your fate by yourself. Rather, your freedom consists in that you subjugate yourself to your fate. Your fate and the self-declared masters of your fate reward you with the promise that only in submitting to your fate will you become a mighty master. As will become clear, the same redefinition of the notion of freedom can be found in Heidegger and in Scheler.

18. Martin Heidegger, *The Metaphysical Foundations of Logic*, trans. M. Heim (Bloomington: Indiana University Press, 1984), 50; *Metaphysische Anfangsgründe der Logik im Ausgang von Leibniz*, GA 26 (Frankfurt: Klostermann, 1978), 62. At a crucial point in his analysis of being-with in *Being and Time*, Heidegger refers to Scheler (SZ 116, n. 1; BT 152, 491).

19. He uses this phrase with regard to the English people throughout the book. At the end of his book, there is an appendix: "On the Psychology of the English Ethos and the Cant" (PPS 218), at the end of which Scheler gathered all his reflections in a "Table of Categories of the English Thinking" (PPS 249f.). The English people mix up, to name just a few, «culture {Kultur} with comfort; . . . the warrior {Krieger} with the robber; thinking {Denken} with calculating; . . . character with narrow-mindedness; . . . the good with the useful; reverence of virtue with cant; . . . Bildung with mental isolation; honesty and uprightness with organic mendacity that makes actual lying superfluous; promise with the bonds of mutual contracts; loyalty {Treue} with exactness with regard to keeping of contracts,» and, of course, they mix up «Gemeinschaft with Gesellschaft» and «Gemüt with sentimentality» (PPS 249f.). The editor notes that Scheler had never been to England (PPS 692). On Heidegger's usage of the distinguished German words with the prefix «ge-» see my paper "On Brinks and Bridges in Heidegger," 133–135.

20. Thanks to the possibilities of the definite article in German, the German text

is much shorter: «Das Maßlose fordert eine maßlose Quelle» (PPS 99; for similar usages of the definite article in Heidegger see my paper "On Brinks and Bridges in Heidegger," 148, 167, n. 37, 183f., n. 59; see also above chapter 1, n. 17). In fact, Scheler even offers a new proof of God's existence using the same medieval means as Descartes in the third of his *Meditations*. Descartes finds among the ideas in him the idea of a substance that is infinite, independent, all-knowing, and all-powerful and that has created him as well as all other existing beings. Since nothing can come out of nothing, and since something perfect cannot be brought about by something inferior, the idea of God cannot have been created by any finite being. Scheler experiences in himself a power for sacrifice that is beyond measure:

> It is only at this point that the idea of war as an ordeal from God becomes fully clear. If God is a God of love, he will give the victory to that Volk in which the love is the most rich, the most profound, and the most noble.
> It is precisely at this point that the genius of war becomes a religion, as though a matter of course—it becomes the guide to God, even for those who were previously unbelievers. For the power of sacrifice {Opferkraft} that thus, nourished by love, grew out of the soul, is too great, too boundless to be understood by reason {Verstand} as representing the sum of all natural and limited motives that reason perceives and whose power it can add up. The experience of this welling up of the power of sacrifice from the soul's roots directs the amazed gaze back to an origin {Ursprung} that is deeper and more universal than anything consciousness of one's natural powers and of the objects and contents attracting these powers can present. What is boundless requires a source that is boundless! By pursuing the origin of this source, . . . the inner gaze perceives effortlessly the sea of grace and love that nourishes the soul and within this sea it perceives the deity. In peace, only very few perceive it, and the majority just "believes" in it. Now, however, many perceive it, and many do so for the first time so that they will never be able to forget it again.—It is in this way that war as an ordeal from God becomes an experience {Ereignis} (PPS 98f.; see also another, in some sense very moving, passage in ibid., 106f.)

21. Note that Scheler's phrases «zurücktönen,» «to echo» —literally «to sound back, to resound» —and «antworten» («answer») are precisely the same as Heidegger's phrase «erwidert.» Fate calls out its demand. Either one does not listen, as those do who remain liberals or pacifists and thus become inauthentic Daseine. Or one listens to fate and reacts as fate demands, that is, one «echoes,» «answers,» or «erwidert,» that is, gives to fate the answer it wants to hear. Note that in Scheler's usage of «antworten» one has an Erwiderung, an Antwort, which is already in the dative (I «antworte jemandem») (and not only in the accusative; see above, chapter 1, sections B and C) a compliance with a demand.

22. Scheler says «no longer allein, alone.» «Allein» can mean «einsam» (lonely). However, he could not have said «no longer einsam,» for this would have reduced the entire event to a mere psychological problem of needy individuals. In addition, a phrase like «no longer einsam» would not have conveyed appropriately what his phrase «no longer allein» does communicate, namely, that «we» are no longer isolated from the «real» powers of life and history, for God is with us.

23. See Scheler's typology of the reactions of German liberals to the beginning of World War I in the introduction of *Der Genius des Krieges und der Deutsche Krieg* (PPS 12). According to Scheler, prior to WWI liberals made up «the largest group in the intellectual sphere.» After the beginning of the war, only a few still adhered to their liberalism, and they did so, according to Scheler, in the same way Schelling responded to

the observation that newly discovered facts contradicted his system of natural philosophy: «all the worse for nature» («Um so schlimmer für die Natur!»). The majority of the
liberals vacillated and considered, as Scheler puts it, «to explode a standpoint that new
great facts have proved to be impossible.» It is to the latter that his book is addressed.

24. The second edition of *Abhandlungen und Aufsätze* was published in 1919 under
the title *Vom Umsturz der Werte* (Subversion of Values). By that time, the war itself,
its result (the defeat of Germany), the «November-Revolution,» and the Weimar Republic in Germany had pretty much disillusioned Scheler. In the preface to the second edition, he points out that he had already suggested the new title to the publishing house
one year before the end of the war and that he hopes readers will not take the new title
to refer to the outcome of the war and to the revolutions in its wake (UW 8). Similarly
to the later Heidegger's assessment of the empirical National Socialism of the thirties
and forties, in the preface to the second edition Scheler regards the war no longer as the
decisive step out of Gesellschaft and the beginning of the rerealization of Gemeinschaft,
but rather as a manifestation of Gesellschaft itself, which, however, at the same time
might be the consummation in which the new order announces itself. The new title,
«Subversion of values,» does not refer to the war and the revolutions, but rather to the
beginning of the modern era when the emerging capitalist spirit subverted the order of
values that was realized in earlier ages. Also since Scheler in this context provides a
good formulation of the motif of «re-,» I quote almost the entire passage.

> If these huge events {the war, its loss, and the revolutions in its aftermath} have any
> essential meaning at all for the mode and structure of the European preferences of val-
> ues—and not only for the distribution of life goods among people, nations, and states
> according to the old preferences of values—(so far, for the answer to this question we
> have only conjectures), this meaning could only be the outward historical *effect*, widely
> visible, of that "upheaval" that is meant by the title of the book; an upheaval that not by
> event and deed {Tat} but rather in form of a silent process enabled the world view and
> ethics of the bourgeois-capitalist age to emerge more and more clearly out of an order of
> life and world that had been guided by the Christian religion and church. However, {these
> huge events} . . . *quite possibly* can be—together with their being the highest outcome of
> bourgeois spirit—the sublime peripetia, in which a reestablishment {Wiederaufrichtung}
> of the eternal order of the human heart, which has been overthrown by the bourgeois-
> capitalist spirit, announces itself. (UW 8f.)

25. Scheler gives no reason for his thesis that the parties of the working class remain
within the confines of selfish interest. Already in *Abhandlungen und Aufsätze,* in the
essay "Die Zukunft des Kapitalismus" (The future of capitalism), written in February
1914 (UW 385, n. 1), Scheler talks about the disadvantages of social politics and insur-
ance politics by the state—the major achievements of the political struggle of the working class during the Kaiserreich and the Weimar republic—and lists «decrease of personal responsibility» (UW 383). Scheler emphasizes that, in his view, for the time being
the advantages outweigh the disadvantages. Heidegger talks only about what he regards
as the disadvantages. He develops «*solicitude*» (BT 157; «*Fürsorge,*» SZ 121) as an
existentiale. Concern with food and clothing and the nursing of the sick body are forms
of solicitude. However, this is not what is meant by «solicitude» as an existentiale (BT
158; SZ 121). Solicitude as an existentiale has a deficient mode and two positive modes.
Heidegger begins with one of the two positive modes: «For example, 'welfare work'
["Fürsorge"], as a factical social arrangement {"Fürsorge" als faktische soziale Ein-
richtung}, is grounded in Dasein's state of Being as Being-with» (BT 158; SZ 121). The

need for this positive mode of solicitude emerges out of the deficient mode of solicitude. Heidegger continues: «Its factical urgency gets its motivation in that Dasein maintains itself proximally and for the most part in the deficient modes of solicitude. Being
for, against, or without one another, passing one another by, not "mattering" to one
another—these are possible ways of solicitude. And it is precisely these last-named deficient and Indifferent modes that characterize everyday, average Being-with-one-
another» (BT 158; SZ 122). Of the two positive modes the one, namely, «'welfare work'
["Fürsorge"] as a factical social arrangement» is inauthentic:

> With regard to its positive modes, solicitude has two extreme possibilities. It can, as it were,
> take away 'care' from the Other and put itself in his position in concern: it can *leap in* for
> him {für ihn *einspringen*}. This kind of solicitude takes over for the Other that with which
> he is to concern himself. The Other is thus thrown out of his own position; he steps back
> so that afterwards, when the matter has been attended to, he can either take it over as some-
> thing finished and at his disposal, or disburden himself of it completely. In such solicitude
> the Other can become one who is dominated and dependent, even if this domination is a
> tacit one and remains hidden from him. This kind of solicitude, which leaps in and takes
> away 'care', is to a large extent determinative for Being with one another, and pertains for
> the most part to our concern with the ready-to-hand. (BT 158; SZ 122)

Of the deficient mode and the first of the two positive modes Heidegger says also:
«Being with one another is based proximally and often exclusively upon what is a matter of common concern in such Being. A Being-with-one-another which arises [ent-
springt] from one's doing the same thing as someone else, not only keeps for the most
part within the outer limits, but enters the mode of distance and reserve. The Being-
with-one-another of those who are hired for the same affair often thrives only on mistrust» (BT 159; SZ 122). Of the second positive mode of solicitude Heidegger doesn't
say much: «In contrast to this, there is also the possibility of a kind of solicitude which
does not so much leap in for the Other as *leap ahead* of him [ihm *vorausspringt*] in his
existentiell potentiality-for-Being, not in order to take away his 'care' but rather to give
it back to him authentically as such for the first time {erst eigentlich als solche zurück-
zugeben}. This kind of solicitude pertains essentially to authentic care—that is, to the
existence of the Other, not to a "*what*" with which he is concerned; it helps the Other
to become transparent to himself *in* his care and to become *free for* it» (BT 158f.; SZ
122). And, following the sentence ending with «mistrust,» he writes on authentic solicitude: «On the other hand, when they devote themselves to the same affair in common,
their doing so is determined by the manner in which their Dasein, each in its own way,
has been taken hold of. They thus become *authentically* bound together, and this makes
possible the right kind of objectivity, which frees the Other in his freedom for himself»
(BT 159; SZ 122). The passage on authentic Dasein as the conscience of the other (see
above p. 66) refers to the authentic mode of solicitude. By becoming the conscience of
ordinary Daseine, authentic Dasein throws them, so to speak, out of welfare and drags
them out of the parties that have fought for the welfare system: «In the light of {Aus}
the "for-the-sake-of-which" of one's self-chosen potentiality-for-Being, resolute
Dasein frees itself for its world. Dasein's resoluteness towards itself is what first makes
it possible to let the Others who are with it 'be' in their ownmost potentiality-for-Being,
and to co-disclose this potentiality in the solicitude which leaps forth and liberates.
When Dasein is resolute, it can become the 'conscience' of Others. Only by authentically Being-their-Selves in resoluteness can people authentically be with one another
{Aus dem eigentlichen Selbstsein entspringt allererst das eigentliche Miteinander}—

not by ambiguous and jealous stipulations {zweideutigen und eifersüchtigen Verabre-dungen} and talkative *frater*nizing {redseligen Ver*brüder*ungen} in the "they" and in what "they" want to undertake» (BT 344f.; SZ 298; italics mine, J. F.). The last sen-tence is indeed a good example of rightist polemics against the parties on the Left and against those in the Center. The phrase «ambiguous and jealous stipulations» targets Kant's notion of «*unsocial sociability* {*ungesellige Geselligkeit*}» (*Idea for a Univer-sal History with a Cosmopolitan Purpose*, in: H. Reiss, ed., *Kant's Political Writings*, trans. H. B. Nisbet [Cambridge: Cambridge University Press, 1980], 44) and the notion of contract in modern political philosophy. The phrase, «talkative *frater*nizing» (italics mine, J. F.) targets the leftist notion of solidarity («*Brüder*, zur Sonne, zur Freiheit!» as the song of the social democrats had it). Note that in this passage, Heidegger uses «aus» as well as «entspringt» in the sense I mentioned above (see pp. 49f.). Authenticity and heritage is the spring «from» which stable identity entspringt without silting up some-where and without covering up its origin.

The entire passage on Fürsorge mirrors numerous passages in the literature on Gemeinschaft and Gesellschaft. Gesellschaft is «bad» (or, in Heideggerian terms, Dasein in its «downward plunge»), because in it Daseine act as isolated and selfish Daseine that mistrust each other and because liberal Gesellschaft has «always already» led into social welfare, social democracy, and socialism. Thus, authentic Dasein has to counteract, or, in terms of section 74 of *Being and Time*, it has to widerrufen Gesellschaft. In the sec-tion on solicitude, Heidegger merely points to «*authentically* bound together» («*eigent-liche* Verbundenheit»). In section 74, he will reveal the subject that makes possible this «*eigentliche* Verbundenheit,» namely, the Volksgemeinschaft («of the community, of {the} people,» BT 436; 384). Listening to this («*erwidert,*» SZ 386; BT 438), authentic Dasein cancels Gesellschaft in order to make room for the rerealization of the Volksge-meinschaft. As to the terminology, Heidegger starts with Sorge and Fürsorge. Moving toward the Being-with-one-another Dasein encounters the Sozialfürsorge (the technical term as well as everyday language word for the institutions of social welfare; «Die "*Für-sorge*" als faktische *soziale* Einrichtung,» SZ 121; italics mine, J. F.; «'*welfare*' work' {"Fürsorge"}, as a factical *social* arrangement,» BT 158; note that the phrase «Die "Für-sorge" als faktische soziale Einrichtung» is like «community, of {the} people» ; in both cases, Heidegger avoids using well-known words—«Sozialfürsorge» and «Volksge-meinschaft» —by placing their first parts [«Sozial» and «Volks»] after the noun [«Für-sorge» and «Gemeinschaft»]; the occurrence of such thoroughly worldly and political notions like «Sozialfürsorge» and «Volksgemeinschaft» might have embarrassed some readers of a book on fundamental ontology). Authentic Dasein cancels Gesellschaft and Sozialfürsorge in the name of the proper Sorge of the Gemeinschaft. Notably, it was not a philosopher, but rather a sociologist and philosopher who pointed out Heidegger's pol-itics in the passage on «Fürsorge» (see Pierre Bordieu, *The Political Ontology of Mar-tin Heidegger,* 70–87).

English readers might wonder what it means that the authentic mode of solicitude leaps ahead of Dasein «not in order to take away his 'care' but rather to give it back to him authentically as such for the first time» (BT 159; «sondern erst eigentlich als solche zurückzugeben,» SZ 122). Does this imply or leave open the possibility that, prior to the moment of being given back, care was already given, or could have already been given, back to Dasein, though in an inauthentic way? The phrase «erst eigentlich» prob-ably does not refer to the notion of authenticity but emphasizes the conjunction «son-dern» («but») so that one might translate, «but rather to give it back to him as such.»

This sentence seems to exclude the possibility that at an earlier time care was already, or could have already been, given back to Dasein, albeit inauthentically. It might be possible, though, that the phrase «als solche» («as such») is supposed to mean «authentic,» and that the translators meant the phrase «authentically» as an explication of «as such.» In that case, they might have understood the phrase «erst eigentlich» as «for the first time,» which is not impossible. (Unless she means «to first» in the sense of «first and foremost,» Stambaugh seems to have worked with both options and in the final editing not to have sufficiently clarified which of them she prefers: «not in order to take "care" away from him, but to first to give it back to him as such» [*Being and Time: A Translation of* Sein und Zeit, 115].) Probably, such vaguenesses in Heidegger's text go back to his assumption that somehow the vanished beginning never disappears but is covered up by Dasein in Dasein's downward plunge.

Still, on both interpretations Heidegger's sentence is an example of his usage of the preposition and prefix «zurück» («back») (see chapter 2, n. 35). In this instance, it is not just an allusion to the need of repetition but—at least, for those familiar with the literature on society and community—an explicit statement on the issue of repetition. Something, *a*, can be given «back» to Dasein only if Dasein had already possessed *a* but lost it at a later point. In the deficient mode of solicitude, Dasein does not have care, or it only has inauthentic care. In the first positive mode of solicitude, care is even actively taken away from Dasein («This kind of solicitude, which leaps in and takes away 'care'» [BT 158; SZ 122]; «to take away his 'care'» [BT 159; SZ 122]). Thus, in the authentic mode of solicitude authentic Daseine give back to Dasein something that Dasein had prior to being in the deficient mode of solicitude. The deficient mode of solicitude is society or liberalism. The first positive mode of solicitude is social democracy as the «truth» of liberalism. (The factical urgency for Sozialfürsorge «gets its motivation in that Dasein maintains itself proximally and for the most part in the deficient modes of solicitude» [BT 158; SZ 121].) Thus, in the authentic mode of solicitude authentic Daseine give back to Dasein the care that Dasein had prior to its downward plunge into society and socialism. That is, authentic Dasein cancels society and repeats or gives back community to Dasein.

The English sentence, «The being-with-one-another of those who are *hired for* the same affair often thrives on mistrust» (BT 159; italics mine, J. F.), reads in German: «Das Miteinandersein derer, die bei derselben Sache *angestellt* sind, nährt sich oft nur von Mißtrauen» (SZ 122; italics mine, J. F.). The noun «Angestellte(r)» with its adjective «angestellt» designates clerks in the offices of companies. While a typist in Berlin-Mitte or on Wall Street is a «kleine Angestellte,» a person in a high management position is a «leitender Angestellter.» Especially in a decade plagued by high unemployment, Heidegger's sentence is a clear and realistic statement about capitalist economy. In this sense, one might even translate the phrase «bei derselben Sache angestellt» as «employed by the same company.» Authentic Daseine, however, «devote themselves to the same affair in *common*» (BT 159; italics mine, J. F.). This phrase reads in German: «das *gemein*same Sicheinsetzen für dieselbe Sache» (SZ 122; italics mine, J. F.). One might even translate it as: «when they form a *Gemein*schaft and devote themselves to the same issue.»

Heidegger says that only the second positive mode of Fürsorge «makes possible the right kind of objectivity [die rechte Sachlichkeit]» (BT 159; SZ 122). As one sees, the adjective «right» presents the same problem as the subordinated clause with «as such.» Is there only one objectivity or are there several ones? So to speak, a right, a left, and a liberal objectivity with the two latter being the wrong objectivities? (On the «magical» character of «rechts,» right, and «links,» left, see above, chapter 2, n. 15.) The «rechte Sachlichkeit» refers to the mentality and attitude of authentic Daseine. However, from the beginning of this passage on Heidegger speaks about «Einrichtung[en]» (instead of «arrangement» in «'welfare work' ["Fürsorge"], as a factical social arrangement {Einrichtung}» [BT 158; SZ 121], one might also say «institution»). In addition, he labels a capitalist company as well as die Sache of the advocates of Gemeinschaft, the issue of the authentic Daseine, a «Sache» (SZ 122; «affair,» BT 159). (One should keep in mind that in German the noun «die Sache» can have a very emphatic meaning, as for instance in Hegel [«die Sache selbst»] or in a title of a book of Heidegger's: *Zur Sache des Denkens* [Tübingen: Niemeyer, 1969]; the rallying cry of the phenomenological movement was «'To the things themselves!'» [BT 50; «"Zu den Sachen selbst!",» SZ 27].) For these two reasons, one might also hear «Sachlichkeit» as the abstract noun to «Sache.» Only authentic Dasein provides Daseine with the right institutions, namely, the ones of Gemeinschaft. The (right) Sache has been toppled by the Sache that employs Angestellte. The Sache that employs Angestellte leads to the socialist Sache, the institutions of social welfare. Authentic Daseine recover the right Sache, as they recover Sorge from its various Fürsorgen.

As Lucien Goldmann observed, it can hardly be a coincidence that Heidegger refers to Lukács's term «Verdinglichung des Bewußtseins» in a programmatic passage at the beginning (SZ 46; «'reification of consciousness',» BT 72) as well as on the last page (SZ 437; BT 487) of *Being and Time* (L. Goldmann, *Lukács and Heidegger: Towards a New Philosophy*, trans. W. Q. Boelhower [London: Routledge, 1979], 27ff.). Heidegger also uses a term of the young Marx, namely, «Entfremdung» and its corresponding verb «entfremden» («alienation, to alienate») (SZ 178ff., 254, 347f; BT 222ff., 298, 399). It is interesting that in German philosophical literature Meister Eckhart was apparently the first to use the notion of Entfremdung as the German translation of the Latin word «alienatio,» and he used it in the sense of, in Heidegger's terms, «to become authentic.» In order to hear God speaking one must be alienated from all that is one's own (see E. Ritz, "Entfremdung," Joachim Ritter, ed., *Historisches Wörterbuch der Philosophie*, vol. 2 [D–F] [Basel: Schwabe, 1972], 512). However, the notion lends itself to a romantic understanding. In acquiring what is one's own and engaging in idle talk, etc., one lives in an Ent-fremdung (see on the prefix «ent-» above pp. 32ff.) from one's origin; one has become entfremdet, alienated, from it. One better cancel one's Entfremdung from it and return to it. Heidegger reconstructs the notion of Entfremdung with the conceptual means of his theory. Entfremdung is the result of falling. In the downward plunge into idle talk, curiosity, etc., Dasein «drifts along towards an alienation [Entfremdung] in which its ownmost potentiality-for-Being is hidden from it» (BT 222; SZ 178). The notions of falling and downward plunge in turn are reduced to a primordial activity for which Heidegger uses another term with the prefix «ent-,» namely, «Entspringen» in its pejorative usage. Thus, in the passage on «Entspringen» from which I quoted above (see above, pp. 34f.) «alienation» occurs: «In the 'leaping-away' {Im "Entspringen"} of the Present, one also forgets increasingly. . . . Even when it makes present in the most extreme manner {Auch im extremsten Gegenwärtigen}, it remains temporal—that is, awaiting and forgetful. In making present, moreover, {Auch gegenwärtigend} Dasein still understands itself, though it has been alienated {entfremdet ist} from its ownmost potentiality-for-Being, which is based primarily on the authentic future and on authentically having been» (BT 399; SZ 348; the second «Auch» is probably parallel to the first one; thus, Stambaugh translates: «Even in making present» [*Being and Time: A Translation of Sein und Zeit*,

319]). Such appropriations of Marxist terms by right-wingers and romantics were certainly one of the reasons why Adorno was always skeptical about the usage of Verdinglichung and Entfremdung and even seemed to have basically disliked the latter notion (see for instance, Theodor W. Adorno, *Negative Dialectics,* trans. E. B. Ashton [New York: Continuum, 1992], 189ff.). Adorno always preferred the Marx of *Capital* over the Marx of the *Economic and Philosophical Manuscripts.*

As one can see, Heidegger's argument against social welfare is similar to the arguments of Republicans in the United States against welfare in the 1990s. From the perspective of Scheler and Heidegger in the debates I address in this book, Republicans in the United States are classical liberals, and Democrats are social democrats or liberals who maintain that classical liberalism no longer works.

26. The English translator has left out the quotation marks at «society,» which is understandable given the huge number of quotation marks and italics in Scheler's text. One might regret the omission, however, since the passage is a good example of the polemical use of quotation marks. In the entire passage, «society» is the only word put into quotation marks. With them and with the addition of «so-called,» Scheler denigrates society, since, as he puts it, society «zersetzt» the Gemeinschaften.

27. See above, this chapter, n. 25; see also the last section of this chapter and section B of chapter 4.

28. As one can already see and as will become clearer in what follows, one might say that there is a contradiction, tension, or confusion, in Scheler or just simply an anachronistic ontology. In the realm of values, each of the four communal forms of togetherness has its specific rationality or style of synthesis of the individuals involved in it. Each of the types of community is free of the rationality of society. Society is one of the four communal forms of togetherness, but it is not a community. If the realm of values is properly preferred, the same holds true for each of the empirical communities. Each empirical family, state, etc., is free of the rationality of society. In this sense, each of the notions of society and the different communities designates an object or an area— an entity in the realm of values or an empirical group—distinct from all the other areas. At the same time, however, each of these notions designates a peculiar rationality that is independent of any area, and that can occur in any of the empirical communities designated by the notions taken in their first way of designation. Without the second way of designation, Scheler could not claim that in the modern age the rationality of society has invaded and taken over empirical families, states, etc. (see esp. section D). (This tension forces or allows Scheler to develop his project within, as it were, the historicized framework of Christian original sin and recovery. Scheler leaves out the theological veto upon the realization of recovery here on earth through human achievement. This is the first step of the alignment of his theory with the political Right.) In *The Theory of Social and Economic Organization,* trans. A. M. Henderson and T. Parsons (Glencoe, IL.: The Free Press, 1947), 136–139 (section 9); *Wirtschaft und Gesellschaft* (Tübingen: Mohr, 1972), 21–23 (section 9), in its first edition published in 1922, Max Weber uses, not just the concepts of Gemeinschaft and Gesellschaft. Rather, he adds the prefix «ver-» and the suffix «-ung»—«'Vergemeinschaftung'» («'communal' social relationship,» or communitization, as it were) and «'Vergesellschaftung'» («'associative' social relationship,» or societalization). This slight modification expresses his theoretical program; namely, to de-ontologize the concepts. In Weber they don't designate different areas or inherent ontological features of certain activities (childraising, love in matrimony, economic activities, etc.) but rather types of synthesis that can occur in every area or activ-

ity, without fixed ontological features of this or that activity being stipulated. This is an instance of the way politics is implied in Weberian science. This theoretical maneuver pulls the rug out from under the feet of any rightist politics, at least concerning the pretension to place rightist politics on a scientific basis. (In this context, Weber mentions only Ferdinand Tönnies's seminal book *Gemeinschaft und Gesellschaft;* Tönnies himself deplored the use right-wingers made of his book; see my book *Society, Community, Fate, and Decision: From Kant to Benjamin.*) Weber points out that there is no purity. The great majority of social relationships is informed by both forms of synthesis. (The awareness of the impossibility of the pure allows, one might add, a non-ontological mode of critique according to pragmatic points of view or according to, say, the liberal notion of human rights.) In addition, many sociologists regard the communal type of relationship as the most radical antithesis of conflict, which, in contrast, is considered to be inherent in the associative type of relationship. «This should not, however,» as Weber points out, «be allowed to obscure the fact that coercion of all sorts is a very common thing in even the most intimate of such communal relationships.» Furthermore, «the possession of a common biological inheritance by virtue of which persons are classified as belonging to the same 'race,' naturally implies no sort of communal social relationship between them.» Rather, as one would say nowadays, race is a social construct. Thus, there is no scientific basis for maintaining that every individual is a priori part of this or that Gemeinschaft, and for calling upon people to form that Volksgemeinschaft they already belong to in order to rerealize alleged biological features and the Gemeinschaft shaped by the latter. In the same way, a common language does not imply any sort of communal social relationship between the speakers. Furthermore, Weber writes: «No matter how calculating and hard-headed the ruling considerations in such a social relationship—as that of a merchant to his customers—may be, it is quite possible for it to involve emotional values which transcend its utilitarian significance. Every social relationship which goes beyond the pursuit of immediate common ends, and which hence lasts for long periods, involves relatively permanent social relationships between the same persons, and these cannot be exclusively confined to the technically necessary activities. Hence in such cases as association in the same military unit {Vergesellschaftung im gleichen Heeresverband}, in the same school class, in the same workshop or office, there is always some tendency in this direction, although the degree, to be sure, varies enormously.» With this passage, Weber makes indeed politics against the Right in two ways. A military unit should be regarded as in the first place a Gesellschaft—«a rationally motivated . . . agreement» of interests («Interessen*verbindung,*» thus, maybe better «union of interests»)—and not as a Gemeinschaft. The first sentence may be understood as an implicit call to withdraw one's emotional energies from Gemeinschaft and to «re-gather» them on Gesellschaft. A Gesellschaft is constituted by an «Interessen*verbindung*» and/or by an «Interessen*ausgleich*» («rationally motivated adjustment of interests» ; when Scheler abandons any rightist politics, his key term will be «Ausgleich,» see this chapter, section F). The fact that, on these two out of the thirty pages on the basic concepts of sociology, in a book of more than nine hundred pages, the most urgent themes and problems—race, language, military, and the economy—are presented shows that the two concepts of Gemeinschaft and Gesellschaft were indeed the major framework within which political problems were discussed at the time.

29. One must not think that here Scheler propagates socialism or communism. See the remainder of this chapter.

30. This is my own translation of the German sentences, «Denn Gerechtigkeit fordert—sofern ihr Wesen rein erfaßt wird—durchaus nicht Vergeltung des Bösen mit Üblem. Nur aus einem Teil des Wesenskernes der Gerechtigkeit, nach dem es gut ist und sein soll, daß unter *gleichen Wertverhalten* auch *gleiches Verhalten* wollender Personen stattfinde, folgt—*wenn* es Vergeltung gibt—, daß diese auch Gleichwertiges gleich zu treffen habe. Nicht aber folgt aus ihr die Forderung einer "Vergeltung" selbst» (FE 363). In brief, in my opinion the sentence, «nach dem . . . Personen statt- finde» («according to which . . . should occur») is a general formulation of a sentence like this one: «"From consideration of" this area of tasks, e.g., "as" economic sub- jects, "as" bearers of civil rights and duties, etc., ultimate bearers can and must "obtain" as "equal" in a given case (which would be the object of a special investigation)» (FEe 509; FE 500). I leave it open whether one gets the same meaning as in my trans- lation in the English translation: «Insofar as the pure essence of justice is grasped, it does not require the reprisal of evil through bad deeds. Only from that part of the cen- tral essence of justice according to which the occurrence of the *same comportment* on the condition of the *same value-complexes* is good and ought to be does it follow that *if* there is reprisal, it must aim equally at factors of equivalent value. But from this no demand for "reprisal" follows» (FEe 363). In the English translation the phrase «wol- lender Personen» («of willing persons») doesn't occur. It might be the case that the translator wasn't quite sure that, indeed, the German expression «Vergeltung trifft» simply means «reprisal (targets you and) punishes (you),» and that the «[V]erhalt» in «*Wertverhalten*» is used with a view to the German noun «Sachverhalt» .

31. As indicated in the quote, the English translator has rendered the German phrase «so bunt gegliedert sie ist» with «mixed as it is.» For whatever reasons, for instance, the benefits of the American melting pot, the translator chose to prefer «mixed» over words like «structured,» which recommend themselves quite easily and convey the required sense. The translation is not just more or less inexact. Rather, it conveys pre- cisely the opposite of Scheler's theories and political intentions. Like other rightist authors, he argues against mixtures, against processes in which distinctions and rank- ings he considers essential are leveled or confused. For Scheler, the liberal assump- tion that all human beings are equal is the most prominent expression of the «essence» of the modern age, that is, to mix up and level the essential differences in the realm of values that have been realized by the «right» acts of preferring in an earlier period. Processes of mixture are not—as the English translation suggests—a productive source and a means to realize the values. Rather, they are the processes by which the right order of values is overthrown and which terminate in socialism, chaos, and anarchy. In direct opposition to the disappearing of differences and rankings by processes of mixture, the German word «gegliedert» conveys the idea of «being ranked within a hierarchy of values and ranks, within which each of the different ranks and each of the individuals and groups related to one of them is clearly distinguished from all the others and the individuals and groups belonging to the latter.» The different peoples and races in history are part of mankind. Mankind, however, entails a hierarchy of the different peoples and races that liberalism and social democracy have done away with. One might also say that the mistranslation of the German phrase is a projection of the later Scheler onto the earlier Scheler (see section F of this chapter).

32. See this chapter, n. 20.

33. See, however, Scheler's critique of Sombart's interpretation of Thomas Aquinas and Protestantism in his *Der Bourgeois und die religiösen Mächte,* where he

summarizes his view as follows: «Neither Protestantism nor Calvinism has "produced" the bourgeois spirit. Rather, in Calvinism also in the sphere of religion and church the bourgeois spirit *broke through* the limitations for the bourgeois spirit posited by the Catholic Church and also Thomas Aquinas» (UW 378). In its spirit, the ethics of Thomas Aquinas belong to the hierarchic and vertical ethics of the «good old world» and by no means to the limitless and horizontal ethics of capitalism.

34. In this passage, Scheler doesn't say more about «mixture of blood» in Sombart. In the essay on ressentiment, he says in a note that in «Sombart's opinion, the "Jewish spirit" is one of the chief causes of the development of the capitalist social structure. It is quite in agreement with my thesis that this spirit, which has had a lien on *ressentiment* for a long time, plays a major role in this process» (RE 194, n. 27; UW 129, n. 2). Sombart wrote a book of almost 500 pages—*Die Juden und das Wirtschaftsleben* (Leipzig: Duncker & Humblot, 1911)—in which he wanted to show that the Jews have established capitalism and which certainly has its place in the history of anti-Semitism.

35. Scheler adds a note to this passage: «This was written in February 1914, that is, long before the war» (UW 385, n.). By this, he probably acknowledges that he has underestimated the anticapitalist potential of the conservatives, which, for Scheler they proved through their support of the war. The note is interesting because, as will become clear in what follows, according to Scheler the bourgeois ethos is bound to die out. However, this takes time. In the meantime, it is possible to speed up the process, among other things through World War I, sent by God as a gift.

36. Since I began with Scheler's war at the «Heimatfront» (the home front), let me just mention a further detail. According to rightists, in Gesellschaft we encounter selfish individuals, and we are lonely. It was part of the rightist ideology concerning war that, since this is the case with society, war is one of the few opportunities when we have an authentic relation to others; in the situation of combat, «face to face with the other,» we encounter «the other as other,» as one finds it, for instance, in Ernst Jünger's writings on war. We all know that killing in wars is not regarded as murder. However, one need not, and should not, justify this thesis in terms of the anachronistic framework of war as a fight between knights or as a duel between Prussian aristocrats, as Scheler does: «Whenever persons are given in war, the intention toward the negation and annihilation of these persons is so little given that, on the contrary, the principle of *chivalry* demands not only that the person expose himself to the same kind and degree of danger as he affords but also that he *affirm the favor* of the *person* of the enemy, in its value and its existence, the better and more courageously he fights and defends himself. A certain measure of positive valuation of the enemy is connected with the very agreement to duel» (FEe 314; FE 317f.). After Scheler had abandoned any rightist politics and turned to the Center in the 1920s (see above this chapter, section F), he worked in the last two years of his life, 1926–28, among other texts, on a book *On the Idea of Eternal Peace and Pacifism,* published only in the Nachlaß volume, in which he defended the idea of eternal peace and refuted reasons for war (in *Gesammelte Werke 13: Schriften aus dem Nachlaß 4,* ed. M. S. Frings [Bonn: Bouvier Verlag, 1990]). On p. 86 one finds as one of his reasons against war the notion that through modern technology the principle of chivalry has become anachronistic. On the same page, he writes a sentence that Heidegger, as one would put it in German, sich hinter die Ohren hätte schreiben sollen, that is, should have read carefully and kept in mind. In his de-cision-

istic phase, Scheler wrote much on the Held, that is, on the right-wing notion of Vorbild, example to follow. For instance, in the passage on the «power of war to forge communities {gemeinschaftsbildnerische Kraft des Krieges}» (PPS 77) from which I quoted above (see pp. 88f.), he says that «the common memory of war is the core of {each nation's} community of fate» and continues by saying that «the shared images of {a nation's} heroes {Helden} represent the strongest force of {its} holding together and of {its} unity» (PPS 77). The Catholic Scheler continues in a way Hitler would not have: «This power forms a bond that in terms of strength by far surpasses belonging to the same race, language, and spiritual culture» (PPS 77). That is, the soldier is higher than the heroes, or paradigms, of the state and the Volksgemeinschaft, and he is higher than the other heroes of a Kulturgemeinschaft; the soldier is only below the hero, or paradigm, of the love-community, Jesus Christ, since for Scheler, prior to his Kehre, the soldier fights for Jesus Christ and the love-community. After his Kehre, Scheler refinds the general term Vorbild and dismisses the right-wing notion of Held: «It is not at all the case that the "Held" is the highest example {Vorbild} of man. Rather, the highest example is the kind-hearted man {der Gütige}, the saint {der Heilige}, the genius of a great and strong heart {das Genie des großen kraftvollen Herzens}» (*On the Idea of Eternal Peace and Pacifism*, 86). Also such a sentence shows that only for rightists was the Held the highest example to follow and that, as I suggested in chapter 1, section A, the paradigm of the «German» Held after World War I was not, as it is assumed in the American literature, any distinguished individual, but rather the Helden von Langemarck (see chapter 5, section C).

37. See above, n. 24.

38. See above, n. 25.

39. On the entire passage see this chapter, n. 25.

40. On all the mentioned points see my book *Fate, Community, and Society: From Kant to Benjamin*.

41. See above, n. 8.

42. See above, p. 38.

43. The flag is an Erwiderung and Widerruf in Heidegger's sense. It erwidert the past, or what-has-been-there, insofar as it brings back the Aryan race, which has been spoiled and forgotten. This step requires that one widerruft the Weimar Republic and its flag, whose colors were black, red, and gold.

44. See Winfried Franzen, "Die Sehnsucht nach Härte und Schwere: Über ein zum NS-Engagement disponierendes Motiv in Heidegger's Vorlesung 'Die Grundbegriffe der Metaphysik' von 1929/30," in Annemarie Gethmann-Siefert and Otto Pöggeler (eds.), *Heidegger und die praktische Philosophie* (Frankfurt: Suhrkamp, 1988), 78–92; see also above, chapter 1, n. 33.

45. Hegel, *Philosophy of Right*, 107 (section 324, n.)

46. On the occurrence of «Eigentum,» property, in the later Heidegger, see my paper "On Brinks and Bridges in Heidegger," 153, n. 59.

47. See above, pp. 107f.

48. For the details see above, pp. 1–7, 43–50.

49. For the details see above, pp. 50–67.

50. For the phrase «is determinative for it» see above, this chapter, n. 3.

51. For the details see above, pp. 60ff. Even after his personal Kehre with regard to Heidegger's philosophy, Caputo repeats the deconstructive interpretation, in which

the Parisian deconstructive mood happily merges with the American idol of the self-made man: «Dasein gives itself a fate» (John Caputo, *Demythologizing Heidegger,* 81). On «setzt sich . . . zusammen» and «the handing down of a heritage constitutes itself in resoluteness» (BT 435; SZ 383f.) see above, pp. 55ff. The notion «Konstitution» is crucial and omnipresent in Husserl, and he also uses the verb «konstituieren» and its reflexive form «sich konstituieren.» Scheler develops four types of social units, namely, the mass, the life-community, society, and the love-community (see above, pp. 97ff.), and he distinguishes between four types of large-scale communities, namely, the church, the nation, the state, and the Volksgemeinschaft (see below, pp. 136ff.). He always stresses that a community is ontologically prior to its individual members, whereas society is ontologically posterior to its individual members. In that context, he uses the reflexive verb «sich konstituieren» («to constitute itself») frequently (FE 509ff.; FEe 519ff.) as a term for the ontological order of the elements of a social unit and the relationship between the whole and its parts. It would lead too far to inquire whether in some of its occurrences he also uses the notion in the sense Heidegger employs it, namely, in the sense of «to become active» (see above, pp. 57ff.). Having used «konstituiert sich» (SZ 383; «constitutes itself,» BT 435) in the sense of «becomes active» Heidegger uses its German translation («sich zusammensetzen» [«setzt sich nicht aus einzelnen Schicksalen zusammen,» SZ 384; «not something that puts itself together out of individual fates,» BT 436]) in the ontological sense and offers a German translation of «sich konstituieren» in the sense of «to become active,» namely, «wird . . . frei» (SZ 384; «become free,» BT 436).

52. On «Ausgleich» as Scheler's key term after his Kehre see section F of this chapter.

53. For the details see above, pp. 43–68. On «communicating» see below, chapter 6, n. 24.

54. For the details see above, pp. 13–21.

55. For the details see above, pp. 7–13, 21–28.

56. See above p. 25.

57. In German, one might say, here Heidegger «läßt die Katze aus dem Sack,» that is, he lays his cards on the table. As one might expect, neither Birmingham nor Guignon quote this sentence. For the terminological difference between «past» and «what-has-been-there» see BT 373ff., 432; ST 325ff., 380. Heidegger will always make the distinction between a past in whose rerealization he is not interested and a past that is supposed to recur, and he will always label the former «Vergangenheit» or «Vergangenes» («past») and the latter «Gewesenes» or «Gewesendes,» see above, this chapter, n. 12, and, for instance, the preface of the volume *Vorträge und Aufsätze:* «Denkwege, für die Vergangenes zwar vergangen, Gewesendes jedoch im Kommen bleibt, warten, bis irgendwann Denkende sie gehen. Während das geläufige und im weitesten Sinne technische Vorstellen immer noch vorwärts will und alle fortreißt, geben weisende Wege bisweilen eine Aussicht frei auf ein einziges Ge-birg./Todtnauberg, im August 1954» (VA 7). Without all its subtleties, this might be translated as: «[There are] ways of thinking, for which what-has-past is indeed past, but for which something-which-has-been-there remains still to come, [and these ways of thinking] wait, until at some point in the future thinkers will go these ways. While the ordinary and, in the broadest sense, technological representation even now wants [to move] forward and sweeps along all {all human beings? all the beings? all things?}, in con-

trast revealing/instructing/commanding ways sometimes grant a view of a single mountain range. Todtnauberg, August 1954.» One finds the shortest formulation of this notion in the following sentence: «Denn was gewesen, verharrt im Wirken, übersteht das Vergehen» ("Wink in das Gewesene," *Aus der Erfahrung des Denkens, 1910–1976*, GA 15 [Frankfurt: Klostermann, 1983], 201; «For what-has-been-there persists in being active and rides out corruption» ; see also above, chapter 2, nn. 5 and 33). This sentence and Heidegger's etymology of vorläufig (see above, chapter 1, n. 11) both confirm the impression that, in the sentence «*Widerruf* dessen, was im Heute sich als "Vergangenheit" auswirkt» (SZ 386, «*disavowal* of that which in the "today", is working itself out as the 'past',» BT 438) the verb «auswirkt» («working itself out») is supposed to have the connotation of «aus» in the sense of «zu Ende,» that is, «coming to an end» (like the rivulet, see above, p. 33; thus one says a rivulet «läuft aus,» silts up, or a product «läuft aus,» that is, it is no longer produced), similar to Nietzsche's saying that what is falling already should also be pushed.

58. On openness and Entschlossenheit see above, chapter 1, section A. In the light of Heidegger's notorious statement on the German and the Greek language (IM 57; EM 43) it is interesting that, with regard to the words used by Heidegger, the Latin and the English languages have a clear advantage over Greek and German. For in German and Greek one can make Heidegger's point by listening properly to the word «erwidern» (see chapter 5, n. 70), not however by listening to the key term of the entire passage, namely, «Wiederholung» (repetition). For except for romantics «Wiederholung» has no normative connotations or aura. However, in English one can make Heidegger's point already by listening to the words «repetition,» or «to repeat.» For they go back to the Latin words «repetitio» and «repetere.» «Petitio» means «an attack, thrust, blow» and also «demand» (or «re-quest» !). Accordingly, «petere» means «to make for, to attack, to assail» and also «to ask for, to beg» or «to request.» The prefix «re-» means «back.» Thus, the repetitor is one who demands something back from someone or who demands someone back. A repetitio is a re-clamation, the demand of something or someone back. Accordingly, «repetere» means «to ask back, to claim back, to trace back» and also the obedience to the request, namely, «to return to, to renew, to begin again.» Properly heard, therefore, in contrast to the German word «Wiederholung» the English word «repetition» already entails the normative aspect, which Heidegger develops in his formula of the «vorrufenden Rückruf» (SZ 280; the call «which calls us back in calling us forth,» BT 326) and in his usage of «entspringen» (see pp. 32ff.) and «erwidern.» Heritage, the past, «repeats» us, that is, it demands us back, it calls upon us to come back, since we sind ihr entsprungen, have jumped out of it and away from it into society. We «repeat» the call, that is, we obey it, kehren um, turn back, and return to the past. By this, we ourselves become the «*repetition* of a possibility of existence that has come down to us» (BT 437; SZ 385). We «repeat» the past, that is, rerealize, renew, begin again the past. In order to do so, we act onto the inauthentic Dasein the way the past has acted upon us, that is, we carry the call over to the inauthentic Daseine. We «repeat» the inauthentic Daseine, that is, we demand from them also that they «repeat» the past, that is, that they return to the past and rerealize it. That is, we make a «*disavowal*» (BT 438; SZ 386), not of the past, which has called upon us, but rather of Gesellschaft, which has entsprungen the past.

Inauthentic Dasein does not listen to, and does not respond to, the call, whereas authentic Dasein does so. Thus, one might perhaps translate Heidegger's phrase «*erwidert* vielmehr» (SZ 386; «Rather, the repetition makes a *reciprocative rejoinder* to the possibility of that existence which has-been-there,» BT 438) with «Rather, the repetition responds to the possibility of that existence which has-been-there,» in the sense that it responds to the call, that is, complies with the demand raised by the past while the meaning Guignon sees in the sentence would be expressed by «Rather, the repetition responds to the possibility of that existence which has-been-there with *x*,» with *x* being the placeholder for the specific answer of authentic Dasein to the past, which in fact in Heidegger's text does not occur. In Birmingham's interpretation, the *x* is authentic Dasein's polemos against the past, this polemos being even more radical than a military counterattack with equal weapons (TP 31). Thus, she writes: «The reply or response to historical possibilities is precisely that which disrupts identity and continuity» (TP 31).

59. One might speculate what it would say about Heidegger, and in general about problems of intellectual and political mentality, if indeed it were coincidental.

60. See section F of this part.

61. See Ott, *Martin Heidegger: A Political Life,* 136; German edition, 134. If he had joined the party just one year earlier, his Tat, deed, would have been a good instance of the kind of activity called for by the sentences on Erwiderung and Widerruf. For 1 May was the holiday in honor of the working class. Thus, to make one's stand for the Volksgemeinschaft on any 1 May prior to 1933 (or, for that matter, on any other day of the year) meant that one helped the Volksgemeinschaft in its call for help and repetition by actively disavowing, fighting against, expelling, (the holiday in honor of) the working class. On 1 May 1933, however, the working class and its special day was already forbidden, and its leaders were already arrested. Thus, to join the Nazis on 1 May 1933 was an act of, as one puts it in German, sich ins schon gemachte Bett zu legen; an act of lying down in a bed prepared by someone else, in Heidegger's case also by his major work *Being and Time.*

62. Another advantage of Heidegger's distinction is that it allows him to insert the entity designated by the term Geschick into the series of distinguished entities and modes the German language and Heidegger have the privilege to call by words with the prefix «ge-» such as «Gebirg,» «Gemüt,» «Gestell,» «Gewissen,» «Geschichte,» «Geschehen,» «Geschenk,» «Gelassenheit,» «Gewesenheit,» «Geviert,» «Geschlecht,» «Gemächte,» «Geworfenheit,» «Gemeinschaft,» and also its Zersetzungsprodukt, «Gesellschaft.» On Heidegger's use of «Gestell» see my paper "On Brinks and Bridges," 133ff.

Some commentators maintain that Geschick was attractive for Heidegger because it goes back to «geschickt» in the sense of «können,» «to be capable of.» However, the subject of «können» in Heidegger is not the individual but rather the Volk. The Dasein owes its Geschicklichkeiten, its capacities, not to itself but rather to the Volk (and, at least for Heidegger in 1933, this includes its soil, as Schlageter is capable of the hardness of the will because the Black Forest has worked on the Daseine living in it for a long time, see chapter 1, n. 33). The Volk as Geschick gives to the individuals their capacities. In this sense, Heidegger might have said that each Dasein is geschickt, «geschickt» meaning «skillful» and also «(has been) sent.» Prior to the crisis, ordinary Dasein is egocentric, selfish, and vacillates between equally insignificant possibilities. There is no real purpose in its life, and it does not respect its past. More or less consciously, Dasein realizes that there is no meaning in its life, no wholeness, and no «Ständigkeit» (SZ 375; «constancy,» BT 375). In brief, Dasein is geworfen, thrown into a naked facticity of inauthentic possibilities as it realizes upon becoming authentic. Once authentic Dasein has taken over its thrownness, it realizes that, now, it is no longer geworfen, thrown, but geschickt, sent. For Geschick has sent it to realize the Geschick, the mission, namely, to rerealize Gemeinschaft. In addition, Geschick has provided Dasein with the necessary Geschicklichkeiten, has made Dasein geschickt to fulfill its mission. However, in *Sein und Zeit* Heidegger does not use the adjective «geschickt» (see Bast and Delfosse, *Handbuch zum Textstudium von Martin* Heideggers '*Sein und Zeit*,' 128).

As to the above-mentioned «Ständigkeit,» it is worth noting that «Ständigkeit» is not just «constancy.» In section 64, Heidegger writes: «Selfhood {Selbstheit} is to be discerned existentially only in one's authentic potentiality-for-Being-one's-Self—that is to say, in the authenticity of Dasein's Being *as care*. In terms of care the *constancy of the Self* {Ständigkeit des Selbst}, as the supposed persistence {Beharrlichkeit} of the *subjectum*, gets clarified. But the phenomenon of this authentic potentiality-for-Being also opens our eyes for the *constancy of the Self* in the sense of its having achieved some sort of position {Standgewonnenhaben}.[1] *The constancy of the Self*, in the double sense of steadiness and steadfastness, is the *authentic* counterpossibility to the non-Self-constancy which is characteristic of irresolute falling[2]» (BT 369; SZ 322). In note 2, the translators comment on Heidegger's use of the root «sta.» The explanation in note 1 reads: «Here our usual translation of 'Ständigkeit' as 'constancy' seems inadequate; possibly 'stability' would be closer to what is meant» (BT 369, n. 1). Ständigkeit is associated with Güte (see above, chapter 2, n. 25). However, in the discourse of the rightists it also has, as in Heidegger's sentence in section 64, an aggressive component directed against Enlightenment and the supposed vacillations of the city-dwellers. In section 74, Heidegger shows that the subject of Enlightenment is inauthentic Dasein and that Dasein can have «Selbstständigkeit» (SZ 375; «Self-constancy,» BT 427, with the translators' note 3; see also BT 369 with the translators' note 2)—the key term of Enlightenment and liberalism—only if it strikes through its «Self» and gains «constancy» (BT 427; SZ 375) by accepting the gift of «some sort of position» («Standgewonnenhaben,» thus, better: «stable stand») that the Volk offers to Dasein, or forces upon Dasein, in order to free Dasein from Dasein's loneliness. The intensified stage of Ständigkeit is Bodenständigkeit (having a stable stand on or in the soil), as it was used by the rightists in their polemics against the «wurzellosen» (rootless) city-dwellers, liberals, and Jews. Heidegger roots Dasein in the Volk by striking through its Selbständigkeit. This paves the way to replace the «Selbst» in «Selbstständigkeit» with «Boden» in order openly to use the rightist term «Bodenständigkeit,» as he has done already in *Being and Time:* «Things are so because one says so. Idle talk is constituted by just such gossiping and passing the word along—a process by which its initial lack of grounds to stand on [Bodenständigkeit] becomes aggravated to complete groundlessness [Bodenlosigkeit]» (BT 212; SZ 168). In the *Rectorate Address,* the vocabulary of roots is present from the second sentence on: «The teachers and students who constitute the rector's following {Gefolgschaft der Lehrer und Schüler} will awaken and gain strength only through being truly and collectively rooted in the essence of the German university {aus der wahrhaften und gemeinsamen Verwurzelung im Wesen der deutschen Universität}» ("The Self-Assertion of the German University," in Wolin (ed.), *The Heidegger Controversy*, 29;

see MH 5; SB 9). Or, «the first bond is the one that binds to the ethnic and national community [*Volksgemeinschaft*]. It entails the obligation to share fully, both passively and actively, in the toil, the striving, and the abilities of all estates and members of the Volk. This bond will henceforth be secured and rooted in student existence [*Dasein*] through *labor service* {*Arbeitsdienst*}» (ibid., 35; see MH 10; SB 15; see how—in analogy to the switch from «handing down to itself» to «handing itself down to,» above, p. 16ff.—the root nourishes the Dasein that has been forced to root itself in the Volk). Becoming rooted in the Volk, the German Daseine submit to «the power that comes from preserving at the most profound level the forces that are rooted in the soil and blood of a Volk {erd- und bluthaften Kräfte}, the power to arouse most inwardly and to shake most extensively the Volk's existence. A spiritual world alone will guarantee our Volk greatness» (ibid., 33f.; see MH 9; SB 14). In the *Rectorate Address*, Heidegger does not use the word «Bodenständigkeit.» He probably does not do so, because quite often the word smacks of immobility, which does not fit the ecstatics of struggle and danger prevalent in the *Rectorate Address*.

63. Or become master of fate; see above, pp. 85ff.

64. Why do Daseine run forward into death? At the beginning of section 74, Heidegger points out that the notion of «*anticipatory* resoluteness» (BT 434; «*vorlaufende Entschlossenheit*» ; thus, literally «resoluteness *running forward*,» SZ 382) in which resoluteness goes «right under the eyes of death» (BT 434; SZ 382) has already been developed in sections 60ff. (BT 434; SZ 382; see BT 341ff.; SZ 295ff.; «*anticipation* of death,» BT 350; «*Vorlaufen* zum Tode,» SZ 302). Section 60 is the last section in the chapter on conscience and its call. Daseine run forward into death because they are called upon to do so by the call of conscience. Does the call of conscience call upon all Daseine or only on some? At any rate, not each Dasein hearing the call listens and obeys to it. For the «they» redirects, so to speak, the «*direction it* {*the call of conscience*} *takes*» (BT 318; SZ 274; «*Einschlagsrichtung*,» a military term, see below, chapter 4, n. 7) and transforms the call «into a soliloquy in which causes get pleaded {in ein verhandelndes Selbstgespräch gezogen}, and it {the call of conscience} becomes perverted in its tendency to disclose» (BT 319; SZ 274). Why do some Daseine listen to the call while others don't? Heidegger gives an answer in the chapter on conscience. In the context of that chapter as well as of the chapter on historicality, the metaphor in which he coins his answer can be taken literally. In the chapter on conscience, he argues against the universalism of Enlightenment. Liberals, social democrats, and communists don't listen to the call because they want to move forward on the road of society (see above, chapter 4) and don't want to be called back (the call of conscience as that «to which we are called back,» BT 326; «Zurückrufen,» SZ 280; on the preposition «zurück» in Heidegger see above, this chapter, n. 25, and chapter 2, n. 35). Only those Daseine listen that want to be brought back: «The call is from afar unto afar. It reaches him who wants to be brought back» (BT 316; SZ 271; «Vom Ruf getroffen wird, wer zurückgeholt sein will» ; thus, literally: «[Only] one who wants to be brought back is hit by the call» ; «getroffen» [«hit»] is also used in books on war: «Getroffen von der Kugel des Feindes, sank er dahin,» hit by the bullet of the enemy he sank down). In contrast to the «they» in the Weimar Republic—liberals, social democrats, and communists—the authentic Daseine choose as their «hero» (BT 437; «Helden,» SZ 385) the «heroes of Langemarck» (see above, chapter 1, section A). The authentic Daseine want to be brought back to the battlefields of

World War I, because already their heroes wanted to be brought back to and rereal-ize the communities that had existed prior to Enlightenment and society and were top-pled by Enlightenment and society. The authentic Daseine want to be brought back to community in order to bring back («*erwidert*» [SZ 386; BT 438] in the sense of «erwiderbringen,» «to bring back,» see below, chapter 5, n.70) community by can-celing society («*Widerruf,*» SZ 386; «*disavowal,*» BT 438). Being called upon by the Volksgemeinschaft to rerealize the Volksgemeinschaft by canceling society, the authentic Daseine repeat a decision that they failed to make earlier, namely, the deci-sion to prevent society from emerging and from replacing community: «{The down-ward plunge into the "they"} can be reversed {rückgängig gemacht werden} only if Dasein specifically brings itself back {zurückholt} to itself from its lostness in the "they." But this bringing-back {Dieses Zurückholen} must have that kind of Being *by the neglect of which* Dasein has lost itself in inauthenticity. When Dasein thus brings itself back {Das Sichzurückholen} from the "they," the they-self is modified in an existentiell manner so that it becomes *authentic* Being-one's-Self. This must be accomplished by *making up for not choosing* {*Nachholen einer Wahl*}. But "making up" for not choosing signifies *choosing to make this choice*» (BT 312f.; SZ 268). Still, the decision to cancel society does not prevent the authentic Daseine from taking over modern technology and capitalism as an economic system.

65. See Karl Löwith, "Last Meeting with Heidegger," in Wolin (ed.), *The Hei-degger Controversy,* 142 (see also MH 158; see above chapter 6, section A).

66. Karl Jaspers, *Philosophische Autobiographie: Erweiterte Neuausgabe* (Munich: Piper, 1977), 101f.; printed also in Martin Heidegger/Karl Jaspers, *Briefwechsel,* ed. W. Biemel and Hans Sauer (Frankfurt, Munich, Zurich: Klostermann, Piper, 1990), 257.

As was mentioned above, Scheler and Heidegger do not need to elaborate on the notion of fate, for they just make use of the meaning of the everyday usage of Schick-sal in their explanation of history. Only those who wanted to redefine the notion of fate had to comment on it as, for instance, Benjamin in his essay "Fate and Charac-ter" (Walter Benjamin, *Reflections,* trans. Edmund Jephcott [New York: Schocken, 1986], 304–311). (Around 1916 Scheler wrote an unpublished essay in which he inter-preted the notion of fate in the light of his philosophy, "Ordo Amoris," *Schriften aus dem Nachlaß I,* GW 10 [Bern: Francke, 1957], 347–376; translation in *Selected Philo-sophical Essays,* trans. D. R. Lachtermann [Evanston: Northwestern University Press, 1973], 98–135.) A sentence such as that—in the «clash» of fates of different people—it was the «fate» of the Jews to be removed from the public and finally killed in Nazi Germany is in line with the everyday meaning of fate and, thus, with the usage of fate in Scheler and Heidegger. In an article in the weekly *Die Zeit* ("Das deutsche Volk war eingeweiht," *Die Zeit,* no. 22, 2 June 1995, overseas edition, p. 16), Siegfried Maruhn quotes an article of Reichsminister Dr. Goebbels on the front page of the weekly *Das Reich,* "Die Juden sind schuld!" (The Jews are to blame) (*Das Reich,* no. 46, 16 November 1941; the usual print run was about 500,000 copies), of which Maruhn says that it is «a remarkably frank document, in which the mass murdering was announced to the German public without any pretense of secrecy.» Goebbels refers to Hitler's prediction in the speech of 30 January 1939 in the Reichstag that, «if the international finance Jewry {Finanzjudentum} should manage to throw the nations once again into a world war, the result will be not the bolshevikization of the earth and thus the victory of the Jewry, but rather the annihilation {Vernichtung} of the Jewish race in Europe.» Goebbels then goes on: «We witness the execution {Vollzug} of this prophecy, and by the execution a fate is fulfilled with regard to the Jewry, which, indeed, is hard but which is more than earned {und es erfüllt sich damit am Judentum ein Schicksal, das zwar hart, aber mehr als verdient ist}. Compassion {Mitleid}, not to mention regret {Bedauern}, is completely inappropriate in this case.» Only cowards try to evade their fate. Thus, Goebbels makes fun of Jews who try to evoke compassion or who try to hide their Judenstern by carrying a newspaper.

With regard to the (hopeless) effort to escape one's fate, Hitler uses a common expression when he says: «Man wollte dem Schicksal enteilen und wurde von ihm ereilt» (MK 156; «They wanted to run away from destiny, and it caught up with them,» MKe 142). «Ent-eilen» is a verb expressing motion, as in the discussion of the prisoners above who «ent-laufen» the prison (see above, pp. 33ff.). The police eilt ihnen nach, runs after them, and, if successful, er-eilt sie, that is, holt sie ein, overtakes them, catches up with them, and re-arrests them.

Only some of the Jews had left Germany early enough to evade their fate. However, several of them were eingeholt by their fate at a later point. Walter Benjamin left Germany on the 18 March 1933 for Ibiza, a Spanish island in the Mediterranean Sea. In autumn 1933, he went to Paris where he would live for most of the coming years to work on the unfinished book on Paris in the nineteenth century, named «Passagenarbeit» (Gesammelte Schriften, V.1 and V.2, ed. R. Tiedemann [Frankfurt: Suhrkamp, 1982]). In June 1940, when German troops invaded Paris, Benjamin fled to Lourdes and Marseille. In Marseille he managed to get a transit visa to Spain. However, on 26 September 1940, when the group of people with whom he had made the escape wanted to cross the border in the small Spanish border town Port Bou, they were told that the day before the border had been closed and that their visas were no longer accepted. The Spanish customs officers told them that the next day Spanish police officers would take them back to France, which meant that they would be deported to German concentration camps. Benjamin killed himself that night. In the aftermath of his suicide, the Spanish customs officers let the rest of the group pass into Spain. In summer 1933 on Ibiza, Benjamin had fallen in love with a woman from the Netherlands. In a letter from that summer, one apparently never sent to her, he wrote «In Deinem Arm würde das Schicksal für immer aufhören, mir zu begegnen. Mit keinem Schrecken und mit keinem Glück könnte es mich mehr überraschen» (Gesammelte Schriften, VI, [Frankfurt: Suhrkamp, 1985], 810; italics mine, J. F.; «In your arms, fate would for ever cease to mir begegnen. By no horror and by no luck could it any longer surprise me.» Benjamin probably did not intend that a deconstructionist might read the last sentence as «It could not surprise me with more horror and more luck.»). «Begegnen» means «to encounter» or «to approach.» I walk along Houston Street, and all of a sudden a friend whom I haven't met for a long time begegnet mir, encounters me, approaches me. «Begegnen» is symmetrical. Thus, by the same token as he begegnet (to) me I begegne (to) him. Often «Mein Schicksal begegnet mir» means «my fate holt mich ein» in the sense of that it catches hold of me and threatens to crush me. Benjamin's sentence was written in the awareness that, sooner or later, his fate will indeed einholen him. All that is left to him is the hope that the arms of the woman will give him the virtue of ataraxia such that even in the moment when fate holt ihn ein and crushes him, at the same time it does not einholen ihn. In the same summer of 1933 on Ibiza, Benjamin wrote a short autobiographical text, "Agesilaus Santander," which begins as follows: «When I was born the thought came to my parents that I might perhaps become a writer. Then it would be good if not everybody noticed at once that I was a Jew. That is why besides the name I was called they added two further, exceptional ones, from which one could see neither that a Jew bore them nor that they belonged to him as first names. Forty years ago no parental couple could prove itself more far-seeing. What it held to be only a remote possibility has come true. {Was es nur entfernt für möglich hielt, ist eingetroffen.} {«eintreffen» is «to arrive at, to come to» and, therefore, also «to come true» ; thus, eintreffen is similar to begegnen and einholen.} It is only that the precautions by which they meant to counter fate {die Vorkehrungen, mit denen es dem Schicksal hatte begegnen wollen} were set aside by the one most concerned. That is to say that instead of making it public by the writings he produced, he proceeded with regard to it as did the Jews with the additional name of their children, which remains secret» (quoted according to Gershom Scholem, "Walter Benjamin and His Angel," in G. Smith [ed.], *On Walter Benjamin: Critical Essays and Recollections* [Cambridge, Mass.: MIT Press, 1991], 58; *Gesammelte Schriften,* VI, 521f.). As mentioned above, a Begegnung itself is symmetrical. If two people sich begegnen, it is not yet determined what happens next. When one says «the creditor begegnet the debtor on the market (and vice versa),» nothing is said as yet about what followed upon this encounter. It is possible to continue with «the debtor paid back his debt» as well as with «the debtor ran away» or «the debtor beat up the creditor.» The phrase «fate begegnet me» may leave open whether it holt mich ein in the sense of «it beats me» or whether I am capable of resisting fate. Also, «I begegne fate» leaves open what happens. Thus, it allows for the possibility «I begegne fate by *x*» in the sense of «I counter fate and try to evade it by *x*,» as Benjamin could have used the other two first names in order to counter the fate his parents vorhersahen (anticipated) and with regard to which they had provided him with precautions in order to «dem Schicksal . . . begegnen,» that is, in order to counter fate and try to evade it (on «vorhersehen,» «vorlaufen,» and «to anticipate» see above, chapter 1, section A).

In the way Hitler and Benjamin use the term, the encounter between me and my fate is hostile, insofar as my fate wants to crush me (and, thus, being the coward I am, I try to evade it or counteract it). As mentioned above, however, there are, so to speak, friendly Begegnungen as well (see chapter 1, nn. 34 and 35). The most distinguished use of «begegnen,» «Begegnung,» in Heidegger occurs probably in his lecture course on Hölderlin of 1934–35. Not two years after the Machtergreifung, Heidegger comments on a line in Hölderlin: «Now that we are a conversation, we are exposed to the being that reveals itself; it is only from that point on that the Being of the being as such can encounter {begegnen} and determine us.» («Seit ein Gespräch wir sind, sind wir ausgesetzt in das sich eröffnende Seiende, seitdem kann überhaupt erst das Sein des Seienden als solchen uns begegnen und bestimmen,» HH 72; see also chapter 5, section B.) Section 74 of *Being and Time* suggests, as it were, a friendly Begegnung between Gemeinschaft and authentic Dasein that includes a hostile Begegnung between authentic Dasein and Gesellschaft, insofar as authentic Dasein has to expel, to destroy, Gesellschaft. In the thirties, Heidegger labeled the same imperative of authentic politics logos (see chapter 5, section B). The Germans begegneten their fate and each other, that is, gathered themselves. This Begegnung demanded that they begegneten, that is, expelled and killed Jews and other «foes of the people.» In his

*Jargon der Eigentlichkeit* ([Frankfurt: Suhrkamp, 1969], 14f.), Adorno mentions that in Germany in the fifties many houses run by the state or the churches were named «Haus der Begegnung,» «house of encounters» (*Jargon of Authenticity,* trans. K. Tarnowski and F. Wille [Evanston: Northwestern University Press, 1973], 13; note that in the German phrase «Begegnung» is singular). In them you would have discussions, or rather Gespräche, Dialoge, dialogues, on and among people of different nations in order, as it was said, «die Hindernisse aus dem Weg zu räumen, die sich geschichtlich aufgetan haben,» or in order to «sich zu verständigen und zu versöhnen.» In light of this history of the word «Begegnung,» it is as natural as disturbing that in 1955 a volume, including a contribution by Heidegger, in honor of the sixtieth birthday of the great hero and bard of hostile Begegnungen, the old warrior Ernst Jünger, was published under the title *Freundschaftliche Begegnung* (Friendly Encounter) (see WM 398; see also above, chapter 1, n. 35, below, chapter 5, n. 60). If Heidegger had wanted to say what Guignon and Birmingham assume he did, he could have used the word «Begegnung,» «begegnen.» In some way or other, he could have made clear whether he meant it as an encounter whose outcome is not yet determined, or as an encounter in which authentic Dasein resists the past. Obviously, when translating the sentence with «*erwidert* vielmehr» in *Sein und Zeit* (SZ 386; BT 436) the French translator of Division Two of *Sein und Zeit,* Emmanuel Martineau, had thought of the German verb «begegnen» and its various meanings as indicated above in connection with Benjamin. For the French noun and verb «rencontre» and «(se) rencontrer» have the same meanings as the German verb «begegnen.» Martineau translated as follows: «Bien plutôt la répétition *ren-contre*-t-elle la possibilité de l'existence ayant été Là. La ren-contre de la possibilité dans la décision est cependant en *même temps, en tant qu'instantanée,* le *rappel* de ce qui se déploie dans l'aujourd'hui comme "passé"» (*Etre et Temps,* trans. Emmanuel Martineau [Paris: Authentica, 1985], 266). By using «rencontre,» he can take up the general implication of the scenario in *Being and Time,* section 74, namely, that Dasein «meets» its fate, or fate «meets» Dasein. By adding the hyphen, Martineau obviously wants to suggest that this rencontre is a hostile encounter in which Dasein acts contre (against) fate and, thus, neither performs a repetition of the past nor complies with the call of the past but breaks with the past and the past's call for repetition. For by adding the hyphen Martineau reads Heidegger's verb «*erwidert*» (SZ 386) as the French verb «contrer» (to counter, to resist, to launch a counterattack). In this way, Martineau's translation can be regarded as a translation of Macquarrie and Robinson's phrase «*reciprocative rejoinder*» (BT 438) that reduces that phrase to Birmingham's interpretation of it, who treats Heidegger's phrase «*erwidert*» (SZ 386) in the same way as Martineau does (see chapter 1, n. 14). Thus, probably in the French literature on Heidegger one finds interpretations of the sentence similar to those of Guignon and Birmingham, especially since deconstructionism is strong in France.

67. Let me repeat a subtle observation of mine concerning the play of language: «Pain and suffering are the very *Mitgift,* the dowry of Being. The *Mitgift* makes the bride—so speaks the English language!—a person "of substance." The word *Mitgift* is a composite of the prefix *mit* (with) and the noun *Gift,* which means "poison." The noun *Gift,* when read as an English word—such is the play of language in *Übersetzungen!*—is used to translate a term in the later Heidegger which finds its analogy in *Being and Time* as "Geschick" and "Schicksal"» ("On Brinks and Bridges in Hei-

degger," 150). For two instances of «Opfer» as the gift of Being in the later Heidegger see ibid., 150ff.

68. Scheler's phrasing, «Man is a being whose essence itself is the decision, still open, what this being wants to be and to become» (WA 150), is very precise in its opposition to the rightist notion of de-cision. As I have tried to show, the rightist concept of de-cision is not a decision. The call calls us out of our living in the mode of the «they.» It is only in this moment that we see an «either-or.» However, in the very same moment the call tells us that it is our duty to rerealize the possibility presented by the «either» (the rerealization of Gemeinschaft) and to cancel the possibility presented by the «or» (to continue living in society).

Close to the beginning of his lectures on the history of philosophy, Hegel says that the tradition, the history of philosophy, has preserved what the past has produced. However, the tradition has not just faithfully preserved; rather, it is «alive, swelling like a mighty river {Strom} which grows the further it has advanced from its source {Ursprunge}» (*Introduction to the Lectures on the History of Philosophy*, trans. T. M. Knox and A. V. Miller [Oxford: Clarendon Press, 1985], 10; *Vorlesungen über die Geschichte der Philosophie, Werke in zwanzig Bänden*, vol. 18 [Frankfurt: Suhrkamp, 1971], 21). He already used the metaphor of a Strom, river, on the first page. The time of the Napoleonic Wars was good for philosophy, and it was also not good for philosophy, «because the world spirit was so much busied with the objective world that it could not turn within and concentrate itself within itself. Now {i.e., after the end of the wars}, however, that flow of the objective world has been broken {dieser Strom der Wirklichkeit gebrochen ist}» (ibid., 1; German edition, 11). At the end of the river of world history, Hegel makes philosophy turn within and back to the past. However, philosophy is not supposed to turn back to the past in order to cancel the present and to rerealize the past. Rather, Hegel recognizes that the past is past beyond recall but is sublated in the «mighty river» that has emerged from it. I have pointed out the logic in Hitler and in Scheler prior to the latter's Kehre. There is something great—the Aryans—and there is something small—the Jews. History is decline, because what-is-small drags down what-is-great and is unable to elevate itself. The small remains small, and its «greatness» consists in dragging down what-is-great and by this producing the «great» monstrosities of modernity. The «greatness» of the small, society, has to be canceled in order to rerealize community. I have also shown the same general motif of history as decline, downward plunge, and rerealization in Heidegger whose metaphor of origin and that which entspringt the origin, jumps out of it, sets the tone for his concept of historicality (see above, chapter 2, section A; also chapter 2, n. 35). In an especially ugly passage of 1935 that may have intentional anti-Semitic allusions Heidegger says: «But what is great can only begin great. Its beginning is in fact the greatest thing of all. A small beginning belongs only to the small, whose dubious greatness it is to diminish all things; small are the beginnings of decay, though it may later become great in the sense of the enormity of total annihilation» (IM 15; EM 15). It is interesting to note how, after his Kehre, Scheler returns to Hegel's metaphors. Man is «a direction of the *movement of the universe* itself, nay, of its ground {Grundes}» (WA 151). World history is «a system of rivers. For centuries a large number of rivers {Flüssen} each followed its own course. However, nourished by numerous tributary rivers they strive towards uniting into *one single* great river {Strom}» (WA 154). This river, Strom, is «Ausgleich that produces an ever increasing flourishing and

refinement of the spiritual individual man» (WA 152). However, the relation of the
«great river» to the past is not as it is in Hegel. Rather, the «great river» is a «tendency» (WA 152) that has to be realized against those who want to stop it (WA 153
and *passim*). (See Hitler's metaphor above, p. 82).

69. See in addition to his other books also his biography of Heidegger, Ernst Nolte,
*Martin Heidegger: Politik und Geschichte im Leben und Denken* (Berlin: Propyläen,
1992).

70. A Menschenfresser is someone who eats human beings, that is, a cannibal.
Thus, a Sozialistenfresser, in a political analogy to a Menschenfresser has an appetite
for those on the Left.

71. Heidegger, *The Metaphysical Foundations of Logic*, 51; *Metaphysische
Anfangsgründe der Logik im Ausgang von Leibniz*, 63.

72. Ibid., 50f. (German text, 62f.).

73. Ibid., 51 (German text, 63).

74. Ibid.

75. Ibid., 52 (German text, 64).

### Chapter 4

1. In light of the passages on utopian ideals I quoted at length in section B of
chapter 1, I take him to say: Christians, Marxists, liberals, and conservatives all live
in the same tradition and present. Each group has specific utopian ideals. Due to the
particular utopian ideal of each group, they each interpret the past differently. The
Christians interpret it in terms of a lost state prior to original sin, communists discover a state prior to private ownership of the means of production, and so on. Thus,
each of them «creatively reinterpret[s]» (HC 138) the past in the light of its particular utopian ideal. Similar to Macquarrie and Robinson's «conversation with the past,»
guided by some utopian ideal, we can discover several possibilities inherent in the
past, some of which we can reject and others adopt, depending on our utopian ideals.
A Christian might either deny that there was a state prior to private ownership of the
means of production or maintain that this state is identical with the state prior to original sin or not a relevant possibility to choose.

It might be possible that Guignon means that authentic Dasein's «projection onto
future possibilities» (HC 141) and its encounter of a «future as a "destiny"» (HC 141)
are identical with Dasein's «utopian ideals» (HC 138). For his comments on the
passage on destiny and fate in *Being and Time* (BT 436; SZ 384) he writes: «To say
that our communal past is a "heritage" that points to a "destiny" is to say that we can
find insights in our past as to what we should accomplish as a community. . . . It is
because we have the resources of our shared past available to us that we have a basis
for selecting the life-defining possibilities that help us "simplify" and focus our lives»
(HC 136). If he means that Dasein acquires its utopian ideal by choosing one of the
possibilities offered by the past, my claim that, according to Guignon, Dasein selects
the possibility relevant to it in light of its utopian ideal (see above, chapter 1, section
B), would be wrong. On the other hand, from the beginning on («the pool of possibilities from which we draw our concrete identities as agents of particular types,» HC
130) Guignon presents the past authentic Dasein draws upon as containing several different possibilities. Thus, authentic Dasein needs some criterion to choose its possi-

bility from the pool offered by the past. Presumably because of this problem, after the passage on destiny quoted in this note, Guignon continues: «In so far as the past gains its sense from its possible ways of making a contribution to the future, . . . the future has priority in authentic historicity. Our commitments towards the future "destiny" of our community first let the past become manifest as counting or mattering in some determinate way» (HC 136). According to this passage, Dasein's choice of its possibility seems to presuppose a commitment toward the future that is independent of the past and its offerings, even if Dasein becomes aware of this commitment only in the moment when it is confronted with the several possibilities offered by the past; a moment that in turn is made possible by Dasein's commitment to the future. Since Guignon introduces Dasein's «utopian ideals» (HC 138; see already HC 137) only after the passage on Dasein's commitment toward the future, it might be possible that Dasein's «utopian ideals» (HC 138) is just another name for Dasein's «commitments towards the future "destiny" of our community» (HC 136) that enable Dasein to choose its possibility from the pool of possibilities offered by the past.

Especially since Guignon uses Wolin's interpretation as the backdrop of his own interpretation (HC 130), he is certainly aware of the charge of circularity in Heidegger's reasoning with regard to this point (see below, chapter 5, section C). In the light of this, I assume that he means that Dasein's utopian ideal enables it to make its choice from the pool offered by the past. However, even if he assumes that Dasein's utopian ideal is identical with the possibility it chooses, my two main points with regard to Guignon remain valid, namely, that, according to him, Dasein finds a plurality of offers in the past and is in a free distance to all of them (see above, chapter 1, section B), and that all political parties at Heidegger's time work with a «*mythos* of pristine beginnings, a time of "falling," and a final recovery of origins» (HC 141) (see this chapter). Probably, Guignon isn't quite clear on the issue of Dasein's utopian ideals, because he is unwilling to distinguish between «the way of interpreting Dasein which has come down to us» (BT 435; SZ 383) and «heritage» (BT 435; SZ 383) (see above, chapter 2, section C) and he too assumes that Dasein chooses its fate (see below, chapter 5, section C).

2. Benjamin, *Illuminations*, 258. See Scheler's metaphor, chapter 3, n. 68.

3. Ibid., p. 260. On the Spartacists, the translator comments: «Leftist group, founded by Karl Liebknecht and Rosa Luxemburg at the beginning of World War I in opposition to the pro-war policies of the German Socialist party, later absorbed by the Communist party» (ibid., 260, n.). Heidegger's notion of historicality is not identical with that of history in the Spartacist group or in Benjamin, if only for the reason that the many «generations of the downtrodden» or the «enslaved ancestors» lived in worlds in which they were enslaved and which thus should not be repeated. Also, there is a difference between the rightist and the leftist use of the word «Opfer.» See on both points my book *Society, Community, Fate, and Decision: From Kant to Benjamin.*

4. See on this my book *Society, Community, Fate, and Decision: From Kant to Benjamin.*

5. Even if all parties used Guignon's schema in the same way, Heidegger's concept would be rightist, since liberals and leftists simply don't interpret history in terms of Gemeinschaft and Schicksal but in terms of reason, class, and class-struggle. Guignon might object that Heidegger uses «heritage,» «community,» and «fate» as

examples of possible choices. As Christians believe in a state prior to original sin, and as Marxists assume a state prior to private property, others select «heritage,» «community,» and «people» as the relevant categories to interpret history. One might easily replace this example with, say, the vocabulary of a communist choice. Thus, the logic of choice itself remains free of any specific political implications. However, in Heidegger's text there is no hint that «community, of {the} people» (BT 436; SZ 384) is meant just as an example. Rather, the development within section 74 suggests the opposite. Thus, if Heidegger had wanted to make this distinction between a general structure and the examples for it, he would have been an extremely poor writer. Furthermore, leftists and rightists negate society in different ways, for the leftists intend an Aufhebung of society whereas the rightists cancel society. First and foremost, however, liberals and leftists just simply opposed any return of a past. This is one of the few points concerning which Hitler, Scheler, Heidegger, Lukács, and Tillich agree, as I have already pointed out in chapter 3 and will make clearer in this chapter. There were some liberals or leftists of whom one might say that they used Guignon's schema. (One of them was Ferdinand Tönnies, the author of *Gemeinschaft und Gesellschaft* [1887], who later in his life joined the Social Democratic Party. He hoped that the future development of society would reintegrate to some extent the Gemeinschaften that had been pushed aside by liberal society. However, this is not the revitalization of Gemeinschaft by way of a cancellation of society but rather a dialectical sublation of Gemeinschaft and Gesellschaft in which the main end is the establishment of a rational society. See my book *Society, Community, Fate, and Decision: From Kant to Benjamin*.) However, in regard to the basic distinctions they were opposed to the Right. For that reason, Hitler, Scheler, Heidegger, Lukács, or Tillich could include them in their classifications.

Lukács quotes a passage from Marx: «"The present generation," says Marx, "resembles the Jews whom Moses led through the wilderness. It must not only conquer a new world, it must also perish in order to make room for people who will be equal to a new world"» (HI 315; GK 318). Rightist authors say that people must stop the march of mankind to Israel and go back to, or rerealize, Egypt. Romantic rightists say that people should leave behind in the desert society and all its luggage. Revolutionary rightists say that Egypt will really flourish only if it can take advantage of achievements, such as private property and modern technology, that happened to emerge in the desert. Liberals, social democrats, and communists say that mankind has to go to Israel. The Social Democrat Tönnies says that hopefully Israel has some features mankind knows from Egypt, and Tillich agrees with him in principle (see section B of this chapter). However, both Tönnies and Tillich agree with liberals, social democrats, and communists that mankind should not go back to Egypt; even if mankind wanted to do so, it could not, for the desert is about to take over Egypt or has already done so. For liberals, social democrats, and communists the emphasis is on the fact that in Israel the individuals can behave rationally and without the constraints of the Gemeinschaften in Egypt. For liberals, Israel is a fully developed liberal society. For social democrats and communists, it is a socialist society. Social democrats and communists disagree, however, as to what the last steps toward Israel will be like. For social democrats, they will be smooth or at least they consider the chances for this good. For communists, however, those steps entail violence. Lukács is familiar with the literature on community and society. He comments on Marx's sentence in a way any rightist author might do: «For the 'freedom' of the men who are alive now is the freedom of the individual isolated by the fact of property which both reifies and is itself reified. It is a freedom *vis-à-vis* the other (no less isolated) individuals. A freedom of the egoist, of the man who cuts himself off from others, a freedom for which solidarity and community {Zusammenhang} exist at best only as ineffectual 'regulative ideas'» (HI 315; GK 318). Some pages later, he writes, «Only when action within a community {Gemeinschaft} becomes the central personal concern of everyone involved will it be possible to abolish {aufgehoben} the split between rights and duties, the organisational form of man's separation from his own socialisation {Vergesellschaftung} and his fragmentation at the hands of the social forces {gesellschaftlichen Mächte} that control him» (HI 319; GK 322; note that also in this passage the basic theoretical term is not Gemeinschaft but rather Ver-Gesellschaftung [see above, chapter 3, n. 28], and that even in this passage Lukács uses aufheben, and not widerrufen or something similar). However, this is one of the very few times that he uses the word «Gemeinschaft,» which in his work never has theoretical status. For what is at stake is not the rerealization of a Gemeinschaft, but rather the Aufhebung of capitalist Gesellschaft into a socialist Gesellschaft.

Since Lukács uses the notion of form, and since I comment on Heidegger and Lukács in terms of that notion, some remarks on it might be useful. The notion of form (εἶδος) was introduced by Aristotle in his theory of principles and of the becoming of natural (and technical) beings (*Physics* I:7). Each being consists of matter and a form, and it comes into existence from them. A house consists of wood, bricks, etc. and the peculiar order, form, that makes them a house and not, say, a bridge. Clay is the matter of a statue, and the peculiar shape that makes it a statue of, say, Socrates, is its form. The matter of an animal, according to Aristotle, is most often female menstruation and, later on in its development and existence, its bones, flesh, etc., and its form is that entity within the animal itself that causes the bones and flesh to be ordered and to operate in such a way that we can identify the being as such-and-such an animal, say, a human being. Aristotle distinguishes between the coming into existence of a substance itself (an individual human being, cat, dog, etc.) and accidental changes—local motion, quantitative changes, and qualitative changes—of an existing substance (*Physics* I:7; V:1). With the exception of the coming into existence of the four elements (fire, air, water, and earth), at the beginning of the coming into existence of a substance there is only matter, which thereupon is informed by the form, which «enters» matter and «informs» it. (In other words, a human being comes into existence out of female menstruation and the male seed [the form], and not out of, say, a pig and the male seed.) In accidental changes, however, it often happens that an arriving form replaces its opposite form in the respective substance (*Physics* V:1f.). The latter also holds true for the elements. Each element consists of prime matter and a form. When air comes into existence, it does not come into existence exclusively out of prime matter and the form air. Rather, it comes into existence out of water; that is, out of prime matter informed by the form water; the form water is replaced in prime matter with the form air (*On Generation and Corruption*). Recently the notion that Aristotle assumes the existence of prime matter has been challenged (see, for instance, Charlton's appendix in his translation of *Aristotle's* Physics, *Books I and II*, trans. W. Charlton [Oxford: Clarendon, 1985], 129ff.). Different beings can be ordered according to their different degrees of complexity and the «dignity» of their forms. At the

bottom are prime matter and the four elements (or only the latter), followed by entities like stones, etc., up to human beings (see Montgomery Furth, *Substance, Form,
and Psyche: An Aristotelian Metaphysics* [Cambridge: Cambridge University Press,
1988], 76ff.). Beings of a relatively «low» level can function as the matter of beings
of a «higher» level, as for instance the four elements, if combined in a certain ratio,
are the matter of flesh, which in turn is the matter of an animal. Thus, only prime matter is in itself devoid of any forms, while all other matters have certain forms though
not the ones they acquire in the respective becomings. Since the most general definition of «matter» is «something that can be informed, determined, by a form,» a substance can be labeled «matter» in regard to its accidents. No form transforms itself
into its opposite. The form water does not transform itself into the form air. Rather,
the form water has to be expelled from a piece of prime matter (through heating) in
order for the form air to «enter» that piece of prime matter. With regard to beings of
«higher» levels, this means that a sentence such as «a pig came into existence out of
a human being» can mean only the following: a human being has died; that is, the
form human being has been expelled from some pieces of flesh and bones; these pieces
disintegrate into beings of a «lower» level down to the level of the four elements
(either under the influence of the weather or in the digestion system of, say, a pig);
these pieces of beings of a lower level thereupon become parts of the process of the
reproduction of pigs. That is, a matter has to be deformed to a higher or lesser degree
in order for a new form to arrive in it and determine it (see *Metaphysics* VIII:5).

One might say that, except for the hypothesis of the existence of ideas, Aristotle simply worked out in detail Plato's outline of a theory of becoming in *Phaedo*. At least
according to the traditional interpretation of Plato, which goes back to Aristotle (*Metaphysics* I:9), if not to Plato himself, and which is shared by Heidegger (IM 180ff.; EM
137ff.), Plato's ontology contains three kinds of beings, namely—to quote Vlastos—
«(1) Forms {or ideas, that is,} entities endowed with the following set of categorical
properties: they are immutable, incorporeal, divine; they cannot be known by means of
sense-experience, but only by "recollection." (2) The individual persons and objects of
ordinary experience, designated by proper names and definite descriptions. (3) The
immanent characters of these individuals, designated by adjectives, abstract nouns, and
common nouns. The very same words *also* name Forms. This becomes strikingly clear
on those rare occasions on which Plato explicitly juxtaposes the Form with the cognate
character to bring out the fact that, though closely connected, they are ontologically distinct. He does so twice in our passage, contrasting "Greatness itself" with "greatness in
us" (102 D), and again "the Opposite itself . . . in the nature of things" (τὸ ἐν τῇ φύσει)
with "the opposite itself . . . in us" (τὸ ἐν ἡμῖν), and both with "the opposite thing" (τὸ
ἐναντίον πρᾶγμα), i.e., the individual that has one of two opposite characters (103 B)»
(G. Vlastos: "Reasons and Causes in the *Phaedo*," *Platonic Studies* [Princeton: Princeton University Press, 1981], 83f.). Beings of the second kind—and space in *Timaeus*
(48 eff.)—correspond to matter in Aristotle, and beings of the third kind to forms in
Aristotle. An idea does not admit, and does not change into, its opposite. However, also
an idea «in us» does not change into its opposite. Rather, if it can no longer resist its
approaching opposite, it will leave those in whom, or in which, it is instead of transforming itself into its opposite (*Phaedo* 102 a 10ff.).

In late medieval philosophy, Aristotle's conceptual framework was taken over by
Christian philosophers. The eucharistic host involved several ontological problems.

The official doctrine of the Catholic Church adopted a mythological notion of change. The accidents of the bread (its size, its taste, etc.) and of the wine remain after the consecration but their substances disappear, and the latter do so by their conversion, transubstantiation, into Jesus Christ. However, there were heretics who, in the name of the metaphysics of substance and form, replaced the miracle of transubstantiation with a different miracle. God annihilates the bread and wine, or he deforms their matters, cleansing them of forms down to the level of prime matter or the four elements (see Thomas Aquinas, *Summa theologiae* [Rome: Editiones Paulinae, 1962], 2262ff. [part 3, question 75, articles 3ff.]; Duns Scotus, *Opera omnia* 8, ed. Wadding [Lyon, 1639; reprint Hildesheim: Olms, 1968], 657ff. [*In lib. IV Sententiarum*, dist. 11, question 4]). The accidents of bread and wine remain through God's providence since it is terrible for human beings to eat and drink the flesh and the blood of a human being, since the pagans might mock people who quite openly eat the flesh of their lord, and since the sacrament in that form is more conducive to faith (see Thomas Aquinas, *Summa theologiae*, 2265 [article 5]).

A house and a bridge both made out of wood differ not qua being made out of wood but insofar as the wooden pieces of the house have an arrangement, a form, that differs from the one of the wooden pieces of the bridge. A clay statue of Socrates is refashioned into a statue of Plato. The latter differs from the former not qua consisting of clay but through the different arrangement, form, of the parts of the clay. Socrates being educated differs from the uneducated Socrates not qua being Socrates but through the form educatedness being present in the former and absent in the latter. In this sense, one might define a form as something that makes a difference in regard to something else. The form does so by organizing matter in a certain way. In this sense, a form is the cause of a certain structure or order imposed onto something. In cases such as the statue the form is indeed nothing but the spatial arrangement of the parts of the clay itself. In this sense, the notion of form can be used in regard to beings that are not individuals in the sense in which Socrates, Plato, this dog over there, etc., are individuals. A democratic constitution establishes structures, relationships between individuals, and habits of individuals that differ from those imposed by an aristocratic constitution. In general, Aristotle talks about a constitution in the same way as about a form and regards the constitution «as, in effect, the formal cause . . . of the polis» (Fred D. Miller, Jr., *Nature, Justice, and Rights in Aristotle's* Politics [Oxford: Oxford University Press, 1995], 79]. He does not, however, ever say so explicitly. He might have hesitated because in his ontology the form always exists as part of an individual. However, in light of his «political naturalism» (ibid., 27ff.) he might have taken for granted that everyone understood that he regarded the constitution as form, and he might have said so explicitly in his lectures, especially since, if the «realistic» reading of Aristotle is right, a form—say, the form human being—exists in each individual human being. Kant labels time a «form of sensible intuition» (*Critique of Pure Reason*, trans. Norman K. Smith [New York: St. Martin's Press, 1965], 75 [B 47]), since it imposes the order of succession and simultaneity onto the objects of intuition. He writes that the concepts matter and form «underlie all other reflection, so inseparably are they bound up with all employment of understanding. The one [matter] signifies the determinable {das Bestimmbare} in general, the other [form] its determination {dessen Bestimmung}—both in the transcendental sense, abstraction being made from all differences in that which is given and from the mode in which it is determined» (ibid., 280 [B 322]).

For Marx, in human labor humans cannot but «work only as Nature does, that is by changing the form of matter {die Formen der Stoffe ändern}» (*Capital: A Critique of Political Economy*, revised and amplified according to the fourth German edition by Ernest Untermann [New York: Random House, n.d.], 50; *Das Kapital: Erster Band* [Berlin: Dietz, 1970], 57). Each product of human labor has a (possible) use value and a value. It has the latter insofar as it is an «expenditure of human labour-power» (ibid., 51; German edition, 58). However, only under a certain system of exchange and distribution of products—namely, one in which each labor is «carried on independently and for the account of private individuals» —do products of human labor acquire «the form of commodities» (ibid., 49; German edition, 57; note that the word «community» in phrases such as «in a community of commodity producers» reads in German «Gesellschaft»). Marx speaks of the «form of value {Wertform}» (ibid., 54; German edition, 62). This formulation indicates the similarities and differences between the use of the notion of form in Marx on one side and Aristotle and Plato on the other. In Aristotle and Plato, a form or an idea is a definite being that is different from other beings, and it is the cause of certain phenomena. In becoming, a form presences and manifests itself in the realm of phenomena. (A beautiful body is a manifestation of the idea of beauty in bodies, and it doesn't matter whether one labels this the «παρουσία {presence of the idea in the body}» or the «κοινωνία {communion of the body and the idea through beauty in us}» [Plato, *Phaedo* 100 d 5f.]; a human being is the result of the presencing [«παρουσία {through presence},» Aristotle, *Physics* 1:7, 191 a 7] of the form human being in female menstruation and flesh and bones.) (For Heidegger, this is the beginning of metaphysics. In the pre-Socratics, forms and shapes were the effects of physis as coming forth or emerging as a process without a definite actor or form. In metaphysics, however, coming forth is thought of as a means through which a preexisting form manifests or realizes itself. This is an upheaval in Scheler's sense: «But if the essential *consequence* {Wesen*folge*} is exalted to the level of the essence itself and takes the place of the essence, what then? Then we have a falling-off {Dann ist der Abfall da}, which must in turn produce strange consequences. And that is what happened. The crux of the matter is not that *physis* should have been characterized as *idea* but that the *idea* should have become the sole and decisive interpretation of being» [IM 182; EM 139].) Similarly, Marx uses the vocabulary of presencing or manifestation («human labour in the abstract has been embodied {vergegenständlicht} or materialised {materialisiert} in it» [*Capital*, 45; German edition, 53]; «embodiment of human labour {Verwirklichungsform}» or «the form under which its opposite, abstract human labour, manifests itself {Erscheinungsform ihres Gegenteils, abstrakt menschlicher Arbeit}» [ibid., 67, German edition, 73]). However, what manifests itself is not a definite form but abstract human labor as the value of products. Abstract human labor is a sheer activity that can be quantified and is constantly quantified in the exchange of commodities. Though human labor as an activity never appears as such but always «in the form {in der Form} of tailoring,» «in the form of weaving» (ibid., 51; German edition, 58), etc., in commodity producing societies abstract human labor as quantifiable human labor manifests itself in a product of human labor—say, gold and whatever serves as money—that functions as the equivalent of all other commodities (ibid., 79ff.; German edition, 83ff.). In this sense, being informed by the form of commodity a product is «changed into something transcendent {sinnlich übersinnliches Ding}» (ibid., 83; German edition, 85). In German, it reads: «into something sensible and suprasensible» or «into something sensibly suprasensible.» A commodity is a sensible thing insofar as it is an extended thing with certain properties. It is a suprasensible thing insofar as, in exchanges, it counts as a manifestation of a quantity of abstract human labor, and this quantity of abstract human labor exists as another sensible thing that is socially accepted as the universally valid manifestation of abstract human labor and as the general equivalent of all other commodities. (For the same reason, it can also be called «a sensibly suprasensible thing,» since in exchanges of commodities its suprasensible aspect is experienced and practiced.) Since abstract human labor as such is sheer activity without definite form, Marx uses the notion of form not as designator of abstract human labor (as the principle or «substance» [ibid., 45; German edition, 53] of the products) but as designator of the ways, forms, in which and as which abstract human labor is manifested. (At least on these two accounts—being a no-thing, a process and being the cause of various forms as results of its activity—«Being» in Marx fulfills Heidegger's notion of Being in the pre-Socratics.) Since a commodity is a sensible thing that manifests something suprasensible, Marx uses the theological notion of «visible incarnation {sichtbare Inkarnation}» (ibid., 77; German edition, 81), or he says that a commodity is «abounding in metaphysical subtleties» (ibid., 81; German edition, 85). When saying that it is abounding in «theological niceties {theologischer Mucken}» (ibid., 81; German edition, 85) he thinks of Feuerbach's and his theory of religion (ibid., 83; German edition, 86) in regard of the phenomenon that the exchange of commodities makes up a system of «action of objects, which rule the producers instead of being ruled by them» (ibid., 86; German edition, 89), and he probably thinks also of the phenomenon that this system produces ruptures, economical crises, comparable only to God's activities in regard of the eucharistic host and other miracles. Note that a capitalist economy is not simply a commodity producing society but one in which a large number of individuals don't own means of production and thus have to sell their labor power as commodity to the owners of the means of production, the labor power thus being the only source of surplus value. As Kant in his definition of the notion of form, in what follows above I will also use the notion of determination.

6. Plato, *Sophist*, 242 e 3. This is Benardete's translation (see *The Being of the Beautiful: Plato's Theaetetus, Sophist, and Statesman*, translated and with commentary by Seth Benardete [Chicago: University of Chicago Press, 1984], II.35). For what follows above see the preceding note.

7. As was mentioned above, for both Hitler and Scheler a liberal society is just a step on the way toward socialism and communism; an assumption that was probably shared by many rightists. From this point of view, one can indeed not rely on any inner tendencies of development in society—be they dialectical or not—for one assumes that there are such inner tendencies but that they carry society precisely into the direction that one wants to avoid. If one cannot rely on society and its inner tendencies, it must be an entity outside of society (though it or its representatives can reside in the same world [see above, chapter 2, section C]) that initiates the political activities in order to «den Karren aus dem Dreck zu ziehen» (to pull the cart out of the muck), since, if left to itself, the car would just continue sinking into the mire. Thus, fate raises its voice and sends Hitler (MKe 510; MK 570) (see above, pp. 86f.), or God raises his voice and calls for a turning back (PPS 646) (see above, pp. 123f.). This is the political aspect of the background of Heidegger's theory of conscience and

anxiety. He chooses a very precise metaphor, which has the additional advantage of reminding readers of the heroes of Langemarck: «While the content of the call {of conscience} is seemingly indefinite, the *direction it takes* {*Einschlagsrichtung*} is a sure one and is not to be overlooked» (BT 318; SZ 274). «Einschlagsrichtung» is a military term. Each bomb or shell has its specific Einschlagsrichtung, that is, angle of hitting the target in which it is most effective. Of course, only the heroes of Langemarck and authentic Daseine are willing to expose themselves and the world in which they live to a bomb that might annihilate or transubstantiate their world as God does the bread. All the other Daseine try to deal with the call according to the mode of society. Heidegger continues: «The call does not require us to search gropingly for him to whom it appeals, nor does it require any sign by which we can recognize that he is or is not the one who is meant. When 'delusions' arise in the conscience, they do so not because the call has committed some oversight (has miscalled), but only because the call gets *heard* in such a way that instead of becoming authentically understood, it gets drawn by the they-self into a soliloquy in which causes get pleaded {verhandelndes Selbstgespräch}, and it becomes perverted in its tendency to disclose» (BT 318f.; SZ 274). As was mentioned (see chapter 2, n. 32), in *An Introduction to Metaphysics* Heidegger uses the same metaphor. Being breaks into the world of the «they» like a bomb or an assault party into the lines of the enemy (IM 163f.; EM 125). Heidegger is so preoccupied with the metaphor that he forgets that, from the viewpoint of ordinary and inauthentic Dasein, authentic Dasein's behavior—namely, from within the world of ordinary and inauthentic Dasein to move toward the line and place itself into the breach in order to help Being burst into the world of ordinary and inauthentic Dasein (IM 163f.; EM 125)—is high treason. It is much more probable, though, that he was very well aware of the implications of the comparison and used it to emphasize as strongly as possible the need to cancel society. Heidegger's sentence in *An Introduction to Metaphysics* goes against the common understanding sedimented in language. «*A* springt in die Bresche für *B*» (*A* fills the breach on behalf of *B*) is a proverbial saying to indicate that *A* helped *B* in a difficult situation. *A* fills the breach in order to avoid that something hostile enters and cancels *B*'s world.

8. The quote is from a letter of 1843. With the term «Auflösung» Marx referred to the material impoverishment of the workers in, so to speak, Manchester Capitalism as well as a certain dissolution of bourgeois ethics consequent upon it. One might wonder whether Lukács thought that his theory of proletarians becoming self-conscious worked, as it were, better under circumstances of increasing material impoverishment of the workers.

9. «Reine Wunder,» Lukács, *Geschichte und Klassenbewußtsein: Studien über marxistische Dialektik, Werke,* vol. 2 (Berlin and Neuwied: Luchterhand, 1968), 21.

10. Marx and Engels, *The Communist Manifesto,* 121.

11. Ibid., 83.

12. To develop a notion of the totality of society and history and to relate one's experience to that totality is the capacity of the proletariat and is what dialectics is about (HI 1ff., 149 ff.; GK 13ff., 164 ff.). The supposed gap between the factical development of history and the empirical consciousness of the workers gives rise to Lukács's theory of class-consciousness and the party (HI 46ff.; GK 57ff.), which is often regarded as Lukács's entrée to Stalinism. Since I am concerned only with Heidegger's concept of historicality, I cannot go into this issue. For the same reason, I

cannot discuss the problem of theory and praxis in regard to my bright picture of dialectics near the beginning of this section.

13. An English reader might perhaps think that Lukács says that history produces a crisis but leaves it to the proletariat how to solve it. However, Lukács uses «Entscheidung» («decision») and not «crisis.» History confronts the proletariat with an issue to decide or to solve. Lukács's «Entscheidung» is a shorthand for «to solve in the way history intends it to be solved.» For—to quote just one passage—«praxis cannot be divorced from knowledge. A praxis which envisages a genuine transformation {wahren Veränderns; not a Widerruf, disavowal} of these forms {= the forms of bourgeois society} can only start to be effective if it intends to think out the process immanent in these forms to its logical conclusion, to become conscious of it and to make it conscious» (HI 177; GK 194). Lukács quotes here section 81 of Hegel's *Encyclopedia* as one of the numerous passages in which Hegel reflects on the dialectical method and stresses that in dialectics a new state does not come about as a result of a Widerruf of the preceding state; the latter is not canceled by an entity that interferes from outside and replaces it with the former; instead the former transforms itself into the latter through an «*immanent* process of transcendence» (HI 177; GK 194).

14. Or, consider: «Thus the economic development of capitalism places the fate of society in the hands of the proletariat» (HI 312; «So legt die Entwicklung der ökonomischen Kräfte des Kapitalismus die Entscheidung über das Schicksal der Gesellschaft in die Hände des Proletariats,» GK 315). Such a statement, too, shows why Lukács never says that an individual or a group produces its own fate. The proletarians have not produced their power to be the fate of society. Rather, it was given to them by the economic development of capitalism or by history. History has given them the task to decide the fate of society in the way history intends it to be decided. The proletarians don't act for the sake of themselves. Rather, they realize a mission, given to them by someone else, for someone else, namely, society as a whole. Also Lukács's statements in which someone is the fate of someone or something else operate, so to speak, within a deontic logic of an assignment of tasks.

15. «Gesellschaftslehre,» «Sozialphilosophie,» Lukács, *Geschichte und Klassenbewußtsein*, 18.

16. English readers might wonder what «the 'we' of the genesis» is. The relative clause reads in German: «jener Klasse vorbehalten geblieben, die das identische Subjekt-Objekt, das Subjekt der Tathandlung, das "Wir" der Genesis von ihrem Lebensgrund aus in sich selbst zu entdecken befähigt war: dem Proletariate» (GK 164). Probably, «der Genesis» is not genitive and does not go with «das "Wir"» but is dative. «Aus» goes with either «der Genesis» or «von ihrem Lebensgrund.» In both cases one can translate: «was reserved for the class that was able to discover within itself as emerging (or, in regard of/due to the emergence) from out of the ground of its own life the identical subject-object, the subject of action, the "we": namely the proletariat.» Possibly, Lukács used «we» in quotation marks as an ironic reference to the abundance of the use of «we» in authors of the Right. Note that «vorbehalten geblieben» («was reserved for» or, literally, «remained to be reserved for») is the language of history—or, in Heidegger's terms Geschick, Being—that «gives» and «withholds.» History has «given» to German idealism the method, the formulation of the way; or it has given to German idealism the first part of the way, namely, the formulation of the method. However, it has «zurückbehalten,» withholds, from German idealism the continuation of the way. History «behält für

sich,» keeps to itself—as «verborgen,» concealed, in itself—the continuation of the way because history has «vorbehalten,» reserved, the continuation of the way for the proletariat, to which it will give the continuation of the way at a later point.

17. The subsequent clause in the second sentence reads in German: «so daß sich gerade in ihrer menschenfernen, ja unmenschlichen Objektivität der gesellschaftliche Mensch als ihr Kern enthüllen kann» (GK 193). It should better be translated as: «so that it is precisely in the objectivity of the forms of society, remote from or even opposed to humanity, (or, precisely in that state of the development of the forms of society in which they have an objectivity that is remote, etc.) that socialized man can be revealed as at the core of the forms of society.»

18. Within the framework of the literature on Gemeinschaft and Gesellschaft the notorious class consciousness in Lukács is just another hypostasized superentity, which is to say that, in terms of rightist thinking, not Marxism but the peculiar thinking in terms of Gemeinschaft is to «blame» for it, even though its realization is not its rerealization. In Heideggerian terms, it is not something which has-been-there; it approaches us from out of the future without having followed us out of the past. In addition, as was already mentioned and as the textbooks have it, the proletarian revolution is the «*self-annihilation*» (HI 71; «*Selbstaufhebung*,» GK 84) of the class of the proletarians and, indeed, of all classes. Rightist revolutions of that time, on the other hand, don't take place for the sake of the Selbstaufhebung of the victorious party, and they rerealize a past with all its hierarchies and ranks, which have been leveled by the modern age. A socialist revolution is supposed to do away with all these differences. Thus, in contrast to the leftist revolution the rightist revolution is not the self-annihilation of the winners, but rather their, so to speak, self-reproduction by the annihilation of the other. Only once, namely in the sentence on distancing (HI 172; GK 188), does Lukács use the concept of human «essence.» The essence of human beings is to determine themselves by themselves. Prior to capitalism this was not yet a reality. Though in capitalism natural limits no longer exist for the self-determination of humans, the essence is not yet realized because of reification. It begins to be realized in the moment when the proletarians distance themselves from the commodity form, for in that moment all existing determinations, including the commodity form, have become, as Hegel used to say, fluid. Furthermore, in regard to Lukács's use of the motif of «socialism or new barbarism» (HI 306; GK 308), it is certainly the case that, according to him, the proletarians have to prevent society from the threat of the revitalization of the past.

19. See my book *Society, Community, Fate, and Decision: From Kant to Benjamin.*

20. See my book *Society, Community, Fate, and Decision: From Kant to Benjamin.*

21. In the famous chapter "The Fetishism of Commodities and the Secret Thereof" (*Capital: A Critique of Political Economy*, 81ff.; German edition, 85ff.), Marx uses the metaphor of the umbilical cord in the same way as Lukács does. He maintains that Christianity is the most fitting form of religion for societies based upon the production of commodities, and that ancient Asiatic societies «are, as compared with bourgeois society, extremely simple and transparent» (ibid., 91; German edition, 93). He continues:

> But they {Asiatic societies} are founded either on the immature development of man individually, who has not yet severed the umbilical cord {Nabelschnur} that unites him with his fellow men in a primitive tribal community {natürlichen Gattungszusammenhangs}, or upon direct relations of subjection. They can arise and exist only when the

development of the productive power of labour has not yet risen beyond a low stage, and when, therefore, the social relations within the sphere of material life, between man and man, and between man and Nature, are correspondingly narrow. This narrowness is reflected in the ancient worship of Nature, and in the other elements of the popular religions. The religious reflex of the real world can, in any case, only then finally vanish, when the practical relations of everyday life offer to man none but perfectly intelligible and reasonable relations with regard to his fellowmen and nature.

The life-process of society {gesellschaftlichen Lebensprozesses}, which is based on the process of material production, does not strip off its mystical veil until it is treated as production by freely associated men {frei vergesellschafteter Menschen}, and is consciously regulated by them in accordance with a settled plan. This, however, demands for society {Gesellschaft} a certain material groundwork or set of conditions of existence which in their turn are the spontaneous {naturwüchsige} product of a long and painful process of development. (ibid., 91f.; German edition, 93f.)

22. On «Gemächte» in Heidegger see chapter 5, section A.

23. Schmitt, *The Concept of the Political,* 27; German edition, 27.

24. See above, chapter 1, n. 33.

25. *«Der Feind ist unsere eigne Frage als Gestalt,»* Carl Schmitt, *Ex Captivitate Salus* (Köln: Greven, 1950), 90.

26. «Romantic reaction» and «political romanticism» (SD 27ff.; SE 34ff.) are Tillich's names for the political Right. He distinguishes between two forms, a conservative and a revolutionary form. See what follows. Incidentally, on the dedication tablet in the lobby of the Graduate Faculty Building of the New School for Social Research Paul Tillich is listed as one of the individuals, foundations, and business organizations whom the New School for Social Research thanks for their support and «devotion to higher education in a democratic society.»

27. Of course, I do not maintain that Tillich or Heidegger copied Hitler, Scheler, or someone else. Their agreement on the crucial differences between Left and Right and on the characteristics of the Right just shows that each of them had sufficient analytical skills in these matters.

28. Literally, «das Schicksal wenden» is «to turn fate around,» like Umkehrruf in Scheler and Heidegger; see above, p. 124; see also p. 174. According to rightists, fate demanded that Gesellschaft and «the other» have to be expelled to revitalize Gemeinschaft. The leftist notion of decision required that the various Gemeinschaften have to be expelled in order finally to expel the antagonistic relation to «the other.» As many others, Tillich and the late Scheler realized that in this mutual decision the extreme Right, the National Socialists, would win, and that their victory would lead to the death of the European nations. The course of rightist fate itself was the downward plunge that had to be canceled, «averted,» or «turned around.» In the «spirit» of the late Scheler, Tillich suggested to end the politics of de-cision, expulsion, on both sides and to forge an alliance between the proletarians and «these groups» (mainly, the peasants and the middle class); to form a *Gemeins*chaft «in *gemeins*amer socialist decision» (SE 11; «*common* socialist decision» , SD xxxii; italics mine, J. F) of the groups that, according to rightists and leftists, had to expel the other. From 1942 onward, the Christian Catholic Carl Schmitt referred to «ὁ κατέχων {the one who restrains}» (2 *Thessalonians* 7) and the «ἄνομος {the lawless one}» (2 *Thessalonians* 8) (see Heinrich Meier, *Die Lehre Carl Schmitts: Vier Kapitel zur Unterscheidung Politischer Theologie und Politischer Philosophie* [Stuttgart/Weimar: Metzler, 1994], 244, n. 106). In the small

book *Land und Meer* (Land and sea) from 1942, he writes: «I believe in the Katechon; to me, he is the only possibility to understand history and find meaning in it as a Christian» (quoted according to Heinrich Meier, *Die Lehre Carl Schmitts,* 245; Meier's reference might be wrong; the quote cannot be found in *Land und Meer* [Köln-Lövenich: Hohenheim, 1981], and probably there was no reason for Schmitt to leave it out in editions after the war; however, he left out an anti-Semitic passage; compare Meier, *Die Lehre Carl Schmitts,* 237f., with *Land und Meer,* 16f.; when reading the passage one must keep in mind that Schmitt says of *Land und Meer* that it was «told to my daughter Anima» [ibid., 5], and that in fact it almost reads like a bedtime story for children). Since Luther translated «the one who restrains» with «der es jetzt aufhält,» Schmitt also uses the German noun «Aufhalter» (for instance, *Land und Meer,* 19) for «the one who restrains.» In the first edition of *Land und Meer,* he seems to have introduced as his translation of «the lawless one» (2 *Thessalonians* 8) the word «Beschleuniger,» the one who speeds up, and Schmitt seems to have characterized the Jews as «Beschleuniger» (see Meier, *Die Lehre Carl Schmitts,* 97; this passage has also been left out in the edition of 1981; compare *Land und Meer,* 16f. with Meier, *Die Lehre Carl Schmitts,* 97; in terms of the metaphor of falling, the Jews speed up the cart's drive into the muck). Sometimes, Schmitt seems to suggest that in the twenties and during his engagement with National Socialism after Hitler's Machtergreifung he himself acted as «the one who restrains.» However, in an entry in his diary from 10 October 1947 Schmitt considers that he was not the Aufhalter but the Beschleuniger («Die Freude an der Beschleunigung, Beschleuniger der Beschleuniger wider Willen; war es das, was mich trieb und trug?» [«The enjoyment of speeding things up; the one who speeds up, the one who speeds up against his will. Was it this that drove me and carried me?»]; deconstructionists might point out that Schmitt does not say «wider meinen Willen» ; thus, he might also or even only mean, «against the will of liberals, Social Democrats, and communists.» *Glossarium: Aufzeichnungen der Jahre 1947–1951* [Berlin: Duncker & Humblot, 1991], 31; at a later point, he added in the margin: «Trog?» , «And deceived me?» , ibid., 31, n. 1). Deconstructionists might not be surprised that Schmitt was not the Aufhalter but the Beschleuniger of National Socialism. For the German word «Aufhalter» is indeed used in the sense of «the one who restrains,» the one who prevents something from emerging within or breaking into history or, say, into one's house. However, it is also used in the sense of «to keep open,» say, the door of one's house. In this sense, Heidegger and Schmitt—if his remark also refers to the time prior to the Machtübernahme—were Aufhalter of National Socialism. Both lived within the house of the Weimar Republic, both erwiderten the call of destiny (BT 438; SZ 386), and both went to the door, and opened it for National Socialism. In this way, they were «historical» men for they «posited {themselves} as the breach into which the preponderant power of being {Übergewalt des Seins} bursts in its appearing» (IM 163; EM 124). Keep in mind that the «historical man» regards going to the door of the house as his task not because he himself made up this task by himself but because he hears the command of Being: «The strangest {das Unheimlichste} (man) is what it is because, fundamentally, it cultivates and guards the familiar {das Einheimische}, only in order to break out of it {um aus ihm auszubrechen} and to let what overpowers it break in {und das hereinbrechen zu lassen, was es überwältigt}. Being itself hurls man into this breaking-away» (IM 163; EM 125). (Note that Heidegger plays with the words «Unheimlich» and «Einheimisch.» Those are «einheimisch,» the familiar ones, who live in the same apartment, house, or city; in the same «Heim,» house. Historical man is «unheimlich,» that is, the negation of «heimlich,» of native, homelike, home, etc., because he opens the door of the Heim and lets someone, or something, into the Heim whom the «they,» the inauthentic inhabitants, want to keep outside the Heim; for the «breach» in Heidegger see this chapter, n. 7.) In colloquial German, the person who screens prospective guests at the entrance of a bar and opens the door for the ones he admits is called «Türsteher» or «Türaufhalter.» Since he is also in charge of discharging guests inside the bar who are considered troublemakers, he his also called «Rausschmeißer,» «the one who throws out.» The call of destiny calls for a reentrance of Volksgemeinschaft into the city and for a *«disavowal {Widerruf}»* (BT 438; SZ 386) of Gesellschaft and its bearers. The Erwiderung acts «for» the Volksgemeinschaft by a Widerruf of Gesellschaft or by acting «against» Gesellschaft. On 3 October 1936, Schmitt delivered the inaugural address of a conference on Jewry and the science of law ("Das Judentum in der Rechtswissenschaft"). Close to the beginning, he quoted a sentence from Hitler's *Mein Kampf* that—in the context of the concept of history of the revolutionary Right—presents the structure of Heidegger's sentence on Erwiderung and Widerruf (BT 438; SZ 386) in the shortest form possible. Schmitt said: «The most profound and ultimate meaning of this struggle {Kampf} and thus also of our task today is expressed in the sentence of the Führer: "by defending myself against the Jew, I am fighting for the work of the Lord {MKe 65; indem ich mich des Juden erwehre, kämpfe ich für das Werk des Herrn, ME 70}"» (quoted according to Meier, *Die Lehre Carl Schmitts*, 235).

The politics of «the one who restrains» may be the only kind of politics allowed to a Christian as a Christian. In the kairos of the twenties and thirties, it was certainly the Jew and converted Christian Catholic Scheler and the Christian Protestant Tillich who displayed the faculty of judgment necessary to decide when and how to engage in the politics of «the one who restrains.»

29. See, for instance, SD 66ff., 127ff., SE 62ff, 104ff. On Gesellschaft and Gemeinschaft see SD 75ff., 85ff., 137ff., 150ff.; SE 69ff., 76ff., 112ff., 122ff.

30. Derrida, "Violence and Metaphysics: An Essay on the Thought of Emmanuel Levinas," *Writing and Difference*, trans. A. Bass (Chicago: University of Chicago Press, 1978), 79–153. See, for instance, Caputo, *Demythologizing Heidegger*, 6ff.

31. Of course, it all depends on what one means by «the Greeks.» Today, probably only few interpret Anaximander like Tillich did. Maybe, none of the Greek philosophers was a «Greek» in Tillich's sense. However, in the presentation of his «Greeks» in *An Introduction to Metaphysics* Heidegger interpreted Heraclitus and Parmenides precisely along the lines of his notion of historicality and authentic Dasein in *Being and Time* and thus in the sense of Tillich's «Greeks» (see my book *The Birth of Tragedy out of the Spirit of National Socialism: Heidegger on Heraclitus and Parmenides* [in preparation]).

### Notes to Chapter 5

1. Quoted according to H. Ott, *Martin Heidegger: A Political Life,* 243. The passage reads in German:

> Wir Heutigen stehen in der Erkämpfung der neuen Wirklichkeit. Wir sind nur ein Übergang, nur ein Opfer. Als Kämpfer dieses Kampfes müssen wir ein hartes Geschlecht haben, das an nichts Eigenem mehr hängt, das sich festlegt auf den Grund des Volkes.

Der Kampf geht nicht um Personen und Kollegen, auch nicht um leere Äußerlichkeiten und allgemeine Maßnahmen. Jeder echte Kampf trägt bleibende Züge des Bildes der Kämpfenden und ihres Werkes. Nur der Kampf entfaltet die wahren Gesetze zur Verwirklichung der Dinge, der Kampf, den wir wollen, ist: wir kämpfen Herz bei Herz, Mann bei Mann. (*Martin Heidegger: Unterwegs zu seiner Biographie*, 231).

As one sees, throughout the quote Heidegger uses «Kampf» and derivatives of «Kampf» («fighting» = «Erkämpfung» ; «warriors in this struggle» = «Kämpfer dieses Kampfes» ; all occurrences of «struggle» are in German «Kampf» ; «of the combatants» = «der Kämpfenden»). In the place of the English phrase «shoulder to shoulder» the German text has a more intimate expression: «heart to heart.» (Soldiers of the same army are said in English as well as in German to fight «shoulder to shoulder,» while one is, as it were, only with one's «sweetheart» «heart to heart.») The English translation, «that cares for nothing of its own, that rests firmly on the foundation of the people and the nation,» lacks connotations and a certain dynamic aspect of the German text. «Hängen an» is often used in a spatial sense and means «to hang on,» as a hat hangs on a wall or a lamp hangs on the ceiling. One also «hängt an» or «krallt sich an» the edge of a reef or a plank in the sea in order not to fall down and be drowned. «Hängen an» is also used in the sense of «to cling to, to be emotionally attached to.» In the latter sense, it can also be used ironically or critically. Person *A* loves her cat or dog very much; so much so that *A*, to translate word-by-word a German saying, «has eyes and ears for hardly anything else.» Person *B* doesn't appreciate *A*'s attachment but thinks that *A* should «have eyes and ears» for other things or persons, say, *B*. Thus, *B* can ironically express his or her disappointment or disapproval by saying to person *C*: «*A* hängt wirklich sehr an ihrer/seiner Katze» (*A* is really very attached to his/her cat). One can also use «hängen an» to indicate that *A* has no stable identity and uses the cat, an ideology, etc., as a surrogate without which *A* would fall into the abyss, or Ab-Grund (hyphens mine, J. F.), of loneliness, inner emptiness, etc. Heidegger uses the phrase in the latter sense. All what is our own, the traditional university and—in general—Gesellschaft, are surrogates. We should not «hängen an» them, for they are surrogates, and to «hängen an» is not a safe position to begin with, especially since what we hang on to is already falling apart (see also chapter 6, section A). Instead, we have to be a Dasein «das sich festlegt auf den Grund des Volkes,» that—quite literally—lays itself/attaches itself firmly on/to the ground of the people or on/to the ground that the people is. On a ground one has a safe stand (see chapter 3, n. 62; see also my paper "On Brinks and Bridges in Heidegger," 149ff.). Thus, one no longer hangs on something that will fall apart anyway. Having reached a safe ground to stand on, one can «stehen in der Erkämpfung der neuen Wirklichkeit,» that is, «stand in the struggle to bring about the new reality» (on the preposition «in» see chapter 1, n. 10, and chapter 6, n. 24). Even linguistically, the entire passage testifies to what Paul Tillich named

the inner contradiction of the return to the myth of origin. The creation of a *national tradition* must, in the context of life in the metropolis and its influence throughout the country, pass over all special traditions, the very traditions so important to the myth of origin. Nothing is more untraditional, in the national sense, than this struggle for a national tradition. What really has been handed down in Germany, and what has remained unbroken down to the present time, is the struggle of the various religious, political, and regional traditions with one another. A struggle of traditions, however, so long as it still has reality and has not been reduced to literature, can only be handed down by the protagonists, i.e., *not* as a unified national tradition. (SD 34; SE 39; these sentences conclude the passage on tradition I quoted above, pp. 180f.)

Hitler takes an entire chapter ("Federalism as a Mask," MKe 554–579; "Föderalismus als Maske," MK 621–649) to explain at length that what Tillich calls «the struggle of the various religious, political, and regional traditions with one another,» is a means for the Jews to achieve domination over Germany. In the völkisch state, the individual provinces will have no political rights, but only some rights in the area of cultural policy (MKe 576; MK 645). However, at the same time «even here time will have a leveling effect. The ease of modern transportation so scatters people around that slowly and steadily the tribal boundaries are effaced and thus even the cultural picture gradually begins to even out» (MKe 576; MK 645f.). In January 1934 Heidegger gave up his efforts to go to Berlin and announced in the speech, "Why do We choose to stay in the Province?" which was broadcast over the radio and printed in the local National Socialist newspaper, that he would not go to Berlin but stay in the provinces. It is not necessary to have read the above-mentioned chapter in Hitler's book to know that there was «something fishy» about Heidegger's speech. See Victor Farías's brilliant analysis of it in *Heidegger and Nazism*, 170–177; German edition, 237–244.

2. Jacques Derrida, *"Geschlecht,* Sexual Difference, Ontological Difference," *Research in Phenomenology* 13 (1983): 65, note.

3. Jacques Derrida, *"Geschlecht* II: Heidegger's Hand," John Sallis, ed., *Deconstructing and Philosophy: The Texts of Jacques Derrida* (Chicago and London: University of Chicago Press, 1987), 162. Both texts are part of Jacques Derrida, *Psyché: Inventions de l'autre* (Paris: Éditions Galilée, 1987).

4. Derrida, *"Geschlecht* II: Heidegger's Hand," 162f.

5. On an occurrence of «Eigentum» (private property) in Heidegger see my paper "On Brinks and Bridges in Heidegger," 153, n. 59.

6. Heidegger uses the word «entfalten» («reveals»). «Entfalten» is not «to create» but to actualize a potential. The leaves of a flower entfalten sich, open, and they can do so only because they already exist prior to the moment in which they open. An entire plant or animal entfaltet sich, emerges and grows, only because this Entfaltung is the Entfaltung of the potential contained in the seed or the embryo. In this way, Heidegger's phrase on the true laws corresponds to the phrases with «constitutes itself» (BT 435; SZ 383) and with «become free» (BT 436; SZ 384) (see above, chapter 2, section C).

7. As is known, the most prominent Opfer at the university of Freiburg was Edmund Husserl (see Ott, *Martin Heidegger,* 172ff.; German edition, 167ff.). Having become Rektor of the university of Freiburg, Heidegger «asked Stieler to draft a code of honour for the soon-to-be-established university lecturers' association, which he submitted to the authorities in Karlsruhe and Berlin with his recommendations. It was based on the military officers' code of honour» (ibid., 155; German edition, 151). The beginning of the document repeats in simple repetition exactly the sentences with erwidert and Widerruf in section 74 of *Being and Time*. In *Being and Time* authentic Dasein erwidert the call of the Volksgemeinschaft and brings the Volksgemeinschaft back—or «erwiderbringet» (see below, n. 70) it. In doing so authentic Dasein brings itself back, or it re-duces, leads back, itself to its true «selbst» (SZ 384; the second «itself» in *«hands* itself *down* to itself,»* BT 435; see above, pp. 62ff.) that has been

pushed aside and covered up by Gesellschaft. Since Gesellschaft is a downward plunge, in re-ducing itself to its «true» self it moves upward again. The first sentence of the document reads: «We lecturers seek to rise up {aufwärts} and come to ourselves again {wieder zu uns selbst kommen}» (Ott, *Martin Heidegger*, 155; German edition, 151). In *Being and Time* authentic Dasein can erwider~~bringen~~ the Volksgemeinschaft only by canceling, expelling «from {Europe's} blood like a foreign poison» (PPS 153), Gesellschaft. This requires that authentic Dasein expels the individuals who are, so to speak, the incarnations of Gesellschaft. The document continues: «We seek to cleanse our ranks of inferior elements {von minderwertigen Elementen reinigen} and thwart the forces of degeneracy in the future» (Ott, *Martin Heidegger*, 155; German edition, 151). Beginning to move upward authentic Dasein must take measures not to fall down again. The third sentence of the document reads: «By nurturing our sense of honour, we seek to teach and instruct each other, thereby ensuring that there is no possibility of falling back into the old ways {Rückfall in die früheren Zustände}» (ibid., 155; German edition, 151). Note that at that time «minderwertige Elemente» («inferior elements») was used in regard to human individuals and not that much, if at all, in regard to intellectual or spiritual influences, which, in Heidegger's text, occur as «the forces of degeneracy.» Even in summer 1935, in a public lecture, Heidegger uses the official National Socialist term—namely, «Säuberung» —and complains that the Säuberung was not radical enough: «The state of science since the turn of the century— it has remained unchanged despite a certain amount of house cleaning {der heute trotz mancher Säuberung unverändert ist} —is easy to see» (IM 48; EM 36; for «complains» see the context of the quote).

    8. See Ott, *Martin Heidegger: A Political Life*, 242; German edition, 231.

    9. See my paper "On Brinks and Bridges in Heidegger."

    10. As is already evident from the examples I have given, if «Geschlecht» is used in the sense of lineage, family, or generation, the accompanying verb is not «haben» (to have) but «sein» (to be), as in «ein altes Geschlecht sein,» «von altem Geschlechte sein,» or «We are the Geschlecht, generation, of World War I Fighters.» In the passage quoted from the speech "The University in the National Socialist State," the translator chose to render «Geschlecht» as «race,» a term that has no connotations of sex organs. He also replaced Heidegger's verb «haben» (to have) with «are.» For Heidegger does indeed not say, we must «be a hard Geschlecht,» but rather that we must «ein hartes Geschlecht haben {have}.» This makes the sentence pretty awkward since it invites associations that Heidegger certainly did not intend. For when one says, «someone hat a Geschlecht,» one refers to vagina or penis and not to family or lineage. Thus, as one can easily imagine, in everyday language, «ein hartes Geschlecht haben,» as Heidegger in fact says, means «to have an erection, an erected, hard, penis.» In light of the examples of heroes to choose from in English literature (see chapter 1, section B, and chapter 5, section C), in the remainder of the book I will promote my own hero, Erwin Szymanski, the prototype of a Berlin proletarian of the twenties. From his perspective, one might say that the phrase «I have a hartes Geschlecht» is, as it were, a bourgeois expression. It bashfully covers up through the work of ambiguity the fact to which Erwin Szymanski might refer with the phrase «I have 'ne Latte» (I have a woody). The phrase «'ne Latte» radically individualizes this event in the sense of Heidegger's «Da» (SZ 12, 132, 263; BT 92, 171, 308) of Division One and does not, as in Heidegger in Division Two, lead it back to the common nature, the

universal. «Hartes Geschlecht,» on the other hand, deindividualizes this event from the outset, subsumes it under some nebulous generality, and forces it into the service of the Volk or the Gemeinschaft.

Due to Heidegger's tendency to use as the grammatical subject of a sentence not a particular Dasein but rather an abstract quality or essence of something (BT 15), things get even worse. Grammatically, the relative pronoun «das» («that») in both of its occurrences («we must be a hard race {ein hartes Geschlecht}, that {das} cares for nothing of its own {an nichts Eigenem mehr hängt}, that {das} rests firmly on the foundation of the people and the nation {auf den Grund des Volkes}») refers unambiguously not to «we» but to «Geschlecht.» As was mentioned (n.1), «hängen an» often means «hang on.» If, as Heidegger claims (BT 134ff.; SZ 101ff.), spatiality is a fundamental existentiale, one might even say that «hang on» is the primary meaning of «hängen an.» Thus, eigentlich, in truth, the first relative clause («ein hartes Geschlecht haben, das an nichts Eigenem mehr hängt») says that the hard Geschlecht no longer hangs on its own, its body; that is, it has been cut off. In that case, the Geschlecht can no longer be hard. If it is still on the body, it «hängt runter» (droops). Erwin Szymanski would refer to this by saying «My Schwanz hängt runter, droops,» or «I have a Hänger,» that is, he has the opposite of an erection in a situation where he as well as the other have looked forward to the erection of his Geschlecht. (The opposite of «hängen» is «stehen,» to stand; thus «I have einen stehen,» «Mir steht einer,» or «I have a Ständer,» are synonymous with, and as colloquial as, «I have 'ne Latte.»)

No one would have these associations if Heidegger had used «sein» instead of «haben» and, instead of the two relative clauses, two paratactic main clauses with «we» as subjects («As fighters in this fight we must be a/of hard Geschlecht; we must no longer cling to our own; and we must attach ourselves firmly to the basis of the Volk»). This sentence, however, would then have lacked the staccato rhythm it has in its current form and thus would be rhetorically weaker. Also his sentence as it is but with «are» instead of his verb «have» would have made sense. One would have understood the «Geschlecht» as generation, and it would have been in line with National Socialistic language that the «Geschlecht» becomes the grammatical subject. It would have invited the association with the sex organ, if at all, to a significantly lesser degree than Heidegger's «haben.» Why did he say «haben?» It cannot have been an instance of common political rhetoric, namely, just to allude to something else in order to mobilize affective energies. For since the sentence in its current form invites all the associations I spelled out, the entire passage becomes just ridiculous, and laughter is the enemy of the sublime and the tyrants. Maybe it was just a—Freudian or not Freudian—slip of the tongue. Or perhaps Heidegger, consciously or not, thought of Geschlecht in terms of blood since one says «er ist (von)» (he is [of]) as well as «er hat» (he has) «good blood» ; or perhaps he was thinking of fate in *Being and Time,* since one «has» a fate (not used with «sein» in either everyday language or *Being and Time*; SZ 384; BT 436), and in *Being and Time* «fate» is related to «Geschick» and «Volk» in the same way in which, in the speech, «Geschlecht» is related to «Volk.» Maybe what happened here was simply a collapse of his otherwise excellent ability to let a sentence or phrase work on different semantic levels at the same time (see Bourdieu, *The Political Ontology of Martin Heidegger*)—a collapse of the sublime into the ridiculous that might have provided comic relief, at least for short time, to some of those who were not Nazis to the degree that they ignored this moment. Some deconstructionists may claim that Heidegger's «haben» subverts the entire speech and thus shows that, also in this speech, Heidegger was a fighter against Nazism. However, this seems highly improbable. After all, even in 1936 Heidegger «hing an» (past tense of «hängen an»), clung to, National Socialism and Adolf Hitler (see Löwith, "My last Meeting with Heidegger," in Wolin, ed., *The Heidegger Controversy: A Critical Reader,* 142; see also MH 158; see above, chapter 6, section A). Furthermore, Heidegger seemed not to be the person for that kind of joke.

Still, this quote is not taken from a text published by Heidegger, but rather from a report on his speech in a newspaper. Thus, maybe somewhere on its way from the journalist to the press the manuscript fell into the hands of a Kasper (see nn. 29 and 31) who changed Heidegger's «sein, be» into «haben, have.» It should be noted that in Latin the verb used in this context is not «have» but «be.» Deucalion and Pyrrha are the only survivors of the deluge. Upon the advice of Themis, they throw stones backward, which become human beings, among them Hellen, the originator of the Hellenes. Ovid summarizes the story by saying «inde genus durum sumus» (*Metamorphoses* I, l. 414; «Hence, we are a hard stock»). However, the sentence is similar in Greek : «ἐξ Ἰθάκης γένος εἰμί, πατὴρ δέ μοί ἐστιν Ὀδυσσεύς» («I am of the stock from Ithaca, and my father is Ulysses,» *Odyssee* XV, l. 267).

11. Hesiod, *Sämtliche Gedichte,* translation with commentary by W. Marg (Zurich: Artemis, 1971), 36, 37.

12. Martin Heidegger, "On the Being and Conception of ΦΥΣΙΣ in Aristotle's Physics B, 1," *Man and World* 9 (1976), 230 (WM 320). «Gemächte» is an old word for the products of God, nature, or humans. Apparently from the eighteenth century on, it has been used in a derogatory way (see *Deutsches Wörterbuch von Jacob und Wilhelm Grimm,* vol. 5 [Gefoppe-Getreibs] [Leipzig: Hirzel Verlag, 1887; reprint Munich: Deutscher Taschenbuch Verlag, 1984], 3144ff.). Probably, Heidegger's advice refers to this fact and not so much to the «male sex organ.»

13. As Heidegger says: «That which produces itself, i.e., places itself into the appearance, needs no fabrication {bedarf nicht erst einer Mache},» Martin Heidegger, "On the Being and Conception of ΦΥΣΙΣ in Aristotle's Physics B, 1," 261 (WM 360).

14. Note that «zusprechen» is different from the compound verb «sprechen zu (jemandem),» to talk to (someone). «Zuspruch» means speaking, admonition, consolation, exhortation, claim, and it is often used precisely to convey all these meanings at the same time. According to Heidegger, Plato «entspricht dem, was sich ihm zusprach.» «Ent-sprechen» consists of «sprechen,» to talk, and the prefix «ent-.» It can mean «to correspond, to be in accordance with, to be equivalent to» and also—as in Heidegger's sentence—«to meet, answer, fulfill, a request or expectation» ; thus, the «entsprochen» in Heidegger's text entspricht the verb «erwidert» in *Being and Time* in my interpretation in chapter 1; note that this verb, too, does not require an accusative object. There is a sentence in which Heidegger regards even a widersprechen in the sense of erwidern ihm etwas (to contradict someone) as entsprechen: «When man, in his way, from within unconcealment reveals that which presences, he merely responds {entspricht er nur} to the call {dem Zuspruch} of unconcealment even when he contradicts it {wo er ihm widerspricht}» (BW 300; VA 22).

15. G. W. F. Hegel, *Philosophy of Right,* section 273; *Grundlinien der Philosophie des Rechts,* ed. B. Lakebrink (Stuttgart: Reclam, 1970), 428. Kant uses two other words. Parents must not regard their children as their «Gemächsel,» or as their «Mach-

werk (res artificialis).» There are several products of nature that at the same time, however, have to be regarded as «Gemächsel (artefacta)» of the state (*Metaphysics of Morals, First Part,* section 28, appendix, section 55). By the way, «Gemachte» is never used to refer to sex organs.

16. See above, chapter 2, n. 25. In contrast to a Gemachtes, the Gemächte has Güte. For while a Gemachtes is produced by human beings and is at their disposal, the Gemächte has priority over them, is in regard to its presencing and its possible disappearance independent of them, and determines their comportment toward beings. One might object that, in contrast to heritage, the Gemächte does not give anything «good.» However, even the Gestell, enframing, in "The Question Concerning Technology" contains «das Rettende» (VA 32; «the saving power,» BW 310). Enframing does so because it remains related to Greek producing and truth as unconcealment (VA 24; BW 302 and often). Thus, enframing contains «das Rettende» only because—despite of the differences between it and Greek producing—it has, so to speak, «come a long way,» as the christening basin in Thomas Mann's novel *The Magic Mountain* has.

17. Martin Heidegger, "On the Being and Conception of ΦΥΣΙΣ in Aristotle's Physics B, 1," 266.

18. Ibid., 250 (WM 346).

19. Ibid., 234 (WM 325).

20. Ibid., 235 (WM 327).

21. Ibid., 235 (WM 327).

22. Ibid., 234 (WM 324).

23. The first occurrence reads: «But the unconcealment itself, within which ordering unfolds, is never a human handiwork {menschliches Gemächte}, any more than is the realm man traverses every time he as a subject relates to an object» (BW 300; VA 22). The second reads: «Where and how does this revealing happen if it is no mere handiwork of man {wenn es kein bloßes Gemächte des Menschen ist}» (BW 300; VA 22). The third occurrence reads: «Meanwhile, man, precisely as the one so threatened, exalts himself to the posture of lord of the earth. In this way the illusion comes to prevail that everything man encounters exists only insofar as it is his construct {ein Gemächte des Menschen}» (BW 308; VA 30f.).

24. On "The Question Concerning Technology" as a discourse on Auschwitz and how to forget about it see my paper "On Brinks and Bridges in Heidegger."

25. A Gespräch is often «serious,» or «deep.» In his interpretation of Hölderlin, Heidegger interprets it as the form of communication among authentic Daseine, while calling communication among ordinary or inauthentic Daseine «Verständigung,» that is, information, notification, agreement, or communication.

26. On «Begegnung» see above, chapter 3, n. 66.

27. As one sees, I have translated Heidegger's phrase «überhöhend» with the rather awkward phrase «in a superelevating manner.» In this context «überhöhend» belongs to the vocabulary of a logic of transformation (see below, this chapter, section C) and of enthusiasm (see below, chapter 6, section A). Community and «that which keeps bound and determines each individual» —which is either community itself or community and that which, so to speak, binds community, namely, death (see what follows above)—«erhöht,» elevates, the individual «über,» above, itself. In this way, the individual has become «überhöht,» that is, has become higher than it was before, so to speak. By being bound into the community the individual is able to step «über,»

to transcend, and leave behind the confinements of its being a subject, an actor in society. In this sense, the community acts similar to the way grace acts, for grace, too, «erhöht» and «überhöht» the individual.

Both dialectical philosophy and Heideggerian phenomenology have reservations concerning the word «is,» as it invites reifying thinking. In light of this, there is no more reifying usage of the copula as in Heidegger's phrase «Gemeinschaft is» (see above, chapter 2, n. 33). However, this use is not the breakdown or absence of thinking in Heidegger, but rather one of its points of fulfillment. In one way or another, Heidegger always tried to stipulate a sphere free of the mediation of the subject; a sphere of immediacy that, in turn, demands of the subject and the individuals to cancel themselves in a gesture for which the next quote above provides the proper term, namely, Opfer, sacrifice. Adorno has always criticized this stipulation as mythical and metaphysical thinking in terms of origin.

28. Note the occurrence of «entspringt»; see above pp. 32ff., and chapter 3, n. 25. As to the presence of the Hand (hand) in Heidegger's vocabulary, I have translated with «catch hold of» the German «angreifen.» «Greifen» is to seize, grasp, grab, grip (by hand and only later also by grab dredgers). «Angreifen» is to «touch,» «handle,» «tackle,» but more often «to attack» (and in some contexts «to weaken or impair one's health,» «corrode,» «bite,» etc.). In combination with «an» or «at» it means that, if one wants to conquer a town or, in court, refute an alibi, one has to, so to speak, launch one's Angriff by angreifen, attacking it/the defendant at its/his weakest point.

29. See pp. 21f. Erwin Szymanski might have asked: «Na, wat denn nu? Nu soll'r uns doch ooch sachen what det authentische Dasein, oder wie det heeßt, sacht zu de Vachangenheet? Oder sacht's janischt und haut's ihr eenfach eenen uff de Rübe? Emma, erinnerst'e dir? Letztes Wochenende in de Hasenheede? Det Kasperletheater da? Haha! Det war'n Ding!»

30. See above, chapter 1, n. 36, and chapter 2, n. 15. Quite literally, an Auseinandersetzung is a spatial sorting out, a separating. Any sort of confrontation—a battle in war, a sports competition, a heated debate—can be called an Auseinandersetzung. In a philosophical Auseinandersetzung, one makes clear the differences between one's own position and the one with which one takes up an Auseinandersetzung in order to show that one, so to speak, does not side with but is «miles away» from the standpoint of the other party or philosopher. The word is used in this sense by Heidegger in *Being and Time* once: «This is not the place [Ort] for coming to terms critically {für eine kritische Auseinandersetzung} with Bergson's conception of time or with other Present-day views of it» (BT 484, n. xxx; SZ 433, n. 1). Heidegger could have used this word, if he had wanted to convey what Guignon and Birmingham think he said. Heidegger used the word Auseinandersetzung ever since the early twenties. In fact, it is one of his pet terms. See Gregory Fried's paper on Heidegger's use of Auseinandersetzung and Kampf, "Heidegger's *Polemos*," *Journal of Philosophical Research* 16 (1990–91), 159–195. Since a philosopher might also say, «For twenty years I had an Auseinandersetzung with Hegel. Now, however, he has convinced me, and I have become a follower of his,» Heidegger might even have used this word, if he had wanted to leave open how authentic Dasein reacts to the call of what-has-been-there. In that case he could have used the word in the same way he might have used the word Begegnung, encounter (see chapter 3, n. 66). If he had wanted to say what Birmingham thinks he said, he could have used «Widerstreit,» for «Widerstreit»—

like «Widerruf»—definitely indicates a gesture of separation. Thus, in principle, Birmingham is not wrong, when she quotes in support of her interpretation of section 74 of *Being and Time* a passage with «Widerstreit» from Heidegger's lectures on Nietzsche (see below, n. 71).

31. Erwin Szymanski would have said: «Emma, weeßte wat det authentische Dasein macht? Det läßt sich eenfach uffschluck'n von de Vachangenheit! Det also isset! Det authentische Dasein läßt sich eenfach einsacken von de Vachangenheet! Und denn macht's den Kaspa for de Völkischen, de Nazis! Emma, det is too much! Gib' ma doch noch 'ne Pulle Bier rüber, ick kann den Schiet nich länga lesen! Diesa ganze Nazi-Scheiß kommt mir nich noch mal ins Haus!» The reader will have noticed that in this note, the Kasper (Punch) acts differently from the way he acts in note 29. In the earlier note, he acts like inauthentic Dasein insofar as he either does not listen at all to the call of the Volksgemeinschaft or actively resists the call by keeping his distance and fighting against it. Here, however, he acts like authentic Dasein, that is, he subjugates himself to the call. However, we don't know whether this is, so to speak, authentically authentic or, as Erwin Szymanski and, to some extent, Wolin maintain (see section C of this chapter), sheer opportunism. Thus, the Kasper vacillates even more than ordinary and inauthentic Daseine. For the Kasper vacillates not only between different inauthentic possibilities but also between inauthentic and authentic possibilities, and regarding the latter he wavers between taking them authentically and taking them opportunistically. Or rather, he doesn't vacillate but demonstrates the sad truth that in hard times—that is, when authentic Daseine pressure those whom they regard as inauthentic Daseine—people sometimes use unusual means, such as cunning and conformism, to survive as an inauthentic Dasein. Kasper does so without bad conscience and with a good sense of wit. Thus, the Kasper is humane as well as inhumane. He is humane insofar as he is able to listen to all the different voices and would do whatever he can to save the life of this or that inauthentic Dasein. (He is like the chorus in Greek tragedies and the incorporation of Heraclitus's concept of soul as presented in Martha C. Nussbaum's *The Fragility of Goodness* [Cambridge: Cambridge University Press, 1986], 23–85.) He is inhumane insofar as he is ready to betray each and everyone just to save his own life. And we can hardly ever be sure which path he will take. For an interpretation of a prominent German Kasper, Till Eulenspiegel, see Klaus Heinrich's *Versuch über die Schwierigkeit nein zu sagen* (Frankfurt: Suhrkamp, 1964), 87ff.

32. In these situations, one talks, so to speak, like the oracle at Delphi which «neither speaks nor conceals but indicates,» as Heraclitus says, fragment B 93. However, the three nouns Heidegger employs («Widerklang,» «Einklang,» and «Vorklang») might be used as well when it comes to direct speech, that is, to a declaration of love. A lover who feels that way, might say to his or her beloved: «I feel strongly the Widerklang of my soul in you; our hearts are in deep Einklang; this is a marvelous Vorklang of the wonderful life we will have if you marry me!» However, this direct use often takes its toll, which is that—and not only for listeners today—these as well as Heidegger's sentences sound somewhat narcissistic and kitschig. On «innigst» (in «im innigsten Einklang,» «intimately bound up») see my paper "On Brinks and Bridges in Heidegger," 164, n. 28.

33. "Warum bleiben wir in der Provinz?" (Why do we stay in the provinces) was broadcast in March 1934 and published in the National Socialistic newspaper *Der Ale-*

*manne: Kampfblatt der Nationalsozialisten Oberbadens.* See Farías's brilliant analysis of this speech in *Heidegger and Nazism,* 170–177; German edition, 237–244.

34. On the entire sentence see my paper "On Brinks and Bridges," 152.

35. On «hörig» in *Being and Time* see above, chapter 1, n. 36. For Heidegger in 1935 the National Socialist revolution seems to have lost its momentum. However, in *An Introduction to Metaphysics* Heidegger interprets the pre-Socratics as paradigmatic National Socialists (see above, chapter 4, n. 31), and one aspect of this seems to be that he wanted to breathe new life into the National Socialism of his days. Thus, at a later point in *An Introduction to Metaphysics*—namely, in his interpretation of Heraclitus—he uses «hörig» again (IM 129; EM 99; see above, chapter 1, n. 36).

36. Heidegger says: «im Vollzug der Sammlung» (EM 133). The English translator has left out the «Vollzug» («in collecting,» IM 174; thus, better: «in the execution of the collecting toward the collectedness of being»). The noun Vollzug is a strange word, which is rarely used in everyday language. It is used in political and theological contexts, in the professional language of judges, lawyers and business people, and it is also used in Husserl. However, it has its distinguished place in the vocabulary of authoritarian bureaucracies. Due to this and to his notion of gathering, «Vollzug» in Heidegger sounds more or less violent. As in the case of «Geist,» one is not well advised to use the occurrence of «Vollzug» in Heidegger, Husserl, and, say, Benjamin to «deconstruct» their differences.

As to the prisoners on the run (see above, chapter 2, section A), the bureaucratic term for Gefängnis (prison) is «Strafvollzugsanstalt» ; that is, an «Anstalt» (institute) for the «Vollzug» (carrying out) of a «Strafe» (penalty). Thus, in thieves' cant an ironic expression for «to be imprisoned» is «to be im (= in dem = in the) Vollzug.» The Anstalt is, so to speak, the Kropf (see below, n. 38) into which the bad ones disappear.

There are two reasons for Heidegger saying «im Vollzug der Sammlung» and not just «in der Sammlung.» In general, he always carefully distinguishes between the actual taking place (the presencing, Anwesen, παρουσία, Advent, or ἐντελέχεια) of something (a form, Jesus Christ, an existentiale, Being, or Wesen) and the something itself. Thus, there is not just a gathering, but the Vollzug of the gathering. In particular, the usage of «Vollzug» allows him in the heat of the years after the Machtübernahme to take over the emotional force of the Christian expectation of the Advent of Jesus Christ and claim it for his peculiar project, while investing this project with the authority of the bureaucratic machinery. In this sense, Heidegger's «Vollzug» is the Heideggerian neopagan version of the παρουσία, the Advent, of Jesus Christ. It is even literally the bureaucratic translation of «Advent.» «Advent» is in German Advent, or (Wieder-)Ankunft. Kunft (Nieder-, An-, Wieder-, Her-, Zu-Kunft, Ein-künfte = income) and Zug stem from verbs of motion. The prefix «voll-» corresponds to the prefix «an-» («ad-»). Both designate the fulfillment of a motion and the arrival of Christ, etc. In this sense, Heidegger's «Vollzug» is closely related to his term «Ereignis» («event»).

37. See chapter 1, n. 36.

38. Actually, «Kröpfchen» is the diminutive of «Kropf» (crop). The entire sentence is Aschenputtel's request to the two white doves in the Brother Grimm's fairy tale "Aschenputtel" ("Cinderella," or "Ashputtel"). There we find the same expressions and the same three aspects as in Heidegger's notion of Logos as «Sammlung»

and «auslesende "Lese".» (For what follows keep in mind that in later editions several fairy tales were changed; none of the English translations I have looked at give the fairy tale in the version of the first edition from 1812, a reprint of which I quote. All hyphens and italics mine, J. F.) When the stepsisters poured peas and lentils into the ash, Aschenputtel had to sit the entire day and had to «sie wieder *aus-lesen*» («sort them out again») (*Kinder- und Hausmärchen der Brüder Grimm:* Vollständige Ausgabe in der Urfassung, ed. F. Panzer [Wiesbaden: Emil Vollmer, n. d.], 112). On the night of the first ball, the stepsisters give Aschenputtel a basin of lentils and say that the bowl must be «ge-*lesen* seyn» («be sorted») (ibid., 113) by the time they come back. The doves offer to help Aschenputtel «Linsen *lesen*» («to sort the lentils») (ibid., 113). The next morning the stepsisters see that Aschenputtel has «die Linsen *rein ge-lesen*» («sorted the lentils cleanly») (ibid., 113). All these formulations assume a mixture that has to be segregated and purified. The first phrasing takes as the object of the Auslese the good elements of the mixture, and it says that the Auslese takes place such that the good ones leave the basin, the city, thereby leaving it to the bad ones. Also, all the other formulations focus on the good ones as the object of the Lese, but they leave open whether the good ones will leave the city (to the bad ones) or whether the bad ones will be forced to leave the city. Each Lese is an Aus-Lese, and in each Lese, explicitly or implicitly, the bad ones are also, if not mainly, the object of the Lese. On the second evening, the oldest of the stepsisters commands Aschenputtel: «*lese* die guten und bösen *aus-einander!*» («separate the good ones and the bad ones from each other!») (ibid., 114). Here, the bad ones are explicitly the objects of the Lese as Auslese. (The verb in the infinitive, «to lesen lentils,» gives rise to the noun «the Lese of the lentils.» This Lese is an Aus-einander-Lese, thus, an Aus-lese of the good ones and the bad ones. Readers familiar with Heidegger will notice that the Aus-einander-Lese, or the «auslesende "Lese",» are variations on one of Heidegger's pet words, namely, «Aus-einander-Setzung» ; see above, n. 30.) However, the question is still open as to which ones will have to leave the city. The actual Auslese, however, unambiguously takes place in such a way that the bad ones are taken out of the mixture and annihilated: the doves began to peck and «fraßen die schlechten weg und ließen die guten liegen» («ate away the bad ones and let the good ones lie [where they have always already been all the time, namely, in their city which, as the Lesenden claim, is theirs, and which they don't leave to the bad ones]») (ibid., 113; see also 114, 116). A quarter of an hour later, the lentils were «so rein» («that cleanly sorted») that not a single bad one was among them, and Aschenputtel could put them into the cooking pot, i.e., the purified city, which can then act (ibid., 113).

39. On «brink» and the move toward the brink and along the brink until the point of death see my paper "On Brinks and Bridges in Heidegger."

40. John D. Caputo, *Heidegger and Aquinas* (New York: Fordham University Press, 1982), 175.

41. Ibid., 175f.

42. Ibid., 176.

43. Ibid., 176.

44. Ibid., 177.

45. Ibid., 188.

46. Ibid., 179.

47. Ibid., 180.

48. Ibid., 180. The accompanying note 18 reads: «This is the remarkable argument of "Die Kehre" in *Die Technik und die Kehre*. In the recognition of the *"Gestell"* as *Gestell*, as the withdrawal of Being, there is already the "saving." In this recognition there is a flash of truth (*Blitzen*) in the midst of the dark night of technology. In the withdrawal, we see what is withdrawn. The difficulty with Thomas Aquinas, then, is that his times were not altogether dark enough, rather the way one cannot yet see the stars in the late afternoon because it is not yet dark enough! That is why Heidegger wrote of the "clear night of the Nothing" (*Weg*, 2d ed., 114/115)» (ibid., 184, n. 18; on Auschwitz as the *extremum* in Heidegger's "The Question Concerning Technology" see my paper "On Brinks and Bridges in Heidegger," esp. 167, n. 38). Note that Caputo here offers another metaphor conveying that the lost beginning remains constantly present (see above, for instance, chapter 2, n. 33, and chapter 3, n. 7).

49. Caputo, *Heidegger and Aquinas*, 180f.

50. Ibid., 185.

51. Ibid., 187.

52. Ibid., 187.

53. Ibid., 190.

54. Equally, one might read the preceding passage on the «so-called "private existence",» which is by no means «essential, that is to say free, human being» (BW 197; WM 149) as Heidegger's veto against nonpolitical, individualistic interpretations of authentic Dasein and as a confirmation of my thesis that section 74 of *Being and Time* contains the twofold movement out of Gesellschaft and then back into it in order to cancel it. Having mentioned the passage in the English translation of *Brief über den "Humanismus,"* about which—regarding the notions that are important in my book, namely, Gesellschaft and Gemeinschaft—deconstructionists might say, a «trace» has been erased, I would like to point to another passage in the English translation of which the same has happened. In the lecture "Das Zeitalter des Weltbildes" ("The Age of the World Picture"), delivered on June 9, 1938, Heidegger raised a question whose English translation reads as follows: «Only because and insofar as man actually and essentially has become subject is it necessary for him, as a consequence, to confront the explicit question: Is it as an 'I' confined to its own preferences and freed into its own arbitrary choosing or as the "we" of society {Gesellschaft}; is it as an individual {Einzelner} or as a community {Gemeinschaft}; is it as a personality within the community or as a mere group member in the corporate body {Körperschaft}; is it as a state and nation and as a people {Volk} or as the common humanity of modern man, that man will and ought to be the subject that in his modern essence he *already* is?» ("The Age of the World Picture," *The Question Concerning Technology and Other Essays*, trans. W. Lovitt [New York: Harper & Row, 1977], 132f.). Reading this passage one assumes that the opposition is between two groups; the first group comprises the «'I' confined to its own preferences and freed into its own arbitrary choosing,» the «individual,» the «mere group member in the corporate body,» and «the common humanity of modern man» ; the opposing group includes «the "we" of society,» «community,» «personality within the community,» and «state and nation and as a people» ; that is, one supposes that both «community» as well as «society» belong to the same group, the «good» group. Indeed, the same seems to be said in the German text: «Nur weil und insofern der Mensch überhaupt und wesentlich zum Subjekt geworden ist, muß es in der Folge für ihn zu der ausdrücklichen Frage kommen, ob der Mensch

als das auf seine Beliebigkeit beschränkte und in seiner Willkür losgelassene Ich oder als das Wir der Gesellschaft, ob der Mensch als Einzelner oder als Gemeinschaft, ob der Mensch als Persönlichkeit in der Gemeinschaft oder als bloßes Gruppenglied in der Körperschaft, ob er als Staat und Nation und als Volk oder als die allgemeine Menschheit des neuzeitlichen Menschen das Subjekt sein will und muß, das er *als neuzeitliches Wesen schon* ist» ("Das Zeitalter des Weltbildes," *Holzwege* [Frankfurt: Klostermann, 1952], 85). However, as the evidence I adduced shows, Heidegger was aware of the basic opposition between Gesellschaft and Gemeinschaft at his time, and he could take for granted that his listeners were so too, if only because of the propaganda of the National Socialists. Those hearing the speech understood the passage differently from the way one has to read the English translation. For «an "I" confined to its own preferences and freed into its own arbitrary choosing» and «the "we" of society» belong not to different groups but to the same. They are the two modes of being «an individual.» (Or the «and» is explicative, and the phrase «the "we" of society» only explains the phrase «an "I" confined to its own preferences. . . . ») Thus, the first group includes the «"I" confined to its own preferences and freed into its own arbitrary choosing,» «the "we" of society,» «individual,» «mere group member in the corporate body,» and «the common humanity of modern man»; the «good» group comprises «community,» «personality within the community,» and «state and nation and as a people.» That is, «society» and «community» belong to different groups, «society» to the «bad» group and «community» to the «good» group. In 1938 Heidegger could be sure that every listener would understand the terms and the pertinent oppositions. In addition, by his intonation he could easily emphasize that «als Einzelner» («individual») is the common denominator of the «"I" confined to its own preferences and freed into its own arbitrary choosing» and «the "we" of society.» When he printed the text, he did not take into consideration that anyone who had not heard him speaking and was not familiar with the usage of the notions at Heidegger's time would think that «the "we" of society» and «community» belong to the same group, the «good» one. After the passage quoted, Heidegger continues: «Only where man is essentially already subject does there exist the possibility of his slipping into the aberration of subjectivism in the sense of individualism. But also, only where man *remains* subject does the positive struggle against individualism and for the community {Gemeinschaft} as the sphere of those goals that govern all achievement and usefulness have any meaning» ("The Age of the World Picture," *The Question Concerning Technology and Other Essays*, 133; *Holzwege*, 85). The last sentence is the only explicit statement about politics in the essay, and it is from the viewpoint of National Socialism «politically correct,» at least at first sight. It has been discussed whether in this essay and his other writings on technology Heidegger criticizes National Socialism or, as Rockmore argues, only the empirical National Socialists without abandoning his commitment to National Socialism itself (see Rockmore, *On Heidegger's Nazism and Philosophy*, 204ff.). In the context of that question, the quoted passages probably have additional aspects. However, I cannot discuss this issue here.

One might also point to a passage in the essay "Vom Wesen des Grundes," written in 1929, in which Heidegger interprets himself and points out that his notion of Dasein is tailored precisely so as to conceptualize the transition from Gesellschaft to Gemeinschaft: «The sentence: *The Dasein exists for the sake of itself*, does not include any ego-istic-ontic positing of an end for a blind self-love of the factical human being. Thus, it cannot be "refuted" by pointing out that many human beings sacrifice themselves *for the others,* and that, in general, the human beings don't exist for themselves but rather in Gemeinschaft. In the mentioned sentence is entailed neither a solipsistic isolation of Dasein nor an egoistic intensification of it. Rather, the sentence points out the condition of the possibility {Bedingung der Möglichkeit} that man can comport himself *either* in an "egoistic" *or* "altruistic" way» (WM 53f.). In 1929 Heidegger published the lecture "Was ist Metaphysik?" ("What is Metaphysics?," BW 91–112). When it was published in its fourth edition in 1943, Heidegger added an afterword that was revised in all the editions that appeared after World War II (WM 397). Still, even in its revised form the afterword sounds pretty rough. Heidegger again uses the fascist formula of sacrifice— it is only through sacrifice of oneself that one becomes free—and he writes about «wesentliches Denken» («essential thinking») or «anfängliches Denken» («original thinking»):

Instead of counting *on* what-is *with* what-is, it expends itself *in* Being for the truth of Being {verschwendet es sich *im* Sein für die Wahrheit des Seins}. This thinking answers to the demand of Being {antwortet dem Anspruch des Seins} in that man surrenders his histori- cal being {überantwortet dem} to the simple, sole necessity whose constraints do not so much necessitate as create the need (*Not*) which is consummated *in* the freedom of sacri- fice {die sich *in* der Freiheit des Opfers erfüllt}. The need is: to preserve the truth of Being no matter what may happen to man and everything that "is." Freed from all constraint, because born of the abyss of freedom, this sacrifice is the expense of our human being *for* {Verschwendung des Menschenwesens *in*} the preservation of the truth of Being in respect of what-is. In sacrifice there is expressed {ereignet sich} that hidden *thanking* which alone does homage to the grace {Huld} wherewith Being has endowed the nature of man, in order that he may take over *in* his relationship to Being the guardianship of Being {damit dieser *in* dem Bezug zum Sein die Wächterschaft des Seins übernehme}. Original thanking is the echo {Widerhall} of Being's favor *wherein* it clears a space for itself {Gunst des Seins *in* der sich das Einzige lichtet} and causes the unique occurrence: that what-is is. This echo {Widerhall} is man's answer {Antwort} to the Word of the soundless voice of Being. . . . But how else could humanity attain *to* original thanking {fände . . . *in* das ursprüngliche Danken} unless Being's favour preserved for man, through his open relationship to this favour, the splendid poverty *in* which the freedom of sacrifice hides its own treasure {*in* der die Freiheit des Opfers den Schatz ihres Wesens verbirgt}. . . . Sacrifice is rooted *in* the nature of the event through which Being claims man *for* the truth of Being. {Das Opfer ist heimisch *im* Wesen des Ereignisses, als welches das Sein den Menschen für die Wahrheit des Seins *in* den Anspruch nimmt.} Therefore it is that sacrifice brooks no calculation, for calculation always miscalculates sacrifice in terms of the expedient and the inexpedient, no matter whether the aims are set high or low. Such calculation distorts the nature of sacri- fice. The search for a purpose dulls the clarity of the awe, the spirit of sacrifice ready pre- pared for dread, which takes upon itself kinship with the imperishable. ("What is Meta- physics?" in *Existence and Being* [Chicago, Ill.: Henry Regnery, 1949], 357f.; WM 105f.; all italics with the occurrences of «in» and «im» in the German text and the corresponding occurrences of «in,» «to,» «for,» and «wherein» mine, J. F.; on «in» in Heidegger see below, chapter 6, n. 24)

Note that sacrifice is «heimisch» («at home,» not «rooted») in the «Wesen» («essence» or «presencing,» not «nature») of the event. Heidegger understood the noun «Wesen» from the verb «anwesen» or «wesen» ; that is, the «Wesen des Ereignisses» is the presencing, the advent, of the event (see this chapter, n. 36). Prior to the advent of the event man is not at home, and he can come home only through sacrifice. The afterword, as mentioned, was added in 1943, that is, shortly after the famous defeat and loss of a huge German army at Stalingrad, which in military history is regarded as the turning point in the war between Germany and the Soviet Union. After the lost battle of Stalingrad thinking realizes that the death of the German soldiers is a sacrifice that Being demands in order to presence itself. Thinking thanks Being for its advent. It gives up its pretensions to autonomy and is transformed into thanking that «ereignet sich» («presences itself,» not «is expressed»). Only through sacrifice of the German soldiers and of thinking can man be brought back into the realm of Being so as to become the agent («guardianship of Being») of Being.

No matter whether this passage was supposed to be a consolation for the people at home or an advertisement for philosophy since the Denker stands im Sturm, in the storm, no less than the soldiers though much safer—it certainly marks the consummation of the effort of the rightists to redefine the vocabulary of Enlightenment for their own purposes (see above, chapter 3, n. 17). (On a similar passage from summer 1941 see my paper "On Brinks and Bridges in Heidegger," 147ff.) Note the play with «antwortet dem Anspruch» and «überantwortet dem.» Both phrases as well as «echo» correspond to the words «erwidert» and «überliefert sich» in section 74 of Being and Time, and the sacrifice of the German soldiers corresponds to the «disavowal» (BT 438; SZ 386). Again, it is the same story as in Being and Time, the only difference being that, as in the passage taken from an Introduction to Metaphysics, essential thinking no longer insists on immediate realization.

55. With the exception of a sentence near the end of section 74 (PB 61f.), Wolin's commentary on section 74 ends with his interpretation of the sentence on the «choice which makes one free for the struggle of loyally following in the footsteps of that which can be repeated» (BT 437; SZ 385) (see PB 53–66).

56. After the sentence on «Widerruf,» Heidegger goes on, «Die Wiederholung überläßt sich weder dem Vergangenem, noch zielt sie auf einen Fortschritt. Beides ist der eigentlichen Existenz im Augenblick gleichgültig» (SZ 386; «Repetition does not abandon itself to that which is past, nor does it aim at progress. In the moment of vision authentic existence is indifferent to both these alternatives,» BT 438). Commentators who maintain that, in this or that way, Dasein distances itself from the past will interpret the sentences as a summary of authentic Dasein's capacity to distance itself from any specific content offered by the past and, by extension, any commitment for the future entailed in it, or as authentic Dasein's incapacity to identify with or to subjugate itself to some content. Especially Guignon would probably interpret «progress» as the expectations of ordinary or inauthentic Dasein. However, Heidegger said that repetition is not a simple reproduction of the past because it is an endangered past that calls upon Dasein to destroy the false present in order to rerealize the past. In the context of this idea and the possible charge of nostalgic romanticism against which he has to defend his concept, «sich überlassen» means a specific attitude of indulging in an alleged past without drawing any inferences for the present from this. «Ich überlasse mich einer Stimmung» is «I give myself over to a mood» without doing anything else besides indulging in that mood. The proverbial romantic and nostalgic person indulges in, or gives himself or herself over to, fairy tales of the Middle Ages or so, or he «geht auf in ihnen,» is absorbed in them, in his leisure time, or he leaves—or tries to leave—society in this or that way in order to keep himself free from its

alienating impact. Thus, those who überlassen sich to the past do not follow the past's command to cancel and destroy the present (or they do so only in a private act without consequences for the community or society). Also, «nor does it aim at progress» may mean that authentic Dasein is not engaged in the Enlightenment project of progress, whether of the liberal or social democratic variety. In this way, the sentence summarizes precisely the move of authentic Dasein against liberals and leftists on one hand as well as against the romantic Right on the other. Because of the second sentence («In the moment . . . alternatives»), however, one might also read the two quoted sentences differently, namely, within the context of the distinction between the German notions of Tat and Handlung. Within Heidegger's framework, Handlung is the type of action that ordinary and inauthentic Daseine constantly perform, namely, simply to repeat what the «they» offer. A Tat, however, is an action that makes a difference and brings about a different state of affairs (see, for instance, «sei eines Tages wirklich in die Tat umgesetzt,» SZ 173; «should some day be actually translated into deeds,» BT 218; see, for instance, above pp. 91, 162). (See «Like the theological conception of *kairos*, there is a right time, a propitious instant when things come together, so to speak—a moment when an important action is possible, such as the transition to authenticity in practice through the grasp and reenactment of one's heritage on both the levels of the individual and the group,» Rockmore, *On Heidegger's Nazism and Philosophy*, 48.) A Tat is different from, and superior to, a Handlung. The person performing a Handlung most of the time keeps a keen eye on the consequences, his benefits from this action, his reputation in the eyes of others, etc. The one carrying out a Tat, however, abstracts from all these egocentric concerns. Within a Tat, all the distinctions between subject and object, means and ends, step-by-step realization of intermediate ends, etc. disappear. (In Heidegger, the «true» Tat is sacrifice; one who is capable of sacrificing his or her Eigenstes no longer asks for the purpose and the benefit of his sacrifice; see above, pp. 189ff., and this chapter, n. 54.) Or, to put it differently, these sentences represent Heidegger's appropriation of the Kantian «good will» for which the consequences don't matter as long as the will is good. This passage too suggests the above-mentioned (see pp. 18f., 127ff.) interpretation of the sentences explaining that repetition is not just a simple bringing back of some past («But when one has . . . formerly actual, may recur,» BT 437f.; SZ 385f.). Ordinary and inauthentic Dasein just simply repeats the choices of the «they» or is «persuaded» («überrede{t}») (BT 437; SZ 386) by the choices of the «they.» Authentic Dasein, however, having gone «under the eyes of death» (BT 434; ST 382) and having been called upon by the call of the people, knows that there is something at stake, namely, the struggle.

57. See the quotes above and others, for instance, PB 63. Wolin mentions only in passing that for Heidegger «fate possesses a distinctly *ennobling* character for him or her it envelops» (PB 62). This vocabulary differs from the vocabulary of autonomy, nihilism, fatalism, and subjugation that Wolin applies to Heidegger in order then to distill what he regards to be the crucial contradiction between autonomy and fatalism. Maybe, with this remark Wolin wants to pay tribute to the fact that, with regard to the relationship between call and the Dasein called upon by the call, Heidegger exploits motifs developed in the context of Christian rapture and grace. For the relationship between will and grace is not the negation of autonomy by fatalism, neither is it the reconciliation between two opposites, nor a Hegelian Aufhebung of opposites. Rather,

being informed by grace, the will becomes the free will it essentially is or it becomes transformed, transfigured, or—in Wolin's words—«ennobl{ed}» into love. What Heidegger employs is a logic not of reconciliation or of dialectical mediation but rather one of transfiguration. Hermeneutically, it is highly reasonable and shows Heidegger's sensitivity to the needs of the time that in contrast to Cassirer and other Neo-Kantians, he felt it necessary to develop such a logic of transfiguration to interpret the mood of the young people in the Youth movement or that of the conservatives of his time. It is this transfiguring power of the call, of the origin, the promise entailed in the passive aspect of Entschlossenheit I mentioned at the beginning (see chapter 1, section A) that would lead adherents of the Youth movement to answer a criticism such as Wolin's by saying either that Wolin's framework is completely alien to their own self-experience or that getting rid of autonomy was precisely what they had hoped for. One might say that Paul Tillich's *The Socialist Decision* presents a criticism of Heidegger and the rightists that takes the desire of the rightists for a logic of transfiguration seriously without abandoning the need for autonomy.

58. In light of the above-mentioned advertisement as well as of what follows, it is truly remarkable that one of the notes of the translators on the very first and programmatic page of *Being and Time*—Heidegger's comments on a sentence within the passage on the battle of giants in Plato's *Sophist* (BT 19; SZ 1) preceding the "Introduction" (BT 21; SZ 2)—reads as follows: «Throughout this work the word 'horizon' is used with a connotation somewhat different from that to which the English-speaking reader is likely to be accustomed. We tend to think of a horizon as something which we may widen or extend or go beyond; Heidegger, however, seems to think of it rather as something which we can neither widen nor go beyond, but which provides the limits for certain intellectual activities performed 'within' it» (BT 19, n. 4). It follows from the logic of the American dream that precisely by realizing it one renders oneself as well as one's heirs inauthentic. In his book *Old Money*, Nelson W. Aldrich, Jr. writes: «The old-money rich, the hereditary rich, are totally out of sync with the dominant theology or ideology of American life. They have no place in the American dream. The American dream is 'to make it.' The American dream is a dream of self-making—not just self-moneymaking. But the inheritor of wealth is already made. So the only thing he or she can do is to somehow make a virtue out of the syntax of his wealth. In other words, he or she *is,* everybody else is *becoming*» (quoted according to *The New York Times Magazine,* 19 November 1995, pp. 66f.).

59. See above, this chapter, n. 57.

60. See also «sacrifice» above, this chapter, n. 54. Heidegger does not comment on his usage of «Held.» Thus, he quite obviously uses it in line with the common usage of the word. The paradigmatic case of a German Held in the twenties, however, were the «Helden von Langemarck,» who subjugated themselves to and sacrificed themselves for what they regarded to be the common good, higher than themselves and an end in itself, the Volksgemeinschaft, which will reward them for their sacrifice. I noted above that Scheler—as probably everyone else—was obviously aware that, in the twenties, the core meaning and connotation of the word Held was the courageous soldier. For after his Kehre he replaced the notion of Held with the more general and neutral one of Vorbild and denied that the Held was the highest Vorbild (see above, chapter 3, n. 36). There was also, in the Kaiserreich as well as in the Weimar Republic, the «Heldengedenktag,» a festive day in memory of the fallen

German soldiers, the Helden. The Left had its own festive day, the 1st of May (see above, chapter 3, n. 61). Others welcomed a Heldengedenktag as Memorial Day is appreciated by many here in the USA, namely, as just a day off. For conservatives and especially right-wingers, however, it was a very important day. As in the case of «Vorlaufen in den Tod» (see above, chapter 1, section A), instead of «Held» Heidegger could have used—like Scheler after his Kehre—neutral terms such as «Beispiel» or «Vorbild.» However, German readers probably intuitively feel that these notions just don't fit into the atmosphere or mood built up by Heidegger's strong rightwing vocabulary in section 74.

In his article "Held" in *Historisches Wörterbuch der Philosophie* (vol. 3 [Basel and Stuttgart: Schwabe, 1974], col. 1048), O. F. Best adduces three quotes from the second edition (1922) of Ernst Jünger's novel, *In Stahlgewittern* (In the thunderstorms of steel). Readers of the only edition that is easily available—the one in volume 1 of his *Werke in zehn Bänden* (Stuttgart: Ernst Klett Verlag, 1960ff.)—should know that Jünger suffered, as he himself put it in a letter, a «mania of revisions and versions {Manie der Bearbeitungen und Fassungen}» (quoted according to U. Böhme, *Fassungen bei Ernst Jünger* [Meisenheim am Glan: Verlag Anton Hain, 1972], 3). He never indicated that he made revisions, omitted long passages, revised others, and added new ones. The edition of *In Stahlgewittern* in *Werke in zehn Bänden* is identified on p. 10 simply as «First edition 1920.» According to Böhme, this was the fifth or sixth version (ibid., 3 and 7). The second of the three quotes in *Historisches Wörterbuch der Philosophie* defines Held as «a man who achieves the almost divine stage of perfection, the unselfish devotion to an ideal, including sacrificial death {die selbstlose Hingabe an ein Ideal bis zum Opfertode}.» This passage as well as the first quote in Best's article has completely disappeared in the edition in *Werke in zehn Bänden*. On p. 235 of the latter edition, Jünger writes: «Of all the exciting moments in war none is as strong as the encounter {Begegnung, see above, chapter 3, n. 66} of two leaders of raiding parties {Stoßtruppführer} in between the narrow clay walls of the front lines {Kampfstellung}. There is no {move} back and no mercy {Erbarmen}. This much everyone knows who has seen them in their empire {Reich}; the sovereigns {Fürsten} of the trench with the hard, decided {entschlossenen} faces, daredevil {tollkühn}, lissomely jumping forth and back, with sharp, blood-thirsty eyes; men who were up to the task of the moment and of whom no report tells.» The phrase «men who were . . . and» replaces the phrase «Helden» of the second edition as quoted by Best. In the entire text of *In Stahlgewittern* as printed in *Werke in zehn Bänden*, the word «Held» occurs just twice. (I should note that I used the text in volume 1 of Ernst Jünger's *Auswahl aus dem Werk in fünf Bänden* [Stuttgart: Klett-Cotta Verlag, 1994]; spot checks show that the text is identical with the one in *Werke in zehn Bänden*.) On p. 231 Jünger reports a deed of a private, saying that he kept in mind «this hero of the moment {diesen Helden des Augenblicks}.» It was not the greatest deed, and—at least for all those who no longer live in the Augenblick, the kairos, of the twenties—«Held des Augenblicks» doesn't sound that impressive. Combined with the demonstrative pronoun, it even looks slightly ironic. Right at the beginning, on p. 19, Jünger speaks of «heroism {Heldentum}.» Jünger begins with the enthusiasm he and his fellow soldiers felt on the way to the front. However, the days in the communications zone didn't bring the dangers they had hoped for, but just «mud, work, and sleepless nights . . . {and} boredom.» It was mastering of these facts that required «a

kind of heroism that was not precisely our cup of tea {ein uns wenig liegendes Helden-
tum}.» Readers should also know that neither the *Werke in zehn Bänden* nor the
*Auswahl aus dem Werk in fünf Bänden* (nor, for that matter, any other edition or book
of Jünger's) contain any of the around 140 articles Jünger published in journals of the
extreme Right between 1920 and 1933. For instance, a few weeks prior to Hitler's
putsch in November 1923 Jünger wrote: «The true revolution has not yet taken place;
it marches along irresistibly. It is not a reaction, but rather a real revolution with all
its marks and expressions. Its idea is the völkische {idea} honed to a sharpness hitherto unknown. Its banner is the swastika. Its essence is the concentration of the will
into one single point—the dictatorship! It will replace the word with the deed {Tat,
see above, this chapter, n. 56}, ink with blood, the empty phrase with sacrifice {Opfer},
the pen with the sword» (quoted according to Renate Haßel and Bruno W. Reimann,
*Ein Ernst Jünger-Brevier: Jüngers politische Publizistik 1920 bis 1933. Analyse und
Dokumentation* [Marburg: BdWi-Verlag, 1995], 199). (Due to copyright restrictions,
they couldn't publish an edition of any of Jünger's articles; ibid., 13). The omission
of Jünger's articles from the twenties in all later editions and the omission of the word
«Held» combine to show that, indeed, in the twenties the Helden von Langemarck
were the German Helden par excellence. Still, even without the occurrence of the word
«Held» the novel *In Stahlgewittern* as it appeared in *Werke in zehn Bänden* as well
as other (revised) texts in *Werke in zehn Bänden* provide good examples of the
encounter of men «face to face» in Kampf, encounters in which the true character of
a man becomes «free» (BT 436; SZ 384). They also show what I called the logic of
transfiguration (see above, this chapter, n. 57). By fighting for the Volksgemeinschaft
to the point of death, the brave soldiers leave behind their supposed isolation as bourgeois subjects, and their individuality is transformed, transfigured, into a beloved and
loving member of the Volksgemeinschaft who, after his death, will be remembered
as a Held.

Note that in German there is a difference between the Held and the Heros, which
is not rendered in English. If one of them distances himself from a tradition and establishes something new without repeating a past, it is the Heros, and not the Held. Thus,
in German Heracles or Prometheus are usually called Heroen and not Helden. However, according to the «German» understanding of tragedies also Heroen perform their
actions, not for the sake of their glorious self-affirmation, but for the sake of a group.
Like Heracles, the Heros Prometheus caused one of the major ruptures in history not
in order to indulge in self-affirmation but to bring fire to human beings. A Held, and
also a Heros, neglects his self-realization for the sake of a higher good. Or, rather, he
finds his self-realization, which is his self-transfiguration, by complying with a higher
order. After World War II, the word Held pretty much disappeared from public political speech. («The Helden of Bern!» was used for the members of the German soccer team that won the soccer world championship in Bern 1954 and thus made Germany respectable again.) It is used ironically in phrases such as, «Das sind/Ihr seid
mir Helden!» (These/you are some kind of Helden!). Sometimes, mothers say this to
or about their children—or adults say it to and about other adults—if the children
haven't complied with orders but have done some nonsense instead; this use is ironic,
and it can be so, because a Held is concerned not with self-realization but with compliance with an order. As to the «Held» in section 74 of *Being and Time,* Rockmore
is right: «The conception of the hero (*Held*) is evoked in relation to the authentic rep-

etition of a possibility. We can speculate that the hero is one willing to sacrifice or even die for this cause, that is, the destiny of the *Volk*» (*On Heidegger's Nazism and Philosophy,* 48).

Within the, so to speak, nonpolitical interpretations of authenticity and historicality in Heidegger, Dreyfus pushed the aspect of distancing in authentic Dasein to the extreme. He writes: «In Chapter V, "Temporality and Historicality," Heidegger introduces a culture's history as source of *superior* possibilities» (Hubert L. Dreyfus, *Being-in-the-World: A Commentary on Heidegger's* Being and Time, *Division I* [Cambridge, London: MIT Press, 1991], 328). The possibilities Heidegger is interested in, are «*marginal practices* that have *resisted leveling*» (ibid., 329). As examples, Dreyfus adduces «Christian caring in the early Christian communities and absolute commitment at the height of romantic chivalry, or Greek mentoring of adolescent boys» (ibid., 329), «John Muir» (ibid., 331), «Martin Luther King, Jr.,» «Jesus, Florence Nightingale, or Mentor himself» (ibid., 330), and—«for our generation»—«ecology . . . adapting past practices of preserving and respecting nature. (Such practices will, of course, subsequently be leveled to banality by the one {his translation of Heidegger's Man})» (ibid., 331). Even if one regards, as Dreyfus does (ibid., 361, n. 65), section 74, and *Being and Time* in general, as politically neutral, the very tone of Heidegger's vocabulary in section 74 should have led one at the very least to look for some instance of rightist politics to add it to such a long list of possible choices. However, it is not by chance that Dreyfus does not do so, for people like the heroes of Verdun contradict his entire interpretation of section 74. According to him, the main interest of authentic Dasein is to make a choice that is too marginal and uninteresting for the «they» to level it. It is only a mild exaggeration to say that from Dreyfus's analysis one gets the impression that Heidegger was analyzing the strategies of an ironic Romantic or of a dandy who distances himself not only from the «they» but from the content of his own choice as well, since to identify oneself with the content of one's choice would already level it as well as oneself (see ibid., 330–333). For Dreyfus, under the gaze of authentic Dasein all traditional practices bleach out and lose their «*intrinsic meaning*» (ibid., 331). Thus, «no possibilities can have *intrinsic* or *enduring* meaning» with the effect that the heritage becomes «available as a source of *meaningless* differences. These nonbanal, nonleveled possibilities can still serve as a source of unique possibilities as long as Dasein does not take them up with the pseudoseriousness of everyday conscience or the unconditional seriousness of {Kierkegaard's} Religiousness B» (ibid., 331). Heidegger himself would surely have subsumed such behavior under «*Abständigkeit*» (SZ 126; «*distantiality,*» BT 164) as a mode of ordinary and inauthentic Dasein. In Dreyfus's picture of section 74, the only disturbing phenomenon is Heidegger's vocabulary, which, as it were, even Dreyfus cannot avoid quoting. Of the paragraph with the «*Geschick*» and the «Gemeinschaft, des Volkes» (SZ 384; BT 436) at its core, Dreyfus quotes only the last sentence in order to recommend, as already mentioned, ecology as the «issue for our generation,» and in order to place the following apodictic statement in a note: «One can perhaps see here Heidegger's philosophical justification of his political engagement in support of the National Socialists in 1933. It is important to realize, however, that even if one believed that the issue for Heidegger's generation was whether or not to support the Nazis, nothing in *Being and Time* suggests that the Situation demanded a positive response. Of course, nothing suggests that it required a negative response either» (*Being-in-the-World,* 331, n.

65). If this sentence is not simply the result of indifference to the historical and political context of *Being and Time,* it is a nice example of that dandyism, mixed with the authoritarianism of elegant brevity, which Dreyfus sees in Heidegger.

Dreyfus works out the authentic Dasein as dandy in order to meet and partly agree with a possible criticism of Heidegger concerning an opposition between anxiety and authentic Dasein's choices, a criticism similar to Wolin's regarding autonomy versus fatalism (ibid., 331–333). Again, it seems to me he too misses the logic of transfiguration that is at work in these passages.

61. See above, chapter 4, n. 1.

62. Christopher Fynsk, *Heidegger: Thought and Historicity* (Ithaca and London: Cornell University Press, 1986), 40f.

63. Ibid., 24.

64. Ibid., 24f.

65. Ibid., 26.

66. Ibid., 28–54.

67. Ibid., 49.

68. Ibid., 47.

69. Ibid., 55.

70. I mentioned that Birmingham seems to assume that the root «wider» in «*erwidert*» is, so to speak, the verbalization of the prefix «wider-» in «*Widerruf*» (see chapter 1, n. 14). In fact, she might be right in that there is a prefix in erwidern. However, it would be, not the prefix «wider-,» but rather «erwider.» The spacious house of German language, the *Deutsches Wörterbuch,* says: «ERWIDER in place of *herwider,* Old High German *hëra widar,* back here, back again; used in inauthentic {uneigentlichen} composites in cases where, today, one just uses *again,* or *back*» (*Deutsches Wörterbuch von Jacob und Wilhelm Grimm,* vol. 3 [E—Forsche] [Leipzig: S. Hirzel Verlag, 1862; reprint Munich: Deutscher Taschenbuch Verlag, 1984], 1062). The first example of these inauthentic composites is «ERWIDERBRINGEN (bring back again), *referre, reportare, reducere*» (ibid., 1062). Thus, in his sentence with «*erwidert,*» Heidegger has just crossed out «BRINGE» in «ERWIDERBRINGEN» («ERWIDER~~BRINGEN~~») and by this has erwider gebracht, brought back again, the authentic verb «erwidern» from its fallen and inauthentic life as the prefix «erwider-» as in erwiderbringen. The first example of «ERWIDERBRINGEN» is Luther's translation of *Baruch* 5, 9: «denn gott wird Israel erwider bringen mit freuden» (ibid., 1062; «For, God will bring back again/restore Israel with joy»). Thus, Heidegger says that authentic Dasein will bring back or restore the Volksgemeinschaft, and at the same time he points implicitly to those whom he has declared to be its foe and against whom the Widerruf is directed. Thus, on this path among the Holzwege of the German language one gets the impression that Heidegger has expressed his anti-Semitism in this sentence.

In my interpretation, Heidegger's «*erwidert*» is tailored precisely along the lines of the general comment in the *Deutsches Wörterbuch* according to which the word «wider» in the sense of «toward» or «against» is not the opposite of «wieder» in the sense of «bringing back,» but rather is entailed in «wieder» as bringing back: «To distinguish in writing ERWIDERN and ERWIEDERN is a mistake since also the notions *wider* and *wieder* belong together. For, each which is brought back {das wieder gebrachte} is at the same time something which is brought toward {ein entgegen, dagegen gebrachtes}» (ibid., 1062). Thus, «erwidern» is «to bring back» to some person A what one owes A (a call, a gift, a visit in return, or help as the proper Erwiderung of A's call for help); this meaning of «wider» —namely, «wieder» in the sense of «back to» A—entails a «wider» in the sense of «entgegen/dagegen» (toward) A, insofar as in order to bring back (wieder) to A what I owe A I have to bring it toward (wider) A. In this sense, one might say, Heidegger's «erwidert» equals the verb «erwiderbringen.»

There are a lot of usages of the prefix or adverb «wider» in the sense of «toward» that have no hostile sense whatsoever. «I lean my head wider a wall» (*Deutsches Wörterbuch von Jacob und Wilhelm Grimm*, vol. 29 [Wenig—Wiking] [Leipzig: S. Hirzel Verlag, 1960; reprint Munich: Deutscher Taschenbuch Verlag, 1984], 873) means «I lean my head against a wall» and thus provide my head, and myself, with a firm support, namely, the wall. There is also an old German translation of the Holy Scripture in which St. Paul's formula «πρός-ωπον πρὸς πρός-ωπον» (1 Cor 13, 12; hyphens mine, J. F.; «face to face») is translated as «face wider face» (ibid., 873). Thus, having been called upon and having opened itself for the call, authentic Dasein turns around and toward (wider) the past, that is, the Volk; leaning toward (wider) the Volk authentic Dasein achieves a firm stand—or «Ständigkeit» (see above, chapter 3, n. 62)—against the vacillations of inauthenticity; turning toward (wider) and leaning toward (wider) the Volk are parts of the move within which authentic Dasein brings back (wieder) to (wider) the Volk what it owes to the Volk, namely itself as the gift in return, a gift that will never equal the gift received from the Volk; in the process, authentic Dasein brings back (wieder) the Volk, that is, it performs a «Wiederholung,» or an Erwiderbringung, of the Volk; however, in this process, authentic Dasein realizes that in the Wiederholung more is at stake. It is only at this point that a prefix «wider-» in Birmingham's sense occurs; for the task to bring back (wieder) itself to (wider) the Volk and to. bring back, to rerealize, the Volk with joy entails a hostile stance against (wider) inauthenticity, against Gesellschaft, namely, the order to destroy it so as to make room for the proper realization of the Volk; this «wider,» however, is not the «wider» in Heidegger's verb «erwidert» but rather the prefix «wider-» in his word «*Widerruf.*» Thus, also in language the «Wiederholung des Möglichen» (SZ 385; «repeating of that which is possible,» BT 437) is not a simple repetition, since Heidegger's «Wiederholung des Möglichen» includes several activities that are described by verbs with the adverb «wider» and by the verbs «erwidern» and «widerrufen.» Ordinary and inauthentic Daseine, however, perform a simple repetition. For they don't turn around and toward (wider) a vanished past; they don't lean toward (wider) the Volk; they don't bring back (wieder) to (wider) the Volk themselves as a gift; they don't erwidern the call of the Volk; they don't bring back (wieder) the Volk; and they don't widerrufen society. For they simply repeat what the «they» instill into them—a Wiederholung without the various activities wieder and wider a vanished past and society that authentic Dasein performs. In some way, the inauthentic Daseine and to some degree also the ordinary Daseine indeed perform an activity that might be described by a verb with the prefix «wider.» For during the Bocksgesang the ordinary Daseine cover up the authentic possibilities. After Being has constituted itself and has called the authentic Daseine into the «Kampf» (SZ 384; «in struggling,» BT 436), the inauthentic Daseine widersetzen sich, resist, oppose, the effort of the authentic Daseine to cancel Gesellschaft and to impose Gemeinschaft onto all Daseine. However, these activities of the ordinary and the inauthentic Daseine are instrumental to their effort to go on with their simple repetition of Gesellschaft.

So far, I have silently corrected something that looks like a misprint but does not need to be one. All words and phrases that are in italics from the seventh edition of *Sein und Zeit* onward were set spaced in editions one through six. Only four pages prior to the passage with erwidern and Widerruf, the sixth edition has a misprint concerning one of these spaced phrases, for in the spaced word «zeitlich» («*temporally*» in «because they exist *temporally in so primordial a manner*,» BT 433) the last two letters are not spaced (*Sein und Zeit* [Frankfurt: Max Niemeyer, 1949], 382). This misprint has been taken over in the seventh edition (*Sein und Zeit* [Frankfurt: Max Niemeyer, 1953], 382) and is still in the twelfth edition («weil es *so ursprünglich zeitli*ch existiert,» SZ 382). Bast and Delfosse note this misprint and say that, as most other misprints, it has been corrected from the fifteenth edition (*Sein und Zeit* [Frankfurt: Max Niemeyer, 1979], 382) on (*Handbuch zum Textstudium von Martin* Heideggers *'Sein und Zeit,'* 400, 401). In the sixth edition the word «erwidert» on page 386 was correctly spaced (*Sein und Zeit* [Frankfurt: Max Niemeyer, 1949], 386). However, in the seventh edition the letter «t» in «erwidert» has not been set in italics, for the seventh edition has «*erwidert*» (*Sein und Zeit* [Frankfurt: Max Niemeyer, 1953], 386). The same mistake can be found in the twelfth edition (SZ 386) as well as in the seventeenth edition (*Sein und Zeit* [Frankfurt: Max Niemeyer, 1993], 386) and thus probably occurs in all editions following the seventh. Bast and Delfosse don't list this misprint (see *Handbuch zum Textstudium von Martin* Heideggers *'Sein und Zeit,'* 401). It is of course possible that neither Heidegger nor Bast and Delfosse noticed this misprint. However, since Bast and Delfosse probably worked on the index for several years, it might be possible that they asked Heidegger, and that Heidegger either said that it was no misprint or that it was one of those rare misprints that improve the text and thus should not be corrected. Perhaps the typesetter of the seventh edition was a Kasper (see above, this chapter, nn. 10 and 31); in this case, not one who drags the sublime into the ridiculous but one who emphasizes the meaning of the word and of the entire phrase. For by setting in italics just «erwider» and not the entire word «erwidert» he highlighted a prefix that was old and outdated even at Heidegger's time, the prefix «erwider,» and in this way he also typographically emphasized that Heidegger's «*erwidert*» is meant in the sense of a response to a call for help and in the sense of a revitalization. Heidegger's «*erwidert*» is indeed the verbalization of the prefix «erwider» in the sense of «erwiderbringen,» to bring back, to restore. In this way, Heidegger or the typesetter stressed the continuity between *Being and Time* and Heidegger's later writings (see above, this chapter, section B) and, in addition, gave a further example of Heidegger's alleged capacity to reveal the «true» meaning of a word by reducing it to its forgotten «primordial» meaning. In light of this, it is regrettable that the edition of *Sein und Zeit* as volume two of the Gesamtausgabe has erased the trace by italicizing the entire word («*erwidert*,» *Sein und Zeit* [Frankfurt: Klostermann, 1976], 510).

Maybe Heidegger's formulation that authentic Dasein «dem Tod unter die Augen geht» (SZ 382; «goes right under the eyes of death,» BT 434), is an allusion to St. Paul's formula (1 Cor. 13, 12). In Christianity, the way from being «face wider face» with death leads to the hope of some day being «face wider face» with God. In Heidegger it leads to being «face wider face» with the Volk. Heidegger also wrote the notorious sentence: «For along with German the Greek language is (in regard to its possibilities for thought) at once the most powerful and most spiritual of all languages» (IM 57; EM 43). Perhaps he regarded wider and erwidern as good examples of this claim, since the different meanings of «wider» and «erwidern» parallel the different meanings of the Greek πρός which in the genitive means primarily «that *from* which something comes» (Liddell & Scott, *Greek English Lexicon,* 1496) for which Heidegger uses «aus» (ἐκ) («Der Ruf kommt *aus* mir und doch *über* mich,» SZ 275; «The call comes *from* me and yet *from beyond me and over me,*» BT 320; see also his usage of «aus» in section 74; see above, chapter 2, section C with n. 33). In this way, Heidegger endows the entity πρός, from which the call comes with the nobility of being the origin since πρός in this sense and ἐκ can be close to each other anyway. The call comes from somewhere. In contrast to inauthentic Dasein, authentic Dasein listens to the call and unites itself with it. Πρός in the dative and in the accusative expresses «proximity,» «close engagement,» «union,» and «motion or direction towards» (Liddell & Scott, *Greek English Lexicon,* 1497) as, in the case of the accusative, in St. Paul's formula and, in the case of the dative, for instance in Plato's *Phaedrus:* in recollection the soul turns upward toward that which truly is; through memory the soul is always near those things a god's nearness whereunto makes him truly god («ἀνακύψασα εἰς τὸ ὂν ὄντως. . . . πρὸς γὰρ ἐκείνοις ἀεί ἐστιν μνήμη κατὰ δύναμιν, πρὸς οἷσπερ θεὸς ὢν θεῖός ἐστιν,» 249 C). One finds «4. in hostile sense, against» (Liddell & Scott, *Greek English Lexicon,* 1497) only as one among sixteen meanings of πρός with accusative, which I see only in the «*Wider*» of the «*Widerruf,*» whereas Birmingham seems to see it in both the «*erwidert*» as well as the «*Widerruf.*» However, maybe up to now St. Paul's formulation has been completely misunderstood since in a deconstructivist interpretation it might turn out that actually St. Paul's phrasing says that also and especially in this situation Dasein turns in hostility against God's face and leaps out of the regained paradise. From my point of view, this is what inauthentic Dasein, or the Dasein in the «dwarf»-like place (see below, this chapter, n. 71), does.

Even more pertinent than the Greek πρός is ἀντί. It covers all the different meanings of wider and wieder I have presented. Thus, in German-Greek lexica one finds as translations of German words with the prefixes «wieder-» or «wider-» in all their meanings words with the prefix ἀντί, and in Greek-German lexica vice versa. Correspondingly, under the entries «erwidern» and «Erwiderung» one finds words like ἀντιλέγειν as well as words like ἀνταπόδοσις as in Aristotle (see above, chapter 1, n. 15). Thus, in contrast to inauthentic Dasein, authentic Dasein erwidert the call, that is, brings back to the Volk what it owes the Volk, and what it owes the Volk is its own existence; that is, authentic Dasein ἀντιχαρίζεται itself (accusative) τῷ Volk (dative), that is, authentic Dasein is the «*sich {der* Vergangenheit} überliefernde Entschlossenheit» (SZ 385; «hands *itself* down {*to* the past},» BT 437, emphasis mine, J. F.; see above pp. 16ff.). In this act authentic Dasein realizes that it is called upon to enter into the «struggle» (BT 436; SZ 384)—into the ἀνταγωνία or «γιγαντομαχία» (*Sophist* 246 a 4), as Plato says in the context of the quote right at the beginning of *Being and Time* (BT 19; SZ 1)—against inauthentic Dasein; a struggle in which there are two ἀντικείμενα— namely, authentic Daseine and inauthentic Daseine—that cannot coexist in the same city, the latter being the matter of their struggle (see above, chapter 4, n. 5). Thus, in the vocabulary of Aristotle's *Physics* (I, ch. 7), the presence of inauthentic Dasein in the city as the ἀντικείμενον, ἐναντίον or absence, ἀπουσία, of form, Being, or Volk in the city is replaced with the presence, the παρουσία, of form, Being, or Volk in the city, which entails the destruction, or the expulsion, of the ἐναντίον that inauthenticity is. The «*Widerruf*» (SZ 386; BT 438) anticipates this outcome of the struggle.

In my interpretation the first step in the sentence on Erwiderung and Widerruf is a strong identification, or subjugation, of Dasein; in Guignon and the translators' interpretation the first step is a distancing and only then is there a partial identification; in Birmingham's interpretation there is no identification at all. In contrast to Guignon, Dreyfus and others, Birmingham does not give examples of authentic historicality. Probably, the reason for this is that, strictly speaking, there is no worldly example of her «(*Erwidert*)» (TP 32). Perhaps each action by any worldly actor requires some identification, even the most radical rupture, individual or collective suicide or killing. Compare Dreyfus's list of examples of heroes to choose (see above, this chapter, n. 60) with Guignon's list (see above, p. 8). After having read quite a few of American texts on Heidegger's historicality, in note 60 of this chapter I almost wrote: «As examples of heroes to choose Dreyfus adduces the usual crowd.» Would a sentence like that have revealed that language has already leveled these heroes? Language or me? «Wann ich so schwerz bin, Schuld ist nicht mein ~~allein~~.» («Would I ever!?») Nonetheless, «round up the usual suspects!» Fortunately, Hollywood and TV have preserved for sempiternity some of the authentic heroes. One should wiederholen, repeat, the way, the run, the escape, which Humphrey Bogart, Ingrid Bergman, Paul Henreid, Victor Láslo, Peter Lorre, Benjamin and others did, or tried to do, and then one might recognize the heroes who were around at the time of *Being and Time,* namely, among others, all the Siegfrieds and Brunhildes of Wagner's operas, the Helden von Verdun, the Hitlers and Schlageters (see above, chapter 1, n. 33) on the one hand and, on the other, the workers of the Parisian Commune, the workers and sailors of the Arbeiter- und Soldatenräte in Munich and Kiel, Erwin Szymanski, and Rosa Luxemburg, among others. Rosa Luxemburg was tortured by the Schlageters, stabbed to death, and thrown into the Landwehrkanal, a canal running through downtown Berlin. Landwehr is «territorial army» ; thus, listening to language a rightist might have rendered this event by, «Das Land (countryside, soil) wehrt sich, defends itself (against its foes).» Rick's famous sentence, «Here's looking at you, kid,» reads in the German version of *Casablanca* «Ich seh' Dir in die Augen, Kleines (I look into your eyes, little girl).» This is a slightly false, but precisely for that reason a very good translation. Anyway, in each version Ingrid Bergman does not turn away, but remains face wider face.

71. I have checked only her first two quotes from Heidegger's lectures on Nietzsche. The first is: «Whoever stands in the moment (*Augenblick*) lets what runs counter to itself come to collision, though not to a standstill, by cultivating and sustaining the strife {Widerstreit} between what is assigned him as a task and what has been given him as his endowment. To see the moment means to stand in it. But the dwarf keeps to the outside, perches on the periphery» (TP 34; *Eternal Recurrence of the Same,* trans. D. Krell [New York: Harper & Row, 1984], 57; *Nietzsche I,* [Pfullingen: Neske, 1961], 311f.; on Widerstreit see above, this chapter, n. 30). She leaves something out in this quote und does not quote the immediately preceding sentences, namely: «Und dennoch ist da ein Zusammenstoß. Freilich nur für den, der nicht Zuschauer bleibt, sondern *selbst* der Augenblick *ist,* der in die Zukunft hineinhandelt und dabei das Vergangene nicht fallen läßt, es vielmehr zugleich übernimmt und bejaht. Wer im

Augenblick steht, der ist zwiefach gewendet: für ihn laufen Vergangenheit und Zukunft *gegeneinander.* Er läßt das . . .» (*Nietzsche I,* 311). Whatever these sentences mean and however one might relate them to *Being and Time,* no one should discuss the former passage without the latter. Subsequently, she presents claims concerning Heidegger's concept of the moment and underpins them with the following quote: «Here, then, it is a matter of decision—and of incision—in our lives, a matter of cutting away what has prevailed hitherto, what has by now run its course, from what still "remains." Obviously, the cut is made by the thought of return, which transforms everything» (TP 34; *Eternal Recurrence of the Same,* 75; *Nietzsche I,* 331). This quote, too, cannot be discussed without its context, which Birmingham does not present. Furthermore, the context shows that Heidegger does not develop a theory of decision and incision but rather talks about the impact of the thought of eternal recurrence on Nietzsche's life. The first sentence in her quote is tendentiously, or falsely, translated. For in the German text Heidegger means unambiguously that the theory of eternal recurrence marks a crucial turn in Nietzsche's life.

72. If—to assume the impossible—Erwin Szymanski would have interpreted Heidegger like Birmingham, instead of saying that Heidegger «forgot the *sublime* moment which calls for *Dasein*'s resolute judgment» (TP 44) he would have said, «Dem (Heidegger) iss da Film gerissen!» (his film is torn!) In such a case, one splices the two parts of the film back together and forgets about the Riß. There is, so to speak, a generation of scholars, for instance, Wolin and Lacoue-Labarthe, who under the impact of Heidegger's engagement in National Socialism ask whether this was related to *Being and Time,* and their answer is that it was. They don't deal with a certain passage, namely, the one on erwidert and Widerruf. Thus, the next generation erwidert them by referring to this passage, since at least in its English translation it seems to support the assumption that the main aspect of authentic Dasein is its capacity of distancing itself from tradition, etc. Though for very different reasons, for Wolin and Lacoue-Labarthe *Being and Time* is prone to National Socialism. For Guignon, *Being and Time* is politically neutral, and Heidegger's engagement in National Socialism is just a matter of his conservative habits. For Birmingham, *Being and Time* is antitotalitarian and thus anti-National Socialism; for her Heidegger's engagement in National Socialism is not a matter of some habit but rather a Riß, as she puts it, and thus an inexplicable miracle that has not changed the course of his anti-totalitarian thinking. Though deconstructionists—especially since a seeming move toward theology in recent deconstructionism—should welcome and strengthen the Riß that a miracle represents, in this case the notion of a miracle is used to confirm the supposed continuity of Heidegger's anti-totalitarian thinking. Once the miracle has done its job, one can forget about it and is left with Heidegger as the only philosopher who thought antitotalitarian politics. Even if one does not agree with Wolin that Derrida's «apologetic and relativizing treatment of Heidegger's ties to Nazism . . . raises the question of deconstruction's adequacy as a heuristic for guiding our judgments in the ethicopolitical realm» (PB xviii), one must acknowledge that Heidegger has come a long way.

Fynsk as well as Birmingham have as one of their major «Helden» Lacoue-Labarthe. Strangely enough, as in the case of Wolin as taken up by Guignon, so in Lacoue-Labarthe's interpretation there is something that makes it prone to be turned into Birmingham's interpretation, and that is due to his interpretation of the motif of the «Held,» of which he says in a note that he is «indebted to Christopher Fynsk for

having drawn {his} attention» to ("Transcendence Ends in Politics," *Social Research*
49, no. 2 [Summer 1982]: 432, n. 32; Engl. translation of "La Transcendance finie/t
dans la politique," *L'imitation des modernes* [Paris: Galilée, 1986], 135–175). However, it would lead too far to elaborate on this point, which also spoils Lacoue-
Labarthe's book *Heidegger, Art, and Politics.*

In his book *Daimon Life,* Krell (who does not discuss the passage on Erwiderung
and Widerruf) does not deny the strong nationalism at work in section 74. Thus, he
asks: «By a heavy-handed sleight-of-hand, Dasein now inherits a possibility that allows
it to pick itself up by its own bootstraps and leap over its own shadow. . . . What good
is it if Heidegger reminds himself and us of the *finitude* of proper temporality once
that sleight-of-the-hand has done for Dasein precisely what the relation to the Infinite
has always done for human beings in the past, namely, granted them the license
to perpetrate infinite violence?» (David F. Krell, *Daimon Life: Heidegger and Life-
Philosophy* [Bloomington and Indianapolis: Indiana University Press, 1992], 178). At
first, he has no answer: «What such repeatability can mean in the face of a mortality
that is insurmountable remains unclear. . . . This can only disturb and haunt us» (ibid.,
178). However, a stale joke relieves him of his disturbance: «Dasein natal is Dasein
fatal. Its nativity implies nationality, and its nationality, at least in Heidegger's case,
although certainly not in his alone, entails a nationalism. Heidegger's nationalism, the
inherited hellenized *Deutschtum* of the George-Kreis, the hard and heavy legacy of
what Philippe Lacoue-Labarthe and Jean-Luc Nancy have called a "national aestheti-
cism," will escape unscathed the rigors to which Heidegger almost everywhere else
subjects his heritage» (ibid., 179). The only virtue of this passage is that it does not
wiederholen the notion that one produces one's own fate. In, so to speak, Wiederholung and Erwiderung of Krell's own style (ibid., 157–170), I make the following
remarks: (1) These sentences show that Krell has not understood anything of section
74. (2) In dissimilar similarity to Lacoue-Labarthe, Krell presents Heidegger as the
great hero Heracles who cleaned up the stable of Augias and who did so many things
for us. We cannot blame him for not completing his job. After all, despite all his
achievements Heidegger too is finite. (3) Krell makes nationalism, as it were, into a
fatality of Germans. One doesn't know whether or not one should hope that he is not
aware that these sentences are a slap into the face of all those who back then fought
against National Socialism. Besides, just the sentence in Jaspers in 1945 that Heidegger belonged to the few professors who «helped place National Socialism in the
saddle» (M. Heidegger/K.Jaspers, *Briefwechsel 1920–1963,* 271; see Wolin, ed., *The
Heidegger Controversy,* 149) and Heidegger's own assessment—that he was all alone
in his engagement for National Socialism (see Karl Löwith, "My last Meeting with
Heidegger," in Wolin, ed., *The Heidegger Controversy: A Critical Reader,* 142; see
also MH 158; see chapter 6, section A)—should keep anyone from writing such sentences. (4) Krell hasn't understood anything of the dramatics of *Being and Time* as a
whole. Heidegger was very familiar with Augustine and with Luther. In both Augustine and Luther one finds a criticism of thinking in terms of substances. In both of
them this effort to «soften,» to «weaken,» or to deconstruct the individual is closely
related to their efforts to make room for the Infinite, for God, and to hand over the
individual to God. It is also obvious that in *Being and Time* in his own peculiar
way Heidegger adopts Hegel's stages of consciousness in the *Phenomenology of
Spirit.* Thus, one might surmise that Heidegger combines all these motifs to lead us

to nationalism as the ultimate Stufe of Dasein. It is not, as Krell would have it, that Heidegger arrives at nationalism despite his criticism of substance and subject, but the other way around: he criticizes the substance and the subject to pave the way for nationalism. (5) In the face of the Nazism in *Being and Time,* one might listen to language and hear that only a subject and not an authentic Dasein, in Krell's words, «subjects his heritage» (ibid., 179) to a critical examination and deconstruction. In the light of this one should certainly insist on the subject against its deconstructors. Because of the outrageous pages on Habermas (ibid., 161–163) one feels tempted to redirect his recommendation to Habermas back to the author and suggest that he himself eventually begin—as he himself says nine times—«to *read*» (ibid., 162–163) Heidegger.

In my view, Birmingham and others, as it were, project the benevolent multiculturalism and individualism of the USA onto Heidegger's *Being and Time,* though especially Heideggerian hermeneutics requires breaking through, and freeing oneself from, one's «they»-like assumptions. Admittedly, however, for people in the USA this is not so easy when it comes to section 74. It is not just a matter of the mistranslation of the sentences with Erwiderung and «*disavowal*» (BT 438, n. 1). On page 10 E of the *New York Times,* Sunday, December 22, 1996, Karen de Witt published an article on the movie *Evita,* starring Madonna. Already the title of that review—"Once Villainous, Now Virtuous"—speaks to the point of my book. As is known, in December of that year Bloomingdale's opened an Evita boutique. Karen de Witt quotes Kalman Rutenstein, vice president for fashion at Bloomingdale's («"We've reordered three times."») and comments on the movie: «The reordering is not limited to Evita clothing. The woman herself has been retrofitted as a material girl with a penchant for charity, . . . The real Eva Perón . . . was as corrupt, vengeful and power hungry as her husband.» Neither Bloomingdale's nor Madonna are repeating any what-has-been-there in Heidegger's sense. Rather, the late Heidegger might have said they treat the past, its products, and its heroes as «standing-reserve [*Bestand*]» (BW 298). In the following occurrences of words with the prefix «re-» in de Witt's review the words designate not a Heideggerian revitalization but rather—as in Birmingham—a break with, or move away from, something past toward something new as the first social commandment of life in the USA. (Also Guignon's formula «to creatively reinterpret» [HI 138] the chosen hero does not imply that in this reinterpretation one has to come as close to the hero himself as possible.) «Sociologists, social critics, philosophers and movie makers» say that it is «all part of the American cult of individualism.» David Ruth is quoted: «"Americans have this tremendous faith in the ability to repackage themselves. . . . That's the great American gift to the 20th century. And one of the ways they convince themselves that they have this ability is to repackage historical figures."» Stanley Crouch adds a further note to this. He said «that Americans have problems with complex humans. The remaking of villains into heroes comes from an American confusion about rebels, he said. "There is a very substantial history in America of people who rebelled against the law and were right," he said. "It isn't something that's just romantic. That is what the 13 colonies were all about. But we get confused about the difference between heroic individuality, which makes possible a greater social freedom, and anarchic individuality, which is ruthless, narcissistic, amoral and dangerous."» If one just looks at these occurrences, one might indeed get the impression that the English prefix «re-» is, as it were, the keynote address and flagship of American life and its cheered constant break with as many pasts as possible and that the «origin» of the «re-» («repetition,» see above, chapter 3, n. 58) has been done away with as well. Its German counterpart, the prefix «wieder-» («Wiederholung»), however, most of the time introduces an activity of bringing back. For romantics, «back again» has never lost its aura, and in Heidegger it has had one of its most devastating recurrences.

The note of the translators on the sentence with Erwiderung and «*disavowal*» (BT 438, n. 1) is one of the few in which they offer not just information about Heidegger's use of particular words but also an interpretation of the text. Concerning particularly difficult passages they probably asked the people they thank in the preface (BT 16) for help. Since Hannah Arendt was a native German speaker as well as probably the best expert on Heidegger among them, it is possible that she advised them. In that case, one would have an astounding solution to the problem of the mistranslation. Hannah Arendt read her own political theory—the political as the site of the manifestation of individuals as individuals, the emphasis on the new, which is not a repetition—into the passage. If this is the case, it would certainly be one of the most remarkable slips of the pen in the history of interpretation and translation of philosophical texts. Joan Stambaugh translated the passage differently. In her translation, it reads: «Arising from a resolute self-projection, retrieve is not convinced by "something past," in just letting it come back as what was once real. Rather, retrieve *responds* to the possibility of existence that has-been-there. But responding to the possibility in a resolution is at the same time, *as in the Moment, the disavowal* of what is working itself out today as the "past"» (Martin Heidegger, *Being and Time: A Translation of Sein und Zeit*, 352f.). This translation allows for all the different meanings of erwidern I have adduced: erwidern as counterattack, as response within a conversation, and as response to a call for help (see above, chapter 1, sections B and D). Thus, its only disadvantage is that it does not rule out the first and the second meaning, which one has to rule out for reasons of grammar and context. Unfortunately, however, American readers of her translation will also most likely think more of the first and the second meaning than of the third. For she has translated the phrase «läßt sich . . . nicht . . . überreden» (SZ 386) with «is not convinced.» Most likely, American readers will associate a Dasein that is autonomous and independent of the past and that thus might have a conversation with or launch a counterattack against, the past. As I pointed out, however, «überreden» is not «to convince,» but rather «to talk someone into» ; thus, it stands in the middle between «überzeugen,» «to convince,» on one side and «to subjugate» on the other side. In the sentence on Erwiderung and disavowal, Heidegger definitely moves to the side of «to be subjugated» (see above, pp. 19ff.). Still, in her preface she writes: «The word *Wiederholung*, which I have translated as "retrieval," could also be translated as "recapitulation" since that word is used in music to refer to what Heidegger seems to intend by *Wiederholung*. In music (specifically in the sonata form) recapitulation refers to the return of the initial theme after the whole development section. Because of its new place in the piece, that same theme is now heard differently» (xvf.). From the perspective of my interpretation, one can hardly imagine a comment on section 74 that is at the same time more true as well as more misleading. (In fact, by comparing it to a sonata she makes Heidegger follow the same notion of history he as well as people like Scheler prior to his Kehre oppose; see my *Society, Community, Fate, and Decision: From Kant to Benjamin*.) In the context of the American notion of hero and of the tendency to read *Being and Time* from the

perspective of the work of the late Heidegger—ecology as «the issue for our generation»—one might meditate over the cover of the SUNY-edition a bit like Benjamin
over frontispieces of baroque books: it shows a leaf of a tree and a manuscript, or letter, of the late Heidegger: «der Dank zu-gedacht» («the thanking thought-to»).

I am not the only one to read the two short sentences on Erwiderung and Widerruf
(SZ 386; BT 438) the way I have explained. In summary, in the sentence on Erwiderung
Heidegger calls upon us to listen to the call and to leave the city; in the sentence on
Widerruf he calls upon us to realize the call, that is, to go back into the city and cancel
Gesellschaft in order to rerealize Gemeinschaft. In 1955 one of the major existential-
ists in postwar West Germany and a student of Heidegger and Jaspers, Otto Friedrich
Bollnow, published a systematic summary of existentialism in the early Heidegger and
Jaspers. Because, as the author says, in the time after World War II humanity witnessed
the «at this stage, total collapse of our entire spiritual world» (Bollnow, *Existenzphilosophie*, 6th ed. [Stuttgart: Kohlhammer, 1964], 126f.), Bollnow presents Heidegger's notion of historicality as a matter of inwardness. Listening to and complying with
the call, the authentic Dasein withdraws from or leaves the city and retreats into his
inwardness without going back out into the city to cancel it. Bollnow insists that authentic Dasein is not capable of producing by itself its ends and contents (ibid., 113). Rather,
they are given by the Erbe, heritage, which is «the community {Gemeinschaft} within
which the individual lives, and especially the decisive, historically autonomous unit of
life, the people {entscheidenden, geschichtlich selbständigen Lebenseinheit, dem
Volk}» (ibid., 113). In Lebensphilosophie the individual creatively transforms the heritage. However, existentialism does not allow for such hubristic enthusiasm and belief
in progress (114f.). Summarizing these thoughts, Bollnow quotes the entire passage
beginning with «The repeating of that which is possible does not bring again» (BT 437;
SZ 385) and ending with «In the moment of vision authentic existence is indifferent to
both these alternatives» (BT 438; SZ 386). However, he leaves out the sentence on
Widerruf («But when . . . as the 'past',» BT 438; SZ 386): «Thus, repetition in the strict
existential sense does not exclude a transformation of the outer appearance. However,
repetition just has become unconcerned about such a transformation and cannot derive
its own meaning from it. In this sense, Heidegger situates the notion of repetition
within a broader understanding of history: "Die Wiederholung des Möglichen ist weder
ein Wiederbringen des 'Vergangenen' noch ein Zurückbinden der 'Gegenwart' an
das 'Überholte'. Die Wiederholung läßt sich, einem entschlossenen Sichentwerfen
entspringend, nicht vom 'Vergangenen' überreden, um es als das vormals Wirkliche
nur wiederkehren zu lassen. Die Wiederholung erwidert vielmehr die Möglichkeit der
dagewesenen Existenz. . . . {Bollnow's ellipses} Die Wiederholung überläßt sich weder
dem Vergangenen noch zielt sie auf einen Fortschritt. Beides ist der eigentlichen Existenz im Augenblick gleichgültig" (SZ. 385f.)» (ibid., 117f.).

I owe the reader some translations. The children's verse in n. 70 of this chapter reads:
«I am not ~~the only one who is~~ responsible {Schuld} for the fact that I am so dirty» (as
in the German original strikethrough mine, J. F.). On the absence of Schuld in Heidegger's "The Question Concerning Technology" see my paper "On Brinks and Bridges in
Heidegger" in general and in particular pp. 162f., n. 21. In the first quote in the epigraph
to chapter 1, a poet speaks about ladies in Gesellschaft. According to him, they are inauthentic, insofar as they either don't respond to the call at all or in such a way that the
call becomes «pleaded, and . . . perverted» (BT 319; SZ 274): «With their waists laced

in stays and their faces made up in rouge,/They haven't anything healthy to respond {erwidern},/Wherever you touch them—{they are} decayed in all their limbs.» Also in the second quote, an authentic Dasein speaks about and to an inauthentic Dasein, or rather one that has not yet resolved itself. It is a rhetorical question: «You really want to hamper {erwiedrigen} such love by being insubordinate!?» However, with the third quote we are «in» (see chapter 6, n. 24) the realm of decision, resoluteness, and authenticity: «In the moment of vision, I have become resolved/wild {erwilden}.» Thus, the fourth quote follows: «Each and every man is resolved/has determined {erwillen} his will for war.» Finally, Ernst Jünger does not regard it to be «tragic if a student is not able to differentiate clearly between *wieder* and *wider,* or between *death* and *dead.*»

## Notes to Chapter 6

1. See above, pp. 150f.

2. Karl Löwith, "My last Meeting with Heidegger," in Wolin, ed., *The Heidegger Controversy: A Critical Reader,* 142; see also MH 158; K. Löwith, *Mein Leben in Deutschland vor und nach 1933: Ein Bericht,* 57.

3. Löwith, "My last Meeting with Heidegger," 142 (MH 158; German edition, 57). Löwith goes on:

> He had underestimated only two things: the vitality of the Christian churches and the obstacles to the *Anschluss* with Austria. He was convinced now as before that National Socialism was the right course for Germany; one had only to "hold out" long enough. The only aspect that troubled him was the ceaseless "organization" at the expense of "vital forces." He failed to notice the destructive radicalism of the whole movement and the petty bourgeois character of all its "power-through-Joy" institutions, because he himself was a radical petit bourgeois.
>
> In response to my remark that there were many things about his attitude I could understand, with one exception, viz., how he could sit at the same table (at the Academy of German Law) with someone like J. Streicher, he remained silent at first. Then, somewhat uncomfortably followed the justification . . . that things would have been "much worse" if at least a few intelligent persons [*Wissenden*] hadn't become involved. And with bitter resentment against the intelligentsia {"Gebildeten"} he concluded his explanation: "If these gentlemen hadn't been too refined to get involved, then everything would be different; but, instead, now I'm entirely alone {aber ich stand ja ganz allein}." To my response that one didn't have to be especially "refined" in order to renounce working with someone like Streicher, he answered: one need not waste words over Streicher, *Der Stürmer* was nothing more than pornography. He couldn't understand why Hitler didn't get rid of this guy—he must be afraid of him.
>
> These responses were typical, for nothing was easier for the Germans than to be radical when it came to ideas and indifferent in practical facts. They manage to ignore *all individual Fakta,* in order to be able to cling all the more decisively to their *concept of the whole* and to separate "matters of fact" from "persons." In truth, the program of "pornography" [e.g., embodied in anti-Semitic publications such as *Der Stürmer*] was fulfilled and became a German reality in November 1938; and no one can deny that Streicher and Hitler were in agreement on this matter. (Karl Löwith, "My last meeting with Heidegger," 142f.; MH 158f.; German edition, 57f.)

The English translation («but, instead, now I'm entirely alone») sounds as though Heidegger said that initially he had allies among «these gentlemen.» However, in the

German text he said that he was alone from the beginning on. In German, there is a strong difference between «die Intelligentsia» (or «die Intelligentzia») and «die Gebildeten.» The former word is a polemical term used by conservatives or right-wingers to denote left-wing—or just liberal—intellectuals and «wurzellose,» rootless, Asphalt-Literaten and artists; in 1936, all of them had already been exiled or silenced. The latter word, however, refers to bourgeois individuals educated in the humanities, most notably, in the culture of antiquity and that of Goethe and his time. (This distinction of course does not imply that an «Intelligenzler» cannot be educated in the humanities, or it implies that only for conservatives or right-wingers.) Heidegger is polemicizing against the members of the «humanistic culture,» or against humanism, as he did throughout his career. The word Hitler uses, «Intelligenz» (see above, p. 82), is neutral toward that distinction.

Both English translators point out that Julius Streicher (1885–1946) was a notorious National Socialist demagogue and politician, who was the founder and editor of the rabidly anti-Semitic periodical Der Stürmer, and that Löwith's allusion to November 1938 must be a reference to the so-called «Kristallnacht,» the «Crystal night,» 9 November 1938, the night in which synagogues were burned, the windows of Jewish businesses were shattered (the broken glass giving that night its name), Jews were killed, and thousands of Jews were sent to concentration camps.

In retrospect, Karl Löwith characterized Heidegger's clothing in the twenties as a picture-puzzle: «a kind of Black Forest farmers jacket with broad lapels and a semi-militaristic collar, and knee-length breeches, both made from dark-brown cloth—a "one's ownmost" style of dress, which was supposed to antagonize the 'they' and amused us then, but at that time we did not recognize it as a peculiar temporary compromise between the conventional suit and the uniform of the SA» (My Life in Germany, 45; Mein Leben in Deutschland, 43).

4. See below, this chapter, n. 5.

5. The title of Gadamer's essay ("Superficiality and Ignorance: On Farías' Publication"; in German "Oberflächlichkeit und Ignoranz: über Victor Farías Buch") was chosen by the German editors, Kettering and Neske, of the German edition of MH in 1988 (MH 141). It is somewhat misleading insofar as it implies that the essay is dealing with Farías's book. However, the essay is not about Farías's book but about its reception in France and about Heidegger. According to Altwegg, it was originally published in Le Nouvel Observateur, 22 January 1988, as "Comme Platon à Syracuse" (J. Altwegg, ed., Die Heidegger Kontroverse [Frankfurt: Athenäum, 1988], 246). Altwegg himself published Gadamer's essay under the title "Zurück von Syrakus?" (ibid., 176), that is, the famous «Back from Syracuse?» mentioned by Gadamer (MH 143) with which one colleague greeted Heidegger when he met the latter for the first time after Heidegger had resigned from the rectorate.

It doesn't come as a surprise that Birmingham doesn't quote Löwith at all. Guignon quotes from Löwith's entire account twice just the phrase «his concept of historicity was the basis for his political engagement» (HC 131, 141; see above, pp. 150 and 151), and doesn't comment on the notions. Wolin finds Heidegger's claim «far from unambiguous» (PB 75) in order thereupon to summarize his interpretation, and in order «once again» to find «a tantalizing contradiction» (PB 76), namely, the one between Being and Time's neutral formalism, conformism, and the presence of components of the conservative revolutionary worldview. However, Löwith as well as Heidegger definitely meant something more simple than in Wolin's interpretation and less general than in Guignon's. For Löwith would not have used the formulations «im Wesen seiner Philosophie» («in the essence of his philosophy») and «stimmte mir ohne Vorbehalt zu» («agreed with me without reservation»), if Heidegger had answered something that amounted to Wolin's interpretation of historicality in Heidegger. Furthermore, someone who stumbled into all this just due to his strongly conservative attitudes, and who soon became disappointed, (or a disappointed opportunist, if this is not a contradiction in itself) would not have politicized the way Heidegger did in Rome, especially if he regarded himself to be the only one of his milieu (see this chapter, n. 3; he could have remained opportunistic in regard to his peer group). Löwith as well as Heidegger definitely meant more than Guignon reads out of their words, otherwise Löwith would not have spoken about «in seinem Wesen,» «stimmte mir ohne Vorbehalt zu,» and «Grundlage» («basis»). For if *Being and Time* just formulates the context of all possible decisions and is neutral toward each of them, none of these possible decisions lies in the «Wesen» («essence») of *Being and Time*. Rather, each of them would be accidental to *Being and Time*, precisely because the essence of *Being and Time* does not allow to prescribe or privilege any of them. Furthermore, most of the time—and definitely in an affirmative answer to a question framed in terms of the «essence»—the word «Grundlage» means more than a neutral basis on which one can built whatever one likes. A Grundlage is laid for a specific purpose. For instance, a foundation of a building is laid for building one particular house, and not any other. Or, conversely, on a given foundation one cannot erect just any kind of house. In a text published in 1934, in which he explicates the National Socialist understanding of state, people, and the National Socialist movement, and in which he rejects all efforts to interpret the so-called Ermächtigungsgesetz, Enabling Act, of 23 March 1933 within the framework of the constitution of the Weimar Republic, Carl Schmitt argues that to interpret the Ermächtigungsgesetz in terms of the Weimar constitution means not to realize the fact «that the law of the present National Socialist state does not rest on a basis {Grundlage} that is alien and hostile toward its essence {wesensfremden und wesensfeindlichen}, but rather on its own basis {Grundlage}» (*Staat, Volk, Bewegung* [Hamburg: Hanseatische Verlagsanstalt, 1934], 7). The fact that the preliminary constitution of 23 March 1933 was passed legally, namely, according to Article 76 of the constitution of the Weimar Republic, «does not mean that one is justified today in regarding the Weimar constitution as the basis {Grundlage} of the present state {Staatswesens}; rather it merely means that {the Ermächtigungsgesetz} represents a bridge from the old state to the new state, from the old basis {Grundlage} to the new basis {Grundlage}» (ibid., 7f.). Also, in 1925 Hitler said that «when not even memory will reveal the names of the entire present-day state conception and its advocates, the fundamentals {die Grundlagen} of the National Socialist program will be the foundations {Fundamente} of a coming state» (MKe 369; MK 404).

6. Maybe, there was not much of a need to conceal a general rightist tendency. After all, a «great philosopher» might enjoy some privileges, especially since many professors and students shared an indifference toward and ignorance of politics and opposition against liberalism and leftist ideas. (In his report on his life in Germany, written in 1940, Karl Löwith writes about the years prior to 1933: «I was indifferent to the political situation, and for years I did not even read a newspaper. It was only much later that I became aware of the growing threat from Hitler's movement. I was innocent

{ahnungslos} about politics as were most of my colleagues» [Löwith, *My Life in Germany*, 69; German edition, 66].) However, concealment was probably required in the case of the more specific option for National Socialism. It could be significant in this context that Heidegger's English translators translated «erwidert» as though it were followed by a dative. After all, there is a sense of «erwidern» with the accusative which comes close to «erwidern» with the dative (see above, chapter 1, sections B, C, and D); and, on a first reading, the context itself seems to suggest the dative. Heidegger never gave a seminar on Division Two of *Being and Time;* section 74 is close to the end of the book; the attitude of many students was—as even Hans Jonas, by no means a minor figure in the philosophy of this century, put it in his recollection "Heidegger's Resoluteness and Resolve"—«I don't understand it, but that must be it» (MH 198; Jonas is asked: «But what is the connection between these two components, the magnificent thinker and teacher Heidegger and the chauvinist, who came out of his hiding place in 1933? Or were these components always connected subterraneously?» He answers: «Yes, one must say the latter. But it took a long time for me to realize it. In 1933, when he gave that infamous rectorial address, justifiably called treacherous in a philosophical sense and actually deeply shameful for philosophy, I was simply appalled and spoke with friends about it and said: "That from Heidegger, the most important thinker of our time." Whereupon I heard the reply: "Why are you so surprised? It was hidden in there. Somehow it could already be inferred from his way of thinking." That was when I realized, for the first time, certain traits in Heidegger's thinking and I hit myself on the forehead and said: "Yes, I missed something there before"» [MH 200f.]). Perhaps Heidegger wrote section 74 intentionally in such a way that on a somewhat careless reading it could be read in as many ways as there are senses of «erwidern,» and that each could take out of it whatever he or she liked. As an expert on the history of categories, Heidegger, of course, was aware that the commentators in late antiquity wondered why, in *Categories,* Aristotle maintained that individual substances were primary substances whereas in some of his other writings Aristotle regarded the forms as common natures to be primary substances. The commentators' answer was that *Categories* was written for beginners and that for us the individual substances were first substances. Progressing in philosophy, talented students would recognize that, by nature, the common natures had priority over the individual substances (see, for instance, Philoponus, *In Aristotelis Categoriae Commentarium,* ed. A. Busse, *Commentaria in Aristotelem Graeca,* vol. 13.1 [Berlin: De Gruyter, 1897], 34.16ff.). In a similar way, Heidegger may have meant the passage on «erwidert» as a shibboleth. Arriving at the section on historicality, readers have finally reached the most «primordial» (BT 424; SZ 372) level of interpreting Dasein. For those who are able to read and listen, via the accusative «diese Möglichkeit» (SZ 386; «this possibility,» BT 438) behind the tortured, alienated, and often lonesome Daseine of the sections 1–71 there steps out of the «obscure» (BT 424; «Dunkel,» SZ 372) das Volk and das Völkische and presents itself as the one and only substance of the individual Daseine that will redeem them. Those who regard this suggestion as infamous should keep in mind that, given his love for the Greeks, Heidegger might have had reasons to adopt techniques of initiation from antiquity in his pedagogy; Löwith characterizes Heidegger's style in lectures in the following way: «His lecturing method consisted in constructing an edifice of ideas, which he himself then dismantled again so as to baffle fascinated listeners, only to leave them up in the air. This art of enchantment sometimes had the most disturbing effects in that it attracted more or less psychopathic personalities, and one female student committed suicide three years after such guessing games» (*My Life in Germany*, 45; *Mein Leben in Deutschland*, 43; the English translation might sound as though the student committed suicide three years after she stopped taking courses with Heidegger; in the German, however, he says that she committed suicide at the end of the three years of courses with Heidegger). Furthermore, Heidegger himself interpreted his rectorate speech that way. For by saying, «I did not name Military Service {"Wehrdienst"} in either a militaristic or an aggressive sense but understood it as defense in self-defense {Wehr in der Notwehr}» ("The Rectorate 1933/34: Facts and Thoughts," MH 20; SB 27), he probably does not deny that several or even all of his listeners related this to the National Socialist «Aufbruch,» and did not understand it as a «Wehr in der Notwehr.» Heidegger wrote the text in 1945 and later gave it to his son, Hermann Heidegger, who published it in 1983 along with the *Rectorate Address* (see MH 4, SB 6).

The talented students join their master to form the invisible church of those Daseine that are «*authentically* {*themselves*} in the primordial individualization of the reticent resoluteness which exacts anxiety of itself» (BT 369; SZ 322), and whose «reticence» (BT 318; SZ 273) has been stressed throughout the section on conscience as a characteristic of authentic Dasein in contrast to the idle talk that passes among ordinary and inauthentic Dasein (BT 434; SZ 382). The talented students then wait for the situation to unconceal themselves and to turn the heads of the fallen Daseine. According to Caputo (*Demythologizing Heidegger*, 52f.), it was in his lecture course of 1929–30, *Grundbegriffe der Metaphysik: Welt—Endlichkeit—Einsamkeit* that Heidegger became explicit, and it was in that same lecture that Heidegger quite clearly stated that the task of philosophy was to produce a «Grundstimmung» (GA 29/30 [Frankfurt: Klostermann, 1992], 89ff.), a basic, fundamental, or original mood. In this way, *Being and Time* might be a picture-puzzle: everything is already there and becomes visible when the situation is ripe.

7. "The Self-Assertion of the German University," in Wolin, ed., *The Heidegger Controversy: A Critical Reader*, 38 (see MH 13; SB 19). Note the use of «Schein» («pseudo») (see above, pp. 200ff.). «Fuge» will become important for Heidegger. In his interpretation of Anaximander, he does not use «In den Fugen krachen» but rather «aus den Fugen sein» : «The word ἀ-δικία immediately suggests that δίκη is absent. We are accustomed to translate δίκη as "right." The translations even use "penalties" to translate "right." If we resist our own juridical-moral notions, if we restrict ourselves to what comes to language, then we hear that wherever ἀδικία rules all is not right with things {nicht mit rechten Dingen zugeht}. That means, something is out of joint {etwas ist aus den Fugen}. . . . How can what is present without jointure {ohne Fuge} be ἄδικον, out of joint? . . . That which lingers perseveres in its presencing. In this way it extricates itself from its transitory while. It strikes the willful pose of persistence {Es spreizt sich in den Eigensinn des Beharrens auf}, no longer concerning itself with whatever else is present. It stiffens—as if this were the way to linger—and aims solely for continuance and subsistence. . . . What is present then comes to presence without, and in opposition to, the jointure of the while {ohne und gegen die Fuge der Weile}» (Martin Heidegger, *Early Greek Thinking: The Dawn of Western Philosophy*, trans. D. F. Krell and F. A. Capuzzi [San Francisco: Harper, 1984], 41–43; *Holzwege*, 326–328). As the Greek alpha-privativum, the German prefix «un-» is used to indicate the privation of something. As Heidegger notes (*Early Greek Thinking*, 46; *Holzwege*, 332), the German

word «Unfug» most of the time, if not always, is used in the sense of «nonsense.» Still, Heidegger uses it to translate ἀδικία in Anaximander's fragment: «they let order belong, and thereby also reck {Ruch}, to one another (in the surmounting) of disorder {Un-Fugs}» (*Early Greek Thinking*, 47; *Holzwege*, 333).

8. See "The Self-Assertion of the German University," in Wolin, ed., *The Heidegger Controversy*, 38; see also MH 11.

9. On «sich überliefern» see above, pp. 16ff.

10. "The Self-Assertion of the German University," in Wolin, ed., *The Heidegger Controversy*, 38 (see MH 13; SB 19).

11. See above, p. 66, and chapter 3, n. 25.

12. "The Self-Assertion of the German University," in Wolin (ed.), *The Heidegger Controversy*, 38 (see MH 13; SB 19).

13. Ibid., 38; see MH 13; SB 19.

14. Ibid., 39; see MH 13; SB 19.

15. «Wir waren alle verblendet» («We all have been deluded») is what many Germans of Heidegger's generation say when asked about their experiences concerning National Socialism. Of course, as to the German professors in the twenties there were— to continue the somewhat floppy way of speaking—in addition to the «absentminded professors» and those whom I labeled the «non-absentminded» professors also liberals and/or social democratic professors. As to philosophers (also) concerned with Plato, the liberals and/or social democrats were represented by the Neo-Kantians Hermann Cohen and Paul Natorp. They focused on the theory of science and knowledge in Plato. The main representative of the non-absentminded professors was Werner Jaeger (before he left Germany in 1936). Unlike the Neo-Kantians, the non-absentminded professors focused on Plato's *Republic* as the countermodel to the Athenian democracy and to the Weimar Republic, and they paved the way for National Socialism. In his *Platons Staat und Hitlers Kampf* (Plato's State and Hitler's Kampf) (Berlin 1933), Joachim Bannes even explicitly parallels Plato and Hitler. Hitler is the repetition of the gewesene Plato, this time successfully. The basic motif is identical with Heidegger's. In liberalism and in the Weimar Republic, people have fallen away from Gemeinschaft. Living in Gesellschaft, the Neo-Kantians have distorted and covered up the «true» Plato. Looking through the work of ambiguity of the Neo-Kantians, the non-absentminded professors realize that Plato is not vergangen, but rather gewesen, and that Hitler will repeat the «true» Plato by destroying Gesellschaft and by rerealizing Gemeinschaft. In the last sentence of the *Rectorate Address,* Heidegger also caters to these non-absentminded professors and declares their victory in their and his Auseinandersetzung with the Neo-Kantians. On the German non-absentminded Platonists of that time see T. Orozco, *Platonische Gewalt: Gadamers politische Hermeneutik der NS-Zeit* (Hamburg: Argument-Verlag, 1995), 32–90. In his short chapter on Plato in *The Myth of the State* (New Haven and London: Yale University Press, 1946, reprint 1979), the Neo-Kantian Ernst Cassirer, who had to emigrate from Germany in 1933, mentions this contrast briefly (ibid., 62). His interpretation of Plato as «the founder and the first defender of the Idea of the Legal State» (ibid., 65) is also an implicit Erwiderung to the Plato of the non-absentminded professors.

16. See above, p. 12.

17. Aristotle, *Categories,* ch. 1, 1 a 14.

18. *Metaphysics* IV:2, 1003 a 33ff. Since Gwil E. L. Owen ("Logic and Metaphysics in some Earlier Works of Aristotle," I. Düring and G. E. L. Owen, editors,

*Aristotle and Plato in the Mid-Fourth Century* [Göteborg: Elanders Boktryckeri Aktiebolag, 1960], 163–190; reprint in Owen's *Logic, Science, and Dialectic: Collected Papers in Greek Philosophy* [Ithaca: Cornell University Press, 1986], 180–199) Aristotle's notion of πρὸς ἕν is called «focal meaning.» Heidegger takes advantage of the rhetorical possibilities of the notion of focal meaning when he speaks of «us» «als Kämpfer dieses Kampfes» (see above, chapter 5, n.1), fighters in this fight, «as the warriors in this struggle» (see above, p. 189).

19. In marriage, wife and husband are united also im Fleische, in the flesh, as the ultimate subject in which we are here on earth. The flesh is ennobled by the Geist in it, as our human Geist is ennobled by the presence of the divine Spirit in it. Thus, divine Geist, human Geist, and Fleisch are related, so to speak, like Volk, Gemeinschaft, and Gesellschaft. Volk inspires Gemeinschaft. The result of their union, the Volksgemeinschaft, in turn inspires the Gesellschaft to liberate it from all its supposed foes and to transform it into a proper manifestation of the Volksgemeinschaft.

20. For these reasons, one says someone commits an extraordinary deed «in stürmischer Leidenschaft,» in stormy passion, but one does not say, «in windhafter/windischer Leidenschaft» or «im Wind seiner Leidenschaft.» For the same reasons and also because «Wind» can be used in the sense of «Furz» (fart), it would have been ridiculous, a slip of the tongue, truly «deconstructionist,» or a subversive joke, if in the presence of the Sturm Abteilung (see what follows above) Heidegger had concluded his speech with saying, «All that is great stands in the wind.»

21. Aristotle, *Categories,* ch. 1, 1 a 20ff.

22. As is known, the sentence in *Republic* 497 d 8–10 comes toward the end of the sixth book. The ideal city has been developed. Socrates maintains that only this city as developed in the first books is the appropriate one for philosophers. He then points out that no city nor any constitution or individual will be good unless there arises a necessity for the philosophers to take care of the city and to impregnate it with true philosophy and that the realization of the ideal city is not impossible. This is followed by the theory of the idea of the good and the similes of the sun and the line and, in the seventh book, by the simile of the cave and the theory of education of the philosophers.

23. See the accounts and analyses of Heidegger's becoming Rektor and the *Rectorate Address* in Farías, *Heidegger and Nazism,* 72ff., German edition, 131ff.; and Ott, *Martin Heidegger: A Political Life,* 133ff., German edition, 131ff.; for the "Horst-Wessel-Lied" see Ott, ibid., 152, German edition, 149.

24. Can Heidegger have been unaware of the fact that his choice of the quote and its peculiar translation not only invited the, so to speak, regular extreme National Socialists such as my relative, but also, and especially, had to be understood as the subjugation to the extremely extreme National Socialists, namely to the members of the SA and to their vanguard, the editors and readers of the widespread journal that, according to his statement in Rome 1936, he regarded to be pornography (see this chapter, n. 3)? Deconstructionists might say that Heidegger meant that the university is «im Sturm» of National Socialism as in a danger against which it had to defend itself, and/or that precisely by falsely translating Plato he was able to implicitly point toward the obscureness of National Socialism. In German, rather colloquially one might erwidern, «wer's glaubt, wird selig» (You can tell that to the marines). See also the «buoyant storm» (IM 113; EM 86, «beflügelnder Sturm,» literally: a storm that gives one wings [and thus enables one to fly, not against, but rather with the storm])

that a «truly sapient man» —that is, the poet, the thinker, and the statesman; Hölderlin, Heidegger, and Hitler—has experienced on the path of being (see also above,
chapter 3, n. 14). In his interpretation of amor fati, love of fate, in Nietzsche, Heidegger has nicely pointed out the emotional benefit the Right promised to all those it
called upon to submit to fate. It is the transformation of need and desperation into
love and enjoyment. We move into fate, because we are forced to open ourselves to
it, to be de-cided upon as «one who is ever resolute {als Entschiedener}» (*Eternal
Recurrence of the Same*, 207; *Nietzsche I*, 471; for the passive see above, p. 5), such
that fate enters us, is within us, and rewards us with love and joy. In this section I
have pointed out the enthusiastic quality of many occurrences of the German preposition and prefix «in,» which led Heidegger to his peculiar translation of line 497 d 9
in Plato's *Republic*. In the course of the book, the enthusiasm of the preposition «in»
has already occurred several times. Scheler alludes to it by placing «in» into quotation marks in his elaboration on the notion of the highest community, the love-
community (see above, p. 98). Heidegger draws on it when, in the winter of 1934–35,
he replaces the line «and are able to hear from (of) each other» in Hölderlin with «we
are placed into and at the mercy of the being as it reveals itself» (see above, p. 195).
In the speech "The University in the National Socialist State" on 30 November 1933,
he says: «We of today are in the process of fighting to bring about the new reality»
(see above, p. 189). The emphatic use of «in» is also present in Heidegger's formulas «in collecting» (see above, p. 200 with n. 36 of chapter 5, «Advent») and «active
in Logos» (see above, p. 202). Its soteriological quality is extensively exploited in the
passage on sacrifice in "What is Metaphysics?" (see above, chapter 5, n. 54). See also
his obituary on Scheler above, p. 146. Indeed, in this perspective also the preposition
«in» in Heidegger's formula of «Vorlaufen in den Tod» (running forward into death)
has enthusiastic aspects. See also the frequent occurrences of «in» in section 74 (to
quote just a few, «to take over in its thrownness that entity which,» «The situation is
one which has been resolved upon {Entschluß in die Situation},» «Existing fatefully
in the resoluteness which hands itself down,» see above, chapter 1, n. 10, «the handing down of a heritage constitutes itself in resoluteness,» «brings Dasein into the {in
die} simplicity of its *fate*,» «Only in communicating and in struggling does the power
of destiny become free,» BT 434ff.; SZ 382ff.; though, of course the section also
includes nonenthusiastic uses of «in»). It is always the same situation. Dasein has
fallen away from, or out of, the origin. Thus, Dasein has to move back into the origin when the latter raises its voice to claim its proper rerealization. Through obeying
the call of the origin, Dasein has become authentic and is already back in the origin
even though the origin is not yet fully realized. (In the forties it is «essential thinking» that is already «in the indestructible» even though the latter will be fully realized only in a remote future; see my paper "On Brinks and Bridges in Heidegger,"
150, «das schon vorausgesprungene Stehen im Unzerstörbaren,» «the standing in the
indestructible» ; this standing has achieved itself by already leaping ahead into the
realm of the indestructible.) In summer 1931—that is, after his lecture course *Grundbegriffe der Metaphysik* (see above, this chapter, n. 6)—Heidegger gave a lecture
course on book IX, chapters 1–3, of Aristotle's *Metaphysics*. In German, there is the
adjective «imstande.» It means «to be capable of, to be able to.» In some contexts it
has a somewhat aggressive or threatening overtone («I am imstande to beat up this
person, if he doesn't return the money within the next twenty-four hours.»). However,

it can also convey enthusiasm («I am imstande to embrace the world—just out of sheer happiness!»). Heidegger resolves the adjective «imstande» into its components and thus has another formula of enthusiasm and inspiration, namely, «im Stand sein zu.» One who is im Stand is so because he is, or has, his Stehen im (the indestructible, authenticity, origin, etc.; see above in this note; see, however, also chapter 5, n. 10). Heidegger's interpretation artfully culminates in an interpretation of lines 1047 a 24–26. As he points out, normally these lines have been taken as the definition of the notion of the possible: possible is that whose realization doesn't entail something impossible; i.e., it does not entail a contradiction. Heidegger derides this interpretation as a typical example of the way philosophy professors read. He himself illustrates his own interpretation with reference to a runner waiting for the call at the starting line:

> Let us consider a sprinter who, for example, has (as we say) taken his or her mark {ange-treten ist} in a hundred-meter race just before the start. What do we see? . . . Face and glance do not fall dreamily to the ground, nor do they wander from one thing to another; rather they are tensely focused on the track ahead, so that it looks as though the entire stance is stretched out towards what lies before it {sind gespannt in die Bahn nach vorn gehalten, so daß es so aussieht, als sei diese ganze Haltung von dem her, was da vorne liegt, ge-strafft}. No, it not only looks this way, it is so . . . he is poised for the start {Er ist im Stand loszulaufen}. The only thing needed is the call "go!" {des Rufes "los!"}. Just this call and he is already off running {im Lauf}, hitting his stride, that is, in enactment {d.h. im Voll-zug}. . . . The one who enacts is just that one who leaves nothing undone in relation to his capability, for whom there is now in the running actually nothing more of which he is capa-ble {für den es jetzt im Laufen wirklich nichts mehr gibt, was er nicht vermag}. This, of course, is then the case only if the one who is capable comes to the running in full readi-ness, if in this readiness he extends himself fully {in der vollen Bereitschaft zum Laufen antritt, sich in dieser Bereitschaft voll ausbreitet}. But this implies that he is then genuinely in a position to run {im Stande zu laufen} only if he is in good condition, completely poised, in full readiness {gut im Stand, vollkommen im Stand ist, in voller Bereitschaft stehend}. *In a position to* {*Im Stand sein zu*} . . . , this means first: he is fit for it. Yet not simply this, but at the same time it also means: he ventures himself, has already become resolved. . . . The full preparedness of being in a position to, which lacks only the *releasement* into enact-ment {das bereitschaftserfüllte Im-Stand-sein-zu, dem nur noch die *Enthemmung* in den Vollzug fehlt} . . . 1047 a 24–26: . . . In this concise statement, every word is significant. With Aristotle {An diesem knappen Satz . . . . Mit ihm} the greatest philosophical knowl-edge of antiquity is expressed, a knowledge which even today remains unappreciated and misunderstood in philosophy. (*Aristotle's* Metaphysics Q *1–3: On the Essence and Actu-ality of Force*, trans. W. Brogan and P. Warnek [Bloomington and Indianapolis: Indiana University Press, 1995], 187–188; instead of «nothing more of which he is capable» one has to read «nothing left of which he is not capable»; instead of «Aristotle» in «is signifi-cant. With Aristotle» read «it» [= the concise statement]; instead of «stretched out towards» in «the entire stance is stretched out towards what lies before it» read «stretched out by and toward,» for in Heidegger's German text «stretched out» is passive, and «what lies before it» is at the same time that which stretches out the runner, and that toward which the run-ner is stretched out; for the German text see GA 33, 217–219)

Only a nostalgic Rightist, as it were, lets his «face and glance . . . fall dreamily to the ground,» while ordinary and inauthentic Daseine «wander from one thing to another» in curiosity, idle talk, etc. (BT 211ff.; SZ 167ff.). Authentic Dasein, however, cancels both sorts of behaviors and «has already become resolved.» On «im Vollzug» see above, chapter 3, n. 66, and chapter 5, n. 36. Heidegger's use of the phrase «im Stande sein» and his peculiar formulation «von . . . gestrafft» («stretched out by and toward») belong to the language of conservatives, right-wingers, soldiers, and adherents of the Turnvater Jahn, the authoritarian forerunner of gymnastics at the time. In the military the command for lining up was, and probably still is, «Antreten!» (or «Angetreten!» ; in the quote from Heidegger occurring as «taken his or her mark») followed by «Stillgestanden!» and «Augen geradeaus!» Even in the fifties and early sixties in gymnastic clubs «Antreten!» was followed by «Brust raus!» ; that is, already standing in line like in a military unit you had—like in the military through the commands «Stillgestanden!» and «Augen geradeaus!»—to stretch your chest out and forward. In following the command you could no longer «dreamily» look downward or «wander from one thing to another.» The command of the instructor «stretched out» your chest, and it stretched you «toward» the Sache the commander represented. Your chest «has already resolved {itself}» («hat sich bereits entschlossen»); that is, your chest has opened, unlocked, itself for the Sache the commander represents, which in this case means that your chest has been resolved upon (see above, p. 5). On Heidegger as the representative of the Sache of National Socialism toward whom, from summer 1933 onward, Dr. Georg Stieler—professor of philosophy and pedagogy and enthusiastic member of «Der Stahlhelm» (Ott, *Martin Heidegger: A Political Life*, 151; German edition, 148; «The Steel Helmet,» an extreme right-wing organization of World War I soldiers) whom the rector Heidegger asked to draft the code of honor mentioned above (see chapter 5, n. 7)—stretched out the chests of the students and to whom Stieler «made his 'report' in the correct military manner, as if the rector {Heidegger} was the commander-in-chief of his military forces,» see Ott, *Martin Heidegger: A Political Life*, 151f.; German edition, 148f.

To be sure, all the other words in the quote from Heidegger are also used, though by no means often, in everyday language («antreten,» «in Bereitschaft sein» was certainly used in the exercises of the SA, by Professor Dr. Georg Stieler, and by the young boys in the voluntary fire brigades, who were proud to have such an important job). In light of Heidegger's authoritarian language as well as of the abundance of the enthusiastic preposition «in,» however, the militaristic component is predominant. This was the end of the entire lecture course. It is remarkable that, in the very first example of his definition, Aristotle himself adduces just the opposite situation: «I mean, e.g., if [a thing] is capable of sitting and it's open to it to sit, there will be nothing impossible [in this]» (*Metaphysics: Books Zeta, Eta, Theta, Iota (VII–X)*, trans. M. Furth [Indianapolis: Hackett, 1984], 63 [1047 a 26–28]; «give me a break,» so to speak). Heidegger refers to this passage in a longer note (*Aristotle's* Metaphysics Q *1–3*, 189–193; GA 33, 219–224) that was written either during the lecture course or later, but at any rate was not part of the lecture itself (see ibid., 195; read «bottom of p. 188» instead of «bottom of p. 189» ; see GA 33, 225).

At the beginning of the race the runner has a vision of the goal, but he does not yet see it clearly. In order to be able to do the latter he must first «ins (= in das) Ziel kommen,» to come into the finish, to finish. In this usage of «in» its spatial and its enthusiastic use coincide. At the beginning of the race the runner sees the goal only in a fragmented way, so to speak, only as «Gemeinschaft, des Volkes» (SZ 384; «the community, of {the} people,» BT 436). When Heidegger gave his rectorate address, the origin had already «become free» (BT 436; SZ 384). Thus, the listeners of his address are forced to see the origin clearly; the «*direction {the call} takes {Einschlagsrichtung}*» (BT 318; SZ 274; see chapter 4, n. 7) can no longer be «overlooked» and «perverted» (BT 318f.; SZ 274) by them: «The first bond is the one that binds *to* the ethnic and national community [*Volksgemeinschaft*] {Die erste Bindung ist die *in* die Volksgemeinschaft}. It entails the obligation to share fully, both passively and actively, in {Sie verpflichtet zum mittragenden und mithandelnden Teilhaben am} the toil, the striving, and the abilities of all estates {Stände} and members {Glieder} of the Volk. This bond will henceforth be secured and rooted in student existence [*Dasein*] through *labor service*. The second bond is the one that binds *to* the honor and the destiny of the nation {Die *zweite* Bindung ist *an* die Ehre und das Geschick der Nation} . . . *military service*. The third bond is the one that binds the students *to* {Die *dritte* Bindung der Studentenschaft ist die *an*} the spiritual mission {geistigen Auftrag} of the German Volk» ("The Self-Assertion of the German University," in Wolin, ed., *The Heidegger Controversy*, 35; see MH 10; SB 15; emphasis with the prepositions mine, J. F.). Heidegger could certainly assume that not all listeners to his address were already National Socialists. Heidegger's phrase in the first sentence, «Bindung . . . in» («first bond . . . to»), is unusual. Normally one says, as Heidegger does in the context of the second and the third bond, «Bindung an.» A Bindung an A—say, the Volksgemeinschaft—is a state in which one is bound to and by the Volksgemeinschaft. The Volksgemeinschaft keeps one in its grip. The state of the Bindung an the Volksgemeinschaft has to be established, and the «Bindung in» is the activity of the Volksgemeinschaft and its representative, Heidegger, to bind one to it in order from now on to be in the state of the Bindung an it. For in this case Heidegger's «Bindung . . . in» is an abbreviation of «Einbindung.» «Einbindung in» and Heidegger's «Bindung in» is a variation of «jemanden in die Fügung/Verfügung fügen,» that is, to command someone to submit to (the command of) destiny. Like «ins Ziel kommen,» «Bindung in» combines the spatial and the enthusiastic use of «in.» In addition, «Bindung in» instead of «Einbindung in» allowed him to use the phrase three times and thus to strongly emphasize the «Bindung.»

«To share fully, both passively and actively» translates Heidegger's «mittragenden und mithandelnden Teilhaben;» that is, a «participation {Teilhaben} (in the toil, the striving, and the abilities of all estates and members of the Volk) that co-carries and co-acts (the toil, etc., of the Volk).» Normally, one has not produced what one co-carries. For instance, Mitleid, compassion, is a Leid, suffering, of someone else that one co-carries; a Mittäter is an accessory to the crime; a Mitläufer, co-runner, is a conformist (see also my remarks on Aristotle's notion of συμβεβηκότα καθ᾽ αὐτά, per se accidents, "Genus and τὸ τί ἦν εἶναι (Essence) in Aristotle and Socrates," *Graduate Faculty Philosophy Journal* 19:2–20:1 (1997), 186f., 198, n. 13). The sense that one has not produced what one is made to co-carry is confirmed by the word «Teilhaben.» «Teilhabe» or «Anteilhabe» are the usual German translations of Plato's term μέθεξις, participation. When Socrates participates in the idea of beauty, he has not produced the idea of beauty. The idea of beauty does not lose anything, if someone or something participates in it, and it exists, even if nothing participates in it. «Stände» («estates») is the conservative and right-wing term for «classes.» In the political language at Heidegger's time, a Glied is part of a Gemeinschaft as of an organism, and it is the latter's organ or instrument. The «spiritual mission of the German Volk» exists prior to the moment in which it «become{s} free» (BT 436; SZ 384). In the moment in which it «become{s} free» it calls upon the Daseine to co-carry it, and it claims them as its mere organs. Heidegger's «mittragenden und mithandelnden» corresponds to the proliferation of the preposition and prefix «mit» in the passage on destiny in section 74 of *Being and Time* («Mitsein mit Anderen» [«Being-with Others»], «Mitgeschehen» [«co-historizing»], twice «Miteinandersein» [«Being-with-one-another»], and «Mitteilung» [«communication»] [SZ 384; BT 436]). Already in *Being and Time* the actors and co-actors don't produce their fates. Rather it is destiny and the «community, of {the} people» (BT 436; SZ 384) that calls upon them, and destiny «is not something that puts itself together out of individual fates» (BT 436; SZ 384). Rather «our fates have already been guided in advance» (BT 436; SZ 384) by destiny and the Volksgemeinschaft. At some point in the downward plunge, destiny or Volksgemeinschaft raises its voice, puts itself together, steps out of the background onto the main stage, and becomes the main historical actor (see chapter 2, section C) that, as Heidegger develops in the passage ending with the sentences on Erwiderung and Widerruf, demands a rerealization of the Volksgemeinschaft (see chapter 1, section C). The rerealization of the Volksgemeinschaft requires the disavowal of Gesellschaft and of the inauthentic Daseine, who want to go on living in Gesellschaft. Thus after the sentence on destiny guiding our fates in advance, Heidegger continues: «Only in communicating {In der Mitteilung} and in struggling {im Kampf} does the power of destiny become free» (BT 436; SZ 384).

This is already the second step in Heidegger's scenario. In the first step, authentic Dasein obeys the call and is brought «from the endless multiplicity of possibilities ... of comfortableness, shirking, and taking things lightly ... into {in} the simplicity of its *fate*» (BT 435; SZ 384). This is the moment in which «heritage constitutes itself» (BT 435; SZ 383f.) and becomes the main actor, for authentic Dasein «hands itself down» (BT 436; SZ 384) to heritage and its claims. The second step either follows immediately upon the first, or between the first and the second there is a time in which the authentic Daseine live «in reticence {in der Verschwiegenheit}» (BT 343; SZ 296). At any rate, in the first step destiny has communicated itself to the authentic Daseine, and in the second step the authentic Daseine communicate destiny to the inauthentic Daseine, that is, to those Daseine that «'have' no fate» (BT 434; SZ 384). Authentic Dasein «brings {inauthentic} Dasein into the simplicity of its *fate*» (BT 435; SZ 384). Since inauthentic Dasein covers up heritage and clings to Gesellschaft, this communication cannot but take place «in struggling {im Kampf}» (BT 436; SZ 384) for authentic Dasein cancels Gesellschaft and forces inauthentic Dasein to do so too. Close to the end of the chapter on conscience, Heidegger already gave the shortest possible formulation of this thought: Authentic Dasein «can become the 'conscience' of Others.» This is followed by the sentence: «Only by authentically Being-their-Selves in resoluteness can people authentically be with one another {das eigentliche Miteinander}—not by ambiguous and jealous stipulations and talkative fraternizing in the "they" and in what "they" want to undertake» (BT 344f.; SZ 298; see chapter 3, n. 25). Having been brought into its fate by the «Mitteilung» inauthentic Dasein has become authentic and «hat Teil an,» partakes in, destiny and has been made a co-carrier of destiny. Destiny «teilt sich mit,» communicates itself to, the authentic Daseine, and the authentic Daseine «teilen mit,» communicate, destiny to the inauthentic Daseine. Thus, in the *Rectorate Address* Heidegger fully spells out the Platonic implications of the term «Mitteilung.» A successful Mitteilung results in that those who receive the Mitteilung partake in it and become its co-carriers. Thus, in the *Rectorate Address* the Volksgemeinschaft commits the Daseine «zum mittragenden und mithandelnden Teilhaben am» («to share fully, both passively and actively, in») «the toil, the striving, and the abilities of all estates and members of the Volk.» In this way, the inauthentic Daseine «werden eingebunden in,» are bound to, the Volksgemeinschaft and are promoted to being its co-carriers.

The translation of «Mitteilung» with «communicating» (BT 436; SZ 384; Stambaugh has «communication,» *Being and Time: A Translation of* Sein und Zeit, 352) is misleading, if «to communicate» is normally understood as a mutual process, as a back and forth between several individuals or groups, that is, as an Auseinandersetzung or Erwiderung in Guignon's and the translators' understanding of the sentence with «*erwidert*» in *Being and Time* (SZ 386; «*reciprocative rejoinder,*» BT 438). Heidegger did not say «Gespräch,» «Verständigung,» «wechselseitige Mitteilung,» «Unterhaltung,» or «Auseinandersetzung.» He chose «Mitteilung» because in that way he could use a further word with the—in this context—emphatic prefix «mit-.» As I already indicated, however, the main reason for his choice was certainly a different one. «Gespräch,» «Verständigung,» «wechselseitige Mitteilung,» «Unterhaltung,» and «Auseinandersetzung» are all words for verbal exchanges, and none of them implies that the participants are unequal. A Mitteilung, however, is by definition not an exchange but a one-way-street-communication, as it were. In addition, often the one who issues a Mitteilung is in a superior position to the recipient of the Mitteilung. An «Amtliches Mitteilungsblatt» is a brochure in which a bureaucratic or administrative institution announces its «binding» decisions to the public. Or, «herewith, I teile Ihnen mit, inform you, that you are dismissed from your job,» «yesterday, I received the Mitteilung that my lease was not renewed.» A Mitteilung often amounts to a command or is one. In most other cases, the logic of a Mitteilung follows the logic of Platonic participation. I already have something, and when I teile es mit to someone else, I make him share, or I impose onto him, something that I already have. In the Mitteilung, I don't lose what I already have. That which I teile mit to someone is not diminished by the fact that I and later on the one to whom I mitteile it have it. On the contrary, by passing it on to others so they have it, I help it communicate, spread, itself and enlarge its dominion. (In regard to this aspect, the Mitteilung corresponds to the programmatic sentence 105 a 3–5 in Plato's *Phaedo*; see my paper "Genus and τὸ τί ἦν εἶναι (Essence) in Aristotle and Socrates," 192ff., n. 7.) In sum, quite appropriately in dictionaries one finds as translations of «Mitteilung» «announcement,» «notification,» «(administrative) communication,» «memo,» and as translations of «mitteilen» «impart a thing to a person,» «communicate a thing to a person,» «inform someone of something,» «pass on something to someone,» «spread something.» All these expressions designate one-way communications. None of them implies that the recipient of a Mitteilung argues with its sender. To the contrary, often a Mitteilung implies that the recipient, as is said in bureaucratic and administrative language, «die Mitteilung zur Kenntnis nimmt und entsprechend danach handelt,» takes notice of the Mitteilung and acts accordingly, that is, obeys without arguing with the sender. Note also that Heidegger does not use the plural, and he does not add Daseine in the plural as those who conduct communications. Instead, he uses the singular with definite article («In der Mitteilung und im Kampf,» SZ 384; BT 436) (on the definite article see above, chapter 1, n. 17). This further emphasizes the Platonic structure of communicating something from «the haves» down to «the have-nots.»

Some Mitteilungen are «fürchterlich,» dreadful, and others are «freudig,» joyful, «überraschend,» surprising. In any case, a Mitteilung is almost by definition «wichtig,» important. In section 74 of *Being and Time*, Heidegger responds to the kairos of the twenties in Germany. In that context, Heidegger's «Mitteilung» (SZ 384; BT 436) might be his pagan rendering of the Christian «Verkündigung,» Annunciation, «Frohe Botschaft,» gospel. As I showed, Scheler pursued a certain Christian platonism. In World War I, God breaks into the fallen world and reveals the true order of things that «we» have to realize at the expense of the Gesellschaft we have lived in up to that point. As the example of Hitler shows, the same motif can be used in conjunction with an ontology that was not acceptable according to usual philosophical standards. The motif itself was probably shared by many rightists. For if one assumes that Gesellschaft is a downward plunge, the salvation must come from something outside of Gesellschaft (see above, chapter 4, n. 7). Heidegger did not accept Scheler's ontology. Still, he shared the general motif present in Scheler and Hitler. Thus it is not coincidental that he finished his *Rectorate Address* with a quote from the metaphysician Plato, and that, in section 74 of *Being and Time*, he did not choose a word of the early Socrates but took advantage of a word that belongs to Plato's metaphysics of participation.

The Platonic structure of Heidegger's «Mitteilung» in section 74 is already present in Division One of *Being and Time*. For in sections 33 and 34 Heidegger interprets «assertion» as a «*"communication"* [*Mitteilung*]» and reads the word «Mitteilung» in the Platonic sense (BT 197; SZ 155). His main concern in both sections is whether those who receive an authentic Mitteilung hear it properly or not (BT 197f., 206f., 207f.; SZ 155, 163, 164f.). In section A of chapter 1 I pointed out that the English phrase «anticipation of death» reverts the meaning of Heidegger's «Vorlaufen in den Tod.» For anticipating something, I, so to speak, stay within the wall of the city and rely on a temporal interval between the moment of anticipation and the moment in which the anticipated event occurs. In running forward into death, however, I cancel both the spatial security zone and the temporal interval. In addition, I discussed Heidegger's notion of the second positive mode of solicitude according to which authentic Dasein «*leap{s} ahead*» (BT 158; «*vorausspringt,*» SZ 122) (see above, chapter 3, n. 25; see also chapter 2, n. 5), and I also quoted several times the passage with the call of conscience as a call that «calls us back in calling us forth» (BT 326; «vorrufenden Rückruf,» SZ 280). In the English translation one cannot see that all German phrases have the same prefix, namely, «vor-.» The prefix «vor-» functions like a focal meaning in Aristotle (see above, p. 222, with n. 18). Native German speakers are probably slightly amused about Heidegger's notion of «vorausspringen» as the only way of becoming «*authentically* bound together» (BT 159; SZ 122). However, the notion fits well into the extensive vocabulary of falling and leaping in *Being and Time*. In addition, in the light of the *Rectorate Address* the focal meaning of «vor-» in *Being and Time* amounts to the focal meaning of «Sturm-» in the *Rectorate Address* as the Sturmtrupp runs ahead of the other troops. Running vor one is «schon,» already, or «bereits,» already, at a site where the others are not yet or never want to be. In this sense, Heidegger says in the *Rectorate Address*: «But it is our will that our Volk fulfill its historical mission. We will ourselves. For the young and youngest elements of the Volk, which are already {schon} reaching beyond us, *have* already {bereits} *decided* this» ("The Self-Assertion of the German University," in Wolin, ed., *The Heidegger Controversy,* 38 [see MH 13; SB 19]). Having already achieved the historical mission they mitteilen, communicate, it to the others. In this way, they become the conscience of the others and force them into their fate. Guignon remarks that it «is important to keep in mind that the term "Dasein" does not refer simply to individual human beings» (HC 131). Since the notion of fate was polemical against liberals and leftists, it might be possible that Heidegger's notions of «vorausspringen» and «vorlaufen» are his version of the notion of the proletariat as the vanguard of the proletarians in Lukács. Both the proletariat and the authentic Dasein run vor all the others. The major difference on which the other differences hinge is that the proletariat only moves forward while authentic Dasein runs vor in order to be called «back» (BT 326; SZ 280) since it «wants to be brought back» (BT 316; SZ 271) (see above, chapter 2, n. 35, and chapter 3, n. 25). For authentic Dasein wants to cancel Gesellschaft and to rerealize the «Gemeinschaft, des Volkes» (SZ 384; «the community, of {the} people,» BT 436; see above, chapter 1, n. 17).

As was mentioned above, «Mitteilung» can easily be regarded as the general notion for «participation,» «Frohe Botschaft» (gospel), and bureaucratic ways of communication. In the kairos of the twenties, each group wanted to establish its notions as the commonly accepted ones or to «fill» the general notions with its meaning. In other words, the art of political propaganda consists in offering phrases that many individuals and groups can recognize as their own. Heidegger's gathering of Platonists, Christians, and bureaucrats under the umbrella of a National Socialist «Mitteilung» might serve as an example of Heidegger's capacity I mentioned in note 13 of the preface.

Note finally that in the passage from the *Rectorate Address* Heidegger says quite openly what, as I tried to show, is the «finish» of *Being and Time*: «The first bond is the one that binds to the ethnic and national community [*Volksgemeinschaft*] {and not a bond that binds to, say, Scheler's love-community}.» To carry out the *"Task of Destroying the History of Ontology"* (BT 41; SZ 19) Heidegger also destroyed one of the most prominent representatives of ontology at his time, namely, Scheler.

25. Thomas Mann, *The Magic Mountain,* 715. The song reads in German: «Und seine Zweige rauschten, als riefen sie mir zu.» Thus, a literal translation would be: «And its branches rustled, as if calling to me.»

26. Ibid., 145 (section 9 of chapter 4 ["Mounting Misgivings; of the Two Grandfathers and the Boat-ride in the Twilight"]; the German text has «durch Mark und Bein»).

27. Ibid., 716.

28. In the second sentence of the short text *Der Feldweg,* published in 1953, Heidegger mentions «the old lime-trees of the palace gardens» in Meßkirch (*Der Feldweg,* 1). However, the moral of the text is conveyed, not through them, but rather through «the oak-tree by the path» (ibid., 2). On the moral of the text see my paper "On Brinks and Bridges in Heidegger," 152ff.

29. St. Augustine, *Confessions,* trans. R. S. Pine-Coffine (London: Penguin, 1961), 177 (book 8, ch. 6).

30. Walter Benjamin, "The Work of Art in the Age of Mechanical Reproduction," *Illuminations,* 222f.

31. Walter Benjamin, *One-Way Street, Reflections,* 68.

32. On the slight irony of the sentence with the «good ground» see Winfried Menninghaus, *Walter Benjamins Theorie der Sprachmagie* (Frankfurt: Suhrkamp, 1980),

238; see, however, also Marleen Stoessel, *Aura: Das Vergessene Menschliche. Zu Sprache und Erfahrung bei Walter Benjamin* (Munich: Hanser, 1983), 49ff. I made no effort to translate the rhythm, the alliterations, and the onomatopoetic quality of these sentences. Thus, here is the original:

### DER BAUM UND DIE SPRACHE

Ich stieg eine Böschung hinan und legte mich unter einen Baum. Der Baum war eine Pappel oder eine Erle. Warum ich seine Gattung nicht behalten habe? Weil, während ich ins Laubwerk sah und seiner Bewegung folgte, mit einmal in mir die Sprache dergestalt von ihm ergriffen wurde, daß sie augenblicklich die uralte Vermählung mit dem Baum in meinem Beisein noch einmal vollzog. Die Äste und mit ihnen auch der Wipfel wogen sich erwägend oder bogen sich ablehnend; die Zweige zeigten sich zuneigend oder hochfahrend; das Laub sträubte sich gegen einen rauhen Luftzug, erschauerte vor ihm oder kam ihm entgegen; der Stamm verfügte über seinen guten Grund, auf dem er fußte; und ein Blatt warf seinen Schatten auf das andre. Ein leiser Wind spielte zur Hochzeit auf und trug alsbald die schnell entsprossenen Kinder dieses Betts als Bilderrede unter alle Welt. ("Kurze Schatten," *Gesammelte Schriften*, IV.1, 425f.)

In July 1911, in the journal *Der Akademiker,* a poem, "Auf stillen Pfaden" (On still paths) was published by someone who signed his name only as «-gg-.» Ott attributes it to Heidegger (*Martin Heidegger: A Political Life,* 68; German edition, 71). Given Heidegger's strong love for the mountains of the Black Forest (for instance, ibid., 125; German edition, 123), one is almost inclined to assume that this poem could not have been written by Heidegger since it centers on the «weisse Birken in der Heide» («white birches on the heath») in the context of a nocturnal experience of relief from sorrows and complaints. Those who love the mountains in the Black Forest usually don't like birches on the heath that much, and vice versa. Birches often evoke (at least for city-dwellers) pretty much the opposite of that «Härte des Willens» that, according to Hei-degger, the Black Forest calls forth (see above, chapter 1, n. 33). Perhaps, however, it was the special situation of the summer 1911, Heidegger's struggle with Catholi-cism, his insecure professional future, and his delicate health, that had «alienated» him somewhat even from the mountains of the Black Forest and made him refer to birches. In this case, this short poem would be, so to speak, the analogue to Goethe's journey to Italy.

33. Walter Benjamin, *One-Way Street, Reflections,* 76.
34. Ibid., 92–94.
35. Ibid., 88–90.

# Index of Names

354     Index of Names

Dallmayr, Fred, viii
Delfosse, Heinrich. See Bast, Rainer A.
Derrida, Jacques, viii, 187, 189, 230, 232f.,
    243, 256, 309, 332
Descartes, René, 110, 273
Descombes, Vincent, VII
Deucalion, 312
Dietrich, Marlene, 236
Don Quixote, 143
Dostoyevsky, Fyodor M., 90
Dreyfus, Hubert L., 326f., 331
Duns Scotus, John, 299

Ebert, Friedrich, 123
Eckhart, Meister, 58, 278
Engels, Friedrich, 156, 161, 166, 260
Eulenspiegel, Till, 315
Ewing, Patrick, 56

Farías, Victor, viif., 245–247, 264, 309, 316,
    343
Feick, Hildegard, 32, 254
Feuerbach, Ludwig, 301
Fichte, Johann G., 1f., 89, 169, 189, 232,
    254
Fontane, Theodor W., 248
Foucault, Michel, vii, 58, 232
Francis, Saint, 123
Franzen, Winfried, 283
Freud, Sigmund, 110, 242, 265, 267, 311
Fried, Gregory, 314
Fritsche, Johannes, 232f., 237, 265, 273,
    292f., 307, 313, 347, 349
Furth, Montgomery, 298
Fynsk, Christopher, 213f., 332

Gadamer, Hans-Georg, 218, 338, 342
Galilei, Galileo, 26, 150
George, Stefan, 250, 255, 333
Goebbels, Joseph, 289f.
Goethe, Johann W. von, 74, 79, 127, 242,
    338, 352
Goldmann, Lucien, 278
Guignon, Charles, viii, 7–10, 12f., 19, 23,
    25–27, 35, 45f., 48–50, 52–54, 60f., 62f.,
    138f., 149–152, 159, 171, 177, 198, 205,
    207–214, 216f., 220, 241, 251, 254, 256f.,
    266, 268, 284, 286, 292, 294f., 314, 321,
    331f., 334, 338f., 349, 351

Habermas, Jürgen, 7, 137, 233, 334
Hades, vii
Hartmann, Nicolai, 147
Haßel, Renate, 325
Hauptmann, Gerhart, 90
Hegel, Georg W. F., 19, 42, 74, 97, 102,
    123, 130, 154, 156, 159, 164–166, 170f.,

173, 192, 230, 247f., 254, 270, 278, 293f.,
    303f., 314, 322, 333
Heidegger, Martin, vii–xvi, 2–69, 71f., 83,
    87f., 93, 101, 112, 121, 124–143, 146f.,
    149–154, 157–159, 162f., 169, 171–175,
    177, 181f., 185–227, 229–270, 272–279,
    282–289, 291–293, 295–298, 300–324,
    326–352
Heine, Heinrich, 225
Heinrich, Klaus, 267, 315
Hellen, 312
Henreid, Paul, 331
Heracles, 325, 333
Heraclitus, 252, 307, 315f.
Herder, Johann G., 238
Hesiod, 191
Hillel, Rabbi, 226
Hitler, Adolf, xi–xiii, 70–88, 108–110, 112,
    123, 126–130, 132–136, 138, 141f., 144,
    152–154, 159, 172, 185f., 189f., 194, 196,
    199f., 203, 215, 217f., 222, 224, 241,
    246–249, 267, 269–271, 283, 289–291,
    293f., 296, 301, 305–307, 309, 312, 325,
    331, 337, 339, 342, 344, 350
Hitler, Alois, 77, 249
Hitler, Klara, 76, 249
Hölderlin, Friedrich, xiii, 58, 194f., 197,
    253, 291, 313, 344
Homer, 153, 312
Hume, David, 100
Husserl, Edmund, 232, 284, 309, 316

Ignatius, Saint, 123
Isenschmidt, Andreas, 7

Jaeger, Werner, 342
Jahn, Friedrich L., 346
Jannings, Emil, 236
Jaspers, Karl, 142, 333, 361
Jesus Christ, 108, 153f., 240, 283, 299, 316,
    326
Jonas, Hans, 7, 14, 140, 218, 340
Jünger, Ernst, 1, 133, 222, 224, 226, 282,
    292, 324f., 337

Kant, Immanuel, 100, 105, 123, 169, 220,
    230, 254, 276, 299, 301, 312, 322
Kepler, Johannes, 226
Kierkegaard, Søren, 326
King, Martin Luther, Jr., 8f., 26, 241, 326
Klee, Paul, 15
Krebs, Engelbert, 254
Krell, David F., viii, 230, 333f.

Lacan, Jacques, 233
Lacoue-Labarthe, Philippe, 214f., 229,
    332f.

Compositor:    Braun-Brumfield, Inc.
Text:    10/12 Times Roman
Display:    Helvetica
Printer and Binder:    Maple-Vail Book Mfg. Group